The Cadfael Companion

Also by Robin Whiteman
(with Rob Talbot)

THE COTSWOLDS
THE ENGLISH LAKES
SHAKESPEARE'S AVON
CADFAEL COUNTRY
THE YORKSHIRE MOORS AND DALES
THE HEART OF ENGLAND
THE WEST COUNTRY
WESSEX
THE GARDEN OF ENGLAND
ENGLISH LANDSCAPES

The Cadfael Companion

The World of Brother Cadfael

ROBIN WHITEMAN
Introduction by Ellis Peters

Containing people, places, properties and herbs mentioned in Chronicles 1 to 20

THE MYSTERIOUS PRESS
Published by Warner Books
A Time Warner Company

Mysterious Press books are published by Warner Books, Inc.,
1271 Avenue of the Americas, New York, NY 10020.

A Time Warner Company

First published in Great Britain in 1991 by
Macdonald & Co. (Publishers) Ltd
This revised edition published in 1995 by
Little, Brown and Company
Reprinted 1995

10 9 8 7 6 5 4 3 2

Library of Congress Cataloging-in-Publication Data

Whiteman, Robin.
The Cadfael companion : the world of Brother Cadfael / Robin Whiteman : introduction by Ellis Peters.
p. cm.
Originally published: Macdonald and Co., 1991.
Includes bibliographical references (p.)
ISBN 0-89296-513-4
1. Peters, Ellis, 1913– —Characters—Brother Cadfael—Encyclopedias. 2. Cadfael, Brother (Fictitious character)—Encyclopedias. 3. Detective and mystery stories, English—Encyclopedias. 4. Shrewsbury (England)—In literature—Encyclopedias. 5. Historical fiction. English—Encyclopedias. 6. Middle Ages in literature—Encyclopedias. 7. Monks in literature—Encyclopedias. I. Title.
PR6031.A49Z96 1995 95–15435
823′.912—dc20 CIP

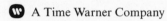

Contents

To Tricia

The Chronicles of Brother Cadfael

by Ellis Peters

1 A Morbid Taste for Bones, 1977
2 One Corpse Too Many, 1979
3 Monk's-Hood, 1980
4 Saint Peter's Fair, 1981
5 The Leper of Saint Giles, 1981
6 The Virgin in the Ice, 1982
7 The Sanctuary Sparrow, 1983
8 The Devil's Novice, 1983
9 Dead Man's Ransom, 1984
10 The Pilgrim of Hate, 1984
11 An Excellent Mystery, 1985
12 The Raven in the Foregate, 1986
13 The Rose Rent, 1986
14 The Hermit of Eyton Forest, 1987
15 The Confession of Brother Haluin, 1988
16 The Heretic's Apprentice, 1989
17 The Potter's Field, 1989
18 The Summer of the Danes, 1991
19 The Holy Thief, 1992
20 Brother Cadfael's Penance, 1994

Published by Little, Brown (1–13) and Headline (14–20) in hardback and Warner Futura in paperback

A Rare Benedictine, 1988 (Headline)

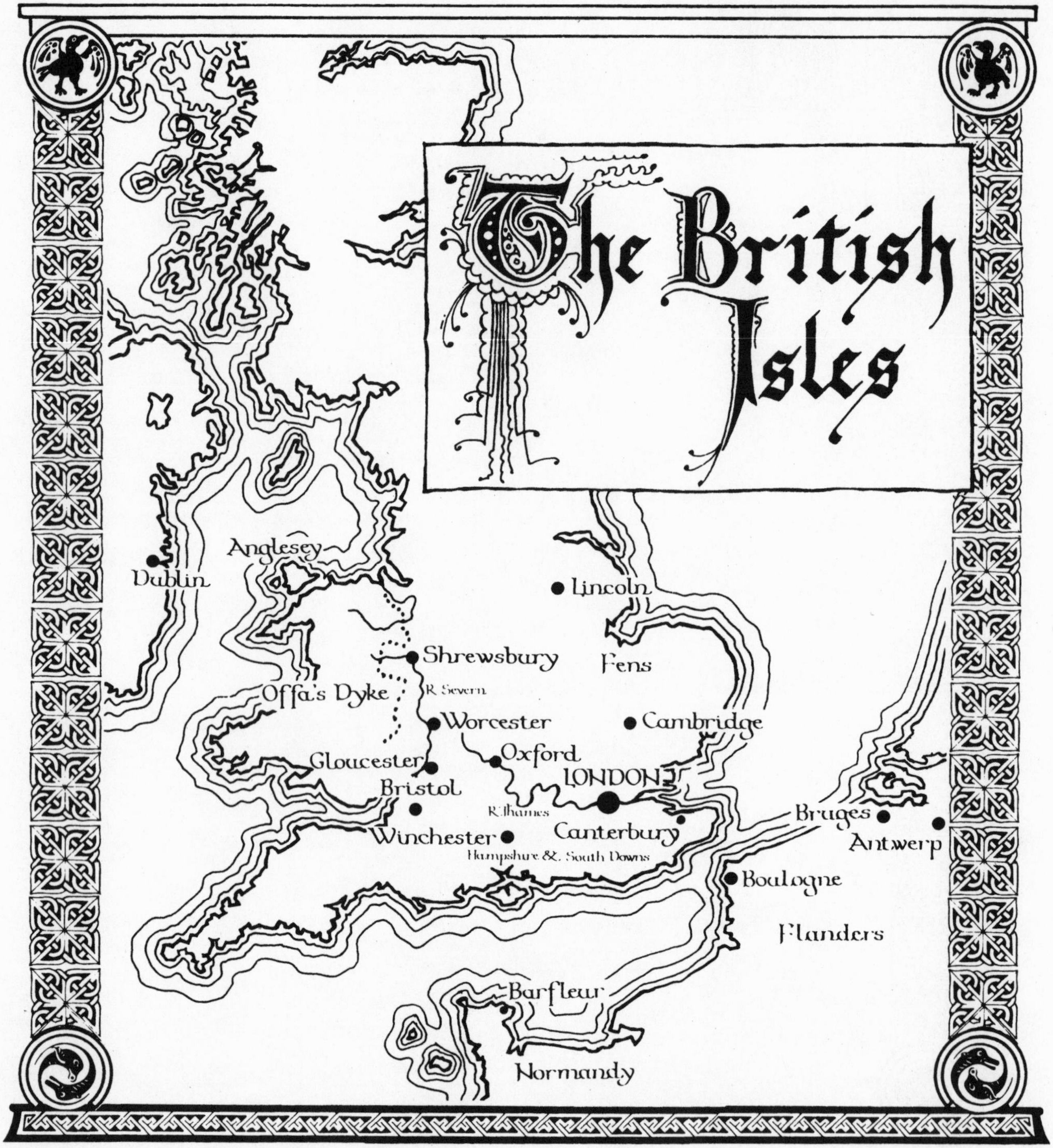
The British Isles
Anglesey
Dublin
Lincoln
Shrewsbury
Fens
R. Severn
Offa's Dyke
Worcester
Cambridge
Oxford
Gloucester
LONDON
Bristol
R. Thames
Winchester
Canterbury
Hampshire & South Downs
Bruges
Antwerp
Boulogne
Flanders
Barfleur
Normandy

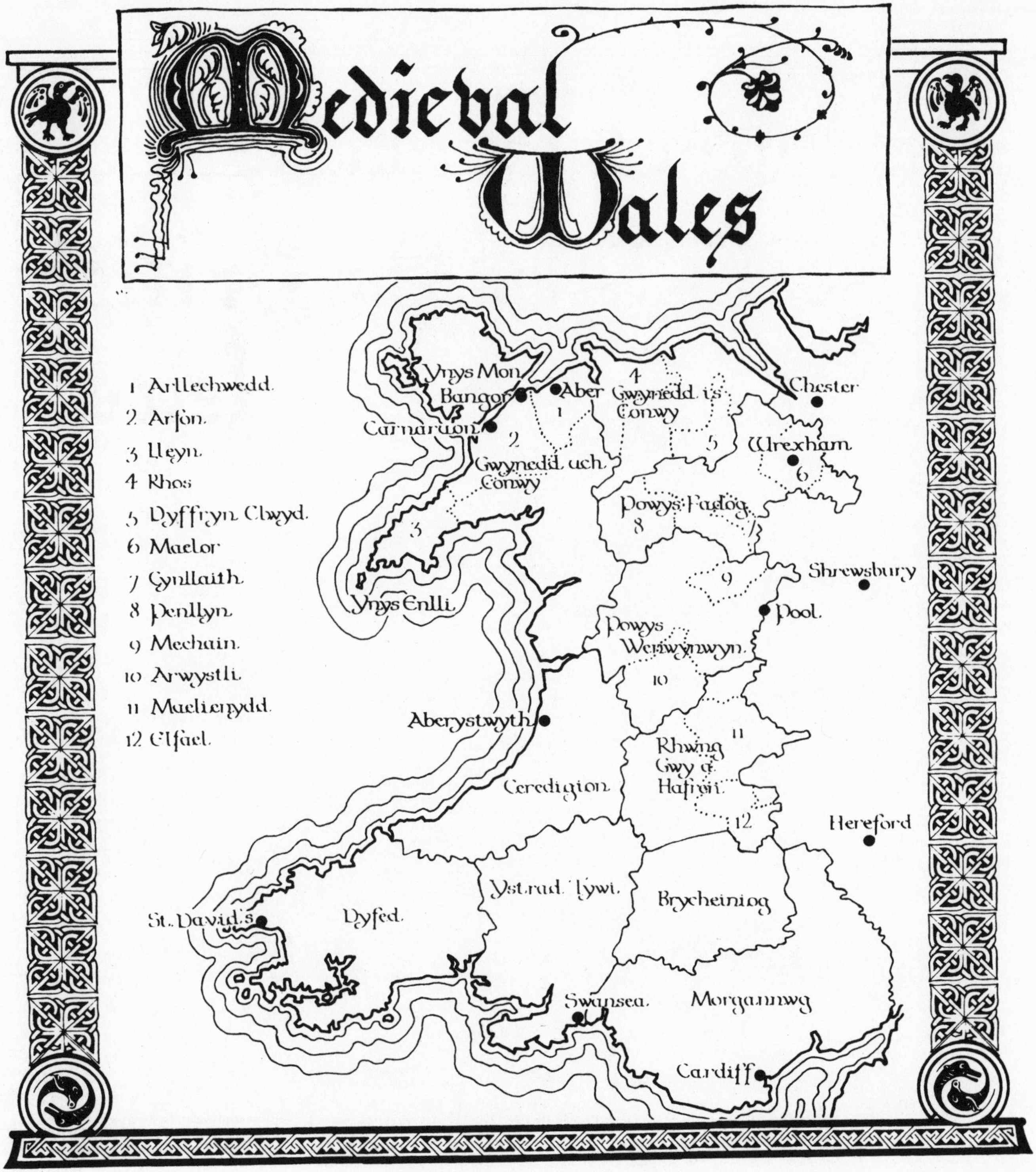
Medieval Wales
1 Arllechwedd.
2 Arfon.
3 Lleyn.
4 Rhos
5 Dyffryn Clwyd.
6 Maelor
7 Cynllaith.
8 Penllyn
9 Mechain.
10 Arwystli.
11 Maelienydd.
12 Elfael.
Ynys Mon
Bangor
Aber
Carnarvon
Gwynedd is Conwy
Chester
Wrexham
Gwynedd uch Conwy
Powys Fadog
Shrewsbury
Ynys Enlli
Pool.
Powys Wenwynwyn
Aberystwyth
Rhwng Gwy a Hafren
Ceredigion
Hereford
Ystrad Tywi
Brycheiniog
St. Davids
Dyfed.
Swansea.
Morgannwg
Cardiff

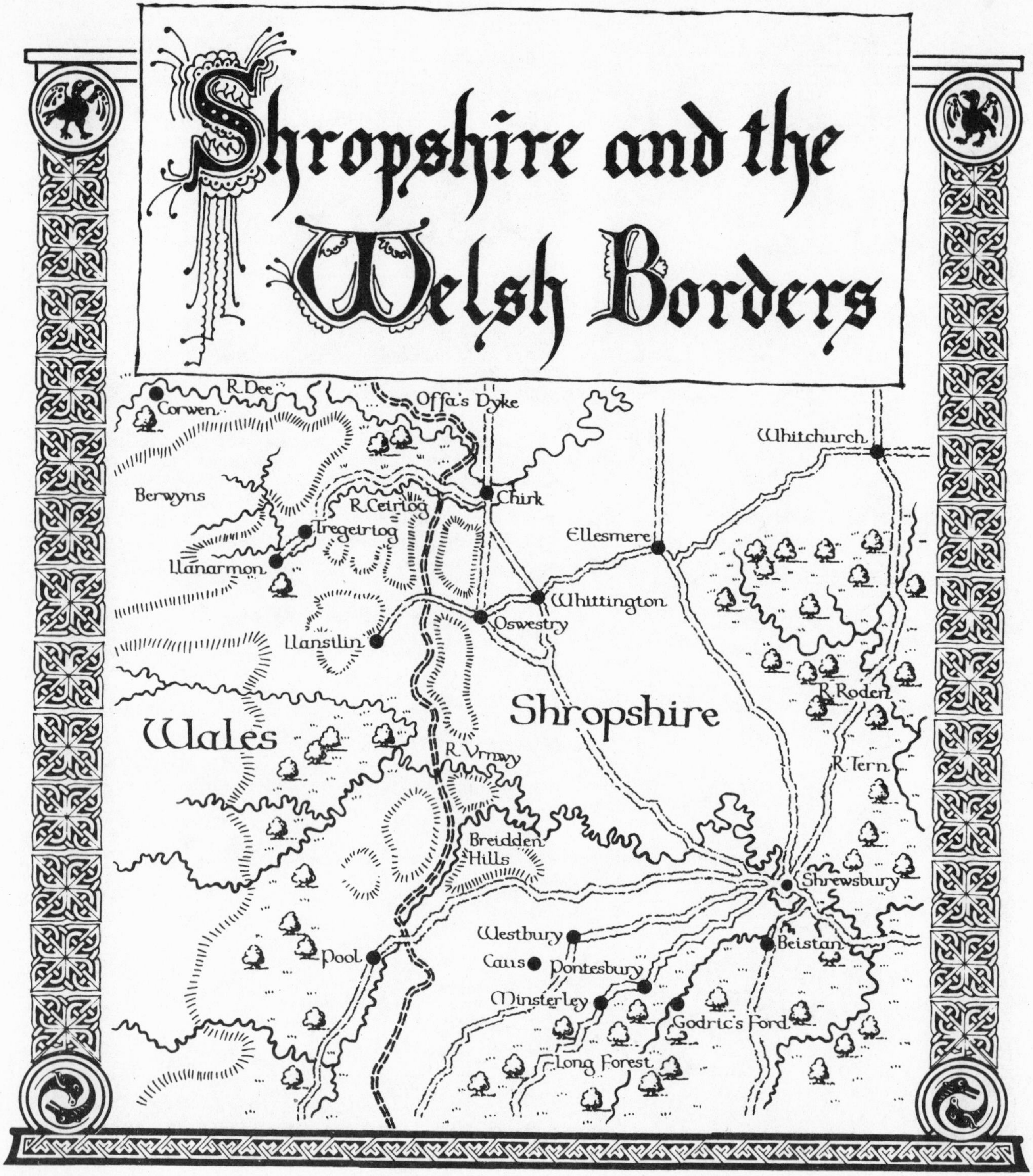
Shropshire and the Welsh Borders
R. Dee
Corwen
Offa's Dyke
Whitchurch
Berwyns
R. Ceiriog
Chirk
Tregeiriog
Llanarmon
Ellesmere
Whittington
Oswestry
Llansilin
Shropshire
R. Roden
Wales
R. Vrnwy
R. Tern
Breidden Hills
Shrewsbury
Westbury
Beistan
Caus
Pontesbury
Pool
Minsterley
Godric's Ford
Long Forest

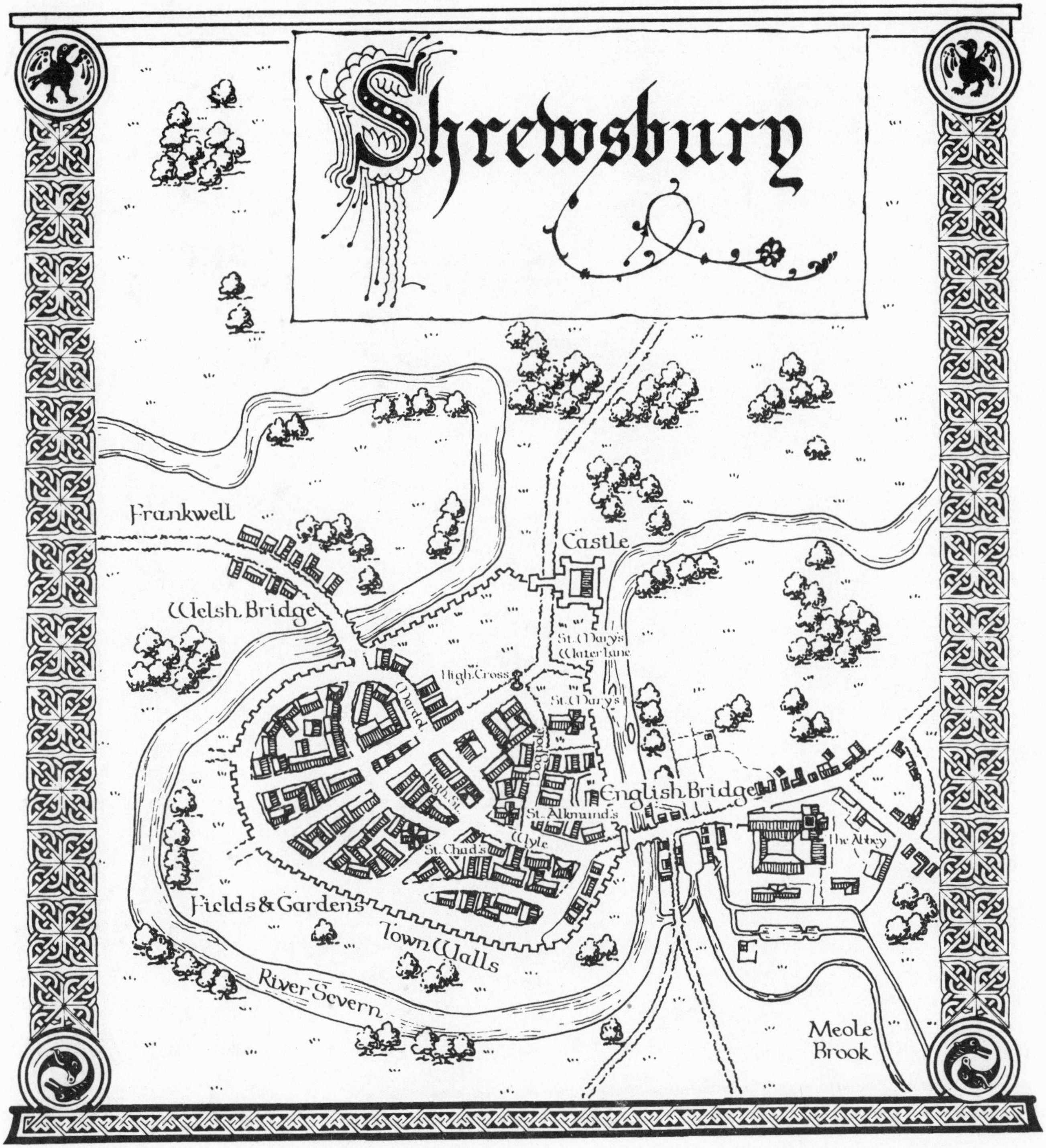
Shrewsbury
Frankwell
Castle
Welsh Bridge
St. Mary's Water Lane
High Cross
Marldot
St. Mary's
Dogpole
High St.
English Bridge
St. Alkmund's
Wyle
St. Chad's
The Abbey
Fields & Gardens
Town Walls
River Severn
Meole Brook

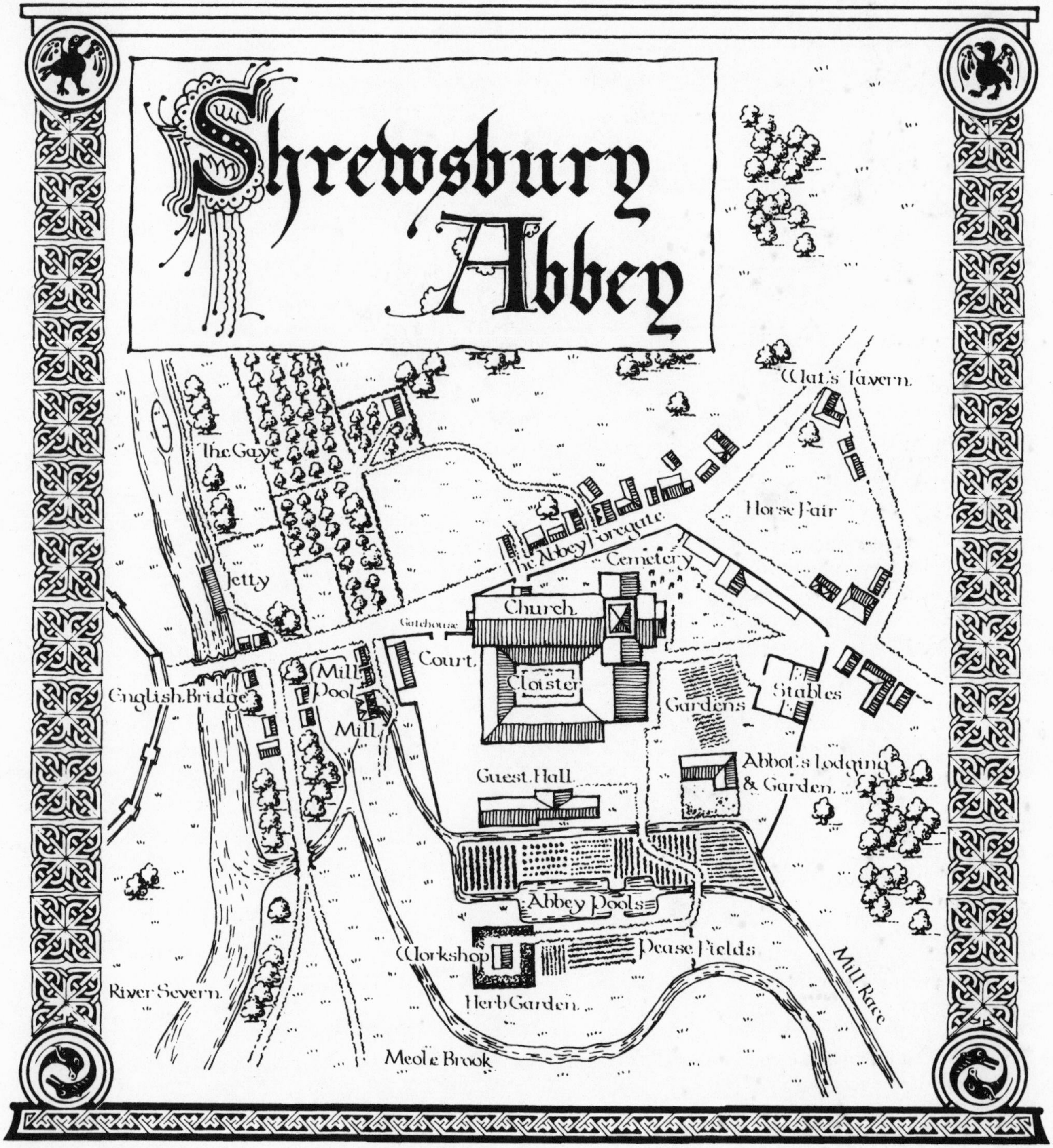
Shrewsbury Abbey
Wat's Tavern
The Gaye
Horse Fair
The Abbey Foregate
Cemetery
Jetty
Church
Gatehouse
Court
English Bridge
Mill Pool
Mill
Cloister
Gardens
Stables
Abbot's Lodging & Garden
Guest Hall
Abbey Pools
Workshop
Pease Fields
River Severn
Herb Garden
Mill Race
Meole Brook

Introduction

by Ellis Peters

The landscape of the Brother Cadfael Chronicles, with its distant prospect of all too genuine turmoil, warfare and rivalry, and its foreground of fictional characters and imagined lives, interwoven into and shaped by that turbulent background, is a complex field for mapping and documentation.

What I have created is an amalgam of stark fact and derived fiction. The fictional element is devised always with due respect to the known, recorded and agreed facts of English and Welsh history in the twelfth century. I have not tampered with anything that is accepted as authentic. These kings, earls, bishops, abbots, Welsh princes, Danish settlers and marauders, really did exist, intermarry, rule, engender their successors, and die. All that is known of them I have respected. But the teeming thousands whose names are not recorded in the histories – the merchants, labourers, peasants, housewives, who inhabited towns and villages, farmed the land, made the artifacts, managed the small manors and coppiced the woodlands – these I am entitled to imagine, to name, and to fit into the trellis of history, representatives of the common stock.

As with people, so with places. I have not altered the location of any event in recorded history, but I have felt free to place my little people in imagined hamlets, whenever no actual village offered a suitable domicile. Nor have I ever placed a fictional tenant in any real manor, where the name of the actual incumbent at the time is known, whether from Domesday or any other authority. But all the properties subject to FitzAlan, for instance, had passed into crown hands by reason of the earl's adherence to the opposing cause, and many of his former vassals were dispossessed with their lord, so that room is left among the Shropshire manors for imaginary crown nominees to take over the tenancies. And them I may create, and endow with a local habitation and a name.

Nor need even the most literal-minded reader wonder that these imagined settlements – they are few – have vanished from the modern face of England. Scattered through the English counties can be found dozens of sites known to archaeologists as DMVs – Deserted Medieval Villages. Not all are utterly deserted, but there are many where only certain ordered patterns on the ground indicate the overgrown house-platforms that were once the dwellings of families. Even planned towns, larger and more recent, sometimes failed to establish themselves and decayed into the earth, leaving only the plan of their symmetrical streets faintly discernible by a slanting light in the turf.

In this territory, in its totality true but in detail elusive, I have been at home for so long that both the historical highways and the domestic byways are familiar to me. But I am reminded that there are now eighteen of the Cadfael novels, and that they are not merely a sequence of individual stories, but an unfolding history of England, and especially of Shropshire and the Marches, through seven years, recorded season by season, and that there may well be need of signposts here and there to link up past acquaintances, and to define what is history and what is imagination, which of these inhabitants of shire and realm actually lived and died in twelfth-century England, and which of them might well have done so unrecorded and unknown, among our anonymous Salopian ancestors.

So here they are, in someone else's painstaking and meticulous work, not mine, the entire catalogue of those figures that played a part in the shaping of the world in time long past – the Crusader-kings of Jerusalem and the Atabegs of Mosul, the corsairs of the Mediterranean and the Norse adventurers who planted temporary roots in Dublin, the solitary saints of Wales and the powerful princes of the Roman Church, the magnates who took up arms for Stephen and for Maud, the demon-earls of the Fenlands and of Chester, who made regional hells about them for a few months or years, the abbots and obedientiaries of Cluny who played host to the pilgrims crossing Europe to the most celebrated shrines of the Western world, the Knights Hospitallers who housed the pilgrims to Jerusalem, all real, all deserving of remembrance.

And moving in the nearer ground before them, closer yet smaller and more shadowy, in a denial of perspective, the humble people who might have been you or me, had we been born eight centuries earlier – the shopkeepers and artisans of Shrewsbury, the small gentry of the Shropshire manors, the pedlars, the craftsmen, the humble brothers and sisters of the monastic Orders, the villeins bound to the land, the younger sons who cut out assarts from the forests, the men-at-arms, the ambivalent souls with one foot in England and one in Wales, like me, like you, the continuity of humanity inhabiting these islands, and especially this shire. I may have given them their names, within the covers of my books, I may have given them a local habitation and a history, but they existed, as surely as did the kings, then and in every age since, and exist still today, and will continue into future centuries. They are you and me, and the ones who come after us.

I produced the novels, yes, but I could not have produced this book; it had to come from another, for others, if it was to come at all. Robin Whiteman, who provided the meticulous text for *Cadfael Country*, to accompany Rob Talbot's beautiful photographs, has here tackled an even more testing task with the same patience and thoroughness, to supply a guide to this complex literary landscape. If it is of help to you who read, I am glad and grateful. I feel a part of a progression which is England. I hope you may feel the same, and be glad of it, as I am glad.

Ellis Peters.

Preface

I have to confess that when it was first suggested that I became involved in the production of an illustrated book based on *The Chronicles of Brother Cadfael*, I was in total ignorance of the existence of this fictional monk, nor had I heard of his creator Ellis Peters. That was in early 1987, the year the Twelfth Chronicle *The Raven in the Foregate* was published in Futura paperback. I read the book, enjoyed it, but was faced with serious misgivings about the wisdom of producing a book entitled *Cadfael Country*. The major question, for the photographer Rob Talbot, was how to capture the world of the twelfth century over eight centuries later? Surely, given the massive changes in the environment, it would be better to use drawn illustrations? No, the publishers wanted Rob's photographs and, if we were to take on the project, he had to find an acceptable solution to the problem. As the writer of *Cadfael Country*, however, I was faced with a different and almost insurmountable set of problems. Essentially, I had to disentangle the facts from the fiction. Which places were real or imagined? Which characters were fictional or historical? Which properties existed? And, of those that did, how many had managed to survive the ravages of time and the whims of changing generations?

Since the publication of *A Morbid Taste for Bones* in 1977, millions of readers throughout the world have been captivated and enthralled, delighted and intrigued by the exploits and adventures of Brother Cadfael, the twelfth-century Welsh monk and herbalist of Shrewsbury Abbey who uses his skills, knowledge and considerable powers of deduction to solve murder mysteries. As soon as it became clear that this fictional and worldly-wise detective had an enthusiastic following, Ellis Peters concentrated, almost exclusively, on writing further chronicles in the series. The first novel was set in the spring of 1137, the second in the summer of 1138. Thereafter, the *Chronicles* have progressed steadily, season by season, year by year, until they now number eighteen. Set in England and Wales during the turbulent reign of King Stephen, the novels are a rich blend of historical fact and derived fiction: people and places, real and imagined, are woven with such skill and confidence into the fabric of the whole that without access to the author's mind or knowledge of her references it becomes almost impossible to disentangle. That this should be necessary may at first seem questionable. But, like Cadfael, many of his fans are endlessly curious and have demonstrated that they are eager for more information about the lively and jostling throng of people, properties and places appearing in the *Chronicles*.

While writing and researching *Cadfael Country*, I unearthed a fascinating collection of material relating to Cadfael and his colourful world. Indexing all eighteen novels, plus the three short stories in *A Rare Benedictine*, produced a list of over one thousand characters and locations, some appearing in only one story, others recurring again and again. These, combined with a list of all the plants and herbs mentioned in the *Chronicles* and a glossary of archaic words, form the basis of *The Cadfael Companion*. Now, after two years of detailed research, with the full support, encouragement and endorsement of Ellis Peters herself, I have managed to answer nearly all those questions posed during the writing of *Cadfael Country*. I say nearly all, because three references have evaded all my best endeavours to pin them down (and in this even Ellis Peters has been unable to help). Perhaps you, dear reader, will be able to throw some light on these baffling and intriguing references (two are listed in the main body of the Companion as 'untraced'; while the third appears in Appendix I as 'unidentified').

The Cadfael Companion grew out of my researches into *Cadfael Country*. It is my sincere hope that it will prove to be an invaluable work of reference, not only for the Cadfael reader but for all those interested in the medieval period in which he lived. For two whole years Brother Cadfael filled almost every waking hour of my life. I am a convert. Now, like you, I am one of this rascally-loveable monk's devoted fans. But, whilst working on these books, I count myself fortunate to have received a further blessing. I have had the privilege of meeting and befriending Cadfael's creator, Ellis Peters (Edith Pargeter), and discovering, within her lively, knowledgeable and enlightened mind, all the characters and places that feature in the *Chronicles*. If nothing else, I number myself one of the luckiest of all her countless fans.

Robin Whiteman

Note to the Second Edition

Since the first edition of *The Cadfael Companion*, Ellis Peters has written two further *Chronicles of Brother Cadfael*, bringing the total to twenty. With the publication of the *Companion* in the United States of America and the launch of a major television series (based on the *Chronicles*) an update seemed appropriate. It also provides a welcome opportunity to correct errors and mention that one of the three 'baffling and intriguing' references, 'gilvers' appearing in Appendix I, was solved by a kind reader from Wales. The other two, however, remain unsolved.

Acknowledgements

Robin Whiteman would like to acknowledge the generous co-operation he received from the following individuals and organisations: the Reverend Ian Ross, Vicar of the Parish of the Holy Cross, for his help and advice regarding Shrewsbury Abbey; Michael Holmes for the information on the Parish of Holy Cross, Shrewsbury; Dr Jane Renfrew and the President and Fellows of Lucy Cavendish College, Cambridge, for information regarding Anglo-Saxon herbs; Nigel Baker and Simon Buteux, Shrewsbury Heritage Project (Birmingham University Field Archaeology Unit); Shrewsbury and Atcham Borough Council; and Shropshire County Council.

The staff in the reference departments of the following public libraries were particularly helpful: Chester; Coventry; Huntingdon; Leamington Spa; Lichfield; Northampton; Ramsey; Salisbury; Shrewsbury; Warwick; and Wilton. Thanks also to Tim Morland for access to the reference to the battle of Wilton in his manuscript, 'A Capital Town', and to Colin Hutchens, who had the unenviable task of editing the substantial manuscript.

Special thanks to: Deborah Owen and Judith Dooling; Arthur Fielder (Beringar Ltd.); and last but by no means least, Edith Pargeter (Ellis Peters), without whose writings, guidance, patience and warm encouragement this book would not have been possible.

Abbreviations

AD	*anno Domini*, in the year of Our Lord
b.	born
BC	before Christ
bib.	biblical
C.	century
c.	*circa*, about
Cul	*Culpeper's Complete Herbal*
d.	died
DB	Domesday Book
f.d.	feast day
fict.	fictitious
fl.	*floruit*, flourished
ft.	feet
hist.	historical
MP	Member of Parliament
myth.	mythological
OS	Ordnance Survey
RB	*A Rare Benedictine*
Refs	References
St	Saint

Note to the Reader

Entries are in word-by-word alphabetical order. Commoners are arranged according to their surname (e.g. 'Aspley, Meriet'); if their only form of identification is a place, then that place is used as a surname (e.g. 'Bristol, Thomas of'); otherwise they are arranged under their first name (e.g. 'Thomas the Farrier'). Nobles are also arranged according to their surname (e.g. 'Mandeville, Geoffrey de, Earl of Essex'). All ecclesiastics are arranged according to their first name (e.g. 'Henry of Blois, Bishop of Winchester'; 'Radulfus, Abbot'). All monarchs, monarch-types and immediate members of their families are arranged according to their first names (e.g. 'Stephen, King of England'; 'Geoffrey, Count of Anjou'; 'Robert, Earl of Gloucester'). Cross-references are used where appropriate.

In an entry, any text after the word 'Novels' denotes that the information refers to *The Chronicles of Brother Cadfael*. At the end of an entry, references are given to the relevant *Chronicle* and chapter numbers (e.g. 'Refs: **12** (7, 10–12)' refers to *The Raven in the Foregate*, Chapters 7, 10, 11 and 12). In the case of references to *A Rare Benedictine*, '**RB** (1, 2, 3)' refers to each tale, i.e. 'A Light on the Road to Woodstock', 'The Price of Light' and 'Eyewitness'.

Place entries in Shropshire and in part of Staffordshire include information which appears in the Domesday Book (referred to as 'DB'), the survey of most of England carried out in 1086 under the orders of William I.

A

Aachen (Germany). Also called Aix-la-Chapelle. CHARLES THE GREAT, the first Holy Roman Emperor, built his palace here in the 8th C. and made it the northern capital of his empire. The city became the centre of a cultural rebirth in Europe, known as the Carolingian renaissance.

Novels: Aachen is mentioned alongside Byzantium (see CONSTANTINOPLE) in connection with the Caesars.

Refs: **16** (11).

Abbey Foregate (Shrewsbury, Shropshire). Formerly called Monks' Foregate. The old Abbey Foregate, stretching from the English Bridge eastward towards ST GILES and LONDON, lies to the north of SHREWSBURY ABBEY. In 1836 the few remaining monastic buildings to the south of the abbey church were demolished to make way for Thomas Telford's new road linking London to CAERGYBI. Part of this new road included the construction of a new and straighter Abbey Foregate, passing immediately south of the church where the cloisters would have been. In addition to the abbey church, there are several buildings of interest dating from the 16th–19th C. These include the timber-framed Merival house, built in *c.*1601; the Hospital of Holy Cross, built by Pountney Smith in 1853; the early 18th C. Abbey House; and Whitehall, built of red sandstone for Richard Prince in 1578–82. At the eastern end of the Abbey Foregate is Lord Hill's Column, erected by Thomas Harrison in 1814–16. On top of the column is a statue of the distinguished soldier, Rowland Hill (1772–1842), by Joseph Panzetta.

Novels: 'The Foregate . . . was bustling with life, every shop-front and house-door opened wide to the summer, and a constant traffic of housewives, urchins, dogs, carters and pedlars on the move, or gathered in gossiping groups. In this belated but lovely burst of summer, life quitted the confines of walls and roof, and moved into the sunshine.' At the eastern end of the Abbey Foregate lay the Hospital of St Giles; while at the western end stood the English Bridge, leading across the River SEVERN to one of the main gates of SHREWSBURY. Essentially beaten-earth with deep ruts, the broad, straight highway was partly cobbled. ERWALD THE WHEELWRIGHT was reeve of the Abbey Foregate and unofficially used the title of provost. Among the buildings in the Abbey Foregate were: Bishop ROGER DE CLINTON'S HOUSE; Niall BRONZESMITH'S HOUSE AND SHOP; THOMAS THE FARRIER'S MESSUAGE; the bakehouse of Jordan ACHARD; the premises of Erwald the Wheelwright; and a few ale-houses. Behind the Abbey Foregate was a 'tangle of narrow lanes', while on the south side, near the English Bridge, lay the abbey mill pool, ranged by six houses in the abbey's grant. The west door of the abbey church, which was the parish door, opened on to the Abbey Foregate, outside the convent walls. The low ground of the Abbey Foregate (from the English Bridge to the abbey enclave) was flooded when the Severn burst its banks in February 1145.

Refs: **2** (2, 6, 9); **3** (1, 6); **4** (1:1, 1:3, 2:3, 4:1–2, 4:5); **5** (1, 4–5); **7** (3, 5, 11); **8** (7, 12); **9** (1–2, 5, 8–9); **10** (3); **11** (1, 5, 13); **12** (1, 3–6); **13** (1–2, 5–6); **14** (1, 9); **15** (3); **16** (1, 3–4, 6–9, 12–13); **17** (6, 10); **19** (1–3, 5–8, 11–13); **20** (2, 16).

Abel (bib.). The son of Adam and Eve, he was murdered by his elder brother, CAIN. According to Genesis 4:1–8, Abel was a shepherd, whose sacrifice to God of the firstborn of his flock was accepted. In Christian tradition he is regarded as the first martyr and as a hero of faith.

Novels: '"The first murderous warfare in the world, we are told, was between brothers."'

Refs: **20** (8).

Abelard, Pierre (1079–1142) (hist.). The eminent French scholar, philosopher and theologian whose teachings brought him into controversy with the medieval Catholic Church. His love for Heloise, one of his pupils, ended in tragic separation and a famous correspondence. He was to encounter considerable opposition from conservatives in the Church, led by the Cistercian Abbot of Clairvaux, SAINT BERNARD. Abelard died at the Cluniac priory of ST MARCEL on 21 April 1142.

Novels: William of LYTHWOOD and ELAVE spoke with Abelard at ST MARCEL in 1142.

Refs: **16** (2).

Aber or Abergwyngregyn (Gwynedd, Wales). Situated at the mouth of the River Rhaeadr-fawr, 4 miles east of BANGOR, the village of Aber lies about half-a-mile from the coast. By the 13th C. it was the royal seat of the commote of ARLLECHWEDD Uchaf and the favourite residence of the princes of Gwynedd.

Novels: Prior ROBERT's party located OWAIN GWYNEDD at Aber in May 1137. It was from there that his clerk, URIEN, set out to guide the monks to GWYTHERIN. In Spring 1144 CADFAEL and Deacon MARK journeyed to the royal seat and tref of Aber in the company of Owain. Bledri ap RHYS was murdered within the high stockade of the llys.

Refs: **1** (2); **18** (1–6, 8, 11, 14).

Aberdaron (Gwynedd, Wales). A fishing village, situated at the tip of the LLEYN PENINSULA 'fronting the wild sea and the holiest island of the Welsh church'. Pilgrims to the island of YNYS ENLLI came to Aberdaron, the last staging-post on their journey, and stayed in the hospice of Y Gegin Fawr. (The small cottage is now a café.) They also worshipped in St

Hywyn's Church, dating from the 12th C., which stands almost on the seashore.

Novels: In the spring of 1141 the pilgrim CIARAN stated, untruthfully, that his avowed intention was to walk barefoot to Aberdaron.

Refs: **10** (3–6, 8, 11, 14).

Abermenai (Gwynedd, Wales). At the southernmost tip of ANGLESEY, a long sand and shingle bar stretches out into the south-western entrance of the MENAI STRAIT. At the very end of this thin peninsula, opposite Fort Belan on the mainland, is Abermenai Point. Although there are public rights of way across the expansive sand dunes of Newborough Warren Nature Reserve to Abermenai and its lighthouse, warnings stress the danger of high tides. CADWALADR landed at Abermenai, then a port, with a Danish fleet from Ireland in 1144. Those with him included OTIR, TURCAILL, (*fl.* 1144) and the son of Ischerwlf.

Novels: 'The sands to the north of the strait, where the coast of Anglesey extended into a broad expanse of dune and warren, none too safe in high tides, and terminating in a long bar of shifting sand and shingle.' A great fleet of Danish ships from DUBLIN landed on the peninsula opposite Abermenai in May 1144. CADWALADR promised the Irish Danes, under OTIR, a sum of 2,000 marks if they would help him regain the Welsh lands OWAIN GWYNEDD had taken from him.

Refs: **18** (4–7, 12).

Aberystwyth (Dyfed, Wales). This coastal town stands at the mouth of the River Rheidol and in the heart of Cardigan Bay. In medieval times the town was walled and grew up around the 13th C. Norman castle.

Novels: In February 1141, after the battle of LINCOLN, CADWALADR returned to Aberystwyth with his plunder and prisoners.

Refs: **9** (1, 3).

Aberystwyth Castle (Dyfed, Wales). In 1109 Gilbert Strongbow, a Norman, built a castle in the valley of the River Ystwyth, about a mile and a half south of the present town of ABERYSTWYTH. In 1143 HYWEL AB OWAIN burned CADWALADR's castle at Aberystwyth. See also LLANBADARN CASTLE. A second castle was built by Edward I in the 13th C. on the rocky headland overlooking Cardigan Bay, immediately north of the mouth of the River Rheidol. It was slighted by the Parliamentarians during the Civil War and is now in ruins.

Novels: In February 1141 Sheriff Gilbert PRESTCOTE was captured by CADWALADR at the battle of LINCOLN and taken back to Aberystwyth Castle. Two years later, Hywel ab Owain drove Cadwaladr out of CEREDIGION and burned the castle.

Refs: **9** (1, 3); **18** (12).

Abingdon (Oxfordshire, England). Situated on the north bank of the River THAMES and 6 miles south of OXFORD, this market town grew up around the Benedictine abbey, established in 676, and both prospered with the medieval wool trade.

Novels: In 1141 Brother ADAM OF READING lodged at the abbey on his way to SHREWSBURY and LEOMINSTER. There he noticed CIARAN and Matthew (see MEVEREL, Luc). Olivier de BRETAGNE also passed through Abingdon on his way north in search of Luc Meverel. In December 1142 the Empress MAUD, escaping from the siege of OXFORD CASTLE, 'walked the six miles or so to Abingdon'.

Refs: **10** (5, 7, 11, 12); **15** (1).

Achard, Jordan (*fl.* 1141) (fict.). **Novels:** Baker of the ABBEY FOREGATE, he rented his ovens from SHREWSBURY ABBEY and took a professional pride in his work. Although married, he had the reputation of being a womaniser and was thought to have fathered a number of bastards, including Eluned NEST's child. He was publicly accused of the murder of Father AILNOTH in December 1141, but was proven innocent.

Refs: **12** (3, 7, 10–13).

Achard, Wife of Jordan (*fl.* 1141) (fict.). **Novels:** The loyal wife of Jordan ACHARD, she was a poor, subdued creature who would not dare cross her husband. By December 1141 she had borne eleven of his children, but only two were alive.

Refs: **12** (7, 10–12).

Acre (Israel). An ancient city and port with a natural harbour, situated 80 miles north of JERUSALEM. The crusaders first captured the city in 1104, and in the ensuing centuries it changed hands numerous times between Christian and Muslim.

Novels: In 1104, during the First Crusade, CADFAEL fought against the Saracens in the battle of Acre.

Refs: **5** (1); **19** (2).

Acton (now Acton Burnell) (Shropshire, England). DB – Actune: in Condover Hundred; a holding of Roger, son of Corbet, under Roger de MONTGOMERY. Acton Burnell is an attractive village situated some 7 miles south-east of Shrewsbury. The castle (more accurately a partly-fortified manor house) was built towards the end of the 13th C. by Robert Burnell, Bishop of Bath and Wells, and Lord Chancellor under Edward 1, from whom the village takes the latter part of its name. Acton Burnell Castle is now a ruin. St Mary's Church is 13th C.

Novels: Evading the sheriff's men in December 1138, Edwin GURNEY was captured in the woods beyond Acton.

Refs: **3** (6).

Acton Burnell. See ACTON.

Acton Scott. See HENLEY.

Adam (b. 1124) (fict.). **Novels:** 'A dreaming soul, evidently, who saw no use in a sheriff but to bring trouble to lesser men.' Eldest son of WALTER THE COOPER and his wife Elfrid (see HERIET), Adam, who had freckles, was the godson of Adam HERIET. In September 1141 he was helping in his father's business at BRIGGE.

Refs: **11** (8).

Adam, Brother (b. *c.*1073) (fict.). **Novels:** A Benedictine monk of SHREWSBURY ABBEY. In February 1141 Brother Adam, who had a bad chest cold, was allowed to leave the infirmary at his abbey and return to the dortoir.

Refs: **9** (4).

Adam, Brother (*fl.* 1141) (fict.). **Novels:** A Benedictine monk of READING ABBEY, he came to SHREWSBURY on 17 June 1141 to attend St WINIFRED's translation. He was on a mission for his abbot to LEOMINSTER Priory. At Reading he had the same duties as CADFAEL, being a gardener and herbalist. When he left Shrewsbury he had 'a pouch well filled with seeds of species his garden did not possess'. 'Knowing and practical', he alerted Cadfael to the presence in the guest-hall of the rogue Simeon POER.

Refs: **10** (3, 5, 8, 12, 16).

Adam, Father (*c.*1081–1141) (fict.). **Novels:** 'A sad man, because he had been listening to and bearing with the perpetual failures of humankind for seventeen years, a tired man because endless consoling and chiding and forgiving takes it out of any man by the time he's sixty, especially one with neither malice nor anger in his own make-up. A kind man, because he had somehow managed to preserve compassion and hope even against the tide of human fallibility.' A man of humble origins, barely literate and with no pretensions, he became the vicar of the parish of HOLY

CROSS in SHREWSBURY in 1124. LILIWIN and RANNILT were married by him in May 1140. He died in November 1141 and was buried in the cemetery east of the SHREWSBURY ABBEY church.

Refs: **7** (14); **12** (8); **13** (14).

Adela (*c.*1064–1137), Countess of Blois (hist.). Daughter of WILLIAM I, she married Stephen (d. 1102), Count of Blois. Among their children were: THEOBOLD OF NORMANDY, Count of Blois; STEPHEN, King of England; and HENRY OF BLOIS, Bishop of Winchester.

Novels: Referred to as a woman like the Empress MAUD, her niece.

Refs: **2** (1).

Adeney, Fulke (*fl.* 1138) (fict.). **Novels:** Father of Godith (see BLUND), his only child. He was a loyal supporter of MAUD and the greatest of William FITZALAN's vassal lords. He successfully escaped from SHREWSBURY CASTLE, when it was besieged by King STEPHEN in the summer of 1138, and eventually reached safety in NORMANDY.

Refs: **2** (1–10); **12** (6).

Adeney, Godith. See BLUND, Godith.

Adrian, Brother (d. *c.*1138) (fict.). **Novels:** A monk of SHREWSBURY ABBEY, he was confined to the infirmary in 1138, and by December was close to death.

Refs: **3** (1).

Aelfric (*c.*955–*c.*1010) (hist.). Nickname: Grammaticus. A Benedictine monk of Cerne Abbas and also of WINCHESTER, where he was a pupil of St Aethelwold. When he died, Aelfric was abbot of Eynsham Abbey, some 6 miles north-west of OXFORD. He is considered to be the greatest prose writer of his time, writing in both Latin and Old English, and among his numerous works are the *Catholic Homilies* (990–2) and the *Lives of the Saints* (993–8). His *Colloquy* (*Nominum Herbarum*) (995) lists over 200 names of herbs and trees, several of which are unidentifiable.

Novels: CADFAEL obtained a copy of Aelfric's list of herbs and trees in September 1140, and 'wanted peace and quiet to study it'.

Refs: **8** (1).

Aelfric (*fl.* 1138) (fict.). **Novels:** 'Inches above CADFAEL's square, solid bulk, and erect and supple of movement, but lean and wary, with a suggestion of wild alertness in his every motion.' The young manservant of Gervase and Richildis BONEL. Although his father was born free, after his death Aelfric found himself bound villein of Bonel. In December 1138 he carried the food which poisoned and killed his master, and became a possible suspect. Eventually proved innocent, he was made a free man by Edwin GURNEY, Bonel's heir. At the end of December 1138, Aelfric was set, in due course, to marry ALDITH and take on the stewardship of MALLILIE.

Refs: **3** (1–10).

Aelfric, Brother (*fl.* 1143) (fict.). **Novels:** An illuminator and copyist at SHREWSBURY ABBEY, he worked under Brother ANSELM in 1143.

Refs: **15** (14).

Aelgar (*fl.* 1141) (fict.). **Novels:** A free man and parishioner of HOLY CROSS in SHREWSBURY, he 'worked the field strips' of Father ADAM's 'glebe, and cared for the parish bull and the parish boar'. In December 1141 he complained about his new master, Father AILNOTH, who questioned whether he was free or villein. Ordered to plough more closely, Aelgar ploughed up part of EADWIN's headland. Although innocent, for a short while he was under suspicion for the murder of Ailnoth.

Refs: **12** (2, 3, 6,11).

Aelred (b. *c.*1086) (fict.). **Novels:** Married with two 'big' sons, of whom the elder was about thirty and the younger about fifteen in 1141. Tenant of the Marescot manor at SALTON, Aelred warmly received Godfrid Marescot (later Brother HUMILIS) on the latter's visit in August 1141.

Refs: **11** (2, 12).

Aeron, River or Afon (Dyfed, Wales). Rising on the slopes of Mynydd Bach, south-west of Bronnant, the waters of the Aeron sweep in a south-westerly curve to Aberaeron and Cardigan Bay. From source to sea the river is some 18 miles in length. In 1143 it formed the northern boundary of HYWEL AB OWAIN's territory of South CEREDIGION.

Novels: In 1143 Hywel ab Owain was sent by his father, OWAIN GWYNEDD, to 'waft an army across the Aeron and drive CADWALADR headlong out of North CEREDIGION'.

Refs: **18** (2).

Aguilon, Simon (b. 1114) (fict.). **Novels:** 'Curly haired, athletic . . . with a brown, open face.' Nephew and heir of Huon de DOMVILLE, Aguilon came to SHREWSBURY in October 1139 to attend the marriage of his uncle to Iveta de Massard (see LUCY). In order to safeguard his inheritance, he murdered Domville in the woods near BEISTAN. Pretending to help Joscelin LUCY evade the sheriff's men, Aguilon planned to betray him. Aguilon tried to persuade Iveta's guardian, Sir Godfrid PICARD, that he should step into Domville's shoes and 'inherit bride, and honour, and all'. He was eventually given away by the ring he wore on his right hand, and was brought to trial for the murder of his uncle.

Refs: **5** (1–11).

Ailnoth, Father (1105–41) (fict.). **Novels:** Also known as the Raven in the Foregate. 'A man abstemious, rigidly upright, inflexibly honest, ferociously chaste . . . A man with every virtue, except humility and human kindness.' Ailnoth was brought from WESTMINSTER by Abbot RADULFUS to replace Father ADAM as the parish priest of HOLY CROSS, arriving at SHREWSBURY on 10 December 1141. He came highly recommended by Bishop HENRY OF BLOIS, whom he had loyally and efficiently served for four years as a clerk. The new priest soon came to be disliked, even hated, by his parishioners. When he was found dead in SHREWSBURY ABBEY millpond, it was believed that he had been murdered by one of his many enemies. It was established, however, that his death was almost certainly an accident. He died on the night of Christmas Eve 1141, and was buried in the abbey cemetery on New Year's Day 1142.

Refs: **12** (1–13); **16** (4).

Alard the Clerk (b. *c.*1080) (fict.). **Novels:** '"Fifty-seven brothers I had, and now I am brotherless. I begin to miss my kin, now I'm past forty. I never valued them when I was young . . . I was a monk of Evesham, an oblatus, given to God by my father when I was five years old. When I was fifteen I could no longer abide to live my life in one place, and I ran."' Alard the Clerk was with CADFAEL in the employ of Roger MAUDUIT in November 1120. They sailed from BARFLEUR to SOUTHAMPTON, and then travelled north to Mauduit's manor near NORTHAMPTON. Since abandoning the cowl, Alard had travelled throughout Europe, turning his hand to almost anything. At the age of about forty he grew weary of the road. On 22 November, after completing the documents for his employer's case against SHREWSBURY ABBEY, he departed for EVESHAM, unable to resist the call to return to his abbey. '"They will take me back, though in the lowest place. From that there's no falling."'

Refs: **RB** (1).

Alard the Silversmith (*fl.* 1134) (fict.). **Novels:** Villein-born and an excellent silversmith, he ran away from his master, Hamo FITZHAMON of LIDYATE, on St Stephen's Day, 26 December 1134. Fitzhamon had promised Alard his freedom, and marriage to ELFGIVA, in return for making him a pair of silver candlesticks. The promised price was refused, and Alard, leaving Elfgiva behind, made his way to SHREWSBURY. Since Shrewsbury was a charter borough, Alard gained his freedom by working with the town silversmiths for a year and a day. Elfgiva ran away exactly a year later to join him.

Refs: **RB** (2).

Alberic (1080–1147), Cardinal-Bishop of Ostia (hist.). Born in Beauvais, France, he was a monk at the Benedictine abbey at CLUNY before becoming prior of

St Martin-des-Champs. In 1126 Alberic was sent by PETER THE VENERABLE to reform the monastery at Cluny. Between 1131 and 1138 he was abbot at Vezelay. Having been made papal legate and bishop of OSTIA by Pope INNOCENT II, Alberic held, during Advent 1138, a synod at LONDON in which THEOBOLD OF BEC was made Archbishop of CANTERBURY. In April 1139, with the assistance of Queen MATILDA, he ended the war between STEPHEN, King of England, and DAVID I, King of Scotland. Alberic died at Verdun, France.

Novels: Pope Innocent II, in acknowledgement of STEPHEN's claim to the crown, sent Alberic of Ostia over to England with full powers to support the king. In December 1138 Alberic held a legatine council in London for the reform of the Church, during which Abbot HERIBERT of SHREWSBURY ABBEY was removed from office and replaced by Abbot RADULFUS.

Refs: **3** (1, 8).

Albin, Brother (*fl.* 1140) (fict.). **Novels:** Albin the Porter, a Benedictine monk of SHREWSBURY ABBEY, 'was the most consummate gossip in the enclave'.

Refs: **8** (4).

Alcher (*fl.* 1140) (fict.). **Novels:** In May 1140 Alcher, the finest marksman in the garrison at SHREWSBURY CASTLE, was ordered by the sheriff's deputy, Hugh BERINGAR, to put an arrow clean into the hatch of the Aurifaber barn, beyond FRANKWELL. His loosed arrow struck Susanna AURIFABER 'full into her left breast' and killed her.

Refs: **7** (13).

Aldhelm (*c.*1125–45) (fict.). **Novels:** 'A loose-limbed fellow all elbows and knees, but quick and deft in movement for all that. He had a blunt, goodnatured face and a thick head of reddish hair.' A shepherd with 'a half yardland by PRESTON', living 'alone, without a family', Aldhelm worked with the sheep at the manor of UPTON. In February 1145 at SHREWSBURY ABBEY he helped GREGORY and LAMBERT transfer the load of wood from the LONGNER cart to the wagon bound for RAMSEY ABBEY. After helping Brother RICHARD move some of the abbey's treasures out of reach of the rising floodwater, Aldhelm was detained by an unknown monk (Brother TUTILO), who asked him to help carry a 'long, slender burden' out of the abbey church and through the 'heavy double gates' of the cemetery, to the wagon bound for Ramsey. Aldhelm was unaware that he had been tricked into helping Tutilo steal St WINIFRED's reliquary. Later, out at one of the Upton folds, Aldhelm told CADFAEL exactly what had happened that night. Although he was unable to name the unknown monk, the shepherd had seen his face and was positive that by sight, he could 'pick him out from a thousand'. When the party, which included Tutilo, had returned to SHREWSBURY from WORCESTER and HUNCOTE, Cadfael sent Father BONIFACE's errand boy to find Aldhelm, and 'ask him to come down to the abbey when his work for the day was over, and pick out his shadowy Benedictine from among a number now complete.' On his way to the abbey, at 'about a quarter or half of the hour past six', Aldhelm was struck down from behind with a fallen branch by Brother JEROME, who mistook the cowled and whistling figure for Tutilo, similar 'in build, and in age'. While Aldhelm lay senseless, and after Jerome had fled, BÉNEZET (believing that Aldhelm may have seen him rob the coffer for Ramsey Abbey and might possibly recollect it under questioning) coldly and deliberately smashed his skull with a heavy stone. Aldhelm's dead body was discovered in thick woodland, on the narrow path from the Longner ferry, by Tutilo and taken to the mortuary chapel at Shrewsbury Abbey. He was buried 'among his people' in early March by the parish priest of Upton.

Refs: **19** (2–13).

Aldith (*fl.* 1138) (fict.). **Novels:** '"Very pretty, not very tall, round and fair, with a lot of yellow hair, and black eyes. It makes a great effect, yellow hair and black eyes."' A free woman and the maidservant of Gervase and Richildis BONEL, Aldith came to SHREWSBURY from the manor of MALLILIE with her lord and lady in December 1138. She was attracted to Bonel's manservant, AELFRIC, but his villein status prevented him from declaring himself to her. However, when the new lord of Mallilie, Edwin GURNEY, set Aelfric free, they were able to marry.

Refs: **3** (1–5, 9–11).

Aldwin (*c.*1094–1143) (fict.). **Novels:** 'Aldwin had entered the household in Girard's service, and stepped into Elave's shoes when William took his own boy with him on pilgrimage. A man past forty at that time, barely literate but quick with numbers as a gift of nature, Aldwin looked much the same now at nearing fifty, but that his hair had rather more grey in it, and was thinning on the crown. He had had to work hard to earn his place and hold it, and his long face had set into defensive lines of effort and anxiety.' This clerk in the LYTHWOOD household was not 'a man who had many friends, nor one of any great resolution of mind'. In June 1143, when ELAVE returned to SHREWSBURY after a seven-year absence, Aldwin feared that 'he might be elbowed out of office'. Unaware that Elave had no intention of displacing him, and valuing 'himself so low he expected as low a regard from everyone else', Aldwin attempted to remove his seeming rival by going to SHREWSBURY ABBEY and denouncing him 'for abominable heresies'. As soon as he realised that Elave was no threat, Aldwin set out for the abbey intent on trying to undo what he had done, but was knifed in the back by Jevan of LYTHWOOD before he reached the gates. His corpse was found in the SEVERN by CADFAEL. Aldwin was buried on 26 June 1143 in the graveyard of ST ALKMUND'S CHURCH, after his parish priest, Father ELIAS, had finally established that he had died penitent.

Refs: **16** (3–15).

Alexandria (Egypt). Situated on the Mediterranean Sea at the extreme north-western tip of the Nile Delta some 114 miles north-west of Cairo, Alexandria was once the greatest city of the ancient world. It was founded by Alexander the Great in 332 BC. It is reputed that in AD 45 St Mark made his first convert to Christianity in the city, which played a major part in the theological disputes over the nature of Christ's divinity that divided the early Christian church.

Novels: ELAVE heard tell that, in Alexandria, there was once a father of the Christian Church (ORIGEN) who held 'that in the end everyone would find salvation. Even the fallen angels would return to their fealty, even the devil would repent and make his way back to God.'

Refs: **1** (2, 4, 5).

Alice (*fl.* 1140) (fict.). **Novels:** Cousin of Edward REDE. In the spring of 1140, Alice looked after Edward's mother while he went to visit his father, William REDE, in the infirmary of SHREWSBURY ABBEY.

Refs: **RB** (3).

Alison (*fl.* 1142) (fict.). **Novels:** 'A plump, comfortable figure of a woman with some worn traces still of the good looks she had handed on to her son.' Mother of BERTRED, the widow Alison cooked for the VESTIER family and its workers. On the evening of 19 June 1142 her son promised to make her more than a servant in the house, a '"gentlewoman, an honoured dowager!"' The next day Bertred was found drowned in the SEVERN. Had she been asked, Alison could have told the sheriff, Hugh BERINGAR, that Miles COLIAR had given Bertred the boots worn by the murderer of Brother ELURIC. With the death of her son, Alison was left without anyone to look after her. Judith PERLE, however, promised to provide for her.

Refs: **13** (7, 9, 10, 12–14).

Alkington (Shropshire, England). DB – Alchetune: in HODNET Hundred; a holding of William Pantulf, under Roger de MONTGOMERY. A small hamlet close to the Cheshire border, some 17 miles north-east of SHREWSBURY and 3 miles south-west of WHITCHURCH.

Novels: 'The manor of Alkington lay on the edge of this wilderness of dark-brown pools and quaking mosses and tangled bush . . . It was sadly run down from its former value, its ploughlands shrunken.' In October 1140 Hugh BERINGAR visited Alkington in his search for the missing Peter CLEMENCE.

Refs: **8** (3).

Alps (Austria, Slovenia, Germany, Italy, Switzerland and France). The great mountain system of southern and central Europe, they cover all of Switzerland, most of Austria, Slovenia and parts of Germany, Italy and France. The highest peak is Mont Blanc.

Novels: On his way to the east, CADFAEL had observed the blue flowers of gentians (*gentiana verna*) 'in the mountains of southern France'. ALARD, the vagabond clerk turned soldier, claimed that he had seen 'Italy as far south as ROME, served once for a time under the Count [ROBERT] of Flanders, crossed the mountains into Spain, never abiding anywhere for long.'

Refs: **10** (8); **19** (1); **RB** (1).

Ambrose, Brother (*fl.* 1141) (fict.). **Novels:** 'No one knew the abbey rolls as Brother Ambrose did. He had been clerk to Brother MATTHEW, the cellarer, for four years, during which time fresh grants to the abbey had been flooding in richly . . . and there was no one who could match him at putting a finger on the slippery tenant or the field-lawyer, or the householder who had always three good stories to account for his inability to pay.' Brother Ambrose of SHREWSBURY ABBEY fell ill 'with a raging quinsy' in the spring of 1140, 'just a few days before the yearly rents were due for collection'. Consequently, the necessary rolls were left 'uncopied, and the new entries still to be made'. In December 1141 Brother Ambrose was the almoner, 'whose office brought him into contact with the poorest of the poor' throughout the ABBEY FOREGATE.

Refs: **12** (1, 5); **17** (1); **RB** (3).

Ambrosius, Father (*fl.* 1143) (fict.). **Novels:** 'A rare man and a scholar . . . who studied some years in Brittany.' Parish priest at WITHINGTON, he was the friend of Brother ANSELM.

Refs: **17** (10).

Amicia (*fl.* 1120), Countess of Leicester (hist.). The wife of Robert de BEAUMONT (the younger) and daughter of Ralph de Wader, Earl of Norfolk, by Emma, daughter of William Fitz-Osbern, Earl of Norfolk. For her dowry, she brought Robert the fief of BRETEUIL.

Novels: Robert Beaumont (the younger) was 'lord of half Leicestershire, a good slice of Warwickshire and NORTHAMPTON, and a large honour in NORMANDY brought to him by his marriage with the heiress of Breteuil.' The Countess of Leicester remained in Leicester while Robert went to HUNCOTE, from where he journeyed to SHREWSBURY to investigate the discovery of St WINIFRED's reliquary within his woodlands.

Refs: **19** (4, 11).

Anarawd ap Griffith (d. 1143), Prince of Deheubarth (hist.). Also called Anarawd ap Gruffudd ap Rhys. Eldest son of Griffith ap Rhys and brother of Cadell (d. 1175), Maredudd (d. 1155) and Rhys (d. 1197), Anarawd was either betrothed or married to OWAIN GWYNEDD's daughter (or possibly his niece). In 1137 he killed Letard Little King in a campaign against Flemish settlers in the cantref of Rhos. He was ambushed and killed himself in 1143 by followers of CADWALADR. Anarawd was described in the *Brut y Tywysogyon* as 'the hope and glory of the men of DEHEUBARTH'. His son, Einon, died in 1163.

Novels: 'Nor could all these lost this year call into life again Anarawd, dead last year in the south, at

Cadwaladr's instigation, if not at his hands.' Prince of Deheubarth, Anarawd was betrothed to OWAIN GWYNEDD's daughter. He was ambushed and killed in 1143 on Cadwaladr's orders. The sword stroke that took his life also cut off Cuhelyn ab EINION's left arm.

Refs: **18** (1–3, 11, 14).

Andover (Hampshire, England). Originally named after the river (now called Anton), on which the present town stands, Andover is situated about 12 miles north-west of WINCHESTER. An ancient town, it was a municipal borough under John and a centre for the medieval wool trade.

Novels: When Julian CRUCE of LAI rode south in 1138, under the pretext of joining the convent at WHERWELL, she stayed overnight at Andover in a lodging with 'a merchant's household'. It was during the three- or four-mile ride between Andover and Wherwell that she vanished with her valuables. In August 1141 a beggar, 'able-bodied but getting old', arrived at the Hospital of ST GILES, SHREWSBURY, and stayed overnight to rest. He came from the south, from the STACEYS, near Andover, and brought the first news that Winchester was in flames. In the same month Nicholas HARNAGE came to Shrewsbury from Andover, where his troops had 'burned the town'. During his visit to SHREWSBURY ABBEY to see Brother HUMILIS, Harnage assured the monk that his command could do very well without him for a while: '"I've left them snug enough, encamped near Andover, living off the land, and my sergeants in charge."'

Refs: **11** (1, 3–8, 11).

Andrew, Brother (*fl.* 1138) (fict.). **Novels:** A monk of SHREWSBURY ABBEY, he took the readings in chapter sometime in December 1138.

Refs: **3** (6).

Andrew, Father (*fl.* 1142) (fict.). **Novels:** The parish priest of EATON, he buried Richard LUDEL (the elder) in Eaton churchyard in October 1142. Richard's mother, Dame Dionisia LUDEL, sent the priest to SHREWSBURY ABBEY to deliver 'a gift of money to pay for Masses in the Lady Chapel for her son's soul'. Father Andrew willingly allowed Hugh BERINGAR and his men to search his house and went with them round the manor at Eaton looking for young Richard LUDEL, who had been abducted. The priest, who was 'an honest man', was therefore not party to Dionisia's plans to marry young Richard against his wishes to Hiltrude ASTLEY.

Refs: **14** (1, 2, 8, 10).

Andrew the Apostle, Saint (d. *c.*60) (hist.) (f.d. 30 November). A fisherman of Bethsaida in Galilee and elder brother of St PETER, Andrew was a disciple of St JOHN THE BAPTIST before becoming an apostle of Christ. Although he is mentioned in the Gospels, notably in relation to the feeding of the 5,000, accounts of his later life are unreliable. He is said to have preached in Asia Minor and Greece, where he is supposed to have been crucified at Patras. He is the patron saint of Scotland, Russia and Greece.

Novels: 'Young Brother FRANCIS . . . fumbled a pious commentary on the ministry of St Andrew the Apostle, whose day was just past.'

Refs: **3** (1).

Angers (France). An ancient town which pre-dated the Romans, it was formerly the capital of ANJOU.

Angers, Sir Laurence d' (*fl.* 1139) (fict.). **Novels:** Guardian and uncle of the orphans Yves and Ermina HUGONIN, this 'knight of Angevin blood' arrived in England in November 1139, having 'long been overseas in the HOLY LAND'. A 'Crusader of unblemished repute', a baron of Gloucestershire and loyal 'liegeman to the Empress', he joined MAUD and her forces at GLOUCESTER after her soldiers had attacked and ransacked the city of WORCESTER, and bore 'no blame for it, as he took no part in it'. From Gloucester, d'Angers requested the permission of Gilbert PRESTCOTE, Sheriff of Shropshire, to make a search in his county for the Hugonin orphans, who had gone missing after the 'Worcester panic'. When it was refused, d'Angers secretly sent Olivier de BRETAGNE into STEPHEN's territory to find his nephew and niece, and escort them safely back to him in Gloucester. Rainald BOSSARD was in the following of Laurence d'Angers. In September 1141 d'Angers was still in Gloucester. Still serving Maud, d'Angers was with his 'force' in DEVIZES in November 1145. From there he made widespread enquiries about the missing Olivier de Bretagne, but without result.

Refs: **6** (1, 3, 5–6, 8–9, 12–13, 15); **10** (2, 7–8, 10, 15–16); **11** (5); **20** (1–3, 6, 9–10).

Angharad (1093–1127) (fict.). **Novels:** Welsh maidservant at the manor of MALLILIE, she was the daughter of Ifor ap MORGAN and his wife, MARARED, and the niece of Brother RHYS. Angharad was the mother of Gervase BONEL's illegitimate child, MEURIG.

Refs: **3** (1, 7–9).

Angharad (d. 1162) (hist.). She was the blonde wife of GRIFFITH AP CYNAN and the mother of Cadwallon, OWAIN GWYNEDD and CADWALADR. Angharad was the daughter of Owain ab Edwin, a chieftain of eastern Gwynedd. She married Griffith in *c.* 1095: and, in addition to their three sons, had two daughters by him: Gwenllian and Susanna (who married MADOG AP MEREDITH). It is not clear whether Griffith's three other daughters, MARARED, RANNILT and ANNEST, were by her.

Refs: **9** (3); **18** (2).

Anglesey or Ynys Mon (Gwynedd, Wales). A large island, it is separated from the north-west mainland of Wales by the Menai Strait. There are numerous prehistoric remains on the island and, before the arrival of the Romans, it was a major centre of the Druids: the Celtic prophets and mystics of Welsh and Irish legend. In contrast to the rest of Gwynedd, Anglesey is relatively flat and extremely fertile and, during medieval times, the area was important as a grain-growing centre. Edward I succeeded in his conquest of Wales in the 13th C. by first capturing the island and, thereby, starving the mainland of cereals. Aberffraw, situated in the south-west, was the capital of the Princes of Gwynedd from the 7th to the 13th C. Anglesey's largest town is CAERGYBI (or Holyhead).

Novels: 'The coast of Anglesey stretched out northward, to end in the tiny island of YNYS LANOG.' In 1141 it was CIARAN's avowed intention to walk barefoot to BANGOR, 'to the bishop there, who would see me to Caergybi in Anglesey, and have me put aboard a ship for DUBLIN'. In 1144, Ieuan ab IFOR held lands on the island. The rich, fertile plain of Anglesey was 'the cornfield of Wales'.

Refs: **10** (14); **18** (2–4, 6–8, 10–11, 14).

Anjou (France). The ancient district of western France that gave its name to the Angevin empire. Its capital was ANGERS and, during medieval times, the region was ruled by the powerful counts of Anjou, including FULK (1092–1143) and GEOFFREY (1113–51).

Novels: There are several mentions of Anjou, such as sending the boy Henry Plantagenet (HENRY II) back there. The references to Anjou are not always complimentary: Hugh BERINGAR called Ninian BACHILER one of those '"imps of Anjou"'.

Refs: **6** (1, 4, 11); **12** (4, 6, 10); **14** (1); **15** (1); **19** (11); **20** (3–4, 13); **RB** (1).

Anjou, Countess of. See MAUD, Empress.

Anjou, Count of. See GEOFFREY, Count of Anjou.

Annest (*fl.* 1137) (fict.). **Novels:** 'Her hair a great, heavy braid over her shoulder, the colour of polished oak, a light silken brown, even with silvery dashes in it like the grain of oak.' Brother JOHN, when he arrived at GWYTHERIN with Prior ROBERT's party in May 1137, immediately noticed the Welsh girl, Annest. She was SIONED's tire-woman or waiting-woman and the niece of BENED THE SMITH, in whose loft John was lodged. On her frequent visits to her uncle's house, she and John got to know one another. When John was put under nominal captivity at RHISIART's holding, Annest tried to teach him Welsh and, while they were alone together, John forgot his 'too-hasty' vows and kissed her. They fell in love and when OWAIN GWYNEDD's bailiff of RHOS, Griffith ap RHYS, came to arrest John, Annest helped him slip away. More than two years later, in June 1139, Bened arrived at SHREWSBURY ABBEY and informed CADFAEL that Annest and John had married late in 1137, some eighteen months earlier. He also reported that Annest was pregnant.

Refs: **1** (2–5, 7–9, 11–12); **12** (13).

Annet (*fl.* 1142) (fict.). **Novels:** 'She was small but sturdy, and very trimly made, with a straight blue gaze, the fresh colouring of a wild rose, and smoothly-braided hair of a light brown sheen like the grain of polished oak.' Daughter of EILMUND THE FORESTER, Annet lived with her father in a small cottage in the heart of EYTON FOREST, some 6 miles south-east of SHREWSBURY. She first met HYACINTH in October 1142, after he had brought her injured father home. They were immediately attracted to each other. When his master, Drogo BOSIET, came looking for him, Annet hid the runaway villein and they became lovers. In November, Hyacinth declared that, once he had gained his freedom, he would get work in Shrewsbury, and make Annet his wife.

Refs: **14** (3–6, 8–10, 12–13).

Anselm, Brother (b. 1090) (fict.). **Novels:** 'The precentor, [of SHREWSBURY ABBEY] who also presided over the library, was ten years younger than CADFAEL, a vague, unworldly man except where his personal enthusiasms were concerned, but alert and subtle enough in anything that concerned books, music or the instruments that make music, best of all the most perfect, the human voice. The blue eyes that peered out beneath his bushy brown eyebrows and shock of shaggy brown hair might be short-sighted, but they missed very little that went on, and had a tolerant twinkle for fallible human creatures and their failings, especially among the young.' 'And Brother Anselm the precentor, who acknowledged few disruptions other than a note off-key, or a sore throat among his best voices, accepted all other events with utter serenity, assumed the best, wished all men well, and gave over worrying.' Brother Anselm agreed to mend LILIWIN's broken rebec in May 1140 (see Brother ANSELM'S WORKSHOP). In March 1141 the precentor compiled 'the sequence of music for the burial of Gilbert PRESTCOTE' (the elder). Even as 'a man past fifty, who spoke in a round, human voice deeper than most', Anselm could 'sing at will' in the upper register of 'the most perfect of boy cantors'. In June 1143, Cadfael suggested that FORTUNATA show her box to Anselm: '"He's well versed in all the crafts, and may be able to say where it came from, and how old it is."' Anselm was an 'excellent precentor'.

Refs: **1** (10); **3** (1); **7** (1, 3–7, 9, 11, 14); **9** (8); **10** (1, 8–10); **11** (2, 9); **12** (4, 8, 10); **13** (1–2 ,4–6, 12); **14** (2, 5); **15** (1, 14); **16** (5–7, 9–13, 15); **17** (1, 10–11); **19** (1–2, 11); **20** (2).

Anselm, Lay Brother (b. *c.* 1083) (fict.). **Novels:** 'huge and muscular, like an oak of his own fifty-five years.' In August 1138 this giant of a man looked after the SHREWSBURY ABBEY grange in the LONG FOREST,

A

beyond PULLEY, with Lay Brother LOUIS. He helped Godith and Torold BLUND get safely away with William FITZALAN's treasury.

Refs: **2** (7, 9–10).

Anselm, Saint (*c.*1033–1109), Archbishop of Canterbury (hist.) (f.d. 21 April). Born at Aosta in northern Italy, Anselm was the son of a Lombard nobleman with whom he quarrelled as a young man. In *c.*1059 he entered the monastery at Bec in NORMANDY where he became a pupil, disciple and friend of LANFRANC, whom he eventually succeeded as prior. He was elected abbot of Bec in 1078, after the death of the founder, Abbot Herluin. In 1093, four years after the death of Lanfranc, Archbishop of Canterbury, Anselm reluctantly accepted the appointment to his former teacher's vacant see. From then on he became involved in dissensions, first with WILLIAM II and then with HENRY I, over the interference of the crown in affairs of the church. Attempts by William II to get rid of the archbishop resulted in Anselm going to ROME in 1097, where he remained in exile for three years, returning to England when Henry I came to the throne in 1100. Quarrelling with the king over the question of investitures, Anselm found himself in exile abroad for a second time from 1103 to 1106–7, when a compromise was reached. Thereafter, he remained in England, dying at Canterbury. He wrote many theological and philosophical works including the *Monologion*, *Proslogion* and *Cur Deus Homo*.

Novels: 'Brother ELURIC was a child of the cloister, not long a full brother, and entrusted with his particular charge by reason of his undoubted deserving, tempered by the reserve that was felt about admitting child oblates to full office, at least until they had been mature for a number of years. An unreasonable reserve. CADFAEL had always felt, seeing that the child oblates were regarded as the perfect innocents, equivalent to the angels, while the conversi, those who came voluntarily and in maturity to the monastic life, were the fighting saints, those who had endured and mastered their imperfections. So Saint Anselm had classified them, and ordered them never to attempt reciprocal reproaches, never to feel envy. But still the conversi were preferred for the responsible offices, perhaps as having experience of the deceits and complexities and temptations of the world around them. But the care of an altar, its light, its draperies, the special prayers belonging to it, this could well be the charge of an innocent.'

Refs: **13** (1).

(Brother) Anselm's Workshop (Shrewsbury Abbey, Shropshire) (fict.). Although it never existed, Brother ANSELM's Workshop was in a corner carrel of the north walk of the cloister. Although the cloisters have not survived, a few small arches can be found on the south side of the abbey. It is thought that these Norman remains may have formerly housed monastic cupboards.

Novels: Brother Anselm 'kept the manuscripts of his music in neat and loving store' in his workshop. In May 1140 he agreed to mend LILIWIN's broken rebec: '"Come," said Brother Anselm, taking him firmly by the arm, "I will show you my workshop and you and I between us, after High Mass, will try what can best be done for this rebec of yours. I shall need a helper to tend my resins and gums. But this will be slow and careful work, mind, and matter for prayer, not to be hastened for any cause. Music is study for a lifetime, son – a lifetime however long."'

Refs: **7** (4); **11** (2); **16** (11); **19** (2).

Antioch (Turkey). A thriving city and trading centre in ancient SYRIA, it was founded in 300 BC. One of the earliest centres of Christianity, Antioch was the headquarters of the missionary St PAUL THE APOSTLE in about AD 47–55. The city was almost destroyed by a series of earthquakes during the 6th C. and was also sacked by the Persians. In the 7th C., when Syria was overrun by the Muslims, Antioch declined. Taken by the Byzantines in 969 and the Seljuk Turks in 1084, it was captured by the crusaders in 1098. It remained in Christian hands until the Mamluk Turks took the city in 1268. Now in Turkey, Antioch is situated near the mouth of the Orontes river on the Mediterranean Sea, nearly 60 miles west of Aleppo, Syria.

Novels: CADFAEL 'had good cause to remember Antioch, for it was there he had begun and ended his long career as a crusader, and his love affair with PALESTINE, that lovely inhospitable, cruel land of gold and sand and drought'. Cadfael was with GODFREY OF BOUILLON at Antioch, when the Saracens surrendered it in 1098. He also met MARIAM in the city, and stayed there for a whole year before moving on to JERUSALEM in 1099. He returned to Antioch and Mariam in *c.*1113. Unbeknown to him, when he finally left, Mariam was pregnant, and in 1113 his son, Olivier de BRETAGNE, was born. Mariam lived and died in Antioch.

Refs: **1** (1); **6** (1, 8, 15); **10** (7); **16** (2); **20** (1–2, 8); **RB** (1).

Antwerp (Belgium). The main seaport of Belgium, Antwerp (founded in the 8th C.) is situated at the mouth of the River Scheldt some 55 miles from the North Sea. One of the largest and busiest ports in the world, it was a busy trade and shipping centre even in the Middle Ages.

Novels: '"In Antwerp," said Canon GERBERT, "a certain TACHELM has drawn deluded thousands after him to raid churches and tear down their ornaments."'

Refs: **16** (5).

Apollo (myth.). In Greek mythology, he loved HYACINTH. Son of Zeus and Leto, Apollo was the god of archery, prophecy, music, medicine, poetry, and the sun. He was represented as the perfect embodiment of youthful manhood.

Refs: **14** (3).

Arald the Groom (b. *c.*1120) (fict.). **Novels:** 'A fresh-faced country youth', the young groom of Ivo CORBIÈRE came to SHREWSBURY on 30 July 1139. He went to STANTON COBBOLD with Corbière, Turstan FOWLER and Emma Vernold (see CORVISER) on 4 August. It was thought unlikely that Arald was involved in Corbière's and Fowler's crimes.

Refs: **4** (1:1, 2:2, 3:4–5, 4:1–2).

Arfon (Gwynedd, Wales). The medieval Welsh cantref of Arfon in ancient Gwynedd Uch Conwy (or Gwynedd Above Conwy) lay on the mainland opposite ANGLESEY, and included BANGOR, BEDDGELERT and CLYNNOG. It was bounded by the cantrefs of ARLLECHWEDD and Lleyn, and the commotes of Nant Conwy, Ardudwy and Eifionydd.

Novels: 'They had their first snow before us, up there in Arfon, and there was no chance of getting a messenger through overland.'

Refs: **3** (11); **18** (1, 5–6, 10, 14).

Arianna (*fl.* 1098) (fict.). **Novels:** CADFAEL met this Greek boat-girl in his roving youth. In 1138 he was reminded of her by Godith Adeney (see BLUND): 'Long ago, skirts kilted above the knee, short hair a cloud of curls, leaning on her long oar and calling across the water to him.'

Refs: **1** (1, 9); **2** (6); **3** (5).

Arllechwedd (Gwynedd, Wales). This medieval Welsh cantref lay in the north-eastern corner of ancient Gwynedd Uch Conwy (or Gwynedd Above Conwy). It was subdivided into two commotes, Arllechwedd Uchaf (or Upper) and Arllechwedd Isaf (or Lower), and was associated with the commote of Nant Conwy. Arllechwedd was bounded by the River CONWAY, by the Irish Sea, by ARFON, and beyond Nant Conwy, by the commote of Ardudwy. The royal court of Arllechwedd was at 'ABER of the White Shells' (or Abergwyngregin). The church had little influence in Arllechwedd until the foundation of the Cistercian abbey at Aberconwy (see CONWY) in 1186. There was no important 'clas' within its bounds. However, the church of St Tudclyd at Penmachno (see PENMACHMO), founded in the 5th or 6th C., was probably the one of most repute.

Novels: In May 1144 at Aber, on hearing of the approach of a great fleet of Danish ships, OWAIN

GWYNEDD sent couriers to raise a Welsh fighting force: '"Six couriers I want, one to go before us now, the others to carry my summons through the rest of Arlechwedd [sic] and Arfon."'

Refs: **18** (5).

Arnald, Master (*fl.* 1140) (fict.). **Novels:** Master Arnald of SHREWSBURY was Walter AURIFABER's own physician, doctoring the goldsmith in May 1140 after he had been attacked and robbed.

Refs: **7** (2).

Arnald the Fishmonger (*fl.* 1142) (fict.). **Novels:** Arnald lived 'under the WYLE' at SHREWSBURY.

Refs: **13** (7).

Arnulf the Chamberlain (b. *c.*1075) (fict.). **Novels:** 'A man well past sixty, grey-haired and staid, with illusionless eyes and the withdrawn, resigned dignity of most old servants.' Huon de DOMVILLE's chamberlain came to SHREWSBURY in October 1139 for his lord's marriage to Iveta de Massard (see LUCY). He informed CADFAEL that his master had a permanent mistress, Avice of Thornbury (see MAGDALEN, Sister).

Refs: **5** (1, 5, 7).

Arnulf the Steward (*fl.* 1141) (fict.). **Novels:** 'A grey elder dried and tanned like old leather, but very agile and sinewy', he was the Saxon steward of Reginald CRUCE, Lord of the manor of LAI, and had previously served Reginald's father, Humphrey.

Refs: **11** (7).

Arundel (West Sussex, England). Situated in the valley of the River Arun, where it had cut a gap in the SOUTH DOWNS, and some 3 miles north of Littlehampton, Arundel grew up on the slope between the river and the castle. Records confirm that the town was of some importance by the 9th C. After the Norman Conquest, it became a major administrative centre for Sussex. It was once a river port and as such was used by ROBERT of Gloucester and the Empress MAUD, during their war with King STEPHEN.

Novels: 'The Empress Maud had landed at Arundel . . . with her half-brother ROBERT, Earl of Gloucester, and a hundred and forty knights, and through the misplaced generosity of the king, or the dishonest advice of some of his false friends, had been allowed to reach BRISTOL, where her cause was impregnably installed already.'

Refs: **4** (5:3, 5:6); **5** (1); **12** (1); **14** (1).

Arundel Castle (West Sussex, England). Although there had been an earlier fortification on the site – erected to protect a gap in the SOUTH DOWNS formed by the River Arun – the first stone castle was built by Roger de MONTGOMERY soon after the Norman Conquest. Built of stone and flint, it was destroyed by the Parliamentarians during the English Civil War and fell into ruin. Later it was restored and twice almost completely rebuilt. The castle is today the ancestral home of the dukes of Norfolk.

Novels: On 30 September 1139 'the Empress MAUD and her half-brother ROBERT of Gloucester landed near ARUNDEL and entered into the castle there.'

Refs: **4** (5:6).

Arwystli (Powys, Wales). The medieval Welsh cantref of Arwystli in ancient Powys Wenwynwyn lay in the centre of Wales, and included Talgarth (near Trefeglwys), Carno, Caersws, Llandinam and Llangurig. The cantref itself was divided into two commotes: Arwystli Uwch Coed and Arwystli Is Coed. It was bounded by the commotes of Ceri, Gwerthrynion, Cymwd Deuddwr, Mefenydd, Creuddyn, Perfedd, Cyfeiliog, and Caereinion; and the two cantrefs of MAELIENYDD and Cydewain. The source of the River SEVERN lay in the mountains just inside Arwystli's western border with CEREDIGION.

Novels: OWAIN GWYNEDD's wife, GWLADUS, was the daughter of LLYWARCH AP TRAHAEARN, Prince of Arwystli.

Refs: **1** (4).

Arwystli, Prince of. See LLYWARCH AP TRAHAEARN, Prince of Arwystli.

Ascalon (Israel). Situated on the Mediterranean coast, just over a mile to the south-west of today's modern city of Ashquelon (or Ashkelon) and 40 miles east of JERUSALEM, Ascalon dates back to at least 2000 BC. On 19 August 1099, during the First Crusade, the Christians under GODFREY OF BOUILLON managed to take the city from the Arabs, who had captured it in 636. But victory was short-lived, and it was not until 1153, after a long struggle, that it was finally conquered. From then until 1191, when it was taken by Saladin, it was one of the crusaders' major ports and strongholds in the HOLY LAND. By the end of the 13th C. the inhabitants had gone and the city was in ruins. The site was excavated in the early 1920s.

Novels: CADFAEL 'had seen battles, too in his time in the world, as far afield as ACRE, and Ascalon and Jerusalem in the First Crusade'. 'Guimar de MASSARD, wounded and captive after Ascalon, had learned from the doctors who attended him in captivity that he was already a leper.'

Refs: **5** (1–2, 11).

Aspley (Shropshire, England) (fict.). Although it never existed, the manor of Aspley was situated some 6 miles south-east of SHREWSBURY, 'towards the fringes of the LONG FOREST' and to the west of the old Roman road. It stood in the general location of Pitchford Hall, near the village of Pitchford.

Novels: The manors of Aspley, LINDE and FORIET grew '"from what began as one assart. They all held from the great earl [Roger de MONTGOMERY], they all hold from the crown now."' On 8 September 1140 Peter CLEMENCE visited Aspley on his way to CHESTER.

Refs: **8** (1, 3–13).

Aspley, Avota (d. 1138) (fict.). **Novels:** The Norman wife of Leoric ASPLEY, and the mother of Nigel and Meriet ASPLEY. On her marriage she brought her husband a manor near NEWARK. Peter CLEMENCE was the son of one of her cousins.

Refs: **8** (1, 3, 6, 10).

Aspley, Leoric (b. *c.*1085) (fict.). **Novels:** Leoric came from 'a family older than ETHELRED'. His '"grandsire was Saxon to the finger-ends, but a solid man, and Earl Roger [de MONTGOMERY] took him into favour and left him his land. They're Saxon still, but they'd taken his salt, and were loyal to it and went with the earldom when it came to the crown. This lord took a Norman wife and she brought him a manor somewhere to the north, beyond NOTTINGHAM, but ASPLEY is still the head of his honour . . . His reputation and word stand high."' Saxon husband of Avota and father of Nigel and Meriet ASPLEY, Leoric was also the legal guardian of the orphan, Isouda FORIET. He was the lord of two manors, ASPLEY and one near NEWARK. In 1140, misguidedly believing that Meriet had murdered Peter CLEMENCE and to protect his ancient honour, Leoric buried the body within a charcoal-burner's stack in the LONG FOREST and fired it. He also forced Meriet to take the cowl and escorted him personally to SHREWSBURY ABBEY. The dead man's horse was let loose in the mosses near WHITCHURCH. Discovering his son's innocence, Leoric confessed his part to Abbot RADULFUS and was given absolution. To make part amends, he bequeathed his manor at Aspley to Meriet, and promised to pay whatever monies were needed for Brother MARK to become a priest.

Refs: **8** (1–13); **10** (10).

Aspley, Meriet (b. 1121) (fict.). Also known as the Devil's Novice. **Novels:** '"Meriet's father took precious little pleasure in anything Meriet ever did, and Meriet took precious little pains to please him. They waged one long battle. And yet I dare swear they loved each other as well as most fathers and sons do."' Younger son of Leoric and Avota ASPLEY, Meriet idolised his elder brother, Nigel ASPLEY, and believed himself to be in love with his brother's fiancée, Roswitha Linde (see ASPLEY). Jealous of his father's affections for Nigel, Meriet rebelled. On 9 September 1140 he found a 'busy and bloodied' Nigel over the body of Peter CLEMENCE. Convinced that his brother had murdered the envoy, Meriet told Nigel to go away while he disposed of the body. Leoric discovered Meriet trying to drag the dead man into cover and, believing that he was guilty of the murder, forced his son to take the cowl. Meriet entered SHREWSBURY ABBEY as a novice a week or so later, ostensibly 'at his own earnest wish'. Tormented by nightmares, Meriet was 'feared by his fellows for bringing a demon into the abbey with him', and was called the Devil's Novice. In October, Meriet was questioned by Canon ELUARD OF WINCHESTER about the disappearance of Clemence. Brother JEROME found a lock of Roswitha's red hair in the novice's bed and, after he had set it alight, Meriet attacked him. The penalty for assaulting a priest was the lash and some ten days in solitary confinement. After completing his penance, Meriet went to help Brother MARK tend the sick at the Hospital of ST GILES. On an expedition into the LONG FOREST to collect wood, Meriet innocently led MARK to the partly fired charcoal-burner's hearth where his father had hidden the body of CLEMENCE. Troubled by further bad dreams, Meriet was startled awake by MARK while he was sleep-walking and fell from the loft of the barn, injuring his head and twisting his right foot badly. Events confirmed his innocence and he was reconciled with his repentant father. Meriet returned home at the end of December 1140 and was made the heir to the manor of ASPLEY. Although he did not know it at the time, Isouda FORIET was determined to make him her husband and the lord of her inheritance at FORIET.

Refs: **8** (1–13).

Aspley, Nigel (b. 1115) (fict.). **Novels:** 'Lissome and light-footed with youth, and the light brown hair and ruddy, outdoor skin of the Saxon. Such a son as any man might rejoice in. Healthy from birth, as like as not, growing and flourishing like a hearty plant, with every promise of full harvest.' Elder and favourite son of Leoric and Avota ASPLEY and brother of Meriet ASPLEY, Nigel was heir to the ASPLEY estates. In midsummer 1140, accompanied by Janyn LINDE, he visited his father's northern manor near NEWARK, which Leoric had promised to give him to manage after his marriage to Roswitha Linde (see ASPLEY). While there, Janyn persuaded him to join the rebellion plotted by William of ROUMARE. When Peter CLEMENCE arrived at Aspley on 8 September 1140, Nigel asked Janyn to send a rider north to CHESTER to warn Roumare of the envoy's impending arrival. To Nigel's horror, Janyn murdered Clemence shortly after he had left Aspley. Nigel was discovered by Meriet, 'busy and bloodied', over the dead body. Despite his pleas of innocence, Meriet told him to wash off the blood, go back to Roswitha and remain at LINDE while he tried to dispose of the body. Nigel married Roswitha on 21 December 1140 and, immediately after the ceremony, before he could be arrested, fled north. South-west of STAFFORD, he was knifed from behind by Janyn and left to die. Found by the sheriff's men, he was taken back to SHREWSBURY where he confessed to his part in the crime. Instead of bringing him to trial, Hugh BERINGAR, the deputy sheriff, set him free. Unable to go north to the Aspley manor near Newark as planned, Nigel went with Roswitha to the manor of Linde, which he eventually inherited through his marriage. In November 1143 Nigel was among the company of men supplied by Hugh Beringar to help STEPHEN oust Geoffrey de MANDEVILLE's 'marauders' from their stronghold in the FENS.

Refs: **8** (1, 3–8, 10–13); **17** (9).

Aspley, Roswitha (née Linde) (b. 1118) (fict.). **Novels:** 'The image of her brother, but everything that in him was comely and attractive was in her polished into beauty. She had the same softly rounded, oval face, but refined almost into translucence, and the same clear blue eyes, but a shade darker and fringed with auburn lashes . . . and reddish gold hair, a thick coil of it, and curls escaping on either side of her temples.' Daughter of Wulfric LINDE and the twin sister of Janyn LINDE, Roswitha flirted with Peter CLEMENCE, when he stayed overnight at the ASPLEY manor on 8 September 1140, much to the annoyance of her fiancé, Nigel ASPLEY. On the eve of her wedding, the murdered CLEMENCE's ancient ring-brooch was found by Isouda FORIET in Roswitha's possession. She married Nigel on 21 December 1140 at the high altar of SHREWSBURY ABBEY. Reunited with her husband, after his capture near STAFFORD, they inherited her dispossessed brother's manor of LINDE.

Refs: **8** (3–6, 10–13).

Astley, Sir Fulke (b. *c.*1094) (fict.). **Novels:** A 'gross, self-important man in his late forties, running to fat, ponderous of movement'. Father of Hiltrude ASTLEY and the lord of the manors of LEIGHTON and WROXETER, he attended the funeral of his neighbour, Richard LUDEL the elder, on 20 October 1142. Astley conspired with Dame Dionisia LUDEL to abduct young Richard LUDEL, and force him into marriage with Hiltrude. When Richard escaped from Leighton, Astley followed in hot pursuit, catching up with him at the gates of SHREWSBURY ABBEY. He was thwarted from taking the fugitive back to his manor by Abbot RADULFUS and Hugh BERINGAR. Astley was present when Cuthred (see BOURCHIER, Renaud) was found dead in his hermitage in November 1142. When it was revealed that Cuthred was not a priest and that the marriage of Hiltrude and Richard was invalid, Astley protested vehemently. But, in the end, it was a truth that he had to accept.

Refs: **14** (1–2, 8, 10–13).

Astley, Hiltrude (b. *c.*1120) (fict.). **Novels:** 'She had a clear, pale skin and large, guarded brown eyes, and if her hair was straight and of a mousey brown colour, she had a great mass of it, plaited in a thick braid that hung to her waist. She did not look ill-natured, but she did look bitterly resigned and wretched.' Daughter of Sir Fulke ASTLEY, Hiltrude was heiress to both the manors of LEIGHTON and WROXETER. Although she wanted EVRARD, her father's steward, she was forced to marry young Richard LUDEL in November 1142. The marriage, however, was proved invalid when Cuthred, who performed the ceremony, was found not to be a priest (see BOURCHIER, Renaud). She helped Richard escape from Leighton.

Refs: **14** (1–3, 10–13).

Aston (Shropshire, England). DB – Estune: in HODNET Hundred; a holding of William Pantulf under Roger de MONTGOMERY. Aston is a hamlet on the River RODEN, some 10 miles north-east of SHREWSBURY and 1 mile east of WEM.

Refs: **4** (1:1).

Aston, Reginald of (*fl.* 1139) (fict.). **Novels:** This SHREWSBURY silversmith, who was a man of substance, was 'well known' to CADFAEL. On 30 July 1139 he was among the delegation from the Guild Merchant who requested from Abbot RADULFUS a percentage of the tolls from the SHREWSBURY ABBEY fair to help pay for repairs to the town walls and streets.

Refs: **4** (1:1).

Aston-under-Wrekin or Aston (Shropshire, England). This small village is situated some 8 miles east of SHREWSBURY and is to the north-west of the WREKIN.

Novels: The land belonging to the LUDEL manor of EATON 'falls between the [SHREWSBURY] ABBEY holdings of EYTON-BY-SEVERN on the one side, and Aston-under-Wrekin on the other'.

Refs: **14** (1).

Atcham (Shropshire, England). DB – Atingeham: in

Wrockwardine Hundred; a holding of ST ALKMUND'S CHURCH in SHREWSBURY. Situated on the east bank of the River SEVERN, some 4 miles south-east of Shrewsbury and at the south-western corner of ATTINGHAM Park, Atcham was an ancient river-crossing settlement. The name 'Atcham' is a shortened version of Attingham, representing 'the home of Eata's people'. Eata, who was the patron saint of the village, formed a small religious community at a ford of the Severn in the 7th C. Ordericus Vitalis, the medieval historian and chronicler, was born at Atcham in 1075 and was baptised in the church. The earliest record of St Eata's Church – the only one dedicated to the saint in England – was in 1075.

Novels: '"There are men who live by the river traffic and fishing, yes, and poaching, too, and they'll know every bend and beach from here to Atcham where things fetch up on the current."' In December 1138 Edwy BELLECOTE, pursued by the sheriff's men, led them through Atcham. Thomas of BRISTOL's body was found, by a late boat coming up the River Severn from BUILDWAS, in a cove at Atcham on 31 July 1139. Father EADMER (the elder), the parish priest, lived at Atcham.

Refs: **2** (7, 9); **3** (5–6, 9, 11); **4** (1:4); **5** (7); **11** (13); **17** (11); **19** (3).

Athanasius, Brother (*fl.* 1138) (fict.). **Novels:** 'The only relief they had to offer him [CADFAEL] was Brother Athanasius, who was deaf, half-senile, and not to be relied upon to know a useful herb from a weed, and the offer had been firmly declined. Better by far manage alone.' A monk of SHREWSBURY ABBEY, Athanasius was 'as blind as a mole'. In August 1138 Cadfael advised Godith Adeney (see BLUND) to stay with Athanasius because 'he wouldn't know a stag from a hind'. Nor would he have 'noticed a thunder-clap right behind him'.

Refs: **2** (1, 5).

Attingham (Shropshire, England). Situated some 4 miles south-east of SHREWSBURY, Attingham Park contains a large Georgian mansion, which belongs to the National Trust. 'Atingeham' was recorded in the Domesday Book survey of 1086, but the name for the village has since been shortened to ATCHAM.

Novels: Attingham and Atcham are interchangeable in the Chronicles. In November 1142, on his return from SHREWSBURY ABBEY, HYACINTH 'crossed the river [SEVERN] by the bridge at Attingham, waded the watery meadows of its tributary the TERN, and turned south from WROXETER towards EYTON. On their journey from Shrewsbury Abbey to Hales in early March 1143, CADFAEL and Brother HALUIN rested with the older Father EADMER at Attingham. In June of the same year, Cadfael walked the 4 miles to Attingham to speak to young Father EADMER.

Refs: **14** (3); **15** (3); **16** (7, 9).

Augustine of Hippo, Saint (354–430) (hist.) (f.d. 28 August). Also called Austin. Born at Tagaste in Numidia (Algeria), Augustine was the eldest son of the pagan, Patricius, and his Christian wife, St Monica. Although his mother instructed him in the Christian religion, he was not baptised. He went to Carthage to study rhetoric at the age of sixteen, and was soon living with a woman, who in 372 bore him an illegitimate son, Adeodatus. Intending to become a lawyer, Augustine abandoned the idea in order to devote himself to study and teaching. For some time he was strongly influenced by the teachings of Manichaeism, which led to his virtual abandonment of the Christian faith. In 383 he went to lecture in ROME and, between 384 and 386, he taught in Milan.

There he came under the influence of St Ambrose, Bishop of Milan, and, having suffered long and agonising inward conflict, he was converted to Christianity and baptised at Easter 387. Augustine returned to Africa in 388, living with a few friends in a sort of monastic community, until he was ordained priest at Hippo (Hippo Regius, near Annaba, Algeria) in 391. Four years later he became coadjutor-bishop to Valerius, whom he succeeded soon after as Bishop of Hippo. For much of the remainder of his life Augustine found himself defending the Catholic faith against one form of heresy or another, particularly Manichaeism, Donatism and Pelagianism. He died of a fever, during the siege of Hippo by the invading Germanic Vandals. The most important of his many works are the *Confessions* and the *City of God*.

Novels: There are many references to St Augustine. For example, RHUN recites a prayer of St Augustine, which Brother PAUL had taught him, while Meriet ASPLEY is given the sermons of the saint to study when in his punishment cell at SHREWSBURY ABBEY in September 1140. 'The readings during the meal, probably chosen by Prior ROBERT in compliment to Canon GERBERT, had been from the writings of Saint Augustine, of whom CADFAEL was not as fond as he might have been. There is a certain unbending rigidity about Augustine that offers little compassion to anyone with whom he disagrees.' Among the relics possessed by COVENTRY Priory was an arm of St Augustine.

Refs: **3** (1); **8** (6); **11** (4); **16** (2, 4–6, 9, 13, 15); **20** (2).

Aurifaber, Daniel (b. *c.*1116) (fict.). **Novels:** 'He was tall and well-made and assured of manner, a little too well aware of a handsome face, and he was very elegant in festival finery, even if his best cotte was now somewhat crumpled and disordered from the turmoil of pursuit, and his countenance red and slack from the effects of a good deal of wine drunk. Without that induced courage, he would not have faced the lord abbot with quite so much impudence.' Son and heir of Walter AURIFABER, Daniel married Margery Bele (see Margery AURIFABER) in May 1140, more for her money than for her looks. He was one of the leaders of the mob which hounded LILIWIN out of SHREWSBURY and forced him to seek sanctuary in SHREWSBURY ABBEY church. It was Daniel who accused Liliwin of striking down his father and plundering his strong-box. A goldsmith like his father, Daniel was a womaniser and, although newly married, continued his affair with Cecily CORDE. Liliwin saw him slip out of the AURIFABER house on the night of Baldwin PECHE's murder. After Hugh BERINGAR had enquired about his whereabouts that night, Daniel was forced by Margery – who knew of his unfaithfulness – to go and see his mistress and persuade her to tell the deputy-sheriff the truth: that he had been with Cecily until the early hours of the morning. Cecily, however, ordered him out of her house and out of her life. Desperate to establish his innocence, Daniel turned to Margery for help and, from that moment on, she had a 'tamed husband who would dance henceforth to her piping'. On the night of 21 June 1141, Daniel was captured by Olivier de BRETAGNE, while attempting to flee from the sheriff's men after he had been gambling under the arches of the English bridge. He was found to have CIARAN's stolen ring, which he had bought in good faith from Simeon POER. No charges were brought against him.

Refs: **7** (1–12, 14); **10** (7, 13).

Aurifaber, Dame Juliana (*c.*1060–1140) (fict.). **Novels:** 'So she would, thought CADFAEL ruefully, seeing her life-blood spilled if a prized possession was broken, she who hoarded every groat that was not spent on her perverse tenderness for her soul, which brought alms flowing to the abbey altars, and rendered Prior ROBERT her cautious friend.' Mother of Walter AURIFABER and grandmother of Daniel and Susanna, Juliana had a reputation 'for tartness, obstinacy and grim wit, and for taking always, with her kin, the contrary way. Whoever said black, Juliana would say white'. She was a parsimonious, grey-haired old woman and set in her ways. In May 1140, at Daniel's wedding-feast, she lashed out in fury at LILIWIN with her stick when he accidentally smashed her best pitcher while juggling. And when he complained, she had him thrown out of the house. Thinking that her son, Walter, had been murdered as well as robbed, she 'fell into a seizure' and, although she recovered, it left her unwell. She sent for Cadfael, having more faith in his remedies than in all the physicians. It was said that the only person on whom she doted was Daniel, and 'even he had never yet found a way to get her to loose her purse-strings'. Although she gave Susanna the keys to the household, Juliana retained a set of her own. With them, she discovered Walter's stolen valuables hidden in Susanna's locked store-room. Later, while confronting her granddaughter with the knowledge that she knew of her guilt, the old woman noticed that Susanna was pregnant. The shock brought on her third and final seizure, causing her to fall from the top of the stairs. She was buried in the grounds of ST MARY'S CHURCH in May 1140.

Refs: **7** (1–5, 8–12).

Aurifaber, Margery (née Bele) (b. *c.*1120) (fict.). **Novels:** 'A small, round, homely girl . . . perhaps twenty years old, with fresh, rosy colouring and a great untidy mass of yellow hair. Her eyes were round and wary. No wonder if she felt lost in this unfamiliar and disrupted household, but she moved quietly and sensibly.' Daughter of Edred BELE and heiress to his fortune, Margery married Daniel AURIFABER in May 1140. On the Monday night, three days after their marriage, Daniel slipped out of their marriage-bed to visit Cecily CORDE. When Hugh BERINGAR came to the house enquiring after Daniel's whereabouts that night, Margery turned the situation to her advantage. Having removed Cecily from the scene, Margery then persuaded Daniel to let her replace Susanna AURIFABER as mistress of the house. Successfully forcing Susanna to hand over her keys, Margery became the undisputed mistress of the AURIFABER household.

Refs: **7** (1–5, 8–12, 14); **10** (7).

Aurifaber, Susanna (*c.*1108–40) (fict.). **Novels:** 'Walter's daughter Susanna had a cool dignity about her that went very ill with violence and crime.' Daughter of Walter AURIFABER, granddaughter of Juliana and sister of Daniel AURIFABER, Susanna felt deep down that she was despised by her family. In May 1140, on the night of Daniel's wedding-feast, IESTYN, her secret lover and father of her unborn child, struck Walter on the head and robbed him of his valuables. The booty was hidden in the well and, later, when all was quiet, Susanna removed it and secreted it in her store-room. Her father had 'grudged' her a dowry, so she had taken it for herself. Baldwin PECHE reasoned that Susanna had stolen her father's treasure and attempted blackmail. Susanna, however, killed him. Forced to relinquish her role as mistress of the AURIFABER household, Susanna left SHREWSBURY with Iestyn, taking the stolen valuables and Rannilt with her. Having committed one murder, Susanna had no qualms about committing another, and was prepared to kill RANNILT to stop her from talking. She was killed at FRANKWELL in May 1140, protecting her lover from an arrow loosed by ALCHER, one of the sheriff's archers.

Refs: **7** (1–5, 7–14), **10** (7).

Aurifaber, Walter (*fl.* 1140) (fict.). **Novels:** The 'one thing that haunted him day and night was his lost treasury, of which he had rendered an inventory piece by piece, almost coin by coin, in loving and grieving detail . . . Walter's head might be healed now without, but his loss might well have done untold harm to the mind within'. A wealthy SHREWSBURY goldsmith, the balding Walter Aurifaber was the son of Juliana AURIFABER and the father of Daniel and Susanna. In May 1140, after the marriage of his son, he was struck over the head and his strong-box robbed by the Welsh journeyman, IESTYN. After his recovery, he accompanied CADFAEL and Hugh BERINGAR to his FRANKWELL stables, where his daughter was killed and his valuables recovered.

Refs: **7** (1–14); **19** (1).

(Walter) Aurifaber's Burgage (Castle Street, Shrewsbury, Shropshire) (fict.). **Novels:** 'The goldsmith's burgage was situated on the street leading to the gateway of the castle, where the neck of land narrowed, so that the rear plots of the houses on either side the street ran down to the town wall, while the great rondel of SHREWSBURY lay snug to the southwest in the loop of the SEVERN. It was one of the largest plots in the town, as its owner was thought to be one of the wealthiest men; a right-angled house with a wing on the street, and the hall and main dwelling running lengthwise behind. [Walter] AURIFABER, ever on the lookout for another means of making money, had divided off the wing and let it as a shop and dwelling to the locksmith Baldwin PECHE . . . A narrow passage led through between the two shops to the open yard behind, with its well, and the separate kitchens, byres and privies. Rumour said of Walter Aurifaber that he even had his cesspit stone-lined, which many considered to be arrogating to himself the privileges of minor nobility. Beyond the yard the ground fell away gradually in a long vegetable-garden and fowl-run to the town wall, and the family holding extended even beyond, through an arched doorway to an open stretch of smooth grass going down to the riverside.'

Refs: **7** (2).

Aylwin, Brother (*fl.* 1141) (fict.). **Novels:** A monk of SHREWSBURY ABBEY. On 25 May 1141 CADFAEL was in his workshop 'mutely stirring his brew for Brother Aylwin's scouring calves'.

Refs: **10** (1).

Aylwin, Walter (*fl.* 1138) (fict.). '"There is no reason to hurry in the matter of the Aylwin grant, he is an old friend to our order, his offer will certainly remain open as long as needs be."' In December 1138 HERIBERT was suspended as abbot. One of those charters which could not be sealed was 'the grant made by Walter Aylwin'.

Refs: **3** (1).

B

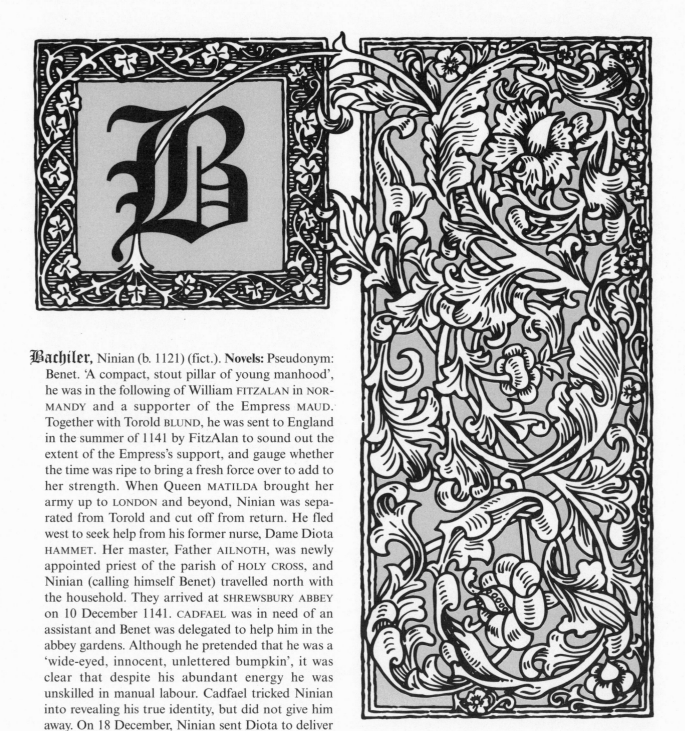

Bachiler, Ninian (b. 1121) (fict.). **Novels:** Pseudonym: Benet. 'A compact, stout pillar of young manhood', he was in the following of William FITZALAN in NORMANDY and a supporter of the Empress MAUD. Together with Torold BLUND, he was sent to England in the summer of 1141 by FitzAlan to sound out the extent of the Empress's support, and gauge whether the time was ripe to bring a fresh force over to add to her strength. When Queen MATILDA brought her army up to LONDON and beyond, Ninian was separated from Torold and cut off from return. He fled west to seek help from his former nurse, Dame Diota HAMMET. Her master, Father AILNOTH, was newly appointed priest of the parish of HOLY CROSS, and Ninian (calling himself Benet) travelled north with the household. They arrived at SHREWSBURY ABBEY on 10 December 1141. CADFAEL was in need of an assistant and Benet was delegated to help him in the abbey gardens. Although he pretended that he was a 'wide-eyed, innocent, unlettered bumpkin', it was clear that despite his abundant energy he was unskilled in manual labour. Cadfael tricked Ninian into revealing his true identity, but did not give him away. On 18 December, Ninian sent Diota to deliver a letter to Ralph GIFFARD the elder asking for his help, and suggesting a secret rendezvous by the abbey mill. Giffard betrayed him. Sanan BERNIÈRES, Giffard's step-daughter, however, decided to help him escape. Ninian and Sanan fell in love and pledged themselves to each other in marriage. They left SHREWSBURY together on 1 January 1142 with the intention of crossing the border into Wales, and then making their way south to join the empress's army in GLOUCESTER.

Refs: **12** (2–13).

Bagendon (Gloucestershire, England). Some 3 miles north of Cirencester, this ancient COTSWOLD village lies in a small tributary valley of the River Churn. In the 1st C. AD it was the fortified capital of the British Dobunni tribe. Remains of their defensive Iron Age earthworks, known as Bagendon Dykes, lie to the east and south-east of the village. Standing near the junction of two ancient trackways – the White Way and the Welsh Way – Bagendon declined after the founding of *Corinium Dobunnorum* (see CIRENCESTER). St Margaret's Church, remodelled in the Perpendicular style in the late 15th C., retains fragments of the Anglo-Saxon and Norman structures. Attempts at limiting the damage from flooding, including raising the nave floor, have proved ineffective. Manor Farm, near the church, possesses a disused waterwheel.

Novels: In December 1145 CADFAEL and Olivier de BRETAGNE, travelling together as father and son from Cirencester to GLOUCESTER, spent 'the first night in a shepherd's hut near Bagendon'.

Refs: **20** (15).

Bagot, Walter (*fl.* 1141) (fict.). **Novels:** He had a face 'rounded and glossy, as if oiled with the same dressing he used on his leathers'. One of a gang of tricksters, he arrived at SHREWSBURY ABBEY on 17 June 1141, claiming to be a glover by trade. On 21 June he and his companions (Simeon POER, John SHURE and William HALES) were surprised by Hugh BERINGAR and his men while gambling with loaded dice under the arch of the English Bridge. All, except HALES, managed to escape, fleeing west into the LONG FOREST. The gang attacked CIARAN and Matthew (see MEVEREL, Luc) in the woods, but were foiled by CADFAEL, Olivier de BRETAGNE, Hugh and his men. They fled, but were eventually captured and taken back to SHREWSBURY CASTLE 'to answer for more, this time, than a little cheating in the marketplace'.

Refs: **10** (4, 7,14).

Baldwin I (1058?–1118), King of Jerusalem (1100–18) (hist.). Also called Baldwin of Boulogne. Son of Eustace II, Count of Boulogne, and younger brother of GODFREY OF BOUILLON, he was crowned king of the crusader state of JERUSALEM in December 1100 after Godfrey's death. He fought in the First Crusade, and campaigned against the Seljuk Turks in Anatolia, becoming Count of EDESSA in 1098. He married Arda, the daughter of an Armenian nobleman, and in 1113 forced her to enter a convent so that he could marry Adelaide of Saona, dowager countess of Sicily. He died without an heir and was succeeded by his cousin, Baldwin II.

Refs: **1** (1); **5** (11); **8** (2).

Bampton Castle (Oxfordshire, England). In the upper THAMES valley, some 12 miles west of OXFORD, this small market town contains the remains of a moated castle (or fortified house) built by Aymer de

B

Valence, Earl of Pembroke, in *c.*1315. The remains, including a fragment of the west gatehouse, are part of Ham Court farm. St Mary's Church, much rebuilt in the 12th–13th C., and restored in the 19th C., dates from late Norman times. Its octagonal spire stands on a square tower with sculptured supports at each corner. In 1142 the Empress MAUD erected a castle in the village 'right on the church tower, which had been built in olden times of wondrous form and extraordinary skill and ingenuity.' (*Gesta Stephani*, ed. Potter, 1976). The castle was taken by King STEPHEN shortly after. In medieval times the town prospered on the manufacture and sale of gloves, sheepskin jackets and gaiters.

Novels: Bampton Castle was one of a circle of castles, centred on CRICKLADE, and held by King Stephen in December 1145, 'among which safe harbours his fighting men and his wounded could be comfortably distributed.'

Refs: **20** (10, 14).

Bangor (Gwynedd, Wales). The cathedral city of Bangor lies on the northern coast of the Welsh mainland at the eastern entrance to the Menai Strait, 9 miles north-east of CARNARVON and 13 miles south-west of CONWY. The cathedral, which is dedicated to ST DEINIOL, the first Bishop of Bangor, who founded a Celtic monastery on the site in the 6th C., contains the tombs of a number of Welsh princes, including the stone coffin of OWAIN GWYNEDD. The town originally grew up around a Norman castle, of which few traces remain.

Novels: In 1137 Prior ROBERT and his party set out for GWYTHERIN to acquire the bones of St WINIFRED for SHREWSBURY ABBEY. They arrived at Bangor in the third week of May and received Bishop DAVID's consent for the proposed translation. After CIARAN had murdered Rainald BOSSARD on 9 April 1141, Bishop HENRY OF BLOIS offered him passage under his protection to Bangor, to the bishop there, who would see him to CAERGYBI in ANGLESEY, and have him put aboard a ship for DUBLIN. Bishop MEURIG was consecrated in his own home diocese of Bangor in 1140. Deacon MARK and CADFAEL went to see the bishop and to present him with a letter and gift from Bishop ROGER DE CLINTON in May 1144.

Refs: **1** (1–2); **3** (11); **10** (14–15); **18** (1–8).

Bangor, Bishop of. See DAVID, Bishop of Bangor; MEURIG, Bishop of Bangor.

Barbary (fict.). **Novels:** Also called Russet. The bay horse of Peter CLEMENCE, who was murdered in the woods near the manor of ASPLEY on 9 September 1140. Leoric ASPLEY turned the horse loose on the mosses near WHITCHURCH, where it was eventually found.

Refs: **8** (3–4, 11).

Bardsey Island. See YNYS ENLLI.

Barfleur (France). Some 80 miles south of Portsmouth, across the English Channel, this small port in NORMANDY lies at the north-eastern tip of the Cotentin Peninsula. The *White Ship* (see BLANCHE NEF), carrying Prince WILLIAM THE AETHELING, son of HENRY I and the heir to the English throne, sank after leaving Barfleur on 25 November 1120.

Novels: CADFAEL and ALARD THE CLERK were among those who sailed from Barfleur to SOUTHAMPTON in November 1120. ELAVE brought the body of his master, William of LYTHWOOD, back to England through the port of Barfleur.

Refs: **16** (2); **20** (3); **RB** (1).

Bari (Italy). In south-eastern Italy, Bari is a port on the Adriatic Sea, some 65 miles north-west of Brindisi. From 1096, when Peter the Hermit preached the First Crusade at Bari, many crusaders embarked from its port.

Novels: 'There are plenty of Greek and Italian merchant ships plying as far as THESSALONIKA, some even all the way to Bari and VENICE.'

Refs: **16** (3).

Barnabas, Lay Brother (*fl.* 1138) (fict.). **Novels:** A 'big, massive man, all muscle and bone, with reserves of fight in him that needed only a little guidance'. Lay Brother of SHREWSBURY ABBEY, Barnabas looked after the abbey sheepfolds near RHYDYCROESAU. In December 1138 he fell ill with a bad chest and CADFAEL was despatched north from Shrewsbury to doctor him. By the end of the month Barnabas was wholly restored.

Refs: **3** (7–8, 11).

Barrow Gurney. See MINCHINBARROW PRIORY.

Barton Stacey. See STACEYS, The.

Bath (Avon, England). Some 12 miles south-east of BRISTOL, the city of Bath lies on the banks of the River Avon, at the southernmost tip of the limestone hills that stretch northward to become the COTSWOLDS. Bath is famous for its Roman baths and its unique wealth of Georgian architecture.

Novels: Bishop HENRY OF BLOIS spent much of the year 1140 trying to get King STEPHEN and Empress MAUD to come to a peaceful settlement in their dispute over the throne of England. By September, 'he had done his best, and even managed to bring representatives of both parties to meet near Bath only a month or so ago. But nothing had come of it.'

Refs: **8** (1).

Bayston Hill. See BEISTAN.

Beaumont (now Beaumont-le-Roger) (France). Some 9 miles south of BRIONNE, on the banks of the River Risle, Beaumont-le-Roger contains the 13th C. ruins of a priory built by the monks of Bec (or Le Bec Hellouin). St Nicolas' Church, dating from the 14th–16th C., was restored after World War II damage.

Novels: Robert de BEAUMONT (the elder) had 'died in possession of the earldom of Leicester in England, Beaumont, Brionne and PONTAUDEMER in NORMANDY, and the county of MEULAN in France.'

Refs: **19** (4–5).

Beaumont, Robert de (the elder) (d. 1118), Count of Meulan (hist.). The son of Roger de Beaumont by Adeline, the daughter of Waleran de Mellente, Count of Meulan, and father of Robert de BEAUMONT (the younger) and Waleran de BEAUMONT. He fought with WILLIAM I at the battle of Senlac Hill, near Hastings, on 14 October 1066. Having distinguished himself in the fighting, Robert was rewarded with large grants of land in Warwickshire; his brother, Henry de Beaumont (or Newburgh), was given WARWICK Castle (see also BEAUMONT, Roger de). Robert succeeded to the title Count of Meulan in *c.*1079. On William I's death in 1087, he and his brother supported WILLIAM II. Having angered ROBERT, Duke of Normandy, by demanding the castellanship of Ivry (now Ivry-la-Bataille), Robert was imprisoned and the castellanship of BRIONNE taken from him. He was eventually released after the payment of a heavy fine. Although Brionne was returned to him, he was forced to recover the castle by siege. Robert succeeded to the family fiefs of BEAUMONT and PONTAUDEMER when his father entered the abbey of St Peter at Preaux. Both he and his brother were present at William II's death in 1100. Robert became HENRY I's 'specially trusted counsellor' and, shortly after, by the use of cunning, added the rebellious Ivo de Grantmesnil's lands in Leicestershire (including the town of LEICESTER) to his already large estates in NORMANDY and England. With great diplomatic skill and ingenuity, he opposed ANSELM in the quarrel over the question of investitures. In 1103 he went to Beaumont to look after Henry's interests in Normandy. In 1106 he fought alongside Henry at the battle of Tinchebrai, in which Robert, Duke of

Normandy, was captured. On his deathbed in 1118, it is said that he was urged to restore the lands he had unjustly acquired. Characteristically, Robert's response was to say that he would leave them to his sons in order for them to provide for his salvation. He died on 5 June and was buried with his father at Preaux.

Novels: Father of the twin Beaumont brothers, Waleran and Robert, Robert de Beaumont (the elder) was 'one of the most reliable props of old King Henry [I]'s firm rule'. He had died in 'possession of the earldom of Leicester in England, Beaumont, Brionne and Pontaudemer in Normandy, and the county of MEULAN in France'.

Refs: **19** (4–5, 11).

Beaumont, Robert de (the younger) (1104–68), Earl of Leicester (hist.). Also called Robert Bossu (or the Hunchback). Son of Robert de BEAUMONT (the elder) by his wife Elizabeth (or Ysabel), daughter of Hugh the Great of Vermandois and niece of Philip I, King of France. He was also the younger twin brother of Waleran de BEAUMONT and first cousin of Roger de BEAUMONT, Earl of Warwick. In 1118, on the death of his father, Robert inherited the English lands, while Waleran inherited those in NORMANDY and France. Brought up and educated with his brother in the royal household of HENRY I, he and his twin were considered to be infant prodigies. When Robert married AMICIA, daughter of Ralph de Wader, Earl of Norfolk, he received the fief of BRETEUIL for her dowry. Both twins accompanied the king to Normandy and, after Henry's death in December 1135, supported STEPHEN in his seizure of the English throne. The twins, who hated HENRY OF BLOIS, instigated the brawl at OXFORD in 1139, which led to the arrest of ROGER, Bishop of Salisbury, and his fellow bishops. Under the king's orders, Robert escorted the Empress MAUD to BRISTOL in October 1139. Robert was in Normandy in 1141, acting as Stephen's principal lieutenant, and after the king's defeat at LINCOLN on 2 February secured from GEOFFREY of Anjou a truce for Waleran and himself. In 1143, two years after his return to England, Robert founded the Augustinian abbey of St Mary de Pratis (or de Pré) at LEICESTER. Sometime between 1149 and 1153 he signed a disarmament treaty with his powerful neighbour RANULF of Chester, agreeing to 'final peace and concord'. In 1153, when Henry Plantagenet (later HENRY II) invaded England, Robert, like many powerful magnates, adopted an attitude of neutrality by remaining loyal to Stephen, while refusing to fight the lawful heir to the kingdom. He soon transferred his allegiance to Henry and, after Henry became king in December 1154, Robert was made his chief justiciar. Between 1158 and 1163, and also in 1165, when the king was absent in Normandy, Robert was left in charge of the kingdom. He was buried at the abbey of St Mary de Pratis in 1168.

Novels: 'No sane malefactor would want to settle and conduct his predatory business in territory controlled by so active and powerful a magnate as Robert Beaumont, earl of Leicester', 'lord of half Leicestershire, a good slice of Warwickshire and Northampton, and a large honour in Normandy brought to him by his marriage with the heiress of Breteuil.' 'Squarely built and no more than medium tall, dark of hair and darker of eyes, rich but sombre in his attire, and carrying the habit of command very lightly, not overstressed, for there was no need. He was cleanshaven, in the Norman manner, leaving open to view a face broad at brow and well provided with strong and shapely bone, a lean jaw, and a full, firm mouth, long-lipped and mobile, and quirking upward at the corners to match a certain incalculable spark in his eye. The symmetry of his body and the smoothness of his movements were thrown out of balance by the slight bulge that heaved one shoulder out of line with its fellow. Not a great flaw, but insistently it troubled the eyes of guests coming new to his acquaintance.' 'Robert Bossu they called him, Robert the Hunchback, and reputedly he made no objection to the title', 'for the flaw neither embarrassed him nor hampered the fluency of his movements.' On his father's death Robert inherited 'the English lands'. In February 1145 St WINIFRED's reliquary was found within the earl's woodlands near ULLESTHORPE and taken to Robert at HUNCOTE. Hugh BERINGAR, Prior ROBERT, Sub-Prior HERLUIN, Brother TUTILO and NICOL lodged overnight at the manor. The following day, Robert, who 'in earnest or in mischief' laid a claim to the saint's relics, accompanied them (together with the reliquary) to SHREWSBURY ABBEY to settle the matter by a 'more disinterested tribunal'. Abbot RADULFUS decided that the 'neutral assessor' should be the *sorts Biblicae* at which the earl received John 7:54 (see JOHN THE EVANGELIST) and, eventually, withdrew all claim to St Winifred. Robert agreed to take into his household RÉMY of Pertuis and his two servants, BÉNEZET and DAALNY; but events transpired that only Rémy went back to Leicester with him. In early November 1145 Robert sent a courier to Shrewsbury Castle to inform Hugh Beringar of the planned meeting in COVENTRY between King Stephen and the Empress Maud. He also sent Hugh a list of 'some thirty young men of quality, knights and squires' captured and held for ransom after Stephen's forces had taken FARINGDON Castle. Among the list was Olivier de BRETAGNE. At the council in Coventry on 30 November, attended by Stephen and Maud, Robert sat 'shoulder to shoulder' with Hugh. 'Robert Beaumont, secure in his earldom since the age of fourteen, intelligent, witty and wise', 'was trying to bring together all the wisest and most moderate minds from both factions, to force a compromise which would stop the fighting by agreement.' '"Nothing will come of it," said Robert Bossu resignedly in Hugh Beringar's ear, when the two monodies had declined at last into one bitter threnody. "Not here. Not yet. This is how it must end at last, and in an even bleaker desolation. But no, there'll be no end to it yet."'

Refs: **19** (4–13); **20** (1–4, 6–8, 16).

Beaumont, Waleran de (1104–66), Count of Meulan (hist.). Also called Earl of Worcester. He was the son of Robert de BEAUMONT (the elder), Count of Meulan, twin brother of Robert de BEAUMONT (the younger), Earl of Leicester, and half-brother of William de WARENNE, Earl of Surrey. On his father's death in 1118, Waleran succeeded to the feudal estates of MEULAN (on the River Seine near Mantes, France) and BEAUMONT (near Bernay, NORMANDY). One of the most prominent barons of the period, he supported William Clito, the son of ROBERT, Duke of Normandy, in the movement against HENRY I. In 1123 he was present at the conspiracy of Croix St Leufroi. Captured by Ranulf of Bayeux in 1124, Waleran was kept in close confinement by the English king for five years and forced to surrender his castle at Beaumont. He was present at Henry's deathbed on 1 December 1135 and, shortly afterwards, supported STEPHEN's seizure of the English throne. Having been promised the hand of Stephen's infant daughter in 1136, he fought against the king's opponents in Normandy. The *Gesta Stephani* (ed. Potter, 1976) says that Waleran, together with his twin brother, instigated the brawl which led to the arrest of Bishop Roger of Salisbury (see ROBERT, Bishop of Salisbury) and his fellow bishops at OXFORD in June 1139. This violent act and Stephen's seizure of the bishop's castles are said to have given 'the signal for the civil war'. Towards the end of the year, Stephen rewarded Waleran for his loyalty by making him Earl of Worcester. At the battle of Lincoln on 2 February 1141, however, he fled, along with the Earls of Richmond, Norfolk, Northampton (see SENLIS, Simon II de), and Surrey (see WARENNE, William de), and left the king to his fate. In 1143 he helped GEOFFREY of Anjou besiege ROUEN. After joining the Second Crusade in 1146, Waleran returned to England to support the Empress MAUD and held

B

WORCESTER against Stephen in 1152. He was captured in Normandy by his nephew, Robert de Montfort, and imprisoned in Orbec for a while. He was in attendance at the court of HENRY II in 1157 and was a witness to the treaty of 1160, between the English king and LOUIS VII, King of France. Waleran was succeeded by his son, Robert.

Novels: Earl Waleran of Meulan was overlord of the manors of LAI, HARPECOTE and IGHTFELD. In about September 1138, he demanded twenty men-in-arms from Reginald CRUCE for reinforcements in the contention against the bishops. In September 1141 he supported Queen MATILDA at the siege of WINCHESTER. Having inherited 'Beaumont, BRIONNE and PONTAUDEMER in Normandy, and the county of Meulan in France', Waleran was in Normandy in February 1145, protecting his own and his twin brother Robert's interests. He had been there four years. '"The French and Norman lands matter most to Waleran, who can wonder that he's gone over there and made himself at least acceptable to Geoffrey [of Anjou], rather than risk being dispossessed. It's more than the lands. He got the French possessions, the heart of the honour, when their father died, he's count of Meulan, and his line is bound up with the title. Without Meulan he'd be nameless."' Although Waleran was Anjou's man in 1145, it was reckoned that '"he will do Stephen as little harm as he can, and give Geoffrey as little active support."'

Refs: **4** (4:1); **11** (7–8, 11); **19** (4–5).

Beddgelert (Gwynedd, Wales). Some 12 miles south-east of CARNARVON and 7 miles west of Blaenau Ffestiniog, Beddgelert lies in the heart of the Snowdonia National Park. The village – formerly an inland port – stands at the confluence of two mountain streams, the Afon Glaslyn and the Afon Colwyn. The ancient Celtic monastery at Beddgelert, founded in the 6th C., became an Augustinian priory in the late 12th or early 13th C. All that remains of the priory are parts of the church.

Novels: MEURIG rode into one of the granges of the monastery of Beddgelert in the winter of 1138 and left his horse there, for it to be returned to RHYDYCROESAU.

Refs: **3** (11).

Beistan or Beiston (now Bayston Hill) (Shropshire, England). DB – Begestan: in Condover Hundred; a holding of William Pantulf under Roger de MONTGOMERY. Just over 2 miles south of SHREWSBURY, Bayston Hill is a large village with its church and green situated to the east of the A49. LYTHWOOD Hall is 1 mile to the west of the village.

Novels: 'CADFAEL went on briskly, emerging on to a highroad at the village of Beistan, where the path he was following crossed and moved on, dead straight, past a few scattered holdings beyond, and then into fitful stretches of rising heathland and copses between two gentle slopes.' In October 1139 Huon de DOMVILLE was found 'thrown from his horse on the woodland path that leads out towards Beistan'.

Refs: **5** (5, 7–8); **9** (13); **17** (6).

Bele, Edred (*fl.* 1140) (fict.). **Novels:** A wealthy SHREWSBURY cloth-merchant, he was the father of Margery (see AURIFABER), who married Daniel AURIFABER in May 1140.

Refs: **7** (2).

Bele, Margery. See AURIFABER, Margery.

Bellecote, Alys (b. 1127) (fict.). **Novels:** Elder daughter of Martin and Sibil BELLECOTE, she was, in December 1138, 'about eleven, very house-wifely and prim', and also 'bright'.

Refs: **3** (3-4).

Bellecote, Diota (b. 1134) (fict.). **Novels:** Younger daughter of Martin and Sibil BELLECOTE, she was, in December 1138, 'an elfin miss no more than four'.

Refs: **3** (3).

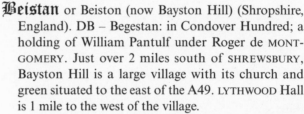

Bellecote, Edwy (b. 1124) (fict.). **Novels:** 'CADFAEL had known him well since the boy, turned eighteen now, was a lively imp of fourteen, tall for his years and lean and venturesome, with a bush of chestnut hair, and light hazel eyes that missed very little of what went on about him.' Elder son of Martin and Sibil BELLECOTE, Edwy was, in looks, almost the twin of his uncle Edwin GURNEY, who happened to be the younger of the two. Edwy helped Edwin escape from the sheriff's men in December 1138 by leading them on a wild-goose chase around the outlying villages to the south-east of SHREWSBURY. On 31 July 1139, the eve of St Peter's Fair, Edwy was among the twenty or so youngsters of the town who caused a riot at the SHREWSBURY ABBEY jetty. In June 1142 Edwy, who worked for his father, brought CADFAEL a pair of odd shoes from the VESTIER household .

Refs: **3** (3–4, 7); **4** (1:2–3, 2:2); **13** (13).

Bellecote, Martin (b. *c.*1100) (fict.). **Novels:** 'A pleasant, square-built, large-handed man with a wide, wholesome face, and a deep reserve in his eyes, which CADFAEL was glad to see. Too much trust is folly, in an imperfect world.' Master-carpenter of SHREWSBURY, Martin Bellecote married Sibil Gurney (see BELLECOTE) in 1122 while he was the journeyman of her father, Eward GURNEY. After Eward's death in 1133, Martin inherited the shop and business. He was the father of four children, Edwy, Alys, Thomas and Diota. On 30 July 1139 Martin was among the delegation, from the Guild Merchant of SHREWSBURY, which asked Abbot RADULFUS if a percentage of the tolls, taken at St Peter's Fair, could be granted to the town for repairs to its walls and streets. The carpenter's many commissions included: fitting the carved oak panelling in Gervase BONEL's manor house at MALLILIE; making a cradle, and later a horse, for Hugh BERINGAR's son, Giles; and building coffins for Thomas of BRISTOL, Huon de DOMVILLE, BERTRED the foreman-weaver, Drogo BOSIET and Juliana AURIFABER.

Refs: **3** (3–4, 8); **4** (1:1, 2:2–3); **5** (6); **7** (11); **12** (4); **13** (9, 12); **14** (9).

Bellecote, Sibil (née Gurney) (b. 1105) (fict.). **Novels:** 'A woman like enough to be known for her mother's daughter, but softer and rounder and fairer in colouring, though with the same honest eyes.' Elder sister of Edwin GURNEY and daughter of Richildis (see BONEL) and Eward GURNEY, Sibil married Martin BELLECOTE in 1122. She was the mother of Edwy, Alys, Thomas and Diota.

Refs: **3** (3–4); **13** (13).

Bellecote, Thomas (b. 1130) (fict.). **Novels:** Younger son of Martin and Sibil BELLECOTE and brother to Edwy, Alys and Diota.

Refs: **3** (3–4); **4** (3:2).

(Martin) Bellecote's House and Shop (Wyle, Shrewsbury, Shropshire) (fict.). Although they never existed, the house and shop of Martin BELLECOTE stood halfway up and on the north side of the steep, curving WYLE.

Novels: 'After his [CADFAEL's] knock at the closed door there was a longish silence, and that he could well understand, and forbore from knocking again. Clamour would only have alarmed them. Patience might reassure.'

Refs: **3** (3–4, 8); **4** (2:1).

(Martin) Bellecote's Wood-Yard (Shrewsbury, Shropshire) (fict.). Although it never existed, the wood-yard of Martin BELLECOTE stood on the town side of the English Bridge, on the steep bank between the town wall and the SEVERN, directly opposite the present Abbey Gardens.

Novels: 'Several of the businesses in town that

needed bulky stores had fenced premises here for their stock, and among them was Martin Bellecote's wood-yard where he seasoned his timber.' The wood-yard was an old refuge for Edwy BELLECOTE and Edwin GURNEY when either or both of the boys happened to be in trouble.

Refs: **3** (3–4).

Bened the Smith (b. *c.*1095) (fict.). **Novels:** A 'thickset, muscular man of middle years, bearded and brown' with a 'grizzled head'. The smith of GWYTHERIN 'was a highly respected man, like all of his craft'. In May 1137 Bened, a widower, secretly hoped to marry SIONED, an ambition that was never realised. In 1139 he set out on a pilgrimage to the shrine of Our Lady of WALSINGHAM, and in June called in to see CADFAEL at SHREWSBURY ABBEY.

Refs: **1** (2–3, 9, 12); **12** (13).

Benedict, Brother (*fl.* 1137) (fict.). **Novels:** 'Brother CADFAEL came to chapter in tranquillity of mind, prepared to be tolerant even towards the . . . long winded legal havering of Brother Benedict'. A Benedictine monk of SHREWSBURY ABBEY, Brother Benedict, the sacristan, had a 'fine, sonorous voice' which filled the 'whole vault as he read the lessons in between the spoken psalms'.

Refs: **1** (1); **3** (1); **12** (10); **14** (1, 5); **16** (2).

Benedict of Nursia, Saint (*c.*480–*c.*547) (hist.) (f.d. 11 July, formerly 21 March). The father of Western monasticism was born in the Italian town of Nursia (or Norcia). Little is known of his life, apart from the information contained in the *Dialogues* of Pope Gregory I (590–604). Born into a middle-class family, Benedict was educated in ROME, but abandoned his studies to devote himself to God. He joined a small religious community, which he left shortly after to become a hermit in the mountains of Subiaco, where he spent several years living in a cave. His fame as a holy man grew and in time he was persuaded to become the abbot of a neighbouring monastery. It is said, however, that the monks rebelled against the severity of his discipline and tried to poison him. Returning to Subiaco, Benedict founded twelve monasteries, each containing twelve monks, with himself in overall control. In *c.*529 he established the hilltop monastery of Monte Cassino, where he composed the monastic rules for which he is famous. The Rule, which demanded from the monks a life-long vow of poverty, chastity, obedience and stability, was adopted not only by the Benedictines but also, with modifications, by later orders.

Novels: '"The blessed Benedict wrote in the Rule that even to the third time of straying a man may be received again if he promise full amendment."' 'Of the instruments of good works listed in the Rule of Saint Benedict, second only to the love of God came the love of humankind, and CADFAEL reverenced the Rule above the detailed and meticulous rules.'

Refs: **1** (9); **9** (8); **11** (7); **15** (11); **17** (4); **19** (9, 13); **RB** (1).

Benedicta, Sister. See VIVERS, Bertrade.

Benet. See BACHILER, Ninian.

Bénezet (b. *c.*1110) (fict.). **Novels:** 'Bénezet, naturally curious about anything that might serve his turn or redound to his profit, was not averse to picking up a few crumbs of useful information by the way.' Manservant of RÉMY of Pertuis and a native of PROVENCE, Bénezet arrived at SHREWSBURY ABBEY with his master and DAALNY in February 1145. During the chaos caused by rising floodwaters invading the abbey church, he helped Brother MATTHEW carry what they thought was St WINIFRED's reliquary upstairs to the safety of the north porch. Before he left the church, Bénezet robbed the coffer for RAMSEY ABBEY, which stood on the altar of the Lady Chapel; later, he hid his valuable booty in a large, baked clay storage jar inside the HORSE-FAIR stable. Some days later, seeing Brother JEROME hurrying into the cloister, Bénezet followed and overheard the monk inform Prior ROBERT that CADFAEL had named the holy thief as Brother TUTILO, and also that ALDHELM was coming to the abbey that night to identify Tutilo. Bénezet, in turn, suggested to DAALNY that Tutilo should make himself scarce. Believing that Aldhelm may have seen him rob the coffer on the night of the flood and might possibly recollect it under questioning, Bénezet decided to ambush the shepherd. Hiding in thick woodland on the path from the LONGNER ferry, he saw Brother Jerome strike down Aldhelm with a fallen branch. After Jerome had fled, Bénezet coldly and deliberately smashed the senseless shepherd's skull with a heavy stone, replacing the murder object carefully back in the place that he had found it. Getting ready to leave Shrewsbury with Rémy in early March, Bénezet went to the Horse-Fair stable and removed his booty from the cornjar. Realising that Cadfael may have heard him, he lied about his reason for being in the stable. While Rémy, Robert BEAUMONT and Sub-Prior HERLUIN, together with their respective entourage, were assembling to depart the abbey, Daalny accused Bénezet of theft and possibly murder. When ordered to reveal the contents of his saddlebag, Bénezet made a frantic dash for freedom. Having 'leaped and scrambled' into the saddle of CONRADIN the horse and after swerving to slice at Daalny with his dagger, he galloped out of the gate towards the town. Realising that he was riding straight for Alan HERBARD and three of the sheriff's sergeants, Bénezet veered south-westward into the LONG FOREST. He was eventually captured and taken back to SHREWSBURY CASTLE to stand trial for murder.

Refs: **19** (2–3, 5–8, 10–13).

Benjamin (ib.). Youngest son of Jacob, Benjamin was the brother of Joseph (who unbeknown to him had been sold into slavery by his elder brothers). Benjamin's mother, Rachel, died while giving birth to him in Canaan. She named him Ben-oni, meaning 'son of my sorrow', but Jacob changed the name to Benjamin. The boy was taken to Egypt with his brothers to buy corn. On Joseph's orders, their sacks were filled with food and money. A silver cup, however, was secretly hidden in Benjamin's sack. When it was discovered, Joseph threatened to keep the boy as his slave. After an eloquent appeal by Judah, Joseph relented and sent the boy back to his father with 'three hundred pieces of silver, and five changes of raiment' (Genesis 45:22). In Genesis 44:20 Benjamin is described as 'a little one'; in Genesis 46:21, however, he is the father of ten sons.

Novels: 'Was there not a cup hidden in the sack of the boy Benjamin, in the Bible story, to make it possible to detain him? And had not the same stratagem been used many times since?'

Refs: **5** (4).

Beringar, Aline (née Siward) (b. 1120) (fict.). **Novels:** 'She was as fair as Hugh was black, primrose-fair, and fine-boned, and a shade taller than her husband.' Aline Beringar was the younger sister of Giles SIWARD, wife of Hugh BERINGAR and mother of Giles BERINGAR. At SHREWSBURY in August 1138, shortly after the death of her father, Aline offered King STEPHEN her fealty, together with the keys of her two newly inherited castles. While in the town she met Hugh Beringar, who was shortly to become deputy sheriff of Shropshire. They were married in late August or early September 1138, and on 5 December the following year Aline gave birth to their son, Giles. In 1143, she was 'radiantly content in her fulfilment, happy wife and mother'.

Refs: **2** (1–3, 12); **4** (1:1); **5** (7); **6** (4); **7** (3, 14); **8** (1–2, 7, 8); **9** (1); **10** (1, 5, 7, 15–16); **12** (1); **13** (1, 5); **14** (7); **15** (1, 3); **17** (1); **18** (1, 14); **19** (2, 10–11).

Beringar, Giles (b. 1139) (fict.). **Novels:** 'A large, comely, self-willed child, fair like his mother, and long of limb, some day to dwarf his small, dark, sardonic father,' 'with Hugh's self-reliant nature, but something also of his mother's instinctive sweetness'. Son of Hugh and Aline BERINGAR, and godson of CADFAEL, Giles was born at SHREWSBURY on 5 December 1139 and christened early the following year.

Refs: **4** (1:1, 2:3, 4:2); **5** (7); **6** (1, 4, 8, 15); **7** (3); **8** (7); **9** (1); **10** (1, 5); **11** (10); **12** (4); **13** (1, 5); **14** (7); **15** (1); **16** (1, 9); **17** (1, 10); **18** (1, 14); **19** (2, 11).

Beringar, Hugh, (b. *c.*1114) (fict.). **Novels:** 'A lightweight, not above the middle height and slenderly built, but of balanced and assured movement; he might well make up in speed and agility what he lacked in bulk and reach. Perhaps two or three years past twenty, black-avised, with thin, alert features and thick, quirky dark brows. An unchancy fellow, because there was no guessing from his face what went on behind the deep-set eyes. His forthright speech might be honest, or it might be calculated. He looked quite subtle enough to have weighted up his sovereign and reasoned that boldness might not be displeasing.' 'Hugh's first visit [to SHREWSBURY ABBEY] was always to pay his respects to the abbot. By the same token, he never left the enclave without seeking out Brother CADFAEL in his workshop in the garden. They were old friends, closer than father and son, having not only that easy and tolerant relationship of two generations, but shared experiences that made of them contemporaries. They sharpened minds, one upon the other, for the better protection of values and institutions that needed defence with every passing day in a land so shaken and disrupted.' Son of Robert BERINGAR of MAESBURY, Hugh inherited his father's estate in the first half of 1138. Godith Adeney (see BLUND) was betrothed to him from a child, but they never married. In August 1138 Hugh swore his fealty to King STEPHEN at SHREWSBURY, and, after the death of Adam COURCELLE in a trial by combat, the king made him deputy sheriff of Shropshire. That same month Cadfael tricked him out of William FITZALAN's treasure, and from then on they became good friends. In late August or early September 1138, he married Aline Siward (see BERINGAR) and on 5 December 1139 they had a son, Giles. On 2 February 1141 Hugh fought at the battle of LINCOLN, in which the king was taken captive and Sheriff Gilbert PRESTCOTE badly injured. Hugh returned to Shrewsbury on 7 February. After Prestcote's murder in March, Hugh assumed the office of sheriff. Later that same month, he rode north for a meeting with OWAIN GWYNEDD, in which they formed a peaceful alliance to protect their respective borders. Summoned to the king's court at CANTERBURY in December 1141, Hugh was confirmed in office as sheriff of Shropshire. In early November 1143 he went to CAMBRIDGE and the FENS to help the king put down the rebellion of Geoffrey de MANDEVILLE. By the end of the month the campaign had been postponed and he was back with his levy in Shrewsbury. In February 1145 Hugh accompanied Prior ROBERT to WORCESTER to speak to Sub-Prior HERLUIN and Brother TUTILO about the disappearance of St WINIFRED's reliquary. From there he rode to ULLESTHORPE and HUNCOTE, returning to Shrewsbury not only with the missing reliquary, but also with Robert BEAUMONT (the younger). On 27 November of the same year Hugh accompanied Cadfael to Coventry, where they attended the conference between Stephen and Maud. He returned to Shrewsbury without his friend.

Refs: **2** (1, 5, 7–9, 12); **3** (7–8); **4** (1:1); **5** (7); **6** (1, 4); **7** (2–3); 8 (1–3); **9** (1, 5–8, 10); **10** (1, 5); **11** (8–9); **12** (1–2, 6); **13** (1–2, 4–14); **14** (1, 9, 13); **15** (1); **16** (1); **17** (1–14); **18** (1, 14); **19** (1–13); **20** (1–7, 13–14, 16).

Beringar, Robert (d. 1138) (fict.). **Novels:** Father of Hugh BERINGAR and lord of the manor of MAESBURY, Robert died in the first half of 1138: for, in August, Hugh had inherited his lands 'only some months ago'.

Refs: **2** (1); **12** (6).

(Hugh) Beringar's Town House (St Mary's Close, Shrewsbury, Shropshire) (fict.). Although it never existed, the town house of Hugh BERINGAR was situated near ST MARY'S CHURCH, off St Mary's Street, in what is now called St Mary's Place. At No. 10 is Drapers' Hall, a timber-framed building, built about 1560 and the former meeting place of the medieval Drapers' Guild.

Novels: 'Hugh's house by Saint Mary's Church had an enclosed garden behind it, a small central herber with grassed benches round it, and fruit trees to give shade. There Aline BERINGAR was sitting on the clipped seat sown with close-growing, fragrant herbs, with her son playing beside her.'

Refs: **6** (1, 4); **7** (11); **8** (1, 9); **9** (1); **10** (1, 5, 7); **11** (10, 13); **12** (4); **13** (2, 5); **14** (6–7); **15** (3); **16** (9); **17** (10); **19** (2).

Berkeley (Gloucestershire, England). In the Vale of Berkeley, roughly midway between GLOUCESTER and BRISTOL, the small town of Berkeley was the site of an Anglo-Saxon minster. St Mary's Church, dating from the 12th C., belonged to the Augustinian abbey at Bristol. It stands on high ground overlooking the essentially 14th C. castle, first erected shortly after 1067 by William FitzOsborn, Earl of Hereford. The home of the Berkeley family since 1153, the castle is famed as the site of Edward II's murder in 1327.

Novels: Guy CAMVILLE was 'a border knight from near Berkeley'.

Refs: **20** (12).

Bernard, Brother (*fl.* 1139) (fict.). A Benedictine monk and apiarist at SHREWSBURY ABBEY, he also looked after the main gardens in the GAYE.

Refs: **4** (3:1); **12** (2).

Bernard, Master (*fl.* 1145) (fict.). **Novels:** '"Here [at DEERHURST] we are building another south-east chapel, and the like to balance it on the northern side. Our master mason is a local man, and the works of the Church are his pride. A good man! He gives work to some unfortunates other masters might find unprofitable."' Master mason, Bernard, who worked 'upon manors and barns and farmsteads as well as churches', took FORTHRED into his employ in 1145. In December of the same year, while working at Deerhurst priory, he was unable to help CADFAEL identify the seal of Geoffrey FITZCLARE.

Refs: **20** (6–7).

Bernard of Clairvaux, Saint (1090–1153) (hist.) (f.d. 20 August). Third son of Tescelin Sorrel, a Burgundian nobleman, Bernard was born near Dijon, France. In 1112 he entered the Cistercian monastery at Cîteaux, founded in 1098, persuading four of his five brothers and some twenty-five friends to join him. In 1115 his abbot, Stephen Harding, sent Bernard to CLAIRVAUX in Champagne to found a new community and, under his influence, the Cistercian Order spread rapidly throughout Europe. Amongst the Cistercian houses established in England during his lifetime were BUILDWAS (originally Savigniac), Fountains, Rievaulx and Tintern. Named after Cîteaux, the Cistercian Order was based on a strict and austere interpretation of the Benedictine Rule. Although Abbot Bernard of Clairvaux was a mystic by nature and preferred to cultivate his inner life within the monastery, he was increasingly drawn into church affairs and eventually became the uncrowned ruler of medieval Christian Europe. In addition to writing and preaching, Bernard's advice was sought and respected by princes and churchmen alike. He was confidant to five popes, including his former pupil, Pope Eugenius III (1145–53). Bernard vehemently opposed and condemned the teachings of Pierre ABELARD. He was appointed by Eugenius to promote the cause of the disastrous Second Crusade (1147–9). Although plagued by ill health, Bernard was Abbot of Clairvaux for thirty-eight years.

Novels: 'The very mention of Bernard of Clairvaux, the apostle of austerity, was a reminder of the rising influence of the Cistercians, to which order Archbishop THEOBALD was sympathetically inclined. And though Bernard might put in a word for popular criticism of the worldliness of many high churchmen, and yearn for a return to the poverty and simplicity of the Apostles, by all accounts he would have small mercy on anyone who diverged from the strictly orthodox where dogma was concerned.'

Refs: **16** (2).

Bernières, John (d. 1138) (fict.). **Novels:** Father of Sanan BERNIÈRES and loyal supporter of the Empress MAUD, he fought for his overlord William FITZALAN at the siege of SHREWSBURY in August 1138 and was killed. His manor, in the north-east of Shropshire, was confiscated by King STEPHEN. Sanan inherited his sword and dagger.

Refs: **12** (4, 6, 8–10).

Bernières, Sanan (b. 1123) (fict.). **Novels:** She had 'a coiled braid of hair of an indefinable spring colour, like the young fronds of bracken when they are just unfolding, a soft light brown with tones of green in the shadows. Or hazel withies, perhaps! Hazel eyes are no great rarity, but how many women can boast of hazel hair?' Daughter of John BERNIÈRES and step-daughter of Ralph GIFFARD the elder, she was a loyal supporter of the Empress MAUD, like her father. After his death in August 1138, her mother married Ralph Giffard. When she died, Sanan moved with her step-father to his town house in SHREWSBURY. In December 1141 Sanan became aware of Ninian BACHILER through the letter that he sent to Giffard asking for help. Although Giffard was no longer willing to take the risk of helping a supporter of the empress's party and decided instead to betray him, Sanan went to SHREWSBURY ABBEY to find Ninian and offer him her assistance. They fell in love, almost at their first meeting. When he was discovered by the sheriff's men, she helped him escape, found him a hideout in Giffard's cattle byre, and secured horses for his escape. Making sure that Ninian should not appear before the 'empress or ROBERT of Gloucester shabby, or without arms or horse', Sanan provided him with clothes and the sword and dagger that had belonged to her father. They both slipped quietly away from Shrewsbury on the night of 1 January 1142, and were married soon afterwards in GLOUCESTER.

Refs: **12** (4, 6–13).

Berton (Cambridgeshire, England). Now spelled Barton. Three miles south-west of CAMBRIDGE, with its origins pre-dating Anglo-Saxon times, Barton is now primarily a detached suburb of the university city. Situated on the Roman road, running north-eastward from Ermine Street through CAMBRIDGE to Stretham, ELY and Littleport, the village contains a 14th C. church, with parts of the chancel dating from *c.*1100. Barton Moats, now covered with grass, have been dated as late Saxon or early Norman, somewhere between the 10th C. and 12th C. The main part of the earthworks consists of a 140 ft. rectangle surrounded by a dry moat 30 ft. wide and 2 ft. deep. On its southern side is a smaller moated area measuring 80 ft. by 60 ft.

Novels: For a 'year or more' before he entered RAMSEY ABBEY, Brother TUTILO was a 'harper to his father's lord at the manor of Berton.'

Refs: **19** (1).

Bertred (*c.*1121–1142) (fict.). **Novels:** 'A youthful body and handsome, perhaps slightly over-muscled for perfection. Not much past twenty, surely, and blessed with features regular and shapely, again perhaps a shade over-abundant in flesh or under-provided with bone . . . Nevertheless, a very comely young man. Face and neck and shoulders, and from elbow to fingertips, he was tanned by outdoor sun and wind.' Son of ALISON, Bertred was foreman of Judith PERLE's weavers and lived with his mother in the VESTIER household in SHREWSBURY. He had 'an eye for a pretty girl' and fancied his chance at marrying his widowed mistress. When she was abducted by Vivian

HYNDE, Bertred discovered her whereabouts and, on the night of 19 June 1142, he slipped out secretly to rescue her. As he tried to break into Hynde's counting-house he was disturbed by the watchman's mastiff and, in his panic to escape, he was half-stunned by 'a glancing blow on the head' from the watchman's long staff. Bertred made a last great leap from the bank of the SEVERN and struck his head 'hard against a sharp edge of stone'. While he was unconscious, Miles COLIAR heaved Bertred out into the river and he was drowned. For a while, it seemed that Bertred was Brother ELURIC's murderer, but his innocence was eventually proven. He was buried in ST CHAD's churchyard on 22 June 1142.

Refs: **13** (1, 5–9, 14).

Berwyns (Clwyd, Powys and Gwynedd, Wales). From the broad SEVERN plain near OSWESTRY, the foothills of the Berwyn mountains of North Wales slope westward for some 15 miles, reaching a height of over 2,000 feet. The Berwyns are sometimes referred to as the 'Foothills of Snowdonia', and stretch in a north-easterly direction from near Bala to Llangollen. The highest mountain of the range is Moel Synch, at 2,713 ft. Among the rivers rising on the Berwyns are the Tanat, VYRNWY and CEIRIOG.

Novels: 'In the distance, as he [CADFAEL] rode due west in the dimming light, the hills of Wales rose blue and noble, the great rolling ridge of Berwyn melting into a faintly misted sky.'

Refs: **3** (8); **9** (2–3).

Betton (now Betton Abbots) (Shropshire, England). DB – Betune: in Condover Hundred; land of the Bishop of Chester. (In the 12th C. lands at nearby Betton Strange [see SUTTON STRANGE] were granted to HAUGHMOND ABBEY and those at Betton Abbots to SHREWSBURY ABBEY. Betton Abbots was sometimes called Little Betton, to distinguish it from Great Betton, near HALES, which was also held by Shrewsbury Abbey.) Betton Abbots, now essentially a farm, lies just over 6 miles to the south-east of SHREWSBURY. Within the area of Betton, to the north of Betton Abbots, there is Betton Pool, Betton Alkmere, Betton Coppice and Betton Strange.

Novels: On 22 June 1143 Father BONIFACE 'was called away to Betton, and missed all but the morning Mass.' JAMES, the master-carpenter, came from Betton.

Refs: **16** (9); **19** (2-4).

Betton Strange. See SUTTON STRANGE.

Beuno Saint (d. *c.*640) (hist.) (f.d. 21 April). Much of the information on St Beuno comes from his Life written in the 14th C. Some sources claim that he was born in Shropshire in *c.*550, while others place his birth in Llanfeuno (now spelled Llanveynoe), Hereford & Worcester. Nevertheless he is considered to be a Welshman. The son of Bugi and Beren (who are both called by a range of alternative names), Beuno is traditionally held to be the uncle of St WINIFRED and is reputed to have brought her back to life after she had been beheaded. He is particularly associated with CLYNNOG Fawr in Gwynedd, where he founded his principal monastery and became abbot. He was buried at Clynnog, and his tomb and nearby well became highly esteemed as healing shrines. He is considered to be the second most important saint in Wales after DEWI SANT.

Novels: St Beuno converted TEVYTH and his household, including St WINIFRED. Seeing CRADOG cut off the head of Winifred, her uncle Beuno 'fitted the head of the virgin onto her neck, and the flesh grew together, and she stood up alive, and the holy fountain sprang up on the spot where she arose'.

Refs: **1** (1); **10** (1).

Bianca (*fl.* 1098) (fict.). **Novels:** 'CADFAEL thought of Bianca, and ARIANNA, and MARIAM and all the others, some known so briefly, all so well.' In his roving youth, Cadfael met Bianca in VENICE and, years later, remembered her 'drawing water at the stone well-head'.

Refs: **1** (1, 9); **3** (4).

Bigod, Hugh (d. 1176/7), Earl of Norfolk (hist.). Second son of Roger Bigod, and younger brother of William Bigod, he succeeded to the family's estates in 1120, after his elder brother was drowned in the wreck of the *White Ship* (see BLANCHE NEF). Little is known about Hugh's youth, but before 1122 he was a constable of Norwich Castle and a governor of the city. The following year he was a steward in HENRY I's court. After the king's death in 1135, Hugh was instrumental in persuading Archbishop WILLIAM OF CORBEIL to crown STEPHEN King of England (he swore an oath that Henry had changed his mind about the succession and designated Stephen). Although Hugh supported Stephen in the early years of his reign, he treacherously seized every opportunity to further his own position and power. In 1140 he is said to have changed his allegiance to the Empress MAUD, but on 2 February the following year he was with Stephen at the battle of LINCOLN, and was among those who fled (see also William de WARENNE, [d. 1148] and Waleran de BEAUMONT). Hugh finally declared for Maud in 1141, but spent most of his time in East Anglia consolidating his own domains, which included castles at Framlingham (the main family seat), Bungay, Thetford and Walton. In 1143/4 Hugh joined with Geoffrey de MANDEVILLE in laying waste to the FENS. In 1148 he supported THEOBALD OF BEC in his quarrel with Stephen, and entertained the archbishop at Framlingham. When Henry Plantagenet (later HENRY II) invaded England in 1153, Hugh seized Ipswich Castle. Although it was recaptured by Stephen, Hugh escaped without punishment. After Henry's accession in December 1154, Hugh received confirmation of his earldom. In 1166 he was excommunicated for refusing to restore lands belonging to the monastery of Pentney, Norfolk. The following year he was absolved, but excommunicated again in 1169, and absolved again in 1170. Further years of rebellion by Hugh and his followers led to the capture and sacking of Norwich, the destruction of his castle at Walton by the king, and the surrender of Bungay and Framlingham, all in 1174. Two years later, the castles at Bungay and Framlingham were destroyed. According to one chronicler Hugh died in the HOLY LAND. This Hugh, however, may have been the earl's younger son. His eldest son, Roger, did not became the 2nd Earl of Norfolk until 1189.

Novels: '"She [Maud] needs all her allies round her, and Hugh Bigod carries more weight than most with the baronage."' Hugh Bigod, Earl of Norfolk, was a loyal supporter of the Empress Maud. On 30 November 1145 he attended the conference at COVENTRY between the empress and King Stephen. While there, he commended Yves HUGONIN to Maud 'for an errand well done'.

Refs: **20** (2–3, 5).

Blanche Nef (or *White Ship*). On the night of 25 November 1120, after leaving the port of BARFLEUR, the *White Ship* sank in the English Channel. Although the ship was one of the finest of its kind, fitted out with many of the latest devices, the crew and passengers were extremely drunk and should never have put to sea. Trying to overtake the main fleet, the ship struck a rock and sank with the loss of all hands except one. Some 300 young noblemen were drowned in the tragedy, including Prince WILLIAM THE AETHELING, son of HENRY I and the heir to the English throne. His death resulted in the period of anarchy which followed Henry I's death, and the fratricidal civil war for the crown of England between King STEPHEN and Empress MAUD.

Refs: **20** (3); **RB** (1).

Blois (France). The city of Blois is situated on the River Loire in north central France, midway between Tours and Orleans. It is first mentioned by Gregory of Tours in the 6th C. By the early Middle Ages it was the seat of the powerful counts of Blois, the ancestors of the Capetian kings of France.

Blount, Donata (1098–1145) (fict.). **Novels:** 'She was past forty-five and long, debilitating illness had aged her into a greyness and emaciation beyond her years.' Wife of Eudo BLOUNT (the elder) of LONGNER and mother of Eudo (the younger) and Sulien, Donata was taken ill in 1135, at the age of thirty-seven, with some form of wasting disease. At one time she had made use of CADFAEL's 'skills at least to dull her pain', but for several years she had refused any medication. Cadfael remembered how she had looked before she 'had shrunk to a dry wand': 'a woman a little taller than his own modest height, slender as a willow even then, her black hair already touched with some strands of grey, her eyes of a deep, lustrous blue.' Towards the end of November 1143 Donata journeyed to SHREWSBURY ABBEY to reveal that GENERYS, her late husband's mistress, had died by poison. As neither of the two women could bear to share him, they agreed to settle the matter by each drinking a cup of wine, one of which contained a fatal draught of hemlock. Having drunk, the women parted to await the outcome of their choice. Donata survived and from then on honoured her pledge never to take any palliatives, whatever the state of her health. 'World-weary and closely acquainted with the ironies of life and death,' she passed peacefully away in March 1145, accompanied by Brother TUTILO's angelic singing. Before she died, as a 'ransom' for Sulien, Donata gave RAMSEY ABBEY some of her valuables. Tutilo was bequeathed her psaltery.

Refs: **17** (3, 6–7, 11, 14); **19** (1–2, 4–5, 7–8, 13)

Blount, Eudo (the elder) (1100–43) (fict.) **Novels:** Eudo, Lord of LONGNER, married Donata in *c.*1118, and they had two sons, Eudo and Sulien. Because of his wife's wasting illness, Eudo was 'forced to be celibate as ever was priest or monk' and, when the opportunity presented itself, he took GENERYS, RUALD's wife, as his mistress. On 28 June 1142, after Donata had told Eudo that GENERYS was dead, 'he went that night, alone, and buried her' at the edge of the POTTER'S FIELD. In early October, he made the gift of the field to HAUGHMOND ABBEY and left LONGNER to join King STEPHEN at OXFORD. Eudo died at the battle of WILTON, and Sulien brought his body home to LONGNER from SALISBURY for burial in March 1143.

Refs: **17** (1, 3, 13–14).

Blount, Eudo (the younger) (b. 1120) (fict.). **Novels:** 'A young man, cheerful and open by nature, a year established now in his lordship, and comfortable in his relationship with his own people and the ordered world around him. The burial of his father, seven months past now, and the heroic manner of his death, though a grief, had also served to ground and fortify the mutual trust and respect the new young lord enjoyed with his tenants and servants.' Elder son and heir of Eudo and Donata BLOUNT, and brother of Sulien. Eudo was left in charge of the manor of LONGNER in the autumn of 1142, after his father had left to join King STEPHEN's army at OXFORD. He became the Lord of Longner on his father's death in March 1143 and married Jehane in the July. By November his young wife was pregnant and he was 'happy in the prospect of an heir'. Eudo gave RAMSEY ABBEY a cartload of wood in February 1145.

Refs: **17** (3, 11); **19** (1–3, 8).

Blount, Jehane (*fl.* 1143) (fict.). **Novels:** 'Sturdy and wholesome as good bread, sure to get sons.' Jehane married young Eudo BLOUNT, Lord of LONGNER, in July 1143 and by November she was expecting their first child. Happy and contented in her marriage, she was 'a pleasant wife'.

Refs: **17** (3, 12–13); **19** (2, 8).

Blount, Sulien (b. 1125) (fict.). **Novels:** 'So this, thought CADFAEL . . . this is the younger brother who chose to enter the Benedictine Order just over a year ago, and went off to become a novice at Ramsey in late September . . . Now why, I wonder, did he choose the Benedictines rather than his family's favourite Augustinians?' He was the younger son of Eudo and

Donata BLOUNT and brother of Eudo. On the night of 28 June 1142, Sulien discovered his father burying the body of GENERYS in the POTTER'S FIELD and concluded, mistakenly, that he was the murderer. Sulien 'chose to take the cowl' and entered RAMSEY ABBEY as a novice in late September. He was given leave by his abbot to return to LONGNER to bring his father's body home from SALISBURY for burial in March 1143. After the monks were expelled from the abbey by Geoffrey de MANDEVILLE, Brother Sulien was ordered to report to Abbot RADULFUS at SHREWSBURY ABBEY. He arrived on 8 October 1143, having been on the road seven days. Sulien confessed to Radulfus that he was no longer sure of his chosen vocation and wanted more time, before he took his final vows. Radulfus admitted him to the abbey and, in order to give him 'some days of quietude', set him to work helping Cadfael in the herb garden. A 'secret child', Sulien heard that Generys' body (then unidentified) had been found in the Potter's Field and went to great lengths to prove that she was still alive, or that those accused of her murder were innocent. RUALD and Generys were close friends of his childhood, and when Ruald left his wife, Sulien found himself in love with her. Instead of revealing his feelings, however, he was prepared to 'give his mind the mastery, set his love up on a pedestal – an altar, rather . . . and worship her in silence.' In mid-October 1143, Sulien abandoned the cowl and returned home to his family at Longner. He discovered GUNNILD, alive and well, at the manor of WITHINGTON and, while there, he first saw Pernel OTMERE. Although not guilty, Sulien confessed to the killing of Generys in order to protect his father. When his mother told him the truth about Generys' death, he was set 'free from every haunted and chivalrous burden that weighed him down'. In February 1145 Sulien and Pernel were 'shortly to marry'; but before, 'to free his conscience', Sulien promised Sub-Prior HERLUIN that he would return to Ramsey and work there with his hands for one month. After his mother's death, having been trained for arms, Sulien was set to join the garrison of SHREWSBURY CASTLE.

Refs: **17** (1, 3–6, 12–13); **19** (1–2, 7–8).

Blund, Godith (née Adeney) (b. 1122) (fict.). **Novels:** Pseudonym: Godric. Nickname: Ganymede. Wife of Torold BLUND and the only offspring of Fulke ADENEY, she was betrothed from a child to Hugh BERINGAR. She was with her father in August 1138 when SHREWSBURY CASTLE was under siege by King STEPHEN, but escaped before it fell. Edric FLESHER gave her refuge and his wife, Petronilla, took her to SHREWSBURY ABBEY, disguised as the boy Godric. She was taken on as a lay servant and set to work helping CADFAEL in the herb garden. Although Cadfael tricked her into giving away her real identity, he kept her secret and also helped her maintain her pretence. She identified the body of Nicholas FAINTREE. Finding the injured Torold Blund in the fields beyond the GAYE, she persuaded Cadfael to doctor his wounds. Thinking she was a boy, Torold nicknamed her GANYMEDE. But, after she had revealed her true identity, they fell in love. With mainly Cadfael's and partly Aline Siward's (see BERINGAR) help, the fugitives managed to escape from SHREWSBURY. Beringar, however, apprehended them in the LONG FOREST. Thinking he had relieved them of William FITZALAN's treasury, he allowed them to go free. Before they parted Beringar kissed Godith and wished her well. It is likely that she and Torold were married before they reached NORMANDY, where she was in December 1141.

Refs: **2** (1–11); **12** (6).

Blund, Torold (b. *c.*1121) (fict.). **Novels:** 'He had a large, generous mouth', hair 'as fair as corn-stalks'. Husband of Godith, liegeman of William FITZALAN and loyal supporter of the Empress MAUD, Torold, a Saxon, came from 'a hamlet by OSWESTRY'. In August 1138 he was among those besieged in SHREWSBURY CASTLE by King STEPHEN. Together with Nicholas FAINTREE, Torold managed to escape, with orders to try and save FitzAlan's treasury. Edric FLESHER hid the fugitives in his barn at FRANKWELL. As soon as it was dark they headed for Wales, but Nicholas's horse fell lame. Torold managed to get a fresh horse from ULF. Returning to ULF'S HUT in the woodland, he discovered that Nicholas had been murdered. He was attacked in the darkness by an unknown assailant (Adam COURCELLE), but managed to escape. Torold fled west, but was forced to turn back towards SHREWSBURY. Being a strong swimmer, he eventually took to the SEVERN, 'saddlebags and all'. Struck in the shoulder by an arrow, he was carried downstream to safety by the current and managed to hide the treasury in the river under the first arch of the English Bridge. The next day Godith, disguised as the boy Godric, discovered him in the fields along the GAYE and informed CADFAEL. Together they hid Torold in the disused SHREWSBURY ABBEY mill where Cadfael tended his injuries. It did not take Torold long to discover that Godric was in fact the daughter of Fulke ADENEY, and was also being hunted by the king's officers. With Cadfael's help, despite Hugh BERINGAR's attempts to intervene, Torold and Godith managed to escape together into Wales with FitzAlan's gold. It is most probable that, between leaving Cadfael in the LONG FOREST and reaching NORMANDY, they were married. Torold returned to England during the summer of 1141 with Ninian BACHILER to sound out the extent of MAUD's support. When Queen MATILDA moved her army up into LONDON and beyond, Torold and Ninian found themselves cut off from return. Although Ninian was forced to flee north, Torold 'slipped overseas again safely, back to his wife'.

Refs: **2** (4–5); **12** (6).

Bohemond I (*c.*1052–1111), Prince of Antioch. (hist.). The Norman son of Robert Guiscard, Duke of Apulia and Calabria, and his first wife, Alberada, Bohemond fought with his father against the Byzantine empire between 1081 and 1085. Bohemond and his small force of Normans joined the First Crusade in 1096, and they took ANTIOCH in 1098 (see also GODFREY OF BOUILLON). When the crusaders set out for JERUSALEM in 1099, Bohemond stayed behind in Antioch and declared himself prince, thereby violating the oath he had given to the Byzantine Emperor, Alexius Comnenus. He was imprisoned by the Emir of Cappadocia between 1100 and 1103. On his return to Antioch he found the city caught between the conflicting interests of the Byzantine empire in the north and the Muslim world to the east. The city was attacked by Alexius in 1104. In the same year Bohemond returned to Europe and his nephew, TANCRED, succeeded to the princedom. In 1106 Bohemond married Constance, the daughter of Philip I of France. She bore him two sons, one of whom eventually became Prince of Antioch. He continued his war against Alexius, but was defeated and forced to agree to terms which brought Antioch under the overlordship of the Byzantine empire.

Novels: 'There are alliances that cross the bloodline of families, the borders of countries, even the impassable divide of religion. And it was well possible that Guimar de MASSARD should find himself closer in spirit to the Fatimid caliphs than to Bohemond and BALDWIN and TANCRED, squabbling like malicious children over their conquests.'

Refs: **5** (11).

Bohun, Humphrey de (d. 1187) (hist.). Son of Humphrey II de Bohun, with whom he appears to have been confused by some historians, he was originally a supporter of King STEPHEN, but changed allegiance in 1139 when the Empress MAUD landed at ARUNDEL, and became one of her two stewards (the other was Robert de Courcy). His stronghold was at Trowbridge, Wiltshire, which he strengthened. He was among those captured at WINCHESTER in 1141, but was released after paying his ransom. Little is heard about him after the accession of HENRY II, except that he was one of the king's loyal baronial supporters. Humphrey married the eldest daughter of MILES, Earl of Hereford, and, in 1199, their grandson, Henry de Bohun, was created earl.

Novels: Steward of the Empress Maud and one of 'the props of her personal household', Humphrey de Bohun was a practical man, encouraging confidence in his fellow men. He attended the conference at COVENTRY between Maud and King Stephen on 30 November 1145. In December he was with the empress at GLOUCESTER when Yves HUGONIN brought news that Philip FITZROBERT was at La MUSARDERIE. Bohun helped the empress take the castle.

Refs: **20** (2–3, 10–12, 14).

Bonde, John (b. *c.*1110) (fict.). **Novels:** '"a simpleton, or little better, but a hard worker and open as the day"', he was a servant in the household of Humphrey CRUCE, Lord of the manor of LAI. After his master's death in 1138, he became subject to a new lord, Reginald CRUCE. Bonde was one of three trustworthy men-at-arms, under Adam HERIET, who escorted Julian CRUCE to the Benedictine Abbey at WHERWELL in 1138. All, except Heriet, went no further than ANDOVER. Bonde was proficient in the use of the short Welsh bow. In September 1141 he was questioned at Lai by Nicholas HARNAGE about Julian Cruce's disappearance, but could tell him nothing.

Refs: **11** (7).

Bonel, Gervase (1078–1138) (fict.). **Novels:** 'Gervase Bonel had surely let his spite run away with his reason, to barter such a property for the simple necessities of life, when he was already turned sixty years, and could hardly expect to enjoy his retirement very long.' Lord of MALLILIE, husband of Richildis, step-father of Edwin GURNEY, and father of the illegitimate MEURIG, Gervase had been a widower for many years and was without legitimate children when he married Richildis Gurney (herself a widow) in 1135, after a long courtship, promising to make her son, Edwin, his heir. Falling out with Edwin in 1138, he decided to cut his step-son off without a penny and grant his inheritance to SHREWSBURY ABBEY. At the beginning of December, however, the 'guestship agreement' between the abbey and Gervase was unable to be ratified because of HERIBERT's suspension from the abbacy. Although the agreement could not be sealed, the move was countenanced 'pending final sanction' and, just before Christmas, the Bonel household moved from Mallilie to a messuage at SHREWSBURY. Gervase died shortly afterwards, poisoned by Meurig. He was buried just before Christmas 1138 in the cemetery at Shrewsbury Abbey.

Refs: **3** (1–3, 6).

Bonel, Richildis (née Vaughan, then Gurney) (b. 1080) (fict.). **Novels:** 'She had married the right man and been blessed, and a late mistake with the wrong man was over without irreparable damage.' Wife of Gervase BONEL and mother of Edwin and Sibil by her first husband Eward GURNEY, Richildis Vaughan of SHREWSBURY was the 'daughter of an honest, unpretentious tradesman'. She was 'affianced' to CADFAEL in December 1097, 'though nobody knew it but themselves, and probably her family would have made short work of the agreement if they had known of it'. The following year, Cadfael left for the HOLY LAND. In 1104, tired of waiting for his return, she married Eward Gurney, 'a solid yeoman with good prospects in the shire, and no intention of flying off to the wars'. She gave birth to Sibil in 1105, and Edwin in 1124. In 1133, after Eward's death, Martin BELLECOTE took over her husband's shop. Richildis married Gervase Bonel, 'out of her kind', in 1135, on the promise that he would make Edwin his heir. In December 1138, just before the Christmas feast, she moved from MALLILIE, with Gervase and two servants, AELFRIC and ALDITH, to a house in the ABBEY FOREGATE belonging to SHREWSBURY ABBEY. Shortly after, Gervase was poisoned and Richildis found herself widowed for the second time. While in Shrewsbury, she met Cadfael, whom she had not seen for forty-two years. In January 1139 Richildis returned to MALLILIE. 'Brother Cadfael heaved a deep sigh that might have been of regret, but might equally well have been of relief.'

Refs: **1** (1); **3** (2–3, 5, 8, 11); **RB** (1).

Bonel's Messuage (Abbey Foregate, Shrewsbury, Shropshire) (fict.). Although it never existed, the Bonel messuage stood on the south side of the ABBEY FOREGATE, just east of the present Railway Bridge.

Novels: The 'first house on the town-side of the mill-pond', it was 'a good house, with three rooms and the kitchen, and a small garden behind, running down to the pond . . . The kitchen door faced away from the pond, towards the prospect of SHREWSBURY beyond the river . . . the strip of garden was narrow here, though the house stood well above the water level'.

Refs: **3** (2, 7).

Boneth, John (*fl.* 1140) (fict.). **Novels:** He 'cast a knowledgeable eye on his master, and withdrew, assured of having work to himself, as he preferred it. By this time John Boneth knew everything his skilled but idle tutor could teach him, and was quite capable of running the business single-handed . . . he was trusted and depended on.' Journeyman locksmith of Baldwin PECHE, John Boneth lived, in 1140, with his widowed mother 'two streets away' from his master's shop in SHREWSBURY. When PECHE was murdered in May 1140, Boneth inherited the business.

Refs: **7** (1–3, 5, 8).

Boniface, Father (b. *c.*1112) (fict.). **Novels:** 'Young, not much past thirty, of unassuming appearance and modest bearing, no scholar like his predecessor, but earnestly cheerful about his duties. The deference he showed to his monastic neighbours disposed even Prior ROBERT to approve of him, though with some condescension in view of the young man's humble birth and scanty Latin.' Father Boniface succeeded Father AILNOTH as priest of the SHREWSBURY parish of HOLY CROSS in May or June 1143. He and young Father EADMER of ATTINGHAM had been students together.

Refs: **16** (9); **17** (9, 11); **19** (1–3, 5–6).

Bosiet (now Bozeat) (Northamptonshire, England). Some 9 miles east of NORTHAMPTON, the ancient village of Bozeat lies close to the borders of Bedfordshire and Buckinghamshire.

Novels: The manor, 'the far side of Northampton, some miles south-east of the town', originally belonged to Drogo BOSIET, but, after his death in 1142, it passed to his son, Aymer.

Refs: **14** (4, 6, 9, 12).

Bosiet, Aymer (b. *c.*1112) (fict.). **Novels:** 'As tall and long-boned as his father, but carried less flesh and was leaner in the face; but he had the same shallowy-set eyes of an indeterminate, opaque colour, that seemed all surface and no depth.' Eldest son of Drogo BOSIET and brother of Roger BOSIET, Aymer had had only one wife 'but she was a sickly thing and died young'. He was 'made to the same pattern' as his father, 'free with his fists' and brutal when dealing with his underlings. He arrived at SHREWSBURY in November 1142, in vindictive pursuit of the runaway villein, Brand (see HYACINTH), to find that his father had been murdered and that he had become the new Lord of BOSIET. After only a few days, he abandoned his search, 'cut his losses, and made off in haste to secure his gains at home'. Aymer took his father's coffined body back to Bosiet with him.

Refs: **14** (4, 9, 12).

Bosiet, Drogo (*c.*1092–1142) (fict.). **Novels:** 'And here just issuing from the stables and crossing the yard in long, lunging strides, the gait of a confident and choleric man, was someone undoubtedly of consequence in his own domain, richly dressed, elegantly booted, and wearing sword and dagger.' Father of Aymer and Roger BOSIET, Drogo held the manor of BOSIET in Northamptonshire 'and a fair bit of the county besides'. According to his groom, WARIN, Drogo's wife was '"a poor pale lady, all the juice crushed out of her . . . but better born than the Bosiets, and has powerful kin, so they have to use her better than they use anyone else"'. A brutal master, 'free with his fists', Drogo arrived at SHREWSBURY in November 1142, in pursuit of his runaway villein, Brand (see HYACINTH).

He was murdered in EYTON FOREST by Renaud BOURCHIER in mid-November. His body was taken back to Bosiet for burial by Aymer.

Refs: **14** (4, 6, 9).

Bosiet, Roger (*fl.* 1142) (fict.). **Novels:** 'Not so loud nor so violent [as his brother], but sharper witted and better able to twist and turn.' Younger son of Drogo BOSIET and 'subtle' brother of Aymer, Roger was 'fully capable of mischief for his own advancement'. In autumn 1142, like Aymer, he was looking for a wife. According to WARIN THE GROOM, '"There's an heiress not far from BOSIET they both fancy now – though by rights it's her lands they fancy. And if Aymer is the heir, Roger's far better at making himself agreeable. Not that it lasts beyond when he gets his way."'

Refs: **14** (9, 11).

Bossard, Juliana (b. *c.*1097) (fict.). **Novels:** '"Now she's widowed she'll have a hard fight on her hands to evade being married off again – for she'll want no other after Rainald. She has manors of her own to bestow."' Wife of Rainald BOSSARD and distant cousin of Luc MEVEREL. Having no children of their own, they took Luc into their household in 1140, meaning 'to make him their heir'. Juliana was widowed on 9 April 1141. That same day Luc disappeared and, when Olivier de BRETAGNE went north on business for the Empress MAUD, Juliana asked him to look out for her kinsman.

Refs: **10** (7, 10).

Bossard, Rainald (1092–1141) (fict.). **Novels:** Husband of Juliana and a knight of the Empress MAUD, in the following of Laurence d'ANGERS, Rainald's chief manor was near WINCHESTER. Olivier de BRETAGNE knew him well through 'a year of service in Palestine, and the voyage home together. A good man he was, and a good friend.' Although he had no children, Rainald intended to make Luc MEVEREL his heir. He was slain in WINCHESTER on the evening of 9 April 1141 by CIARAN, while trying to rescue CHRISTIAN. '"The clerk got no worse than a few bruises. It was the knight who got the knife between the ribs from behind and into the heart. He died in the gutter of a Winchester street."'

Refs: **10** (1–2, 7).

B

Boterel, Evrard (b. *c.*1114) (fict.). **Novels:** 'A fine figure of a young man, fair as his horse's mane, and well aware of his handsome appearance and his dominant nobility', he inherited his father's two manors, CALLOWLEAS and LEDWYCHE, in 1137. Although the Boterels were not a 'great family', they were 'respected'. On 2 December 1139 Evrard received a message from Ermina Hugonin (see BRETAGNE) at DRUEL'S HOLDING. A 'son or nephew' to one of her father's friends, he had visited her 'now and then' at WORCESTER. Late that evening, he arrived at the holding with horses and took her back with him to Callowleas. Ermina and he intended to marry and, with her consent, Evrard sent for a priest. But, on 3 December, the manor was sacked by Alain le GAUCHER's outlaw band. Evrard fled to LEDWYCHE with Ermina, abandoning his people to die. When she told him that she would not marry a coward, he tried to take her by force. Ermina knifed him in the arm and, 'while he was raving and cursing and dripping blood', she slipped out into the night and ran. Evrard followed her and, when he discovered Sister HILARIA alone in a hut, he 'took out his venom' on her and 'avenged himself'. He claimed later that he had not meant to kill her, only to stop her from screaming. He took her naked, lifeless body out into the snow and left it in the brook, hoping to put the blame on GAUCHER's outlaws. In their search for the missing Ermina, CADFAEL, Hugh BERINGAR and Yves HUGONIN visited Evrard at Ledwyche and found him unwell. Later that month, fully restored to health, he rode into BROMFIELD Priory. Cadfael drew him into the church and once inside Ermina tricked him into betraying his guilt. He was arrested for the murder of Hilaria and taken to LUDLOW CASTLE to stand trial.

Refs: **6** (4–6, 15).

Bouldon (Shropshire, England). DB – Bolledone: in Culverstone Hundred; a holding of Helgot under

Roger de MONTGOMERY. Situated some 7 miles north of LUDLOW, near the remains of the 12th C. Corfham Castle, Bouldon lies in the Clee Brook valley at the western foot of BROWN CLEE HILL. One mile to the north-east of the village on the western slopes of Brown Clee Hill is Heath, where, standing in lonely isolation in a field, there is a small chapel that has survived virtually unaltered since Norman times. Evidence of an abandoned medieval village can be found in the fields surrounding the church.

Refs: **RB** (3).

Bouldon, Jacob of (*fl.* 1140) (fict.). **Novels:** 'That paragon of clerks, so quick to learn the value of a rent-roll, so earnest to win the trust and approval of his master, and lift from him every burden, particularly the burden of a full satchel of the abbey's dues.' In 1140 the young Jacob of Bouldon entered the service of SHREWSBURY ABBEY as a lay clerk. When Brother AMBROSE fell ill just a few days before the yearly rents were due for collection, Jacob was installed as a substitute by William REDE. 'Not that he had found any cause to complain of the young man's work. He had copied industriously and neatly, and shown great alertness and interest in his quick grasp of what he copied, making round, respectful eyes at the value of the rent-roll.' After Jacob had robbed Rede of the ABBEY rents and slid his unconscious master's body into the River SEVERN, CADFAEL tricked the lay clerk into giving himself away. Jacob was apprehended in Roger CLOTHIER's loft by the sheriff's sergeant, while attempting to murder, so he believed, the only witness to the crime, the blind beggar, Rhodri FYCHAN (the less).

Refs: **RB** (3).

Boulogne (France). On the coast of northern France, some 50 miles south-west of Calais, the city and port of Boulogne lies at the mouth of the River Liane. The English port of Folkestone is some 28 miles across the Channel to the north-west.

Novels: In 1141, '"She [Empress MAUD] has greatly offended the bishop-legate," said the abbot [RADULFUS], "by refusing to allow STEPHEN's son to receive the rights and titles of his father's honours of Boulogne and MORTAIN, now that his father is a prisoner. It would have been only justice. But no, she would not suffer it. Bishop HENRY [OF BLOIS] quit her court for some time, it took her considerable pains to lure him back again."'

Refs: **10** (2).

Bourchier, Renaud (d. 1142) (fict.). **Novels:** Pseudonym: Cuthred. Also called St Cuthred. Also known as the Hermit of Eyton Forest. A knight of the Empress MAUD, Bourchier 'gained his life and liberty' by escaping from the siege of OXFORD at the end of September 1142. Maud entrusted him with her treasure and also a confidential letter to Brian FITZCOUNT. Bourchier, however, betrayed her trust and, abandoning his horse in the woods near WALLINGFORD, he headed north with his spoils. The evidence seemed to suggest that Bourchier had been robbed and murdered 'for what he carried, and buried somewhere in the woods or slung into the river'. The traitorous knight met HYACINTH at NORTHAMPTON PRIORY. After the runaway villein had stolen a habit from the priory store, they journeyed to BUILDWAS together as priest and servant. In October, calling himself Cuthred, Bourchier arrived at the manor of EATON. CADFAEL first saw the priest on 21 October at the funeral of Richard LUDEL the elder. 'He wore a monastic gown, rusty black and well worn at the hems, but a head of unshorn dark hair showed within his cowl, and a gleam of reflected light picked out two or three metallic gleams from his shoulder that looked like the medals of more than one pilgrimage. Perhaps a wandering religious about to settle for the cloister.' Dame Dionisia LUDEL persuaded him to settle in a disused hermitage on Eaton land in EYTON FOREST. 'Within a month of his coming his discipline counted for more in the manor of Eaton than did either Dionisia's or Father ANDREW's and his fame, banned from being spread openly, went about by neighbourly whispers, like a prized secret to be exulted in privately but hidden from the world.' He soon gained such a reputation for holiness that many of the country folk referred to him as St Cuthred. He interceded on Dionisia's behalf in her attempts to persuade Abbot RADULFUS to return young Richard LUDEL to Eaton. And, although he was not a priest, he married young Richard and Hiltrude ASTLEY, against their wishes, at LEIGHTON. In November, Drogo BOSIET went to visit Cuthred at his hermitage to enquire about his missing villein, Brand (see HYACINTH), and recognised the hermit as being the same man he had played chess with at THAME Abbey two months earlier. As soon as he realised that Drogo had seen through his disguise, Bourchier knifed him from behind and left his body in the forest. Shortly after, Bourchier was killed in a 'fair fight' by Rafe of Coventry (see GENVILLE.).

Refs: **14** (2–6, 9, 11, 13–14).

Bozeat. See BOSIET.

Brace Meole (now Meole Brace) (Shropshire, England). **DB** – Melam: in SHREWSBURY Hundred; land of the Bishop of Chester, where he also had a manor; the church and some land was held by ST MARY'S CHURCH, Shrewsbury; Ralph of Mortimer also had a manor at Meole. Just over a mile south of Shrewsbury, Meole Brace, once a small village, is now part of the town's extensive suburbs. The site of the 12th C. castle, destroyed by fire in 1669, is in the grounds of the manor, Meole Hall. The name Brace comes from de Bracey (or de Braci), lords of the manor in the 12th C.; while Meole means a hill or sandy bank.

Novels: 'The first mile was through the edges of the [LONG] FOREST, the ground opening gradually into heath and scrub, dotted with small groves of trees. Then he [Niall BRONZESMITH] came to the hamlet of Brace Meole, and from there it was a beaten road, widening as it neared the town into a cart-track, which crossed the MEOLE BROOK by a narrow bridge, and brought him into the [ABBEY] FOREGATE.

Refs: **13** (3, 11).

Bradwell Priory (Buckinghamshire, England). Now almost swallowed by the sprawling modern development of Milton Keynes, Bradwell is 8 miles north-east of BUCKINGHAM and 14 miles south-east of NORTHAMPTON. The small Benedictine priory at Bradwell was founded before 1136 and dissolved in 1524–5. Its sparse remains lie to the west of Bradwell, within the narrow triangle formed by the A5 trunk road, the A422, and the LONDON to Birmingham railway line.

Novels: CADFAEL was among those who accompanied Roger MAUDUIT on the journey from SUTTON MAUDUIT to WOODSTOCK in November 1120: 'They set out early, and before BUCKINGHAM made a halt at the small and penurious priory of Bradwell, where Roger elected to spend the night, keeping his three men-at-arms with him, while GOSCELIN with the rest of the party rode on to the hunting-lodge to make all ready for their lord's reception the following day.'

Refs: **RB** (1).

Bran (b. 1131) (fict.). **Novels:** '"Welsh?" asked CADFAEL, eyeing the child thoughtfully. He must surely have been named for BRAN THE BLESSED.' Son of a Welsh father, Bran, a spindly boy of eight years, arrived at the Hospital of ST GILES with his dying mother, a 'beggar woman', in September 1139. He became a favourite of Brother MARK. Within a month Cadfael's medicines had almost healed Bran's sores and considerably reduced the swellings in his neck. He had a 'knock-kneed gait that stemmed from under-nourishment'. A bright child, Bran turned out to be 'thirsty for letters, and drew in learning like his mother's milk, as naturally as breathing'. When Joscelin LUCY hid in the hospice to escape capture by the sheriff's men, Bran became his friend and constant companion. He was orphaned towards the end of 1139. In September or October 1140 he was 'taken into the household of Joscelin and Iveta LUCY on their marriage'.

Refs: **5** (1, 5–7, 9, 11); **8** (6).

Bran the Blessed (myth.). He first appears in the second branch, or story, of the collection of medieval Welsh tales known as *The Mabinogion*. In the story of 'Branwen Daughter of Llyr', he is the King of Britain. Although the tales were not written down until the 14th C., they are based on ancient pre-Christian Welsh legends. Bran is clearly of divine origin, described as being so huge that no house could contain him. He is portrayed as a just and generous king, a patron of the arts, and the possessor of a magic cauldron which could restore the dead to life. When he is fatally wounded in a battle against the Irish, he orders that his head should be cut off, taken to LONDON and buried with his face pointing towards France. The head gained the power of speech and was able to avert invasions and ward off plagues, but its powers were ultimately lost. After the arrival of Christianity, Bran became the father of Caratacus (or Caractacus or Caradoc). He accompanied his son to ROME, was converted to Christianity, and returned to Britain to spread the faith. He is credited as being the first to bring the Gospel to Wales.

Novels: 'Bran the Blessed, who first brought the gospel to Wales.'

Refs: **5** (1).

Brand. See HYACINTH.

Branwen (*fl.* 1142) (fict.). **Novels:** 'Not at all averse to being the desirable bone between two handsome dogs.' Formerly a carder in the VESTIER household at SHREWSBURY, Branwen, in June 1142, was a 'maid' in the personal service of Judith PERLE. Because of her allergy to raw wool, Judith planned to teach her weaving. '"She's a good girl, she would soon learn."' Branwen was 'fond of Judith' and 'proud of her advancement into Judith's personal service, and fondly imagined herself closer to her mistress's confidence than in fact she was'.

Refs: **13** (1, 5–6).

Branwen, Dame (*fl.* 1137) (fict.). **Novels:** Welsh wife of CADWALLON and the mother of PEREDUR, 'Dame Branwen was indeed audible before they even entered the small room where husband and son were trying to soothe her, against a tide of vociferous weeping and lamentation that all but deafened them. The lady, fat and fair and outwardly fashioned only for comfortable, shallow placidity, half-sat, half-lay on a couch, throwing her substantial person about in extravagant distress, now covering her silly, fond face, now throwing her arms abroad in sweeping gestures of desolation and despair, but never for one moment ceasing to bellow her sorrow and shame. The tears that flowed freely down her round cheeks and the shattering sobs that racked her hardly seemed to impede the flow of words that poured out of her like heavy rain.'

Refs: **1** (3, 9).

Breidden Hills (Powys, Wales). Breidden Hill, formed mainly of volcanic rock, is situated 6 miles north-east of Welshpool (see POOL), overlooking the valley of the River SEVERN. In contrast to Middletown Hill, its immediate south-east neighbour, the eastern slopes of Breidden Hill are thickly afforested. On the summit is Rodney's Column – a landmark dedicated to Admiral Lord Rodney, who died in 1792 – as well as a giant telecommunications mast. The north-west face of the hill has been subjected to extensive quarrying. During the Iron Age there were fortresses on both hills.

Novels: 'Hugh and his men had skirted the Breidden hills before the hour of Prime, and left those great, hunched outcrops on the right as they drove on towards WESTBURY.'

Refs: **9** (12–13).

Bretagne, Ermina de (née Hugonin) (b. 1121) (fict.). **Novels:** 'Blessed be Olivier de BRETAGNE, who had somehow found a way to master her, ousting an immature fantasy of love from her heart, and at whose command she would even remain still and inactive, and leave the burden of the day to others, wholly against her nature.' Wife of Olivier de Bretagne, daughter of Geoffrey HUGONIN, sister of Yves HUGONIN and niece of Laurence d'ANGERS. In 1139, orphaned of both parents, she was in the care of the Benedictine nuns of WORCESTER ABBEY. When the city was sacked by the Empress MAUD's men in November, Ermina, Yves and Sister HILARIA fled north into Shropshire. In bitter snow conditions, and after a long detour to avoid bands of roaming soldiers, they managed to reach CLEOBURY. The following day Brother ELYAS of PERSHORE joined the party, travelling with them as far as FOXWOOD. He tried to persuade them to go west with him to BROMFIELD, but Ermina refused and insisted on pressing on over the hills to GODSTOKE. In the afternoon of 2 December the Hugonin pair and Hilaria arrived at DRUEL'S HOLDING. While there Ermina secretly sent DRUEL's son to CALLOWLEAS with a message for Evrard BOTEREL, with whom she thought she was in love. That night he arrived with horses and took her back to his manor, leaving Yves and Hilaria behind. Ermina consented to marry Boterel, and he immediately sent out for a priest to perform the ceremony. Meanwhile, Callowleas was attacked by Alain le GAUCHER's outlaws, and Boterel, forcing Ermina to go with him, fled to his second manor at LEDWYCHE. Unable to marry a coward, Ermina rejected his advances, knifing him in the arm when he tried to take her by force. While Boterel was 'raving and cursing and dripping blood', she slipped out into the night and ran. Although he followed, she managed to evade him, but became lost and 'benighted' in the snow. She was eventually taken in by a forester and his wife, and discovered the following day by Olivier de Bretagne. In the guise of the forester's son, Olivier escorted her to Bromfield Priory and safety. When Boterel later rode into Bromfield, Ermina named him as the killer of Hilaria and tricked him into betraying his guilt. Shortly after, Olivier secretly returned and took Ermina and Yves away with him to their uncle at GLOUCESTER. At Christmas 1140, Ermina and Olivier were married in Gloucester. She was still in the city in December 1145, and imminently expecting their first child, possibly a grandson and godson for CADFAEL.

Refs: **6** (1, 4, 8, 13, 15); **10** (16); **20** (1–2, 6, 10, 13–14).

Bretagne, Olivier de (b. 1113) (fict.). **Novels:** Formerly called Daoud. Pseudonym: Robert the Forester. 'Everything about him was stirring and strange, and yet from time to time CADFAEL caught his breath as at a fleeting glimpse of something familiar, but so long past that the illusion was gone before he could grasp it, and search back in his memory for the place and the time where it belonged.' 'Son of an English crusading soldier in ROBERT of Normandy's following, somehow blown across the world in the service of an Angevin baron, to fetch up here almost more Norman than the Normans.' Illegitimate son of Cadfael and MARIAM, Olivier de Bretagne was born in ANTIOCH in 1113 and given the name Daoud. His mother died when he was fourteen. Attracted to the Christian faith, he made his way to JERUSALEM, where in 1133 he took service with Laurence d'ANGERS. He was baptised a Christian and 'took the name of the priest who stood' as his godfather, Olivier de Bretagne. In November 1139 he arrived in England with his lord, as his 'most trusted squire'. During the severe winter of 1139 he travelled north from GLOUCESTER into Shropshire in search of Ermina and Yves HUGONIN. He was first seen by Cadfael outside the gate of BROMFIELD Priory when, disguised as Robert the Forester's son, Olivier brought Ermina there for safety. After a struggle, Olivier rescued Yves from the outlaw fortress on TITTERSTONE CLEE and slew their leader, Alain le GAUCHER, after a fierce sword fight. Once he knew that Yves was safe, Olivier slipped away to evade capture by the sheriff's men. A few days later, in the disguise of Robert the Forester, he returned to Bromfield to take the Hugonin orphans back with him to Gloucester. Cadfael spotted him in the parish part of the church during Compline, and approached him when the service had ended. While waiting for the brothers to fall asleep, they talked and Cadfael discovered that Olivier was his son. Olivier and Ermina were married in Gloucester at Christmas 1140. Olivier arrived at Shrewsbury on 21 June 1141 to ask Hugh BERINGAR to transfer his allegiance from King STEPHEN to the Empress MAUD. He had been sent by Maud and Bishop HENRY OF BLOIS 'to urge all sheriffs of shires to . . . take the oath of loyalty to her'. He was also under instructions to look out for Luc MEVEREL, whom he found. On 24 June Olivier heard that Maud had been driven out of LONDON. Abandoning his plans, he hurriedly headed south to join his lord. Despite meeting Cadfael several times, Olivier only found out that the monk was his father in December 1145. In the same year he was secretly imprisoned in the dungeons of La MUSARDERIE by his friend, turned traitor, Philip FITZROBERT, after refusing to change his allegiance from Maud to Stephen. Cadfael located Olivier at La Musarderie, 'hidden away out of reach'. It was FitzRobert who informed Olivier that Cadfael was his father. After his eventual release, Olivier, helped by Cadfael and REINOLD, got the injured and unconscious FitzRobert – 'captor turned prisoner, friend turned enemy' – out of La Musarderie, and away from the clutches of the empress's forces, to safety at CIRENCESTER ABBEY. Olivier returned to Gloucester at the close of 1145 accompanied by Cadfael. And there father and son parted.

Refs: **6** (5, 7, 12, 15–16); **8** (6); **10** (2, 7, 10–11, 14–16); **11** (5); **20** (1–16).

Breteuil (France). Some 30 miles south-east of Bernay and 7 miles north of Verneuil-sur-Avre, Breteuil (or Breteuil-sur-Iton) is an old market town almost encircled in a loop of the River Iton. Although there was a medieval castle at Breteuil, the site is now occupied by public gardens. Parts of the church of St Sulpice, including the nave and lantern tower, date from the 11th C. The town is separated from the Forest of Breteuil by an artificial lake, fed by the river.

Novels: Robert de BEAUMONT (the younger)'s wife (see AMICIA, Countess of Leicester) brought him Breteuil, 'a large honour in Normandy', but it was the 'lesser part' of his heart.

Refs: **19** (4–5, 11).

Breteuil, Heiress of. See AMICIA, Countess of Leicester.

Brewood Nunnery or White Ladies Priory (Shropshire, England). DB – Breude: in Cuttlestone Hundred; land of the Bishop of Chester. The remains of White Ladies Priory are situated some 4 miles west of Brewood and 2 miles north of Albrighton. Although not mentioned in DB, at the time of the Norman Conquest there was an extensive forest in the area, known as the Royal Forest of Brewood. White Ladies Priory was located almost in the heart of the forest. The nuns were of the Augustinian Order and were called 'white ladies' because of the colour of their undyed habits. Dedicated to St Leonard, the priory was founded around the beginning of the 12th C., but the foundation was small; in 1377 there were nine nuns and in 1536, at its dissolution, there were even less. By the 17th C. White Ladies Priory was part of a large house belonging to the Roman Catholic Giffards, but it was demolished in the following century. White Ladies Priory is open to the public and administered by English Heritage.

Novel: Asked by Lazarus (see MASSARD, Guimar de) where he would take Iveta de Massard (see LUCY), Joscelin LUCY replied: '"I'd take her to the White Ladies at Brewood, and ask sanctuary for her until enquiry could be made into her affairs, and a proper provision made for her. They would not give her up gainst her will.'"

Refs: **5** (7).

Briar (fict.). **Novel:** Favourite horse of Joscelin LUCY, Briar was 'silvery grey blotched with darker grey'. While he was tethered in the ABBEY FOREGATE, near Bishop ROGER DE CLINTON'S HOUSE, Joscelin knotted a coiled strip of vellum securely in the horse's forelock with a secret message to Simon AGUILON.

Refs: 5 (**8**).

Bridgnorth. See BRIGGE.

Brigge or Bridgnorth (Shropshire, England). Some 18 miles south-east of SHREWSBURY, and also on the River SEVERN, the old market town of Bridgnorth is divided into Low Town and High Town. The lower town, lying on the eastern bank of the river, is linked to the upper town, on the western side, by a six-arched stone bridge. High Town is situated on a red sandstone ridge overlooking the Severn valley with a church at each end and a castle at the southernmost point. There are many half-timbered houses in Bridgnorth, the earliest – Bishop Percy's House – dating back to Elizabethan times. A few of the buildings have cellars or storerooms cut in the rock. There are also a number of caves, some of which were occupied right up until the early 20th C. (the last cave dweller left the Hermitage in 1928). The town was granted the right to hold a market in the early 13th C.

Novels: WALTER THE COOPER'S SHOP was in the hilltop town of Brigge. 'The Danes had reached no further south than Brigge in this shire, but they had left a few of their getting behind when they retreated.' Rhodri ap HUW from MOLD came to Shrewsbury by barge on 30 July 1139. Once his Welsh boatmen had unloaded most of the cargo, he sent the rest downriver to Bridgnorth.

Refs: **4** (1:2, 4:1); **11** (1, 8, 13–14); **13** (10).

Brigge Castle (Shropshire, England). DB – There is no record of Bridgnorth (see BRIGGE), but there is mention that in Alnothstree Hundred Roger de MONTGOMERY had a small 'Borough called Quatford' in which he had a 'new house' and founded a church. At Quatford, 2 miles south-east of Bridgnorth, there are the remains of a fortress, probably the site of Roger de Montgomery's fortified 'new house'. In *c.*1100 his son, Roger de Bellême, transferred the 'Borough' to Bridgnorth, where he built a new fortress on a more strategic site. Situated high up at the southernmost end of the sandstone ridge, the castle was ideally positioned to defend itself against assault, whether from the west or from the east and along the River Severn valley. After a three-month siege, in 1102, the castle was taken from de Bellême by the army of HENRY I and became Crown property. During STEPHEN's reign it was seized by Hugh de MORTIMER, who held it until 1155 when it was once again besieged and taken. By the close of the 13th C., it had declined in importance and was allowed to fall into decay. Today only part of the tower of the keep remains, leaning at a seemingly perilous angle of 17 degrees from the perpendicular. The castle grounds are now a public park.

Novels: WALTER THE COOPER'S SHOP in the hilltop town of Brigge was 'in a narrow alley no great way from the shadow of the castle walls'.

Refs: **11** (8).

Brionne (France). Some 10 miles north-east of Bernay and 30 miles south-west of ROUEN, Brionne was an important market and crossroads town in ancient times. During the Middle Ages it occupied a strategic site guarding the Risle Valley. From 1047–50 the Duke of Burgundy was besieged in Brionne Castle by William of Normandy (later WILLIAM I). Robert de BEAUMONT (the elder) was forced to recover the castle by siege in *c.*1090 after ROBERT, Duke of Normandy, had given it to Robert de Meules. In 1118, on Robert's death, Waleran de BEAUMONT inherited Brionne. Although the Norman fortress is now in ruins, the remains of the square 11th–12th C. keep continues to overlook the town from its commanding hill-top site. Now a sprawling commercial and industrial centre, Brionne is about 5 miles upriver from Bec (or Le Bec-Hellouin), where there are the remains of the once great Benedictine abbey, famed for providing England with two Archbishops of Canterbury, LANFRANC and ANSELM.

Novels: Brionne was among Robert de Beaumont (the elder)'s possessions in NORMANDY at the time of his death. It was inherited by Waleran de Beaumont.

Refs: **19** (4).

Bristol (Avon, England). The medieval town of Bristol, known as Bristowe, was situated at the confluence of the rivers Avon and Frome, some 7 miles upriver from the mouth of the SEVERN (Avonmouth). In 1247 the Frome was diverted to create a harbour and, during the Middle Ages, Bristol became one of the most important ports in England, chiefly involved in the export of wool and woollen cloth. Among its imports were sherry from Spain and wine from Portugal. The city was heavily bombed during World War II, but old buildings still to be seen are: the restored cathedral, founded in 1142 as the church of an Augustinian abbey; and the parish church of St Mary Redcliffe, dating from the 13th C. and described by Elizabeth I as 'the fairest, goodliest and most famous parish church in the kingdom'. The modest remains of Bristol Castle, dating from the end of the early 12th C., are at Castle Green.

Novels: '"Some of the best wines of France come into Bristol, they should have a ready sale as far north as this."' The merchant Thomas of BRISTOL was a man of consequence in the city. 'Empress MAUD had landed at ARUNDEL [on 30 September 1139] . . . with her half-brother ROBERT, Earl of Gloucester, and a hundred and forty knights, and through the misplaced generosity of the king, or the dishonest advice of some of his false friends, had been allowed to reach Bristol, where her cause was impregnably installed already.' 'February [1141] had seen King STEPHEN made prisoner at the disastrous battle of LINCOLN, and swept away into close confinement in Bristol castle by his arch-enemy, cousin and rival claimant to the throne of England, the Empress Maud.' In March 1141 Bishop HENRY OF BLOIS was allowed to speak to Stephen in his prison at Bristol and had 'taken a covey of bishops with him'. At the end of 1142, Henry Plantagenet (see HENRY II) was in Bristol. In June 1143 Hugh BERINGAR commented that '"young Henry is still there in Bristol, but Stephen has no chance of carrying his war that far, and even if he could, he would not know what to do with the boy when he had him"'. In August 1143 it was rumoured that William FITZALAN was back in England and with Maud's forces in Bristol. In February 1145, despite attempts to 'shame it out of England, if not out of the world', slave dealers traded out of Bristol. '"Very quietly, but yes, it's known. But that's mainly a matter of shipping Welsh slaves into Ireland, money seldom passes for humankind here."' The traffic, however, was two ways: DAALNY's Irish mother was sold to a Bristol trader, who sold her again.

Refs: **4** (1:2); **5** (1); **9** (9); **10** (1); **11** (1); **12** (1); **13** (10); **14** (1); **15** (1); **16** (1); **17** (1); **19** (2, 11); **20** (2).

Bristol, Thomas of (d. 1139) (fict.). **Novels:** 'The BRISTOL boat was moored, and her three crewmen beginning to hoist casks of wine on to the jetty, while a big, portly, red-faced elderly gentleman in a long gown of fashionable cut, his capuchon twisted up into an elaborate hat, swung wide sleeves as he pointed and beckoned, giving orders at large. A fleshy but powerful face, round and choleric, with bristly brows like furze, and bluish jowls. He moved with surprising agility and speed, and plainly he considered himself a man of importance, and expected others to recognise him as such on sight.' Uncle and guardian of Emma Vernold (see CORVISER) and a supporter of the Empress MAUD, the merchant, Thomas of Bristol, arrived at SHREWSBURY on 31 July 1139, having brought his barge, laden with goods for the annual fair, up the River SEVERN from Bristol. He was 'one of the biggest importers of wine into the port', and dealt 'in a small way in fancy wares from the east, sweetmeats and spices and candies.' Approached by a delegation of the young men of Shrewsbury, demanding that part of the tolls due to SHREWSBURY ABBEY be paid to the town to help repair the walls, Thomas struck out at the leader, Philip CORVISER, with his staff and knocked him to the ground. In the fight which followed, Thomas was brought down heavily by a rolling cask of wine. He was murdered, stabbed through the heart from behind, on 31 July 1139 by Turstan FOWLER on the orders of Ivo CORBIÈRE. Dying instantaneously and without a struggle, Thomas was stripped, searched and thrown into the river. He was killed because of the letter he was carrying to Euan of SHOTWICK, for eventual delivery to RANULF of Chester. It contained the names of as 'many as fifty . . . secretly bound to the empress, perhaps even the date when ROBERT of Gloucester hopes to bring her to England, even the port where they plan to land'. His naked body was found in a cove near ATCHAM, and brought to Shrewsbury by a boat coming up the Severn from Buildwas on 1 August. Three days later, his coffined body was taken back to Bristol by barge for burial.

Refs: **4** (1:2–4; 2:1; 5:6).

Britric the Pedlar (*fl.* 1143) (fict.). **Novels:** '"They do say there's a good living to be made in pedlary, if you're willing to work at it. Give him a year or two more, and he'll be renting a booth like the merchants, and paying ABBEY fees."' The pedlar of RUITON was a 'big, red-haired', 'powerful fellow' with 'big, sinewy hands'. Since 1137 he had frequented the annual SHREWSBURY ABBEY fair. He met GUNNILD in COVENTRY and from there they travelled to SHREWSBURY together. They stayed in Brother RUALD's deserted croft during the fair of 1142, fighting frequently. Britric deserted her on 4 August, slipping out of the croft while she was asleep and taking 'every penny of her earnings with him as well as his own'. In Autumn 1143 he was suspected of having murdered Gunnild, burying her in the POTTER'S FIELD. He was apprehended near MERESBROOK and taken to SHREWSBURY CASTLE in November 1143, but he was released when the woman was found to be alive and well.

Refs: **17** (6-8).

Bromfield (Shropshire, England). DB – Brunfelde: in Culverstone Hundred; a holding of St Mary's Church, Bromfield (not ST MARY'S CHURCH, SHREWSBURY with which it was confused in the survey). Just over 2 miles north-west of LUDLOW, the village of Bromfield is situated near the confluence of the rivers ONNY and TEME. Little is known about the early history of Bromfield Priory, but by *c.*1115 Osbert was the 'prior'. In 1155 the priory became dependent on the Benedictine abbey at GLOUCESTER, and remained so until the Dissolution, when the monastic buildings were destroyed. The church became the property of Charles Foxe of nearby Ludford, who converted it into a house. In 1658 it was restored once more to being a place of worship. The unique and memorable plaster ceiling was painted in a naive flamboyant style by Thomas Francis in 1672. Near the church, the stone, timbered gatehouse, dating from the 14th C., is all that remains of the priory.

Novels: 'On the fifth day of December [1139], about noon, a traveller from the south, who had slept the night at Bromfield Priory, some twenty-odd miles away, and had the good fortune to find the highroad, at least, in passable condition, brought an urgent message into SHREWSBURY ABBEY. Prior LEONARD of Bromfield had been a monk of Shrewsbury until his promotion, and was an old friend of Brother CADFAEL's, and familiar with his skills.' Cadfael went to Bromfield in December 1139 to tend the injured Brother ELYAS, and while there he discovered that he had a son, Olivier de BRETAGNE.

Refs: **6** (2–15); **10** (2, 7, 11, 16); **20** (2, 9, 13).

Bronzesmith, Avota (d. 1137) (fict.). **Novels:** Wife of Niall BRONZESMITH, Avota died while giving birth to their daughter, Rosalba BRONZESMITH.

Refs: **13** (2, 11).

Bronzesmith, Niall (b. 1102) (fict.). **Novels:** 'Everything about him fitted into the picture of the ordinary, worthy soul almost indistinguishable from his neighbour, and yet the sum of the parts was very simply and positively himself and no other man.' Widower of Avota, father of Rosalba BRONZESMITH and brother of Cecily STURY, Niall the bronzesmith had a house and shop in the ABBEY FOREGATE at SHREWSBURY, which he rented from SHREWSBURY ABBEY. Rosalba lived with her aunt at PULLEY, and every Sunday and some evenings Niall visited her. In June 1142 he was asked by Abbot RADULFUS to take over the responsibility for delivering the rose-rent to Judith PERLE. After all, the rose-bush was in his garden and he had cared for it. One morning Niall discovered that the bush had been damaged. Close by lay the murdered body of Brother ELURIC. After Judith's abduction on 18 June and on his way home from Pulley, Niall recognised her as she rode pillion behind an unidentified horseman, and decided to follow them. He rescued her from an unseen attacker and escorted her safely to GODRIC'S FORD. Although Miles COLIAR had set light to the bush, hoping to prevent the abbey from paying Judith the rent, Niall had picked a rose the day before. On 22 June, the day the rent was due, he went to her house with his daughter and presented her with the rose. As he was about to leave, she called him back. It is highly likely that Niall and Judith were married in the second half of 1142.

Refs: **13** (1–3, 5, 11,14).

Bronzesmith, Rosalba (b. 1137) (fict.). **Novels:** 'A fair creature, with a bright sheen of gold in her cloud of hair, like her mother before her, and a skin like creamy milk, that glowed in sunny weather with the same gilded gloss.' Daughter of Niall and Avota BRONZESMITH (her mother died in childbirth) and niece of Cecily and John STURY, Rosalba was christened with her unusual name by Father ADAM. Unable to care for her on his own, Niall sent her to PULLEY to stay with his sister, Cecily, where she would have other children to play with and a woman's care. Rosalba left the Stury household and returned home with her father on 22 June 1142, the day he delivered the rose-rent to Judith PERLE.

Refs: **13** (2, 11, 14).

(Niall) Bronzesmith's House and Shop (Abbey Foregate, Shrewsbury, Shropshire) (fict.). Although they never existed, the house, shop and yard of Niall BRONZESMITH were in the ABBEY FOREGATE, on the opposite side of the road to SHREWSBURY ABBEY, somewhere in the vicinity of HORSE-FAIR and Holywell Street.

Novels: 'The house in the Foregate stood well along towards the grassy triangle of the horse-fair ground, where the high road turned the corner of the abbey wall. A lower wall on the opposite side of the road closed in the yard where Niall the bronzesmith had his shop and workshop, and beyond lay the substantial and well-built house with its large garden, and a small field of grazing land behind. Niall did a good trade in everything from brooches and buttons, small weights and pins, to metal cooking pots, ewers and dishes, and paid the abbey a suitable rent for the premises.' See also Judith PERLE'S HOUSE.

Refs: **13** (1–5).

Brown Clee Hill (Shropshire, England). Formed of Old Red Sandstone, this hill is situated 8 miles north-east of LUDLOW and 8 miles south-west of BRIDGNORTH. Capped with a tough layer of volcanic rock, known locally as 'dhustone', it is the highest hill in Shropshire. See also BOULDON.

Novels: 'The great, hunched bulk of Brown Clee.'

Refs: **6** (3).

Bruges (Belgium). This city in north-western Belgium is some 7 miles inland from its port, Zeebrugge, on the North Sea, to which it is connected by a canal. During the Middle Ages, Bruges was a leading member of the Hanseatic League and one of the most important commercial centres in Europe, with a monopoly in English wool.

Novels: 'There was a merchant of SHREWSBURY who dealt in fleeces all up and down the borders, both from Wales and from such fat sheep-country as the COTSWOLDS . . . and had good trading relations as far afield as Bruges in Flanders.'

Refs: **11** (5).

Bryn or Bryn Euryn (Clwyd, Wales). Bryn Euryn, 1,424 ft. high, rises above the deep valley of the Afon CLEDWEN, to the east of the village of GWYTHERIN.

Bryn is the plural of the Welsh word *bryniau*, meaning a hill. There are several farms on the hillside with the name of Bryn, for example Bryn-tan, which is the one nearest to Gwytherin.

Novels: In 1137, when asked to account for his movements, and in whose company, ENGELARD replied: '"In no man's company. The byres behind Bryn are in a lonely place, good pasture but apart from the used roads. Two cows dropped their calves today, one around noon, the second not before late afternoon, and that was a hard birth, and gave me trouble. But the young things are there alive and on their legs now, to testify to what I've been doing."'

Refs: **1** (5, 8).

Buckingham (Buckinghamshire, England). Some 18 miles south of NORTHAMPTON and 12 miles west of Milton Keynes, this market town lies on a hill in a loop of the River Ouse, and was once an important medieval wool centre.

Novels: 'There was a merchant of SHREWSBURY who dealt in fleeces all up and down the borders, both from Wales and from such fat sheep-country as the COTSWOLDS . . . Now, in early September, he was on his way home with his purchases, a train of three wagons following from Buckingham, which was as near as he could reasonably go to OXFORD. For Oxford had become as alert and nervous as a town itself under siege, every day expecting that the Empress must be forced by starvation to retreat from WINCHESTER.' Jean de PERRONET, who journeyed to VIVERS in March 1143 to marry Helisende VIVERS, came from Buckingham.

Refs: **11** (5); **15** (7); **RB** (1).

Buildwas (Shropshire, England). DB – Beldewes: in Condover Hundred; held by the Bishop of Chester. The village of Buildwas, on the north bank of the River SEVERN, is situated some 10 miles south-east of SHREWSBURY and 9 miles north-west of Bridgnorth (see BRIGGE). In 1135, on the south side of the river, Bishop ROGER DE CLINTON founded an abbey for Savigniac monks, which was dedicated to Our Lady and St Chad. Buildwas became a Cistercian house when the Savigniac and Cistercian orders were united in 1147; a union that was solemnly promulgated at the Council of Reims in 1148. It was demolished at the Dissolution in 1536. Considered to be one of the finest ruined abbeys in England, Buildwas Abbey is open to the public and managed by English Heritage.

Novels: At the funeral of Richard LUDEL the elder on 21 October 1142, 'There were two grey-habited monks from the Savigniac house of Buildwas, a few miles away down river, to which Ludel had been a generous patron on occasion . . . Savigny had been at Buildwas now for some forty years [in fact, seven years], a foundation of Roger de Clinton, bishop of Lichfield.' Cuthred (see BOURCHIER, Renaud) travelled to Buildwas from NORTHAMPTON in 1142, and it was 'the Savigniac brothers from Buildwas, who brought him into Dame Dionisia LUDEL's house at EATON.'

Refs: **4** (1:4, 2:1); **14** (2, 10, 12–13).

Builth (now Builth Wells or Llanfair-Ym-Muallt) (Powys, Wales). Builth Wells, some 37 miles upstream from HEREFORD, lies on the banks of the River Wye, near its confluence with the rivers Irfon and Ghwerfri. An ancient market town, Builth grew up around a Norman castle, which was partly destroyed by the Welsh, rebuilt by Edward I towards the end of the 13th C., and demolished in the 16th C.

Novels: Alice WEAVER said to CADFAEL: '"It's my young nephew [RHUN], you see, brother . . . my sister's son, that was fool enough to go off and marry a roving Welshman from Builth, and now her man's gone, and so is she, poor lass, and left her two children orphan, and nobody to care for them but me."'

Refs: **10** (3).

Burwell (Cambridgeshire, England). Some 9 miles north-east of Cambridge and 5 miles north-east of Newmarket, the long and winding Fen-edge village and former inland port of Burwell lies at the head of the Burwell Lode waterway. The earthwork remains of King STEPHEN's unfinished moated castle, standing on the site of an earlier settlement, lie at the southern end of the village near the church. Excavations in 1935 uncovered evidence of a large Roman building on the site. It was while besieging the castle in 1144 that Geoffrey de MANDEVILLE was struck in the head by an arrow. The castle was later converted into a manor house by the abbots of RAMSEY ABBEY of which nothing visible now remains. This was replaced in the 14 C. by a new manor house, at what is now Parsonage Farm on Low Road. Although the house was largely rebuilt in the 18th C., the medieval barn and outbuildings survive, but with later, mainly 16th C., alterations. Near the Perpendicular church of St Mary, built of flint and 'clunch' (a soft locally-quarried chalk stone), is a spring – thought to be the original 'Bur-well' or 'spring by the fortified place'. To the south of the village is the Devil's Dyke, a defensive earthwork cut in about the 6th C., which now marks the parish boundary between Burwell and Swaffham Prior.

Novels: 'But this strong-point of Burwell, north-east of Cambridge, irritated [Geoffrey de Mandeville] . . . because it was beginning to interfere with his supply lines, almost the only thing vulnerable about him.' In late August 1144, while besieging King Stephen's castle at Burwell, Mandeville 'discarded his helmet and the curtain of fine mail that guarded his neck' and was 'struck in the head' by an arrow, loosed by 'an ordinary bowman on the wall'. He died of an infection from the wound on 16 September.

Refs: **19** (Prologue).

Bury (also called Bury St Edmunds or St Edmundsbury) (Suffolk, England). The ancient market and cathedral town of Bury St Edmunds is situated on the River Lark, some 14 miles east of Newmarket. It is named after the Saxon king and martyr, St Edmund, who died in 869, and whose body was brought to the monastery at Bury in *c.*903. It was because of his shrine that the town became one of the major centres of pilgrimage in Britain during the early Middle Ages.

Novels: '"Is Torold [BLUND] clean away? Oh, you do me good!" cried Ninian [BACHILER], flushed with joy. "We were separated when they almost cornered us near Bury. I feared for him! Oh, if he's safe home . . ." He caught himself up there, wincing at the thought of calling NORMANDY home.' CUTHRED said: '"I was on my way from St Edmundsbury, by way of the Augustinian canons at CAMBRIDGE, and I lodged two nights over at the Cluniac priory in NORTHAMPTON. He [HYACINTH] was among the beggars at the gate."'

Refs: **12** (6); **14** (6).

Butcher Row (Shrewsbury, Shropshire). Named after the butchers who either lived or traded in the street, old Butcher Row was situated on the southern side of Corviser's of Shoemaker's Row (now Pride Hill). The present Butcher Row (called at one time 'Ffleshomeles' or 'Flesh Shambles' and later, Double Butcher Row) is situated between Pride Hill and Fish Street. In 1828 there were sixteen butcher's stalls in old Butcher's Row, fifteen in Double Butcher Row and nine in Fish Street. The three-storeyed, timber-framed, early sixteenth-century Abbot's House is wrongly reputed to have been the town residence of the abbots of LILLESHALL Abbey.

Novels: 'The street rose steeply, the island town sat high. BERINGAR knew it well, and knew where he was bound. At the summit of the hill the row of the butchers' stalls and shops and houses levelled out, silent and deserted.' Edric FLESHER's shop, the finest in Butcher Row, had 'the sign of the boar's head'.

Refs: **2** (2, 4).

Bwlch y Ddeufaen (Gwynedd, Wales). The old Roman road from ST ASAPH to ABER and CARNARVON crossed the River CONWAY near the legionary fortress of CANOVIUM. From there the road climbed in a north-westerly direction to the mountain pass of Bwlch y Ddeufaen, some 1,400 ft. above sea level. Lying in the gap between Y Drosgl and Foel Llwyd, the pass takes its name from two large standing stones found at its highest point.

Novels: Travelling to Aber in the retinue of OWAIN GWYNEDD in May 1144, CADFAEL and Deacon MARK crossed the barrier of mountains through the 'narrow but wide enough' pass of Bwlch y Ddeufaen.

Refs: **18** (4).

Byzantium. See CONSTANTINOPLE.

C

Cadfael (b. 1139) (fict.). **Novels:** Son of SIONED and ENGELARD, Cadfael was born in March 1139 at GWYTHERIN and named after Brother CADFAEL. BENED brought the news to Cadfael at SHREWSBURY in June 1139. They '"have a fine son – three months old, I reckon he'd be now – dark and Welsh like his mother. And they've named him Cadfael."'

Refs: **1** (12).

Cadfael, Brother (b. 1080) (fict.). **Novels:** Also called Cadfael ap Meilyr ap Dafydd. 'The light encounters and the grave, not one of them had left any hard feelings behind. He counted that as achievement enough, and having known them was part of the harmonious balance that made him content now with this harboured, contemplative life, and gave him patience and insight to bear with these cloistered, simple souls who had put on the Benedictine habit as a life's profession, while for him it was a timely retirement. When you have done everything else, perfecting a conventual herb-garden is a fine and satisfying thing to do. He could not conceive of coming to this stasis having done nothing else whatever.' Benedictine monk, herbalist and apothecary at SHREWSBURY ABBEY. Son of MEILYR and grandson of DAFYDD, Cadfael was born in TREFRIW in May 1080. He had a younger brother to whom he left his share of the land. He entered the service of a SHREWSBURY wool merchant in 1094, and remained in the town until the death of his master in 1097. He fell in love with Richildis Gurney (see BONEL), but left her in the same year, when he took up the Cross and left England for the HOLY LAND. Vowing to return to Shrewsbury to marry her, Cadfael delayed his 'coming far too long; and she for all her pledges to wait for him, had tired at last and succumbed to her parents' urgings, and married a more stable character'. Cadfael joined the mixed army raised by ROBERT of Normandy. Their route to the east took them across Europe by land to Pontarlier, over the ALPS into Italy, and south by ROME to Brindisi, where they embarked for Asia Minor and CONSTANTINOPLE. For some sixteen years he roved as far afield as VENICE, CYPRUS and the Holy Land, fighting in one campaign after another, first as a soldier and later as a sailor. In 1098 he was with GODFREY OF BOUILLON at the fall of ANTIOCH. The following year he was at the siege and storming of JERUSALEM. In August 1099 he fought at ASCALON. And when the Crusader Kingdom of JERUSALEM was established he became a sea captain, engaged along the coast, defending the newly won Christendom. He first met MARIAM at Antioch in 1098 and their relationship lasted 'a whole year' before the forces of the Cross moved on to take Jerusalem. In 1113 he finally left the Holy Land, departing from the port of ST SYMEON by way of Antioch. It was not until twenty-six years later that Cadfael discovered, to his surprise and joy, that he had left Mariam pregnant with their illegitimate son, Olivier de BRETAGNE. It appears that in 1114, Cadfael briefly returned to England to discover, to his relief, that Richildis had married someone else. Shortly after he enlisted in the 'muddled mêlée of a war' in which the English under HENRY I fought to consolidate their earlier conquest of NORMANDY. By the time Henry had brought his campaign to a successful conclusion, Cadfael was in the process of reassessing his life. Realising that he had finally finished with arms, he was looking for 'a new need and a different challenge'. In mid-November 1120 he sailed into SOUTHAMPTON from Normandy in the service of Roger MAUDUIT. At WOODSTOCK that same month, having fulfilled his obligations to his lord, Cadfael decided to become a novice in Shrewsbury Abbey. Gradually, over the years, he worked hard to create one of the finest Benedictine herb gardens in the whole of England, stocked with 'many plants of his own careful raising', collected in his travels throughout Europe and the Holy Land. It was 'his own small kingdom' and within it 'he ruled unchallenged'. In November 1145 Cadfael betrayed his vow of obedience to Radulfus, discarding his vocation in order to find Olivier, who had been imprisoned in some unknown location. Having accomplished his duty as a father, he returned to Shrewsbury where he was received back into the monastery.

Refs: **1-20**; **RB** (1–3).

(Brother) Cadfael's Workshop (Shrewsbury Abbey, Shropshire) (fict.). Although it never existed, Brother CADFAEL's Workshop stood within the herb garden, on the south side of the abbey church and beyond the monastic buildings. To the south and west of his wooden hut, the fields led down to the MEOLE BROOK. To reach Cadfael's herbarium from the main courtyard, a path led between the guest-hall and the abbot's lodging, across the mill leet by a small footbridge, through the gardens and round the southern perimeter of the fish-ponds. The site of the Gardens, including the workshop, is now occupied by a car park. 'The Shrewsbury Quest', adjacent, contains a replica of Cadfael's workshop and gardens.

Novels: 'And in his wooden work-shed in the herbarium, his own particular pride, he had half a dozen preparations working in glass vessels and mortars on the shelves, all of them needing attention at least once a day, besides the herb wines that bubbled busily on their own at this stage. It was high harvest time among the herbs, and all the medicines for the winter demanding his care.' Hugh BERINGAR often visited Cadfael in his workshop, where they spent many a pleasant hour together, talking, reminiscing and drinking wine. It was inside the workshop that Cadfael did his best thinking. Solid and squat, the hut was built of wood and well oiled to prevent cracking. In it Cadfael stored and brewed his mysteries. The shelves were neatly arrayed with flagons, bottles, jars and pots: some filled with wines and medicines; others empty. From the deep eaves hung fragrant bunches of dried herbs. The floor was of beaten earth. On it stood a brazier, used to brew Cadfael's preparations and to keep the place warm in winter. Along the wall opposite the door stood a long wooden bench. Among those who used the sweet-scented workshop to secretly meet were: Lady FITZHAMON and MADOC; Joscelin LUCY and Evita de Massard (see LUCY); Sanan BERNIÈRES and Ninian BACHILER.

Refs: **2** (1, 4, 8); **3** (1–2, 4, 7); **4** (3:1, 4:3, 5:4); **5** (1–2, 10); **6** (1); **7** (6); **8** (1, 3, 9, 13); **9** (2, 8); **10** (3, 6, 12); **11** (5); **12** (2, 4–8); **13** (13); **14** (1, 9, 14); **15** (1); **16** (1, 3, 7, 12); **17** (10); **18** (1); **19** (2–3, 5, 7–8, 12); **20** (1, 9); **RB** (2–3).

Cadwaladr (d. 1172), Prince of Gwynedd (hist.). He was the son of GRIFFITH AP CYNAN, king of Gwynedd, by his wife ANGHARAD, and brother of OWAIN GWYNEDD and Cadwallon. In 1136, accompanied by Owain, Cadwaladr invaded CEREDIGION in the south, taking five northern castles, including ABERYSTWYTH. On the death of their father in 1137, Owain became the ruler of North Wales, while Cadwaladr, from his castle at ABERYSTWYTH, laid claim to northern CEREDIGION. In order to strengthen his hold on the region, Cadwaladr married Alice de Clare, sister of Gilbert, Earl of Clare, and daughter of Richard, Earl of Clare (Lord of Ceredigion before his death in 1136), and niece of RANULF of Chester. On 2 February 1141 he was with Ranulf at the battle of LINCOLN, in which King STEPHEN was captured and the town sacked. It was not long before Cadwaladr became involved in feuds with his family and his Welsh neighbours in the south. In 1143 his men murdered ANARAWD AP GRIFFITH, to whom Owain had promised his daughter in marriage. Owain sent his son, HYWEL AB OWAIN, to attack Aberystwyth Castle, and Cadwaladr was forced to flee to Ireland. He returned the following year with a Danish army to wreak vengeance on Owain. The two brothers, however, were reconciled, and the Danes, considering that they had been treacherously deceived, seized Cadwaladr. (The claim that he was blinded by the Danes is due to a mistranslation of the *Brut* by John Williams ab Ithel.) He was released only after the payment of a heavy ransom. In 1146 further hostilities broke out between Cadwaladr and his family and, eventually, Owain drove him into exile in England. In 1157, during the reign of HENRY II, Cadwaladr and MADOG AP MEREDITH joined forces with the king against Owain. Forced eventually to pay homage to Henry, Owain became 'prince' instead of 'king' of Gwynedd, and Cadwaladr regained his Welsh lands and possessions. A great benefactor to HAUGHMOND ABBEY, Cadwaladr was buried, alongside OWAIN, in BANGOR Cathedral.

Novels: 'A handsome man, this Cadwaladr, CADFAEL reflected, approving the comeliness of the shape, if doubtful of the mind within. This man was not so tall as his brother, but tall enough to carry his firm and graceful flesh well, and he moved with a beautiful ease and power beside the squat and muscular Dane. His colouring was darker than Owain's, thick russet hair clustered in curls over a shapely head, and dark, haughty eyes well set beneath brows that almost met, and were a darker brown than his hair. He was shaven clean, but had acquired some of the clothing and adornments of his DUBLIN hosts during his stay with them, so that it would not have been immediately discernible that here was the Welsh prince who had brought this entire expedition across the sea to his own country's hurt. He had the reputation of being hasty, rash, wildly generous to friends, irreconcilably bitter against his enemies. His face bore out everything that was said of him. Nor was it hard to imagine how Owain could still love this troublesome brother, after many offences and repeated reconciliations.' In February 1141, after the battle of LINCOLN, Cadwaladr took Gilbert PRESTCOTE the elder back to Aberystwyth Castle as his prisoner. He agreed to exchange the sheriff for Elis ap CYNAN. In Autumn 1143 a party of men under Cadwaladr's orders ambushed and killed Anarawd ap Griffith. Owain Gwynedd responded swiftly. His son, Hywel ab Owain, drove Cadwaladr out of Wales, and burned his castle of LLANBADARN. In the spring of the following year, Cadwaladr returned with a Danish fleet to avenge himself and restore his lands. He made peace with Owain, however, and reneged on his promise to pay OTIR and the Irish Danes the sum of 2,000 marks. In retaliation, they secretly invaded Owain's camp and took Cadwaladr prisoner. He was released only after he had paid the Danes their fee. Unable to totally discard Cadwaladr, Owain restored him to part of his lands, on probation.

Refs: **9** (1, 3); **18** (1–14).

Cadwallon (*fl.* 1137) (fict.). **Novels:** Husband of Dame BRANWEN, father of PEREDUR and a man of 'substance' in GWYTHERIN, he was a 'peaceable man' who liked 'his comfort and his hunting'. He was neighbour to RHISIART, with whom he had been 'friends from youth'. In May 1137 Brother JEROME and Brother COLUMBANUS stayed at his holding, which was one of the biggest in the parish.

Refs: **1** (2–3, 6).

Caergybi or Holyhead (Gwynedd, Wales). This large port and industrial town lies on the north coast of Holy Island (Ynys Gybi), at the western extremity of ANGLESEY. Named after St Gybi (6th C.), Caergybi was a Christian centre for many hundreds of years.

Novels: '"Where do you suppose he [MEURIG] was bound Hugh? CLYNNOG or Caergybi, and oversea to Ireland?"' 'CIARAN would surely reach his journey's end safely, however long it might take him. Not the journey's end of his false story, a blessed death in ABERDARON and burial among the saints of YNYS ENNLI, but a return to his native place, and a life beginning afresh. He might even be changed. He might well adhere to his hard terms all the way to Caergybi, where Irish ships plied, even as far as DUBLIN, even to his ransomed life's end. How can you tell?'

Refs: **3** (11); **10** (14–15).

Caerhun. See CANOVIUM.

Cai (*fl.* 1137) (fict.). **Novels:** 'Dark, squat and powerful, with a salting of grey in his shaggy locks.' RHISIART's ploughman and a Welshman from GWYTHERIN. In May 1137, when Brother JOHN was taken to Rhisiart's house to be kept under lock and key, Cai volunteered to be his gaoler. He helped John escape when Griffith ap RHYS came to arrest him.

Refs: **1** (2–3, 6, 10).

Cain (bib.). The son of Adam and Eve and the elder brother of ABEL. According to Genesis 4, Cain was a tiller of the soil, whose sacrifice to God was refused, while his brother's offering was accepted. In a jealous rage Cain murdered Abel, and was banished by God to live as a fugitive, 'cursed from the earth', unable to settle and farm the land again. For his protection, God gave Cain a mark or sign, promising that if he were slain, his death would be avenged sevenfold.

Novels: '"The first murderous warfare in the world, we are told, was between brothers"'.

Refs: **20** (8).

Callowgate. See CALLOWLEAS.

Callowleas (now Callowgate) (Shropshire, England). Callowgate is a small farmstead lying on the northern slopes of TITTERSTONE CLEE, approximately midway between Cleestanton and CLEETON St Mary, and some 6 miles north-east of LUDLOW.

Novels: '"There is a manor known as Callowleas, a quarter-circle round the flank of [Titterstone] Clee from [John] DRUEL's place, and much on the same level." Hugh [BERINGAR] paused to frown over his own choice of words. "There was such a manor! It has been wiped out, drained, filleted like a fish. What we found was Druel's homestead over again, but to

C

another degree. This was a thriving manor, and now it's a snowy waste, a number of bodies buried or frozen there, nothing living left to speak."' Once part of 'the old LACY writ', the manor of Callowleas was held by Evrard BOTEREL from Josce de DINAN in 1139. On 2 December, Boterel escorted Ermina Hugonin (see BRETAGNE) from DRUEL'S HOLDING to the manor. The following day, it was destroyed by Alain le GAUCHER's outlaws.

Refs: **6** (4–6, 8, 14–15).

Calvary, Mount (Israel). Also called Golgotha, meaning 'the place of a skull'. The small hill outside the walls of ancient JERUSALEM where Jesus Christ was crucified. The hill is now occupied by the Church of the Holy Sepulchre. Some authorities, however, claim that the location of Calvary is near the Damascus Gate. Legend says that the skull of Adam was buried on the hill.

Novels: Among the 'somewhat dubious' relics belonging to SHREWSBURY ABBEY were: 'Stones from Calvary and the Mount of OLIVES – well, stones are stones, every hill has a scattering of them, there is only the word of the purveyor as to the origin of any particular specimen.'

Refs: **19** (2).

Cambridge (Cambridgeshire, England). Some 60 miles north of LONDON and 45 miles east of NORTHAMPTON, the famous university city of Cambridge lies in East Anglia on the banks of the River Cam. Originally a Celtic river-crossing settlement, Cambridge grew from a Roman outpost, with a bridge across the Cam, to a thriving Saxon market town. In the 9th C., it was occupied by the Danes and, towards the end of the 11th C., by the Normans, who built a castle on a hill overlooking the river. A small Augustinian priory was founded in 1092 by William Picot, Sheriff of Cambridgeshire, on the site of the Saxon church of St Giles, near the castle. It was moved to a new site at Barnwell in 1112 and it was there that the canons built a new church, dedicated to St Giles and St Andrew. The church was rebuilt in 1190, but in 1287 it was struck by lightning and almost completely destroyed. By the close of the 13th C., the priory buildings had been considerably altered and improved. It was dissolved in 1538 and, over the next two centuries, its stones used in the construction of various college buildings. The remains of the priory belong to the Cambridge City Council and may be visited by appointment. The Benedictine priory of St Radegund was founded *c.* 1135, but, after a series of scandals and misdemeanours involving the nuns, it was suppressed in 1496. The following year, John Alcock, Bishop of ELY, founded Jesus College on the site of the nunnery. It was decided, however, to adapt the buildings of the 12th C. priory, and not demolish them and rebuild anew. There were two further monastic houses at Cambridge during the Middle Ages: a Benedictine priory which, after its suppression, became Magdalene College, refounded in 1542; and a large house of Dominican Friars, demolished after the Dissolution and its site occupied by Emmanuel College, founded in 1584.

Novels: Renaud BOURCHIER lodged with the Augustinian canons at Cambridge in 1142 on his way from St Edmundsbury (see BURY) to NORTHAMPTON PRIORY. Geoffrey de MANDEVILLE sacked and burned Cambridge in Autumn 1143. In November, Hugh BERINGAR was ordered to supply a company of men to join King STEPHEN's muster at Cambridge.

Refs: **14** (6); **17** (3, 8, 10); **19** (Prologue).

Campden (now Chipping Campden) (Gloucestershire, England). On the northern edge of the COTSWOLDS, some 19 miles west of Banbury and 11 miles south-west of Stratford-upon-Avon, this ancient market town is dominated by the elegant pinnacled tower of its church. In the Middle Ages it was one of the richest wool-trading centres in the Cotswolds, and its prosperity is not only reflected in the magnificent 'wool' church of St James but also in the town itself.

Novels: Alice WEAVER, who was at SHREWSBURY in June 1141, came from Campden, where she continued her late husband's weaving business.

Refs: **10** (3–4).

Camville, Guy (*fl.* 1145) (fict.). **Novels:** 'A border knight from near BERKELEY', Guy Camville was Philip FITZROBERT's deputy. After his lord had been injured in the attack on La MUSARDERIE castle Camville found himself in command: 'the burden of leadership heavy on him'. Under FitzRobert's orders he surrendered the castle to the forces of the Empress MAUD, and, negotiating terms, was allowed to lead the garrison, fit and wounded, safely to CRICKLADE. The dead he was allowed to bury. FitzRobert he had to leave behind.

Refs: **20** (12–14).

Cannock. See CHENET.

Canovium (now Caerhun) (Gwynedd, Wales). The earthwork remains of the Roman fort of Canovium lie on the west bank of the River CONWAY, near Caerhun, just over 4 miles south of CONWY. It was strategically situated on the ancient military road from CHESTER to CARNARVON, guarding a tidal crossing of the river. The medieval church at Caerhun stands on the site of the fort.

Novels: '"An old, old road," said CADFAEL. "It starts from Chester, and makes straight for the head of Conwy's tidal water, where once, they say, there was a fort the like of Chester. At low tide, if you know the sands, you can ford the river there, but with the tide boats can ply some way beyond."'

Refs: **18** (4).

Canterbury (Kent, England). Some 16 miles north-west of Dover, Canterbury originated as an Iron Age settlement beside the River Stour. After the Roman invasion of 43, the town became a trading centre between the mainland of Europe and LONDON. The arrival of St AUGUSTINE, on his mission from ROME, in 597 led to the founding of St Augustine's Abbey outside the city walls. The remains of the once-great centre of learning and burial place of Augustine himself in *c.*604, include: the foundations of the abbey church; the tombs of several Saxon kings; and Abbot Wulfric's uncompleted rotunda started in the 11th C. Augustine, who became the first Archbishop of Canterbury, founded the cathedral inside the city walls which eventually became the primary ecclesiastical administrative centre of England. The building was severely damaged in 1011 by the Danes, and destroyed by fire in 1067. Three years later, Archbishop LANFRANC began work on completely rebuilding the cathedral, shipping in stone from France. Since then the cathedral has been considerably altered and rebuilt. After the murder of Archbishop Thomas à Becket in 1170 and HENRY II's penance there four years later, Canterbury became an important place of pilgrimage.

Novels: '"King STEPHEN means to keep Christmas at Canterbury this year [1141], and put on his crown again, for all to see which of two heads is the anointed monarch here. And he's called all his sheriffs to attend him and render accounts of their shires."' Hugh BERINGAR attended Stephen's Christmas feast at Canterbury in 1141 and returned confirmed in his office as sheriff. While there, he was given orders to look out for the fugitive Ninian BACHILER. GERBERT was a canon of the Augustinian abbey at Canterbury.

Refs: **12** (1, 4, 6); **16** (1, 11); **18** (1–2, 6).

Canterbury, Archbishop of. See THEOBALD OF BEC, Archbishop of Canterbury.

Carnarvon or Caernarfon (Gwynedd, Wales). Situated on the Welsh mainland, near the western end of the MENAI STRAIT, opposite ANGLESEY, the town and port of Carnarvon is the county seat of Gwynedd. In *c.*75, south-east of the town at Llanbeblig, the Romans built the fort of Segontium on a low hill overlooking the River Seiont (a second and later Roman fort can be found lower down the hill). Nearby is St Peblig's Church dating from the 13th C. At the end of the 11th C. the Norman Earl of CHESTER, Hugh the Wolf, constructed a motte-and-bailey castle near the mouth of the river, overlooking the Menai Strait. The princes of Gwynedd later established a royal residence at Carnarvon. In 1283, after his conquest of North Wales, Edward I began building the present castle and town walls. The stone fortress was erected on the site of the earlier Norman stronghold, but was sacked by the Welsh in 1294. It was strengthened the following year and finally completed in 1322. Edward's son, the first English Prince of Wales (later Edward II), was born there in 1284. It was captured by the Parliamentarians in 1646. The medieval fortified town lay to the north of the castle and within its walls, which survive almost complete, are many old houses, shops and inns linked by a maze of narrow streets. St Mary's Church, dating from the 14th C., stands inside the northernmost corner of the walls.

Novels: In May 1144 a messenger from Carnarvon brought word to OWAIN GWYNEDD at ABER of an imminent Danish invasion. Couriers were dispatched through ARLLECHWEDD and ARFON to call all available Welshmen to Carnarvon. Owain and his force set out the next day. The road from Aber to Carnarvon was direct, and had been built by the Romans to link their great forts. Deacon MARK informed Owain at his Carnarvon stronghold that CADFAEL and HELEDD had been taken prisoner by the Danes.

Refs: **18** (1, 4–8, 10, 13–14).

Carrog, River or Afon (Gwynedd, Wales). Rising on the hills near Rhosgadfan, the Afon Carrog meanders west past the settlements of Rhostryfan and Dolydd. After only a 4 mile journey, the river enters FORYD BAY, where it meets the Afon GWYRFAI before debouching into the MENAI STRAIT, opposite ABERMENAI.

Novels: 'The anchorage at the mouth of the Menai was separated from the broad sandy reaches of the bay to southward by a long spit of shingle beyond which the water of two rivers and their tributaries wound its way to the strait and the open sea, in a winding course through the waste of sands.' TURCAILL (*fl.* 1144) and his companions sailed up the River Carrog to raid the camp of OWAIN GWYNEDD and abduct CADWALADR.

Refs: **18** (10).

Castle Foregate (Shrewsbury, Shropshire). The continuation of the street called Castle Gates, the Castle Foregate stretches northwards from SHREWSBURY CASTLE towards WHITCHURCH. It is one of only two roads into SHREWSBURY which do not have to cross the River SEVERN, either by ford or bridge. Both lead north and occupy the dry neck of land which was formerly guarded by the castle.

Novels: 'Outside the northern gate of Shrewsbury the Castle Foregate housed a tight little suburb of houses and shops, but it ended very soon, and gave place to meadows on either side the road. The river twined serpentine coils on both sides, beyond the fields.'

'Across the swift and sinuous currents of the SEVERN sparkling in sunlight, the hill of the town rose sharply, its long enfolding wall terminating . . . in the thick sandstone towers of the castle, and giving place to the highroad launching away to the north from the Castle Foregate towards WHITCHURCH and WEM.'

Refs: **2** (1, 3, 12); **9** (1, 11); **13** (7, 9); **16** (6, 8).

Castle Street (Shrewsbury, Shropshire). Running from HIGH CROSS, at the junction of Pride Hill and St Mary's Street, to Castle Gates, Castle Street was once part of High Street or High Pavement. In the 18th C. it was known as Raven Street, after the Raven Hotel. It was not until the mid-19th C., however, that the present name was finally fixed. During the 12th and 13th C. the street was the most fashionable residential part of the town. The timber-framed Castle Gates House, built in the early 17th C., was originally in Dogpole, but was dismantled by the Earl of Bradford and re-erected on its present site in 1702. The bay windows were added in 1912 when the building was restored. The Library, originally Shrewsbury Grammar School, was built of stone in 1630. Riggs Hall, one of the original buildings of the School founded in 1552, dates from 1500 and has been recently restored. The Old Council House dates from the early 16th C. and was once the meeting place of the Council of the Welsh Marches. Dated 1618, the timber-framed Council House Gatehouse, Gateway House, is reputed to have been used as a prison.

Novels: 'On the way through the town, up the steep street to the high cross, and down the gentler slope beyond the ramp which led to the castle gateway.' Walter AURIFABER'S BURGAGE 'was situated on the street leading to the gateway' of SHREWSBURY CASTLE.

Refs: **4** (2:2); **7** (2).

Caus Castle (Shropshire, England). Soon after the Norman survey of 1086, Roger Fitz Corbet (1086–1121) built a castle high up on the eastern foothills of the Long Mountain, less than 2 miles south-west of WESTBURY, and named it Caus in honour of his birthplace, Pays de Caux in NORMANDY. Anderson, in *Shropshire: Its Early History and Antiquities* (1864) writes, 'The castle of Caux was one of those border fortresses which, throughout the Anglo-Norman period, was called on alternately to serve the purposes of aggression and defence. Planted in a position of inherent strength, it commanded a wide extent of country; and from its battlements the warder might descry from afar every danger that approached by way of the valley of the Rea.' (See also MINSTERLEY and MINSTERLEY VALLEY.) After Fitz Corbet's death his eldest son, William CORBETT, inherited the castle. In 1134 it was reputedly captured and burnt by the Welsh. It was of such strategic importance, guarding the route from MONTGOMERY to SHREWSBURY, that it continued to play an important role in the defence of the borders for centuries afterwards. Towards the close of the 13th C., there was even a town in the large outer bailey. Caus Castle was finally destroyed in 1645, during the English Civil War. All that now remains are its stone foundations and fragments of the keep.

Novels: 'The first thing that happened was a lightning raid from Caus along the valley towards Minsterley, the burning of an isolated farmstead and the driving off of a few cattle. The raiders drew off as rapidly as they had advanced, when the men of Minsterley mustered against them, and vanished into Caus and through the hills into Wales with their booty.' The border castle of Caus was in the hands of the Welsh of Powys until April 1141, when Hugh BERINGAR managed to recapture it.

Refs: **9** (9, 12–14); **10** (13).

Cecilia, Saint (*fl.* 3rd C.?) (hist.) (f.d. 22 November). Also called Cecily or Celia. Almost nothing is known about Cecilia except that she was a Roman martyr of some unknown date, probably 3rd C., and was buried in the cemetery of St Callistus. According to her late 5th C. legend, she was betrothed to Valerian, a pagan; but, having vowed to give herself to God, she refused to consummate the marriage. Both her husband and his brother, Tiburtius (who were historical people), became Christians and were arrested and martyred in ROME. Cecilia herself was sentenced to be suffocated in the bathroom of her own house, but was partially beheaded, dying three days later. She is the patron saint of musicians.

Novels: 'Brother CADFAEL saw them in church together at the sung Mass for Saint Cecilia's day, the twenty-second of November.'

Refs: **17** (11).

Cegin, River or Afon (Gwynedd, Wales). Rising on the hills north-west of Deiniolen, the Afon Cegin flows north to Glasinfryn and BANGOR, where it enters the MENAI STRAIT at Abercegin. The river is some 6 miles in length.

Novels: The Roman road from ABER to CARNARVON crossed the Afon Cegin, south of Bangor.

Refs: **18** (5).

Ceiriog, River (Clwyd, Wales). Rising on the southern slopes of Moel Fferna, 2,067 ft. high, the waters of the 19-mile-long river flow south to enter the Ceiriog valley near Pentre. Sweeping in a north-easterly direction, it passes the villages of LLANARMON Dyffryn Ceiriog, TREGEIRIOG, Pandy and GLYN CEIRIOG, before it swings east to Llwynmawr, Pontfadog and CHIRK. At Chirk Thomas Telford and William Jessop constructed a ten-arched, 70 ft. high aqueduct to carry the Shropshire Union Canal over the Ceiriog. Nearly 4 miles downstream from their remarkable feat of engineering, the river joins the DEE. The name Ceiriog is derived from a Celtic word meaning 'favoured' or 'loved'.

Novels: 'Tudur ap RHYS's maenol lay in a cleft where a mountain brook came down into the river Ceiriog . . . Beyond the river, with its fringes of forest and the few stony fields and huddle of wooden cots about the maenol, the hills rose again brown and bleak below, white and bleak above, to a round snow-summit against a leaden sky.'

Refs: **9** (3).

Centwin (*fl.* 1141) (fict.). **Novels:** 'a decent poor soul', he lived with his wife, ELEN, in the ABBEY FOREGATE, near the HORSE-FAIR. He was as 'quiet a creature as breathes, never a trouble to any'. In December 1141, because he had a grudge against AILNOTH concerning the burial of his unbaptised son, Centwin was one of those briefly under suspicion for the priest's murder.

Refs: **12** (3, 7, 9).

Ceredigion (Dyfed, Wales). The territory of Ceredigion appears, for much of its history, to have had the same borders as the old Welsh county of Cardigan. It was bounded to the east by the Cambrian Mountains, to the west by the sea, and to the north and south by the rivers Dovey (or Dyfi) and Teifi, respectively. Itself part of DEHEUBARTH, Ceredigion was divided into four cantrefs. These in turn were subdivided into ten commotes: Geneu'r Glyn, Perfedd, Creuddyn, Mefenydd, Anhuniog, Pennardd, Mabwnion, Caerwedros, Gwinionydd and Iscoed. For one brief period in its history Ceredigion included the commote of Cemais.

Novels: 'So this was the young fellow who had been sent by his father to waft an army across the AERON and drive Cadwaladr headlong out of North Ceredigion with his castle of LLANBADARN in flames behind him'. In 1143 HYWEL AB OWAIN drove CADWALADR 'bodily out of every furlong of land he held in Ceredigion'. Some men, however, remained loyal to their dispossessed lord. On reaching manhood Hywel had been granted land in South Ceredigion, but after Cadwaladr's flight he possessed the whole of the region. After Cadwaladr had made peace with OWAIN GWYNEDD, he was restored to part of his former lands.

Refs: **18** (1–3, 5–6, 9–12).

Chad, Saint (d. 672) (hist.) (f.d. 2 March). Also called Ceadda. Brother of St Cedd, Chad was educated at Lindisfarne under St Aidan, and later in Ireland. After his return to England, he succeeded his brother as abbot of Lastingham, North Yorkshire. From there he was made bishop of York, but humbly returned to Lastingham when in 669 Theodore, Archbishop of Canterbury, ruled that his consecration had been irregular. Theodore, however, reconsecrated him as bishop of the Mercians, with his see at LICHFIELD. After his death Chad was buried in St Mary's Church. Almost immediately, he was venerated as a saint and in 700 his relics were enshrined in the first cathedral of St Peter. Although the shrine of St Chad no longer exists, some of his bones are said to be in the possession of St Chad's Roman Catholic Cathedral, Birmingham.

Novels: The silver pectoral cross given to Bishop GILBERT by Bishop ROGER DE CLINTON in 1144 was 'blessed at the shrine of St Chad. One of the canons made it, he's a good silversmith.' Chad was the first bishop of Lichfield.

Refs: **18** (2); **20** (2).

Chalons on the Saône (now Chalon-sur-Saône) (France). Some 40 miles south of Dijon, on the banks of the Saône, this industrial and commercial town in Burgundy is also a busy river port. The former cathedral, now St Vincent's Church, dates from the 11th C.

Novels: '"SAINT MARCEL is close by Chalons on the Saône. It is a daughter house of CLUNY."'

Refs: **16** (2).

Charles III (839–88), Holy Roman Emperor (881–87) (hist.). Also called Charles the Fat. Youngest son of Louis II the German, King of the East Franks, and great grandson of CHARLES THE GREAT. When Louis the German died in 876 his kingdom was divided between his three sons: Carloman (d. 880), Louis the Younger (d. 882) and Charles. In 879 Charles took over the lands and titles of Carloman because of the latter's ill health. He was crowned Holy Roman Emperor at ROME by Pope John VIII in February 881, and, the following year, on the death of Louis the Younger (or Louis III) – who like Carloman had no heir – Charles found himself King of all the East Franks. In 885, after the death of Carloman, King of the West Franks and son of Louis the Stammerer, Charles became the ruler of the reunited empire of Charles the Great. He was deposed in 887, and died in January the following year amid a general state of anarchy which heralded the final disintegration of the Carolingian Empire.

Novels: '"Great pity," said King Charles – Charles the Fat, they called him – "that ever such a genius [as St TUTILO] should be made a monk." He called down a malediction on the man that did it.'

Refs: **19** (1).

Charles the Great (*c.*742–814) (hist.). Also called Charlemagne. Eldest son of Pepin III (also called Pepin the Short), he became King of the Franks in 768 and King of the Lombards in 774. As a military leader he eventually united, by conquest, practically all the Christian lands of western Europe into one empire, except Britain, southern Italy and a large part of Spain. On Christmas Day 800 he was crowned emperor by Pope Leo III. Charles died at AACHEN and his tomb is in the cathedral.

Novels: '"There is traffic between the two courts [ROME and CONSTANTINOPLE], as there has been since Charles the Great."'

Refs: **16** (11).

Charon (myth.). In Greek mythology, he was the aged boatman of hell who ferried the souls of the dead across the Styx, the river separating the lands of the living and the dead. It was, therefore, customary to place a coin in the hand or mouth of the dead to pay the ferryman's fare.

Novels: 'There was a ferryman called Charon, CADFAEL recalled from his forays into the writings of antiquity, who had the care of souls bound out of this world. He too, took pay from his passengers, indeed he refused them if they had not their fare. But he did not provide rugs and pillows and cerecloth for the souls he ferried across to eternity. Nor had he ever cared to seek and salvage the forlorn bodies of those the river took as its prey. MADOG OF THE DEAD BOAT was the better man.'

Refs: **11** (12).

Chenet (now Cannock) (Staffordshire, England). DB – Chenet: in Cuttlestone Hundred; land of WILLIAM I. Cannock is a large industrial town situated 8 miles north-east of WOLVERHAMPTON, and some 31 miles due east of SHREWSBURY to which it is almost linked by the old Roman road of Watling Street. Cannock was originally a royal preserve and its forest was used by the Plantagenet kings for hunting. Stretching to the north and east of the town is Cannock Chase – only a part of the once extensive forest – where there is now a Country Park. At Castle Ring, east of the town, are the remains of an Iron Age hill fort, which occupies the highest point of Cannock Chase and from it there are extensive views. The remains of what was probably a medieval hunting-lodge can be seen in a corner of the 9-acre site.

Novels: In March 1143 CADFAEL and Brother HALUIN spent the night at the manor of Chenet, 'in the king's holding'. Adelais de CLARY, with her maid and two grooms, rode through Chenet Forest on her way to ELFORD. Hugh BERINGAR and Cadfael rode through the forest on the way to LICHFIELD, and eventually COVENTRY, in November 1145.

Refs: **15** (4–5); **20** (2).

Chester (Cheshire, England). Some 34 miles north-west of SHREWSBURY, this city lies on a sandstone ridge at the head of the River DEE estuary, close to the border with Wales. Because of its strategic position, it became the headquarters of the Roman 20th Legion and grew from a military base to a flourishing Anglo-Saxon town. Following the Norman Conquest, in 1071 Chester became a county palatine, virtually independent of royal government. Chester reached the height of its prosperity during the 13th and 14th C., trading with Ireland, Scotland and parts of Europe. Chester Cathedral stands on the site of an Anglo-Saxon church, founded in the 10th C. Hugh d'Avranches, WILLIAM I's nephew and Earl of Chester, made it a Benedictine abbey in 1092 and, a year after its dissolution in 1540, it became a cathedral and bishopric. Considered to be the best-preserved walled city in England, Chester contains a wealth of ancient remains.

Novels: In July 1139 Euan of SHOTWICK, who was 'an important man' about the court of RANULF of Chester, attended the annual Shrewsbury fair. Bishop HENRY OF BLOIS sent Peter CLEMENCE north to Chester in September 1140. The following month, Canon ELUARD also visited the town. In December Ranulf of Chester and William of ROUMARE seized King STEPHEN's castle at LINCOLN. The plot had been hatched three months earlier at Chester. On his way north to Chester in June 1143, Canon GERBERT's horse fell lame and he was forced to stay at SHREWSBURY ABBEY. The old Roman road from Chester headed west into North Wales, to ST ASAPH and eventually CARNARVON.

Refs: **1** (1); **3** (11); **4** (1:2, 3:2); **8** (2–3, 5, 12); **9** (2); **16** (1, 15); **18** (1, 4); **19** (2–3, 11); **20** (1).

Chester, Bishops of. The bishoprics of CHESTER and COVENTRY originated as the gigantic see of Mercia. The first bishop was St CHAD with his seat at LICHFIELD. In 1075 Archbishop LANFRANC moved it to Chester. Peter, who had been consecrated Bishop of Lichfield in 1072, became Bishop of Chester, where he already owned considerable property. Peter died in 1085 and was succeeded by Robert de Limesey, who transferred the see to COVENTRY in 1102. The see remained at Coventry under Bishop Robert Peche (1121–6) and Bishop ROGER DE CLINTON (1129–48). These two contributed to the revival of Lichfield, particularly de Clinton who rebuilt the cathedral church and fortified the town. The see may have moved, temporarily, to Lichfield in 1143, when the cathedral-priory at Coventry was converted into a fortress. Despite the fact that the see was in Coventry, both Peche and de Clinton used the title Coventry and Lichfield indiscriminately. But, like de Limesey, they also thought of themselves as bishops of Chester. De Clinton's successor, Walter Durdent (1149–59), was the first to use the title Bishop of Coventry, exclusively. Although the title Bishop of Chester was officially abandoned in the 12th C., it continued to be used unofficially for some time afterwards. The

Benedictine Abbey at Chester was dissolved in 1540. In 1541 the former abbey church was made the cathedral of the newly formed diocese of Chester. Its first bishop was also appointed.

Novels: 'SALTON was formerly held by [Peter] the Bishop of Chester, and granted to the church of SAINT CHAD, here within the walls [of SHREWSBURY].' 'Parochially, the situation of the whole demesne of LONGNER was peculiar, for it had belonged earlier to the bishops of Chester, who had bestowed all their local properties, if close enough, as outer and isolated dependencies of the parish of Saint Chad in Shrewsbury.'

Refs: **11** (2, 4); **17** (3).

Chester, Earl of. See RANULF, Earl of Chester.

Chipping Campden. See CAMPDEN.

Chirk or Y Waun (Clwyd, Wales). A large village 5 miles north of OSWESTRY, Chirk lies mainly on the north bank of the River CEIRIOG, from which it takes its name. Housing development across the river to the south, however, has pushed a small part of the village (Chirk Bank) over the border and into Shropshire. The oldest part of the village is centred around the church, with its 15th C. tower and timbered roof. It contains a number of memorials to the Myddleton family of CHIRK CASTLE. South of the church, above the river, are the remains of what is thought to have been a 12th C. castle.

Novels: In Spring 1144 Deacon MARK and CADFAEL rode from SHREWSBURY to ST ASAPH by way of OSWESTRY and Chirk.

Refs: **18** (1).

Chirk Castle (Clwyd, Wales). Situated in parkland just over a mile west of CHIRK village, Chirk Castle is a unique example of a Marcher, or border, fortress. Built on the site of an earlier castle, it was started in the reign of Edward I by the powerful Marcher lord, Roger Mortimer, and completed in 1310. In 1595 the castle was purchased by Sir Thomas Myddleton, a merchant and later Lord Mayor of London, and has been lived in continuously by the Myddleton family ever since. The property is now owned by the National Trust.

Novels: 'Brother CADFAEL arrived in Oswestry by evening, to find town and castle alert and busy, but Hugh BERINGAR already departed. He had moved east after his meeting with OWAIN GWYNEDD, they told him, to WHITTINGTON and ELLESMERE, to see his whole northern border stiffened and call up fresh levies as far away as WHITCHURCH. While Owain had moved north on the border to meet the constable of Chirk and see that corner of the confederacy secure and well manned.'

Refs: **9** (10, 12)

Christian (*fl.* 1141) (fict.). Although the name of the clerk, Christian, is fictional, it is a historical fact that at WINCHESTER on 8 April 1141 a clerk did hand Bishop HENRY OF BLOIS a petition from his liege lady, Queen MATILDA, on King STEPHEN's behalf.

Novels: '"And if any ask my name, it is Christian, and true Christian I am as any here, and true to my salt."' Clerk in the service of Queen Matilda. On 8 April 1141, at Winchester, Christian presented Bishop Henry of Blois with a petition from the queen urging the legatine council to support Stephen. When the bishop refused to read the parchment aloud, the clerk snatched it back and read it aloud to the assembly himself. That evening, setting out to return to the queen, Christian was attacked in the street close to the Old Minster by five or six ruffians, including CIARAN. He was rescued by Rainald BOSSARD and escaped with only a few bruises.

Refs: **10** (2, 7, 11, 14–15); **12** (2).

Church Stretton. See STRETTON.

Ciaran (b. *c.*1116) (fict.). **Novels:** '"My name is Ciaran, I am of a Welsh mother, and I am going back to where I was born, there to end my life as I began it. You see the wounds on my feet, brother, but what most ails me does not show anywhere upon me. I have a fell disease, no threat to any other, but it must shortly end me."' Born in DUBLIN of an Irish father and a Welsh mother, he was in the service of Bishop HENRY OF BLOIS until 8 April 1141, when he attacked CHRISTIAN and murdered Rainald BOSSARD at WINCHESTER. Dismissed by Bishop Henry for the crime, Ciaran was sentenced to banishment in Dublin. He was condemned to go barefoot every step of the way, carrying a heavy cross around his neck. To ensure that he had the protection of the Church to BANGOR, the bishop gave Ciaran his ring. On the journey north he was joined by Matthew (see MEVEREL, Luc) near NEWBURY. They arrived together at SHREWSBURY ABBEY on 17 June 1141. Although Ciaran's ring was stolen by Simeon POER, it was eventually retrieved and returned. Ciaran, with the help of Melangell (see MEVEREL), managed to slip away from SHREWSBURY without Matthew's knowledge on 22 June, the day of St WINIFRED's festival. On his way west through the LONG FOREST, the barefoot pilgrim was attacked by POER, Walter BAGOT and John SHURE. MATTHEW, who had been in hot pursuit of his runaway companion, heard Ciaran's cries for help and attempted to hold his attackers at bay. CADFAEL, in turn, came to their rescue, and, when Hugh BERINGAR and his men arrived, the outlaws fled. During the fighting, the heavy cross was torn from Ciaran's neck. The terms of his penance broken, his life forfeit, Ciaran, nevertheless, found himself spared: for in the end Matthew was unable to kill him. After he had confessed to the murder of Bossard, Ciaran was allowed to continue his penitential journey into Wales, alone.

Refs: **10** (3–8, 12, 14–15).

Cirencester (Gloucestershire, England). Beside the River Churn, some 15 miles south-east of GLOUCESTER, Cirencester occupies the site of *Corinium Dobunnorum*, the administrative capital of the Romano-British Dobunni tribe. After LONDON, it was the largest town in Roman Britain. The name was changed back to *Coryn Ceastre*, or Cirencester, by the Saxons, who destroyed the town and church in 577. It benefited from the prosperity of the medieval wool trade, of which it was an important market centre. All roads in the region converge on the town, including the Roman Fosse Way, Akeman Street and ERMIN WAY. The town contains many fine buildings, dating back to medieval times.

Novels: 'And King STEPHEN, like a giant breaking loose from some crippling enchantment, surged out of his convalescence into vigorous action, and bearing down on the port of WAREHAM, the most easterly still available to his enemies, seized both town and castle with hardly a graze to show for it. "And is making north again now towards Cirencester," reported Hugh BERINGAR, elated by the news, "to pick off the Empress's outposts one by one, if only he can keep up this storm of energy."' 'It was late afternoon [in 1145] when he [CADFAEL] reached Cirencester, a town he did not know, except by reputation as a very old city, where the Romans had left their fabled traces, and a very sturdy and astute wool trade had continued independent and prosperous ever since.'

Refs: **13** (1); **20** (10, 13–15).

Cirencester Abbey (Gloucestershire, England). The abbey at Cirencester, founded by HENRY I in 1117 and dedicated to St MARY, stood on the site of an Anglo-Saxon church, erected about the beginning of the 8th C. Becoming one of the wealthiest Augustinian houses in England, it was demolished at the Dissolution and survives only in street names, a Norman gatehouse and a few sparse remains. The Hospital and Chantry of St John the Evangelist, in Spitalgate, dates from the 12th C. Some 80 yards to the south-west of the old Saxon church, the Normans built another church, dedicated to St John the Evangelist. In 1180 the chancel was widened and between 1235 and 1250 it was extended further and the nave rebuilt. Originally intended to carry a spire, the 162 ft. high tower was built in the 15th C. The church became one of the largest and most magnificent in England. The unique three-storey south porch was the administrative headquarters of the medieval abbey, and later served as the Town Hall.

Novels: In December 1145 Olivier de BRETAGNE took the badly injured Philip FITZROBERT to safety at Cirencester Abbey, where he could 'recover from his wounds'; for the canons there had a 'good name as physicians'. CADFAEL followed shortly after. 'He had to stop and ask his way to the Augustinian abbey, but there was no mistaking it when he found it, and no doubt of its flourishing condition. The old King Henry had refounded it upon the remnant of an older house of secular canons, very poorly endowed and quietly mouldering, but the Augustinians had made a success of it, and the fine gatehouse, spacious court and splendid church spoke for their zeal and efficiency. This revived house was barely thirty years old, but bade fair to be the foremost of its order in the kingdom.' ROBERT of Gloucester was reconciled with Philip, his younger son, in the infirmary. Cadfael rode from the abbey to GLOUCESTER with Olivier.

Refs: **20** (13–15).

City of God. See JERUSALEM.

Clairvaux (France). A village near the small market town of Bar-sur-Aube in north-eastern France, Clairvaux is some 35 miles east of Troyes. Under the influence of its abbot, BERNARD OF CLAIRVAUX, the abbey, founded in 1115, became a great centre of the Cistercian Order.

Novels: '"You'll not tell me Robert BEAUMONT is thinking of taking the Cross? There are some powerful sermons coming out of Clairvaux, I'm told, that will be hard to resist."'

Refs: **16** (2); **20** (1).

Clare (Suffolk, England). Some 25 miles west of Ipswich and 19 miles south-east of CAMBRIDGE, this town contains the 13th C. remains of a castle, first erected soon after the Conquest by Richard de Clare, grandfather of Richard de CLARE. The de Clare family, who founded some fifteen religious houses in England, took their name from this, their chief lordship. The 'wool' church of St Peter and St Paul is mainly 15th C., with earlier parts, including a 13th C. tower. In 1248, at Clare, the Augustinian Friars (or Austin Hermits) founded their first English house.

Refs: **20** (7).

Clare, Gilbert FitzRichard de (d. 1151/3), Earl of Hertford (hist.). Son and heir of Richard FitzGilbert de CLARE, by Adeliz (or Alice), sister of RANULF of Chester, he succeeded to the great family estates, which included CLARE and Tonbridge Castle, in 1136. King STEPHEN created him Earl of Hertford in *c.*1138, and from then on he was variously known as the Earl of Hertford or of Clare. He was with Queen MATILDA's army at WINCHESTER in 1141; but later it seems that he may have changed his allegiance from Stephen to the Empress MAUD, for when the king arrested Ranulf, his uncle, in 1146, Gilbert gave himself, together with his castles, as hostage for the earl. Some authorities claim, however, that he was not a supporter of the empress, but was simply defending his family's rights. Although he revolted against Stephen, they subsequently made peace. It is generally thought that he did not get married.

Novels: Earl of Hertford, Gilbert de Clare was the son of Richard de CLARE and half-brother of Geoffrey FITZCLARE, Jovetta de MONTORS' son. '"Gilbert, for all I know, is a good man, too. At least he and his half-brother have always respected and liked each other, seemingly, although all the Clares are absolute for STEPHEN."' Gilbert remained good friends with Geoffrey, despite his support for the Empress MAUD.

Refs: **20** (7–8, 15).

Clare, Richard FitzGilbert de (d. 1136), Earl of Hertford (hist.). Son and heir of Gilbert FitzRichard de Clare (d. 1115?), he married Adeliz (or Alice), sister of RANULF of Chester, and was the father of Gilbert FitzRichard de CLARE and Roger FitzRichard de Clare (d. 1173). Lord of CEREDIGION, Richard owned large possessions in Wales and is generally thought to have been the 1st Earl of Hertford. He was ambushed and killed by the Welsh, near Abergavenny, and was buried at GLOUCESTER. His death signalled a general Welsh uprising in which a number of Norman strongholds were taken, including ABERYSTWYTH CASTLE.

Novels: Father of Geoffrey FITZCLARE, by Jovetta de MONTORS, and Gilbert de Clare, Richard was Earl of Hertford and a loyal supporter of STEPHEN. He brought Geoffrey, '"his bastard home almost newborn, and the grandam took him in care, and they did well by him, and set him up for life when he was grown."' Richard gave Geoffrey 'the salamander in its restoring bath of fire' for his own device.

Refs: **20** (7, 15).

Clary, Adelais de (b. *c.*1077) (fict.). **Novels:** 'Her beautiful, proud face was composed and mute, admitting nothing, denying nothing. Only the burning of her dark eyes in their deep settings was eloquent, and even that in a language he could not quite translate.' Widow of Bertrand de CLARY and mother of Audemar de CLARY and Bertrade (see VIVERS). Adelais remained at HALES, 'her favourite home', after her husband's death in *c.*1131. Attracted to HALUIN, when he was a clerk of eighteen, and jealous of his attentions to her daughter, she exacted a terrible vengeance. Discovering that Bertrade had conceived HALUIN's child, she dismissed the youth from her service and banned him from seeing her daughter again. In 1124, Adelais went to SHREWSBURY ABBEY, where Haluin had become a monk, and informed him of Bertrade's condition. He gave her a potion to 'procure abortion'. Later she lied, telling him that both mother and child had died because of the draught he had concocted. Adelais then hurriedly married off her pregnant daughter to Edric VIVERS. In March 1143, nineteen years later, Haluin returned to Hales to spend a night of vigil at Bertrade's tomb. Although Adelais went to great lengths to conceal the fact that Bertrade and Haluin's daughter (see VIVERS, Helisende) were still alive, she failed to stop the monk from discovering the truth. Having been forced to face the consequences of her actions by CADFAEL, she confessed to her deception. She denied, however, having any part in the killing of EDGYTHA. Audemar, in consequence, banished her to Hales for ever.

Refs: **15** (2–5, 7, 11–14).

Clary, Audemar de (b. 1104) (fict.). **Novels:** 'In the yard the flickering torchlight flared and guttered and flared again on the strongly-boned countenance and massive body of Audemar de Clary, as he swung himself down from the saddle and tossed his bridle to a scurrying groom.' Son of Bertrand and Adelais de CLARY and brother of Bertrade (see VIVERS), Audemar inherited the de Clary honour after his father's death in *c.*1131. Ruling from the family's chief seat at ELFORD, he was 'married to a Staffordshire wife' and had 'a young son to succeed him'. He was overlord to Cenred VIVERS at the manor of VIVERS. In Winter 1142 Audemar, with a company of men, supported King STEPHEN at the siege of OXFORD. In March 1143, after the revelation that HALUIN was the father of Helisende VIVERS and that Adelais had deliberately deceived the family, Audemar banished her for ever to HALES.

Refs: **15** (3, 5–6, 8–10, 13–14).

Clary, Bertrade de. See VIVERS, Bertrade.

Clary, Bertrand de (d. *c.*1131) (fict.). **Novels:** Husband of Adelais de CLARY and father of Audemar de CLARY and Bertrade (see VIVERS), BERTRAND became the Lord of ELFORD on his father's death in *c.*1112, inheriting a 'large and scattered' honour in Staffordshire and also the manor of HALES in Shropshire. During, at least, the years 1118 to 1122, Bertrand was, like his father before him, a crusader in the HOLY LAND. Although his father was buried at Hales, Bertrand was buried in the great family vault of the church at Elford. He was succeeded by his son, Audemar.

Refs: **15** (3–5).

Cledwen, River or Afon (Clwyd, Wales). It rises on the north-west slopes of the 1,746 ft.-high Mwdwl-eithin, and flows north past GWYTHERIN to Llangernyw, where it merges with the waters of the Afon Gallen to become the ELWY.

Novels: 'They turned aside from the CONWAY valley at LLANRWST, climbing away from the river into forested country. Beyond the watershed they crossed the Elwy where it is young and small, and moved steadily south-eastwards through thick woods, over another ridge of high land, to descend once again into the upland valley of a little river, that provided some marshy watermeadows along its banks, and a narrow band of tilled fields, sloping and sturdy but protected by the forests above these lush pastures. The wooded ridge on either hand ran in oblique folds, richly green, hiding the scattered house-steads.'

Refs: **1** (2).

Clee Forest (Shropshire, England). The royal forest of Clee lay immediately to the north of LUDLOW, and stretched in a broad swathe from the CLEE HILLS westward towards the River CORVE. Compared to other Shropshire forests it was small, only 24,000 acres in extent. It ceased to belong to the Crown in 1155, when HENRY II gave it to Hugh de Periers. By the 16th C., it was noted by the historian, John Leland, that 'there is no great plenty of wood in Clee Hills'. Today, except for a few surviving pockets of woodland, the area consists of farmland, with numerous small villages and hamlets scattered among the fields and pastures.

Novels: 'Clee was a royal forest, but neglected now, as much of England was surely being neglected, left to rot or to be appropriated by opportunist local magnates, while king and empress fought out their battle for the crown. Lonely country, this, and wild, even within ten miles of [Ludlow] castle and town. Assarts were few and far between. The beasts of the chase and the beasts of the warren had it for their own domain, but in winter even the deer would starve without some judicious nursing from men. Fodder too precious to be wasted by the farmer might still be put out by the lord to ensure the survival of his game in a bad season.' In the vicinity of HOPTON BROOK, Clee Forest 'was broken by scattered holdings and fields, and occasionally a sheep shelter, roughly propped with its back to the wind.' In December 1139, CADFAEL found Yves HUGONIN in THURSTAN'S ASSART in Clee Forest. Olivier de BRETAGNE pretended that he was '"Robert, son to one of the foresters of Clee Forest."'

Refs: **6** (3–4, 12, 15); **20** (2).

Clee Hill (Shropshire, England). Some 5 miles east of LUDLOW, the Clee Hills – comprising Clee Hill, TITTERSTONE CLEE and BROWN CLEE – are the highest in Shropshire rising to almost 1,800 ft. The rocks of these hills are formed of Old Red Sandstone and are capped with a hard protective layer of volcanic rock known locally as 'dhustone'. The hills were once mined for coal, ironstone, limestone and copper and, although the scars have long been overgrown, the abandoned workings (some dating back to at least the 13th C.) are still in evidence. High up on the southern slopes of Clee Hill, approximately 1,150 ft. above sea level, is the 19th C. mining village of Clee Hill. Since ancient times the hills have been the subject of superstition and legend. Clee Hill, allegedly, was the haunt of fairies and witches, and also the home of the Devil. On the summits there are numerous prehistoric sites.

Novels: In December 1139, on their way from WORCESTER to SHREWSBURY, Yves HUGONIN and Ermina Hugonin (see BRETAGNE) and Sister HILARIA travelled over 'those bleak hills', the Clee Hills. CADFAEL passed the hills on his penitential journey back to Shrewsbury from La MUSARDERIE and CIRENCESTER in December 1145.

Refs: **6** (2–3, 5, 15); **20** (16).

Cleeton (now Cleeton St Mary) (Shropshire, England). DB – There is no record of Cleeton, but some authorities have suggested that it may have been a member of LEDWYCH, and, if so, in Culverstone Hundred; held by William Pantulf under Roger de MONTGOMERY. Some 6 miles north-east of LUDLOW and high up on the north-east slopes of TITTERSTONE CLEE, Cleeton St Mary is a tiny village with a church dedicated to its patron saint. To the north, well away from the present village and a few hundred yards north-east of the moated earthwork marked on the OS map, is the site of an abandoned medieval settlement.

Novels: 'A hard place, bleak to farm, meagre to crop, but good for sheep, the rangy upland sheep that brought the leanest meat but the longest fleeces. Across the uphill edge of the settlement there was a crude but solid stockade, and someone was on watch for strangers arriving, for a whistle went before them into the huddle of horses, shrill and piercing. By the time they rode in there were three or four sturdy fellows on hand to receive them. Hugh [BERINGAR] smiled. Outlaws living wild, unless they had considerable numbers of sufficient arms, might be wise to fight shy of Cleeton.' In December 1139, after his holding had been sacked by Alain le GAUCHER's outlaws, John DRUEL and his family sought shelter and safety at the village of Cleeton. Olivier de BRETAGNE, enquiring after Yves HUGONIN and Ermina Hugonin (see BRETAGNE), made 'an impression upon the women of Cleeton'. After the capture of Gaucher's stronghold the stolen animals were taken down to Cleeton.

Refs: **6** (3–6, 8, 10, 14–15).

Clemence, Peter (*c.*1113–40) (fict.). **Novels:** 'A young man marked for advancement.' Scholar and cleric in the personal household of Bishop HENRY OF BLOIS, he was a distant cousin of Avota ASPLEY. He was sent north to CHESTER in September 1140 on a civil diplomatic mission to secure the allegiance of RANULF of Chester and William of ROUMARE. On 8 September Clemence stayed at the ASPLEY manor. He was murdered the next day, shortly after leaving Aspley, by Janyn LINDE in order to prevent him from reaching Chester and discovering that Ranulf and William were plotting treason. Clemence's body was secretly buried in a charcoal-burner's hearth by Leoric ASPLEY and the stack partly fired. His horse, BARBARY, was taken north towards WHITCHURCH and set loose on the mosses. The charred remains of the envoy's body were discovered by Meriet ASPLEY in November and taken to SHREWSBURY.

Refs: **8** (3–10, 12).

Cleobury (now Cleobury Mortimer) (Shropshire, England). DB – Claiberie: in Condertree Hundred; a holding of Ralph of Mortimer under Roger de MONTGOMERY. Cleobury Mortimer is a small town beside the River Rea, 10 miles east of LUDLOW on the Bewdley road and just over a mile from the western edge of the Wyre Forest. St Mary's Church, built of greenish sandstone, has outward leaning walls, and a spire with a notable twist caused by warping of its oak frame. The east window is dedicated to William Langland, the medieval poet, and depicts the vision of *Piers Plowman*. According to tradition, Langland was born in the town in *c.*1330.

Novels: 'Cloud was settling low overhead. CADFAEL turned and made his way back to his mule, and with heightened care led him, still in the shelter of the trees, down to the opening of the ravine, and waited and listened for a while before mounting and riding. He went back the way he had come, and never encountered a living soul until he was well down towards the lowlands. There he could very well have branched left and descended to the highroad from Cleobury, but he did not do it, preferring to retrace his course all along the road the reivers used.' In December 1139 Sister HILARIA, Yves HUGONIN and Ermina Hugonin (see BRETAGNE), stayed one night at Cleobury in their flight north from WORCESTER. While in the village they met Brother ELYAS, who travelled with them as far as FOXWOOD.

Refs: **6** (2–4, 7, 10).

Clinton, Roger de. See ROGER DE CLINTON, Bishop of COVENTRY and LICHFIELD.

Clothier, Roger (*fl.* 1140) (fict.). **Novels:** A SHREWSBURY clothier who lived near ST MARY'S WATER-LANE, he let the blind beggar, Rhodri FYCHAN (the Less), sleep in the loft above his cart-house and barn.

Refs: **RB** (3).

(Roger) Clothier's Cart-House and Cart-Yard (St Mary's Water-Lane, Shrewsbury, Shropshire) (fict.). Although it never existed, Roger CLOTHIER's cart-yard opened onto ST MARY'S WATER-LANE.

Novels: In 1140 William REDE was attacked in the passage above the water-gate, right under Roger Clothier's cart-yard. Jacob of BOULDON was arrested in the loft above the cart-house and barn while attempting to murder Rhodri FYCHAN (the Less).

Refs: **RB** (3).

Cluny (France). Some 15 miles north-west of Mâcon in Burgundy, this town gave its name to the Cluniac order of monks, who returned to a strict observance of the Benedictine Rule. Founded in 910 by William the Pious, Duke of Aquitaine, and placed under direct papal control, the abbey became the mother house of around 1,500 monasteries in Europe. The abbey church, built between 1088 and 1130, was once the largest in the Christian world. In the early 12th C. many felt that Cluny itself was in need of reform and the numbers attracted to the order began to decline in favour of the Cistercians. The abbey suffered during the religious wars of the 16th C., was suppressed during the French Revolution, was closed in 1790, and was almost entirely demolished in the early 19th C. Parts of the abbey buildings to survive include the ruins of the south transept and its great belfry tower. The Abbot's House contains a museum.

Novels: 'GERBERT sniffed loudly and turned up his masterful nose at the mention of Cluny. That great house had taken seriously to the pilgrim traffic and had given aid and support, protection along the roads and shelter in their houses to many hundreds not only from France, but of recent years from England, too. But for the close dependants of Archbishop THEOBALD it was first and foremost the mother-house of that difficult colleague and ambitious rival, Bishop Henry of Winchester.' In Spring 1142 ELAVE and William of LYTHWOOD made the pilgrimage to St JAMES at COMPOSTELA with a party from Cluny. Bishop HENRY OF BLOIS was brought up and educated in the monastery at Cluny, and is referred to as the 'Monk of Cluny'. After being convicted of heretical writings at the Council of SENS, Pierre ABELARD was 'allowed to retire peacefully into Cluny at the request of the abbot'.

Refs: **10** (1); **16** (2)

Clwyd, River or Afon (Clwyd, Wales). Rising in Clocaenog Forest, north-east of Llanfihangel Glyn Myfyr, the Clwyd flows in a north-easterly direction from Melin-y-Wig to RUTHIN. From there it heads north-north-west, past Denbigh (or Dinbych), ST ASAPH and RHUDDLAN, to enter the Irish Sea at Rhyl. Between Rhuddlan and St Asaph it is joined by the River ELWY. From source to sea the course of the river is some 30 miles.

Novels: 'In May 1144 CADFAEL and Deacon MARK crossed the river, and climbed over the treeless uplands from the valley of the DEE to the valley of the Clwyd, and there followed the stream at ease the length of a bright morning and into an afternoon of soft showers and wilful gleams of sun. Through Ruthin, under the outcrop of red sandstone crowned with its squat timber fortress, and into the vale proper, broad, beautiful, and the fresh green of young foliage everywhere. Before the sun had stooped towards setting they came down into the narrowing tongue of land between the Clwyd and the Elwy, before the two rivers met above Rhuddlan, to move on together into tidal water. And there between lay the town of Llanelwy and the cathedral of SAINT ASAPH, comfortably nestled in a green, sheltered valley.'

Refs: **18** (1–2).

Clynnog or Clynnog Fawr (Gwynedd, Wales). On the north-west coast of the LLEYN PENINSULA, Clynnog Fawr is some 9 miles south-west of CARNARVON. The village today, set back from the shore, is small and remote; yet, it was once an important religious centre, founded by St BEUNO at the beginning of the 7th C. The present church stands on the site of the saint's original monastery. The waters from St Beuno's Well, just outside the village, are reputed to have curative properties.

Novels: '"Where do you suppose he [MEURIG] was bound, Hugh? Clynnog or CAERGYBI, and oversea to Ireland?"'

Refs: **3** (11).

Coliar, Agatha (*fl.* 1142) (fict.). **Novels:** '"She talks of the peace of the cloister, and release from the cares of the world. But she always talks so, though I know she's well content with her comfortable life if the truth were told."' Widow of Will COLIAR, mother of Miles COLIAR and aunt of Judith PERLE, Agatha had been widowed for many years, although she was 'ever lamenting it'. In 1142 she looked after the VESTIER house at the head of MAERDOL, owned by her niece. On 22 June 1142 Hugh BERINGAR called at the Vestier household to question Miles about the boots he had given BERTRED. By blurting out the truth before her son could speak, Agatha unwittingly undermined his story, and revealed him to be not only a liar but also a murderer.

Refs: **13** (1, 3, 13).

Coliar, Miles (b. 1115) (fict.). **Novels:** 'CADFAEL, always vulnerable to curiosity, his prevalent sin, halted, wavered and turned aside, recognising Miles Coliar, that tidy, practical, trim young fellow a great deal less trim than usual, his hair blown and teased erect in disorder, his bright blue eyes dilated beneath drawn and anxious copper brows.' Son of Agatha and Will COLIAR, Miles was the cousin of Judith PERLE and the 'conscientious foreman and manager' of her flourishing clothier's business in SHREWSBURY. In 1142 he was betrothed to ISABEL, whom he planned to marry later that year. Harbouring ambitions to repossess Judith's former house in the ABBEY FOREGATE and live in it himself, Miles tried to break the abbey's hold on the property by preventing payment of the annual rose-rent. On 16 June 1142, while trying to destroy the rose-bush, Miles was surprised by Brother ELURIC, whom he unintentionally killed. However, he deliberately helped BERTRED to his death in the SEVERN, and tried to implicate him in ELURIC's murder. After Judith's abduction, fearing that he might lose his inheritance if she was forced into marriage, Miles turned 'the town upside-down hunting for her'. Attacking Judith in the LONG FOREST, he was driven off, unrecognised, by Niall BRONZESMITH. Miles later set fire to the rose-bush, destroying it completely. He was arrested on 22 June 1142, and brought to trial for murder and attempted murder.

Refs: **13** (1, 3, 5–7, 9, 11, 13–14).

Coliar, Will (*fl.* 1115) (fict.). **Novels:** Husband of Agatha COLIAR and father of Miles COLIAR, he died while his son was a young child.

Refs: **13** (3).

Collen, Saint (*fl.* 7th C.) (hist.). (f.d. 21 May). Also spelled Colan or Gollen. Little is known about this Welsh saint, except that he gave his name to LLANGOLLEN and through legend has connections with Wales, ROME and GLASTONBURY Tor. He seems to have taken on the proportions of an epic hero, and among his exploits is reputed to have slain a cannibalistic ogress in the Vale of Llangollen.

Novels: In May 1144 CADFAEL and Deacon MARK, on the journey from SHREWSBURY to ST ASAPH, lodged overnight with the parish priest of Llangollen, where the church was dedicated to St Collen.

Refs: **18** (2).

Columbanus, Brother (*c.*1113–37) (fict.). **Novels:** 'Who knew what this badly-balanced saint, half-idiot would do next?' Benedictine monk at SHREWSBURY ABBEY, Brother Columbanus came from 'a formidable, aristocratic Norman family, a younger son despatched to make his way in the monastic ranks as next-best to inheriting land'. An ambitious man, he entered the Order in 1136, but was given to feigning violent fits for his own advancement and holiness. In early May 1137, after a particularly severe attack, Columbanus was taken, delirious, to HOLYWELL, where he was miraculously cured. Shortly after, he joined Prior ROBERT's party to GWYTHERIN, to acquire the bones of St WINIFRED. Fearing that RHISIART might stand in the way of his plans, Columbanus killed him, drugging JEROME with a dose of CADFAEL's poppy-juice. While Columbanus was keeping watch with Cadfael at St Winifred's chapel, Columbanus had another fit. When he regained consciousness, he claimed to have seen St Winifred, who had charged him with being her messenger 'of reconciliation and peace'. SIONED tricked him into confessing to the murder of her father, with Cadfael as witness. As soon as Columbanus realised that he had been deceived, he attempted to silence Sioned with his dagger. She fled from the church. ENGELARD came to her rescue and, in the ensuing struggle, Columbanus's neck was accidentally broken. Cadfael secretly placed his lifeless body in St Winifred's reliquary and resealed it. The next morning Columbanus was found to have vanished. All that remained of the monk were his clothes, neatly spread before the altar and reliquary, and strewn with white may petals. The reliquary, containing his body and not the saint's, was ceremoniously taken back to Shrewsbury Abbey. In February 1145, when the reliquary was stolen by TUTILO, there was a danger that it could have been opened to reveal '"the body of a young man about twenty-four, instead of the bones of a virgin saint. And mother naked, at that!"' Had that happened, Cadfael's 'goose' would have been '"finely cooked!"'

Refs: **1** (1, 4, 6–11); **10** (1); **19** (2–4, 7, 11).

Compostela (now Santiago or Santiago de Compostela) (Spain). Also spelled Compostella. In north-western Spain, Compostela lies near the confluence of the rivers Sar and Sarela, some 30 miles south-west of the city of La Coruna. 'Santiago' is Spanish for St JAMES. In 813, at nearby Padron, the reputed tomb of the martyred apostle was discovered. A church was built over the tomb, first of earth and later of stone, and by the end of the 11th C. it had become one of the most important pilgrimage centres in the Christian world. Construction of the present cathedral, dedicated to St James, patron saint of Spain, began in 1078 on the authority of Alfonso VI, King of Leon and Castile. It was consecrated in 1128 and completed in 1211.

Novels: '"It is a silver scallop-shell medal. Whoever owned it made the pilgrimage to Compostella, to the shrine of St James."' Joscelin LUCY's father made the pilgrimage to Compostela. In 1142, William of LYTHWOOD and ELAVE journeyed to the shrine of St James with a party from CLUNY. In February 1145 TUTILO felt that, if RAMSEY ABBEY had a patroness like St WINIFRED, 'pilgrims would come by the thousand' and the monastery could be 'another Compostela'.

Refs: **5** (3); **16** (2, 10); **19** (2).

Conan (b. 1116) (fict.). **Novels:** '"He liked the daughter, did Conan, in a cool sort of way, but he began to like her much better when she had a dowry to bring with her."' Head shepherd of Girard of LYTHWOOD. In 1143, when FORTUNATA came into her dowry, Conan suddenly began to take an interest in her. Considering

ELAVE a threat, he and ALDWIN connived together to remove him from the LYTHWOOD household. He was called before the SHREWSBURY ABBEY tribunal as a witness to Elave's heresy. A prime suspect for Aldwin's murder, Conan spent some time in SHREWSBURY CASTLE under lock and key, but was released when his alibi was substantiated.

Refs: **16** (3–6, 8, 10–12, 14–15).

Conrad III (1093–1152), Holy Roman Emperor (1138–52) (hist.). Son of Frederick I, Duke of Swabia, and grandson of Emperor Henry IV, Conrad became Duke of Franconia in 1115. After the death of Emperor Lothair II in 1137, Conrad was elected his successor and crowned at AACHEN in 1138. He joined the Second Crusade in 1147. Eventually returning to Germany, he was succeeded after his death by his nephew, Emperor Frederick I (or Frederick Barbarossa).

Novels: 'The monks of CLUNY have hospices all across France and down through Italy, even close by the emperor's city they have a house for pilgrims. And as soon as you reach the HOLY LAND the KNIGHTS OF SAINT JOHN provide shelter everywhere.'

Refs: **16** (3).

Conradin (fict.). **Novels:** The horse of the youngest of Robert de BEAUMONT (the younger)'s two squires. BÉNEZET made his escape from the great court of SHREWSBURY ABBEY on Conradin and fled south-westward into the fringes of the LONG FOREST, chased by Alan HERBARD and three of Hugh BERINGAR's sergeants. Startled by a hind, the horse baulked, reared (after Bénezet had used his dagger) and swept him against a low branch to the ground. Riderless and with his owner's gear in the saddlebags, Conradin bolted. Perhaps, 'with the luck of the saints, or the devil himself', Brother TUTILO and DAALNY, fleeing south-westward by the same road as Bénezet, happened across the horse in the forest. If so, Tutilo would have been able to exchange his habit and cowl for the clothes of the squire. As CADFAEL said: '"Finding is not thieving."'

Refs: **19** (13).

Conradin, Brother (b. *c.*1038) (fict.). **Novels:** Benedictine monk of SHREWSBURY ABBEY, he had been 'one of the first child oblates, and worked as a boy under the monks of SEEZ'. In 1143 he was in charge of building-work and repairs to the fabric of the abbey.

Refs: **15** (1).

Constance (b. *c.*1109) (fict.). **Novels:** Maid of Aline BERINGAR, Constance, who from childhood had been a loyal friend and servant to Aline, accompanied her mistress to SHREWSBURY in August 1138. She was an 'expert seamstress' and remained in her mistress's service after Aline's marriage to Hugh. As soon as their son, Giles, was born, she became his 'devoted slave'. Constance had a cousin in the WYLE, whom she visited.

Refs: **2** (1); **4** (2:1, 2:3, 3:2); **6** (15); **8** (1, 7); **9** (1); **11** (10); **12** (14); **18** (1); **19** (11).

Constantinople (now Istanbul, Turkey). Lying on either side of the Bosporus Strait and strategically situated at the entrance to the Black Sea, Istanbul is the largest city and chief port of Turkey. It has a long and important history, stretching back to the 8th C. BC when it was first settled by the Greeks and called Byzantium. Three centuries later it was part of the Persian Empire and in 330 it became the New Rome, second capital of the Roman Empire. It was later renamed Constantinople, after Constantine the Great, the first Roman ruler to be converted to Christianity. At its height it was one of the major religious, cultural and commercial cities of the Christian world, its art and architecture bringing about a fusion between the styles of both East and West. The golden age of Byzantium – with an empire extending from southern Italy to Syria and Armenia – lasted for about two hundred years, from the mid-9th C. to the mid-11th C. In 1203 the city was captured and sacked by the armies of the Fourth Crusade. Latin rule, which commenced in 1204, lasted until 1261 when the Christians were expelled by the Greek emperor of Nicaea. In 1453 Byzantine Constantinople was captured by the Turks, and became the capital of the Ottoman Empire, popularly known as Istanbul. In 1923 the Turkish Republic moved the capital of Turkey from Constantinople to Ankara and, seven years later, Constantinople was officially renamed Istanbul.

Novels: ' "The ivory [on FORTUNATA's box] was carved by a craftsman from Constantinople or near it, but it need not have been made there. There is traffic between the two courts [ROME and Constantinople], as there has been since CHARLES THE GREAT. Strange that the box brings the two together as it does, for the carving of the wood is not eastern. The wood itself I cannot fathom, but I think it must be from somewhere round the Middle Sea. Perhaps Italy? How all these materials and talents come together from many places to create so small and rare a thing!" '[Brother] ANSELM turned back to the dedication page, and read aloud slowly from the golden Latin: Made at the wish of OTTO [I], King and Emperor, for the marriage of his beloved son, OTTO [II], Prince of the Roman Empire, to the most Noble and Gracious THEOFANU, Princess of Byzantium, this book is the gift of His Most Christian Grace to the Princess. DIARMAID, monk of SAINT GALL, wrote and painted it."' On their pilgrimage to the HOLY LAND, ELAVE and William of LYTHWOOD visited Constantinople in *c.*1137.

Refs: **16** (3, 11, 15).

Conway, River (Gwynedd, Wales). Also called Afon Conwy. The source of the River Conway lies at Llyn Conwy, a lake over 1,600 ft. high in the Cambrian Mountains, 5 miles west of the mining town of Blaenau Ffestiniog and just below the peak of Pen y Bedw. From the lake the river flows south for almost a mile to Pont a Conwy, plunges over a waterfall, turns abruptly north-east and rushes downhill towards Pentrefoelas. A mile before reaching the village, the Conway swings sharply to the north-west and heads for Betws-y-Coed. On its tumbling downward journey towards the popular tourist centre, it is joined by the Afon Machno, near the spectacular Conwy Falls. Within a mile of their meeting, the waters are swelled further by the Afon Lledr and, shifting its direction to the north, the river enters the Vale of Conwy. Beyond Betws-y-Coed, where there is a celebrated collection of bridges, the river is joined by the Afon Llugwy. At LLANRWST – no longer a mountain torrent but a wide shallow stream – the Conwy sweeps past Gwydyr Castle and flows on to TREFRIW, becoming tidal as it heads for the walled town of CONWY and the open sea. The distance from the river's source, in the mountains of Snowdonia, to its mouth at Conwy Bay is little more than 31 miles.

Novels: 'They came over the crest of a high ridge before noon, and there below them the valley of the Conwy opened, and beyond, the ground rose at first gently and suavely, but above these green levels there towered in the distance the enormous bastions of Eryri [see SNOWDON, Mount], soaring to polished steel peaks against the pale blue of the sky. The river was a winding silver thread, twining a tortuous course through and over shoals of tidal mud and sand on its way northward to the sea, its waters at this hour so spread and diminished that it could be forded without difficulty. And after the crossing, as Cadfael had warned, they climbed.' CADFAEL was born in the Vale of Conway, near Trefriw. In May 1137, on their way to GWYTHERIN from BANGOR, Prior ROBERT's party travelled through the Conway valley and LLANRWST. In May 1144 Cadfael and Deacon MARK travelled to ABER from ST ASAPH in the retinue of OWAIN GWYNEDD, crossing the river near Caerhun (see CANOVIUM).

Refs: **1** (2); **3** (8); **18** (4).

Conwy (Gwynedd, Wales). Also spelled Conway. Situated on the broad estuary of the River CONWAY and 12 miles north-east of BANGOR, Conwy is a fortified town with a castle built by Edward I in 1283–87. It became the English king's headquarters during some of his campaigns against the Welsh, and formed an important link in the great chain of Anglo-Norman fortresses, stretching from Flint to ABERYSTWYTH. During the English Civil War, the Royalists were besieged in the castle before they eventually yielded to the Parliamentarians. In 1665 the castle was partly dismantled for its iron, timber and lead by Edward Conway, Earl of Conway, who had been granted the castle by Charles II. The walls of the town – with three gates and twenty-one semi-circular towers – have survived almost complete. Conwy is considered to be one of the best-preserved examples of a medieval fortified town in Britain. The 14th C. St Mary's Church stands on the site of the Cistercian abbey founded in 1186, of which nothing else now remains.

Novels: '"Even here we must be a good mile or more the Welsh side of the old boundary dyke. I never was here before, not being a sheep man. I'm from Gwynedd myself, from the far side of Conwy. But even these hills look like home to me."'

Refs: **3** (8); **18** (4).

Corbett, William (*fl.* 1121) (hist.). Also spelled Corbet. Eldest son of Roger Fitz Corbet (1086–1121), who was born at Pays de Caux in NORMANDY, William inherited the barony of Caus in *c.*1121. In 1134, according to Odrericus Vitalis, CAUS CASTLE was captured and burnt by the Welsh. William died childless, sometime between 1136 and 1155, and the honour of Caus passed to his younger brother, Ebrard (*fl.* 1140).

Novels: 'It was some years since the men of Powys had captured and partially burned the castle of Caus, after the death of William Corbett and in the absence of his brother and heir, and they had held on to this advanced outpost ever since, a convenient base for further incursions.'

Refs: **9** (9).

Corbière, Isabel (*fl.* 1139) (fict.). **Novels:** Sister of Ivo CORBIÈRE and wife of one of RANULF of Chester's knights. '"If you behave sensibly now you may yet meet, some day, the only sister I have . . . [She] keeps me informed of what goes on in Ranulf's court. But devil a nun she'd ever have made, even if she were not already a wife."'

Refs: **4** (5:1–3).

Corbière, Ivo (*c.*1110–1139) (fict.). **Novels:** '"My name," said the rescuer blithely, "is Ivo Corbière, of the manor of STANTON COBBOLD in this shire, though the main part of my honour lies in Cheshire."' Lord of the manor of Stanton Cobbold, brother of Isabel CORBIÈRE, and a distant kinsman of RANULF of Chester, Ivo's main estates lay in Cheshire. He arrived at SHREWSBURY ABBEY on 30 July 1139, with his three retainers, Turstan FOWLER, ARALD THE GROOM and EWALD THE GROOM. During a riot on the jetty, Corbière saved Emma Vernold (see CORVISER) from falling in the SEVERN. Although Emma was attracted to him, Ivo paid no real attention to her until he realised that she might have the very thing he was seeking: a letter from ROBERT of Gloucester to Ranulf of Chester. In his desperate search for the letter, Fowler and Ewald murdered Thomas of BRISTOL and Euan of SHOTWICK. When Ewald hecame a suspect for the killings, Corbière ordered his death in case he should talk. He persuaded Emma to allow him to escort her first to his manor at Stanton Cobbold and from there to BRISTOL, pretending that his sister, Isabel, was about to enter a convent nearby. They left SHREWSBURY for the south on 4 August 1139. On their arrival at Stanton Cobbold, Corbière tried to take the letter from Emma by force. She overturned the brazier over his ankles and feet, setting the manor alight. Ivo was consumed in the fire.

Refs: **4** (1:1–4, 3:2, 4:2, 5:1–3, 5:6).

Corde, Ailwin (b. 1080) (fict.). **Novels:** '"I'd keep your tongue within your teeth," he [CADFAEL] advised amiably. "Wool merchants are a power in this town, and not every husband will thank you for opening his eyes."' Elderly husband of Cecily CORDE, Ailwin was a wealthy SHREWSBURY wool merchant. After the death of his first wife, he married Cecily, a third his age, 'against his grown son's wishes'. He attended the wedding of Daniel and Margery AURIFABER in May 1140. Later that month he journeyed on business to OXFORD.

Refs: **7** (3–4).

Corde, Cecily (b. 1117) (fict.). **Novels:** Young wife of Ailwin CORDE, she was 'a fine, flaunting beauty' a third her husband's age. In May 1140 Cecily and Daniel AURIFABER were secret lovers. Their relationship ended abruptly when Daniel asked her to admit to the sheriff that they had spent the Monday night together. Not wanting to jeopardise her marriage and blight her good name, she threw him out.

Refs: **7** (3–4, 8).

Corve, River (Shropshire, England). Rising on the south-eastern slopes of WENLOCK Edge near Bourton, the River Corve flows south-west for some 18 miles to LUDLOW, where it merges with the River TEME. The broad fertile valley of the Corve, known as Corve Dale, runs from Much Wenlock to Ludlow and is flanked by CLEE HILLS to the east and Wenlock Edge to the west. In the early Middle Ages Corve Dale was a major line of communication between the Midlands and the Welsh border, with castles like Corfham strategically placed to guard the route.

Novels: 'Blundering blindly ahead with a burly young novice beside him, northwards across the Corve, CADFAEL groped through a chill white mist, and knew that they were all wasting their time. They might probe the drifts as they would, but the weather had the laugh on them, covering everything in the same blank pall.' In Winter 1139 Brother ELYAS left his warm bed at BROMFIELD Priory, and headed like a madman into a blinding snowstorm, doggedly followed by Yves HUGONIN. On their northward ordeal, they crossed the River Corve. The manor of WHITBACHE lay 'to the west and on the near side of the Corve'.

Refs: **6** (6–9).

Corviser, Emma (née Vernold) (b. 1121) (fict.). **Novels:** '"I am a stone-mason's daughter, and niece to a merchant. No landed lord is likely to become a suitor for someone like me."' Wife of Philip CORVISER, Emma was the daughter of a master-mason of BRISTOL and a 'famous embroidress'. She was orphaned when her mother died in 1129. Then only eight, she was taken in by her uncle, Thomas of BRISTOL, becoming his heiress. In July 1139 she went to SHREWSBURY with him, arriving by barge on the 31st. After her uncle's murder, she moved from her living quarters on the barge to SHREWSBURY ABBEY guesthall, lodging with the BERINGARS. Pretending she wanted to replace her lost gloves, Emma tried to slip away from Aline to find Euan of SHOTWICK and give him the letter her uncle had been charged to deliver. She was unaware of its contents. On 3 August Euan was found murdered. The following day, believing that Ivo CORBIÈRE – to whom she was attracted – was going to escort her home to Bristol, Emma willingly went with him to his manor at STANTON COBBOLD. When Corbière tried to take the letter from her by force, she thrust it into the fiery heat of the brazier, badly burning her hand. With her good hand, she overturned the brazier, setting fire to Corbière and the house. She was rescued from the blazing inferno by Philip Corviser, and returned with him to his home at Shrewsbury. By March 1141 Emma and Philip were man and wife.

Refs: **4** (1:3–4, 2:1, 2:3, 3:1–2, 4:1–2, 5:1, 5:3–6); **9** (8).

Corviser, Geoffrey (b. *c.* 1090) (fict.). Novels: 'Master Geoffrey Corviser, named for his trade, was a big, portly, vigorous man not yet fifty, clean-shaven, brisk and dignified. He made some of the finest shoes and riding-boots in England, and was well aware of their excellence and his own worth.' Husband of Mistress CORVISER and father of Philip, Geoffrey Corviser was a master-shoemaker and the provost of SHREWSBURY from, at least, 1139. On 30 July 1139 he led the ten-strong delegation from the Guild Merchant, who requested, of RADULFUS, that a proportion of the SHREWSBURY ABBEY fair tolls should go to the town to repair the damage caused by King STEPHEN's siege. A 'decent and respected' man, he was present when LILIWIN was accused of striking and robbing Walter AURIFABER in May 1140. As a wedding present he made Liliwin a 'fine new pair' of shoes. In 1141, Corviser attended the funeral of Gilbert PRESTCOTE (the elder) in March, and that of Brother HUMILIS in September. Hugh BERINGAR informed the provost, in February 1145, of Sub-Prior HERLUIN's intention to preach at the HIGH CROSS to ask the 'whole of Shrewsbury' to help in the restoration of RAMSEY ABBEY.

Refs: **4** (1:1, 2:3, 5:5); **7** (1–2, 14); **8** (9); **9** (4, 8); **10** (7); **11** (14); **12** (11); **13** (5); **15** (3); **19** (1–2); **RB** (3).

Corviser, Mistress (*fl.* 1139) (fict.). **Novels:** 'Mistress Corviser had undoubtedly been fulminating for hours about her errant son, a good-for-nothing who was no sooner bailed out of prison than he was off in mischief somewhere else until midnight. Probably she had said at least a dozen times that she washed her hands of him, that he was past praying for, and she no longer cared, let him go to the devil his own way. But for all that, her husband could not get her to go to bed, and at every least sound that might be a footstep at the door or in the street, steady or staggering, she flew to look out, with her mouth full of abuse but her heart full of hope.' Wife of Geoffrey CORVISER and the mother of Philip, she 'was large, handsome and voluble'. In August 1139, when her son returned home from STANTON COBBOLD with Emma Vernold (see CORVISER), she accepted Emma into the household with open arms.

Refs: **4** (4:2, 5:5).

Corviser, Philip (b. 1123) (fict.). **Novels:** 'The Corviser sprig was known for a wild one, clever, bursting with hot and suspect ideas, locked in combat with his elders half of his time, and occasionally liable to drink rather more than at this stage he could carry.' Son of Geoffrey and Mistress CORVISER, Philip was a shoemaker like his father. On 31 July 1139, the day after his father had failed to persuade the Abbot RADULFUS to grant a proportion of the SHREWSBURY ABBEY fair tolls to the town, Philip took matters into his own hands. Leading his own delegation, he tried to win the direct support of the merchants themselves. After he was knocked to the ground by Thomas of BRISTOL, a riot broke out on the jetty. Although Philip managed to avoid arrest, he was eventually captured and brought before the sheriff's court. He was accused of being the ringleader and also of assaulting the merchant. Emma Vernold (see CORVISER), however, spoke up in his defence. On Turstan FOWLER's testimony, however, Philip was detained in a cell at SHREWSBURY CASTLE on suspicion of Thomas's murder. He was released on his father's warranty on 2 August. Determined to prove his innocence, he tried to retrace his movements that fatal night, and discovered Ivo CORBIÈRE's involvement in the events surrounding the BRISTOL merchant's murder. Suddenly Philip realised that Emma was in terrible danger. He rushed to the guest-hall to find that she had left for STANTON COBBOLD with Corbière. Stealing the saddled horse of a WORCESTER merchant, he rode out of the court in hot pursuit. Arriving at the manor, he found it ablaze with Corbière's men trying desperately to quench the flames. Nevertheless, he managed to rescue Emma from the blazing solar, and took her back home to his parents, who were proud and full of praise that he had vindicated himself. Between August 1139 and March 1141 Philip and Emma were married, probably sometime in 1140. In June 1142 CADFAEL took the waxen footprint of Brother ELURIC's murderer to Philip, who offered to show it to the cobbler in FRANKWELL. In January 1143 he used his skills to make a pair of special boots for the crippled Brother HALUIN.

Refs: **4** (1:2–4, 2:1–3, 3:1, 4:1–5, 5:1–2, 5:4–6); **9** (8); **13** (5); **15** (3).

(Geoffrey) Corviser's House and Garden (Pride Hill, Shrewsbury, Shropshire) (fict.). Before the 13th C., when the whole street was renamed Pride Hill, the northern side was known as Corviser's or Shoemaker's Row and the southern side opposite as BUTCHER ROW. At one time the street, including CASTLE STREET, was referred to as High Street. Although it never existed, it is most likely that the house of the CORVISER family was in Corvisor [*sic*] Row. Their garden was somewhere upstream from the 18th C. Welsh Bridge, below the town wall. The 13th C. remains of Bennet's Hall, the old SHREWSBURY MINT, are incorporated into a shop in Pride Hill.

Novels: The Corvisers had 'a garden upstream, below the town wall, as many of the burgesses had, for growing their own fruit and vegetables, and there was a small hut there, and a sward'.

Refs: **4** (4:2).

Corwen (Clwyd, Wales). On a bend of the River DEE, near its confluence with the Afon Alwen, the small Welsh market town of Corwen is some 10 miles west of LLANGOLLEN. It lies in the shadow of the BERWYNS and is reputed to be entirely sunless throughout the winter months. Corwen is derived from *Corfaen*, meaning 'sacred stone', which is thought to refer to the ancient stone known as *Carreg-y-Big yn y fach Rewlad*, or 'the pointed stone in the icy nook'. Originally a freestanding monolith, the stone is now built into the porch wall of the church. The town was associated with Owen Glendower or Owain Glyndwr (*c.*1354–*c.*1416), self-proclaimed Prince of Wales.

Novels: In February 1141 OWAIN GWYNEDD, 'they said, had come east out of his eyrie to keep a weather eye upon RANULF of Chester, who might be so blown up with his success as to mistake the mettle of the prince of Gwynedd. He was patrolling the fringes of CHESTER territory, and had reached Corwen on the Dee.'

Refs: **9** (3).

Cotswolds (Gloucestershire, Oxfordshire, Avon, Wiltshire, Hereford & Worcester, and Warwickshire, England). Stretching in a broad swathe across south-west England, the range of limestone hills known as the Cotswolds were famous, during the Middle Ages, as the major wool-producing area in England. The name itself is derived from the Anglo-Saxon *cote*, meaning a 'sheepfold', and *wold*, a 'tract of uncultivated land'. At the height of the region's prosperity vast flocks of sheep, known as 'Cotswold Lions', bred for their long wool, roamed the open hills. The medieval merchants made fortunes from the export of the raw wool (and later cloth), and their wealth is reflected in the magnificent houses, manors and churches found throughout the wolds. The most northerly point is Meon Hill, a few miles north of Chipping CAMPDEN; the most southerly point is BATH. The Cotswolds lie mainly in Gloucestershire, where the escarpment rises abruptly from the River SEVERN valley to dip down gently into Oxfordshire. In the south the wolds extend into Avon and Wiltshire, while in the north they include a small corner of Warwickshire and an even tinier portion of Hereford & Worcester – namely Broadway. The highest point in the Cotswolds is Cleeve Hill.

Novels: 'There was a merchant of SHREWSBURY who dealt in fleeces all up and down the borders, both from Wales and from such fat sheep-country as the Cotswolds.' CADFAEL journeyed through the Cotswolds in December 1145. 'After this last rise the ground levelled into the Cotswold plateau, wide and flat on top of its elevated world, with great, straight roads, big open fields and rich villages fat with sheep.'

Refs: **11** (5); **20** (7, 10, 15).

Cound (Shropshire, England). DB – Cuneet: in Condover Hundred; a holding of Reginald the Sheriff under Roger de MONTGOMERY. Cound is a small village situated on rising ground 6 miles south-east of SHREWSBURY, near the confluence of the Cound Brook and its tributary the Coundmoor Brook, and about a mile west of the SEVERN. Originally a Saxon foundation, St Peter's Church dates mostly from the

13th C., although the north aisle, chancel and vestry were rebuilt in Victorian times.

Novels: In December 1138 the sheriff's men were led on a wild-goose chase by Edwy BELLECOTE through the countryside around Cound, including ATCHAM, CRESSAGE and ACTON. After his capture, Edwy tried hard 'to suppress a smile when he contemplated the one who had gone head over heels in the meadows near Cound'.

Refs: **3** (6).

Courcelle, Adam (1108–38) (fict.). **Novels:** 'The young man had bright chestnut hair, and eyes of the same burning brown, and knew that he stood well with his king.' King's officer and deputy sheriff of Shropshire under Gilbert PRESTCOTE the elder, Adam was with STEPHEN at the siege of SHREWSBURY in August 1138. The night before the fall of SHREWSBURY CASTLE, he received the traitor, Giles SIWARD, into his tent and learned of William FITZALAN's plans for his treasury. Letting his informer believe that his life would be spared, Courcelle sent him back into the castle. After its fall, however, he gave orders that Siward should be hanged. Despite his attempts to find and capture FITZALAN and Fulke ADENEY, both managed to escape. He was also under orders to search for Godith Adeney (see BLUND). While the prisoners, including Siward, were being hanged, Courcelle slipped away alone to intercept Nicholas FAINTREE and Torold BLUND, who were attempting to flee with the treasury. Knowing their route in advance, he sprinkled the forest ride with 'caltrops'. He managed to halt the fugitives and kill Faintree with a 'strangler's cord'. But Blund escaped. In order to conceal the fact that Faintree had been murdered, Courcelle dumped the body with the ninety-four who had been hanged. After Aline Siward (see BERINGAR) had identified the corpse of her brother, Courcelle presented her with Giles's cloak. Giles's broken dagger he disposed of in the River SEVERN. Courcelle was accused of Faintree's murder by Hugh BERINGAR and, after proclaiming his innocence, he was challenged before the king to trial by combat. In a fight that went on for 'two full hours, with never a break for breath', Courcelle was killed, after falling on 'his own upended poniard'. He was succeeded as deputy sheriff by Beringar.

Refs: **2** (1–3, 5, 6–12).

Coventry (West Midlands, England). This city is situated some 9 miles north-east of WARWICK and 20 miles east of Birmingham city centre. The name Coventry, meaning 'Cofa's tree', is derived from *Cofa*, a personal name, and the Anglo-Saxon *treo*, meaning a 'tree'. Some authorities, however, argue that the name is derived from 'convent town', since a convent or nunnery was founded on the site in the 7th C. (see St OSBURG). The convent was destroyed by the Danes in 1016 and, twenty-seven years later, LEOFRIC, Earl of Mercia and husband of Lady Godiva (or Godgifu), founded on the site a Benedictine monastery, which was dissolved in 1539. Today only fragments survive of what was once one of the richest houses in the midlands. Godiva is famous for her legendary ride, naked and on a white horse, through the town. From *c.*1043 until 1355 the government of the town was divided between two distinct lordships: the northern half belonged to the priory; while the southern half belonged to the earls of Chester and their heirs. By the mid-15th C. Coventry was the midland centre of the woollen textile industry, and the fourth important city in England after LONDON, York and BRISTOL.

Novels: 'A marvel, CADFAEL considered, that any bishop had ever contrived to manage so huge a see as the original bishopric of Mercia, successively shifting its base from LICHFIELD to CHESTER, back again to Lichfield, and now to Coventry, in the effort to remain in touch with as diverse a flock as ever shepherd tended.' In 1140, Bishop ROGER DE CLINTON appointed Mother PATRICE from Coventry as Abbess of FAREWELL. In 1142 BRITRIC met GUNNILD at

Coventry and travelled with her from there to SHREWSBURY. Deacon SERLO left Shrewsbury for Coventry in June 1143 to report to Roger de Clinton about the accusation of heresy brought against ELAVE. Roger de Clinton took THEOFANU's precious psalter, given to him by FORTUNATA, back with him to the library at Coventry. On his way to join King STEPHEN's muster at CAMBRIDGE in November 1143, Hugh BERINGAR and his company picked up fresh horses at Coventry. On their homeward journey, towards the end of the month, the soldiers halted a while in the town. 'Approaching the city from the north, they found Earl Leofric's old defences still in timber, but sturdy enough, and the tangle of streets within well paved and maintained since the bishops had made this city their main base within the see.' 'The earl of Chester's small timber castle [was] within the town'. 'The city was divided between two lordships, the prior's half and the earl's half, and from time to time there was some grumbling and discontent over privileges varying between the two, but there was a shared and acknowledged town moot for all, and by and large they rubbed shoulders with reasonable amity. There were few more prosperous towns in England, and none more resilient and alert to opportunity. It was to be seen in the bustle in the streets.' Hugh Beringar and Cadfael travelled to Coventry in 1145 to attend the conference between King Stephen and the Empress MAUD. 'The day of the council at Coventry was fixed as the last day of November. Before that date there had been certain evidences that the prospect of agreement and peace was by no means universally welcome, and there were powerful interests ready and willing to wreck it.' (Ellis Peters says: 'The conference did take place at about that time, without result, but there's no record of where, or exactly when. I thought Coventry a likely venue, as the bishops were active in the move, and it made a credible central spot.') Among others who also attended the council – presided over by the bishops HENRY OF BLOIS, Roger de Clinton and NIGEL – were: Robert de BEAUMONT (the younger); Hugh BIGOD; Humphrey de BOHUN; Philip FITZROBERT; William FITZROBERT; Reginald FITZROY; Yves HUGONIN; William MARTEL; RANULF of Chester; ROBERT of Gloucester; ROGER of Hereford and WILLIAM OF YPRES. Brien de SOULIS was murdered in St Mary's Priory. Cadfael attended to seek news of Olivier de BRETAGNE, taken prisoner at FARINGDON. The conference ended 'with nothing settled, nothing solved, peace as far away as ever.'

Refs: **15** (10–11); **16** (5–6, 13, 15); **17** (7, 9, 11); **20** (1–3, 5–11, 14–15).

Coventry, Bishop of. See ROGER DE CLINTON, Bishop of Coventry and Lichfield.

Coventry, Rafe of. See GENVILLE, Rafe de.

Cowley (Gloucestershire, England). Some 5 miles south of Cheltenham, the COTSWOLD village of Cowley lies on rising ground to the west of the River Churn. St Mary's Church, standing in the grounds of Cowley Manor, dates from the 12th C. At the time of the Domesday survey the church, manor and mill belonged to PERSHORE Abbey.

Novels: In December 1145 CADFAEL and Olivier de BRETAGNE spend one night, on their journey from CIRENCESTER to GLOUCESTER, 'in the hospitable mill at Cowley'.

Refs: **20** (15).

Cradoc, Prince (*fl.* 630, (hist.). Also spelled Caradoc, Caradog, Chradocus, Karadoc or Karadauc. Reputed to have murdered St WINIFRED for refusing his lustful advances, Prince Cradoc of Hawarden, Clwyd, was the son of a Welsh chieftain and lived in the 7th C. He is probably a historical character, although the circumstances of his death have been obscured by the St Winifred legend. In *A History of Shrewsbury* (1825), Owen and Blakeway quote from the Cottonian MS, regarding the Life of St Winifred: 'Karadauc, son of Alauc, of the royal blood comes to the house tired with hunting, and seeking refreshment. He falls in love with her. She declines his addresses, and having recourse to a stratagem escapes through her chamber, and runs to the valley. Karadoc, mounts his horse, overtakes her before she reaches the door of the church, and cuts off her head.' In Prior ROBERT Pennant's *Life of St Winifred*, the Bodleian MS states that: 'Chradocus, the king's son came to the house for the sole purpose of gratifying his desires.'

Novels: 'Remember what befell Prince Cradoc, whose flesh watered away into the ground like rain, so that he vanished utterly, as to the body expunged out of the world, as to the soul, the fearful imagination dared not guess.' In May 1137, at chapter, Brother RHYS told the story of St Winifred and Prince Cradoc.

Refs: **1** (1, 4, 8); **10** (9).

Cressage (Shropshire, England). DB – Cristesache: in Condover Hundred; a holding of Ranulf Peverel under Roger de MONTGOMERY. Some 8 miles south-east of SHREWSBURY and on the south bank of the SEVERN, Cressage is an ancient village, now dominated by modern housing. It derives its name from the Saxon *Cristesac*, meaning 'Christ's Oak'. 'About a quarter of a mile from the village of Cressage,' wrote John Corbet Anderson in *Shropshire: Its Early History and Antiquities* (1864), 'on the road to Shrewsbury, is the shattered trunk of an old oak tree. Tradition has it, that under the once wide-spreading branches of this identical oak, Christian missionaries preached to our pagan Saxon forefathers the unsearchable riches of Christ.' The tree later became known as the Lady Oak, in honour of the Virgin Mary. There is still a 'Lady Oak' at Cressage, standing in a field near Lady Oak Leasowe, just north of the Shrewsbury road. But the one referred to by Corbet no longer exists. It is thought to have grown on the site of the present War Memorial. The ancient church of St Samson stood on a site that was subject to persistent flooding by the River Severn. It continued to serve the village until 1841, however, when a new church (Christ Church) was built on a safer and drier site. The old church was then demolished. At Castle Mound, on the south bank of the Severn, are the earthwork remains of a Norman motte and bailey castle, built to guard the river crossing.

Novels: In December 1138 Edwy BELLECOTE led the sheriff's men on a wild-goose chase through Cressage and the surrounding countryside, including ATCHAM, COUND and ACTON. In October 1143 Sulien BLOUNT's search for GUNNILD took him 'as far afield as Cressage'.

Refs: **3** (6); **17** (8).

Cricklade (Wiltshire, England). On the south bank of the River THAMES, 7 miles south-east of CIRENCESTER and 6 miles north-west of Swindon, Cricklade is an ancient wool market town, dating back to Romano-British times. Lying just to the west of the Roman ERMIN WAY, the town was fortified during the reign of Alfred the Great (871–99), and in the 11th C. it possessed a mint. The parish church, dedicated to St Sampson, dates from Anglo-Saxon times. The pinnacled and richly decorated tower was completed in 1553. Although much restored, the smaller St Mary's Church, in High Street, is essentially Norman. The Old Town Cross in the churchyard is 14th C. The nearby priory contains the remains of a 13th C. hospital. Nothing remains of the castle built in 1144 by William Peverel of Dover, a supporter of the Empress MAUD. The *Gesta Stephani* (ed. Potter, 1976) says that the castle 'was inaccessible because of the barrier of water and marsh on every side'. After Peverel had left England for the HOLY LAND, the castle was placed in charge of Philip FITZROBERT, who surrendered it to King STEPHEN in Summer 1145. In late 1146 or early 1147 the castle withstood an assault by Henry Plantagenet (later HENRY II).

Novels: In the 'dangerous and explosive battlefield of the Thames valley', the castle at Cricklade was held for the Empress Maud by Philip FitzRobert. In

Summer 1145, however, FitzRobert 'handed over Cricklade whole and entire to King Stephen, himself, his garrison, arms, armour and all.' It became the centre of a ring of royal fortresses that included BAMPTON, FARINGDON, MALMESBURY and PURTON. In December of the same year Guy CAMVILLE led his garrison away from La MUSARDERIE to safety at Cricklade.

Refs: **20** (1–3, 5–7, 10–12, 14).

Cristina (b. 1123) (fict.). **Novels:** '"A small, sharp dark creature, quite handsome in her way . . . Her hand is regarded as a great prize."' Her father was Tudur ap RHYS, while her mother was 'a woman of Gwynedd'. Although she was betrothed to Elis ap CYNAN from a child, Cristina did not love him. CADFAEL first met her on a visit to TREGEIRIOG in February 1141. On a return visit, the following month, she revealed to him her secret love for Eliud ap GRIFFITH. She also told her father that she would marry no one but Eliud. When Elis fell in love with Melicent PRESTCOTE, Cristina was finally free to marry the man of her choice. She was unaware, however, that Eliud had murdered Gilbert PRESTCOTE the elder. Nevertheless, despite the crime, she eventually married Eliud.

Refs: **9** (2–5, 10–12, 14–15).

Croesau Bach (Shropshire, England). Some 3 miles south-west of OSWESTRY and 18 miles north-west of SHREWSBURY, Croesau Bach is a tiny farming hamlet nestling in the foothills of the BERWYNS. It is pleasantly situated, above the valley of the River Morda, between the ancient boundary of OFFA'S DYKE and the present border separating England and Wales.

Novels: In December 1138 CADFAEL passed through the hamlet of Croesau Bach on his way from RHYDYCROESAU to MALLILIE. On his return to SHREWSBURY he made a detour to visit Ifor ap MORGAN, before 'cutting due east from Croesau Bach to strike the main road well south of the town' of OSWESTRY.

Refs: **3** (8, 11).

Cruce, Cecilia (*fl.* 1141) (fict.). **Novels:** 'His lady sat aloof and quiet, a pale-haired woman in green.' She married Reginald CRUCE in *c.*1123, bringing him a manor and lands in Staffordshire, where they settled until 1138. She gave birth to a boy in *c.*1126, and a boy and girl in *c.*1132. In August 1141 she was pregnant again.

Refs: **11** (4).

Cruce, Humphrey (d. 1138) (fict.). **Novels:** 'The child of Humphrey's age had plainly usurped his whole heart, even though his son would inherit all when that heart no longer beat. "He lived barely a month longer," said Reginald. "Only long enough to see the return of her escort, and know she was safely delivered where she wished to be. He was old and feeble, we knew it. But he should not have dwindled so soon."' Father of Reginald CRUCE by his first marriage and Julian by his second, Humphrey was Lord of LAI until his death in September 1138. He also held the manors of IGHTFELD, HARPECOTE and PREES, from the Bishop of CHESTER, and lands in Staffordshire. His overlord was Earl Waleran of Meulan (see BEAUMONT). Humphrey's first wife died in 1110. He married again in 1118, but his second wife died the same year while giving birth to Julian. While she was still a child, he arranged his daughter's betrothal to Godfrid MARESCOT. In August 1138, when Julian decided to become a nun at WHERWELL Abbey, Humphrey reluctantly agreed and gave her an escort of three men-at-arms. Saddened by the loss of his dearly loved daughter, he died the following month. He was succeeded by his son, Reginald.

Refs: **11** (4–5, 7).

Cruce, Julian (b. 1118) (fict.). **Novels:** Also called Brother Fidelis. '"What she wanted and held to be hers she took, the whole of it, to the end, to the last

C

moment. His company, the care of him, the secrets of his body, as intimate as ever was marriage – his love, far beyond the common claims of marriage. No use any man telling her she was free, when she knew she was a wife. I wonder she is free even now."' Daughter of Humphrey CRUCE by his second wife and half-sister of Reginald, Julian was affianced to Godfrid MARESCOT (see HUMILIS) in 1124, when she was six years old. Severely wounded while in the HOLY LAND, Godfrid was unable to fulfil the betrothal contract. Setting Julian free to marry whom she would, Godfrid entered the Benedictine Priory at Hyde Mead (see HYDE ABBEY), changing his name to Humilis. Julian, however, was determined that they would not be separated. In 1138, pretending that she was entering the nunnery at WHERWELL, she travelled south from LAI – with the sole intention of joining Godfrid. Assisted by Adam HERIET, she sold her belongings, disguised herself as a boy and entered Hyde Mead on 20 August, calling herself Brother Fidelis. She also maintained that she was dumb, and therefore unable to speak. Soon, she became the ailing Humilis's faithful friend and constant companion. In August 1141, after Hyde Mead had been burned to the ground, Fidelis and Humilis travelled north together to enter SHREWSBURY ABBEY. Brother URIEN discovered that Fidelis was a girl, not a boy, and attempted blackmail. But RHUN, who had soon become her friend, helped to protect her from Urien's unwanted advances. While Humilis and Fidelis were returning to the abbey from a visit to SALTON, their boat capsized in a torrential rainstorm and Humilis was drowned. To all appearances, Fidelis died also, casting off the shadowy cowl of a monk to re-emerge into the light as the lady, Julian Cruce. Shortly after, she returned to LAI. It is most probable, once she had come to terms with Humilis's death, that she married Nicholas HARNAGE.

Refs: **11** (1–10, 12–14).

Cruce, Reginald (b. *c.*1101) (fict.). **Novel:** 'A big, black-haired man of austere features and imperious manner, but well-disposed, it seemed, towards chance travellers.' Son of Humphrey CRUCE, elder half-brother of Julian, and husband of Cecilia. Reginald's mother died in 1110, when he was nine years old. He married Cecilia in *c.*1123 and went to live in Staffordshire. Reginald inherited his father's manors in 1133, and became Lord of LAI, holding an additional three manors from Earl Waleran of Meulan (see BEAUMONT). In August 1141 he had three children, two boys and a girl, and 'another sibling on the way'. In September he went to SHREWSBURY with Nicholas HARNAGE to see Hugh BERINGAR, the sheriff, to demand justice for the alleged murder of his sister. Finding, on a later visit, that she was alive and well, Reginald took her back to LAI.

Refs: **11** (4, 6–7, 14).

Cuthred, Saint. See BOURCHIER, Renaud.

Cuthred's Hut (Eyton Forest, Shropshire) (fict.). Although it never existed, Cuthred's stone hut was situated in a clearing midway between the present-day villages of Eyton-on-Severn (see EYTON-BY-SEVERN) and EATON Constantine.

Novels: 'The stone hut . . . was stoutly built but small and low-roofed, and showed signs of recent repair after being neglected for years. There was a little square garden enclosure round it, fenced in with a low pale, and part of the ground within had heen cleared and planted . . . the door of the hut stood open, and from deep within a steady gleam of light showed.' In Octoher 1142 Cuthred (see BOURCHIER, Renaud) moved into the disused stone hermitage belonging to Dionisia LUDEL of EATON.

Refs: **14** (5–6).

Cynan, Elis ap (b. *c.*1120) (fict.). **Novels:** 'He was an engaging youth . . . readable like a book, open like a daisy at noon.' Nephew of Griffith ap MEILYR and cousin of Eliud ap GRIFFITH, Elis ap Cynan was placed in his uncle's fosterage after his father's death. He grew up with Eliud as brothers: they were of the same age and had been born within half an hour of each other; Eliud being the elder. Elis's mother was cousin to OWAIN GWYNEDD, who was also his overlord. Although he was betrothed to CRISTINA while they were children, neither loved each other. Elis fought alongside CADWALADR at the battle of LINCOLN on 2 February 1141. Among a Welsh raiding party on their way home from Lincoln, he was captured at GODRIC'S FORD. He was taken back to SHREWSBURY CASTLE, where arrangements were made to exchange him for Gilbert PRESTCOTE the elder. Giving Hugh BERINGAR his word not to escape, Elis was given free run of the castle. While there he met Melicent PRESTCOTE and fell helplessly in love. When the injured Gilbert Prestcote was alone in the infirmary, Elis went to see him, to plead for his daughter's hand. But he was unable to speak with the sheriff because the latter was asleep. As soon as Melicent heard that Elis had entered her father's chamber, she accused him of his murder. Shortly after, Melicent went with Sister MAGDALEN to Godric's Ford intent on taking the veil. Elis overheard talk of an attack on Godric's Ford and, fearing for Melicent's safety, he slipped out of the castle, breaking his parole. Armed with only his tongue and a long, two-tined pikel lashed to a six-foot pole, Elis faced his fellow countrymen. In the ensuing battle he was wounded, pinned together with Eliud by an arrow. Besides the wound in the arm, his injuries included a twisted knee and a cracked rib. Proven innocent of murder, he and Melicent were reconciled. Elis eventually returned to TREGEIROG, while Melicent returned to her stepmother – until such time as Elis could formally ask for her hand in marriage.

Refs: **9** (1–11, 13–15).

Cynan, Rhys ap (*fl.* 1137) (fict.). A landowner and man of substance in GWYTHERN, he was waiting in May 1137 to be taken to court by RHISIART over a disputed boundary. In the same month, he attended the council, held by Father HUW, which agreed to withdraw all opposition to Prior ROBERT's plans to translate the relics of St WINIFRED to SHREWSBURY.

Refs: **1** (6).

Cynllaith, Commote of (Clwyd, Wales). The medieval Welsh region of Cynllaith in ancient Powys Fadog lay to the west of OWESTRY. It was bounded in the east by the English border; to the north by the cantref of Nanheudwy; to the west by Edeyrnion; and to the south by Mochnant and MECHAIN. The commote was centred on St Silin's Church in LLANSILIN.

Novels: Brother RHYS of SHREWSBURY ABBEY was born just to the west of the manor of MALLILIE, 'nearby the church of Llansilin'. In December 1138 CADFAEL travelled to Mallilie in Cynllaith. MEURIG claimed before the Welsh court, held at Llansilin, '"that Welsh law has never lost its right in any part of that land [of Mallilie], for whatever its ownership, it is part of the commote of Cynllaith"'. In Febuary 1141 OWAIN GWYNEDD was rumoured to be in Cynllaith or GLYN CEIRIOG, keeping a watchful eye on RANULF of CHESTER. In 1141 Tudur ap RHYS was the Lord of TREGEIRIOG in Cynllaith.

Refs: **3** (7–9); **9** (2).

Cynllaith, River (Clwyd, Wales). Rising on the southern slopes of the 1,457 ft. high Pen y Gwely, the waters of the Cynllaith enter the Pen-y-Gwely Reservoir, flow south-east to RHYDYCROESAU and from there sweep south-west in a mile arc to join the Afon Tanat at Pen-y-Bont Llanerch Emrys. The main village on its 9-mile course to the Tanat is LLANSILIN, nestling on high ground to the west of the Cynllaith valley.

Novels: '"To the house of Cynfrith ap RHYS it is but half a mile . . . You'll see his white goats in the little paddock. For Ifor ap MORGAN you must go further. Keep to the same track again until you're through the hills, and looking down into the valley, then take the path to the right, that fords our river before it joins the Cynllaith."'

Refs: **3** (8).

Cynllaith, Valley of (Clwyd, Wales). This valley sweeps in a south-westerly arc from RHYDYCROESAU, past LLANSILIN to Pen-y-Bont Llanerch Emrys. It is a fertile and attractive valley with numerous small farms scattered along the partially-wooded hillsides.

Novels: 'He came through the defile, and saw the valley of the Cynllaith open before him, and the track to the right weaving a neat line through the rising grass to ford the little tributary. Half a mile beyond, woodland clothed the slope of the ridge, and in the full leaf of summer it might have been difficult to detect the low wooden house within the trees; but now, with all the leaves fallen, it stood clear behind the bare branches like a contented domestic hen in a coop.' In December 1138 CADFAEL left the holding of Cynfrith ap RHYS near Llansilin, to ride to the house of Ifor ap MORGAN. The journey took him through the Valley of the Cynllaith.

Refs: **3** (7–9).

Cynric (b. *c.*1090) (fict.). **Novels:** 'It was rare enough for Cynric to utter thirteen words together, except by way of the responses learned by heart in the holy office. Thirteen words of his own had the force of prophecy.' Verger of the parish church of HOLY CROSS in SHREWSBURY since *c.*1126, Cynric, who never married, came 'of a country family of free folk, and had a brother somewhere north of the town with a grown family'. In 1141, he had been with Father ADAM through most of his years of office and 'had absorbed, in the years of his service, something of the same qualities without the authority'. He lived in one of the two tiny upper rooms over the north porch of SHREWSBURY ABBEY, where 'Father Adam robed and kept his church furnishings'. In December 1141 he alerted CADFAEL to baby Winifred NEST's sickness. On 31 December he began to dig the grave for Father AILNOTH's body. The following day, after the coffin had been lowered into the grave, Cynric admitted that he alone had witnessed Ailnoth's death. He established that it had been accidental, but had made no attempt himself to save the drowning man. In June 1143 Cynric approved of the appointment of Father BONIFACE as Ailnoth's successor. During the flood of February 1145, Cynric temporarily 'surrendered his small dwelling above the porch to the housing of the church treasures'. These included St WINIFRED's 'swathed and roped' reliquary, which turned out to be a 'log of wood'.

Refs: **12** (1, 8–13); **16** (4, 9); **19** (2–3, 6, 13).

Cyprus (Mediterranean Sea). The third largest island in the Mediterranean, it lies about 40 miles south of Turkey and 60 miles west of Syria. The island has had a turbulent history. For example, Richard I, King of England, conquered the island in 1191 and sold it to the Knights Templar, who resold it to the dispossessed King of JERUSALEM, Guy de Lusignan. Increasing trade between Cyprus and Italy, especially from Genoa and VENICE, led to the island becoming part of the Venetian Empire in the 15th C. In 1571 it became part of the Ottoman Empire.

Novels: 'Here, in the enclosed garden within the walls . . . Brother CADFAEL ruled unchallenged. The herbarium in particular was his kingdom, for he had built it up gradually through fifteen years of hard labour, and added to it many exotic plants of his own careful raising, collected in a roving youth that had taken him as far afield as VENICE, and Cyprus and the HOLY LAND. Amongst other goods, the merchant Thomas of BRISTOL dealt 'in a small way in fancy wares from the east, sweetmeats and spices and candies', which the Venetians brought in from Cyprus and SYRIA. On their way home to England from the HOLY LAND, ELAVE and William of LYTHWOOD 'took ship for Cyprus and THESSALONIKA' from TRIPOLI.

Refs: **1** (1); **4** (1:2); **16** (3).

Daalny (b. 1127) (fict.). **Novels:** 'Her Provençal master, apparently, made no demands on her body, and the use he made of her voice provided her considerable pleasure. It is essentially pleasure to exercise the gifts of God. He clothed, warmed and fed her. If she had no love for him, she had no hate, either, she even conceded, very fairly, that his teaching had given her a means to independent life, if ever she could discover a place of safety in which to practise it. And at her age she could afford a few years of waiting. RÉMY [of Pertuis] himself was in search of a powerful patron. In the court of some substantial honour she might make a very comfortable place for herself. But still, CADFAEL reflected ruefully at the end of these practical musings, still a slave.' '"I am more interested," said [Brother] ANSELM . . . "in where he got the girl. For she is not French, not Breton, not from Provence. She speaks the English of these borders, and some Welsh. It would seem she is one property he got this side of the ocean."' 'He had never seen her close before, nor expected to, for she kept herself apart, taking no risks, perhaps, with an exacting master. Her head was uncovered now, her face, oval, thin and bright, shone lily-pale between wings of black, curling hair.' Born a slave and sold to Rémy of Pertuis, Daalny, who was unable to read or write, was highly valued by her troubadour master for her 'lovely voice', and was 'an important part of his stock in trade'. Daalny's Irish mother had been sold by her own father, having 'one daughter too many to feed', to a BRISTOL trader, 'who sold her again to the lord of a half-waste manor near GLOUCESTER. He used her as a bedmate till she died.' Nevertheless, Daalny was not his offspring; her father was someone her mother 'liked'. In February 1145 Rémy, Daalny and BÉNEZET were on their way north to CHESTER in search of a wealthy patron, when one of their horses fell lame and they were forced to stay at SHREWSBURY ABBEY. There Daalny met Brother TUTILO from RAMSEY ABBEY and found that they both shared an interest in music. After Bénezet had told her that ALDHELM was on his way to the abbey to identify the Holy Thief, she warned Tutilo, suggesting that he make himself scarce. That evening she joined Tutilo in the loft of the HORSE-FAIR stable, where they talked, 'nothing more', until they 'heard the Compline bell', after which she returned alone to the abbey. Her first attempt to free Tutilo from the penitentiary cell failed, because the porter, prompted by Cadfael, had swapped the keys. The second time, on the night before Rémy's departure for Leicester, she was successful; urging Tutilo to go 'westward, into Wales'. After talking to Cadfael, she came to suspect Bénezet of some sort of crime; a suspicion strengthened by her discovery of what sounded like coins in his saddlebag. As Rémy was about to leave Shrewsbury with Robert de BEAUMONT, Daalny publicly accused Bénezet of theft and possibly murder. She received a long graze down her arm from Bénezet's dagger as he slashed at her, before fleeing the abbey enclave. In a state of shock, Daalny ran blindly into the church followed by Cadfael. Realising that Tutilo was there in hiding, she asked Cadfael to ask the others to leave her alone in private for a little while. Her wishes were respected. When due time had passed, she was found to have vanished; fled with Tutilo south-westward into the LONG FOREST and possibly Wales.

Refs: **19** (2–3, 5, 7–8, 11–13).

Daalny, Queen (myth.). Also spelled Dealgnaid. Wife of PARTHOLAN, Daalny had an affair with Todga, her servant, while her husband was away. Discovering her infidelity on his return, he accepted that the fault was his for neglecting her.

Novels: 'Daalny, Partholan's queen, a demi-goddess from the western paradise.'

Refs: **19** (2, 11–13).

Dafydd (*fl.* 1040) (fict.). **Novels:** A Welshman, the father of MEILYR and grandfather of CADFAEL.

Refs: **18** (3); **RB** (1).

Dafydd, Brother (*fl.* 1144) (fict.). **Novels:** Benedictine monk of SHREWSBURY ABBEY, he was born in DYFFRYN CLWYD. In 1144 Brother Dafydd was confined to the abbey infirmary. Although he had not seen his native cantref for forty years, he 'was still convinced he knew it like the palm of his ancient hand'.

Refs: **18** (1).

Damascus (Syria). Capital of Syria, the city lies on the Barada river in the south-west of the country. Many authorities claim that it is the world's oldest city. Called the 'Pearl of the East', it was the capital of the Islamic empire from 661 to 750. A Saracen stronghold during the crusades, Damascus became part of the Ottoman Empire in 1516. The Great Mosque of Damascus was built between 705 and 715, on the site of a Christian church and a 1st C. Hellenic temple. An ancient shrine in the mosque is said to hold the head of St JOHN THE BAPTIST.

Novels: 'JERUSALEM had been shaken to its foundations' by Atabeg ZENGHI's defeat of FULK, King of JERUSALEM, 'but the kingdom had survived through its alliance with the emirate of Damascus'.

Refs: **11** (2).

Daniel (*fl.* 1139) (fict.). **Novels:** Lay servant at SHREWSBURY ABBEY. On 4 August 1139 Daniel, who was loading a collecting cart, was 'all but brained' when a large bottle fell from the top of one of the fair stalls.

Refs: **4** (5:2).

Daniel (*fl.* 1139) (fict.). **Novels:** Servant of Sir Godfrid and Lady Agnes PICARD, he arrived at SHREWSBURY ABBEY with his master in October 1139 for the wedding of Iveta de Massard (see LUCY) to Huon de DOMVILLE. He was ordered not to let Iveta out of the abbey gate.

Refs: **5** (1).

Daniel, Abbot (*fl.* 1143) (hist.). Formerly called Brother Daniel. In 1143, having induced or compelled Abbot WALTER of RAMSEY ABBEY to resign his office, Daniel became abbot. Shortly after, the abbey was seized by Geoffrey de MANDEVILLE, and all the monks expelled. Daniel went to ROME, where he found that his rival, Walter, had been restored to his abbacy by the Court.

Novels: '"For a time Abbot WALTER gave up his office to Brother Daniel, who was no way fit to step into his sandals. That is resolved now, but it was disruption and distress."'

Refs: **17** (4).

Daniel, Brother. See DANIEL, Abbot.

Daoud. See BRETAGNE, Olivier de.

Davey (*fl.* 1140) (fict.). **Novels:** '"I hit Davey with that when he tripped me in the water, but it broke. I threw it away."' Urchin of the parish of HOLY CROSS at SHREWSBURY, Davey was struck with LILIWIN's discarded rebec in May 1140.

Refs: **7** (3).

David (*fl.* 1137) (fict.). **Novels:** A Welshman of GWYTHERIN, he was visited by his cousin, Griffith ap RHYS, in May 1137.

Refs: **1** (11).

David (d. 1139), Bishop of Bangor (hist.). Also called David the Scot. A famous teacher at Wurzburg in Germany, and chaplain of HENRY I's son-in-law Emperor HENRY V, David, a Welshman, became Bishop of BANGOR in 1120. His appointment was supported not only by the clergy but also by GRIFFITH AP CYNAN, King of Gwynedd, and approved by Henry. Although David's see was in North Wales, his allegiance was to England and the archbishop of CANTERBURY. There are records of his presence at various ecclesiastical occasions: including the removal of the relics of St Elgar and St Dubricius from YNYS ENLLI in 1120; the consecration of Gregory as Bishop of DUBLIN in 1125; and the council of Archbishop WILLIAM OF CORBEIL at WESTMINSTER in 1127. Little is known of the later years of his life. He is thought to have died in 1139, as his successor, Bishop MEURIG, was consecrated on 3 December 1139. He may, as one authority asserts, have returned to Wurzburg, to become a monk in the abbey of St James, founded in 1139.

Novels: 'In the third week of May they came to Bangor, and told their story to Bishop David, who was sympathetic, and readily gave his consent to the proposed translation, subject only to the agreement of Prince OWAIN, who was regent of Gwynedd, owing to the illness of the old king, his father.' In May 1137 Prior ROBERT's party to GWYTHERIN first went to see Bishop David at Bangor, to obtain permission to remove the bones of St WINIFRED. On 9 April 1141 Bishop HENRY OF BLOIS offered CIARAN passage under his protection to Bangor, to the bishop there, who would see him to CAERGYBI, and have him put aboard a ship for DUBLIN.

Refs: **1** (1–2); **10** (14).

David (d. *c.*962 BC), King of Israel (bib.). Second of the Israelite kings of JERUSALEM after Saul, David, who was the youngest son of Jesse and grandson of Boaz, reigned *c.*1000–*c.*962 BC. Succeeding where Saul had failed, he united all the tribes of Israel under one rule and thereby established an enduring dynasty. His story is fully told in the Old Testament. He is the boy David who killed the Philistines' champion, Goliath of Gath, with a stone from his sling. Not only was he considered to be a just and patriotic ruler, but he also became the symbol of Israel's fulfilment in the future. He is often depicted as a king playing the harp.

Novels: 'The lid rose on a binding of purple-dyed

vellum, bordered with a rich tracery of leaves, flowers and tendrils in gold, and bearing in the centre, in a delicate framework of gold, a fellow to the ivory on the box. The same venerable face and majestic brow, the same compelling eyes gazing upon eternity, but this one was carved on a smaller scale, not a head but a half-length, and held a little harp in his hands. . . . With reverent care [Brother] ANSELM tilted the box, and supported the hook on his palm as he slid it out on to the table. . . . "Not a saint," he said, "except that they often showed him with a halo. This is King David, and surely what we have here is a psalter."'

Refs: **16** (15).

David I (1084–1153), King of Scotland (1124–53) (hist.). Youngest son of MALCOLM III and St Margaret of Scotland, David married Maud (or Matilda), daughter of Waltheof, Earl of Huntingdon, and widow of Simon I de Senlis, Earl of Northampton, in 1113. By this marriage he received the honour of Huntingdon and became an English baron. His sister, MATILDA, married HENRY I, King of England. David became King of Scotland after the death of his brother, Alexander I. Recognising the claim of his niece, the Empress MAUD, to the throne of England, he supported her against King STEPHEN. He made a brief peace with Stephen in 1136. Fighting for Maud again, he was defeated by Stephen at the battle of the Standard, near Northallerton, Yorkshire, on 22 August 1138. After Stephen's capture at LINCOLN in February 1141, he rejoined the war on Maud's behalf, and was with her in LONDON. Later the same year, fleeing from WINCHESTER, he was almost captured by the armies of Queen MATILDA. One of the most powerful Scottish kings, David made some of the greatest political and ecclesiastical reforms in the history of Scotland. He knighted the empress's son, Henry Plantagenet (see HENRY II), in 1149. After his death, David was succeeded by his grandson, Malcolm IV.

Novels: David swore a solemn oath of allegiance to Maud at King HENRY I's Christmas court in 1126. '"They're gone! Marched out at dawn, that woman and her royal uncle of Scotland and all her lords!"' In September 1141 Maud and her forces, including David 1, King of Scotland, were besieged in WINCHESTER CASTLE by the armies of Queen Matilda. On 14 September, due to lack of provisions and disease, they decided to retreat. David was with Maud in GLOUCESTER in December 1145, when Yves HUGONIN brought news that Philip FITZROBERT was at La MUSARDERIE. 'Beside one darkening window King David of Scotland stood, drawing in the chilling air, half turned away from his imperial niece. He had been at her side through most of the years of this long warfare, with staunch family loyalty, but also with a shrewd eye on his own and his nation's fortunes. Contention in England was no bad news to a monarch whose chief aim was to gain a stranglehold on NORTHUMBRIA, and push his own frontier as far south as the TEES. Able, elderly and taciturn, a big man and still handsome for all the grey in his hair and beard'. David was present at the siege of La Musarderie.

Refs: **11** (6); **20** (10–11).

David, Saint. See DEWI SANT.

Dee, River (Cheshire, England; Gwynedd and Clwyd, Wales). Also called Afon Dyfrdwy. Rising on the slopes of the 2,156 ft. high Dduallt in Snowdonia National Park, the River Dee tumbles rapidly downhill into Bala Lake (or Llyn Tegid). From the lake it flows north-east to CORWEN and then east past Carrog, Glyndyfrdwy and LLANGOLLEN. Leaving the mountains of North Wales, the river enters the Cheshire plain and meanders northward to CHESTER, where it is artificially channelled, in a straight line, north-west to Flint and the sea. From its source high up on the slopes of Dduallt to the town of Flint the river traces a course of approximately 80 miles. The estuary is extremely shallow and is 12 miles long by over 5 miles wide at its mouth.

Novels: 'They had halted at the crest of the ridge overlooking the lush green valley of the Dee. The sun was westering, and had mellowed from the noon gold into a softer amber light, gleaming down the stream, where the coils of the river alternately glimmered and vanished among its fringes of woodland. Still an upland river here, dancing over a rocky bed and conjuring rainbows out of its sunlit spray.' In July 1139 Rhodri ap HUW from MOLD shipped his wool-clip up the Dee, before taking it across land to the River VRNWY. In February 1141 it was rumoured that OWAIN GWYNEDD was 'patrolling the fringes of Chester territory, and had reached Corwen on the Dee'. In Spring 1144, on their way from SHREWSBURY to Llanelwy (see ST ASAPH), Deacon MARK and CADFAEL travelled up part of the valley of the Dee. They lodged overnight at Llangollen.

Refs: **4** (1:2); **9** (3); **18** (1–2, 7); **19** (3).

Deerhurst (Gloucestershire, England). On the east bank of the River SEVERN, some 3 miles south-west of TEWKESBURY, Deerhurst was once the chief monastery of the Anglo-Saxon kingdom of Hwicce. It was on an island in the Severn near Deerhurst in 1016 that King Edmund Ironside and King Canute (or Cnut) signed a peace treaty which redivided England between Anglo-Saxons and Danes. The parish church of St Mary, formerly the priory church, dates from the 7th C. or earlier. Odda's Chapel, nearby, was built in 1056 by Earl Odda, a friend of EDWARD THE CONFESSOR. The monastery declined after the Confessor made it a cell of St Denis in PARIS. It became a cell of Tewkesbury Abbey in 1467.

Novels: Yves HUGONIN was captured by the forces of Philip FITZROBERT in woodland near Deerhurst in December 1145. 'At Deerhurst there was an alien priory belonging to St Denis in Paris.' 'An old, old house, centuries old, and refounded and endowed by the Confessor, and bestowed by him upon St Denis.' Brother EADWIN was a Benedictine monk at the priory. CADFAEL visited the house in December 1145. 'And there gleaming through the trees no great way inland from the water was the creamy silver stone of the church tower, solid Saxon work, squat and strong as a castle keep.' 'Within Deerhurst's priory church there was as yet no mark of the Norman style, all was Saxon, and the first walls of the nave centuries old.' FORTHRED, who worked for Master BERNARD, the mason, identified the seal of Geoffrey FITZCLARE for Cadfael.

Refs: **20** (6-7, 10).

Deheubarth (Dyfed, Powys and West Glamorgan, Wales). Originally the territory of Deheubarth embraced the whole of South Wales. In medieval times it only included the territories of CEREDIGION, Ystrad Tywi and Brycheiniog. The region is represented today by parts of the following Welsh counties: Dyfed, roughly excluding the peninsula south-west of Cardigan and Carmarthen; West Glamorgan, west of the Afon Tawe; and Powys, south of Hay-on-Wye and Mynydd Eppynt. The main royal residence of Deheubarth was situated at Dinefwr on the north bank of the Afon Tywi in Cantref Mawr. The remains of the castle can be found in the wooded grounds of Dynevor Castle, Llandeilo.

Novels: ANGHARAD (d. 1162) had been noted 'for her golden hair among the dark women of Deheubarth'.

Refs: **18** (1–2, 5).

Deheubarth, Prince of. See ANARAWD AP GRIFFITH, Prince of Deheubarth.

Deiniol, Saint (d. 584) (hist.) (f.d. 11 September). Also called Daniel or Deiniol Wyn. The first bishop of BANGOR, he was ordained by St DYFRIG or possibly DEWI SANT. Deiniol is reputed to have been a descendant of a Celtic chieftain of Strathclyde and was buried on YNYS ENLLI. The cathedral at Bangor is dedicated in his honour.

Novels: In 1144 Bishop Roger de CLINTON gave Bishop MEURIG a 'very handsome' breviary, containing a picture of St Deiniol, Meurig's founder and patron. The cathedral at Bangor and the church at LLANDEINIOLEN were both dedicated to the saint.

Refs: **18** (6).

Denis, Brother (*fl.* 1137) (fict.). **Novels:** Also spelled Dennis. 'Brother Denis cocked his round, rosy, tonsured head aside and ran a sharp brown eye, very reminiscent of a robin's, down the list.' Hospitaller and Benedictine monk at SHREWSBURY ABBEY from at least May 1137, Denis 'knew every soul who came within the gates', and had an excellent memory and an 'appetite for news and rumours that usually kept him the best informed person in the enclave'.

Refs: **1** (1); **2** (2); **3** (4); **5** (2–3); **6** (1); **9** (5); **10** (1, 7, 10–11); **12** (2); **13** (9, 12); **14** (4); **15** (1); **16** (13); **19** (2, 5).

Derby (Derbyshire, England). This city lies on the River Derwent at the southern end of the Pennines, some 22 miles north-east of LICHFIELD. Its origins date back to at least Roman times. The Danes, who arrived in the 9th C., called it Deoraby, from which the present name is derived. Situated at a major crossroads, Derby became a busy market town and, eventually, a manufacturing centre, making woollen cloth, beer and soap.

Novels: In June 1141 Olivier de BRETAGNE rode north to SHREWSBURY to ask Hugh BERINGAR if he would go back on his sworn fealty to King STEPHEN and accept allegiance to the Empress MAUD. From Shrewsbury, Olivier planned to ride north-east to STAFFORD, Derby and NOTTINGHAM.

Refs: **10** (7).

Devil's Novice. See ASPLEY, Meriet.

Devizes (Wiltshire, England). Some 18 miles east of BATH, this small market town on the Kennet and Avon Canal lies to the west of the Vale of Pewsey. It was the site of a Romano-British settlement. In the 12th C. ROGER, Bishop of Salisbury, built a castle on the boundary between two former hundreds, hence the name Devizes; from the Latin *ad devisas*, meaning 'at the boundaries'. The town grew up around the Norman castle, which played a prominent part in the struggle between King STEPHEN and the Empress MAUD. It was destroyed by the Parliamentarians in 1645, and the present castle was built on the site in the 19th C. Devizes was an important medieval market town.

Novels: In November 1120 ROBERT, Duke of Normandy, was a prisoner in Devizes, 'and unlikely ever to be seen again by the outer world'. After the 'Rout of WINCHESTER' in September 1141, Maud fled with the remnants of her army into GLOUCESTER, 'by way of LUDGERSHALL and Devizes'. In April 1142 Maud and ROBERT of Gloucester met in Devizes and decided to call on GEOFFREY of Anjou's help in the war against Stephen. In 1144/5 Maud maintained her own court there unmolested. Laurence d'ANGERS was in Devizes in 1145, where he was mostly needed.

Refs: **11** (8); **13** (1); **18** (1); **20** (2, 6, 10); **RB** (1).

Dewi Sant (*c.*520–*c.*600) (hist.) (f.d. 1 March). Also called St David. Born near St Bride's Bay on the Pembrokeshire Coast, Dyfed, Dewi was, according to legend, the son of St NONNA, who had been raped by Sant, a Welsh chieftain. He founded a monastery at Mynyw (or Menevia; now called David's or Tyddewi) in the extreme south-west corner of Wales, where he presided as abbot-bishop. He founded numerous churches and monasteries throughout South Wales. He died at Mynyw and was buried in the monastery church. His relics were later transferred to the medieval cathedral at ST DAVID'S. By the end of the 12th C. he had become the patron saint of Wales.

Novels: '"They call me brother CADFAEL, I'm as Welsh as Dewi Sant."'

Refs: **2** (5); **18** (6).

Diarmaid (*fl.* 972) (fict.). **Novels:** 'No fault of Diarmaid . . . who had poured his loveliest art into a gift of love, or at least a gift for a marriage, the loftiest of the age, a mating of empires! No fault of his that this exquisite thing had brought about two deaths, and bereaved as well as endowed the bride to whom it was sent.' An Irish monk of ST GALL, Diarmaid wrote and painted the psalter of THEOFANU, which William of LYTHWOOD gave to FORTUNATA as her dowry.

Refs: **16** (15).

Dinan, Josce de (d. *c.*1166) (hist.). Also spelled Joceas de Dynan. Named after his native town of Dinan in Brittany, north-western France, Josce de Dinan is associated with a number of events which are probably false. For example, the *Fitz-Warin Chronicle* says that Dinan was granted LUDLOW CASTLE by HENRY I: 'The castle of Dynan, and all the country round towards the river of CORVE, with all the Honour, he gave to Sir Joce his Knight; who thenceforth retained the name of Dynan, and was called everywhere Joce de Dynan. This Joce completed the castle which Roger de Belehealme [more probably Roger de Lacy] in his time began; and he was a strong and valiant Knight. Now the town was a very long time called Dynan, which is now called LUDLOW.' (Quoted in Eyton, *Antiquities of Shropshire*, 1857.) According to Eyton, Dinan was appointed castellan of Ludlow Castle by King STEPHEN, and was granted a share of the Lacy estates. Eyton differs from modern historians, however, by affirming that Dinan rebelled against the king and, consequently, Stephen besieged Ludlow Castle in 1139. It is probably true that Dinan fell out with Stephen and defected to the side of the Empress MAUD. Sometime between 1148 and 1154 Dinan and Hugh de MORTIMER waged war against each other. Dinan managed to capture his enemy and, for a while, Mortimer was imprisoned in Ludlow Castle. At his death, Dinan left two daughters and co-heirs, Hawise, wife of Fulk Fitz Warin II of WHITTINGTON, and Sibil, wife of Hugh de Plugenai.

Novels: 'Dinan was too big a man, in every sense, to strain to keep his horse's nose level with that of Hugh's mount, or resent serving under a younger and less experienced man. He had no need to stress his own worth. CADFAEL took to him. He had never before seen this supposedly dubious ally, but he thought him a man to be valued, and lost only with grief.' Josce de Dinan was castellan of Ludlow Castle and overlord of WHITBACHE, CALLOWLEAS and LEDWYCHE. In November 1139 there were rumours that he was thinking of transferring his allegiance from Stephen to Maud. In December Hugh BERINGAR quartered twenty-two men in Ludlow Castle with Dinan, '"to be at hand if I need them, and to give him a salutary jolt if he really is in two minds about changing sides. He cannot be in any doubt now that I have my eye on him."' Dinan went out with Cadfael, Hugh and his men to Callowleas in search of Ermina Hugonin (see BRETAGNE). He also went with Hugh to the manor of Whitbache, sacked by the outlaws of Alain le GAUCHER. Later, he helped Hugh capture Gaucher's stronghold on TITTERSTONE CLEE.

Refs: **6** (1, 4–5, 10–11, 14–15).

Dod, Roger (b. *c.*1109) (fict.). **Novels:** 'He was a burly, well-set-up young man of about thirty, this Roger Dod, and very personable, if he had not been so curt and withdrawn in manner.' Journeyman of Thomas of BRISTOL, he arrived at SHREWSBURY by barge, on 31 July 1139, in the service of his master. He was 'deeply, hopelessly, in love' with Emma Vernold (see CORVISER). In order to avoid giving Dod any opportunity to thrust his attentions on her, Emma decided not to return to BRISTOL with him by barge. On 2 August Dod discovered WARIN THE PORTER bound and gagged in Thomas's booth. Two days later, after the fair, Dod and his two companions left Shrewsbury for Bristol, without Emma.

Refs: **4** (1:4, 2:1–2, 3:1–2, 4:2, 5:1).

Dogditch Brook (Shropshire, England). Never more than a tiny stream, this brook rises high on the slopes of TITTERSTONE CLEE and flows south-westward to Middleton, where it merges with the LEDWYCHE BROOK. Its total length is less than 5 miles.

Novels: 'The track dipped gently to cross the Ledwyche Brook and the Dogditch Brook, its tributary from the north-east threading its way between holdings on either side without ever sighting them, and at once began to climb again steadily. In December 1139 CADFAEL followed the snow-tracks of Alain le GAUCHER's outlaw band. They led across the Ledwyche and Dogditch brooks.

Refs: **6** (5, 10).

Domville Canon Eudo de. See EUDO DE DOMVILLE, Canon.

Domville, Huon de (*c.*1081–1139) (fict.). **Novels:** 'First came Huon de Domville, the muscles of his face set like a wrestler's biceps, his small, black, malevolent eyes alertly bright.' Estranged husband of Isabel de DOMVILLE, whom he married in *c.*1109, uncle of Simon AGUILON and distant cousin of Canon EUDO DE DOMVILLE, Huon de Domville was a Norman lord who was 'in good odour' with King STEPHEN, and held manors in Shropshire, Cheshire, Stafford and Leicester. He arrived at SHREWSBURY for his marriage to the heiress, Iveta de Massard (see LUCY), in October 1139. Bishop ROGER DE CLINTON loaned his house in the ABBEY FOREGATE for the wedding. Domville falsely accused Joscelin LUCY of stealing the wedding gift intended for his bride, 'a collar of gold and pearls', and banished him from his service. On the eve of his wedding-day, after supping with the abbot, Domville dismissed his servants and set out alone into the LONG FOREST to see his 'patient, permanent mistress', Avice of Thornbury (see MAGDALEN, sister), whom he had first met in *c.*1118. On the ride back to his household at SHREWSBURY, Domville was murdered by Aguilon.

Refs: **5** (1, 3–8, 10–11); **11** (14); **13** (1).

Domville, Isabel de (*fl.* 1139) (fict.). **Novels:** '"What, after thirty years of marriage to my Aunt Isabel, and God knows how many passages with how many ladies outside the pale, and never a brat to show for it all?"' Estranged wife of Huon de DOMVILLE, whom she married in *c.*1109, and aunt of Simon AGUILON, she took the veil at WROXALL NUNNERY in *c.*1139. Having had no children, she left Domville without an heir.

Refs: **5** (1, 6).

Downs, See HAMPSHIRE DOWNS; SOUTH DOWNS.

Druel, John (*fl.* 1139) (fict.). **Novels:** 'The lean, wiry husbandman.' Father of Peter DRUEL, he lived with his wife at DRUEL'S HOLDING. Ermina Hugonin (see BRETAGNE), Yves HUGONIN and Sister HILARIA arrived at his tenant-farm on 2 December 1139. Just before dawn on 5 December, the holding was burned to the ground by Alain le GAUCHER's outlaws, and all John's livestock stolen. John managed to get his family safely away to CLEETON, where he was 'sheltered and fed by the village, at least alive if he had lost everything but his life. And his wife and son with him, and the shepherd who laboured for him, all saved.' After the outlaws had been defeated, the prisoners and beasts were taken first to Cleeton, where John identified and claimed his own. He later collected his stolen horse from BROMFIELD.

Refs: **6** (15).

Druel, Peter (*fl.* 1139) (fict.). **Novels:** Son of John DRUEL, Peter went to CALLOWLEAS with a message from Ermina Hugonin (see BRETAGNE) to Evrard BOTEREL on 2 December 1139. When the outlaws of TITTERSTONE CLEE ravaged their farmstead, Peter managed to escape with his family to CLEETON.

Refs: **6** (4–5, 8).

(John) Druel's Holding (Shropshire, England) (fict.). Although it never existed, John Druel's homestead was situated high up on the north-eastern slopes of TITTERSTONE CLEE, above the village of CLEETON St Mary, 6 miles north-east of LUDLOW.

Novels: 'A hard place, bleak to farm, meagre to crop, but good for sheep, the rangy upland sheep that brought the leanest meat but the longest fleeces.' John Druel's Holding was ransacked and burned to the ground, by the outlaws of Alain le GAUCHER, just before dawn on 5 December 1139.

Refs: **6** (5, 8, 10).

Dublin (Dublin, Ireland). Straddling the River Liffey, Dublin lies at the head of Dublin Bay on the Irish Sea. It is the capital city of the Republic of Ireland and the country's main seaport. Although its origins date back to prehistoric times, the earliest historical evidence of occupation dates from the 9th C., when the Danes arrived and settled on the ridge to the south of the river, where Dublin Castle now stands. Despite attempts by the Irish to drive them out, the Danish invaders managed to hold on to the city. In 1170, however, Dublin was taken by the Anglo-Normans from Wales. The following year, alarmed that Ireland might become a rival Norman state, HENRY II landed with his army to impose English sovereignty, and Dublin remained under English rule until 1922.

Novels: 'Not all the centuries of fitful contact between Dublin and Wales had been by way of invasion and rapine, a good many marriages had been made between the princedoms, and a fair measure of honest commerce been profitable to both parties.' OWAIN GWYNEDD's grandmother RAGNHILD, granddaughter of King SITRIC SILKBEARD, came from the Danish kingdom of Dublin. In April 1141 CIARAN set out from WINCHESTER to walk barefoot to BANGOR and CAERGYBI, where he intended to board a ship for Dublin, his home town. In May 1144, attempting to force Owain to restore his lands, CADWALADR landed near CARNARVON with a force of Danish mercenaries from Dublin, under OTIR. HELEDD left Gwynedd for Dublin to be with TURCAILL (*fl.* 1144).

Refs: **9** (3); **10** (14–15); **18** (2, 4–14).

Dunwich (Suffolk, England). On the North Sea coast, barely 4 miles south-west of Southwold and 24 miles north-east of Felixstowe, Dunwich probably originated as a British-Romano cliff-top settlement. It became the most important commercial centre in the region during Anglo-Saxon times. During the Middle Ages the town was a prosperous and thriving port, but severe coastal erosion brought about its ruin and decline. Today, most of old Dunwich lies under the sea.

Novels: In December 1141 it was thought that the fugitive, Torold BLUND, had managed to board a ship for NORMANDY at Dunwich.

Refs: **12** (6).

Dutton, Reyner (*fl.* 1139) (fict.). **Novels:** 'The prior drew his tenant out of the group before it moved off from the gatehouse, and made them acquainted. Clearly Reyner had a warm relationship with his lord, and was ready to fall in cheerfully with whatever course LEONARD suggested.' Tenant of BROMFIELD Priory, Reyner Dutton, 'a good husbandman', had a farmstead near HENLEY. He found the injured Brother ELYAS in the snow and brought him to the priory in December 1139. Reyner helped in the search for the missing Yves HUGONIN, and also took CADFAEL to the spot where ELYAS was found. He discovered Sister HILARIA's bloodied, black habit in the shepherd's hut. While Cadfael followed the tracks of Alain le GAUCHER's outlaws towards TITTERSTONE CLEE, Reyner went back to LUDLOW to warn the deputy sheriff.

Refs: **6** (2, 10).

Dyffryn Clwyd (Clwyd, Wales). This medieval Welsh cantref lay in Gwynedd Is Conwy (Gwynedd below Conwy) and contained three commotes, Dogfeiling or Rhuthyn (see RUTHIN), Llannerch and Coleion. In 1247, after the Peace at Woodstock, the Welsh were forced by Henry III to abandon all claims to the four cantrefs of the 'Middle Country': RHOS, Tegeingl, Rhufoniog and Dyffryn Clwyd. In 1277, however, Edward I granted David ap Gruffudd the last two mentioned cantrefs. Dyffryn Clwyd became a Marcher lordship at the end of the 13th C., and was ruled by the English from the castle at Ruthin.

Novels: Brother DAFYDD was born in the cantref of Dyffryn Clwyd.

Refs: **18** (1).

Dyfrig, Saint (d. *c*.545) (hist.) (f.d. 14 November). Also called Dubricius, Dubric or Devereaux. One of the earliest and most important of the Welsh saints, Dyfrig was Bishop of Llandaff, according to all of his later Lives. He is reputed to have been born at Madley (5 miles west of HEREFORD) and is particularly associated with Gwent and western Hereford & Worcester. According to medieval legend he was Archbishop of Caeleon and crowned Arthur 'King of Britain'. He retired to YNYS ENLLI where he died and his alleged relics were translated to Llandaff in 1120.

Novels: It is reputed that St ILLTUD received the tonsure of a monk from St Dyfrig.

Refs: **17** (9).

D

E

Eadburga of Winchester, Saint (d. 960) (hist.) (f.d. 15 June). Also called Edburga, Iderberga, Idaberga, etc. The daughter of Edward the Elder and granddaughter of Alfred the Great, she was placed as a child in the nunnery at WINCHESTER, founded by Alfred and his wife, Ealhswith. Eadburga supposedly became abbess of Nunnaminster (or Nunminster), where she died. Some of her relics were obtained by PERSHORE Abbey, where her shrine became famous for its miracle-working power.

Novels: In Winter 1139 Brother ELYAS of PERSHORE safely delivered a finger-bone of St Eadburga to BROMFIELD Priory.

Refs: **6** (2).

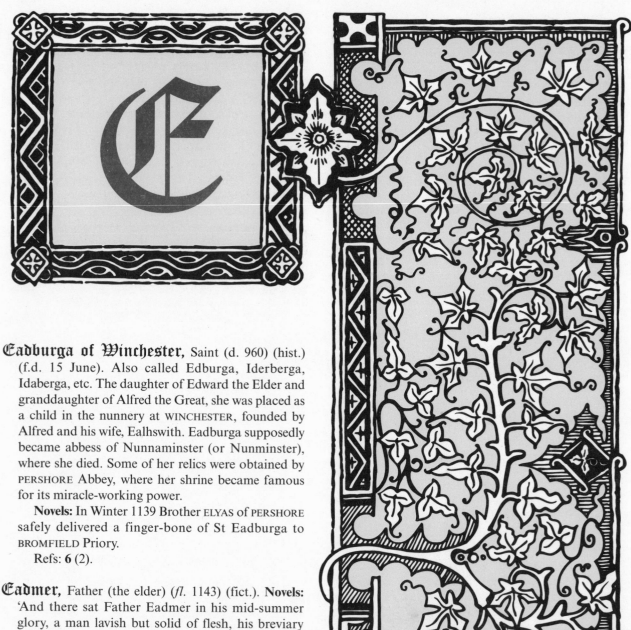

Eadmer, Father (the elder) (*fl.* 1143) (fict.). **Novels:** 'And there sat Father Eadmer in his mid-summer glory, a man lavish but solid of flesh, his breviary unopened on his knees, his considerable weight distilling around him, at every movement, a great aureole of fragrance.' Uncle of young Father EADMER, the elder Father Eadmer was parish priest of St Eata's Church at ATCHAM in June 1143. He lived in the priest's house beside the church. Eudo and Jehane BLOUNT visited him in November 1143.

Refs: **16** (9); **17** (11, 14).

Eadmer, Father (the younger) (*fl.* 1143) (fict.). **Novels:** Also called Eddi. 'The new priest was likely to catch any observant eye, for he was tall, well made and goodlooking, and blessedly unselfconscious about his assets.' Nephew of Father EADMER the elder, and named after him, Eadmer was ordained in May 1143 and in June was still without a cure. He was a fellow-student with Father BONIFACE. On 22 June, while Boniface was away at BETTON, Eadmer confessed ALDWIN and gave him penance and absolution. Going to SHREWSBURY with CADFAEL, he identified Aldwin's corpse.

Refs: **16** (8–10).

(Father) Eadmer the elder's House (Atcham, Shropshire, England) (fict.). Although it never existed, the humble house of Father Eadmer stood beside St Eata's Church, on the east bank of the River SEVERN at ATCHAM.

Novels: 'Father Eadmer had been many years in office here, and worked lovingly upon his garden. Half of it was producing vegetables for his table, and by the look of it a surplus to eke out the diet of his poorer neighbours. The other half was given over to a pretty little herber full of flowers, and the undulation of the ground had made it possible for him to shape a short bench of earth, turfed over with wild thyme for a seat.'

Refs: **16** (9).

Eadwin (*fl.* 1141) (fict.). **Novels:** 'Eadwin, the one whose boundary stone he moved, he's neither forgotten nor forgiven, even if the stone was replaced afterwards.' Eadwin, with his wife and children, lived in the parish of HOLY CROSS at SHREWSBURY. In December 1141 his boundary stone was moved by AELGAR, who had been instructed by Father AILNOTH to plough up part of his headland.

Refs: **12** (3, 6–7, 11).

Eadwin, Brother (*fl.* 1145) (fict.). **Novels:** A Benedictine monk at DEERHURST Priory, Brother Eadwin prided 'himself on knowing the devices of every earl and baron in the land'. Nevertheless, he was unable to identify the salamander badge of Geoffrey FITZCLARE.

Refs: **20** (6).

East Anglian Ports (Norfolk, Suffolk, and Essex, England). Among the ports on the North Sea coast of East Anglia in medieval times were: Great Yarmouth (Norfolk); King's Lynn (Norfolk); DUNWICH (Suffolk); Orford (Suffolk), where HENRY II built a castle in 1165; Ipswich (Suffolk); Harwich (Essex); and Colchester (Essex), the oldest recorded town in England, pre-dating Roman times.

Novels: 'It was a mark of the significance of the SHREWSBURY fair that they [the Flemish merchants] should undertake so long a journey from the East Anglian ports where they put in, and find it worth their while to hire carts or horses for the overland pilgrimage.'

Refs: **4** (1: 2).

Eastcheap (London, England). The site of the medieval meat market. 'Cheap' is derived from the Old English *ceap* or *chepe* meaning 'market'. In Saxon times there was an East Cheap and a West Cheap within the walls of the old Roman city. West Cheap (also called Cheapside) was the principal market place of medieval LONDON. East Cheap (or Eastcheap) – now running between Gracechurch Street and Great Tower Street – once stretched north-westward beyond Gracechurch Street; but this extension was demolished when King William Street was created between 1829 and 1831. The construction work unearthed a Roman road.

Novels: 'No doubt some of the returning pilgrims from the HOLY LAND were genuine, and believed in the genuineness of what they offered, but in some cases CADFAEL wondered whether they had ever been nearer ACRE than Eastcheap.'

Refs: **19** (2).

Eaton (now Eaton Constantine) (Shropshire, England). DB – Etune: in Wrockwardine Hundred; a holding of Reginald the Sheriff under Roger de MONTGOMERY. Eaton Constantine is situated, just over 7 miles south-east of SHREWSBURY, on rising ground to the east of the flood plain of the River SEVERN. St Mary's Church, rebuilt in the mid 19th C. and sited higher than the village, is a landmark that can be seen for miles around. In 1086 there was a fishery on the Severn. The latter part of Eaton's name comes from the Constentin family – named after the Contentin peninsula in NORMANDY – who first became the lords of the manor in 1242 and held it for many years afterwards under the FitzAlans.

Novels: 'The village sat serenely in the meadows, just short of the foothills, the manor within its long stockade raised over an undercroft, and the small church close beside it.' Originally held by William FITZALAN, the manor of Eaton was forfeited to the Crown. As overlord, Hugh BERINGAR allowed Richard LUDEL (the elder) to retain his tenancy. On Ludel's death on 18 October 1142, the manor passed to his heir, young Richard LUDEL. Eaton had its own church and parish priest, Father ANDREW. CADFAEL, Brother PAUL and Brother ANSELM accompanied young Richard to Eaton for his father's funeral. After young Richard's abduction, Hugh went to the Ludel manor 'and set to work to probe every corner of Dionisia LUDEL's hall and solar, kitchens and stores, examined every cask and handcart and barrel in the undercroft, every byre and barn and stable that lined the stockade, the smith's workshop, every loft and larder, and moved outward into the fields and sheep folds and thence to the huts of every tenant and cotter and villein on Richard's land. But they did not find Richard.' John of LONGWOOD was the steward of the manor of Eaton.

Refs: **14** (1–3, 5–11, 13); **19** (4).

Eddi (b. 1131) (fict.). **Novels:** 'A bright boy', son of ERWALD THE WHEELWRIGHT's sister. On 29 December 1141 CADFAEL saw Eddi, amongst half-a-dozen urchins of the ABBEY FOREGATE, playing by the parish priest's house. They were using Father AILNOTH's skull cap as a target, set up on an abandoned fence-post, for their snowballs. He told Cadfael that they had found the cap caught in the reeds by the mill-pond at dawn on Christmas Day.

Refs: **12** (8).

Edessa (Turkey). This ancient city in south-eastern Turkey is some 380 miles south-east of Ankara and 200 miles east of Adana. Lying in the fertile plain of Haran, surrounded on three sides by limestone hills, it commanded a strategic pass on the route between Anatolia and the south. Edessa is traditionally associated with the legendary King Nimrod, and also Abraham, who is said to have been born in a cave under the citadel. It was the chief centre of Christianity by the middle of the 2nd C., when its ruler, Abgar IX (179–216), became a convert. Captured in turn by the Persians and the Arabs, the city was taken by the crusaders in 1098 and Baldwin (later BALDWIN I, King of Jerusalem) was made Count of Edessa. On Christmas Eve 1144, the crusaders suffered their first major disaster. Atabeg ZENGHI of MOSUL seized Edessa and, by so doing, virtually eliminated one of the four crusader states. Edessa became part of the Ottoman Empire in the 16th or 17th C.

Novels: In *c.*1142 mamluk raiders from MOSUL

began to drive Christian monks out of their monasteries, somewhere beyond Edessa, west towards TRIPOLI. One fugitive monk brought with him Princess THEOFANU's psalter, which he eventually sold to William of LYTHWOOD. Edessa fell to the paynims of Mosul at Christmas 1144; since then 'all Christendom has been uneasy about the kingdom of JERUSALEM.' It was ROGER DE CLINTON's aim to recover Edessa from Atabeg ZENGHI.

Refs: **16** (3, 11, 15); **20** (1, 8).

Edgytha, Mistress (*c.*1083–1143) (fict.). **Novels:** 'She was a tall, wiry, active woman probably sixty years old, with the free manner and air of authority habitual in servants who have spent many years in the confidence of lord or lady, and earned a degree of trust that brings with it acknowledged privilege. The younger maidservants deferred to her, if they did not actually go in awe of her, and her neat black gown and stiff white wimple, and the keys jingling at her waist bore witness to her status.' Maidservant of Adelais de CLARY at HALES, until she was sent to VIVERS in 1125 to serve Bertrade de Clary (see VIVERS) on her marriage to Edric VIVERS. Loyal and trustworthy, she was nurse to both Roscelin and Helisende VIVERS. When Bertrade took the veil at POLESWORTH ABBEY in 1135, she left Helisende well mothered, in the care of Edgytha and Emma VIVERS. In March 1143 CADFAEL informed Edgytha that Adelais was at ELFORD. The old maidservant immediately set out for the manor to beg Adelais to reveal the truth about Helisende's real father. On her way back to Vivers, Edgytha was murdered by LUC or LOTHAIR, or both.

Refs: **15** (6–9, 12–14).

Edmund, Brother (b. 1088) (fict.). **Novels:** 'Brother Edmund smiled his quiet, composed smile. "'You at least can question no one's act but your own. I am of a past order, CADFAEL, there'll be no more of me, not under RADULFUS, at any rate."' Benedictine monk and infirmarer at SHREWSBURY ABBEY from at least 1137, Edmund, an obedientiary, had entered the monastery in 1092, at the age of four. In May 1137 Edmund helped Cadfael restrain Brother COLUMBANUS when the latter was seized by a violent fit. Edmund was with Cadfael in the fringes of the LONG FOREST in October 1139, when they discovered Huon de DOMVILLE's corpse. Gilbert PRESTCOTE (the elder) was murdered in the infirmary in March 1141, while in Edmund's care. Edmund had a niece in SHREWSBURY, who joined the sisterhood at GODRIC'S FORD in June 1142.

Refs: **1** (1); **3** (1–2); **4** (4:3); **5** (5, 8); **6** (1); **8** (1); **9** (2, 6–7); **10** (1); **12** (5); **13** (1); **14** (4); **15** (1–3); **16** (2); **17** (8, 11); **18** (1); **19** (2, 5); **20** (2).

Edred the Groom (*fl.* 1140) (fict.). **Novels:** Young groom of Isouda FORIET, he had a sister who lived in a house along the ABBEY FOREGATE. He took two horses to ST GILES on 21 December 1140 to enable Meriet ASPLEY and Brother MARK to attend the marriage of Nigel ASPLEY and Roswitha Linde (see ASPLEY). Leaving them both at the church, Edred went to visit his sister and the girl next door, to whom he had taken a fancy.

Refs: **8** (12).

Edred the Groom (*fl.* 1145) (fict.). **Novels:** A groom at the manor of LONGNER, Edred rode to SHREWSBURY ABBEY in February 1145 with a spare pony to request, on behalf of his mistress, Donata BLOUNT, that Brother TUTILO visit her. He accompanied Tutilo back to Shrewsbury, at least as far as the ferry, before returning to Longner again with the spare pony.

Refs: **19** (2).

Edred the Steward (*fl.* 1143) (fict.). **Novels:** Steward of Cenred VIVERS, Lord of VIVERS, the bearded Edred joined the search party looking for EDGYTHA in March 1143. After the discovery of her corpse, he went on foot to ELFORD with JEHAN (*fl.* 1143) and two other men to enquire if the maidservant had been there. He carried news of Edgytha's death to Audemar de CLARY and Roscelin VIVERS, and also word of the proposed marriage between Helisende VIVERS and Jean de PERRONET.

Refs: **15** (6, 8–9).

Edward the Confessor, Saint (*c.*1003–66), King of England (1042–66) (hist.) (f.d. 13 October, formerly 5 January). Son of ETHELRED II and Emma, daughter of Richard II, Duke of Normandy, Edward was born at Islip, near OXFORD. When the Danes invaded England in 1013, he escaped with his family to NORMANDY. He returned to England the following year, but from 1016 to 1041 he lived in exile abroad. After the death of his half-brother, King Harthacnut (or Hardecanute), in 1142, Edward succeeded to the throne of England. He married Edith, daughter of Godwin (or Godwine), Earl of Wessex, in 1045. Falling out with his powerful father-in-law, Edward drove Godwin and his family into exile in 1051. Being partly Norman himself, Edward strengthened the Norman element in Church and government, and made his cousin, William, (see WILLIAM I), his heir. Godwin returned in 1052, expelled the Normans and forced Edward to return the lands he had given away. After Godwin's death in 1053, his son Harold Godwinson (see HAROLD II) became the dominant power in the kingdom. The king devoted himself to good works and the rebuilding of WESTMINSTER Abbey, where he was buried and where his relics still remain. Edward was canonized in 1161. Although William had been acknowledged Edward's heir, it was Harold who succeeded to the throne.

Novels: '"I've already viewed it in a better light. It's a silver penny of the sainted Edward, king before the Normans came, a beautiful piece minted in this town."' DEERHURST Priory was 'an old, old house, centuries old, and refounded and endowed by the Confessor, and bestowed by him upon St Denis. The Confessor was always more Norman in his sympathies than English.'

Refs: **7** (11); **9** (8); **20** (6); **RB** (3).

Edward the Martyr, Saint (*c.*963–78), King of England (975–8) (hist.) (f.d. 18 March). Son of King Edgar, Edward became king at the age of about twelve. In 978, on his way to visit his half-brother, Ethelred (see ETHELRED II), Edward was assassinated at Corfe, Dorset. He was buried at WAREHAM and, after a number of alleged miracles around his tomb, his relics were solemnly translated to Shaftesbury, Dorset in 979. Although he had not died for religion, he became venerated as a saint and was declared a martyr by Ethelred in 1001.

Refs: **9** (8).

Edwin (b. *c.*1127) (fict.). **Novels:** Native of GWYTHERIN, he was in the service of Father HUW in May 1137. He showed Brothers JEROME and COLUMBANUS the way to St WINIFRED's grave.

Refs: **1** (2, 4, 9).

Edwin (*fl.* 1143) (fict.). **Novels:** Servant in the household of Cedred VIVERS at the manor of VIVERS.

Refs: **15** (6).

Edwin the Novice (b. 1133) (fict.). **Novels:** Novice at SHREWSBURY ABBEY in 1142, and friend and 'devoted ally' of young Richard LUDEL, Edwin fell down the day stairs in November 1142 and hurt his knees. The day after Richard went missing, Edwin fearfully confessed to Brother PAUL that he had seen him ride out along the ABBEY FOREGATE towards ST GILES.

Refs: **14** (4–5, 7, 14).

Eilmund the Forester (b. *c.*1100) (fict.). **Novels:** 'All trace of fever had left him, his colour was good, and he was in no great discomfort, but he was in a glum fury with his own helplessness, and impatient to be out and about his business again, distrusting the abbot's willing but untutored substitutes to take proper care of his forest. The very shortness of his temper was testimony to his sound health.' Father of ANNET and forester of EYTON in the service of SHREWSBURY ABBEY, he went to SHREWSBURY to deliver the abbey's allowance of venison in late

October 1142, and reported that the pilgrim CUTHRED had moved into the disused woodland hermitage of Dame Dionisia LUDEL. The following month, he related a spate of unexplained disasters, and suggested that his forest was 'bewitched'. Two days later, while trying to shore up the banks of a ditch, the earth slipped and brought a tree down on his leg, breaking it below the knee. He was eventually rescued by HYACINTH and taken back to his cottage. CADFAEL straightened the leg, set the bones together and bound them securely in a wooden splint. Eilmund sheltered HYACINTH from Drogo BOSIET and, when his master was murdered, hid the runaway villein from the sheriff's men.

Refs: **14** (2–6, 8, 13).

Eilmund the Forester's Cottage (Eyton Forest, Shropshire) (fict.). Although it never existed, EILMUND THE FORESTER's cottage lay just to the north of Eyton-on-Severn (see EYTON-BY-SEVERN), midway between Watchoak and Halfway House.

Novels: 'The cottage lay in a cleared assart in the forest, with a neat garden about it.' Eilmund lived there with his daughter, ANNET.

Refs: **14** (3, 8).

Einion, Cuhelyn ab (*fl.* 1144) (fict.). **Novels:** 'On CADFAEL's left sat a young man of the prince's party, of the true Welsh build, sturdy and compact, very trim in his dress, and dark of hair and eye. A very black, intense eye, that focused on distance, and looked through what lay before his gaze, men and objects alike, rather than at them. Only when he looked along the high table, to where Owain and Hywel sat, did the range of his vision shorten, fix and grow warm in recognition and acknowledgement, and the set of his long lips soften almost into smiling. One devoted follower at least the princes of Gwynedd possessed.' A native of South Wales, foster-brother of ANARAWD AP GRIFFITH and formerly one of his guard, Cuhelyn ab Einion lost his left hand and much of the forearm in 1143, when his lord, Anarawd, was ambushed and murdered in DEHEUBARTH by CADWALADR's men. The sword stroke which took Anarawd's life also took Cuhelyn's arm from him. He was the only one to survive the slaughter and was taken to Gwynedd by HYWEL AB OWAIN. After his recovery, he was taken into OWAIN GWYNEDD's own service. GWION was Cuhelyn's twin-like, mirror image and enemy, but they became friends. At ABER, Cuhelyn recognised Bledri ap RHYS as one of the men who had murdered Anarawd. He was with Owain Gwynedd at CARNARVON, defending Gwynedd from Cadwaladr's Danish mercenaries.

Refs: **18** (2–6, 10–12, 14).

Einion, Goronwy ab (*fl.* 1144) (fict.). **Novels:** Steward of OWAIN GWYNEDD at ABER, he discovered in May 1144 that HELEDD had taken the missing horse.

Refs: **18** (5).

Elave (b. 1117) (fict.). **Novels:** Also known as the Heretic's Apprentice. 'The rising light cast the young man's face into sharp and craggy relief, fine, jutting nose, strong bones of cheek and jaw, deep shadows emphasising the set of the mouth and the hollows of the eyes under the high forehead.' Girard of LYTHWOOD's clerk, and formerly William of LYTHWOOD's personal clerk and apprentice, Elave left SHREWSBURY to accompany William on a pilgrimage to the HOLY LAND in 1136. The journey out they made the slow way, by land, pausing in CONSTANTINOPLE 'to see the great collection of relics'. In JERUSALEM, they visited 'all the most sacred places', and returned to Europe, by way of TRIPOLI, CYPRUS and THESSALONIKA, staying whenever they could in abbeys and priories. In April 1142 they rested one whole month in the monastery of ST MARCEL, where they met Pierre ABELARD. From there, in early May, they made the pilgrimage to St JAMES at COMPOSTELA. William died at VALOGNES and Elave transported his master's coffined body back to England, embarking from BARFLEUR. He returned to Shrewsbury on 19 June 1143 and lodged at the abbey. At chapter the following day, he asked RADULFUS if William could be buried in the abbey cemetery. After some debate over William's beliefs, Elave's request was granted. Elave also brought with him FORTUNATA's dowry: a carved wooden box containing THEOFANU's psalter (although he was not aware of its contents at the time). After William's funeral, Elave returned to the LYTHWOOD household where, his tongue loosened by drink, he talked to CONAN and ALDWIN. Later, Aldwin went to the abbey and denounced Elave for 'abominable heresies'. He was brought before Radulfus and the assembled chapter to face the charge. While judgement was adjourned, Elave gave the abbot his word that he would not leave his lodging at the abbey until he was free and vindicated. In love with Fortunata, he left the enclave to talk to her. She urged him to run, but he refused. Returning to the abbey, Elave was manhandled by GERBERT's men and struck to the ground by a heavy cudgel. He was locked in one of the abbey's penitential cells. When Aldwin was found murdered, Elave became the prime suspect. Hearing that Fortunata was in danger, Elave broke out of his prison to rescue her. Although he was recaptured, Bishop ROGER DE CLINTON allowed him to leave the enclave, provided he promised to return. Elave was eventually proven innocent of Aldwin's murder and cleared of the charges of heresy. He returned to the Lythwood household as clerk to Girard, and almost certainly married Fortunata.

Refs: **16** (6–15).

Elen (*fl.* 1141) (fict.). **Novels:** Wife of CENTWIN, she gave birth to a boy on 14 December 1141. The infant 'lived barely an hour' and was refused burial in consecrated ground by Father AILNOTH.

Refs: **12** (3).

Elerius, Saint (*fl.* 6th C.) (hist.) (f.d. 3 November). Reputed to have written a Life of St WINIFRED, he is thought to have been abbot of a monastery in North Wales. According to Owen and Blakeway's *A History of Shrewsbury* (1825), by the reign of HENRY II (1154–89) the monks of SHREWSBURY ABBEY had obtained the relics of Winifred's 'friend and director, St Elerius'.

Novels: In May 1140, at Shrewsbury Abbey in the presence of the abbot, LILIWIN swore on the relics of St Elerius that he was innocent of the charges made against him. During the flood of February 1145 the relics of the saint, and 'certain minor treasures' of the house, were temporarily taken for safety to the loft of the HORSE-FAIR stable.

Refs: **7** (1); **19** (3).

Elfael (Powys, Wales). This medieval Welsh cantref lay immediately south of MAELIENYDD. It was bounded to the west and south by the River Wye, and to the east by the English border dyke at Hay-on-Wye. By 1300, after the English conquest of Wales, the cantref had become one of the Marcher lordships under Anglo-Norman baronial control.

Novels: On 4 August 1139, Rhodri ap HUW suggested to CADFAEL that OWAIN GWYNEDD should keep away from Earl RANULF of Chester's borders and aim to enlarge his rule in Maelienydd and Elfael.

Refs: **4** (5:2).

Elfgiva (b. *c.*1108) (fict.). **Novels:** 'A quiet, submissive young woman, perhaps in her middle twenties, perhaps older, in drab homespun, her hair hidden away under a coarse linen wimple. Her face was thin and pale, her skin dazzlingly fair, and her eyes, reserved and weary, were of a pale, clear blue, a fierce colour that ill suited their humility and resignation.' Half-Danish villein of Hamo FITZHAMON of LIDYATE and maidservant of Lady FITZHAMON, Elfgiva loved ALARD THE SILVERSMITH. From *c.*1132 they begged Hamo to allow them to marry, but in vain. On 26 December 1134 Alard ran away. Elfgiva arrived at SHREWSBURY ABBEY with the FitzHamon household on 24 December 1135. She took the silver candlesticks FitzHamon had given to the abbey and hid them inside a sack of lavender, where they were discovered by CADFAEL. Confronted by the sympathetic monk, Elfgiva told him that she was returning them to Alard, from whom they had been stolen by Hamo. CADFAEL helped her run away from FitzHamon's service, and in SHREWSBURY she found Alard – a free man. It is almost certain that they married sometime in 1136.

Refs: **RB** (2).

Elford (Staffordshire, England). DB – Eleford: in Offlow Hundred; land held by WILLIAM I. Some 4 miles east of LICHFIELD, Elford is a small estate village lying on the north bank of the River TAME. St Peter's Church was much restored in the 19th C.

Novels: 'A neat village, with housewives and husbandmen going cheerfully and confidently about their daily business, alert to strangers but civil and welcoming to the Benedictine habit . . . No need to ask how to reach the church, they had seen its low tower before they crossed the bridge. It had been built since the Normans came, sturdy in grey stone, with a spacious churchyard very well stockaded for sanctuary at need, and full of old and handsome trees.' CADFAEL accompanied Brother HALUIN on his journey of expiation to HALES in March 1143. Unable to fulfil his vow to spend a night's penitential vigil at the tomb of Bertrade de CLARY, HALUIN determined to go on to Elford, the chief manor of the Clarys. Cadfael doggedly went with him. After visiting St Peter's Church the two monks went to the manor of Audemar de CLARY.

Refs: **15** (4–14).

Elfrid, Aunt. See HERIET, Elfrid.

Elias, Father (*fl.* 1138) (fict.). **Novels:** 'Small, elderly, grey and fierce in his piety, Father Elias ate like a little bird, whenever he remembered to eat at all, and ran about his flock busy and bothered, like a flustered hen trying to round up alien ducklings under her wings. Souls tended to elude him, every one seeming at the time the only one to matter, and he spent much of his time on his knees apologising to God for the soul that slipped through his fingers. But he would not let even that fugitive in upon false recommendation.' Parish priest of ST ALKMUND'S CHURCH from at least 1136, Father Elias refused to bury ALDWIN in June 1143, without first establishing that the murdered man had died penitent. Eventually satisfied of 'his parishioner's credentials and relieved of all his former doubts', Elias solemnly guided Aldwin 'into the next world' on 26 June.

Refs: **2** (3); **16** (2, 8–9, 12).

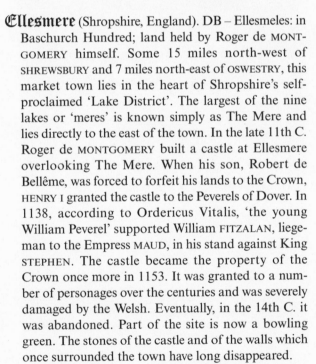

Ellesmere (Shropshire, England). DB – Ellesmeles: in Baschurch Hundred; land held by Roger de MONTGOMERY himself. Some 15 miles north-west of SHREWSBURY and 7 miles north-east of OSWESTRY, this market town lies in the heart of Shropshire's self-proclaimed 'Lake District'. The largest of the nine lakes or 'meres' is known simply as The Mere and lies directly to the east of the town. In the late 11th C. Roger de MONTGOMERY built a castle at Ellesmere overlooking The Mere. When his son, Robert de Bellême, was forced to forfeit his lands to the Crown, HENRY I granted the castle to the Peverels of Dover. In 1138, according to Ordericus Vitalis, 'the young William Peverel' supported William FITZALAN, liegeman to the Empress MAUD, in his stand against King STEPHEN. The castle became the property of the Crown once more in 1153. It was granted to a number of personages over the centuries and was severely damaged by the Welsh. Eventually, in the 14th C. it was abandoned. Part of the site is now a bowling green. The stones of the castle and of the walls which once surrounded the town have long disappeared.

Novels: 'Brother CADFAEL arrived in OSWESTRY by evening, to find town and castle alert and busy, but Hugh BERINGAR already departed. He had moved east after his meeting with OWAIN GWYNEDD, they told him, to WHITTINGTON and Ellesmere, to see his whole northern border stiffened and call up fresh levies as far away as WHITCHURCH.' Hugh Beringar went to Ellesmere to reinforce the castle in March 1141.

Refs: **9** (10).

Eluard of Winchester, Canon (*fl.* 1140) (fict.). **Novels:** 'Eluard of Winchester was a black canon of considerable learning and several masterships, some from French schools. It was this wide scholarship and breadth of mind which had recommended him to Bishop HENRY OF BLOIS, and raised him to be one of the three highest ranking and best trusted of that great prelate's household clergy, and left him now [1140] in charge of much of the bishop's pending business while his principal was absent in France.' In October 1140 the Augustinian Canon Eluard rode north to see RANULF of Chester. On his journey south to LONDON, he spent a night or two at SHREWSBURY ABBEY. While there, he questioned Meriet ASPLEY about the disappearance of Peter CLEMENCE. Having received a warm welcome from Ranulf, Eluard persuaded King STEPHEN to pay a civil diplomatic visit to the north and secure the loyalty of Ranulf and William of ROUMARE. Eluard accompanied the king to LINCOLN, and returned to SHREWSBURY on 18 December in search of further news of Clemence. He attended the wedding of Nigel and Roswitha ASPLEY on 21 December, and spotted Clemence's brooch on the bride's cloak.

Refs: **8** (2–3, 5, 7–8, 10–12).

Eluned. See NEST, Eluned.

Eluric, Brother (*c.*1121–42) (fict.). **Novels:** 'RADULFUS eyed him more sharply, and saw the tension that stiffened the young man's body, and set him quivering like a drawn bowstring. An over-intense boy, always racked by remorse for faults as often as not imaginary, or so venial that to inflate them into sins was itself an offence, being a distortion of truth.' Benedictine monk and oblatus of SHREWSBURY ABBEY and custodian of Saint Mary's altar in the Lady Chapel, Eluric, 'rated normally as a model of virtue', entered the monastery in *c.*1124, when he was three years old, and became a full brother in *c.*1141. In 1138, he was charged with delivering the annual rose-rent to Judith PERLE, which he did for three years. Unacquainted with sin, Eluric found himself haunted by uninvited feelings of love towards the widow and, in June 1142, he went to Radulfus and begged to be relieved of the painful duty. On the night of 16 June, after the task had been lifted from his shoulders, Eluric paid a secret visit to the rose-bush 'to take a last farewell of this wild dream of his, to look for one last time on the roses, and then never no more'. He surprised Miles COLIAR, who was in the process of trying to destroy the tree, and was stabbed to death trying to protect it.

Refs: **13** (1–6, 8).

Elwy, River or Afon (Clwyd, Wales). Its waters rise high up in the Welsh mountains, to the south-east of LLANWRST, and flow rapidly down the hillsides to gather in the Elwy valley near Llangernyw. From the village the river meanders in a north-easterly direction to ST ASAPH, where within a mile it merges with the River CLWYD to flow north-west past RHUDDLAN to enter the Irish Sea at Rhyl. From its source, in the Cambrian Mountains, to its confluence with the River Clwyd, the river traces a course of approximately 20 miles.

Novels: In May 1137 Prior ROBERT's party crossed the Elwy on their journey from LLANWRST to GWYTHERIN. Deacon MARK and CADFAEL journeyed to St Asaph in May 1144. The cathedral of St Asaph and the town of Llanelwy (see St Asaph) lay between the Elwy and the Clwyd.

Refs: **1** (2); **18** (7).

Ely (Cambridgeshire, England). Standing on high ground above the low-lying FENS, and on the west bank of the River Ouse, this city is some 15 miles north-east of CAMBRIDGE and some 13 miles north-west of Newmarket. Before the Fens were drained in the 17th and 18th C., the city – surrounded by treacherous marshes – stood on the eastern side of an island,

7 miles long and 4 miles wide. Etheldreda, daughter of Anna, King of the East Angles, founded a monastery at Ely in the 7th C. It was destroyed by the Danes in 869 and refounded in 970 as a Benedictine monastery (of which there are still remains today). Hereward the Wake, resisting the army of WILLIAM I, held the island fortress against the Normans, until he was driven into hiding in 1071. A Norman abbot, Theodwin of Jumièges, was appointed the following year. At about this time, building probably started on the castle, known as Cherry Hill. The next abbot, Simeon (1081–94), started to erect the present cathedral in 1083. Work on the great building continued over the next hundred years, and by *c.*1200 it was finished. After the central tower's collapse in 1322, the cathedral was extended, and the tower replaced by a remarkable structure known as the Octagon. The Norman cathedral, with its 215 ft. high western tower, dominates the flat fenland for miles around.

Novels: In Autumn 1143 Ely was in danger of being attacked by Geoffrey de MANDEVILLE and his followers.

Refs: **17** (4).

Elyas, Brother (b. *c.*1104) (fict.). **Novels:** '"Prior LEONARD said of him, not long in the cloister. He may well have tried to escape from what was hard to bear alone, and found it no easier among any number of brethren."' Benedictine monk of PERSHORE Abbey, Elyas took the cowl after the death of his beloved wife, HUNYDD, in *c.*May 1139. In November he was sent by his abbot to BROMFIELD Priory with the finger-bone of St EADBURGA. To avoid the trouble at WORCESTER, he took a roundabout route. At CLEOBURY, he met Sister HILARIA, Yves HUGONIN and Ermina Hugonin (see BRETAGNE) and travelled as far as FOXWOOD with them. Although he tried to persuade them to seek shelter with him at Bromfield, Ermina insisted that they push on over the hills to SHREWSBURY. Delivering the sacred relic safely on 1 December, Elyas set out from Bromfield for home two days later. At Foxwood he discovered that Hilaria had gone to DRUEL'S HOLDING and went there to find the nun. On the afternoon of 4 December, she willingly allowed Elyas to escort her to Bromfield. They took shelter from the cold in a hut and, trying to keep her warm, Elyas found himself sorely tempted by the demands of the flesh. He left Hilaria in the hut asleep, and went out into the snow and frost, far away from her, to watch out the night as best he could. He was attacked and left for dead by Alain le GAUCHER and his outlaws. Reyner DUTTON found the badly injured monk and took him to Bromfield Priory. Word was urgently sent to CADFAEL at Shrewsbury to come and doctor him. On 6 December, the day after Cadfael's arrival, Elyas regained consciousness. For some days he was unable to remember what had happened to him, or how he had received his injuries. He was allowed out of bed on 9 December. After being told that Hilaria was dead, Elyas slipped out of the enclave and set out in a snow-storm for the hut where he had left the nun. In frantic pursuit, Yves managed to overtake him. Unable to halt the monk's determined progress, all Yves could do was doggedly follow. On reaching the hut, Elyas knelt in the hay and eventually fell asleep. The next morning Yves was captured by Gaucher's outlaws. Elyas, 'immune from any further onslaughts of cold, pain and fear', followed the outlaws' tracks to their stronghold on TITTERSTONE CLEE, where he faced Gaucher and startled him into letting go of Yves. Elyas was taken back to Bromfield on a litter, wrapped in blankets and brychans. He eventually made a full recovery, in both body and mind, and returned to Pershore.

Refs: **6** (2–4, 7–10, 13–15); **20** (2).

E

Emmanuel, Brother (*fl.* 1138) (fict.). **Novels:** Benedictine monk of SHREWSBURY ABBEY and Abbot HERIBERT's personal clerk, he left SHREWSBURY with the abbot to attend the legatine council in LONDON in December 1138. He returned later the same month with Heribert and the new abbot, RADULFUS.

Refs: **3** (1, 11).

Engelard (*fl.* 1137) (fict.). **Novels:** 'An outlander, a man landless and rootless here in a clan society, where to be without place in a kinship was to be without the means of living. And yet a very pleasing, comely young man, good at his work and feeling for his beasts.' Husband of SIONED and father of CADFAEL (b. 1139), Engelard was the Saxon son of the lord of a Cheshire manor, from the borders of MAELOR. An 'outrageous deer poacher', he was chased out of England by the bailiffs of RANULF of Chester in 1135. An outlander, owning no land and having no kin in Wales, he was taken into the service of RHISIART at GWYTHERIN, who set him up in a croft. Being 'a good man with cattle', Engelard was considered to be the 'finest ox-caller in Gwynedd'. Although Rhisiart refused to allow him to marry his daughter, Sioned, Engelard did not give up arguing and pleading his case. He and Sioned, however, continued to meet in secret. It was from her that Engelard learned to speak Welsh. In May 1137, after Rhisiart had been found murdered, Engelard was accused of the crime. He escaped and went into hiding. Trying to stop the fleeing COLUMBANUS, Engelard accidentally broke the monk's neck and killed him. Engelard was proven innocent of Rhisiart's murder. He became a free man, by dividing all his goods with his new lord, Sioned, and the two finally got married.

Refs: **1** (2–6, 8–10, 12); **10** (1).

Ermin Way (or Ermin Street) (Hampshire, Berkshire, Wiltshire and Gloucestershire, England). The Roman road which stretches from *Calleva Atrebatum* (Silchester, 8 miles south-west of READING) to *Glevum* (GLOUCESTER), passing through *Corinium Dobunnorum* (CIRENCESTER). It should not be confused with Ermine Street, running north from LONDON, through LINCOLN to York.

Novels: 'By the same way that CADFAEL had come, Yves [HUGONIN] departed, out to the great, straight road the Romans had made long ago, arrow-straight across the plateau of the COTSWOLDS.' 'The highroad that went striding out north-west for Gloucester and south-east for Cirencester.'

Refs: **20** (9–10, 13–15).

Erwald the Wheelwright (*fl.* 1141) (fict.). **Novels:** 'The notabilities of the Foregate had begun to appear, Erwald the reeve, sombre-faced and aware of his dignity, as befitted and almost justified the use of the title of provost.' Wheelwright, and reeve of the ABBEY FOREGATE, Erwald unofficially used the title of provost. He and his family lived in a house in the Foregate. On 18 December 1141 Erwald, backed by Jordan ACHARD and several more notables of the parish, complained to Abbot RADULFUS about Father AILNOTH, the new priest. As provost, he attended Ailnoth's funeral on 1 January 1142. EDDI (b. 1131) was Erwald's nephew.

Refs: **12** (1, 3, 6, 10, 12); **19** (2).

Eryri. See SNOWDON, Mount.

Essex, Earl of. See MANDEVILLE, Earl of Essex.

Ethelred II (968?–1016), King of England (978–1016) (hist.). Also spelled Aethelred. Also called Ethelred the Unready or Aethelred Unraed. (Unready is derived from *unraed*, meaning 'evil counsel'.) Son of King Edgar, Ethelred became king after the death of his half-brother, EDWARD THE MARTYR. Ethelred's prestige and authority was weakened from the beginning by the widespread suspicion that he had played a part in his predecessor's assassination. Unable to unify his defences against Danish invasions, which commenced in 980, Ethelred eventually fled to NORMANDY. The Danish King, Sweyn I Forkbeard, became King of England in 1013. After Sweyn's death the following year, Ethelred was restored to the throne. He was succeeded by his son, Edmund II Ironside.

Novels: '"From a family older than Ethelred, and proud as the devil himself, for all he [Leoric ASPLEY] has but two manors to his name."'

Refs: **8** (1).

Eudes de l'Étoile (d. 1148) (hist.). This prophet and preacher called for a return to the asceticism of the early Christians. His disciples soon considered him to be the divine messenger of Christ, if not his reincarnation. William of Newburgh records that Eudes and his followers went on a looting spree in Brittany and gave some of their booty to the poor. Condemned by the authorities as a heretic, Eudes was burned to death at ROUEN.

Novels: In 1143, Canon GERBERT warned Abbot RADULFUS about a wandering preacher in ROUEN, who went about 'preaching poverty and humility and demanding reform'.

Refs: **16** (5).

Eudo de Domville, Canon (*fl.* 1139) (fict.). **Novels:** 'Canon Eudo imperturbably demure and ascetic, like a much younger Prior ROBERT studying for sainthood, but keeping a weather eye on the secular prospects around him all the same.' Distant cousin of Huon de DOMVILLE, Eudo de Domville, canon of SALISBURY, came to SHREWSBURY to perform the marriage ceremony between Huon and Iveta de Massard (see LUCY) in October 1139. While in the town he stayed at Bishop ROGER DE CLINTON'S HOUSE in the ABBEY FOREGATE.

Refs: **5** (1, 4–6).

Eustace (*c.*1130–53), Count of Boulogne as Eustace IV (1150–3) (hist.). Son and heir of King STEPHEN and Queen MATILDA, he married in 1140 Constance, daughter of Louis VI, King of France. He supported his brother-in-law, LOUIS VII, in the war against his Norman rival Henry Plantagenet (see HENRY II). In 1152 Stephen planned to crown Eustace and establish his family permanently on the throne, but Pope Eugenius III intervened and commanded Archbishop THEOBALD OF BEC not to perform the ceremony. His sudden death, while plundering abbey lands near BURY St Edmunds, smoothed the way for a settlement of the civil war between Stephen and the Empress MAUD, by which Henry Plantagenet was designated Stephen's successor. Respected only as a soldier, one contemporary noted that Eustace 'wherever he was, did more evil than good'.

Novels: In May 1141, according to RADULFUS, Maud offended Bishop HENRY OF BLOIS by 'refusing to allow Stephen's son to receive the rights and titles of his father's honours of BOULOGNE and MORTAIN, now that his father is a prisoner. It would have heen only justice. But no, she would not suffer it. Bishop Henry quit her court for some while, it took her considerable pains to lure him back again.'

Refs: **10** (2).

Eutropius Brother (b. 1110) (fict.). **Novels:** 'For what did anyone know about Brother Eutropius? He had come to the Abbey of Saint Peter and Saint Paul of Shrewsbury only two months ago . . . But in two months of Brother OSWIN, say, that young man would have been an open book to every reader, whereas Eutropius contained himself as tightly as did his skin, and gave out much less in the way of information.' Benedictine monk of SHREWSBURY ABBEY, Brother Eutropius worked under Brother MATTHEW, the cellarer. He arrived at the abbey in March 1140 from 'a minor grange of the order'. In the Spring, despairing for the love of a woman, Eutropius tried to drown himself in the River SEVERN. Startled by the act he contemplated, 'dazed by the thunderbolt of revelation', he fled back to the cloister. Having confessed and been absolved, Eutropius found peace of mind.

Refs: **RB** (3).

Everard, Brother (b. *c.*1073) (fict.). **Novels:** Benedictine monk of SHREWSBURY ABBEY. In February 1141 the elderly Everard was allowed to leave the infirmary and return to the dortoir after he had recovered from nothing worse than a chest cold.

Refs: **9** (4).

Evesham (Hereford & Worcester, England). In a tight loop of the River Avon, this market town lies some 12 miles south-west of STRATFORD-upon-Avon and some 14 miles south-east of WORCESTER. The Benedictine monastery, founded in 701 by Egwin, 3rd Bishop of Worcester, became one of the most powerful abbeys in England. When Egwin died in 717, he was buried in the abbey church and his shrine became a place of pilgrimage. The original church collapsed in *c.*960 and was rebuilt in the 11th C. The only section to survive the Dissolution intact was the bell tower.

Novels: ALARD THE CLERK, who entered Evesham Abbey in *c.*1085 and absconded in his youth, returned in November 1120. That same month, Abbot (then Prior) HERIBERT and his party spent the night at Evesham on their way to WOODSTOCK. In February 1145 Sub-Prior HERLUIN, accompanied by TUTILO and a lay servant, rode from SHREWSBURY to Evesham (and then Worcester), where he asked for and received donations for the restoration of RAMSEY ABBEY. On his penitential journey south in December 1145 CADFAEL spent a night on 'a pallet in the common hall' at Evesham Abbey.

Refs: **19** (2, 7, 13); **20** (6); **RB** (1).

Evrard the Steward (*fl.* 1142) (fict.). **Novels:** A younger son with no land to inherit, he was a steward in the service of Sir Fulke ASTLEY at WROXETER. In 1142, Evrard and Hiltrude ASTLEY were in love, despite her forced betrothal to young Richard LUDEL. Whether Evrard and Hiltrude ever married is uncertain.

Refs: **14** (10).

Ewald the Groom (d. 1139) (fict.). **Novels:** 'Ewald had been morose and taciturn, and kept himself apart, and the revelation of his villainy did not greatly surprise his fellows.' Groom of Ivo CORBIÈRE, Ewald came from a Cheshire manor and was of northern ancestry. He arrived at SHREWSBURY with his master on 31 July 1139. Together with Turstan FOWLER, Ewald murdered Thomas of BRISTOL and Euan of SHOTWICK. He received a long gash down his left arm from Euan's dagger. When Gilbert PRESTCOTE the elder informed CORBIÈRE that he suspected the groom of killing Euan, Ivo arranged Ewald's escape and then ordered Fowler to shoot him down. Ewald died with an arrow in his back on 3 August.

Refs: **4** (1:1, 3:2, 4:3–5, 5:2).

Eyton-by-Severn (now Eyton-on-Severn) (Shropshire, England). DB – Aitone: in Wrockwardine Hundred; a holding of St Peter's (i.e. the Abbey of St Peter and St Paul at SHREWSBURY). The land at Eyton was given to SHREWSBURY ABBEY by Roger de MONTGOMERY, and continued to be held by the monastery until the Dissolution. In 1086 there were two fisheries; all the fish from one of them went to feed the monks. Eyton-on-Severn is situated nearly 7 miles south-east of SHREWSBURY on the north bank of the SEVERN.

Novels: 'The land rose on the skyline into the

forested ridge of the WREKIN, a great heaving fleece of woodland that spread downhill to the SEVERN, and cast a great tress of its dark mane across LUDEL land and into the abbey's woods of Eyton-by-Severn. There was barely a mile between the grange of Eyton, close beside the river, and Richard Ludel's manor house at EATON. The very names sprang from the same root, though time had prised them apart, and the Norman passion for order and formulation had fixed and ratified the differences.'

Refs: **14** (1–5, 7–8, 11).

Eyton Forest (Shropshire, England). This forest stretched for some miles from EATON Constantine and the south-western tip of the WREKIN Forest, past Eyton-on-Severn (see EYTON-BY-SEVERN) to WROXETER. Some 6 miles south-east of SHREWSBURY, it lay in a broad sweep on the north bank of the SEVERN, beyond and above the water-meadows.

Novels: 'Late November would soon be tearing away with frost and gales the rest of the quivering leaves. The deserted hermitage in the woods of Eyton would provide winter cover for the small beasts of the forest, and the garden, running wild again, would shelter the slumbering urchins in their nests through the winter sleep.' Cuthred occupied the hermitage in Eyton Forest between October and November 1142 (see BOURCHIER, Renaud and CUTHRED'S HUT). Part of the forest belonged to SHREWSBURY ABBEY and was managed by EILMUND THE FORESTER; another part belonged to the LUDEL family of EATON and was looked after by John of LONGWOOD.

Refs: **12** (5, 8); **14** (1–5, 7–8, 10–14).

Eyton-on-Severn. See EYTON-BY-SEVERN.

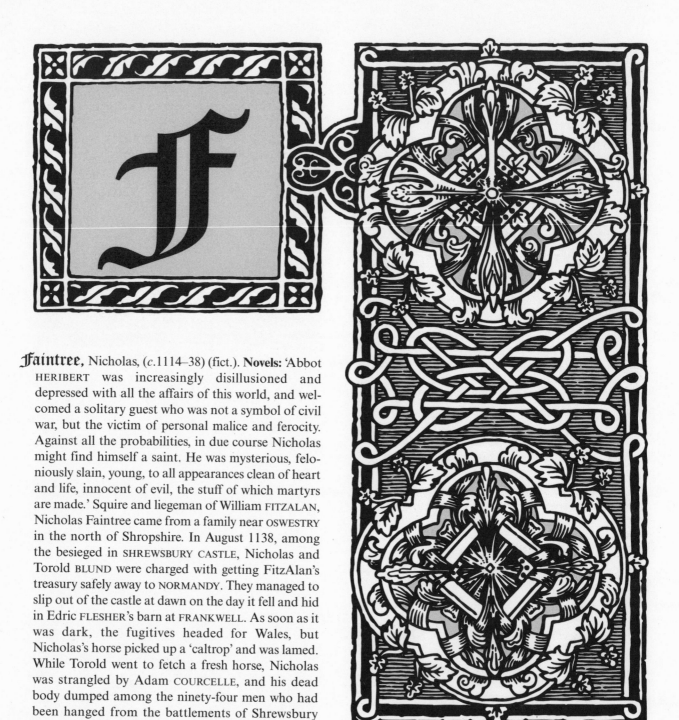

Faintree, Nicholas, (*c*.1114–38) (fict.). **Novels:** 'Abbot HERIBERT was increasingly disillusioned and depressed with all the affairs of this world, and welcomed a solitary guest who was not a symbol of civil war, but the victim of personal malice and ferocity. Against all the probabilities, in due course Nicholas might find himself a saint. He was mysterious, feloniously slain, young, to all appearances clean of heart and life, innocent of evil, the stuff of which martyrs are made.' Squire and liegeman of William FITZALAN, Nicholas Faintree came from a family near OSWESTRY in the north of Shropshire. In August 1138, among the besieged in SHREWSBURY CASTLE, Nicholas and Torold BLUND were charged with getting FitzAlan's treasury safely away to NORMANDY. They managed to slip out of the castle at dawn on the day it fell and hid in Edric FLESHER's barn at FRANKWELL. As soon as it was dark, the fugitives headed for Wales, but Nicholas's horse picked up a 'caltrop' and was lamed. While Torold went to fetch a fresh horse, Nicholas was strangled by Adam COURCELLE, and his dead body dumped among the ninety-four men who had been hanged from the battlements of Shrewsbury Castle. His unidentified body was placed before the altar in SHREWSBURY ABBEY church and recognised by Godith Adeney (see BLUND), who had known him since she was twelve years old. He was buried under a stone in the transept of the church, 'an exceptional privilege.'

Refs: **2** (3–6, 10, 12); **4** (4:4).

Farewell (Staffordshire, England). This tiny hamlet is situated some 2 miles north-west of LICHFIELD and 6 miles east of Cannock (see CHENET). A small abbey of Benedictine nuns was founded here in *c.*1140 by Bishop ROGER DE CLINTON. It declined to a priory in the mid-13th C. and was dissolved in 1527, before the general Dissolution of the Monasteries. The site of the priory buildings is thought to have been where Farewell Hall now stands. From 1527 until 1689, when St Bartholomew's Church was re-opened, there is no record of it being used. The church was pulled down and rebuilt in the mid-18th C., except for the stone chancel of *c.*1300 once used by the nuns.

Novels: 'They were both glad when the path brought them to a small open green flanked by three or four cottages, and they saw beyond these the long pale fence of the new abbey, and the roof of the church above it.' Returning from VIVERS to SHREWSBURY in March 1143, CADFAEL and Brother HALUIN lodged at Farewell Abbey, founded by Bishop ROGER DE CLINTON in *c.*1140, and still in the process of being built. Mother PATRICE, the abbess, received them. Sister URSULA was the hospitaller at the abbey.

Refs: **15** (6, 10–14).

Faringdon (Oxfordshire, England). Some 17 miles east of CIRENCESTER, on the opposite side of the THAMES valley to BAMPTON, Faringdon occupied a site of strategic importance during Anglo-Saxon times. Alfred the Great reputedly built a palace in the ancient market town, and in 1145 ROBERT, Earl of Gloucester, erected a castle, 'strongly fortified by a rampart and stockade' (*Gesta Stephani*, ed. Potter, 1976). It was besieged by King STEPHEN in Summer 1145, 'until those who were chief in command, without the knowledge of the others, sent secretly to the king and made an agreement conceding his demand for the surrender of the castle.' (*Gesta Stephani.*) Stephen's acquisition of Faringdon cut the Empress MAUD's communications between the Thames valley and her strongholds in Gloucestershire, and was regarded by many at the time as a major turning point in the war. All Saints' Church dates from the 12th C. At Great Coxwell, 2 miles south-west of the town, is a 13th C. monastic barn, 152 ft. long, which once belonged to the Cistercians of Beaulieu Abbey, Hampshire. It is now owned by the National Trust.

Novels: 'In the desultory but dangerous and explosive battlefield of the Thames valley Philip [FITZROBERT], the empress's castellan of CRICKLADE, had been plagued by damaging raids by the king's men garrisoned in OXFORD and MALMESBURY, and to ease the load had begged his father to come and choose a site for another castle, to try and disrupt communications between the two royal strongholds, and put them, in turn, on the defensive. And Earl Robert had duly selected his site at Faringdon, built his castle and garrisoned it. But as soon as the king heard of it he came with a strong army and laid siege to the place. Philip in Cricklade had sent plea after plea to his father to send reinforcements at all costs, not to lose this asset barely yet enjoyed, and potentially so valuable to the hardpressed garrison of his son's command. But Gloucester had paid no heed, and sent no aid. And suddenly it was the talk of the south that the castellan of Faringdon, Brien de SOULIS, and his closest aides within the castle, had made secret compact with the besiegers, unknown to the rest of the garrison, let in the king's men by night, and delivered over Faringdon to them, with all its fighting men. Those who accepted the fiat joined Stephen's forces, as most of the ranks did, seeing their leaders had committed them; those who held true to the empress's salt were disarmed and made prisoner. The victims had been distributed among the king's followers, to be held to ransom.' Among those 'overpowered and disarmed' at 'Robert of Gloucester's newly built castle of Faringdon', in Summer 1145, was Olivier de BRETAGNE. Geoffrey FITZCLARE, who refused to put his seal to the agreement to surrender the castle, was murdered on the orders of Brien de

Soulis. Faringdon, held by Philip FitzRobert for Stephen, was one of a ring of royal fortresses surrounding Cricklade, including Bampton, PURTON and Malmesbury.

Refs: **20** (1–7).

Felton (now West Felton) (Shropshire, England). DB – Feltone: in Merset Hundred; a holding of Reginald the Sheriff under Roger de MONTGOMERY. Some 4 miles south-east of OSWESTRY and 13 miles north-west of SHREWSBURY, the village of West Felton grew up around the Norman motte-and-bailey castle. St Michael's Church, standing to the east of the motte, dates from 1140. The tower collapsed in 1782 and was replaced. Further building and restoration to the church was carried out during the 19th C. West Felton is one of the eleven towns of Ruyton Manor (see RUITON).

Novels: In May 1144 CADFAEL, Deacon MARK and Hugh BERINGAR parted from Aline and Giles BERINGAR at Felton: Hugh rode north-west with the monks to WHITTINGTON; while his wife and son rode west to Hugh's manor at MAESBURY.

Refs: **18** (1).

Fens (Cambridgeshire, Norfolk and Lincolnshire, England). Covering about 1,500 square miles of eastern England, between CAMBRIDGE in the south and LINCOLN in the north, the Fens (or Fenland) are characteristically flat and open, with few trees and virtually no hedges. The main rivers – the Witham, Welland, NENE and Ouse – flow eastward into the North Sea, by way of the Wash. Before the land was drained in the 17th and 18th C., the Fens were composed of treacherous expanses of marsh and peat, within which were islands of high ground. These islands were settled from prehistoric times. The Romans not only cultivated the land, but also constructed artificial watercourses for both transport and drainage. In medieval times most of the region was owned by great ecclesiastical institutions, such as the monasteries of ELY, RAMSEY and Thorney. Today, the Fens are one of the richest arable areas in the country.

Novels: 'From Cambridge and the Fens there was no news. No one had yet expected any. But travellers from eastward reported that the weather was turning foul, with heavy rains and the first frosts of the winter. No very attractive prospect for an army floundering in watery reaches unfamiliar to them but known to the elusive enemy.' In 1143, after being stripped of his offices and castles by King STEPHEN, Geoffrey de MANDEVILLE took his revenge on the innocent inhabitants of the Fens, sacking Cambridge and seizing RAMSEY ABBEY. In November, in order to try and quell the anarchy, Stephen ordered Hugh BERINGAR to the Fens with a company of men. Mandeville remained defiant in his watery stronghold until his death at MILDENHALL on 16 September 1144, when Stephen became 'master of the Fens again'.

Refs: **17** (3–6, 8–10, 12–13); **18** (1); **19** (Prologue, 4, 13).

Fidelis, Brother. See CRUCE, Julian.

FitzAlan, William (*c.*1105–60) (hist.). Eldest son of Alan FitzFlaald and his wife Avelina (sister of Arnulf of HESDIN), he inherited his father's estates in 1114 and founded HAUGHMOND ABBEY in *c.*1135. According to William of Malmesbury, Adelaide of Louvain, second wife of HENRY I, who had been granted the county of Shropshire by the king in 1126, appointed FitzAlan as her sheriff. King STEPHEN confirmed him in office. Having married Constantia, a niece of ROBERT of Gloucester, FitzAlan renounced his allegiance to Stephen and took the side of the Empress MAUD. In Summer 1138 Stephen laid siege to the town and castle of SHREWSBURY. One account says that FitzAlan held out for nearly a month, but, in August, he fled. Another says that, having been warned of the king's approach, he slipped secretly away before the siege, with his wife and family. Although he spent some time in exile in NORMANDY, it is known that FitzAlan eventually returned to England to fight for the empress's cause. He was at OXFORD in the summer of 1141 and, shortly after, he was at the siege of WINCHESTER. It is also possible that he found asylum in the court of RANULF of Chester, since his wife was related to MAUD, Countess of Chester. HENRY II, who succeeded STEPHEN in 1154, reinstated FitzAlan's confiscated estates and made him sheriff of Shropshire in 1155. Constantia having died, at about this time FitzAlan married Isabel de Say, Baroness of CLUNY, who sometime between 1155 and 1160, gave him a son and heir, William. FitzAlan was buried in SHREWSBURY ABBEY. Guy le Strange immediately succeeded him as sheriff. In 1165 Isabel married Geoffrey de Vere, who became sheriff in the following year. By Constantia, William left a daughter, Christiana, wife of Hugh Pantulf.

Novels: 'William FitzAlan owed his office as sheriff of Salop to Stephen, and yet had declared and held the castle for his rival.' In August 1138 William FitzAlan was besieged in SHREWSBURY CASTLE by Stephen. Just before the castle fell, he escaped with Fulke ADENEY by swimming across the River SEVERN and eventually reached safety in NORMANDY. His treasury was secreted out of the castle by Torold BLUND and Nicholas FAINTREE. In Summer 1141 FitzAlan sent Blund and Ninian BACHILER to England to sound out the extent of Maud's support. In November 1142 it was rumoured that FitzAlan was back in England and had joined the empress in Oxford. It seemed that in August the following year he was with Maud's forces in BRISTOL.

Refs: **2** (1–2, 4); **4** (1:1); **12** (4, 6–7); **14** (1); **17** (1, 8).

FitzClare, Geoffrey (d. 1145) (fict.). Illegitimate son of Jovetta de MONTORS and Richard de CLARE, and half-brother of Gilbert de CLARE, he was raised with Gilbert, from being almost newborn, and, when grown, was set up for life by his father. Unlike the rest of the Clares, who were 'absolute' for King STEPHEN, Geoffrey supported the Empress MAUD. He and his half-brother, however, 'always respected and liked each other'. Geoffrey was one of six captains under Brien de SOULIS at FARINGDON: he 'carried the most weight' with the common soldiery and was 'the best liked and trusted'. Because he refused to put his seal to the agreement to surrender the castle, he was murdered on de Soulis's orders: his death was attributed to an accidental fall from his horse while riding to CRICKLADE to report to Philip FITZROBERT. Not surprisingly, his forged seal appeared on the agreement. He was buried in Faringdon churchyard.

Refs: **20** (6–8, 13, 15–16)

FitzCount, Brian (*fl.* 1142) (hist.). He was the apparently illegitimate son of Alan Fergant (or Fergan), Count of Brittany, who had served under HENRY I. FitzCount was brought up by the king, who not only gave him a knighthood but also provided for him for life. He married Matilda de Wallingford, the widow or daughter of Miles Crispin, whose lands she brought him. In 1127 FitzCount escorted the Empress MAUD to NORMANDY. By 1130 he held land in at least twelve counties. A loyal supporter of Maud, he rallied to her side when she landed near ARUNDEL on 30 September 1139. FitzCount was briefly besieged in his castle at WALLINGFORD by King STEPHEN. The easternmost fortress of the empress's territory, Wallingford remained a thorn in the king's side throughout the war. Described as MAUD's inseparable companion and lover, FitzCount lost all his lands supporting her cause. He was with the Empress at WINCHESTER in March 1141, LONDON in June 1141, OXFORD in July 1141 and WINCHESTER in September 1141. After her defeat at Winchester, he fled with her to DEVIZES. He was with her at BRISTOL towards the close of the year, and at Oxford in the spring of the following year. After her escape from Oxford in December 1142 she fled to his castle at Wallingford. From 1152, when Stephen failed in his third attempt to take the castle at Wallingford, the rest of FitzCount's life is obscure. One source, though considered unreliable, suggests that he became a crusader.

Novels: 'The lord of Wallingford was the empress's most faithful adherent and companion, next only to the earl, her brother, and had held his castle for her, the most easterly and exposed outpost of her territory, through campaign after campaign and through good fortune and bad, indomitably loyal. Brian FitzCount rallied to support Maud as soon as she landed near Arundel on 30 September 1139, and became her 'most faithful and devoted ally'. After the 'Rout of Winchester' in September 1141, he escorted the empress to safety. Even though Bishop HENRY OF BLOIS made attempts to persuade him to change sides, FitzCount remained loyal to Maud, despite 'beggaring himself for her'. He was with the empress after her escape from OXFORD CASTLE in December 1142.

Refs: **5** (7); **10** (2); **11** (6); **12** (1); **14** (4, 14); **15** (1).

FitzGilbert, John (d. 1165), Marshall (hist.). Son of Gilbert the Marshall, brother of William FitzGilbert (the Empress MAUD's chancellor), and father of William Marshall I, Earl of Pembroke (*c.* 1147–1219), he was HENRY I's marshall, before initially supporting King STEPHEN. After changing his allegiance to the empress in *c.* 1140, he remained loyal to her cause, and was at the siege of WINCHESTER in 1141. The *Histoire de Guillaume le Mareschal* (a Middle French poem celebrating the life of William Marshall I) says that, after the 'Rout of Winchester', John took refuge in WHERWELL abbey church and refused to come out, even when the church was set alight: molten lead was poured from the roof of the tower, causing him severe burns and the loss of an eye. John's principal base was Marlborough, but he also held castles at LUDGERSHALL and NEWBURY. After separating from his first wife, Adelina, John married Sybil, the sister of PATRICK, Earl of Salisbury, thereby ending their family's great rivalry. It was due to the solid backing of both John and Patrick that the empress controlled much of northern Wiltshire. His castle at Newbury was besieged by Stephen in 1152, and eventually taken. After the accession of HENRY II, John retained his marshalship, but lost Marlborough Castle, and his influence in the royal court declined. Shortly before his death he regained the king's favour by supporting him in his persecution of Archbishop Thomas à Becket.

Novels: 'If ROBERT of Gloucester was not available, at least he would rather deal with the marshall than with the lady alone, and it was the marshall who would have to talk good sense into the lady as to how to deal with this opportunity.' Marshall of the Empress Maud and one of 'the props of her personal household', John FitzGilbert was in GLOUCESTER in December 1145. It was his job to deploy the siege force around the castle of La MUSARDERIE, which he did with businesslike efficiency. 'FitzGilbert was too old a hand at the manoeuvrings of civil war to be shaken or diverted by whatever tone was used to him.' A man of his word, he negotiated the terms of the garrison's surrender with Guy CAMVILLE.

Refs: **20** (10–14).

FitzHamon, Hamo (b. 1075) (fict.). **Novels:** 'Dismounting in the great court, the knight of LIDYATE was seen to be a big, over-fleshed, top-heavy man with bushy hair and beard and eyebrows, all grey-streaked from their former black, and stiff and bristling as wire. He might well have been a very handsome man before indulgence purpled his face and pocked his skin and sank his sharp black eyes into flabby sacks of flesh. He looked more than his age, but still a man to be reckoned with.' Lord of Lidyate, he was the elderly husband of Lady FITZHAMON, who was his second or possibly third wife. Hamo was the father of at least one son by a previous marriage. FitzHamon held 'two fat manors' in the north-eastern corner of Shropshire. A 'gross feeder, a heavy drinker, a self-indulgent lecher, a harsh landlord and a brutal master', he had a mild heart attack in 1135, at the age of sixty. In order to secure the welfare of his soul, Hamo decided to present SHREWSBURY ABBEY with two silver candlesticks for the altar of St Mary, and sufficient funds to provide light throughout the year. He arrived at SHREWSBURY, with his wife and servants, on 24 December. The following morning, having been informed that the candlesticks had been stolen, FitzHamon led a vindictive but futile hunt for the culprit. Before he returned to Lidyate on 26 December, CADFAEL found out that, despite promises to the contrary, Hamo had refused to allow ALARD THE SILVERSMITH and ELFGIVA to marry, or give them their freedom.

Refs: **RB** (2).

FitzHamon, Lady (b. *c.*1106) (fict.). **Novels:** 'That frivolous young wife would never really leave her rich husband and easy life, however tedious and unpleasant Hamo's attentions might be, to risk everything with her penniless villein lover. She would only keep him to enjoy in secret whenever she felt it safe. Even when the old man died she would submit to marriage at an overlord's will to another equally distasteful. She was not the stuff of which heroines and adventurers are made. This was another kind of woman.' Second or possibly third wife of Hamo FITZHAMON, she arrived at SHREWSBURY ABBEY with her husband, her maid ELFGIVA, and their two grooms SWEYN THE GROOM and MADOC, on Christmas Eve 1135. Having persuaded CADFAEL to give her a strong sleeping draught for a headache, she used it to drug her husband in order to spend the night with her lover, MADOC.

Refs: **RB** (2).

FitzJohn, Guy (*fl.* 1139) (fict.). **Novels:** Squire of Huon de DOMVILLE, he first entered the baron's service as a page when he was twelve years old. He arrived at SHREWSBURY for his lord's wedding to Iveta de Massard (see LUCY) in October 1139 and reluctantly helped in the fruitless search for his fellow squire, Joscelin LUCY.

Refs: **5** (1–3, 6–7, 9–11).

FitzRobert (*fl.* 1141) (fict.). **Novels:** '"I've thrived, having your commendation. WILLIAM OF YPRES has mentioned me to the queen, and would have taken me among his officers, but I'd rather stay with FitzRobert's English than go to the Flemings. I have a command."' Norman captain in the army of Queen MATILDA, he was with his liege lady at the siege of WINCHESTER in September 1141. Nicholas HARNAGE served under him in 1141.

Refs: **11** (3–4, 11).

FitzRobert, Philip, (b. *c.*1116) (hist.). Younger son of ROBERT of Gloucester, brother of William FITZROBERT and also of MAUD (*fl.* 1139), he was a loyal supporter of the Empress MAUD until Summer 1145, when he mysteriously changed his allegiance to King STEPHEN. His defection seemed to have some connection with the fall of FARINGDON Castle, but it may also be partly explained by the fact that his sister was married to RANULF of Chester. The *Gesta Stephani* (ed. Potter, 1976) describes Philip as: 'a man of strife, supreme in savagery, daring in what should not be dared, in fact a perfect master of every kind of wickedness'. Castellan of CRICKLADE Castle, he also held a 'great many castles, some given to him by grant from the king, others won from the enemy by his own energetic efforts' (*Gesta Stephani*). Among those he captured and held hostage were Robert MUSARD and Reginald FITZROY. In *c.*1146 Philip was suddenly taken ill and, repenting of his former actions, vowed to go on a pilgrimage to JERUSALEM. He was last heard of at ROUEN in 1147, where presumably he was on his way to the HOLY LAND.

Novels: 'For this was certainly Philip FitzRobert, the earl of Gloucester's younger son. There was even a resemblance, though they were built differently. This man was not compact and foursquare, but long and sinewy, abrupt but graceful of movement and

F

dark of colouring. Above the twin level strokes of his black brows, the cliff of forehead rose loftily into thick, waving hair, and below them his eyes were like damped down fires, muted but alive. Yet the likeness was there, stressed most strongly by the set of long, passionate lips and formidable jaw. It was the image carried one generation further into extremes. What would be called constant in the father would be more truly stubborn in the son.' 'He opened his eyes upon a lean, dark figure looming beside him, and a shadowed oval face, high-boned and aquiline, looking down at him impersonally, with a grave and slightly unnerving intelligence. Eyes intent and bright studied him unhurriedly, without reticence, without mercy. Confronted with a mere man, neither ally nor enemy to him, Philip FitzRobert contemplated humanity with a kind of incurious but profound perception, hard to evade.' 'He went in the plainest of dark gear, independent of any manner of ornament or finery. His own bearing was his distinction. Physically, in motion or in stillness, he had an elongated elegance, and a tension like a strung bow.' 'Philip was unmarried and without children, wholly absorbed into the demonic conflict that no one seemed able to end.' Younger son of Robert of Gloucester, brother of William FitzRobert and of Maud (*fl.* 1139), he held three castles: Cricklade, Faringdon and La MUSARDERIE (the latter he had taken from Robert Musard). After begging his father to send reinforcements to Faringdon, without success, Philip, for some inexplicable reason, changed his allegiance in Summer 1145. '"And then," said Yves bitterly, "Philip handed over Cricklade whole and entire to King Stephen, himself, his garrison, arms, armour and all. I can't for my life imagine why, what drove him to it. I've worn my wits out trying to fathom it. Was it a simple calculation that he was labouring more and more on the losing side, and could better his fortunes by the change? In cold blood? Or in very hot blood, bitter against his father for leaving Faringdon to its fate? Or was it he who betrayed Faringdon in the first place? Was it by his orders it was sold?"' '"That," said Hugh flatly, "I shall never understand. He, of all people! Gloucester's own son, and Gloucester has been the empress's prop and stay as good as single-handed throughout, and now his son turns against him and joins the king!"' After the fall of Faringdon, Philip secretly imprisoned his friend Olivier de BRETAGNE, by whom he felt betrayed, in La Musarderie. 'Olivier's fiery scorn would be enough offence. A match for Philip in his towering pride, blazing forth in unrestrained reproach, as if Philip's own mirror image cried out against him. Perhaps the only way to put that mortal wound out of mind had been to bury the accuser out of sight and out of memory.' In October 1145 Philip seized and held prisoner Reginald FitzRoy, whom the king made him release. Philip, 'not yet quite thirty', attended the bishops' conference at COVENTRY on 30 November of the same year: '"if only to confront his father and show that he regrets nothing, but he'll come to destroy, not to placate"'. He captured Yves HUGONIN near DEERHURST and also imprisoned him in La Musarderie, releasing him only after he had been convinced by CADFAEL that the boy was innocent of Brien de SOULIS's murder. 'Philip had fought for King Stephen as relentlessly as ever he had for the empress, but never yet face to face with the father he had deserted. The one enormity, the only one, that had been ruled out in this civil war, was the killing of close kinsmen, and who could be closer kin than father and son. Fratricidal war, they called it, the very thing it was not. When Robert declared himself at the gates of La Musarderie and demanded surrender, his own life in the balance, Philip must give way. Or even if he fought, for very pride's sake, it must be with no more than half his heart, always turning away from confrontation with his own progenitor. Loved or hated, that was the most sacred and indissoluble tie that bound humankind. Nothing could break it.' Under threat of being hanged for treason by the Empress Maud, Philip was badly injured during the siege of La Musarderie. While unconscious, without either his permission or knowledge, Philip was taken by Olivier to safety at CIRENCESTER ABBEY, where – 'his captor turned prisoner, friend turned enemy' – was reconciled with his father. '"I have had time, these last days," said Philip quite gently, "to recall all that happened before I died. It was a hopeless cast," he said with deliberation, "to believe that turning from one nullity to the other could solve anything. Now that I have fought upon either side to no good end, I acknowledge my error. There is no salvation in either empress or king."' From his sickbed, Philip abandoned England and took the Cross.

Refs: **20** (1–16).

FitzRobert, William (d. 1183), Earl of Gloucester (hist.). Eldest son and heir of ROBERT of Gloucester, brother of Philip FITZROBERT and of MAUD (*fl.* 1139), he was a loyal supporter of the Empress MAUD. The *Gesta Stephani* (ed. Potter, 1976) called him 'effeminate and more devoted to bedchambers than to war'. In 1141 William stood as surety for his father (captured at the 'Rout of WINCHESTER') in the exchange with King STEPHEN (captured at LINCOLN). During Robert's absence in NORMANDY, William was governor of WAREHAM. He succeeded to the earldom in 1147, and in the same year took Castle Cary from Henry de Tracy. In 1149 he helped Henry Plantagenet (later HENRY II) escape from DEVIZES, and return to Normandy. Towards the end of Stephen's reign, William made alliances with RANULF of Chester, ROGER, Earl of Hereford, and William de Beauchamp. After inheriting his father's Welsh estates, including the lordship of Glamorgan, William's chief residence became Cardiff Castle, where, in 1158, he and his wife, Hawise, and son, Robert (d. 1166), were captured by Ifor ap Meurig (or Ivor the Little), and only released after the Welshman's grievances against his overlord had been redressed. He was benefactor to numerous religious houses, including Keynsham Abbey in Somerset, which he founded in 1167. In 1183, during Henry II's struggle with his sons, William was one of a number of magnates who were imprisoned because their loyalty was in doubt. His wife, Hawise, whom he married in *c.*1150, was the daughter of Robert de BEAUMONT (the younger).

Novels: 'This one built sturdily, like his father, and resembled him in face.' Eldest son and heir of Robert of Gloucester, brother of Philip FitzRobert and Maud, Countess of Chester, he attended the conference at COVENTRY between King STEPHEN and the Empress MAUD on 30 November 1145. He was a loyal supporter of Maud.

Refs: **20** (2–3, 8).

F

FitzRoy, Reginald (d. 1175), Earl of Cornwall (hist.). Also known as Reginald or Reynold de Dunstanville. Illegitimate son of HENRY I, half-brother of the Empress MAUD and of ROBERT of Gloucester, he was created Earl of Cornwall by Robert, not the empress, in *c.*1141. From 1139 Reginald remained consistently loyal to the empress until his death. He was with her army at the siege of WINCHESTER in 1141, and, with Brian FITZCOUNT, escorted her to safety after the 'rout' which followed. In 1145 he was captured by Philip FITZROBERT, but released on King STEPHEN's orders. He was a witness to the treaty designating his nephew, Henry Plantagenet (later HENRY II), as King STEPHEN's successor. After his death he was buried in READING ABBEY, and his earldom reverted to the Crown.

Novels: Earl of Cornwall, younger half-brother of the Empress Maud and also of Robert of Gloucester, he was seized and held prisoner by Philip FitzRobert in October 1145, but was 'promptly and correctly' released by order of King Stephen. On 30 November, in the same year, Reginald attended the conference at COVENTRY between Stephen and Maud. A loyal supporter of the empress, he was with her at GLOUCESTER, and the siege of La MUSARDERIE, in December 1145.

Refs: **20** (2, 6, 10–11).

Flanders (Belgium, France and Netherlands). This medieval principality of Flanders evolved out of the disintegration of the Carolingian Empire. First appearing in the 8th C., the name is thought to mean 'Lowland'. Lying west of the River Schelde, the region included what are now parts of Belgium,

France and the Netherlands. During the Middle Ages the country was the centre of the prosperous Flemish cloth industry, with its capital, BRUGES, on the Zwijn Estuary. Both England and France had interests in the principality: the former supplied the raw wool for its cloth industry; while the latter tried to bring it under French rule. Flanders disappeared as a political entity during the French Revolutionary Wars of 1789–99.

Novels: Merchants travelling all the way from Flanders attended St Peter's Fair at SHREWSBURY in August 1141. Brother MATTHEW had 'lived for some years in Flanders in his earlier days, and could speak fluent Flemish, to deal with any problems that might arise'. William HYNDE sold his finest fleeces to middlemen for shipping 'to the north and the wool towns of Flanders'. In 1143 Canon GERBERT warned of 'malignant wandering preachers active even now in Flanders, in France, on the RHINE and in LOMBARDY'.

Refs: **4** (1:1–2, 5:2); **11** (1, 5); **13** (5); **16** (5).

Flanders, Robert, Count of. See ROBERT, Count of Flanders.

Flesher, Edric (*fl.* 1138) (fict.). **Novels:** 'And there was her husband, prompt to her call, large and rubicund and competent, the master of his craft in this town, and a councillor.' Husband of Petronilla FLESHER, he was chief of the butchers' guild of SHREWSBURY and a councillor. A good friend to William FITZALAN's house and a loyal supporter of Fulke ADENEY, he and his wife helped Torold BLUND and Nicholas FAINTREE smuggle FitzAlan's treasury out of the besieged town. They also managed to conceal Godith Adeney (see BLUND) in SHREWSBURY ABBEY disguised as a boy. On 30 July 1139 he was among the ten-strong delegation from the Guild Merchant who requested, of Abbot RADULFUS, that a proportion of the abbey fair tolls should go to the town to repair its walls and streets.

Refs: **2** (2, 4–6, 10–11); **4** (1:1).

Flesher, Petronilla (*fl.* 1138) (fict.). **Novels:** 'She was getting old, but still plump, succulent and kindly, the most wholesome thing he had seen in this siege town so far. Her grey hair was tight and neat under its white cap, and her twinkling grey eyes bright and intelligent as ever, welcoming him in.' Wife of Edric FLESHER, and former nurse to Godith Adeney (see BLUND) while she was serving in the household of Fulke ADENEY. In August 1138, pretending that she was her aunt, Petronilla disguised Godith as a boy and hid her in SHREWSBURY ABBEY. On 30 July 1139 Petronilla was among the onlookers on the English Bridge watching Thomas of BRISTOL's barge disembark.

Refs: **2** (1–2, 4–6, 10–11); **4** (1:2).

(Edric) Flesher's Shop (Butcher Row, Shrewsbury, Shropshire) (fict.). Although it never existed, Edric FLESHER's shop was the finest in BUTCHER ROW. It could be easily identified by the sign of the boar's head.

Novels: 'The street rose steeply, the island town sat high. [Hugh] BERINGAR knew it well, and knew where he was bound. At the summit of the hill the row of the butchers' stalls and shops and houses levelled out, silent and deserted. . . . Edric Flesher's shop was the finest of the row, but it was shuttered and still like all the rest.'

Refs: **4** (4:5).

Fomorians (myth.). A race of monstrous and misshapen, violent and cruel creatures, who represented the powers of evil. Led by Cenchos (or Cichol Grinchenghos) the Footless, the Fomorians were driven out of Ireland by PARTHOLAN and his followers. They also battled with the Nemedians and the Tuatha De Danaan, later inhabitants of Ireland. The

Fomorians were finally defeated, and their supernatural powers broken for all time, at the second battle of Mag Tuireadh. Other Fomorian leaders included: Balor of the Evil Eyre, Conann and Morc.

Novels: On Partholan's arrival in Ireland he found it inhabited by 'a race of monsters' which he drove 'northward into the seas and beyond'.

Refs: **19** (2).

Foregates. See ABBEY FOREGATE; CASTLE FOREGATE.

Foriet (Shropshire, England) (fict.). Although it never existed the old manor of Foriet was situated on the fringes of the LONG FOREST and stood in the general vicinity of ACTON Burnell, to the south of the neighbouring manors of ASPLEY and LINDE and across the ancient Roman road.

Novels: Isouda FORIET inherited the manor of Foriet on the death of her parents.

Refs: **8** (3, 5–6, 10–12).

Foriet, Isouda (b. 1124) (fict.). **Novels:** 'No cottar's girl, if she did choose to go plain and scorning finery. She knew she was an heiress, and to be reckoned with.' Orphaned very young, Isouda Foriet inherited the manor of FORIET from her parents. In 1140 it was managed on her behalf by Leoric ASPLEY, with whose family she was brought up, and was 'as well run as any in England'. Also in 1140, Isouda had set her heart on marrying Meriet ASPLEY and was determined that one day he would be hers. On 21 December she attended the wedding of Nigel ASPLEY and Roswitha Linde (see ASPLEY) at SHREWSBURY ABBEY.

Refs: **8** (3, 5–7, 10–13).

Forthred (b. *c.*1115) (fict.). **Novels:** 'The labourer who went heavily on the left leg, surely after some illknit fracture, was otherwise a fine, sturdy fellow, and very agile for all his disability. Probably about thirty years old, with large, able hands, and a long reach.' Forthred, with a 'weathered face, under a thatch of thick brown hair', came from TODENHAM. He took service for the Empress MAUD under Brien de SOULIS, and, in Summer 1145, was a man-at arms at FARINGDON 'the few weeks the castle stood for the cause'. Unwilling to change his allegiance to King STEPHEN, he was letting himself down from the wall of the castle, trying to escape, when someone cut the rope. Left on the ground, 'broken and unaided', Forthred managed to crawl for cover, where he was found by 'decent poor men'. Despite being lame, and 'useless to his lord', he was taken on by Master BERNARD, the mason, at DEERHURST, for whom he worked 'hard and well'. In December 1145, while working at Deerhurst Priory, he informed CADFAEL that the drawing of the salamander seal belonged to Geoffrey FITZCLARE.

Refs: **20** (6–7).

Forton (Shropshire, England). DB – Fordune: in Baschurch Hundred; a holding of Roger of Lacy under Roger de MONTGOMERY. (At Forton there was woodland for fattening one hundred pigs.) The tiny hamlet of Forton, with its red-brick houses and cottages, lies just off the OSWESTRY road, some 4 miles north-west of SHREWSBURY and immediately north of MONTFORD BRIDGE.

Novels: In June 1142 Vivian HYNDE was at Forton with his father, William HYNDE, helping him at their sheepfold. Searching for Girard of LYTHWOOD, CONAN travelled as far as Forton, before giving up and turning back to Shrewsbury.

Refs: **13** (10, 12–13); **16** (4).

Fortunata (b. 1125) (fict.). **Novels:** '"A pretty little thing she was. She had more wit than her mother. It was William named her Fortunata, for he said she'd come into the world with nothing, not even a father, and still found herself a home and a family, and so she'd still fall on her feet lifelong."' Foster-daughter of Girard and Margaret of LYTHWOOD, the illegitimate Fortunata was taken into the household of William of LYTHWOOD from the day she was born.

Her mother was a serving maid, 'who fell foul of a small huckster at the fair one year, and brought forth a daughter'. When her mother died, she was brought up by Margaret, who 'cared for the baby like her own child'. In June 1143 ELAVE brought her a dowry from William, which was to be held in trust by Girard until her marriage. Although she did not know it at the time, the box contained THEOFANU's psalter; but it was secretly stolen and replaced with money by her foster-uncle, Jevan of LYTHWOOD. After Elave had been denounced as a heretic by ALDWIN, Fortunata was forced to give evidence against him. She found herself in love with Elave and was prepared to use her dowry, in whatever way possible, to secure his deliverance from prison. On 26 June, suspecting that Jevan may have exchanged the book inside her box for money, Fortunata searched his workshop at FRANKWELL. She was caught in the act and, when CADFAEL and Hugh BERINGAR arrived, Jevan held a knife against her body to prevent her from denouncing him as Aldwin's murderer. Elave fired the workshop, and Jevan released Fortunata to try and rescue the priceless psalter. Unwilling to keep it, she gave the book to Bishop ROGER DE CLINTON to take back to his library at COVENTRY. She and Elave almost certainly got married, probably in late 1143.

Refs: **16** (3–8, 10–15).

Foryd, River or Afon (Gwynedd, Wales). This tiny stream, some 2 miles in length, rises near Dinas Dinlle to flow north-east into FORYD BAY, where it merges with the rivers CARROG and GWYRFAI. Before it winds across the sandy, tidal bay it forms a small U-shaped lake.

Novels: 'The anchorage at the mouth of the MENAI [STRAIT] was separated from the broad sandy reaches of the bay to southward by a long spit of shingle beyond which the water of two rivers and their tributaries wound its way to the strait and the open sea, in a winding course through the waste of sands.'

Refs: **18** (10).

Foryd Bay (Gwynedd, Wales). Some 2 miles southwest of CARNARVON, this bay lies on the Welsh mainland opposite ABERMENAI. About 2 miles long and just under a mile wide, it is fed by the rivers FORYD, CARROG and GWYRFAI. At low tide the rivers can be seen winding their course across the sand and salt marsh of the bay. To the west is a narrow peninsula, which now accommodates a small airfield. At its tip, to the east of Fort Belan, built by Lord Newborough in the 18th C., is a narrow bar of shingle which almost closes the mouth of the bay.

Novels: 'TURCAILL stood to view the whole sweep of land and water, the long stretch of the bay extending more than two miles to the south, pale gold shoals and sinuous silver water, the green shore of ARFON beyond, rolling back into the distant hills.' In May 1144 Turcaill (*fl.* 1144) and his Danes sailed into the bay, under cover of darkness, and successfully abducted CADWALADR from inside a tent in OWAIN GWYNEDD's camp.

Refs: **18** (10–11, 13).

Fowler, Turstan (*c.*1104–39?) (fict.). **Novels:** 'Sober and recovered from his debauch, he was a well-set-up and comely fellow, with the open face of one who has not a care in the world. Evidently he was long since forgiven, and back in favour.' Villein-born falconer and archer of Ivo CORBIÈRE, Turstan Fowler arrived at SHREWSBURY with his lord on 30 July 1139, accompanied by the two grooms, ARALD and EWALD. Carrying out Corbière's orders, he murdered Thomas of BRISTOL and Euan of SHOTWICK. In order to secure immunity from all suspicion of Thomas's murder, Fowler pretended to drink himself into a stupor and spent the night in one of the abbey's punishment cells. Next day, at the sheriff's court, he testified that Philip

CORVISER, also drunk, had threatened to take his revenge on Thomas of Bristol. At his master's command, Fowler shot and killed Ewald while he was fleeing from the sheriff. On 4 August he accompanied Corbière, Arald and Emma Vernold (see CORVISER) to STANTON COBBOLD. He was arrested at the manor and taken back to Shrewsbury for trial, where he was probably hanged.

Refs: **4** (1:1, 1:4, 2:2, 3:2, 4:1–5, 5:1–2, 5:4, 5 :6).

Foxwood (Shropshire, England). This small village, over 1,000 ft. above sea level, lies on the eastern slopes of TITTERSTONE CLEE and on the north side of the main LUDLOW to Kidderminster road. It is some 7 miles east of Ludlow and 3 miles west of CLEOBURY Mortimer.

Novels: 'To Foxwood was a fairly easy ride, being a used highway, but from Foxwood they climbed by even higher ways, and on tracks more broken and steep.' During the severe Winter of 1139 Sister HILARIA, together with Yves HUGONIN and Ermina Hugonin (see BRETAGNE), met Brother ELYAS at CLEOBURY and travelled with him to Foxwood. After leaving him at Foxwood, they pressed on over the hills to DRUEL'S HOLDING.

Refs: **6** (2–5, 7).

France, King of. See LOUIS VII, King of France.

Francis, Brother (*fl.* 1142) (fict.). **Novels:** Benedictine monk of SHREWSBURY ABBEY and custodian of St Mary's altar by October 1142, he was noted for his 'lame readings in Latin'.

Refs: **3** (1); **5** (2); **14** (2); **17** (7); **18** (1).

Frankwell (Shrewsbury, Shropshire). This suburb lies to the north-west of SHREWSBURY, outside the loop of the River SEVERN which almost encircles the town, but at the mouth of a second and smaller loop. Frankwell begins on the western side of the Welsh bridge and contains numerous 16th and 17th C. timber-framed houses.

Novels: 'The workshop where Jevan of LYTHWOOD treated his sheepskins lay well beyond the last houses of the suburb of Frankwell, solitary by the right bank of the river, at the foot of a steep meadow backed by a ridge of trees and bushes higher up the slope.' In August 1138, after the siege of SHREWSBURY, William FITZALAN's treasury was stowed 'outside the walls of the town, somewhere in the suburb of Frankwell'. It was later revealed that the treasury had been hidden in 'a dry well' in a garden at Frankwell held by Edric FLESHER in readiness for its transfer westward into Wales. Nicholas FAINTREE was 'strangled by night, in a hut in the woods above Frankwell, and thrown among the executed under the castle wall, to cover up the deed'. In 1140 Walter AURIFABER acquired 'a pasture and an old stable across the river, westward from Frankwell'.

Refs: **2** (2, 4, 10); **7** (8, 12); **11** (12–13); **13** (5); **16** (3, 6, 12–14).

Fremund the Steward (*fl.* 1140) (fict.). **Novels:** '"It was the manor steward who came with the word, a solid old countryman, Saxon by his name – Fremund."' Saxon steward of Leoric ASPLEY of the manor of ASPLEY, Fremund was among those who accompanied Peter CLEMENCE on the first mile or so of his journey north to CHESTER on 9 September 1140. He was with ASPLEY, his chaplain and a groom when they found Meriet ASPLEY dragging the dead body of Clemence into the bushes. A week or so later, he asked Abbot RADULFUS, at his lord's request, if Meriet could enter the cloister.

Refs: **8** (1, 3, 5–6, 11–12).

Frome, River (Gloucestershire, England). Rising high on the western escarpment of the COTSWOLDS near Birdlip, 6 miles south of Cheltenham, the river sweeps south past Miserden (see GREENHAMSTED) and the remains of La MUSARDERIE to Sapperton. From here it turns westward, flowing through a deep narrow gorge to Stroud, where it crosses the Vale of BERKELEY to enter the River SEVERN at Upper Framilode. From source to Severn, the Frome threads a semicircular course of some 22 miles. During the Middle Ages, the fast-flowing stream was the source of power for numerous corn- and fulling-mills. By the end of the 16th C. 'Golden Valley', as the Frome valley came to be known, was a major centre of the cloth industry, but declined with the demise of water power at the beginning of the 19th C.

Novels: 'He heard water flowing below, no great flood but the purling sound of a little river with a stony bed; and presently he came out on a narrow slope of grass on its bank, and a narrower tongue of gravel led out into the water, marking the passage of the ford. On the further side the track rose again almost as steeply as on the side where he had descended, and old, established trees hid all that awaited him beyond.' In December 1145 CADFAEL, and others, crossed the River Frome to reach Greenhamsted and La Musarderie. 'When all was done, he [Guy CAMVILLE] led his garrison away eastward, over the river and through WINSTONE to the Roman road (see ERMIN WAY), heading, most likely, for CRICKLADE.'

Refs: **20** (7, 9, 11, 13–15).

Fulchered, Abbot (d. 1120) (hist.). He was appointed the first abbot of SHREWSBURY ABBEY in 1087. He was brought to SHREWSBURY from the abbey of SEEZ in NORMANDY and, according to Owen (*Some Account of the Ancient and Present State of Shrewsbury*, 1808), 'arrived naked and hungry'. He was succeeded by Abbot GODEFRID. He was described by Ordericus Vitalis as an elegant preacher, and is reputed to have prophesied the death of WILLIAM II as a divine punishment for his irreligious conduct and oppression of the Church.

Novels: In November 1120, at the king's court of WOODSTOCK, letters between Fulchered and Arnulf MAUDUIT were produced as evidence in the dispute between Shrewsbury Abbey and Roger MAUDUIT over the ownership of ROTESLEY.

Refs: **RB** (1).

Fulk (1092–1143), King of Jerusalem (1131–43), Count of Anjou and Maine as Fulk V (1109–31) (hist.). Son of Fulk IV and Bertrada of Montfort, Fulk was responsible for laying the foundations of the Angevin Empire. He married Arenburga of MAINE in 1109, and agreed to the marriage of his fifteen-year-old son, GEOFFREY of ANJOU, to the Empress MAUD, daughter of the English king HENRY I, in 1128. Abdicating in favour of Geoffrey, Fulk, who had first visited the HOLY LAND in 1120, returned in 1129 to marry Melisende, daughter and heiress of Baldwin II, King of JERUSALEM. He was proclaimed King of Jerusalem in 1131, on Baldwin's death.

Novels: '"It was not the Atabeg ZENGHI," said Brother HUMILIS, smiling, "whose affairs sent you here so far to seek me out. Leave him to the King of Jerusalem, whose noble and perilous business he is."'

Refs: **11** (2, 4).

Fuller, Godfrey (b. 1092) (fict.). **Novels:** 'Godfrey Fuller himself, his finery shed in favour of stout working clothes, for he was by no means ashamed to soil his hands alongside his workmen, and prided himself on being able to do whatever he asked of them, and possibly as well or better than they could.' A wealthy SHREWSBURY merchant and guildsman, the 'skinflint' Godfrey Fuller had 'buried two wives already and made a profit out of both of them' by 1142. For his third wife, he had designs on the wealthy widow, Judith PERLE, hoping to acquire a profitable spinning and weaving business. Needless to say, his ambition was not realised. See also FULLER'S DYE HOUSE, FULLING-WORKS AND TENTERGROUND and FULLER'S HOUSE.

Refs: **13** (1, 3, 6–8, 10).

(Godfrey) Fuller's Dye-House, Fulling-Works and Tenterground (Shrewsbury, Shropshire) (fict.). Although they never existed, Godfrey FULLER's dye-house, fulling-works and tenterground lay on the west bank of the River SEVERN, outside and under the northern walls of SHREWSBURY

CASTLE. Today the site is occupied by the railway station and a prison.

Novels: 'The open meadows stretched away, widening, into an undulating expanse of field and woodland, peaceful and serene. The only remaining reminders of the town were here close beside the river, Godfrey FULLER's sheds and fulling-troughs and tenterground.'

Refs: **13** (3, 7).

(Godfrey) Fuller's House (Shrewsbury, Shropshire) (fict.). Although it never existed, Godfrey FULLER's house lay not far from SHREWSBURY CASTLE precinct.

Novels: 'CADFAEL looked back along the castle wall to the last wicket giving access to the town, and recalled that Fuller's house lay not far from the castle precinct.'

Refs: **13** (7).

Fychan, Hywel (*fl.* 1138) (fict.). **Novels:** 'Hywel Fychan, the defendant, was a wiry, dark man of belligerent aspect.' A Welshman and neighbour of Owain ap RHYS, Hywel Fychan lived near MALLILIE. In December 1138, at the commote court at LLANSILIN, he was fined for moving one of Owain's boundary stones.

Refs: **3** (8–9).

Fychan, Rhodri (*fl.* 1120) (fict.). **Novels:** Father of Rhodri FYCHAN (the Less), he was a respected beggar of SHREWSBURY, with a pitch outside ST MARY'S CHURCH.

Refs: **RB** (3).

Fychan, Rhodri (the Less) (*fl.* 1140) (fict.). **Novels:** Also called Rhodri the Less. 'He leaned to rattle his begging-bowl at a pious lady who had been putting up prayers in the church. Business was business, and the pitch he held was the envy of the beggars of SHREWSBURY.' A respected beggar like his father, Rhodri FYCHAN, and named after him, and a Welshman, he was blind from birth and begged in a prime spot outside ST MARY'S CHURCH. He slept in the loft above Roger CLOTHIER'S CART-HOUSE and barn and was present when Jacob of BOULDON was arrested. 'In all likelihood Rhodri Fychan, leaning close and recording all, had never heard it, or he would have known it, for his ears could pick up even the shrillest note of the bat.' 'Longest he looked at the little, spry, bowed old man who came forth smiling at CADFAEL's shoulder. For in the wrinkled, lively face the lantern-light showed two eyes that caught reflected light though they had none of their own, eyes opaque as grey pebbles and as insensitive.'

Refs: **RB** (3).

Fychan, Rhodri (*fl.* 1144) (fict.). **Novels:** Steward of CADWALADR, he owned lands at LLANBADARN in CEREDIGION. In May 1144 Rhodri Fychan was ordered by his lord to despatch to the Danes at ABER-MENAI money and stock to the value of 2,000 marks in order to secure Cadwaladr's release.

Refs: **18** (12).

G

Gallus, Saint (*c.*550–*c.*640) (hist.) (f.d. 16 October). Also called Gall, Gallech or Gilianus. An Irish hermit, probably from Leinster, Gallus became a monk at BANGOR and accompanied St Columbanus to Europe, where he helped found the monastery at Luxeuil-les-Bains, Franche-Comté, France. Possibly due to a disagreement, he parted from Columbanus when his superior went to Italy in 612, and established a hermitage in Switzerland. The town which later grew up around it became known as ST GALL. He is venerated as the principal pioneer of Christianity in Switzerland.

Novels: '"Irish script and an Irish name," said the abbot. "Gallus himself was Irish, and many of his race followed him there."'

Refs: **16** (15).

Ganymede (myth.). In Greek mythology, he was the cup-bearer of Zeus (see JOVE). Desiring to make the beautiful youth his favourite, Zeus took the form of an eagle and carried Ganymede up to Olympus where he became immortal.

Novels: When Torold BLUND gave Godith Adeney (see BLUND) the nickname of Ganymede, Godith asked CADFAEL who Ganymede was.

"'A beautiful youth who was cup-bearer to Jove, and much loved by him . . . But some say that it's also another name for HEBE," said Cadfael. "Oh! And who is Hebe?" "Cup-bearer to Jove, and much loved by him – but a beautiful maiden."'

Refs: **2** (5).

Gascony (France). This ancient province in south-western France is bounded by the Atlantic Ocean, and stretches from the mouth of the Gironde to the Spanish border where the Pyrenees meet the sea. The Duchy of Gascony was united with neighbouring Aquitaine in 1052, and in 1073 the duchy passed to the House of Poitiers. Gascony was governed by the dukes of Aquitaine and counts of Poitiers until 1137, when it came under the direct rule of LOUIS VII, King of France, through his marriage to Eleanor of Aquitaine. After the marriage was annulled in 1151, Eleanor married Henry Plantagenet (see HENRY II). This rival claim to Gascony led to warfare between France and England, which continued sporadically, through the Hundred Years' War, to the 15th C. when the French finally drove the English out of the duchy.

Novels: 'He was thrusting boxes and bags of spices aside in his haste, scenting the air, pushing out of his way wooden caskets of sugar confections from the East, come by way of VENICE and Gascony, and worth high prices in any market.'

Refs: **4** (3:1).

Gaucher, Alain le (d. 1139) (fict.). **Novels:** 'Afoot, he might not be a very tall man, but the breadth of his shoulders and breast, and the lion's mane of thick hair that covered his head and flowed down on to his chest in a bushy beard made him look immense. He sat his horse as if they made one powerful body between them. He was all the more frightening because his face was but a shadow, and there was nothing to be read in it.' Illegitimate son of one of the 'Lacy clan' (see LACY FAMILY), Alain le Gaucher served in France for a number of years, fighting against GEOFFREY of Anjou. He received the name 'le Gaucher' because he was left-handed. During the savage winter of 1139, he led the outlaw band on TITTERSTONE CLEE, which attacked and sacked CALLOWLEAS, DRUEL'S HOLDING and WHITBACHE. Gaucher seriously injured Brother ELYAS, leaving him to die in the snow, and also captured Yves HUGONIN. During Hugh BERINGAR's attack on his upland fortress, Gaucher threatened to kill Yves unless his soldiers withdrew. Gaucher was killed during a sword fight in December 1139 by Olivier de BRETAGNE.

Refs: **6** (9–10, 13).

Gaye (Shrewsbury, Shropshire). The lush level land, known as the Gaye, lay outside the loop of the River SEVERN, stretching from the English Bridge in SHREWSBURY to almost opposite SHREWSBURY CASTLE. Today much of the land is occupied by the Gay Meadow, the home ground of Shrewsbury Town Football Club. Shrewsbury station, with its sprawling railway lines and sidings, lies to the north and east. At the southern corner are the Abbey Gardens, a small public park sandwiched between the Football Ground, the Wakeman School and the ABBEY FOREGATE side of the English Bridge.

Novels: 'CADFAEL began the descent to the Gaye. This path was trodden regularly, and bare of grass, and the landward bushes that fringed it drew gradually back from its edge, leaving the level, cultivated ground open. On the river side they grew thickly, all down the slope to the water, and under the first arch of the bridge, where once a boat-mill had been moored to make use of the force of the current. Close to the waterside a footpath led off downstream, and beside it the abbey's gardens lay neatly arrayed all along the rich plain, and three or four brothers were pricking out plants of cabbage and colewort. Further along came the orchards, apple and pear and plum, the sweet cherry, the two big walnut trees, and the low bushes of little sour gooseberries that were only just beginning to flush into colour. There was another disused mill at the end of the level, and the final abbey ground was a field of corn. Then ridges of woodland came down and overhung the water, and the curling eddies ate away the bank beneath their roots.'

Refs: **2** (5–6, 8); **3** (1, 6–7); **4** (1:1–3, 2:2, 4:4–5, 5:2); **5** (3–4, 8); **7** (3, 6, 11); **8** (1–2); **9** (10); **10** (7); **11** (2–3, 8–9, 13–14); **12** (2, 4–6, 10); **13** (2, 6, 8–9, 12); **14** (7); **15** (1–2); **16** (6–7, 15); **17** (3, 5); **RB** (3).

Generys (d. 1142) (fict.). **Novels:** '"Dark, she was, very dark, very beautiful. Everyone would call her so, but now I see that none ever knew how beautiful, for to the world outside it was as if she went veiled, and only I ever saw her uncover her face. Or perhaps, to children – to them she might show herself unconcealed. We never had children, we were not so blessed. That made her tender and loving to those her neighbours bore. She is not yet past all hope of bearing children of her own. Who knows but with another man, she might yet conceive."' Welsh wife of RUALD and lover of the elder Eudo BLOUNT, Generys met Ruald in Wales, where he gave her a silver ring, engraved with a G and R. Married in 1127 and childless, Generys was abandoned by her husband in *c.* May 1142. Bitterly resenting Ruald's sudden departure and unable to take another husband, she took Eudo as her lover by way of revenge. Unable to bear sharing Eudo with each other, Donata BLOUNT and Generys agreed to settle the matter by each drinking a cup of wine, one of which contained a fatal draught of hemlock. Having drunk, the women parted to await the outcome of their choice. Generys lost the wager and died, poisoned, on 28 June 1142. She was buried by Eudo with reverence in a corner of the POTTER'S FIELD. Her remains were uncovered by the abbey plough in early October 1143 and taken back to SHREWSBURY ABBEY, where she was reburied in a 'modest' corner of its graveyard.

Refs: **17** (1–3, 5–6, 9–10, 12–14).

Genville, Rafe de (*fl.* 1142) (fict.). **Novels:** Pseudonym: Rafe of Coventry. Vassal and devoted friend of Brian FITZCOUNT and loyal liegeman to the Empress MAUD. In November 1142, Rafe de Genville arrived alone at SHREWSBURY ABBEY, calling himself Rafe of Coventry, falconer to the Earl of Warwick (see BEAUMONT, Roger de). Although he never announced his mission, he had travelled north from OXFORD in search of the missing Renaud BOURCHIER. As soon as he heard that Cuthred was not a priest, Rafe slipped quietly away and went to his hermitage in EYTON FOREST. Discovering that Cuthred was Bourchier, Rafe challenged him to a fair fight and killed him. He himself was wounded in the arm. Shortly after, he left SHREWSBURY for WALLINGFORD to restore to FitzCount the coins, jewels and letter Bourchier had stolen. 'So quiet, unobtrusive and unremarkable a man, he had hardly been noticed even while he remained here, his stay would soon be forgotten.'

Refs: **14** (7, 9, 11–14).

Geoffrey (1113–51), Count of Anjou as Geoffrey IV (1129–51) (hist.). Also called Geoffrey Plantagenet from the sprig of broom which he wore in his hat. Son of FULK, Count of ANJOU and MAINE and King of JERUSALEM. In 1128, at the age of fifteen, Geoffrey was married to the Empress MAUD, daughter of King HENRY I of England and widow of Emperor HENRY V. Consequently, he acquired a claim to NORMANDY and England. Maud, eleven years older than her Angevin husband, was married against her will and, in 1131, she returned to England leaving Geoffrey behind. When her father died in 1135, she spent the next thirteen years in contention with STEPHEN for the crown of England, a struggle in which Geoffrey gave her little support. He, in fact, was far too busy conquering

Normandy and spent almost all of his life fighting his rivals, and the castellans of his own Anjou. In 1144 he finally conquered Normandy and was accepted as its duke. On his death in 1151 he left to his heir, Henry Plantagenet (see HENRY II), his considerably enlarged empire, which included Anjou, Maine, Normandy and Touraine. He was buried in Le Mans, France.

Novels: There are various references to Geoffrey. Maud detested the title of Countess of Anjou because she felt it belittled her. Maud's half-brother, ROBERT, Earl of Gloucester, went to France in 1142 to ask for help from Geoffrey, who just sent over his nine-year-old son, Henry. In February 1145 Hugh BERINGAR remarked: '"since Geoffrey of Anjou has made himself master of Normandy, on his son's behalf, every man in Stephen's backing fears for his lands over there, and must be tempted to change sides to keep Anjou's favour."'

Refs: **2** (1); **12** (2); **13** (1); **14** (1, 4, 14); **15** (1); **16** (1); **19** (5, 11); **20** (3–4, 13).

Geoffrey, Prior (*fl.* 1140) (hist.). As abbot, Geoffrey of ST ALBANS founded SOPWELL PRIORY for Benedictine nuns in 1140. He allowed a few women living a pious life to settle there without taking vows, or not the full vows.

Novels: 'At Sopwell Priory by Saint Albans a devout woman may live a life of holiness and service short of the veil, through the charity of Prior Geoffrey.'

Refs: **11** (14).

Gerbert, Canon (*fl.* 1143) (fict.). **Novels:** '"I understand you very well," said Canon Gerbert, when he was alone with RADULFUS in the abbot's parlour. Closeted thus in private with his peer, he sat relaxed, even weary, all his censorious zeal shed, a fallible man and anxious for his faith.' Augustinian canon of CANTERBURY under Archbishop THEOBALD OF BEC, Gerbert had rigidly orthodox views. On his way north on a mission of peace and goodwill to RANULF of Chester, his horse fell lame and he was forced to spend a week or so at SHREWSBURY ABBEY. He arrived on 19 June 1143 with his body-servant and two grooms, and Deacon SERLO. When ELAVE asked Abbot Radulfus if William of LYTHWOOD could be buried in the abbey, Gerbert endeavoured to influence the decision, urging a refusal on the grounds that William was allegedly a heretic. After Elave, who had also been denounced for heresy, had left the enclave, Gerbert set his men to search for him and bring him back. He insisted not only that Elave should be brought to trial, but also that he be kept in a cell beforehand. Immediately after Elave had been cleared of the charges against him, Gerbert left SHREWSBURY for Chester.

Refs: **16** (1–7, 10–11, 14–15).

Gerta (b. *c.*1103) (fict.). **Novels:** 'At the door of Adelais's hall he asked for audience, and the woman Gerta came out to him haughtily, protective of her mistress's privacy and assertive of her own office.' Tirewoman of Adelais de CLARY of HALES, Gerta went with her mistress to EATON in March 1143.

Refs: **15** (3–6, 12).

Giffard, Ralph (the elder) (b. 1091) (fict.). **Novels:** 'He had but one cause that mattered to him now, and that was to preserve his own situation and leave his remaining estate intact to his son . . . No, better far to sit still, shun every tempter, and forget old allegiance. Only so could he ensure that young Ralph, busy this Christmas happily playing the lord of the manor at home, should survive this long conflict for the crown without loss, no matter which of the two claimants finally triumphed.' Father of Ralph GIFFARD the younger and stepfather of Sanan BERNIÈRES, Ralph Giffard was the lord of two or three country manors in the north-east of Shropshire and a town house in SHREWSBURY. He had owned more, but certain of his lands were confiscated because of his former allegiance to William FITZALAN and the Empress MAUD. On 22 December 1141 Dame Diota HAMMET delivered a letter from Ninian BACHILER to Giffard asking for his help. In order to safeguard his own position and possessions, Giffard betrayed the fugitive: first to Father AILNOTH and later to Hugh BERINGAR.

Refs: **12** (4, 6–7, 9–13).

G

Giffard, Ralph (the younger) (b. 1125) (fict.). **Novels:** Son and heir of Ralph GIFFARD (the elder) and step-brother to Sanan BERNIÈRES, 'young Ralph' was managing his father's chief country manor in the north-east of Shropshire in December 1141. He was betrothed to a girl in a neighbouring manor.

Refs: **12** (4, 7, 9–11, 13).

(Ralph) Giffard the elder's House (Shrewsbury, Shropshire) (fict.). Although it never existed, the town house of Ralph GIFFARD (the elder) was situated near ST CHAD'S CHURCH: not the 18th C. church overlooking the Quarry but Old St Chad's in Princess Street. Nearby, Belmont (and its continuation, Milk Street) runs between Town Walls and Wyle Cop past Old St Chad's. In medieval times it was known as St Chad's Lane and, from 1350 to 1600, Stury Close after a family of that name. It was once a fashionable street, containing the town houses of various country families. It was widened after the collapse of St Chad's Church in 1791. In Milk Street are a number of timber-framed buildings dating from the 16th C., including the Old Post Office Inn.

Novels: Ralph Giffard mainly spent the winters in his town house in SHREWSBURY, near St Chad's Church.

Refs: **12** (4).

Gilbert (d. 1152?), Bishop of Saint Asaph (hist.). A Norman, he was consecrated at LAMBETH by Archbishop THEOBALD OF BEC in 1143 and, presumably not long afterwards, was installed in the newly revived see of ST ASAPH. Bishop Gilbert was succeeded by Geoffrey of Monmouth.

Novels: 'The tall, dignified Gilbert, self-consciously patrician and austere without, and uneasily insecure within.' Non-Welsh-speaking, Norman bishop of St Asaph at Llanelwy, Gilbert was consecrated at Lambeth by Archbishop Theobald in 1143, and early the following year was finally installed in his see. In May 1144, he was paid a complimentary visit by Deacon MARK on behalf of Bishop ROGER DE CLINTON. Among Bishop Gilbert's clerical reforms was a strict return to celibacy.

Refs: **18** (1–4, 6, 9, 11, 14).

Giles, Saint (d. *c.*710) (hist.) (f.d. 1 September). Also called Aegidius. Although he was one of the most popular saints in western Europe during the Middle Ages, very little is known about St Giles. Probably born in PROVENCE, he founded a monastery on the Rhône, near Arles, where the town of St-Gilles-du-Gard now stands. His shrine became a major centre of pilgrimage and also a stopping-place on the route to both COMPOSTELA and the HOLY LAND. He is the patron saint of cripples, lepers, beggars and the infirm, and in England alone over 160 churches and more than twenty-four hospitals were dedicated to him.

Novels: 'The woman, he knew, had given up all care for the world, and waited only to leave it. Even her son she abandoned thankfully into the hands of Saint Giles, patron saint of the diseased and shunned.' The leper hospital of SHREWSBURY ABBEY was dedicated to St Giles.

Refs: **5** (1, 7).

Glastonbury (Somerset, England). This busy market town lies to the south of the Mendip Hills, some 22 miles south-west of BATH and 12 miles east of Bridgwater. Its origins stretch back to antiquity, when it was an island surrounded by marshes and lakes. Traditionally held to be the site of the Isle of Avalon, the place has long been associated with mystery and legend. In 1191 it was claimed that the graves of King Arthur and Queen Guinevere were discovered nearby, and their bones were reinterred at the abbey. Joseph of Arimathea, the early Christian missionary, is also said to have come to the town from the east, bringing the blood of Christ in a chalice. The first church at Glastonbury was said to have been built in 166 by missionaries from ROME, who came at the invitation of the British King Lucius. According to *The Anglo-Saxon Chronicle*, the monastery was founded by Ine, King of Wessex, in *c.*688. It was enlarged in the 8th C. and again in the 10th C. when, due to Dunstan, Abbot of Glastonbury and later Archbishop of CANTERBURY, it became the most powerful and wealthy of all the religious houses in Britain. The Benedictine abbey, dedicated to St Mary, was destroyed by fire in 1184. Rebuilding commenced immediately and continued for some 300 years. After its dissolution in 1539 many of the buildings were demolished for their stone. Among the monastic remains are the ruins of St Mary's Chapel, the Abbot's Kitchen and a gatehouse.

Novels: HENRY OF BLOIS 'was proof positive that there is a grand career to be made in the world by early assumption of the cowl. Monk of CLUNY, abbot of Glastonbury, bishop of WINCHESTER, papal legate – a rise as abrupt and spectacular as a rainbow.'

Refs: **8** (1).

Gloucester (Gloucestershire, England). Lying to the east of the River SEVERN, in the broad vale between the COTSWOLD Escarpment and the Forest of Dean, this cathedral city and county capital is some 25 miles south of WORCESTER and 33 miles north-east of BRISTOL. By the 10th C. Gloucester had become the capital of the Anglo-Saxon kingdom of Mercia. The abbey of St Peter was founded in *c.*681 by Osric, whose sister was the first abbess (it was a double house for monks and nuns). Although the Benedictine abbey was rebuilt in 1058, having been destroyed by fire, the Normans rebuilt it yet again, but on a grander scale. The main part of the Norman abbey was built between 1089 and 1260, but rebuilding continued through to the 15th C. with the erection of a massive Perpendicular tower. In 1541, after the abbey's dissolution, Henry VIII refounded it as a cathedral, dedicated to the Holy Trinity. Among the many monuments in the cathedral is the tomb of ROBERT, Duke of Normandy. During medieval times Gloucester was a thriving inland port with a seaborne trade in wool, leather and grain.

Novels: 'He [Yves HUGONIN] entered the city by the Eastgate late in the afternoon. The streets seemed to him busier and more crowded than he had ever seen them, and before he reached the Cross he had picked out among the throng the badges or the livery of several of the empress's most powerful adherents . . . At the Cross . . . he turned away from the abbey, and towards the castle, down a busy and populous Southgate towards the river, and the water-meadows that still grew green in the teeth of winter. The great grey bulk of the castle loomed above the streets on this townward side, above the jetties and the shore and the wide steely waters on the other. The empress preferred somewhat more comfort when she could get it, and would certainly have installed herself and her women in the guest apartments of the abbey. Earl Robert was content in the sterner quarters of the castle with his men.' On the journey up the Severn to SHREWSBURY in July 1139, Emma Vernold (see CORVISER) purchased a pair of gloves in Gloucester. MILES, Constable of Gloucester, joined the Empress MAUD when she landed at ARUNDEL on 30 September 1139. Returning to England in the autumn of 1139, Laurence d'ANGERS went to Gloucester to find his nephew and niece, Yves Hugonin and Ermina Hugonin (see BRETAGNE). Gloucester was one of the two main strongholds of the Empress Maud's faction, led by ROBERT of Gloucester. In November 1139 the men of Gloucester attacked and sacked Worcester. After the 'Rout of WINCHESTER' in September 1141, Maud fled with the remnant of her army to the town. Ninian BACHILER and Sanan BERNIÈRES were married there in 1142. In

G

December 1145 the empress and her 'great army' left Gloucester to attack Philip FITZROBERT at La MUSARDERIE.

Refs: **2** (7); **4** (2:3, 4:1–2); **6** (1, 3, 5, 8, 12–13, 15); **8** (1); **10** (16); **11** (8); **12** (4, 6–7, 9–10); **15** (1); **16** (1); **19** (2); **20** (2, 5–7, 9–15).

Gloucester, Constable of. See MILES, Constable of Gloucester.

Gloucester, Earl of. See ROBERT, Earl of Gloucester.

Glover, Mistress (*fl.* 1141) (fict.). **Novels:** One of the 'cronies' of Dame Alice WEAVER, she attended St WINIFRED's festival at SHREWSBURY in June 1141.

Refs: **10** (8, 16).

Glyn Ceiriog, or Llansanffraid Glyn Ceiriog (Clwyd, Wales). This former quarrying village is attractively situated on the wooded hillside above the River CEIRIOG, 7 miles north-west of OSWESTRY and 5 miles west of CHIRK. The church, which stands high on the hillside overlooking the village, was rebuilt in the 18th C., and remodelled in the 19th. It is thought that the churchyard may have originally been circular. Glyn Ceiriog is also the name of the valley of the River Ceiriog.

Novels: In February 1141 OWAIN GWYNEDD was rumoured to be in the commote of CYNLLAITH or Glyn Ceiriog, keeping a watchful eye on RANULF of Chester.

Refs: **9** (2–3, 10).

Godefrid, Abbot (d. 1127) (hist.). Also spelled Godefred. He succeeded FULCHERED as abbot of SHREWSBURY ABBEY in 1120. Ordericus Vitalis says that both men 'were literate and religious pastors, and studied to educate the Lord's flock diligently for forty years'. Godefrid, however, was abbot for only seven of those years, for in 1127 he suddenly died. His successor was HERIBERT.

Novels: In November 1120, due to illness, Godefrid sent Heribert, who was then prior, on his behalf to the king's court at WOODSTOCK.

Refs: **12** (1); **RB** (1).

Godesbrond (*fl.* 1066) (hist.). Also spelled Godesbrand. There were ten recorded minters in SHREWSBURY during EDWARD THE CONFESSOR's reign, and probably there were many more. One of these was Godesbrond, who resided in the town and whose name also appears on coins in HAROLD II's short reign in 1066.

Novels: In May 1140 Hugh BERINGAR showed CADFAEL a silver penny, which had been found wedged in the bucket in Walter AURIFABER's well. It was a beautiful piece minted by Godesbrond in Shrewsbury: '"There are a few of his pieces to be found, but few indeed in the town where they were struck."'

Refs: **7** (11).

Godfrey of Bouillon (1060–1100), Duke of Lower Lorraine (*c.*1082–1100) (hist.). Second son of Eustace II, Count of BOULOGNE and of Ida, daughter of Godfrey II, Duke of Lower Lorraine. Godfrey was rewarded with the duchy in 1082, after proving his loyalty to the Holy Roman Emperor Henry IV in his German and Italian campaigns. A tall, well-built man, with fair hair and a beard, he joined the First Crusade in 1096 with his brothers, Eustace III, Count of Boulogne, and BALDWIN. He led one of the six armies, under BOHEMOND, which took ANTIOCH in 1098 after a long siege. On 13 January 1099, leaving Bohemond behind as self-proclaimed Prince of Antioch, the crusaders, under Godfrey, set out for JERUSALEM, which they laid siege to on 7 June and which fell on 15 July. Godfrey was proclaimed king, but chose instead to be called *Advocatus Sancti Sepulchri*, the dedicated defender of the Holy Sepulchre. The first ruler of Jerusalem, Godfrey died without an heir and was succeeded by his brother, Baldwin I, who assumed the title of king.

Novels: CADFAEL 'was with Godfrey de Bouillon at ANTIOCH, when the Saracens surrendered it' and was also 'in the crusade – with Godfrey of Bouillon at the siege of Jerusalem'.

Refs: **1** (1); **2** (3); **6** (15).

Godric. See BLUND, Godith.

Godric's Ford (Shropshire, England) (fict.). A cell of POLESWORTH ABBEY, the small grange of Benedictine nuns at Godric's Ford was situated beside a small tributary of the Rea Brook (see MEOLE BROOK), in the LONG FOREST 'some miles to the south-west' of SHREWSBURY. Although Godric's Ford never existed, its general location seems to be near the hamlet of Annscroft, midway between BAYSTON HILL and PONTESBURY.

Novels: 'The grange at Godric's Ford was a decent long, low house in a broad clearing, with a small wooden chapel beside it, and a high stone wall enclosing its well-kept kitchen garden and orchard of fruit trees.' In October 1139, after Huon de DOMVILLE's murder, Avice of Thornbury (see MAGDALEN, Sister) entered the Benedictine order at Godric's Ford as a novice. In February 1141, returning from the battle of LINCOLN, Welsh raiders attacked the nunnery and Elis ap CYNAN was taken prisoner. The following month, after a second attack, the raiders were defeated. Julian CRUCE was taken to Sister Magdalen at Godric's Ford after she was almost drowned in the River SEVERN in September 1141. Niall BRONZESMITH escorted Judith PERLE to Godric's Ford one night in June 1142.

Refs: **5** (8–10); **9** (1–2, 4, 8–9, 11, 13–15); **11** (14); **13** (1, 3, 8, 11–14).

Godstoke (now Stoke St Milborough) (Shropshire, England). DB – Godestoch: in Patton Hundred; held by St Milburga's Church itself (it was given to WENLOCK PRIORY by Roger de MONTGOMERY). The village of Stoke St Milborough shelters in a deep valley on the eastern slopes of the CLEE HILLS, 11 miles south-west of Bridgnorth (see BRIGGE) and 6 miles north-east of LUDLOW. It is named after St MILBURGA, the first abbess of Wenlock Priory. It is said that, while being chased by bloodhounds on the Clee Hills, the saint fell from her horse and, at the exact spot where she landed, a spring sprang out of the ground. Known as St Milburga's well, it became a small centre for pilgrimage and the settlement that grew up around it was called 'God's Stoke'. Stoke is derived from the Anglo-Saxon word for an inhabited place or village. There are two wells dedicated to the saint in Shropshire: one at Much WENLOCK and the other at Stoke St Milborough; the waters of the latter are reputed to be good for sore eyes. There was a church at Stoke St Milborough in the 7th C., and the present church, also dedicated to the saint, stands on the original Saxon site. In the Middle Ages the church had a number of dependent chapelries, including the one at Heath (see BOULDON) on the lower slopes of BROWN CLEE HILL.

Novels: 'Godstoke, sunk in its deep, wooded valley between the hills, was held by the priory of Wenlock, a third of the manor farmed in demesne, the rest leased out to life tenants, a prosperous settlement, and well-founded in stores and firing for the winter.' In December 1139 Sister HILARIA, together with Yves HUGONIN and Ermina Hugonin (see BRETAGNE), left FOXWOOD to cross over the Clee Hills towards Godstoke (or Stoke). Shortly after, CADFAEL visited the village in search of the missing party, but found that they had never reached it.

Refs: **6** (2–4, 6); **20** (2).

Goscelin (b. *c.*1095) (fict.) **Novels:** 'For all his mild, amiable and ornamental appearance, combed and curled and courtly, he was a big, well-set-up young fellow, with a set to his smooth jaw.' Squire of Roger MAUDUIT of SUTTON MAUDUIT, Goscelin was the secret lover of Lady Eadwina MAUDUIT, his lord's wife. In November 1120, after Mauduit had returned from a long absence overseas, Goscelin tried to murder him on the way to WOODSTOCK. Although CADFAEL was aware of Goscelin's deceit, he left Mauduit to work it out for himself.

Refs: **RB** (1).

Great Hanwood. See HANWOOD.

Great Ness. See NESSE.

Greenhamsted (now Miserden) (Gloucestershire, England). Also spelled Greenhamstead. DB – Grenhastede: in Bisley Hundred; land held by Erneis under Hascoit MUSARD. Some 7 miles north-west of CIRENCESTER, the COTSWOLD stone village lies on the wooded slopes of the Frome valley. In *c.*1300 it changed its name from Greenhamsted to Miserden, derived from the Musard family who held the manor from the Conquest until the reign of Edward I (1272–1307). (See La MUSARDERIE.) St Andrew's Church, drastically restored in the 19th C., is of late Anglo-Saxon origin. The great house in Misarden Park, on a hillside site overlooking the Golden Valley, was built in *c.*1616. Only the gardens are open to the public.

Novels: 'Beyond, the ground continued to rise steeply in complex folds and levels to a long crest above, where Cadfael could just distinguish above the trees the top of a church tower, and the occasional slope of a roof, marking the village of Greenhamsted.' 'King WILLIAM [I] gave the village to Hascoit Musard some time before the Domesday survey was taken.' Philip FITZROBERT, who took the castle from Robert MUSARD in 1145, left the church and village alone, 'provided neither priest nor reeve gets in his way'. The village was surrounded by a thick belt of woodland. During the siege of the castle in December of the same year, the Empress MAUD 'set up her court in the village' and took 'possession of the priest's house'; for the 'villagers of Greenhamsted fared rather well under the Musards, and felt no inclination at all to send warning to the present castellan of La Musarderie.' It was thought that a 'Musard might yet come back to Greenhamsted. Four generations had left family still acceptable to their neighbours.'

Refs: **20** (6–7, 9–15).

Gregory (b. *c.*1119) (fict.). **Novels:** 'Poor Gregory, who was strong and able of body but very dull of wit.' Servant of Thomas of BRISTOL, Gregory arrived at SHREWSBURY by barge with his master and Emma Vernold (see CORVISER) on 31 July 1139. He set out on the return journey to BRISTOL on 4 August with WARIN THE PORTER and Roger DOD.

Refs: **4** (1:3–4, 2:1–2, 3:1).

Gregory (*fl.* 1145) (fict.). **Novels:** Carter and villein of Eudo BLOUNT (the younger) of LONGNER, Gregory was a good twenty years older than his fellow carter, LAMBERT. In February 1145 Gregory, Lambert and ALDHELM delivered to SHREWSBURY ABBEY the promised load of wood for rebuilding RAMSEY ABBEY. While they were transferring the load to the larger abbey wagon, Brother RICHARD haled them away to help carry some of the abbey's threatened treasures out of the church and out of reach of the rising floodwaters. Unaware that St WINIFRED's reliquary had been placed on the Ramsey wagon, Gregory and Lambert 'hefted another load of timber aboard' and covered it completely. About a week later, after the loss of the reliquary had been discovered, CADFAEL rode out to Longner to talk to Gregory and Lambert: 'Square-built, muscular men both, and weatherbeaten from outdoor living in all seasons, with a good twenty years between them, so that they might have been father and son.' All they could tell him was that Aldhelm had helped an unknown 'close-cowled' brother (Brother TUTILO) 'move some last thing'. Both admitted that they would not recognise the monk, if they saw him again.

Refs: **19** (2–6, 12)

Gregory of Nyssa, Saint (*c.*335–*c.*395) (hist.) (f.d. 9 March). Born at Caesarea in Cappadocia (now Israel), he was the younger brother of St Basil the Great. Gregory was educated in Athens and, after his marriage to Theosebeia, he abandoned his profession as a teacher of rhetoric to become a monk. He was consecrated Bishop of Nyssa in *c.*371 by Basil. In 375 he was accused of maladministration, and the following year he was deposed and banished. Gregory regained his diocese in 378 and, after the death of his brother in 379, he came to the fore as an opponent of Arianism. He took a prominent part in the General Council at CONSTANTINOPLE in 381, and was recognised as the mainstay of orthodoxy throughout Cappadocia. He was one of the three great Cappadocians, the others being St Basil the Great and St Gregory of Nazianzus. He wrote many theological, philosophical and mystical works, and is considered to be a spiritual writer of great authority and depth.

Novels: 'They were past St Gregory and approaching St EDWARD THE CONFESSOR and St BENEDICT himself – the middle days of March, and the blessed works of spring beginning, with everything hopeful and striving ahead.'

Refs: **9** (8).

Gretton (Shropshire, England). DB – Grotintune: in Patton Hundred; a holding of Reginald the Sheriff under Roger de MONTGOMERY. Situated 4 miles north-east of Church STRETTON and some 10 miles south of SHREWSBURY, Gretton is a remote hamlet nestling on the eastern slopes of the Stretton Hills, above Ape Dale. Its nearest neighbour is the village of Cardington, half a mile to the west.

Novels: HARALD the runaway villein, who was taken prisoner by one of Hugh BERINGAR's sergeants in the LONG FOREST, originally came 'from some way south, by Gretton'.

Refs: **8** (9).

Griffin (b. 1127) (fict.). **Novels:** 'Offspring of a maid-servant and a passing tinker. He was well-grown, comely, of contented nature and good with his hands, but he was a simpleton.' Griffin was the locksmith's boy of Baldwin PECHE and, after the latter's death, of John BONETH from late May 1140. Griffin, a simpleton who had a 'gift for picking up practical skills', slept in the PECHE'S SHOP as a watchman. On the morning after Daniel AURIFABER's wedding feast, Griffin discovered a silver coin wedged in the bucket of the well and presented it to PECHE.

Refs: **7** (1–2, 6, 8, 11–12).

Griffith, Eliud ap (b. *c.*1120) (fict.). **Novels:** 'No mistake, the solemn youth could laugh, and laughter lit up his grave face and made his eyes sparkle. It was no blind love he had for his twin who was no twin, he knew him through and through, scolded, criticised, fought with him, and loved him none the less.' Son of Griffith ap MEILYR and foster-brother and cousin of Elis ap CYNAN, Eliud was born on the same day as Elis and was the elder by half an hour. In January 1141 he tried to dissuade Elis from going with CADWALADR to the battle of LINCOLN. The following month, Eliud was with OWAIN GWYNEDD, patrolling the Welsh border with Cheshire. CADFAEL met him at TREGEIRIOG. Eliud accompanied Einon ab ITHEL to SHREWSBURY with the injured prisoner, Sheriff Gilbert PRESTCOTE. While the sheriff was sleeping in SHREWSBURY ABBEY infirmary, Eliud suffocated him. By this action, he hoped that Elis would be detained in England, leaving himself free to marry CRISTINA, whom he had long loved. He and Elis were among those who remained at Shrewsbury under suspicion of the murder. After Elis had slipped out of SHREWSBURY CASTLE and broken his parole, Eliud was taken, under armed escort, to GODRIC'S FORD. Hurling himself between Elis and a loosed arrow, Eliud was struck under his right shoulder-blade. The arrow passed through his body and through the under-flesh of Elis's upper arm, pinning the two together. In the cell at Godric's Ford, Eliud confessed to Prestcote's murder. Before he could be brought for trial, Elis and Melicent Prestcote secretly drugged Eliud and sent him back into Wales in Elis's place. It is most probable that, despite his injuries, Eliud lived to marry Cristina.

Refs: **9** (2–15); **12** (1).

G

Griffith, Rhys ap. (See RHYS, Brother.)

Griffith ap Cynan (*c.*1055–1137), King of Gwynedd (hist.). Also spelled Gruffudd. Husband of ANGHARAD (d. 1162), and father of OWAIN GWYNEDD, Cadwallon and CADWALADR. Rightful heir to Gwynedd, he was born in exile among his Danish mother RAGNHILD's relations in DUBLIN. He was imprisoned in CHESTER Castle in 1087 by Hugh, Earl of Chester. In 1094, after his release, he led the Welsh revolt against the Normans, eventually driving them back towards the River DEE. In 1114, when the armies of HENRY I marched into Gwynedd, Griffith averted a battle by taking an oath of homage to the king. After paying an appropriate fine, Griffith was left in peace to consolidate his gains in North Wales. When he died – a feeble, blind old man – he was succeeded by Owain Gwynedd.

Novels: 'They set out as soon as the fine reliquary for the saint's bones was ready, polished oak ornamented with silver, to serve as proof what honours awaited WINIFRED in her new shrine. In the third week of May they came to BANGOR, and told their story to Bishop DAVID, who was sympathetic, and readily gave his consent to the proposed translation, subject only to the agreement of Prince OWAIN, who was regent of Gwynedd owing to the illness of the old king, his father.'

Refs: **1** (1–2).

Griffri, Anion ap (b. *c.*1114) (fict.). **Novels:** '"A good worker and honest . . . but a surly fellow and silent, and never forgets a benefit nor an injury."' Half-Welsh and half-English, Anion ap Griffri was the illegitimate son of Griffri ap LLYWARCH and half-brother of Griffri ap GRIFFRI. A lay servant and stockman at one of SHREWSBURY ABBEY's granges, Anion broke his leg in Autumn 1140 and was confined to the abbey infirmary. By February 1141 he was hobbling with the aid of crutches. Bearing a grudge against Sheriff Gilbert PRESTCOTE for having hanged his half-brother, Anion was one of those under suspicion for the sheriff's murder. The following month, having taken Einon ab ITHEL's gold pin from PRESTCOTE as a blood-payment, he fled to his father in Wales. CADFAEL noticed Anion at TREGEIRIOG, when Griffri ap Llywarch presented him to OWAIN GWYNEDD. The stockman was warmly acknowledged and admitted into his father's Welsh kinship.

Refs: **9** (4–5, 7–11).

Griffri, Griffri ap (*c.*1115–39) (fict.). **Novels:** 'Young Griffri had killed, yes, but in drink, in hot blood, and in fair fight man against man. He had died a worse death, turned off more casually than wringing a chicken's neck.' Legitimate son of Griffri ap LLYWARCH and half-brother of Anion ap GRIFFRI, Griffri ap Griffri arrived at SHREWSBURY from somewhere in MECHAIN in 1139 to sell his father's fleeces. While in Shrewsbury, in a drunken stupor, he became involved in a street brawl and knifed one of the town gatekeepers, killing him. Even though it was a fair fight, the Welshman was hanged by Sheriff Gilbert PRESTCOTE.

Refs: **9** (4–5, 9–10).

Guarin (*fl.* 1139) (fict.). **Novels:** 'Not one of the worst of them, this Guarin. Yves had taken the measure of many of those close about their chieftain, by this time, he knew those who took pleasure in hurting, in defiling, in making other human creatures writhe and abase themselves. And there were more than enough of them, but this Guarin was none.' Guarin was one of Alain le GAUCHER's band of outlaws, who raided the manors and farmsteads around TITTERSTONE CLEE in Winter 1139. Guarin was ordered to guard their captive, Yves HUGONIN, and told to threaten to kill him should any of the sheriff's men approach. After the robber fortress had fallen, he was either killed or among those captured and taken in chains to LUDLOW CASTLE to stand trial.

Refs: **6** (11).

Guildford (Surrey, England). This cathedral city and county capital lies in the valley of the River Wey, some 34 miles north-east of WINCHESTER. Dating back to at least Saxon times, when it was a river-crossing settlement, the town was first mentioned in a document of *c.*875 as Gyldeforda, meaning the 'golden ford'. Towards the end of the 11th C., the Normans built a motte-and-bailey castle on the site of an earlier fortification. The rectangular stone keep, now in ruins, was probably erected during the reign of King STEPHEN. During medieval times Guildford became a prosperous centre of the wool trade. St Mary's Church, near the castle, was originally built in Anglo-Saxon times, but rebuilt mainly from the 11th to 13th C. The medieval Pilgrim's Way, that led from Winchester to Canterbury, crossed the Wey just south of Guildford. Originally part of the diocese of Winchester, Guildford became a separate diocese in 1927.

Novels: In June 1141, at SHREWSBURY, Simeon POER claimed that he was a merchant of Guildford. In August it was rumoured that Queen MATILDA had met Bishop HENRY OF BLOIS in private at Guildford and managed to lure him back to Stephen's side.

Refs: **10** (5–7, 13–14); **11** (1).

Gunnar (*fl.* 1142) (fict.). **Novels:** 'A very self-assured and articulate person, this Gunnar, CADFAEL reflected, the very image of the intelligent and trusted servant of a commercial house, capable of adapting to travel, and learning from every experience.' Half-Danish and half-Saxon serving-man of Vivian and William HYNDE. While at the VESTIER household in June 1142, Gunnar heard about Judith PERLE's plans to visit SHREWSBURY ABBEY the following day. He told Vivian, and helped him abduct the widow near the English Bridge. She was taken by boat to HYNDE'S COUNTING HOUSE and locked inside.

Refs: **13** (5, 7–8, 10).

Gunnild (b. *c.*1108) (fict.). **Novels:** '"A bold, striding, black-eyed piece, thin and whippy as a withy."' Tirewoman of Pernel OTMERE and former strolling acrobat, tumbler and singer, Gunnild met BRITRIC THE PEDLAR in COVENTRY and travelled with him to Saint Peter's Fair at SHREWSBURY in Summer 1142. They lodged in RUALD's deserted croft in the POTTER'S FIELD at LONGNER. On 4 August Britric slipped away while she was asleep, taking all her valuables with him. Penniless, she barely managed to survive through the autumn months. But, in December, she was taken in by the Otmeres of WITHINGTON. Pernel, the eldest child, took a liking to her, and Gunnild was retained as her tirewoman. In November 1143, as soon as she heard that Britric was in prison, Gunnild went to Shrewsbury to prove him innocent of her murder. Later the same month, she attended Mass at SHREWSBURY ABBEY with Pernel.

Refs: **17** (6–12, 14).

G

Gurney, Edwin (b. 1124) (fict.). **Novels:** '"Edwin had been indulged, I fear, he was used to his freedom and having his own way, and he was for ever running off with Edwy, as he'd always been used to do. And Gervase held it against him that he ran with simple folk and craftsmen – he thought that low company, beneath a young man with a manor to inherit, and that was bound to anger Edwin, who loves his kin.' Son of Eward GURNEY and Richildis (see BONEL), younger brother of Sibil (see BELLECOTE), uncle of Edwy BELLECOTE and step-son of Gervase BONEL, Edwin Gurney became the heir to the Bonel manor of MALLILIE after his mother's second marriage in 1135. Falling out with his step-father, Edwin ran away to his sister and apprenticed himself to her husband, Martin BELLECOTE. He lived in SHREWSBURY with the family. Bonel decided to cut Edwin off from his inheritance and grant Mallilie to SHREWSBURY ABBEY. Bonel was murdered in December 1138, before the charter could be signed, and Edwin became the prime suspect. Learning from Edwy BELLECOTE that he was being sought by the sheriff, Edwin went into hiding.

With Edwy's and MEURIG's help, he managed to get away from Shrewsbury and find refuge with Ifor ap MORGAN, near LLANSILIN. CADFAEL discovered him there by accident and, inadvertently, led the sheriff's men to his door. Although Edwin was arrested and taken back to Shrewsbury, he was proven innocent and released. The agreement between Bonel and the abbey being void, Edwin inherited Mallilie. Being under age, however, RADULFUS became his guardian and also arranged for the manor to be managed by one of the abbey stewards. One of Edwin's first acts as lord of Mallilie was to give AELFRIC (*fl.* 1138) and ALDITH their freedom.

Refs: **3** (2–11).

Gurney, Eward (d. 1133) (fict.). **Novels:** 'A decent, solid man who had nothing of the vagus in him. A guildsman and counsellor of the town of SHREWSBURY, no less.' Guildsman and councillor of Shrewsbury, master-carpenter and carver, Eward Gurney was the first husband of Richildis Vaughan (see BONEL), whom he married in 1104. His children, Sibil and Edwin, were born in 1105 and 1124 respectively. After Eward's death, his journeyman, Martin BELLECOTE, took over the shop and business.

Refs: **3** (3); **RB** (1).

Gurney, Richildis. See BONEL, Richildis.

Gurney, Sibil. See BELLECOTE, Sibil.

Gwion (d. 1144) (fict.). **Novels:** 'Gwion, the last obstinate hostage, who would not forswear his absolute fealty to CADWALADR, sat silent among his peers, and enemies, some of whom, like Cuhelyn [ab EINION], had become his friends.' One of the lesser chiefs of CEREDIGION and liegeman of Cadwaladr, Gwion took no part in the murder of ANARAWD AP GRIFFITH, but was taken hostage by HYWEL AB OWAIN in 1143 to ensure that there should be no further resistance in Ceredigion. By May 1144 most of the hostages had been released, 'having sworn not to bear arms against Hywel's rule or offer service again to Cadwaladr, unless at some time to come he should pledge reparation and be restored'. Gwion, however, refused to forswear his allegiance to Cadwaladr or promise peace to Hywel. He, therefore, remained captive at ABER. While there, Gwion murdered Bledri ap RHYS to stop the latter from betraying him to OWAIN GWYNEDD. Although he had given his parole not to escape, Gwion left Aber to tell Bledri's wife of her husband's death. While there he was persuaded to gather a force of a hundred fighting men still loyal to Cadwaladr and attempt to drive the Danes out of Gwynedd. He was discovered by TURCAILL (*fl.* 1144) inside Cadwaladr's tent in Owain Gwynedd's camp. The Danes took Cadwaladr prisoner, but left Gwion behind, trussed up and gagged. Owain Gwynedd set him free, telling him to stay or go as he pleased, for his word was no longer valued. Gwion went with Hywel to Rhodri FÝCHAN (*fl.* 1144) at LLANBADARN to arrange for payment of Cadwaladr's ransom. While trying to rescue Cadwaladr from the Danes, Gwion was killed. Before he died he confessed to Bledri's murder.

Refs: **18** (3–5, 10–14).

Gwladus (*fl.* 1144) (hist.). She was the daughter of LLYWARCH AP TRAHAEARN, first wife of OWAIN GWYNEDD and mother of IORWERTH AB OWAIN and MAELGWN AB OWAIN.

Novels: Gwladus was the wife of Owain Gwynedd and daughter to a prince of ARWYSTLI. Her two sons, born in *c.*1134 and 1137, had her rich colouring.

Refs: **18** (10).

Gwynedd, King of. See Griffith ap CYNAN, King of Gwynedd.

Gwynedd, Prince of. See CADWALADR, Prince of Gwynedd.

Gwynedd, Regent of. See OWAIN GWYNEDD.

Gwyrfai, River or Afon (Gwynedd, Wales). Rising on the western slopes of Mount SNOWDON, near Llyn y Gader, this river enters the mile-long Llyn Cwellyn. After leaving the lake the river flows north-west to

Waunfawr before heading west to FORYD BAY and the MENAI STRAIT. On its 12 mile journey to the sea, the Gwyrfai passes the settlements of Betws Garmon and Bontnewydd.

Novels: The waters of the rivers CARROG and Gwyrfai unite in Foryd Bay before heading north into the Menai Strait, opposite ABERMENAI. TURCAILL (*fl.* 1144) sailed up the river, under cover of darkness, in May 1144 and successfully abducted CADWALADR from OWAIN GWYNEDD's camp.

Refs: **18** (10).

Gwytherin (Clwyd, Wales). This remote mountain village is situated at the head of the valley of the River CLEDWEN, 5 miles east of LLANRWST and just over 10 miles south of Colwyn Bay (or Bae Colwyn). St WINIFRED, who founded a convent at Gwytherin in the 7th C., was buried in the village. In 1137 (and not 1138 as some histories maintain) Prior ROBERT led an expedition of Benedictine monks from SHREWSBURY ABBEY to Gwytherin to acquire the sacred bones of the saint for their monastery. According to Prior Robert's 12th C. narrative (retold by Owen and Blakeway in *A History of Shrewsbury*, 1825), the cemetery at Gwytherin 'was distinct from that which is now used. It was filled with bodies of many other saints, and held in such reverence, that it was never entered without previous prayer. Any animal which grazes in it immediately drops down dead; and . . . a man endeavouring to cut off a small branch of holy oak which grows there, that he might tie the shoes which, after that country fashion, he had made of raw hide, with some of the inner bark, had soon cause to repent of his temerity. His axe stuck so fast in the tree that no one could move it; his arm became stiff, and immoveably fastened to the handle, nor could he obtain relief from his misery.' In the middle of the cemetery there was a small wooden church 'famed for its sanctity and miraculous cures, and the protection afforded to it by the holy virgin'. The present church of St Winifred stands on a different site to the earlier church mentioned by Prior Robert and was rebuilt in 1867–9. In the churchyard on the north side of the church are four 'pillar' stones dating from the 5th or early 6th C., one with a Latin inscription.

Novels: '"The parish stretches for several miles along the river valley, and a mile or more from the Cledwen on either bank. We do not congregate in villages as you English do. Land good for hunting is plentiful, but good tillage meagre. Every man lives where best suits him for working his fields and conserving his game." "It is a very fair place," said the sub-prior, and meant it, for the fold on fold of well-treed hills beyond the river made a pattern of spring beauty in a hundred different greens, and the water-meadows were strung like a necklace of emeralds along the fringes of silver and lapis-lazuli.' In May 1137 Prior Robert and his party journeyed to Gwytherin to acquire the sacred bones of St Winifred for Shrewsbury Abbey. Properties within the parish included: Father HUW's wooden house; RHISIART's hall; and CADWALLON's holding. A mile or more away from the 'small stone church, whitewashed and shimmering', stood the disused wooden church, containing St Winifred's chapel. The saint herself was buried in the old overgrown graveyard, near the east end of the chapel.

Refs: **1** (1–12); **5** (1); **10** (1, 3, 8); **12** (13); **16** (1); **17** (9); **18** (4); **19** (2–4, 9, 11).

G

H

Hales (now Sheriffhales) (Shropshire, England). DB – Halas: in Cuttlestone Hundred, Staffordshire, but part of the parish was transferred to Shropshire (to Bradford Hundred) soon after 1086; a holding of Reginald the Sheriff under Roger de MONTGOMERY. Sheriffhales derives the first part of its name from Reginald the Sheriff (or Reginald de Balliol) who came from Bailleul-en-Gouffern near Exmes in NORMANDY. Hales means 'a remote valley' or 'a place hidden in the fold of a hill'. The village lies towards the eastern edge of Shropshire, some 16 miles east of SHREWSBURY, 4 miles north-east of Telford and nearly 14 miles west of Cannock (see CHENET). St Mary's Church, in the oldest part of the village, dates from the 13th C. with later additions, including pillars and arches taken from the nearby ruins of LILLESHALL Abbey. Sheriffhales Manor lies to the west of the church and in the late 17th C. became an academy for those who were barred from the major universities because of their nonconformist beliefs.

Novels: 'The church lay a short distance from the manor, where two tracks crossed, and the huddle of village house-plots gathered close about the churchyard wall.' In March 1143 Brother HALUIN went on a penitential pilgrimage to Hales, accompanied by CADFAEL. It was Adelais de CLARY's favourite manor and, after her son, Audemar, had banished her from all his manors except Hales, became her 'hermitage'.

Refs: **15** (2–6, 12–14).

Hales, William (*fl.* 1141) (fict.). **Novels:** 'Master Simeon POER, self-styled merchant of GUILDFORD, was not at all ill-content with the pickings made in SHREWSBURY. In three nights, which was the longest they dared reckon on operating unsuspected, they had taken a fair amount of money from the hopeful gamblers of the town and [ABBEY] FOREGATE, besides the price Daniel AURIFABER had paid for the stolen ring, the various odds and ends William HALES had abstracted from market stalls, and the coins John SHURE had used his long, smooth, waxed finger-nails to extract from pocket and purse in the crowds. It was a pity they had had to leave William Hales to his fate during the raid, but all in all they had done well to get out of it with no more than a bruise or two, and one man short.' Claiming to be a farrier, William Hales appeared at SHREWSBURY ABBEY with John Shure and Walter BAGOT on 17 June 1141. Four days later, they (along with POER) were surprised by Hugh BERINGAR and his men while playing dice, loaded in their favour, under the arch of the English Bridge. All managed to escape, except Hales, who was captured and imprisoned in the castle; however, the others were later caught and brought back to Shrewsbury.

Refs: **10** (4, 6–8, 13).

Haluin, Brother (b. 1106) (fict.). **Novels:** 'Years of remorse and self-punishment had not exorcised the horror that still wrung his flesh and contorted his visage.' Father of Helisende VIVERS and Benedictine monk and priest of SHREWSBURY ABBEY, Brother Haluin was Brother ANSELM's 'best illuminator' and 'lifelong penitent'. Haluin came from a 'landed family' and was heir to a 'good manor'. He was sent to HALES in 1120 as clerk to Bertrand de CLARY, 'being uncommonly bright at learning and figuring.' While his lord was absent in the HOLY LAND, Haluin fell in love with his daughter, Bertrade (see VIVERS). They made love and she conceived their child, Helisende. Adelais de CLARY refused to allow them to marry. Instead, Haluin was dismissed from her service. He entered the abbey as a novice in 1124, assisting CADFAEL in the herb garden until 1127. While there, Adelais persuaded him to give her a potion to provide the means of abortion. Later, she lied, informing him that mother and child were dead. For seventeen years Haluin suffered terrible remorse and self-punishment for his action. From 1127 to 1129, he worked at the Hospital of ST GILES 'among the sick and crippled'. And, before he entered the scriptorium in 1131, he laboured in the gardens of the GAYE and helped with the sheep at RHYDYCROESAU. In December 1142, while working on the roof of the abbey guest-hall, Haluin slipped and fell, seriously injuring himself. Regaining consciousness, he confessed to having given Adelais the potion which killed his lover and their child. He received absolution. Although he was not expected to live, he made a miraculous recovery. The fall, however, left him a lifelong cripple. In March 1143 Haluin, accompanied by Cadfael, set out on a penitential journey to Hales, vowing to spend a night's vigil before the tomb of Bertrade. His journey took him to ELFORD and VIVERS. At FAREWELL Abbey, to his wonder and joy he discovered Bertrade and Helisende alive and well. In June 1143 he was still working in the scriptorium, doing 'good work' with his pens and brushes.

Refs: **15** (1–4); **16** (9, 11)

Hammet, Dame Diota (b. *c.*1101) (fict.). **Novels:** 'A comely, well-kept woman . . . with decent black clothing befitting a priest's house-keeper, and a dark shawl over her neat, greying hair.' Widow of John HAMMET, Dame Diota Hammet was in the service of Ninian BACHILER's mother before her marriage, and became the boy's devoted nurse. Diota's own child had been born dead. After her husband's death in *c.*1138, Bishop HENRY OF BLOIS found her a place as house-keeper to Father AILNOTH. In 1141, the fugitive Ninian sought out her help. She persuaded Ailnoth to let Ninian (calling himself Benet) join them on their journey north to SHREWSBURY, where they arrived on

H

10 December. Ninian was found employment at SHREWSBURY ABBEY and, when Diota visited him on 22 December, he gave her a letter to deliver to Ralph GIFFARD the elder. At Giffard's town house, Diota revealed Ninian's whereabouts to Sanan BERNIÈRES. On the night of 24 December, Diota followed Ailnoth to the mill pond and begged him not to unmask Ninian. He struck her with his staff, knocking her to the ground. Trying to fend off further blows she grabbed the staff, loosed it and somehow managed to flee back to the house. Unknown to her, the priest toppled backwards, hit his head on a tree, fell into the water and drowned. The following morning, having waited in vain for her master to return, Diota went to the abbey to enquire after his whereabouts. CADFAEL noticed the bruises on her forehead and the grazes on the palm of her hand. He insisted on dressing them. After it became apparent that Ailnoth's death was an accident, Diota was allowed to remain in the house until a new priest was appointed. Abbot RADULFUS promised that whatever happened the Church would not abandon her.

Refs: **12** (2–13).

Hammet, John (d. *c.*1138) (fict.). Husband of Dame Diota HAMMET, he was a groom in the service of Bishop HENRY OF BLOIS.

Refs: **12** (2, 6).

Hampshire Downs (Hampshire, England) Part of the extensive rolling, chalk uplands that stretch across most of Southern England, the Hampshire Downs lie to the north of ANDOVER and WINCHESTER. Sweeping across the southern border of Berkshire, they possess some of the highest chalk hills in England. Like the SOUTH DOWNS, the uplands contains numerous prehistoric remains.

Novels: 'North-west along the STOCKBRIDGE road and wavering over the rising downs, the glittering halo of dust rolled and danced, spreading wider as it receded.' The army of the Empress MAUD fled north-west across the Hampshire Downs from WINCHESTER in September 1141.

Refs: **11** (6).

Hampton (now Wolverhampton) (West Midlands, England). DB – Hantone: in Seisdon Hundred; land held by the canons of Wolverhampton from Samson, Chaplain to WILLIAM I and later Bishop of WORCESTER. The so-called 'Capital of the Black Country', Wolverhampton is a large industrial town some 13 miles north-west of Birmingham city centre. Hampton is derived from the Old English word meaning 'high farm'; for the town stands on ground higher than that to the north, west and east. At one time, Wolverhampton was called Wolvrenehamptonia, after Wulfrun (or Wulfruna), the sister of Edgar, King of Mercia. In 994 she refounded a monastery on the site of the present St Peter's Church. The red-sandstone church dates from the 13th C., when Wolverhampton was a prosperous wool town. In the churchyard is a round-shafted, stone cross, dating probably from the mid-9th C.

Novels: In March 1142 Brother HALUIN and CADFAEL, travelling from FAREWELL to SHREWSBURY, 'halted for the night at HARGEDON, where the canons of Hampton had a grange'.

Refs: **15** (14).

Hanwood (or Great Hanwood) (Shropshire, England). DB – Hanewde: in Rhiwset Hundred; a holding of Roger, Son of Corbet, under Roger de MONTGOMERY. Great Hanwood is a residential village some 4 miles south-west of SHREWSBURY, straddling the Rea Brook (see MEOLE BROOK). St Thomas the Apostle's Church, which was rebuilt and enlarged in the mid-19th C., has a Norman font.

Novels: 'In the parcel of old forest north and west of the hamlet of Hanwood there were groves where stray outlaws could find ample cover, provided they stayed clear of the few settlements within reach. Local people tended to fence their holdings and band together to protect their own small ground. The forest was for plundering, poaching, pasturing of swine, all with secure precautions.'

Refs: **9** (13); **10** (13)

Harald (*fl.* 1140) (fict.). **Novels:** '"Not from these parts, some runaway living rough, a poor starving wretch, swears he's never done worse than steal a little bread or an egg to keep himself alive, but the foresters say he's taken their deer in his time. Thin as a fence-pole, and in rags, a desperate case."' Harald had a name that 'once belonged to a king' (see HAROLD II). Runaway villein and farrier from nearby GRETTON, Harald failed in an attempt to avenge the rape of his sister by his lord's steward, and ran away in about August 1140. In November he was living wild in the LONG FOREST, stealing food to survive. He was captured and taken to SHREWSBURY CASTLE. Because Peter CLEMENCE's dagger was found in his possession, Harald became a possible suspect for the envoy's murder. In fact, he had found the weapon in a charcoal-burner's hearth. He was fed and kept warm at the castle, and gradually regained his weight and strength. After his release, he was found employment with a farrier on the town side of the Western Bridge. He became a free man at the end of 1141, after working in the borough for a year and a day.

Refs: **8** (9–11, 13).

Harcourt. See HARPECOTE.

Hardwicke (Gloucestershire, England). Not far from the River SEVERN, in the fertile Vale of Gloucester, 4 miles south-west of GLOUCESTER, Hardwicke contains a number of thatched half-timbered cottages. Like others in the vale, the village was noted in the 18th C. for making 'excellent cheese, and stout cider' (*A New History of Gloucestershire*, Samuel Rudder, 1779). St Nicholas's Church, standing on 12th C. foundations, is mainly 13th C., but was much altered in the 19th C.

Novels: The unnamed cottar, with a woodland holding near DEERHURST, had 'a son married and settled in Hardwicke'.

Refs: **20** (6).

Harefoot, Warin (fl. 1140) (fict.). **Novels:** '"He likes to curry favour with everyone, but that's by way of his trade. A rough-tongued pedlar would not sell many tapes and laces."' Pedlar, packman and travelling haberdasher, Warin Harefoot stayed in the guest-hall at SHREWSBURY ABBEY in Spring 1140. He discovered the money stolen from William REDE sewn into a corner of Jacob of BOULDON's straw pallet. After handing it over to the law, he expected a reward.

Refs: **RB** (3).

Hargedon (now Hatherton) (Staffordshire, England). DB – Hargedone: in Cuttlestone Hundred; land of the clergy of Wolverhampton. Some 28 miles directly east of SHREWSBURY, the hamlet of Hatherton lies just beyond the western outskirts of Cannock (see CHENET) and little more than a mile from the town centre.

Novels: In March 1142 Brother HALUIN and CADFAEL travelled from FAREWELL to Shrewsbury, and stopped for the night at Hargedon, where the canons of HAMPTON had a grange.

Refs: **15** (14).

Harnage, Nicholas (*fl.* 1141) (fict.). **Novels:** 'A neatly-made young man, on a good horse, with an easy seat in the saddle and a light hand on the rein, and a bush of wiry dark hair above a bold, blunt-featured face.' Commander, seasoned crusader and soldier under FITZROBERT, Nicholas Harnage was heir to 'two good manors' from his father and also 'some lands' from his mother. In the service of Godfrid Marescot (see HUMILIS, Brother), he sailed from England to join his lord in the HOLY LAND. He fought against the musselmen of MOSUL. After Godfrid had been severely injured, Nicholas accompanied him home. In 1138 Nicholas was sent to LAI to inform Humphrey CRUCE and his daughter, Julian, that Godfrid was unable to keep his marriage compact. While there, Nicholas was struck by the girl; nor could he forget her. With Godfrid's commendation, he found service with FitzRobert, on the side of King STEPHEN. In August 1141 the troops under Nicholas's command were with the army of Queen MATILDA at WINCHESTER. During a lull in the fighting and after his men had burned ANDOVER, Nicholas rode north intending to ask Cruce for his daughter's hand in marriage. First he went to SHREWSBURY ABBEY to see his former lord. With Godfrid's blessing and consent, Nicholas travelled to Lai where he heard that Humphrey was dead and that Julian had taken the veil at WHERWELL Abbey in August 1138. At SHREWSBURY, in September 1141, Nicholas not only learned that the forces of the Empress MAUD had attacked the town of Wherwell, but also that the abbey church had been burned to the ground. Fearing for Julian's safety, he sped south to try and find her. He was unable to locate Julian at Wherwell or Winchester. Following a suggestion, Nicholas rode to ROMSEY ABBEY and learned from the prioress that no one answering Julian's description had ever reached Wherwell, let alone taken the veil there. All that he could ascertain was that she had disappeared between Andover and Wherwell. He returned north to tell Humilis and Reginald Cruce the dismal news. After long, painstaking enquiries, Nicholas eventually discovered the truth about Julian: that she was alive, and that she had taken the cowl disguised as a dumb boy to be with Humilis. Not long after she had returned to Lai, Nicholas travelled north at her invitation to see her.

Refs: **11** (3–14).

Harold II (*c.*1022–66), King of England (1066) (hist.). Also spelled Harald. Also called Harold Godwinian or Godwineson. The last Saxon king, he was the son of Godwin, Earl of Wessex, and his wife, Gytha. Harold became the Earl of East Anglia in *c.*1044. In 1051 EDWARD THE CONFESSOR drove Godwin and his family into exile, but the following year Harold and Godwin returned to England and forced Edward to return the lands he had given away. After Godwin's death in 1053, Harold succeeded to his father's earldoms, and became the most powerful ruler in England, second only to the king. When the king died in 1066, it was Harold who succeeded to the throne, rather than Edward's promised heir, William, Duke of Normandy (see WILLIAM I). Immediately, Harold was threatened with the rivalry of two royal claimants: William and Harald Hardrada, King of Norway. Harold's brother, Tostig, who had by then become his bitterest enemy, joined forces with Harold Hardrada and invaded England in September, but they were defeated and killed at the battle of Stamford Bridge, near York. A few days later, the Normans invaded, landing at Pevensey on the south coast. On 14 October, at the battle of Senlac Hill, near Hastings, Harold and his two brothers, Gyrth and Leofwine, were killed.

Novels: '"HARALD, my lord. I'm named Harald." The large frame produced a skeletal sound, deep but dry and remote. He had a cough that perforated his speech uneasily, and a name that had once belonged to a king, and that within the memory of old men still living, men of his own fair colouring.'

Refs: **8** (9).

Harpecote (now Harcourt) (Shropshire, England). DB – Hauretescote: in Hodnet Hundred, a holding of William Pantulf under Roger de MONTGOMERY. Harcourt is a tiny hamlet sited on rising ground to the east of the River RODEN, some 9 miles north-east of SHREWSBURY and 4 miles south-east of WEM. On the opposite side of the river, just over 1 mile to the south-west, is the village of Moreton Corbet and the ruins of a medieval castle. Overshadowing the remains of the Norman fortress, and incorporating parts of it; is the shell of a stately mansion, started in the late 16th C. and never finished. It was begun hy Robert Corbet who, it is said, was inspired to build it after returning from a trip to Italy. A Royalist stronghold, the house and castle were besieged by the Parliamentarians during the Civil War and, in consequence, both were extensively damaged. The square castle keep dates from about 1200. Moreton Corbet Castle is open daily throughout the year.

Novels: 'The manor of Harpecote lay in open plain, with a small coppiced woodland on the windward side, and a low ridge of common land to the south.' In 1141 Harpecote was one among several manors held by the CRUCE family of LAI. Edric HERIET, a free tenant, lived with his family in the hamlet.

Refs: **11** (4, 7–8).

Hatherton. See Hargedon.

Haughmond Abbey (Shropshire, England). DB – Uptune: in Wrockwardine Hundred; a holding of Reginald the Sheriff under Earl Roger de MONTGOMERY (the abbey was founded in the half a league of woodland recorded in the Norman survey as being adjacent to UPTON Magna). The extensive ruins of Haughmond Abbey are situated some 3 miles north-east of SHREWSBURY and beneath the wooded north-western slopes of Haughmond Hill. The abbey was founded in *c.*1135 by William FITZALAN for a community of Augustinian canons, and considerably rebuilt as it prospered. Apart from the doorway leading to the western range of the cloister, all that remains of the 12th C. abbey church are the foundations. The chapter house, with its three magnificent carved arches, dates from the late 12th C. The abbey is sited close to Haughmond Hill, and the lower courses of some of the walls on the eastern side are hewn out of solid rock. After its dissolution in 1539, the church and many of the monastic buildings were demolished. Most of the rest were incorporated into a private house, which was burnt down during the Civil War. Haughmond Abbey belongs to English Heritage and is open to the public.

Novels: 'Saint Peter's Fair of that year, 1143, was one week past . . . when Brother MATTHEW the cellarer first brought into chapter the matter of business he had been discussing for some days during the Fair with the prior of the Augustinian priory of Saint JOHN THE EVANGELIST, at Haughmond, about four miles to the north-east of Shrewsbury. Haughmond was a FitzAlan foundation.' In June 1143 Jevan of LYTHWOOD was expecting a canon of Haughmond to visit his workshop and place an order with him for vellum. In September 1143 SHREWSBURY ABBEY acquired the POTTER'S FIELD after an exchange of land with Haughmond Priory. The prior at Haughmond has regular correspondence with one of the canons of CIRENCESTER ABBEY.

Refs: **16** (6); **17** (1, 3–7, 9, 14); **20** (13).

H

Haughton (Shropshire, England). DB – Haustone: in Wrockwardine Hundred; a holding of Roger Hunter under Roger de MONTGOMERY. Haughton is a scattered farming hamlet, nearly 5 miles north-east of SHREWSBURY and on the northern slopes of Haughmond Hill. The little stream which runs down through the hamlet is a feeder of the River RODEN, itself a tributary of the River TERN.

Novels: The land which SHREWSBURY ABBEY exchanged with Haughmond Priory for the POTTER'S FIELD lay 'some mile and a half beyond Haughton', and was 'bounded on all sides by land gifted to the priory. See HAUGHMOND ABBEY.

Refs: **17** (1).

Heath Chapel. See BOULDON.

Hebe (myth.). In Greek mythology, she was the beautiful daughter of Zeus (see JOVE) and Hera, and wife of Hercules. Hebe was the goddess of youth. It is claimed that after exposing herself indecently, she was replaced as cup-bearer to the gods by GANYMEDE.

Refs: **2** (5).

Heledd (b. *c.*1126) (fict.). **Novels:** 'For there was no question but this Heledd, with her gown frayed at the sleeve and crumpled by sleeping in a scooped hollow of sand lined with grass, and her hair unbraided and loose about her shoulders in a mane of darkness burnished into blue highlights by the sun, and her feet as often as not bare in the warm sand and the cool shallows along the seaward shore, was perceptibly closer to pure beauty than she had ever been before, and could have wreaked havoc in most young men's lives here had she been so minded.' Welsh daughter of Canon MEIRION, Heledd greeted Deacon MARK and CADFAEL on their arrival at Llanelwy (see ST ASAPH) in May 1144. A hindrance to her father's advancement in the church, because she was a reminder of a marriage Bishop GILBERT said was unlawful, MEIRION and OWAIN GWYNEDD arranged for her to marry Ieuan ab IFOR of ANGLESEY. Bishop Gilbert wanted to send her to a convent in England to become a nun. Heledd was unwilling to accept either option, and while at ABER, on the way to meet her bridegroom, she ran away. Although Cadfael found her near NONNA's hermitage, south-west of BANGOR, they were both captured by a raiding party of Danes under TURCAILL (*fl.* 1144). She was rescued from the Danish camp by Ieuan ab Ifor. After the Danish fleet had sailed, Heledd returned alone to the dunes. Without prior arrangement, and superbly sure of each other, TURCAILL appeared in his dragon ship and took her away with him to DUBLIN, where they were married.

Refs: **18** (2–14).

Hencot (now Hencott) (Shropshire, England). DB – not mentioned by name but in SHREWSBURY Hundred; a holding of ST ALKMUND'S CHURCH. Hencott is a small hamlet, less than 2 miles north of Shrewsbury, beside the railway line to WREXHAM. To the east are the sprawling suburbs of northern Shrewsbury and to the west Berwick House, built in 1731 for one of the Powys family.

Novels: '"Brother CADFAEL, I think you have need of a helper, and here is a youngster who says he's not afraid of hard work. A good woman of the town has brought him in to the porter, and asked that he be taken and taught as a lay servant. Her nephew from Hencot, she says, and his parents dead."' The 'good woman' was Petronilla FLESHER. 'Her nephew from Hencot' was in fact Godith Adeney (see BLUND), in disguise as the boy Godric. This happened in August 1138.

Refs: **2** (1).

Henley (Shropshire, England). DB – not mentioned by name but Acton (Scott) in Leintwardine Hundred; a holding of Aldred under Roger de MONTGOMERY. Henley is a small village in Ape Dale, nestling between WENLOCK Edge and the Stretton Hills, 9 miles north-west of LUDLOW and 3 miles south of Church STRETTON. Less than 1 mile to the north is Acton Scott.

Novels: '"It seems one of [Josce de] DINAN's archers has an old father at a hamlet south of Henley, a free tenant holding from MORTIMER."' In 1139 the tenanted farmstead of Reyner DUTTON, near Henley, belonged to BROMFIELD Priory.

Refs: **6** (2, 5).

Henry, Brother (*fl.* 1138) (fict.). **Novels:** Benedictine monk of SHREWSBURY ABBEY, he objected to Abbot HERIBERT's demotion in December 1138, and attended the funeral of Father AILNOTH on 1 January 1142.

Refs: **3** (1); **12** (11).

Henry I (1068–1135), King of England (1100–35) (hist.). Also called Henry Beauclerc, or Good Scholar. Youngest son of WILLIAM I and father of the Empress MAUD, he was crowned King of England at WESTMINSTER in 1100, a few days after the death of his brother, WILLIAM II. Henry's eldest brother, ROBERT, Duke of Normandy, who was the rightful heir to the English throne, was in JERUSALEM at the time. Henry married MATILDA, daughter of MALCOLM III, King of Scotland, in 1100, and she gave him a son WILLIAM THE AETHELING, and a daughter, Maud. Henry was, however, the father of a large number of illegitimate children by many mistresses, including ROBERT, Earl of Gloucester. Robert of Normandy invaded England in 1101 with a considerable force, and many of the great Norman barons rallied to his side. Although the two armies met at Alton, near WINCHESTER, Henry and Robert negotiated a peaceful settlement: in return for paying his brother a pension of £2,000 a year and renouncing all claims to land in NORMANDY (except Domfront), Henry was allowed to keep the crown of England. Once Robert had returned to Normandy, Henry set about strengthening his realm by removing any threat of either rebellion or invasion. One by one he confiscated the lands of the prominent Normans who had opposed him. But Henry was not content just to assert his royal authority, he was also determined to take Normandy from his brother. In 1106, at the battle of Tinchebrai, Robert was captured and imprisoned for the remaining twenty-eight years of his life. Although Henry had successfully removed the main threat to his authority and power, the wars in Normandy dragged on intermittently for years. He married his daughter, Maud, to Emperor HENRY V in 1114, and groomed his only legitimate son, William, to be his successor. By 1120 Henry had married William to Matilda, daughter of FULK, Count of Anjou, and forced LOUIS VI, King of France, to accept a definitive peace. On 25 November 1120, after four years' absence, Henry set sail from BARFLEUR for England. Disaster followed shortly after. The *White Ship* (see BLANCHE NEF), carrying William and many young nobles, foundered and sank shortly after leaving port. Henry was left without an heir. Queen Matilda had died in 1118, and in 1121 Henry married Adelaide (or Adela) of Louvain, but she was unable to give him children. His only legitimate daughter, Maud, was summoned back to England after her husband's death in 1125, and Henry made his barons acknowledge her as his heir. Three years later, in order to form an alliance with Fulk of Anjou, Henry forced her to marry the count's fifteen-year-old son and heir, GEOFFREY of Anjou. When Henry died on 1 December 1135 at Lyons-la-Forêt in Normandy, his favourite nephew, STEPHEN, rushed to England, seized the throne and had himself crowned king at Westminster within the month. This action was to herald the start of a long civil war for the crown of England between Stephen and Maud.

Novels: 'The King's court was in no hurry to return to England, that late autumn of 1120, even though the fighting, somewhat desultory in these last stages, was long over, and the enforced peace sealed by a royal marriage. King Henry had brought to a successful conclusion his sixteen years of patient, cunning, relentless plotting, fighting and manipulating, and could now sit back in high content, master not only of England but of Normandy, too. What the Conqueror had misguidedly dealt out in two separate parcels to his elder sons, his youngest son had now put together again and clamped into one. Not without a hand in removing from the light of day, some said, both of his brothers, one of whom had been shovelled into a hasty grave under the tower at Winchester, while the other was now a prisoner in DEVIZES, and unlikely ever to be seen again by the outer world . . . The court could well afford to linger to enjoy victory, while Henry trimmed into neatness the last loose edges still to be made secure. But his fleet was already preparing at Barfleur for the voyage back to England, and he would be home before the month ended.' In November 1120 Henry I set sail from Barfleur for England. His only son and heir, William the Aetheling, put to sea late in the *Blanche Nef* and was drowned when the ship sank. At his Christmas court in 1126, Henry made all the magnates of his realm acknowledge Maud as his heir; a pledge repeated before he died in 1135.

Refs: **2** (1, 8); **8** (1); **10** (2); **12** (1–2); **14** (9); **19** (4); **20** (3–4, 13, 15); **RB** (1).

Henry II (1133–89), King of England (1154–89) (hist.). Also called Henry Plantagenet, Henry of Anjou, Henry FitzEmpress or Henry Curtmantle. Eldest son of the Empress MAUD and GEOFFREY, Count of Anjou, Henry Plantagenet was born at Le Mans, MAINE, on 5 March 1133, and married Eleanor of Aquitaine, the divorced wife of LOUIS VII, King of France, in 1152. Henry invaded England the following year and, after nine months of fighting, reached an agreement whereby STEPHEN would remain king for life, and after his death Henry would succeed to the throne. The first Plantagenet king of England, Henry strengthened and enlarged his vast dominions, and in England brought about lasting reforms in the fields of finance, justice and administration. He is perhaps best known for his friendship with Thomas à Becket, Archbishop of Canterbury. Becket subsequently became his enemy and was murdered in CANTERBURY Cathedral in 1170 by four of Henry's knights.

Novels: In late 1142 Henry was sent over to England by his father in the care of ROBERT of Gloucester. Although Maud had appealed for support from her husband, his only response was to send their nine-year-old son. Both CADFAEL and Hugh BERINGAR made some perceptive comments about this boy who would become king at the age of twenty-one, Cadfael observing: 'No doubt . . . we shall hear more of this Henry Plantagenet who's minding his lessons and biding his time in BRISTOL.'

Refs: **12** (2); **15** (1); **16** (1); **19** (5, 11); **20** (3–4).

Henry V (1081–1125), Holy Roman Emperor (1106-25) (hist.). Son of the Emperor Henry IV, and his first wife, Bertha of Turin, he was crowned joint King of Germany with his father in 1099, after his elder brother, Conrad, was deposed for rebelling against the emperor. During the conflict between the papacy and the emperor in 1104, Henry formed an alliance with Bavarian nobles and revolted against his father. The emperor was captured and imprisoned, and Henry forced him to abdicate in 1105. Although Henry IV died in 1106, his son was not crowned emperor until 1111, when Pope Paschal II was imprisoned and forced to grant the right of investiture. In 1110 Henry was betrothed to MAUD, daughter of HENRY I, King of England, and in the following year they were married. Throughout his reign as emperor, Henry was in conflict with the Church. Supporting his wife's claim to the throne of England, he became involved in the conflict between the English and the French. The last of the Salian dynasty, Henry was succeeded after his death by his former enemy Lothair, Duke of Saxony, who became Emperor Lothair II.

Refs: **12** (1–2); **20** (3–4, 13).

Henry of Blois (*c.*1099–1171), Bishop of Winchester (hist.). Also called Monk of Cluny or Abbot of Glastonbury. Fourth son of Stephen, Count of Blois, by Adela, daughter of WILLIAM I. Henry was the younger brother of King STEPHEN and THEOBALD OF NORMANDY, Count of Blois. He was brought up and educated in the monastery of CLUNY, and in 1126 his uncle, HENRY I, made him Abbot of GLASTONBURY. Although he was consecrated Bishop of Winchester in 1129 at CANTERBURY, he was granted permission (by both pope and king) to retain his abbacy, which he held until his death. In December 1135, with Henry's powerful support, Stephen was able to seize the English throne and crown himself King. In 1136 Henry founded the Hospital of St Cross at WINCHESTER, but very little remains of the original building; he also built a number of castles, including those at Bishop's Waltham, Farnham, Taunton and WOLVESEY. Henry was denied the archbishopric of CANTERBURY in 1138 by Pope INNOCENT II, largely due to the hostility of BERNARD OF CLAIRVAUX, and THEOBALD OF BEC was elected in his stead. Henry's appointment as papal legate in England on 1 March 1139, however, gave him powers superior to those of the Archbishop of Canterbury. In September 1139, while Stephen was besieging the Empress MAUD in ARUNDEL CASTLE, it is reputed that Henry persuaded the king to let the empress join her half-brother, ROBERT of Gloucester, at BRISTOL. It was Henry, together with Waleran de BEAUMONT, Count of Meulan, who escorted her to safety. His attempts to negotiate a peaceful settlement between the two rival claimants to the throne failed. After Stephen's capture at the battle of LINCOLN on 2 February 1141, Henry swore fealty to Maud on the promise that she would leave all ecclesiastical matters in his hands. On the 8 April at the Council of Winchester, the empress was formally elected queen with the bishop's support. The two quarrelled, however, and Henry transferred his allegiance back to Stephen. In August Maud marched on Winchester with a large army and besieged Henry in Wolvesey Castle. In retaliation, the bishop ordered the town to be fired. Among the buildings destroyed were: the royal palace built by William I; HYDE ABBEY; and the Nunnaminster. Maud was forced to retreat when she found herself besieged in turn by the forces of Queen MATILDA and, during the flight, Robert of Gloucester was captured. On 7 December, soon after Stephen's release, Henry held a legatine-council at WESTMINSTER to formally recognise the king's restoration. Henry was with Stephen at the battle of WILTON in 1143; both barely managed to make good their escape. On the death of Pope INNOCENT II on 24 September 1143, Henry ceased to be papal legate. Although he urged the new pope to renew his legatine commission, Celestine II granted it to Archbishop Theobald of Bec. Further attempts by Henry to regain the office failed, and by 1147 he found his influence in ROME had come to an end, for the pope, Eugenius III, and Bernard of Clairvaux favoured Theobald. In 1155, after Stephen's death, Henry secretly shipped his treasure out of the country and, without the permission of HENRY II, went to Cluny. In retaliation, the king seized the bishop's castles, destroying those at Bishop's Waltham and Merdon, and demolishing the tower of Wolvesey. While at Cluny, Henry proved to be a great benefactor to the abbey, using some of his wealth to pay off all its debts. He returned to England, probably in 1157, and in 1162 consecrated Thomas à Becket as Archbishop of Canterbury. In *c.*1168 he gave away much of his wealth to charity, leaving himself the bare minimum means of subsistence. He died at Winchester and was buried before the high altar in the cathedral.

Novels: 'It was no effort to imagine him. Henry of Blois, bishop of Winchester, papal legate, younger brother and hitherto partisan of King Stephen, impregnably ensconced in the chapter house of his own cathedral, secure master of the political pulse of England, the cleverest manipulator in the kingdom, and on his own chosen ground – and yet hounded on to the defensive, in so far as that could ever happen to so expert a practitioner. Hugh had never seen the man, never been near the region where he ruled, had only heard him described, and yet could see him now, presiding with imperious composure over his half-unwilling assembly. A difficult part he had to play, to extricate himself from his known allegiance to his brother, and yet preserve his face and his status and influence with those who had shared it. And with a tough, experienced woman narrowly observing his every word, and holding in reserve her own new powers to destroy or preserve, according to how he managed his ill-disciplined team in this heavy furrow.' Younger brother of Stephen and Theobald of Normandy, cousin of Maud, nephew of Henry I, papal-legate and Bishop of Winchester, Henry of Blois was the ambitious rival of Theobald of Bec, Archbishop of Canterbury, and one of Stephen's best allies. In July 1139 the king 'affronted, attacked and gravely offended the Church in the persons of certain of its bishops' and turned Henry against him. After the empress landed near ARUNDEL on 30 September, Henry was torn between kin, sympathising with both sides in their claim to the throne of England. His attempts to negotiate a peaceful settlement, which included talks with Louis VII, King of France, and his brother, Theobald, came to nothing. In September 1140 Henry sent Peter CLEMENCE north to CHESTER to make sure of RANULF of Chester's and William of ROUMARE's support for Stephen. After Stephen's capture at the battle of Lincoln in February 1141, Henry transferred his allegiance to Maud. He confirmed his support for the empress at a legatine-council held at Winchester on 7 April. As soon as he discovered that CIARAN had murdered Rainald BOSSARD, Henry banished him to DUBLIN, sentencing him to walk barefoot all the way, while wearing a heavy cross round his neck. In June the bishop sent Olivier de BRETAGNE north to try and persuade all sheriffs, including Hugh BERINGAR, to transfer their allegiance to Maud. When Maud was driven out of LONDON in June 1141, Henry withdrew his allegiance and in August he was besieged in Wolvesey Castle by the empress's forces. In retaliation, he set fire to the city. In September, after the 'Rout of Winchester', Henry was unable to help Nicholas HARNAGE in his search for Julian CRUCE's missing valuables. Henry summoned a legatine-council at Westminster on 7 December, to formally bring the Church back into full allegiance to Stephen. When he 'achieved the bishopric' of Winchester, Henry received from the *sortes Biblicae*: '"something from MATTHEW, concerning the latter days when false prophets would multiply among us. Something to the effect that if any man should claim: Here is Christ! do not believe him."' (Matthew 24:23–24.) Henry was one of the three bishops (see NIGEL and ROGER DE CLINTON) who presided over the conference between Stephen and Maud at COVENTRY on 30 November 1145. 'His high, imperious voice CADFAEL had never heard before, though the effects of its utterance had influenced the lives of Englishmen for years, both secular and monastic.'

Refs: **4** (4:1); **8** (1, 3, 6, 8–10, 12–13); **9** (9); **10** (1–2, 6–8, 10, 12, 14–16); **11** (1–8, 10); **12** (1–2, 6, 13); **14** (4); **15** (1); **16** (1–2); **19** (7); **20** (1, 3–5).

Herbard, Alan (b. *c.*1118) (fict.). **Novels:** 'Alan Herbard, younger and less experienced, gritted his teeth and thrust in with all his weight, absolute to make a success of his first command, and perhaps did more execution than was heedful out of pure anxiety.' Son of a knight, Alan Herbard became deputy-sheriff of Shropshire under Hugh BERINGAR in March 1141. When Hugh rode north to reinforce his northern borders and meet with OWAIN GWYNEDD, Alan was left in charge. He gave Eliud ap GRIFFITH a horse and a sword and, coiling a rope around the Welshman's neck, he allowed him to go with them to GODRIC'S FORD. At the battle which followed he helped Hugh defeat the Welsh of Powys. In December 1141, in Hugh's absence, Herbard began the investigation into the death of Father AILNOTH. When Brother ELURIC was murdered in June 1142, he sent a courier north to inform Hugh at MAESBURY. In November 1143 Herbard was left in charge of the garrison when Hugh was summoned by King STEPHEN to CAMBRIDGE. With three of the sheriff's sergeants, he chased and captured BÉNEZET in the LONG FOREST in March 1145.

Refs: **9** (9–14); **10** (7); **12** (5–7, 10); **13** (4–8, 10, 12); **17** (9–10); **19** (13).

Hercules (myth.). In Greek mythology, Hercules, the son of Zeus (see JOVE) and Alcmena (or Alcmene), was a hero of superhuman physical strength. In a fit of madness, inflicted on him by Hera (wife of Zeus), Hercules murdered his wife, Megara, and their children. As penance he was ordered to serve for twelve years the Argive king, Eurystheus, who imposed upon him twelve difficult and dangerous labours. After the completion of the tasks, and many other exploits, he was rewarded with immortality.

Novels: '"By rights he should be paying a small toll for selling here, he brings in as full a man-load as Hercules could have hefted."'

Refs: **17** (7).

Hereford (Hereford & Worcester, England). Some 25 miles south of LUDLOW and 24 miles south-west of WORCESTER, this cathedral city is situated on the banks of the River Wye. It was the Saxon capital of West Mercia and has been a bishopric since 676. The present Norman Cathedral, dedicated to St Mary and St Ethelbert, dates from the 12th C., although parts of the east end are earlier. Further alterations and rebuilding continued throughout the following centuries, including the erection of the Central Tower built between 1300 and 1310. The West Tower collapsed in 1786 and demolished the west end of the nave. Much rebuilding and restoration followed. The West Front was replaced in 1902–08. Among the many treasures of the Cathedral is the famous *Mappa Mundi*, a unique 13th C. vellum map of a flat world with JERUSALEM at its centre. Because of its proximity to the Welsh border, only 7 miles east of OFFA'S DYKE, the medieval city of Hereford was fortified. The Normans built a motte-and-bailey castle on the north bank of the river at Castle Green. After the conquest of Wales at the end of the 13th C., its military importance declined. Today the site, with a few sparse remains, is dominated by a tall column erected in 1809 to honour Lord Nelson.

Novels: 'The manor of STANTON COBBOLD lay a good seventeen miles from SHREWSBURY, in the south of the shire, and cheek by jowl with the large property of the bishops of Hereford in those parts, which covered some nine of ten manors.' Sir Alan LUCY, the father of Joscelin LUCY, had two manors in the Hereford borders. In December 1139, CADFAEL suggested to Olivier de BRETAGNE that he should avoid Hereford. ROBERT of Gloucester was in Hereford with Earl ROGER in December 1145. Olivier rode to the city to bring Robert news that his son, Philip FITZROBERT, had been badly injured.

Refs: **4** (5:3); **5** (2); **6** (15); **20** (10–11, 15).

Heretic's Apprentice. See Elave.

Heribert, Abbot (*fl.* 1127) (hist.). Also spelled Herbert. Heribert became Abbot of SHREWSBURY ABBEY after the sudden death of GODEFRID in 1127. According to Ordericus Vitalis, he 'usurped the rudder of the infant establishment'. He sent Prior ROBERT and a party of six monks to GWYTHERIN in 1137 to bring back the bones of St WINIFRED. Heribert was succeeded by RADULFUS.

Novels: 'And in at the gate ambled Heribert, a small, rotund, gentle elderly man of unimpressive appearance, who rode like a sack on his white mule, and had the grime and mud and weariness of the journey upon him. He wore, at sight, the print of demotion and retirement in his face and bearing, yet he looked pleasantly content, like a man who had just laid by a heavy burden, and straightened up to draw breath. Humble by nature, Heribert was uncrushable.' Benedictine monk of Shrewsbury Abbey and former prior and abbot, Heribert was born in *c.*1075. In November 1120 Heribert, then prior, went to the king's court at WOODSTOCK in place of Abbot GODEFRID. On the way he was seized and captured by Roger MAUDUIT's men, but was rescued by CADFAEL. After judgement had been given in favour of the abbey, Cadfael returned with the prior to SHREWSBURY to become a monk. Heribert was appointed abbot in 1127. In May 1137 he gave Prior ROBERT permission to go to GWYTHERIN to acquire the bones of St WINIFRED. During the siege of Shrewsbury in August 1138, Heribert was slow to support King STEPHEN and acknowledge his sovereignty. In consequence, the king held a lingering grudge against the abbot. Nevertheless, Heribert was invited to the king's table at SHREWSBURY CASTLE. In December 1138, he was summoned to LONDON by Cardinal-Bishop ALBERIC of Ostia to account for his stewardship of the convent. On his return, Heribert informed his brethren that he had been stripped of his office and that Radulfus had been appointed abbot in his place. He spent the remaining years of his life as a simple choir-monk, dying at Shrewsbury in 1140.

Refs **1** (1–2, 10, 12); **2** (2–3, 5–8, 10–12); **3** (1–2, 5–6, 8–9, 11); **4** (1:1); **8** (2); **12** (1); **15** (2); **16** (1–2); **RB** (1, 2).

Heribert, Prior. See HERIBERT, Abbot.

Heriet, Adam (b. *c.*1089) (fict.). **Novels:** 'At a big trestle table sat a solid, brown-bearded, balding man with his elbows spread comfortably on the board, and a beaker of ale before him. He had the weathered look of a man who lives out of doors in all but the bleakest seasons, and an air of untroubled strength about his easy stillness.' Brother of Elfrid HERIET and uncle of Edric HERIET, Adam Heriet was godfather to

ADAM, the eldest of his sister's sons. Born a free man at HARPECOTE, Adam Heriet was a forester and huntsman in the service of Humphrey CRUCE of LAI. He was the devoted servant of Julian CRUCE and 'loved her from a child'. In August 1138 he escorted her south to ANDOVER with WULFRIC, RENFRED and John BONDE. Without telling the others, he helped Julian dispose of her valuables and disguise herself as a boy so that she could enter HYDE ABBEY as a monk. Shortly after returning to LAI, Adam volunteered to join the twenty-strong armed draft demanded by Waleran de BEAUMONT, Earl of Meulan, Cruce's overlord. He was an 'experienced practitioner of sword and bow'. During a lull in the fighting, Adam went to visit his sister at BRIGGE. He was arrested there and taken to SHREWSBURY CASTLE for questioning in connection with Julian's disappearance. Although he denied robbing and killing his mistress, he was locked in a cell and only released when news came that Julian was alive and well.

Refs: **11** (4, 6–11, 13–14).

Heriet, Edric (b. 1111) (fict.). **Novels:** 'A big, tow-headed, shaggy fellow in a frayed leather coat.' Nephew of Adam and Elfrid HERIET, Edric Heriet was in September 1141 a free man, and married with one child. A rent-paying tenant of his lord, Reginald CRUCE, he farmed a yardland at the manor of HARPECOTE.

Refs: **11** (7–8).

Heriet, Elfrid (*fl.* 1141) (fict.). **Novels:** 'She had a round, wholesome, rosy face, and honest eyes.' Wife of WALTER THE COOPER, aunt of Edric HERIET and sister of Adam HERIET, Elfrid gave birth to three sons: ADAM (b. 1124) and two others (b. *c.*1125 and *c.*1131).

Refs: **11** (8, 13).

Herluin, Sub-Prior (b. *c.*1095) (fict.). **Novels:** 'The sub-prior was a big man, long-boned, wide shouldered, carrying flesh once ample, perhaps even excessive, but shrunken and a little flabby now. Certainly no reproach to him; he had shared, it seemed, the short commons on which the unfortunate fen-dwellers had had to survive during this harvestless year of oppression. His uncovered head showed a pale tonsure encircled with grizzled, springy hair more brown than grey, and a long, lantern face, austere of feature, deep-set and stern of eye, with a long straight stroke of a mouth, almost lipless in repose, as though totally stranger to smiling. Such lines as his countenance had acquired, during a lifetime . . . all bore heavily downward, repressed and forbidding.' Sub-Prior Herluin of RAMSEY ABBEY was thrown out of his monastery, along with the rest of his brothers, by Geoffrey de MANDEVILLE in September 1143. Having been forced to find shelter elsewhere, he returned to Ramsey at the end of 1144. In February 1145 Herluin was charged by Abbot WALTER to go to SHREWSBURY, and possibly PERSHORE, EVESHAM and WORCESTER, not only to raise alms for the restoration of their ruined abbey and church, but also to call his scattered brothers home again. For the journey he was accompanied by Brother TUTILO and three lay servants, including NICOL and ROGER. Having received permission of 'sheriff and clergy', Herluin preached in the church of Shrewsbury Abbey and also at the high cross in the town, exacting 'donations from a great many guilty consciences'. While lodging at Shrewsbury, he rode out to LONGNER, with Tutilo and CADFAEL, to exhort Sulien BLOUNT to return to Ramsey with him or, if that was not possible, to get from him or his family 'a conscience fee in silver'. On more than one occasion, at the dying Donata BLOUNT's request, Herluin allowed Tutilo to go to Longner to sing at her bedside. Sending the valuables he had collected and a cartload of timber back to Ramsey, Herluin and Tutilo, accompanied by an unnamed lay brother, rode south-eastward to Pershore and Worcester. While at Worcester, he heard from Hugh BERINGAR and Prior ROBERT of the disappearance of St WINIFRED's reliquary; and from Nicol of the theft of the wagon and team of horses bound for Ramsey. Herluin and Tutilo rode with Hugh, Robert and Nicol to ULLESTHORPE and from there to HUNCOTE, returning to Shrewsbury with Robert de BEAUMONT (the younger) and the missing reliquary. In order to settle the various claims to the reliquary, which included one from Herluin on behalf of Ramsey, Abbot RADULFUS suggested that they consult the *sortes Biblicae* on St Winifred's altar. Herluin received: '"I tell you, I know you not, whence you came. Depart from me, ye workers of iniquity."' (Luke 13:27.) Outraged, he promptly withdrew Ramsey's claim to the saint. Herluin returned to Ramsey in early March without Tutilo, but 'restored to good humour by the recovery of the fruits of his labours in Shrewsbury'.

Refs: **19** (Prologue, 1–13).

Hermit of Eyton Forest. See BOURCHIER, Renaud.

Hertford (Hertfordshire, England). Straddling the River Lea, 20 miles north of the city of LONDON, Hertford is the county town and administrative centre of Hertfordshire. A general synod (council of bishops) was held in the ancient town in 672. The castle, of which the 15th C. gatehouse survives, dates back to Anglo-Saxon times, when Edward the Elder erected two fortifications, one on each side of the river. HENRY II erected a castle on the present site in 1173. It was demolished in the 17th C. by James I, and only parts of the walls remain. The oldest domestic building in the town is the timber-framed Old Verger's House, dating from the 1450s. It stands near St Andrew's Church. There were two religious houses in Hertford: a Benedictine priory, founded before 1093; and a Trinitarian (or Maturin) friary, founded in c.1261.

Refs: **20** (8).

Herward, Brother (*fl.* 1139) (fict.). **Novels:** 'The man who entered beside him was meagre, small and slight of body, grey of tonsure, still tired after his journey, but his ageing eyes were direct of gaze, and his mouth set into lines of patience and endurance.' Sub-prior of the Benedictine monastery of WORCESTER (see WORCESTER ABBEY), Brother Herward arrived at SHREWSBURY ABBEY on 29 November 1139. At chapter the following day, he announced that he had been sent north to enquire after the whereabouts of Yves HUGONIN and Ermina HUGONIN (see BRETAGNE), who had gone missing after the sack of Worcester. Later, he asked Sheriff Gilbert PRESTCOTE if he would allow Laurence d'ANGERS safe-conduct into Shropshire to search for them himself. The request was refused. Shortly afterwards, Herward and his company departed for Worcester.

Refs: **6** (1, 5–6).

H

Hesdin, Arnulf of (d. 1138) (hist.). Also spelled Ernulf de Hesding. It is thought that his father was the Arnulf of Hesding mentioned as a land-owner in Berkshire. Arnulf, his son, was the uncle of William FITZALAN and brother of Avelina, wife of Alan FitzFlaald and mother of William. He is described by Ordericus Vitalis as 'a brave and rash knight' (quoted in Eyton's *Antiquities of Shropshire*, 1858). During the siege of SHREWSBURY in August 1138 Arnulf 'had often rejected with pride the King's offers of peace, and had moreover presumed to utter injurious language against the King, and had constrained some to persist in rebellion who were willing to surrender themselves. So at length when the Castle was reduced, Arnulf, with many others, being taken prisoner was brought before the insulted Prince. But the King, seeing that by his forbearance he only gained the contempt of the contumacious, and that so, many of the Nobles who were summoned to his Court scorned to attend, commanded in his anger that Arnulf and about ninety-three others who had resisted should he hanged or put to other modes of instant death. Arnulf, penitent too late, and several of the rest, entreated the King for mercy, and promised vast sums for their redemption. But the King preferring revenge on wickedness to any weight of gold, they were forthwith executed.' He was hanged by STEPHEN, probably on or *c.*22 August 1138.

Novels: 'Arnulf of Hesdin came in limping heavily, and dragging chains at wrist and ankle; a big, florid man nearing sixty, soiled with dust, smoke and blood. Two of the Flemings thrust him to his knees before the king. His face was fixed and fearful, but defiant still.' Uncle of William FitzAlan and loyal supporter of the Empress MAUD, Arnulf of Hesdin was born in *c.*1079. In August 1138 during the siege of SHREWSBURY, he hurled abuse at King STEPHEN from the towers of SHREWSBURY CASTLE. He was captured and, although tortured by TEN HEYT, refused to reveal the whereabouts of FitzAlan and Fulke ADENEY. He was hanged from the battlements of the castle, the first to die of ninety-three others.

Refs: **2** (1–3, 11).

High Cross (Shrewsbury, Shropshire). High Cross is situated at the junction of Pride Hill, CASTLE STREET and St Mary's Street. In medieval times these streets were called respectively: Corvisor's Row or Butcher's Row; HIGH STREET or High Pavement; and Upper Dogpole. There has been a market cross at High Cross for centuries, certainly until 1705. The present cross was presented to the Corporation of SHREWSBURY by Shrewsbury School and was formally handed over to the town on 19 June 1952. In *Some Account of the Present and Ancient State of Shrewsbury* (1808) Owen wrote: 'All proclamations were made at these market-crosses, and, in considerable towns, they were usually denominated the High Cross, to distinguish them from the smaller buildings of that kind dispersed about. Such was the title of the structure before us, and the street on which it stood was called the High Pavement. On days of solemnity, processions of the Abbot, Monks, and Clergy, attended by the bailiffs and incorporated companies, were used to proceed from one of the churches, generally the abbey, to the High Cross, and from thence to the crosses of the suburbs, at which prayers were offered up, especially on the day of Corpus Christi. Here also the execution of criminals of state, condemned for high treason, took place. On this spot the unhappy David Prince of Wales, with whom expired the ancient race of British Princes, suffered a most cruel fate.' In 1283 David ap Gruffudd was dragged through the streets of Shrewsbury, hung up at High Cross, taken down alive, his heart and bowels torn out and burned before his eyes, then beheaded, and finally quartered. Many other noblemen were executed at High Cross, particularly after the battle of Shrewsbury fought in 1403. The body of Sir Henry Percy (also called Hotspur), who was killed in the battle, was also beheaded and quartered near the cross.

Novels: 'At the High Cross they turned to the right, and were in narrower and darker places, and once, at least, something furtive and swift turned aside from their path, perhaps wary of two, where one might cry out loud enough to rouse others, even if the second could be laid out with the first blow. Shrewsbury was well served in its watchmen, but every solitary out at night is at the mercy of those without scruples, and the watch cannot be everywhere.' In 1135 one of Archbishop WILLIAM OF CORBEIL's canons from ST OSYTH preached in Shrewsbury at the High Cross. Deacon SERLO was with him. In August 1138, CADFAEL gave Giles SIWARD's brown cotte to a feeble-witted beggar at the cross. The house of William HYNDE stood near the cross. Sub-Prior HERLUIN was granted permission to preach at High Cross in February 1145, in order to 'exact donations from a great many guilty consciences' for the restoration of RAMSEY ABBEY.

Refs: **2** (4, 11); **3** (8); **4** (2:2); **7** (6–7); **9** (1, 9); **10** (7); **11** (13); **13** (7, 10); **14** (1); **16** (2); **19** (1–2); **20** (1); **RB** (3).

High Street (Shrewsbury, Shropshire). The medieval High Street (or High Pavement) stretched from Shoplatch to Castle Gates and is represented today by Pride Hill and CASTLE STREET. The present High

Street, running from the summit of WYLE Cop north-west to the junction of Shoplatch and Pride Hill, was, until the 15th C., called Gumblestal Street. It is thought to have got its name from the Gambol or cucking-stool which once stood on the site. Part of the southern side of the street was once known as Bakers or Baxters Row. There are a number of timber-framed houses in High Street, the earliest dating from the 16th C. Two notable examples were built by wool merchants: Richard Owen's Mansion, dated 1592, and Robert Ireland's Mansion, built *c.*1575. One of the passages or 'shuts' leading off the High Street has the particularly graphic name of Grope Lane.

Novels: 'And she shook her bridle and pressed ahead along the High Street. From open doors and shop doorways heads were beginning to be thrust in excited recognition, neighbour nudging neighbour.'

Refs: **2** (11); **13** (12).

High Street (Winchester, Hampshire). Although it never existed, the shop of the WINCHESTER silver-smith, to whom Adam HERIET had sold some of Julian CRUCE's valuables, was in the High Street. St Maurice's Church, in the High Street, has been pulled down, except for the tower (mostly built in 1842).

Novels: 'Thus he came . . . into a small, scarred shop in the High Street, close under the shadow of St Maurice's Church.' On 20 August 1138 Adam Heriet sold some of Julian Cruce's valuables to the silver-smith in the High Street. Three years later, Nicholas HARNAGE walked into the shop and discovered Julian's ring.

Refs: **11** (8, 11, 13).

Hilaria, Sister (*c.*1114–39) (fict.). **Novels:** Also known as the Virgin in the Ice. '"Cold as ice, encased in ice. The first bitter frost had provided her a glassy coffin preserving her flesh immaculate and unchanged to accuse her destroyer."' Benedictine nun of WORCES-TER and tutor to Ermina Hugonin (see BRETAGNE). After the sack of Worcester in November 1139, Sister Hilaria fled north on foot with Ermina and Yves Hugonin, intending to see them safe into shelter. In bitter snow conditions, and after a long detour to avoid bands of roaming soldiers, they managed to reach CLEOBURY. The following day, Brother ELYAS joined the party, travelling with them as far as FOX-WOOD. He tried to persuade them to go west with him to BROMFIELD, but Ermina refused and insisted on pressing on over the hills to GODSTOKE. In the after-noon of 2 December, Hilaria and the Hugonin pair arrived at DRUEL'S HOLDING. Ermina and Yves slipped away, leaving the nun behind at the farmstead. On 4 December, Hilaria allowed ELYAS to escort her to Bromfield. They took shelter from the cold in a hut in CLEE FOREST. But ELYAS, tempted by the demands of the flesh, left her asleep, and went out into the snow and frost to watch out the night as best he could. Hilaria was discovered alone by Evrard BOTEREL. After violating and killing her, he dumped her naked body in a nearby brook. On his way back to Bromfield from THURSTAN's assart, CADFAEL found Hilaria's corpse encased in ice. Once the body had been removed in a block of ice, it was taken back to Bromfield Priory.

Refs: **6** (1–8,10–12, 14–15).

Hinde, John (b. 1093) (fict.). **Novels:** 'Plainly a man of substance in the town, one who might well he a good patron to his favoured religious house, and on excellent terms with abbots.' Silversmith of PETER-BOROUGH and patron of RAMSEY ABBEY, John Hinde was among those tradesmen who refused to leave the town in October 1143, just because Geoffrey de MAN-DEVILLE's forces were in the area. He sheltered Sulien BLOUNT overnight during the novice's journey from Ramsey to SHREWSBURY. The following month,

Hinde was visited by Hugh BERINGAR, who was investigating Blount's claim that he had found GENERYS's ring in the shop. Although he could confirm most of Sulien's story, Hinde knew nothing about the ring.

Refs: **17** (5–6, 10, 12–13).

(John) Hinde's Shop (Peterborough, Cambridgeshire) (fict.). Although it never existed, the shop of John HINDE the silversmith was in Priestgate, not far from the present cathedral.

Novels: 'The shop was there, or at least a flourishing silversmith's shop was there, open for business and showing a prosperous front to the world.'

Refs: **17** (5–6, 10, 12).

Hodnet (Shropshire, England). DB – Odenet: in Hodnet Hundred; land held by Earl Roger de MONTGOMERY himself. Some 12 miles north-east of SHREWSBURY and 5 miles south-west of Market Drayton, Hodnet is a large village with several black-and-white, half-timbered houses. The sandstone St Luke's Church, occupying a hilltop site, is of Norman origin. It has a 14th C. octagonal tower, which is unique in Shropshire. In the grounds of Hodnet Hall are the remains of a motte-and-bailey castle, built by Baldwin de Odenet in the late 11th C.

Novels: 'Over in the tamer country of the hundred of Hodnet the soil was fat and well-farmed, and the gleaned grain-fields full of plump, contented cattle at graze, at once making good use of what aftermath there was in a dry season, and leaving their droppings to feed the following year's tilth.'

Refs: **11** (8).

Holy City. See JERUSALEM.

Holy Cross, Parish Church of (Shrewsbury, Shropshire). Between the founding of SHREWSBURY ABBEY in 1083 and its dissolution in 1540, the parish church of Holy Cross was also the abbey church of Saint Peter and Saint Paul. The Benedictine monks worshipped at the eastern end of the church and the parishioners at the western end, each having their own separate altar. The parish of HOLY CROSS also had its own priest.

Novels: 'He rounded the west end of the church, with its great door ajar outside the enclosure for parish use, and turned in under the arch of the gatehouse.' 'The number of graves as yet was not large, the foundation being no more than fifty-eight years old.' Fathers ADAM, AILNOTH and BONIFACE were parish priests of Holy Cross, while CYNRIC was the verger. The nave of the church was flooded when the River SEVERN and MEOLE BROOK burst their banks in February 1145, and not for the first time: 'The nave had been known to float a raft now and again over the years, once even a light boat.'

Refs: **8** (12); **11** (3); **12** (1, 3–4, 11); **13** (1); **19** (1–2).

Holy Cross, Parish of (Shrewsbury, Shropshire). The present parish of the Holy Cross contains about ten thousand people and includes the areas known as ABBEY FOREGATE, Belvidere Paddocks, Cherry Orchard, Monkmoor, Telford Estate and Underdale. It is bounded to the west, north and east by the great, meandering loop of the River SEVERN. The southern boundary runs from the point where the LONDON to SHREWSBURY railway line crosses the river, at the eastern extremity of the loop; follows the railway to the point where it meets Sparrow Lane; continues down Bell Lane and across the Abbey Foregate to the Rea Brook (see MEOLE BROOK); and finally runs west along the brook to its confluence with the Severn. In medieval times the parish of the Holy Cross also included the present parish of ST GILES. The 6-mile long boundary line enclosed some 1,700 acres, most of which was arable and pasture land. St Giles became a separate parish in the 19th C.

Novels: A big parish, a population made up equally of the craftsmen and merchants of the suburb and the cottars and villagers in the countryside.' 'The relations between cloister and parish here had been harmonious under three abbots in succession.' 'The . . . parish of Holy Cross embraced both sides of the road, on the right stretching well into the scattered hamlets beyond the suburb, on the left as far as the brook.'

Refs: **7** (3); **11** (1); **12** (1–3, 5, 9, 11); **16** (2, 4); **19** (1, 3).

Holy Father. See INNOCENT II, Pope; LUCIUS II, Pope.

Holy Land or Palestine (parts of Israel, Jordan and Egypt). Bounded to the west by the Mediterranean Sea and to the east and south by the Arabian Desert, with mountains to the north, Palestine was an important strategic route between the two ancient civilisations of Egypt and Mesopotamia. It was named after the Philistines who occupied the southern coastal part of the country in the 12th C. BC. Containing sites mentioned in both the Old and New Testaments, the land is held sacred by three religions: Christianity, Judaism and Islam. The majority of holy places are concentrated in and around JERUSALEM, but the districts of Galilee and Hebron are also important. Since early prehistoric times the country has been held by virtually every Near Eastern power, including the Egyptians, Assyrians, Babylonians, Persians, Romans, Byzantines, and Ottoman Turks. The conquest of the Holy Land became the prime objective of the First Crusade, and in AD 1099 the Christians took Jerusalem from the Muslims. Palestine was finally regained by the Saracens, under Saladin, in 1187. It remained Muslim thereafter, except for a brief period in the early 13th C. when Jerusalem, Bethlehem and Nazareth came under Christian rule. The Ottoman Turks conquered Palestine in 1516, and it remained under Ottoman rule for the next four centuries.

Novels: 'Palestine, that lovely inhospitable, cruel land of gold and sand and drought.' CADFAEL's roving youth 'had taken him as far afield as VENICE, and CYPRUS and the Holy Land'. The KNIGHTS OF SAINT JOHN provided shelter everywhere in the Holy Land. Among those who went to the Holy Land either on crusade or pilgrimage were: Laurence d'ANGERS, Rainald BOSSARD, Olivier de BRETAGNE, Bertrand de CLARY, ELAVE, GODFREY DE BOUILLON, Nicholas HARNAGE, LOTHAIR, William of LYTHWOOD, Godfrid Marescot (see HUMILIS, Brother), Guimar de MASSARD and ROBERT of Normandy. 'No doubt some of the returning pilgrims from the Holy Land were genuine, and believed in the genuineness of what they offered, but in some cases Cadfael wondered whether they had ever been nearer ACRE than EASTCHEAP.'

Refs: **1** (1, 6); **2** (2); **3** (2); **6** (1); **8** (1); **9** (7); **10** (2–3, 7, 15); **11** (3–4); **15** (3–5); **16** (2–3, 10); **19** (2, 13); **20** (2).

Holyhead. See CAERGYBI.

Holywell or Treffynnon (Clwyd, Wales). This manufacturing town is situated near the estuary of the River DEE, some 18 miles north-west of CHESTER. The name Holywell refers to the sacred well or spring of St WINIFRED. According to tradition, after Prince CRADOC had cut off the saint's head with his sword, it rolled down the hillside and where it came to rest a fountain of pure water gushed out of the ground. Holywell became a great centre of pilgrimage, and the water from the well was famed for its miraculous healing properties. The present chapel which encloses the well was built at the end of the 15th C. It was drastically altered from the 18th C. onwards and only recently restored. In 1917 the water was cut off when mining operations on nearby Halkyn Mountain diverted the underground stream. Although the supply of water was connected to another source, the flow is now much reduced. Nonetheless, the well is still a place of pilgrimage and is called the Lourdes of Wales. St Winifred founded a nunnery at Holywell in the 7th C. St Winifred's Well, together with the parish church of Holywell, belonged to the Cistercian monks of Basingwerk Abbey from 1240 until the Dissolution. The remains of the abbey are near Greenfield on the Dee estuary.

Novels: '"Saint Winifred, you say, Father? Everyone knows of Saint Winifred. You'll find her spring by the name they gave the place, Holywell, it's no great way in from Chester. But she's not there. You won't find her grave at Holywell."' In May 1137 Brother JEROME dreamt that St Winifred had appeared before him in a great light, telling him that if Brother COLUMBANUS bathed in her healing spring at Holywell he would be cured. That same day a delegation from SHREWSBURY ABBEY escorted the ailing monk to the village, where he was miraculously restored to health. It is said that the water from the well never freezes, however hard the winter. 'No one has ever known it stilled, it bubbles always in the centre.'

Refs: **1** (1); **10** (1); **18** (4).

Hopton Brook (Shropshire, England). DB – Hopton (Hopton Cangeford) not mentioned by name but Stantone (Stanton Lacy): in Culverstone Hundred; land held by Roger de Lacy (see LACY FAMILY). Rising on the slopes of the CLEE HILLS, between the Devil's Mouthpiece and Weston Hill, Hopton Brook flows south, past Hopton Hall Farm to Hopton Cangeford (or Hopton-in-the-Hole). About a mile beyond the tiny village, with its redundant red-brick church of 1776, the tiny stream merges with the waters of the LEDWYCHE BROOK.

Novels: 'They went briskly wherever the forest thinned and the lingering light showed their way clearly. The first floating flakes of new snow drifted languidly on the air as they came down to the Hopton Brook.' In December 1139, having found Yves HUGONIN safe in CLEE FOREST, CADFAEL set out to escort him back to BROMFIELD Priory. A short distance beyond Hopton Brook, in one of its tributary-streams, he discovered the body of Sister HILARIA encased in ice.

Refs: **6** (3, 6).

Horse-Fair (Shrewsbury, Shropshire). Originally, the wide triangular area of open ground lying to the north-east of SHREWSBURY ABBEY and to the north of the ABBEY FOREGATE, Horse-Fair was the site where the monks held their markets and fairs. At its foundation in 1083, Roger de MONTGOMERY granted the abbey all the adjoining land, known as Monks' Foregate. In his charter, quoted in Owen and Blakeway's *A History of Shrewsbury* (1825), Roger de Montgomery 'commanded also, that at the feast of St Peter in the Calends of August, the people of the whole province should meet in the same place at a fair for three days yearly: and that the monks should have the whole toll and profit of it.' The fact that the abbey had the right to hold an independent fair in competition to the town led to frequent and bitter disputes. It was not until the end of the 13th C. that a compromise was reached: during the abbey's fair in early August the townspeople agreed to close their shops and limit their sales to wine and ale in return for a compensatory payment of 38s. a year. Although now occupied by houses, the site of the monastic market-place can be still be traced. It is remembered by the street name of Horsefair, leading off the old Abbey Foregate.

Novels: 'The wide triangle of the horse-fair ground gleamed faintly pallid with light frost. The abbey barn loomed at one corner, close to the enclave wall.' 'The summer darkness of fine nights, which is never quite dark, showed a horse-fair deserted, no trace of the past three days but the trampled patches and the marks of trestles in the grass. All over for another year.' For three days from 1 August, Shrewsbury Abbey held its annual fair of St Peter's in the great triangle of the Horse-Fair. WAT'S TAVERN lay at the northern apex of the fair-ground. The Horse-Fair stable was above the level reached by the flood of February 1145.

Refs: **2** (9); **3** (4, 6); **4** (1:1–2, 4:5, 5:5); **5** (1); **8** (7); **10** (8–9); **11** (1); **12** (7, 11); **13** (2); **17** (7); **19** (2–4, 6, 8, 11–13); **20** (16).

Hugonin, Ermina. See BRETAGNE, Ermina de.

Hugonin, Geoffrey (*fl.* 1121) (fict.). **Novels:** Father of Ermina (see BRETAGNE) and Yves HUGONIN, Geoffrey Hugonin was a Norman baron of the shire of WORCESTER. He died during the 1130s.

Refs: **6** (4, 9).

Hugonin, Yves (b. 1126) (fict.). **Novels:** Pseudonym: Jehan. 'The boy had been well brought up, and felt his status and its obligations. There was much to be said for the monastic education.' Norman son and heir of Geoffrey HUGONIN, brother of Ermina (see BRETAGNE) and nephew of Laurence d'ANGERS, Yves, who was orphaned of both parents, was educated by the Benedictine monks of WORCESTER. After the city was sacked by the men of GLOUCESTER in November 1139, he fled north into Shropshire with Ermina and Sister HILARIA. At CLEOBURY the party were joined by Brother ELYAS, who travelled with them as far as FOXWOOD. Although Yves wanted to go to BROMFIELD with the monk, Ermina insisted on pressing on over the hills to GODSTOKE. In the afternoon of 2 December they arrived at DRUEL'S HOLDING. That night Ermina slipped secretly away with Evrard BOTEREL. Yves followed and became lost in the snow. For fear of wolves, he slept in a tree and, on the second night, he was found by THURSTAN and taken back to his assart. On 7 December, CADFAEL found him with the forester and escorted him to Bromfield. Later, Yves showed Hugh BERINGAR and Cadfael the way from Foxwood to Druel's Holding, finding it a blackened ruin. On another journey, he accompanied them to Boterel's manor of LEDWYCH. Back at Bromfield, on the night of 9 December, Yves discovered Elyas missing from the infirmary and went out into a snow-storm after him. Unable to halt the monk's determined progress, all Yves could do was doggedly follow. Leaving Elyas asleep in a shepherd's hut, Yves slipped out to fetch help. But he was captured by the outlaws of Alain le GAUCHER and taken to their fortress on TITTERSTONE CLEE. Yves claimed that he was Jehan, the shepherd's lad from WHITBACHE. Olivier de BRETAGNE rescued him and, two days later, secretly took Yves and Ermina back to their uncle in GLOUCESTER. Yves was still in the city in June 1141. In November 1145 Yves – 'a young man of birth, and well aware of his value' – rode to Norfolk, to Hugh BIGOD, on an errand for the Empress MAUD. On the way back he met Cadfael and Hugh Beringar at LICHFIELD and accompanied them to the conference at COVENTRY. Yves, like Cadfael, was seeking news of the whereabouts of the captive Olivier. Seeing Brien de SOULIS, the man who had betrayed FARINGDON and also Olivier, Yves hot-headedly challenged him with his sword. The fight was stopped before any harm could be done. The empress, later, called Yves to her apartments and, it seemed, 'quite deliberately instructed' him to kill de Soulis. When de Soulis was murdered suspicion fell on Yves, despite his innocence. Maud, believing that he had carried out her orders, rewarded Yves with a ring, 'so small that it had to be worn on the boy's little finger'. He was allowed to leave Coventry with the empress's forces. But, on the way back to Gloucester, he was abducted by Philip FITZROBERT's men and imprisoned in La MUSARDERIE, where Cadfael secured his release. Realising that Olivier was also imprisoned in the castle, Yves swore to come back for him in arms. Riding to Gloucester, Yves alerted the empress of FitzRobert's presence at La Musarderie, and also drew plans of the castle. He rode with the main body of the empress's army, under John FITZGILBERT, to the assault of the castle. Aware that Maud intended to hang FitzRobert once she had taken the castle, Yves alerted Cadfael of the fact, by re-entering the fortress undetected, risking 'his liberty, and possibly his own life'. 'Yves did not want Philip FitzRobert dead. He had come back in arms for Olivier, certainly, and he would stand by that to his last breath, but he would not connive at his liege lady's ferocious revenge.' He managed to rejoin the empress's army without being missed. After the fighting was over, Yves rode with Cadfael as far as the ford of the river (see FROME, River), where they parted. Still fiercely loyal to the empress, but now wary of her favours, Yves returned to Gloucester.

Refs: **6** (1–15); **10** (2, 7, 16); **20** (1-16).

Humilis, Brother (1094–1141) (fict.). **Novels:** formerly called Godfrid Marescot, Godfrid de Marisco or Godfrid of the Marsh. '"My future," said Humilis reflectively, "I left in Palestine (see HOLY LAND). What remained of me I gave to God, and I trust the offering was not all worthless."' 'A faint grey smile passed slowly over the sick man's face, and left him grave again. "I am the marsh out of which Fidelis must have safe passage. I should have Englished that name of mine, it would have been more fitting, with more than half my blood Saxon – Godfrid of the Marsh for Godfrid de Marisco. My father and my grandfather thought best to turn fully Norman. Now it's all one, we leave here all by the same gate."' Benedictine monk of SHREWSBURY ABBEY from August 1141 and formerly of Hyde Mead (see HYDE ABBEY), Godfrid Marescot – half-Saxon, half-Norman – was born at the manor of SALTON. In 1124, after the death of his father and brother, he felt the need for children to carry on the family line. Planning to go on a long crusade, he drew up a marriage contract between himself and six-year-old Julian CRUCE. He left England for the HOLY LAND with sixty of his own men in *c.*1125. Playing a heroic part in the battle of 1137 against ZENGHI and the men of MOSUL, Godfrid was severely mutilated and, thereafter, unable to father children. His life was saved by Syrian physicians, but the wound continued to plague him for the rest of his life, refusing to heal properly. He returned to England with Nicholas HARNAGE. In August 1138 he sent Nicholas to LAI to release Julian from their marriage contract. Shortly after, he took the cowl and entered the monastery at Hyde Mead. In August 1141, after Hyde Mead had been burned to the ground, Humilis and Brother FIDELIS travelled north together to enter Shrewsbury Abbey. He gave Harnage his blessing and consent to marry Julian. While returning from a visit to Salton with Fidelis, their boat capsized in a torrential rain-storm and he was drowned. Before he died, he realised that Fidelis was in fact Julian. Humilis was buried in the transept of the abbey church in September 1141.

Refs: **11** (1–14).

Huncote (Leicestershire, England). On the north bank of the Thurlaston Brook, the Domesday village of Huncote lies some 5 miles south-west of LEICESTER city centre. The church of St James the Greater was built in 1898, but the planned tower was never erected. The mill, not far from the site of the old chantry, has been converted into a private house.

Novels: 'Huncote was a trim and compact village. There was a thriving mill, and the fields of the demesne were wide and green, the ploughland well tended. It lay clear of the edge of the forest, closely grouped round the manor and its walled courtyard. The house was not large, but built of stone, with a squat tower as solid as a castle keep.' The manor of Huncote was one of the minor properties in Robert de BEAUMONT (the younger)'s 'huge and international honour'. In February 1145 Hugh BERINGAR, Prior ROBERT, Sub-Prior HERLUIN, Brother TUTILO and

NICOL rode from WORCESTER to ULLESTHORPE to investigate the theft of the wagon, laden with timber and treasure for RAMSEY ABBEY. Hearing that St WINIFRED's missing reliquary had been discovered in the woodlands near Ullesthorpe, the party rode on to Huncote, where they found Robert de Beaumont in residence.

Refs: **19** (4-5).

Huntingdon (Cambridgeshire, England). Lying on the northern bank of the Great Ouse some 17 miles north-west of CAMBRIDGE, Huntingdon grew up as an Anglo-Saxon river-crossing settlement, was captured by the Danes and during the Middle Ages became a prosperous market town. All that remains of the Norman castle are extensive earthworks. Oliver Cromwell (1599–1658) was born in the town, and Cromwell House (rebuilt *c.*1830) stands on the site of the Augustinian friary. The Cromwell Museum incorporates part of the old Hospital of St John the Baptist, founded in *c.*1160. Huntingdon Priory, first founded in the 10th C. and becoming Augustinian sometime before 1108, lay to the north-east of the town. Today the site is occupied by a cemetery.

Novels: One of the commissions of Brand the Villein (see HYACINTH) was to specially bind the great codex belonging to the Augustinian canons of Huntingdon. At the end of November 1143, Hugh BERINGAR and his company left Cambridge and headed towards the royal castle at Huntingdon.

Refs: **14** (9); **17** (10); **19** (Prologue).

Hunydd (d. 1139) (fict.). **Novels:** Welsh wife of ELYAS, who became a monk of PERSHORE Abbey after her death.

Refs: **6** (7, 14).

Huw, Father (*fl.* 1137) (fict.). **Novels:** 'And out of the cabbage-patch, freshly planted, in the lee of the wooden cabin, rose a small, square man in a brown sackcloth gown hoisted to the knees, thick brown legs sturdy under him, and a thicket of curly brown hair and beard half-concealing a brown, broad, wondering face round two large, dark-blue eyes. He came out hastily, scrubbing his hands on his skirts. At close quarters his eyes were larger, bluer and more astonished than ever, and as timid as the mild eyes of a doe.' Welshman and parish priest of GWYTHERIN, Father Huw welcomed and looked after Prior ROBERT and his party in May 1137. He gave up his house to Robert and Brother RICHARD, and slept himself in the loft above his cow-byre. During the negotiations for the removal of St WINIFRED's bones, he acted as mediator, particularly between Robert and RHISIART. Although everyone in the parish knew that the coffined body of Brother COLUMBANUS had been taken back to SHREWSBURY ABBEY in place of the saint, it was decided to leave Huw out of the possible scandal.

Refs: **1** (2–12).

H

Huw, Rhodri ap (b. *c.*1089) (fict.). **Novels:** Though ever-present, he had the gift of being unobtrusive until he chose to obtrude, and then could appear from an unexpected direction, and as casually as if only chance had brought him there.' Welsh merchant of MOLD who traded out of the DEE valley, Rhodri ap Huw also served as an intelligencer to OWAIN GWYNEDD. He probably spoke many languages, including French, Flemish, English and Latin. Travelling to St Peter's Fair by way of the rivers DEE, VRNWY and SEVERN, Rhodri arrived at SHREWSBURY on 31 July 1139. In addition to his wool-clip, the other goods he had brought for sale were hides, honey and mead. Pretending not to speak English, he used CADFAEL as his interpreter. He left Shrewsbury by boat on 4 August with a handsome profit and plenty of 'forward information' to report to OWAIN to help 'keep his princedom safe, and add a few more miles to it here and there'.

Refs: **4** (1:2–4, 2:2–3, 3:1, 4:1, 5:2).

Hyacinth (myth.). In Greek mythology, he was the son of the Spartan king of Laconia, Amyclas. Loved by both APOLLO and ZEPHYR, Hyacinth preferred the former. While they were throwing the discus, the jealous Zephyr drove Apollo's discus at the youth's head and killed him. From the blood which gushed from the wound sprang the flower which bears his name, the hyacinth.

Novels: '"I was told, once, that there was a youth of that name in an old story, and two gods fell out over him, and the loser killed him. They say flowers grew from his blood."'

Refs: **14** (3).

Hyacinth (b. 1122) (fict.). Formerly called Brand. **Novels:** 'Brand had been a villein and landless in Northamptonshire, Hyacinth would be a craftsman and free in SHREWSBURY.' Skilled leather-worker and runaway villein of Drogo BOSIET of BOSIET. In 1142 Brand assaulted his master's steward in order to protect the honour of a girl and was forced to run away, changing his name to Hyacinth. In October he met Renaud BOURCHIER at NORTHAMPTON PRIORY, and they agreed to travel west together. Hyacinth stole a habit from the priory store so that Bourchier could disguise himself as the priest, Cuthred. They journeyed to BUILDWAS and on 21 October attended the funeral of Richard LUDEL the elder of EATON. Dame Dionisia LUDEL persuaded Cuthred and his servant, Hyacinth, to take up residence in her disused hermitage in EYTON FOREST. On the orders of Dionisia, Hyacinth caused trouble in SHREWSBURY ABBEY's part of the forest: damming the brook so that seedlings were flooded; undercutting the bank so that deer got into the coppice; and shifting the fence to let out the sheep. In the second week of November, Hyacinth delivered a message from his master to Abbot RADULFUS at the abbey. While in the enclave, he met young Richard Ludel and they immediately became friends and allies. On Hyacinth's return to Eyton, he discovered EILMUND THE FORESTER trapped by a fallen tree. After hoisting it off the forester's leg, Hyacinth went to fetch help. As soon as Eilmund was safely home, Hyacinth ran back to the abbey to fetch CADFAEL. The youth fell in love with the forester's daughter, ANNET. He was warned by Richard that Drogo was in the area looking for him. When Bosiet was found murdered, Hyacinth became the prime suspect and was hidden from Hugh BERINGAR and his men by Annet and Eilmund. Although he was tempted to flee to Wales, Hyacinth stayed for two good reasons: first, to help find Richard who had been abducted; second, because he wanted to earn his freedom in England and marry Annet. At Fulke ASTLEY's manor of LEIGHTON, Hyacinth found Richard and told him the truth about Cuthred. When Aymer BOSIET returned to NORTHAMPTON, Hyacinth came out of hiding and was proven innocent of murder. He went to SHREWSBURY to become a craftsman and work his way to freedom, in a year and a day. It is most probable that Annet became his wife in 1144.

Refs: **14** (2–14).

Hyacinth, Bishop (hist.). Untraced. Ellis Peters says she 'can't find this reference as to a bishop, either, though I know it does exist. There are two saints named Hyacinth, about whom I know nothing, and a Cardinal Hyacinth was one of the curia later arbitrating between Becket and the king. The one I mentioned, to justify what I wrote, was almost certainly much earlier – I think I got him from one of the early Church controversy books, but up to now I can't find him. Yes, he was factual. No, I know no more about him.'

Novels: '"What is your name?" RADULFUS questioned. "HYACINTH, my lord." "I have known a bishop of that name," said the abbot, and briefly smiled, for the sleek brown creature before him had certainly nothing of the bishop about him. "Were you named for him?" "No, my lord. I have never heard of him."'

Refs: **14** (3)

Hyde Abbey (Hyde Mead, Winchester, Hampshire). Edward the Elder, King of Wessex, founded a religious house for secular canons at WINCHESTER in *c.*903. It was called the New Minster to distinguish it from the nearby Old Minster, or Cathedral of St Swithun's. Athelwold, Bishop of Winchester from 963 to 984, refounded it under the Benedictine Rule in 964. In 1110 the monks were forced to move to Hyde Mead, north of the town, because of their monastery's proximity to the new Norman cathedral of Bishop WALKELIN, begun in 1070. The new house was renamed Hyde Abbey; while the New Minster was demolished. The abbey was destroyed during the siege of 1141, when the firebrands of Bishop HENRY OF BLOIS reduced most of the city to ashes. Rebuilding did not begin until 1182. The abbey was dissolved in 1539 and, apart from a few fragments, only the 14th C. gateway survives.

Novels: 'Winchester itself, or as near as made no matter, for the New Minster of that city, always a jealous rival of the Old, where Bishop Henry presided, had been forced to abandon its old home in the city thirty years ago, and banished to Hyde Mead, on the north-western outskirts. There was no love lost between Henry and the community at Hyde, for it was the bishop who had been instrumental in keeping them deprived of an abbot for so long, in pursuit of his own ambition of turning them into an episcopal monastery. The struggle had been going on for some time, the bishop deploying various schemes to get the house into his own hands, and the prior using every means to resist these manipulations.' In August 1141, Hyde Abbey was burned to the ground when Bishop Henry of Blois set light to the city of Winchester. Among the brothers of Hyde who fled were HUMILIS and Fidelis (see CRUCE, Julian).

Refs: **10** (6); **11** (1–2, 6, 8, 11).

Hyde Mead Priory. See Hyde Abbey.

Hynde, Mistress (*fl.* 1142) (fict.). **Novels:** Wife of William HYNDE and the mother of Vivian HYNDE. After her son had abducted Judith PERLE in June 1142, Mistress Hynde received the widow into her house and helped hide her until she could be safely escorted to GODRIC'S FORD.

Refs: **13** (5, 7–8, 10, 13).

Hynde, Vivian (*fl.* 1142) (fict.). **Novels:** 'He was a very personable young man indeed, tall and athletic, with corn-yellow hair that curled becomingly, and dancing pebble-brown eyes in which a full light found surprising golden glints. He was invariably elegant in his gear and wear, and knew very well how pleasant a picture he made in most women's eyes.' Only son and heir of William and Mistress HYNDE, Vivian Hynde squandered his father's money on dice, girls and riotous living. He accumulated debts which his father eventually refused to pay. With his eye on the wealthy Vestier clothing business, Vivian pestered Judith PERLE with offers of marriage which were always refused. Eventually, he took matters into his own hands and in June 1142 he forcibly abducted the widow, hiding her inside his father's disused counting-house. Realising that his cause was hopeless, Vivian bitterly regretted his actions and tried to make amends, entreating Judith to help him undo what he had done. To avoid a scandal, she persuaded him to escort her secretly by night to GODRIC'S FORD. Although Judith refused to bring charges against him, Vivian spent a short while locked in a cell at SHREWSBURY CASTLE under suspicion of BERTRED's murder, a crime of which he was innocent.

Refs: **13** (1, 5–8, 10–14).

Hynde, William (*fl.* 1142) (fict.). **Novels:** Father of Vivian HYNDE and husband of Mistress HYNDE, he was a wealthy SHREWSBURY woolman. In June 1142 he refused to pay any more of his wayward son's debts. Throughout the abduction of Judith PERLE by his son, he was at his sheepfolds by FORTON.

Refs: **13** (1, 5–8, 10, 12–13).

(William) Hynde's Counting-House (Shrewsbury, Shropshire) (fict.). Although it never existed, William HYNDE's counting-house was a part of his warehouse, and was situated downstream from SHREWSBURY CASTLE, in the vicinity of the present Castle Fields.

Novels: After he had abducted Judith PERLE in June 1142, Vivian HYNDE locked her inside his father's counting-house. BERTRED guessed where she was and went secretly, under cover of darkness, to investigate. He was surprised by the watchman and fled.

Refs: **13** (7).

(William) Hynde's Warehouse (Shrewsbury, Shropshire) (fict.). Although it never existed, William HYNDE's warehouse was situated downstream from SHREWSBURY CASTLE, in the vicinity of the present Castle Fields.

Novels: The warehouse of William HYNDE stood in the meadows north of Shrewsbury Castle, beyond Godfrey FULLER's DYE-HOUSE, FULLING-WORKS AND TENTERGROUND: a 'substantial warehouse where William Hynde's best fleeces lay corded and ready, waiting for the middleman's barge to come and collect them, and the narrow, stout jetty where it would draw alongside to load.'

Refs: **13** (5, 7, 10).

Hywel ab Owain (*c.*1122–d. 1170) (hist.). Son of OWAIN GWYNEDD by Pyfog, an Irishwoman, half-brother of RHUN AB OWAIN, IORWERTH AB OWAIN and MAELGWYN AB OWAIN, and nephew of CADWALADR, Hywel ab Owain was a talented poet, singer and harpist as well as a warrior. In 1139 his father granted him South CEREDIGION, the territory between the rivers AERON and Teifi. Four years later, he drove Cadwaladr out of North Ceredigion, burned his castle at ABERYSTWYTH and claimed the whole of Ceredigion for himself. In 1144, however, Cadwaladr made peace with Owain and was given back his lands. In 1145 Hywel and his step-brother, Cynan, raided Cardigan but failed to take the Norman castle. The following year, with Cadell ap Gruffudd of DEHEUBARTH, Hywel succeeded in capturing the Norman castles of Carmarthen and Llanstephan. When Cadwaladr granted his castle at Llanrhystud to his son Cadfan, Hywel seized it in 1150 and reclaimed all of Ceredigion. Cadell and his brothers, however, invaded South Ceredigion and took from him all the territory south of the Aeron. They pushed north and, by 1153, they had conquered North Ceredigion. Hywel fought alongside his father against HENRY II in 1157, but two years later fought on the side of a mixed force of Normans, Flemings, French, English and Welsh against Rhys ap Gruffudd. According to an anonymous poem, he was killed in a battle fought near Pentraeth, ANGLESEY, and was buried at BANGOR.

Novels: 'Hywel ab Owain rose and took the harp, and improvised mellifluously on the women of the north. Poet and bard as well as warrior, this was undoubtedly an admirable shoot from that admirable stem. He knew what he was doing with his music.' On reaching manhood, he was set up honourably in South Ceredigion. In 1143, after driving Cadwaladr out of Wales and burning his castle at LLANBADARN, he possessed the whole of Ceredigion. He greeted CADFAEL and Deacon MARK on their arrival at ST ASAPH in May 1144 and went with them to ABER. He rode south from CARNARVON to Llanbadarn, with GWION, to tell Rhodri FYCHAN (*fl.* 1144) to deliver Cadwaladr's ransom to the Danes.

Refs **18** (1–6, 9, 11–13).

Hywel Dda (d. 950), King of Wales (hist.). Also spelled Howel Dda, and also called Hywel the Good. During his lifetime he was known as Hywel ap Cadell, and only later as Hywel Dda. He became king of virtually all Wales, and during his reign succeeded in maintaining peace with the English by his policy of subservience. Hywel is famous in Welsh history as the great law-giver of medieval Wales. The earliest surviving copies of the *Laws of Hywel Dda* date from *c.*1200, and all agree that they were compiled under his authority. Nevertheless, in the absence of a contemporary record of this work, all that can be claimed with certainty is that Hywel was responsible for the unification and orderly arrangement of pre-existing law. The *Laws of Hywel Dda* governed Wales until the middle of the 16th C. when they were superseded by English law.

Novels: 'Welsh land! That could not be changed, merely because [Gervase] BONEL in WILLIAM [II] Rufus's reign had pushed his way in and got a hold on some acres of it, and maintained his grasp under the patronage of the earl of CHESTER ever since. Why did I never think, wondered CADFAEL, to enquire earlier where this troublous manor lay? "And CYNLLAITH has properly appointed Welsh judges? Competent to deal according to the code of Hywel Dda, not of Norman England?"'

Refs: **3** (7).

I

Ianto (*fl.* 1137) (fict.). **Novels:** Welshman of GWYTHERIN, he helped Father HUW cater for Prior ROBERT's party when they arrived at the village in May 1137.

Refs: **1** (2).

Iestyn (b. *c.*1112) (fict.). **Novels:** 'His face was broad but bony, dark-skinned, thick-browed, deep-eyed, wholly Welsh. A better-humoured man than his master [Daniel], though not so comely.' Welsh journeyman goldsmith of Walter and Daniel AURIFABER, Iestyn slept in the undercroft of the goldsmith's shop. He was the father of Susanna AURIFABER's unborn child. In May 1140, on the night of Daniel's wedding-feast, he attacked and robbed Walter. He hid the valuables in the bucket of the well until Susanna removed them later to her storeroom. When Susanna left the Aurifaber house with RANNILT and the valuables, Iestyn was waiting for her at the stables beyond FRANKWELL. He and Susanna intended to head west and set up a new home together in Wales. Once he realised that Susanna meant to kill Rannilt, he refused to allow her to do it. Before they could leave, they were surprised and surrounded by Hugh BERINGAR and his men. Penned inside the stable, Rannilt was held hostage. Iestyn tried to persuade Hugh to let Susanna go, but she would not leave him. Just as Iestyn was about to knife LILIWIN, ALCHER loosed an arrow. Susanna stepped in the way and was killed. She died in Iestyn's arms. He was arrested and taken back to SHREWSBURY CASTLE to stand trial. It is unlikely that he was hanged as he did not kill anyone.

Refs: **7** (2, 4–5, 8, 10–14).

Ifor, Ieuan ab (b. *c.*1113) (fict.). **Novels:** 'A man perhaps in his middle thirties, square-built and muscular, the first fine salting of grey in his brown hair, his eyes, over-shadowed beneath thick black brows, fixed darkly upon the sand-moulded curves of the naked horizon. He went unarmed, and bare of breast and arms in the sunlight of the morning, a powerful body formidably still in his concentration on distance.' An uchelwr in the service of OWAIN GWYNEDD, Ieuan ab Ifor held land in ANGLESEY. In May 1144 he was betrothed to HELEDD, whom he had never seen. Although he had arranged to meet his reluctant bride at BANGOR, she ran away and was captured by TURCAILL (*fl.* 1144). Ieuan joined Owain at CARNARVON. Combining forces with GWION, he managed to snatch Heledd away from the Danes – only to find that he was not the man she had chosen to marry.

Refs: **18** (2–6, 8–14).

Ightfeld (now Ightfield) (Shropshire, England). DB – Istefelt: in Hodnet Hundred; a holding of Gerard under Roger de MONTGOMERY. Ightfield is a small village situated 17 miles north-east of SHREWSBURY and some 4 miles south-east of WHITCHURCH. St John the Baptist's Church dates from the mid-14th C.

Novels: In 1141 the CRUCE family of LAI held several manors in the north-east of Shropshire, including 'Ightfeld'.

Refs: **11** (4).

Illtud, Saint (d. *c.*505) (hist.) (f.d. 6 November). Also spelled Illtyd, Illtut, Eltut or Hildutus. Much of the information on Illtud is unreliable. Born and raised in Brittany, he is said to have been the son of Bicanus, a nobleman, and Rieingulid, daughter of Amblaud, King of Britain. Some authorities, however, suggest that he was born in central Brecknock, Wales. When he was a young man, Illtud visited 'his cousin King Arthur', and eventually became a chieftain in Glamorgan (sometimes called Illtud the Knight). His marriage to TRYNIHID ended abruptly when an angel warned him to leave her, and immediately he went to St DYFRIG to receive the tonsure of a monk. It is reputed that St Cadoc had also recommended that he leave the world to become a monk. According to the *Life* of St Samson, he was a disciple of St Germanus of Auxerre. Founder and abbot of the great monastic school of Llanilltud Fawr (now Llantwit Major, Glamorgan, Wales), Illtud is one of the most celebrated and learned of Welsh saints. There are two conflicting accounts of his last days: one stating that he died in old age at Llantwit and the other that he died at Dol-de-Bretagne in Brittany.

Novels: 'Now that CADFAEL came to consider the early part of the November calendar, it seemed to be populated chiefly by Welsh saints. RUALD had reminded him that the sixth day was dedicated to Saint Illtud, who had obeyed his dictatorial angel with such alacrity, and so little consideration for his wife's feelings in the matter. No great devotion was paid to him in English houses, perhaps.' St Illtud and his wife, Trynihid, lived simply in a reed hut by the River NADAFAN. After an angelic visitation, he drove his wife out into the night and went to receive the tonsure of a monk from St DYFRIG.

Refs: **17** (10, 14).

Innocent II (d. 1143), Pope (1130–43) (hist.). Born in ROME, as Gregorio Papareschi, he was a cardinal by 1116. On 13 February 1130, the night of Pope Honorius II's death, he was elected pope by a minority. Soon after, the majority elected his rival, Pietro Pierleoni, as Anacletus II. Innocent was hastily consecrated, but by June 1130 Anacletus had forced him to flee to France. Among Innocent's powerful and influential supporters were BERNARD OF CLAIRVAUX, HENRY I, King of England, and St Norbert of Magdeburg. It was through Norbert's efforts that Innocent managed to gain the support of Lothair, King of Germany, and in August 1132 he invaded Italy. By the following June the German army occupied Rome, except for a small area held by Anacletus. Innocent crowned Lothair Holy Roman Emperor. However, when Lothair left Italy, Innocent was forced to flee to Pisa. The Germans reinvaded southern Italy in 1136, driving the forces of Anacletus' chief supporter, Roger II, King of Sicily, into exile. Lothair died in December 1137. Anacletus died the following month and was succeeded by Antipope Victor IV. The influence of Bernard of Clairvaux brought about a reconciliation between the rival popes and, on 29 May 1138, Victor resigned. At the Lateran Council in April 1139, Innocent excommunicated Roger and re-endorsed his support of STEPHEN's claim to the throne of England, first made at Easter 1136. Roger captured the Pope on 22 July 1139 and, three days later, forced Innocent to recognise him as King of Sicily. By the close of the year, they had both acknowledged each other's titles. At the Council of SENS in 1140, Innocent supported Bernard's prosecution of Pierre ABELARD by condemning the latter as a heretic. Innocent died in Rome and was succeeded by Celestine II.

Novels: 'The Holy Father has authority both to bind and to loose, and the same infallible will that can condemn can also with equal right absolve.' In December 1138 Abbot HERIBERT informed the brothers of SHREWSBURY ABBEY that Pope Innocent had acknowledged STEPHEN's claim to the throne of England. By way of support, he had sent over Cardinal-Bishop ALBERIC of OSTIA. When Pierre Abelard was convicted of heretical writings at the Council of Sens in 1140, the sentence was revoked by the pope.

Refs: **3** (1); **11** (1, 11); **12** (1–2); **14** (10); **16** (2, 10).

Iorwerth ab Owain (*fl.* 1144) (hist.). Nicknamed Drwyndwn or Flat-Nosed, he was the son of OWAIN GWYNEDD by his first wife, GWLADUS, and brother of MAELGWN AB OWAIN. Iorwerth married Marared, daughter of MADOG AP MEREDITH, King of Powys. Their son, Llywelyn the Great (d. 1240), married Joan, daughter of King John. There is a strong tradition that Iorwerth was excluded from his inheritance because of his nasal deformity and was driven out of Gwynedd. Lloyd, however, asserts that he was included in the division of his father's estates and probably received the commote of Nantconwy, with its castle of Dolwyddelan, some 5 miles south-west of Betws-y-Coed. His grave is said to be at Penmachno (see PENMACHMO).

Novels: 'The two young boys who came leaping down the steps from the hall door after her were hers, lithe dark imps of about ten and seven years, shrilling with excitement and with a flurry of dogs wreathing round their feet.' Iorwerth ab Owain was the son of Owain Gwynedd and was born in *c.*1134. CADFAEL saw him at ABER in May 1144.

Refs: **18** (4).

Isabeau (b. *c.*1126) (fict.). **Novels:** 'Yves [HUGONIN] recognised the bold, self-assured young woman who had submitted him to such a close scrutiny at COVENTRY before she decided that he would do. Dark hair, with russet lights in its coils, and bright eyes, greenish hazel, that summed up men in sweeping glances and pigeon-holed them ruthlessly, discarding, it seemed, all who were past thirty. Her own age might have been nineteen, which was also Yves' . . . A favourite among the royal gentlewomen, probably; certainly she had adopted some of her mistress's characteristics.' One of the Empress MAUD's gentlewomen, Isabeau was the niece of Jovetta de MONTORS, and 'from the ranks of the baronage'. She was with the empress in COVENTRY on 30 November 1145, and 'had certainly been willing to play a risky game with de SOULIS, but with no intention of letting it go too far'. She was unaware that her aunt, pretending to be her, had killed de Soulis. When Maud returned to GLOUCESTER in December, Isabeau went with her.

Refs: **20** (3–4, 10, 14).

Isabel, Aunt. See DOMVILLE, Isabel de.

Isabel (*fl.* 1142) (fict.). **Novels:** '"She'll bring him a passable dowry, and he's well enough satisfied with his bargain, but there are as good fish in the sea if she slipped off the hook."' In 1142, Isabel was the fiancée of Miles COLIAR but they never married.

Refs: **13** (7, 13).

Ithel, Einon ab (b. *c.*1096) (fict.). **Novels:** 'Einon ab Ithel was a big, muscular man in his forties, bearded, with long moustaches and a mane of brown hair. His clothing and the harness of the fine horse under him spoke his wealth and importance.' Captain of OWAIN GWYNEDD's personal guard, Einon ab Ithel, who spoke some English, arrived at SHREWSBURY in March 1141 with the injured Sheriff Gilbert PRESTCOTE. As soon as he discovered that Prestcote had been murdered, he declared the exchange of prisoners null and void. Einon and his two captains were allowed to return to Wales, but the rest of his party were detained at SHREWSBURY CASTLE. At TREGEIRIOG, Einon recognised as his own the gold pin Anion ap GRIFFRI had given to his father, Griffri ap LLYWARCH. He accused Anion of being a thief.

Refs: **9** (4–7, 9–12, 14).

J

James (*fl.* 1145) (fict.). **Novels:** Master-carpenter from BETTON, with 'broad shoulders' and a 'shaggy head'. In February 1145 James offered to go to RAMSEY ABBEY to help rebuild 'the gutted barns and storehouses'. Bound for Ramsey, he was travelling with MARTIN, PAYNE, NICOL and ROGER through thick woodland near ULLESTHORPE, when they were ambushed by 'eleven or twelve' armed villains and their wagon and team of horses stolen. He returned to SHREWSBURY with Martin more than a week after they had set out, on foot and limping heavily. The experience ended his taste for travelling.

Refs: **19** (2–4).

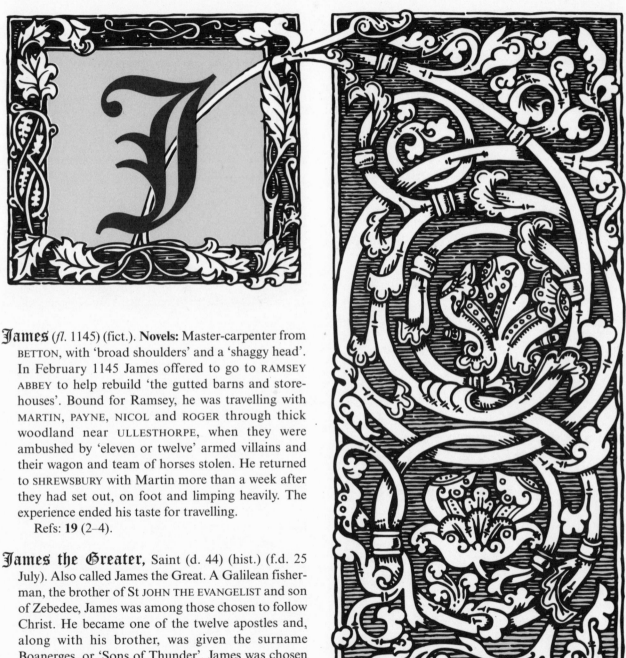

James the Greater, Saint (d. 44) (hist.) (f.d. 25 July). Also called James the Great. A Galilean fisherman, the brother of St JOHN THE EVANGELIST and son of Zebedee, James was among those chosen to follow Christ. He became one of the twelve apostles and, along with his brother, was given the surname Boanerges, or 'Sons of Thunder'. James was chosen by Christ, along with St PETER and St JOHN, to witness his transfiguration and night of agony in the garden of Gethsemane. In order to please the Jewish opponents of Christianity, James was ordered to be put to death by King Herod Agrippa I, and was thereby the first of the apostles to be martyred. Although he was buried at JERUSALEM, there is a tradition that his body was translated to Spain, first to Iria Flavia (now El Padron, in Galicia) and then to COMPOSTELA. During the Middle Ages his shrine at Santiago de Compostela was one of the most important centres of pilgrimage in Christendom. James is the patron saint of Spain and is often depicted as an elderly pilgrim, with a scallop shell.

Novels: "'It is a silver scallop-shell medal. Whoever owned it made the pilgrimage to Compostela, to the shrine of Saint James.'" Among those who made the pilgrimage to the shrine of St James at Compostela were: ELAVE, William of LYTHWOOD, Joscelin LUCY's father and possibly Renaud BOURCHIER.

Refs: **5** (3, 11); **14** (2, 13).

Japhet (fict.). **Novels:** 'A bony old piebald like our Japhet.' Martin BELLECOTE's horse, Japhet, carried the fugitive, Edwin GURNEY, north from SHREWSBURY to the house of Ifor ap MORGAN, near LLANSILIN, in December 1138.

Refs: **3** (7, 8).

Jehan (*fl.* 1139) (fict.). **Novels:** He was man-at-arms serving under Gilbert PRESTCOTE the elder at SHREWSBURY CASTLE in October 1139. During the hunt for the fugitive, Joscelin LUCY, Jehan suggested to his sergeant that they search the house and gardens of Bishop ROGER DE CLINTON. In due course, they found evidence that LUCY had lain in the hay-store. Jehan also suggested that they watch the MEOLE BROOK. It was later revealed that he had been tipped off by Simon AGUILON.

Refs: **5** (5, 10–11).

Jehan (*fl.* 1141) (fict.). **Novels:** Groom of Hugh BERINGAR, he was with his master at SHREWSBURY in September 1141.

Refs: **11** (13).

Jehan (*fl.* 1142) (fict.). **Novels:** He was the groom of Fulke ASTLEY, who was lord of the manors of LEIGHTON and WROXETER.

Refs: **14** (11).

Jehan (*fl.* 1143) (fict.). **Novels:** Servant of Cenred VIVERS of the manor of VIVERS, he was among the search party sent out to look for EDGYTHA in March 1143. After her dead body had been found, he was sent with EDRED THE STEWARD and two other men to ELFORD.

Refs: **15** (8–9).

Jehan (pseudonym of Yves Hugonin). See HUGONIN, Yves.

Jericho (Jordan). Some 6 miles north of the Dead Sea and 15 miles east of JERUSALEM, the ancient city of Jericho, dating from before 8,000 BC, is one of the world's oldest continuous settlements. Sited on a 75 ft. high mound known as Tall as-Sultàn, on the western side of the Jordan valley, above rich arable land and near a perennial spring, the city was defended by a ditch and massive 10 ft. thick dry-stone walls, strengthened at one point by a circular tower almost 30 ft. high. In the Old Testament the Canaanite city was destroyed by the Israelites under Joshua; the city walls having been destroyed by the sound of 'seven trumpets of rams' horns' followed by a 'great shout' from the attackers (Joshua 6:1–27). The Roman and New Testament city of Jericho is about a mile south of Tall as-Sultàn. It was in this area that Herod the Great built his Hellenic-style palace, dying there in 4 BC. The Jericho of the Crusader period, however, stood on a third site, about a mile east of Tall as-Sultàn. It was from this later Jericho that the modern town developed.

Novels: 'All barricades should have fallen like the walls of Jericho at the blast of his trumpet.'

Refs: **19** (1).

Jerome, Brother (b. 1100) (fict.). **Novels:** 'He was Prior ROBERT's closest associate and most devoted hanger-on, and an inevitable choice whenever Robert required strict obedience and meticulous reporting.' Benedictine monk of SHREWSBURY ABBEY and Prior Robert's chaplain and clerk, Brother Jerome accompanied Brother COLUMBANUS to HOLYWELL in May 1137 and, shortly after, went with Prior Robert's party to GWYTHERIN to acquire the bones of St WINIFRED. In August 1138 he attended King STEPHEN's supper at SHREWSBURY CASTLE. After he had set light to a lock of the hair of Roswitha Linde (see ASPLEY) in September 1140, Jerome was attacked and almost strangled by Meriet ASPLEY. In November 1142 he suggested to Drogo BOSIET that his runaway villein, BRAND, might be at CUTHRED'S HUT in EYTON FOREST. Jerome informed Sulien BLOUNT in November 1143 of the discovery of the woman's body in the POTTER'S FIELD. In February 1145 Jerome, prying outside CADFAEL'S WORKSHOP, heard CADFAEL name the Holy Thief as Brother TUTILO and immediately rushed off to tell Prior Robert, who was content to do nothing but wait: '"Retribution may be delayed . . . But it will be certain. A few hours only, and the illdoer will get his due penalty."' Sick and sour with rage, Jerome took matters into his own hands and decided to confront Tutilo, who he knew would be returning to the abbey that evening on the track from the LONGNER ferry. Hiding in thick wooded cover, Jerome mistook ALDHELM for Tutilo and, in a fit of anger, snatched up a fallen branch and struck him on the head. Realising, even in the dark, that his victim was not Tutilo and believing that he had committed murder, Jerome fled in terror, and took to his bed, 'quaking and sick with belly-aches and headaches'. When Prior Robert invited him to approach the altar to undertake the *sortes Biblicae* on behalf of the brothers, Jerome confessed to killing an 'innocent man', not realising that he was not the murderer. Incarcerated inside one of the abbey's two penitentiary cells in March, Jerome, quite clearly, was 'going to take a deal of absolving'. He emerged from a long penance at the end of 1145 'deprived of his office as one of the confessors to the novices, and crushed into surprising humility. For the present, at least, he was much easier to live with, and less vociferous in denouncing the faults of others. In time, no doubt, he would recover his normal sanctimony.'

Refs: **1** (1–9); **2** (11–12); **3** (1–2, 5–6, 11); **7** (3–7); **8** (4–6, 10, 13); **10** (1, 4, 6, 13); **11** (2–3); **12** (1, 3, 7–8, 12–13); **13** (2, 4, 9, 13); **14** (3, 5–7, 14); **16** (1–2, 4–6, 13); **17** (5, 9–10); **18** (1); **19** (2–3, 6, 8–13); **20** (2); **RB** (2).

J

Jerusalem (Israel). Located in the heart of Israel, about 15 miles west of the Dead Sea and some 35 miles south-east of the Mediterranean port of Tel Aviv-Yafo, the ancient city of Jerusalem is of immense historical and religious importance. Inhabited since 1800 BC, it is one of the oldest and holiest cities in the world, held sacred by the three religions of Christianity, Judaism and Islam. The royal city of David in the 10th C. BC, Jerusalem was destroyed by Nebuchadnezzar in 586 BC and subsequently rebuilt. It was occupied by Alexander the Great in 332 BC, captured by the Roman general Pompey in 63 BC, and ruled by Herod the Great, King of Judaea, from 37 to 4 BC. His son, Archelaus, succeeded him, but was deposed by the Romans in AD 6. It was under the fifth Roman procurator, Pontius Pilate, that Jesus of Nazareth was crucified. Many of the famous shrines in the city, including the Church of the Holy Sepulchre, were built after the conversion of Constantine the Great to Christianity in the 4th C. In 614 the Persians captured Jerusalem, massacred the population and destroyed the churches. It remained Muslim until the close of the 11th C., when in 1099 the city was captured by GODFREY OF BOUILLON to become the capital of the Crusader Kingdom of Jerusalem. Saladin reconquered the city in 1187, and it remained in Islamic hands – except for brief intervals during the 13th C. – until 1917, when the British captured it from the Turks.

Novels: 'An ocean as pure and blue and drowningly deep and clear as that well-remembered eastern sea, the furthest extreme of the tideless midland sea of legend, at the end of which lay the holy city of Jerusalem, Our Lord's burial-place and hard-won kingdom.' CADFAEL was with Godfrey of Bouillon at the storming of Jerusalem in 1099. Among those also present were Guimar de MASSARD and ROBERT of Normandy. Godfrey was the first ruler of Jerusalem and was succeeded by his brother, BALDWIN I, who was its first king. When FULK was king, the kingdom came under threat from Atabeg ZENGHI and the men of MOSUL in *c.*1139. Godfrid Marescot (see HUMILIS, Brother) distinguished himself in the battle. Many people made the pilgrimage to the Holy City, including William of LYTHWOOD and ELAVE. In 1127 Olivier de BRETAGNE left ANTIOCH and went to Jerusalem 'to join the faith of his father'. '"Ever since EDESSA fell to the paynims of Mosul, last year at Christmas [1144], all Christendom has been uneasy about the kingdom of Jerusalem. They're beginning to talk of a new Crusade, and there are lords on either side, here at home, who are none too happy about things done, and might welcome the Cross as sanctuary for their souls."' In December 1145 ROGER DE CLINTON's 'heart was already set on playing more than a passive role in the defence of the Christian kingdom of Jerusalem'. See also HOLY LAND.

Refs: **1** (1); **2** (6); **5** (1, 11); **6** (8); **8** (2); **10** (2, 10); **11** (2); **15** (4); **16** (2); **18** (14); **20** (1–3, 8); **RB** (1).

Jerusalem, Kings of. See BALDWIN I, King of Jerusalem; FULK, Count of Anjou and Maine, King of Jerusalem.

John, Brother (*fl.* 1137) (fict.). **Novels:** 'Of Brother John he knew no particular evil, but the redness of his hair, the exuberance of his health and high spirits, the very way he put live blood back into old martyrdoms with his extravagant gusto in the reading, were all offensive in themselves, and jarred on the prior's aesthetic sensibilities.' Former Benedictine monk of SHREWSBURY ABBEY and husband of ANNEST, John took the cowl in 1136 after an unhappy love affair with MARGERY, the daughter of a SHREWSBURY draper. From the beginning, he had doubts about his vocation. In early May 1137, 'barely a year tonsured', he was CADFAEL's assistant in the herb-garden. Together with Cadfael, he joined Prior ROBERT's expedition to GWYTHERIN to acquire the bones of St WINIFRED. Brother John's role was to look after the mules and carry out most of the menial tasks. At Gwytherin he lodged with BENED THE SMITH, sometimes lending him a hand at the forge. John fell in love with Bened's niece, Annest. When ENGELARD was accused of murdering RHISIART, John helped him to escape. In consequence, Prior Robert consigned him to imprisonment at Rhisiart's house until such time as he could be dealt with by Welsh law. When it became known that the bailiff, Griffith ap RHYS, was about to set out for Rhisiart's house and take him to prison, John slipped away and hid in the forest. He only emerged when the bailiff and the monks from Shrewsbury had left. Bened took John on as his apprentice. In about December 1137 he married Annest, and eighteen months later she was carrying his child.

Refs: **1** (1–12); **12** (13); **13** (1).

John the Baptist, Saint (d. *c.*30) (hist.) (f.d. 24 June). John, whose birth was foretold by an angel, was the son of Zacharias, a priest of JERUSALEM, and his wife Elizabeth, who was a cousin of St MARY. He was a forerunner of Jesus Christ, and little is known of him until *c.*27, when he appeared as an itinerant preacher, calling for sinners to 'Repent ye: for the kingdom of heaven is at hand' (Matthew 3:2). He gained many followers, including St PETER THE APOSTLE and St JOHN THE EVANGELIST, and while he was baptising Christ he recognised him as the Messiah. Christ said of him: 'Among those that are born of women there is not a greater prophet' (Luke 7:28). Shortly after, John was arrested for denouncing the incestuous union between King Herod Antipas and Herodias, his niece and half-brother's wife. When, in a moment of weakness, the king promised Herodias's daughter, Salome, whatever she wanted, she demanded the head of John on a dish. The king obliged, and John was executed without trial.

Novels: 'However dull the passages they chose for him in the refectory, and innocuous the saints and martyrs he would have to celebrate at chapter, [Brother] JOHN would contrive to imbue them with drama and gusto from his own sources. Give him the beheading of Saint John the Baptist, and he would shake the foundations.' Among the treasury of relics amassed by SHREWSBURY ABBEY over the years was 'a little flask of the sweat of Saint John the Baptist'.

Refs: **1** (1); **19** (2).

John the Evangelist, Saint (d. *c.* 100) (hist.) (f.d. 27 December). Also called St John the Divine. A Galilean fisherman, John was the son of Zebedee and the brother of St JAMES THE GREATER. He was among those chosen by Christ to be an apostle and, together with his brother, was given the surname Boanerges, or 'Sons of Thunder'. Along with James and St PETER THE APOSTLE he was chosen by Christ to witness his transfiguration and agony in the garden of Gethsemane. He is identified with the unnamed beloved disciple of the Gospel, who was made the guardian of Jesus's mother, St MARY. He was the author of the fourth gospel, and the Book of Revelation, or Apocalypse, is also ascribed to him. After the resurrection, he became a prominent figure in the early Christian Church, and along with Peter and James was considered by St Paul the Apostle to be one of its pillars in JERUSALEM. He was exiled to the island of Patmos (Greece), and was said to have lived to a very great age, eventually dying at Ephesus (Turkey).

Novels: The Augustinian priory at Haughmond (see HAUGHMOND ABBEY) was dedicated to St John the Evangelist. During the *sortes Biblicae*, conducted at SHREWSBURY ABBEY in March 1145, Robert de BEAUMONT (the younger) opened the Gospels to receive John 7:54: '"Ye shall seek me, and shall not find me; and where I am, thither ye cannot come."' (This quote is, in fact, John 7:34.) Prior ROBERT received John 15:16: '"Ye have not chosen me, but I have chosen you."' When WULSTAN, Bishop of Worcester, was 'newly chosen', the *sortes* sent him: '"Behold an Israelite indeed, in whom there is no guile."' (John 1:47.)

Refs: **17** (1); **19** (9–10).

John Chrysostom, Saint (*c.* 347–407) (hist.) (f.d. 13 September, formerly 27 January). The son of Secundus, an officer in the imperial army, by his wife Anthusa, he was born at ANTIOCH. Although he was brought up a Christian by his widowed mother, who gave him the best possible education, he was not baptised till manhood, when he was a law student. In 374 he joined a community of hermits among the mountains south of Antioch and became dangerously ill because of the damp conditions of the cave in which he lived. Forced to return to Antioch in 381, he was ordained deacon and in 386 he became a priest. His fame as a great preacher spread throughout the East and in 398 he was elected Archbishop of CONSTANTINOPLE. He was deposed for his outspoken views in 403, at a gathering of bishops at the Oak, and banished by Emperor Arcadius; but was quickly recalled

J

when a minor earthquake shook the city, terrifying the emperor's superstitious wife, Eudoxia. The following year he was again banished, to Cucusus in Armenia. Then in 407 he was once more banished, this time to Pityus at the eastern end of the Black Sea, but he died from exhaustion while undertaking the journey. He is honoured as one of the four Greek Doctors of the Church (with Athanasius, Basil the Great and Gregory of Nazianzus) and was given the surname of Chrysostom, or 'Golden Mouth', because of his great eloquence.

Novels: '"I wonder what saint is pictured here? An elder, certainly. It could be Saint John Chrysostom."' The saint carved on the lid of FORTUNATA's box may have been John Chrysostom.

Refs: **16** (11).

Jordan, Brother (*fl.* 1135) (fict.). **Novels:** Benedictine monk of SHREWSBURY ABBEY. Towards the end of 1135, old Brother Jordan was going blind and treasured 'the flame of light'. While tending the candles at St Mary's altar in the abbey church, he saw ELFGIVA take ALARD THE SILVERSMITH's silver candlesticks. Unable to see clearly, Jordan mistook her for a vision of St MARY herself. Elfgiva made him promise not to tell anyone of the visitation for three days, but by the time he was able to speak, she had disappeared.

Refs: **RB** (2).

Jove (myth.) In Roman mythology, Jove (or Jupiter) was the brother and husband of Juno, the queen of heaven. Like the Greek Zeus (with whom he was equated), Jove was the supreme god. He was the special protector of ROME. In Italy he was revered as the lord of heaven and bringer of light. He determined the course of human affairs, and his divine will was made known through signs in the heavens, like thunder and lightning, and the flights of certain birds. See also GANYMEDE and HEBE.

Novels: Godith Adeney (see BLUND) said to CADFAEL that Jove must be Torold BLUND).

Refs: **2** (5).

Judas Iscariot (d. *c.*30) (hist.). One of the twelve apostles, he betrayed Jesus for thirty pieces of silver. His surname is probably derived from the Latin *sicarius*, meaning 'murderer' or 'assassin'. There are variant traditions concerning his death. According to Matthew 27:3–10, after seeing Jesus condemned to death, Judas repented, returned the silver and hanged himself. 'And the chief priests took the silver pieces, and said, It is not lawful for to put them into the treasury, because it is the price of blood. And they took counsel, and bought with them the potter's field, to bury strangers in. Wherefore that field was called, The field of blood, unto this day.' In Acts 1:18, however, Judas 'purchased a field with the reward of his wickedness; and falling headlong, he burst asunder in the midst, and all his bowels gushed out'. The field became known as Aceldama, or the Field of Blood.

Novels: '"The POTTER'S FIELD!" said Prior ROBERT, musing. "It was such a field that was bought with the silver of Judas's betrayal, for the burial of strangers. I trust there can be no ill omen in the name."'

Refs: **17** (1).

K

Kentigern, Saint (d. 603) (hist.) (f.d. 14 January). Also called Mungo. There are many legends about Kentigern, but few facts. He is particularly associated with north-west England and south-west Scotland, being the founder of the church at Glasgow and a missionary in Cumbria. He was driven into exile in Wales and is said to have founded the monastery at Llanelwy (see ST ASAPH); authorities, however, claim that he was merely the abbot. He returned to Scotland, living at Dumfries (Hoddam) and particularly Glasgow, where he continued to spread the gospel. He died at Glasgow and his relics are said to be in the cathedral.

Novels: St Kentigern had founded the church at Llanelwy on the monastic principle of the old Celtic clas, a college of canons under a priest-abbot, and with one other priest or more among the members.

Refs: **18** (1–2).

Kettering (Northamptonshire, England). Some 13 miles north-east of NORTHAMPTON, this ancient town dates back to Roman times when a large settlement existed to the north of the present town centre. In

1227 Henry III granted Northampton the right to hold a weekly market. From the 17th C. it became a centre for the production of woollen cloth, and later silk and plush. After the Industrial Revolution the town became associated with the manufacture of boots and shoes, but the footwear industry has now been superseded by more modern industries.

Novels: In November 1143, having been dismissed from further service in the FENS, Hugh BERINGAR sent his men west to Kettering, while he rode north to PETERBOROUGH.

Refs: **17** (10).

King's Chase. See YARDLEY CHASE.

Knights of Saint John (hist.). Also called Knights of St John of Jerusalem, Knights Hospitallers, Knights of Rhodes or Knights of Malta. A religious military order founded in the 11th C. by a group of merchants from Amalfi in Italy, the Knights of St John was re-established in 1099 as a Benedictine hospital for sick pilgrims in JERUSALEM, close to the Holy Sepulchre Church. It was run by a group of monastic brothers under the leadership of a monk called Gerard. Dedicated to alms-giving, hospitality and the care of the sick, the foundation flourished, and was officially confirmed an independent religious order in 1113. During the 12th C. the order was predominantly military, its members literally considering themselves to be soldiers of Christ. Founding hostels in Europe for pilgrims en route to the HOLY LAND, the order was introduced into England in *c.*1114. The headquarters of the Prior of the English and Welsh Knights was at Clerkenwell Priory, north LONDON, founded in *c.*1140. After the fall of ACRE in 1291, the Knights retreated to CYPRUS and in 1307 they conquered Rhodes, defending their occupation against Muslim opposition until 1522. Its headquarters was transferred to Malta in 1530 and remained there until the island was captured by Napoleon in 1798, effectively bringing the order to an end. In 1834, however, the pope established the headquarters of the order in ROME, and today it continues to play a religious and humanitarian role in the world. In England the medieval order was suppressed in 1540. It was revived in 1877 as the St John Ambulance Association, and ten years later the St John Ambulance Brigade was formed, to be merged with the Association in 1971. Today, the order operates mainly through two foundations: St John Ambulance Association, including the Brigade, and St John Ophthalmic Hospital in Jerusalem. Its headquarters is in LONDON.

Novels: '"And as soon as you reach the Holy Land the Knights of Saint John provide shelter everywhere."' While in the Holy Land, ELAVE and William of LYTHWOOD were given shelter by the Knights of St John.

Refs: **16** (3).

Knights Templar (hist.). Also called Poor Knights of Christ and of the Temple of Solomon. A religious military brotherhood, subjected to monastic vows and discipline, founded in *c.*1118 by Hugh de Payens and eight or nine French knights actively to defend the Crusader states of the HOLY LAND and protect pilgrims to JERUSALEM from Moslem hostilities. Baldwin II, King of Jerusalem, allowed them to set up their base in part of his palace – known as the Temple of SOLOMON – from which they derived their name. Among their supporters was BERNARD OF CLAIRVAUX, who drew up their monastic Rule, approved at the Council of Troyes in 1128. In 1137 the Order received its first possessions in England when Queen MATILDA granted them the manor of Cressing in Essex, to which she added Cowley near OXFORD in 1139. After the fall of ACRE in 1291 their purpose in the Holy Land came to an end. Having diversified, the Templars became international bankers and financiers. Immensely wealthy and powerful, autocratic and exclusive, they were eventually destroyed by Philip IV, King of

France. Accused of heresy, sodomy and blasphemy, those Templars who were in France were arrested, tortured, forced to confess their guilt and either imprisoned or burned at the stake. The Order was finally suppressed by Pope Clement V in 1312 and much of its property granted to the KNIGHTS OF ST JOHN. Two years later, the Grand Master Jacques de Molay and Gaufrid (or Geoffroi) de Charney, the preceptor of Normandy, were sent to the stake. The Templars wore a white tunic with a red cross; the naves of their churches were circular, modelled on the Church of the Holy Sepulchre (or possibly the Dome of the Rock on Temple Mount) in Jerusalem. See TEMPLE.

Novels: In September 1144 certain Knights Templar, who were at MILDENHALL when Geoffrey de MANDEVILLE died, took his body back with them to LONDON, 'where for want of any Christian relenting they were forced to let him lie in a pit outside the churchyard in the Temple, in unhallowed ground'.

Refs: **19** (Prologue).

Knockin (Shropshire, England). Some 11 miles north-west of SHREWSBURY and 5 miles south-east of OSWESTRY, this village of brick and sandstone buildings has one long main street. St Mary's Church, hidden among trees, was founded by Ralph le Strange towards the end of the 12th C.; the Norman south doorway of the chancel, through which the priest once entered, still survives. Close by the church are the earthwork remains of a 12th C. castle.

Novels: In November 1143 BRITRIC THE PEDLAR was arrested on the English side of the Welsh border and taken to Knockin. From there he was escorted to a cell in SHREWSBURY CASTLE.

Refs: **17** (7).

L

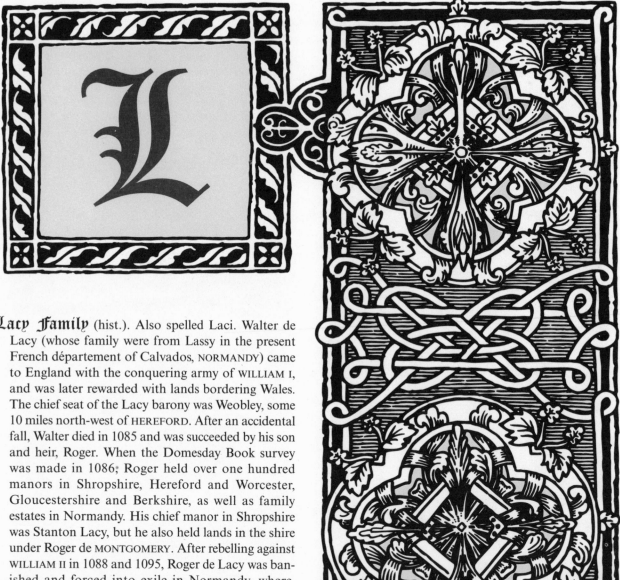

Lacy Family (hist.). Also spelled Laci. Walter de Lacy (whose family were from Lassy in the present French département of Calvados, NORMANDY) came to England with the conquering army of WILLIAM I, and was later rewarded with lands bordering Wales. The chief seat of the Lacy barony was Weobley, some 10 miles north-west of HEREFORD. After an accidental fall, Walter died in 1085 and was succeeded by his son and heir, Roger. When the Domesday Book survey was made in 1086, Roger held over one hundred manors in Shropshire, Hereford and Worcester, Gloucestershire and Berkshire, as well as family estates in Normandy. His chief manor in Shropshire was Stanton Lacy, but he also held lands in the shire under Roger de MONTGOMERY. After rebelling against WILLIAM II in 1088 and 1095, Roger de Lacy was banished and forced into exile in Normandy, where, sometime after 1106, he died. The king gave Roger's forfeited estates to Roger's brother, Hugh, who died without heirs sometime before 1122. His lands passed to the Crown, and HENRY I granted part of the Lacy estate to Pagan FitzJohn. After FitzJohn's death, King STEPHEN granted a large part of the Lacy honour to Josce de DINAN, castellan of LUDLOW. By *c.* 1143 Stephen recognised the title of Gilbert de Lacy, Hugh's nephew, and made him lord of Ewias. Gilbert, who had previously supported the Empress MAUD, was granted his uncle's estates in England as compensation for those Maud had confiscated in Normandy. He died in 1163 and was succeeded by his son, Hugh de Lacy II, who obtained a charter from HENRY II confirming Stanton Lacy, Ludlow, Ewias and other estates to him. Hugh accompanied the king on an expedition to Ireland in October 1172. He was put in charge of the city of DUBLIN, granted the lands of Meath and appointed Judiciary, or Viceroy, of Ireland. After supporting Henry in his Normandy campaigns, Hugh returned to Ireland and married a daughter of the King of Connaught, without the royal licence. Henry suspected that Hugh was intending to found a rival kingdom for himself in Ireland and confiscated the Lacy estates. In 1185 Hugh de Lacy was assassinated in Ireland. By 1189, the year that Henry died, Hugh's lands had been restored to the eldest of his four sons, Walter.

Novels: Alain le GAUCHER was a 'by-blow of the Lacy clan by a younger son of the house'. Stephen granted Josce de Dinan, castellan of Ludlow, the honour of Lacy which included CALLOWLEAS and LEDWYCHE. The lands of Lacy were near Ludlow.

Refs: **6** (1, 5, 11); **20** (16).

Lai (Shropshire, England). DB – Lai: in Hodnet Hundred; a holding of Roger de Lacy under Roger de MONTGOMERY. Lai is thought to be Lowe, which is a small hamlet some 11 miles north of SHREWSBURY and just over 1 mile north-west of WEM.

Novels: 'Nicholas HARNAGE rode between flat, rich fields, unwontedly dried by the heat, into the wattled enclosure of the manor of Lai. Wrapped round on all sides by the enlarged fields of the plain, sparsely tree'd to make way for wide cultivation, the house rose long and low, a stone-built hall and chambers over a broad undercroft, with stables and barns about the interior of the fence.' Although the CRUCE family held several manors in the north-east of Shropshire, they made Lai the head of their honour. Humphrey CRUCE was Lord of Lai until his death in September 1138, and was succeeded by his son, Reginald CRUCE. In September 1141 Nicholas Harnage journeyed to Lai to see Humphrey and ask him for the hand of his daughter, Julian CRUCE.

Refs: **11** (4–8, 11, 13–14).

Lambert (*fl.* 1145) (fict.). **Novels:** Carter and villein of Eudo BLOUNT (the younger) of LONGNER, Lambert was a good twenty years younger than his fellow carter, GREGORY. In February 1145 Lambert, Gregory and ALDHELM delivered to SHREWSBURY ABBEY the promised load of wood for rebuilding RAMSEY ABBEY. While they were transferring the load to the larger abbey wagon, Brother RICHARD haled them away to help carry some of the abbey's threatened treasures out of the church and out of reach of the rising floodwaters. Unaware that St WINIFRED's reliquary had been placed on the Ramsey wagon, Lambert and Gregory 'hefted another load of timber aboard' and covered it completely. About a week later, after the loss of the reliquary had been discovered, CADFAEL rode out to Longner to talk to Lambert and Gregory: 'Square-built, muscular men both, and weatherbeaten from outdoor living in all seasons, with a good twenty years between them, so that they might have been father and son.' All they could tell him was that Aldhelm had helped an unknown 'close-cowled' brother (Brother TUTILO) 'move some last thing'. Both admitted that they would not recognise the monk, if they saw him again.

Refs: **19** (2–6, 12).

Lambeth (London, England). The modern LONDON borough of Lambeth lies south of the River THAMES and stretches as far south as Streatham. Before the 18th C. Lambeth was sparsely populated, consisting mostly of marshland, with the majority of inhabitants

L

living near the river. During Roman times it is thought that the area was covered by a vast shallow lake. The only two buildings to survive in Lambeth prior to the 18th C. are the parish Church of St Mary and Lambeth Palace. The latter, standing almost opposite WESTMINSTER, is the official London residence of the Archbishops of Canterbury. It dates from the end of the 12th C., when Archbishop Hubert Walter built a monastery for Praemonstratensian canons, incorporating a residence for himself. Little is known about these early buildings. The present chapel dates from this period, the vaulted crypt is 13th C., and the Lollard's Tower, originally built as a water tower, was constructed in 1142. The Tudor gatehouse was completed in 1501. The palace was rebuilt and extensively restored in 1828–34 by Edward Blore. The Great Hall now houses an extensive library, including the collection of books bequeathed by Archbishop Bancroft in 1610.

Novels: Bishop GILBERT was consecrated at Lambeth in 1143 by Archbishop THEOBALD OF BEC.

Refs: **18** (1–2).

Lanfranc (*c.*1005–89), Archbishop of Canterbury (hist.). Born at Pavia in LOMBARDY, he was the son of Hanbald and Roza. Like his father, Lanfranc became a lawyer and, while a young man, gained a reputation for knowledge and eloquence. After his father's death, Lanfranc went to France and, eventually, NORMANDY where he established a school at Avranches in 1039. Although he achieved widespread fame as a teacher, he soon determined to become a monk and entered the Benedictine monastery at BEC under Abbot Herlwin. In *c.*1045, after some three years of seclusion, Lanfranc became prior and opened a school in the monastery to which scholars flocked from all over Europe. William of Normandy (see WILLIAM I) made him his councillor, but they fell out when Lanfranc opposed his marriage to Matilda of Flanders. They were soon reconciled, however, and in 1066 William made him abbot of his new monastery of St Stephen's at Caen. In 1070, after Stigand was deposed, William (now King of England) persuaded Lanfranc to become the new Archbishop of CANTERBURY. Lanfranc immediately set about reforming and reorganising the English Church. In 1075, while William was in Normandy, Lanfranc uncovered a conspiracy against the king by the Earls of Hereford and Norfolk which was successfully foiled. On William I's death in 1087, the archbishop crowned WILLIAM II King of England – despite opposition from the partisans of the new king's elder brother, ROBERT of Normandy.

Novels: '"It's been in my mind, since studying the reasonings of Archbishop Lanfranc," said the abbot, "that there must be a change in our thoughts on this matter of child dedication, and I am now convinced that it is better to refuse all oblates until they are able to consider for themselves what manner of life they desire."'

Refs: **8** (1).

Languedoc (France). A historical and cultural region of southern France, Languedoc was named after the *langue d'oc*, or 'oc language' of its inhabitants – 'oc' meaning 'yes'; by the end of the 13th C. the name applied to the entire area in which the language was spoken. From the end of the 9th C. to the middle of the 11th C., under the counts of Toulouse, Languedoc began to develop a culture of its own, more influenced by Provence, Italy and Muslim Spain than northern France. By the mid-12th C., the Cathari, a Manichean sect, had won the support of the counts, and were particularly strong in the region of Albi, from which they became known as Albigensians. This breakaway sect were branded as heretics by the Catholic Church and Pope Innocent III proclaimed a crusade against them. Languedoc was invaded by an army from northern France in 1209, and the ensuing wars, which lasted until 1244, ended its political independence.

Novels: In June 1143 Canon GERBERT warned Abbot RADULFUS about the malignant growth of Manichean heresy in regions like Languedoc and PROVENCE. See also MANES. Brother TUTILO's singing was 'not in English, not even in Norman-French as England knew it, but in the *langue d'oc* CADFAEL remembered imperfectly from long ago.'

Refs: **16** (5); **19** (1).

Lavan Sands or Traeth Lafan (Gwynedd, Wales). At the north-eastern end of the MENAI STRAIT, the Lavan Sands stretch for some 3 miles from the Welsh mainland towards Beaumaris and ANGLESEY. Essentially mud and sand, they are covered by the sea at high tide. There is a tradition that the sands were once dry land, among the fields of which stood the royal palace of Llys Helig.

Novels: 'Immediately below them a village lay in its patterned fields, beyond it narrow meadowland melting into salt flats and shingle, and then the wide expanse of sea, and beyond that again, distant but clear in the late afternoon light, the coast of Anglesey stretched out northward, to end in the tiny island of YNYS LANOG. From the shore towards which they moved the shallow water shimmered pale gold overlaid with aquamarine, almost as far as the eye could distinguish colour, for Lavan Sands extended the greater part of the way to the island shore, and only there in the distance did the sea darken into the pure, greenish blue of the deep channel. At the sight of this wonder about which he had dreamed and speculated all day long, MARK checked his horse for a moment, and sat staring with flushed cheeks and bright eyes, enchanted by the beauty and diversity of the world.'

Refs: **18** (5–6).

Lazarus. See MASSARD, Guimar de.

Ledwyche (now Upper Ledwyche) (Shropshire, England). DB – Ledewic: in Culverstone Hundred; a holding of William Pantulf under Roger de MONTGOMERY. Nearly 4 miles north-east of LUDLOW, Upper Ledwyche is a small upland hamlet lying in the valley of the LEDWYCHE BROOK. The larger settlement of Lower Ledwych lies just over 3 miles downstream, about a mile east of Ludlow.

Novels: 'They came to the manor of Ledwyche over a slight ridge and emerged from woodland to look down an equally gentle slope toward the Ledwyche Brook . . . Beyond the watered valley the ground rose again, and there, directly before them in the distance, hung the vast, bleak outline of TITTERSTONE CLEE, its top shrouded in low cloud. But in between the valley lay sheltered on all sides from the worst winds. Trees had been cleared from round the manor, except for windbreaks left for protection to crops and stock in the most open places. From their ridge they looked down at an impressive array of buildings, the manor-house itself built long and steep-roofed over a squat undercroft, the entire visible sweep of the stockade lined within barn and byre and store. A considerable holding, and surely a temptation to the hungry and covetous, in these lawless times, but perhaps too strongly manned to be easy prey.' In 1139 Evrard BOTEREL held the manors of CALLOWLEAS and Ledwyche from Josce de DINAN. CADFAEL, Yves HUGONIN and Hugh BERINGAR visited Boterel at Ledwyche in December.

Refs: **6** (5–6, 8, 15).

Ledwyche Brook (Shropshire, England). This brook rises on the southern slopes of BROWN CLEE HILL to flow south-west towards LUDLOW. A short distance beyond Upper LEDWYCHE, near Crow Leasow Farm, the stream is joined by the HOPTON BROOK. Threading its sinuous course south, passing to the east of Ludlow, the Ledwyche Brook flows through Middleton Court and the village of Middleton, where it receives the waters of the DOGDITCH BROOK. From there it flows through the landscaped parkland of Henley Hall to Lower Ledwyche. Beyond the village, it tumbles over a weir and turns south-eastward, meandering wildly past Caynham and numerous farmsteads towards Burford. About a mile upstream from Burford, at Burford House Gardens, the Ledwyche Brook joins the River TEME. From its source in the heart of the CLEE HILL to its confluence with the Teme, the length of the brook is some 11 miles.

Novels: Sister HILARIA, encased in ice, was found by CADFAEL in a tributary of the Ledwyche Brook in the severe winter of 1139.

Refs: **6** (6, 10).

Leicester (Leicestershire, England). Some 22 miles south of NOTTINGHAM and 28 miles east of LICHFIELD, this sprawling industrial city lies on the River Soar and the Grand Union Canal. Its origins date back to prehistoric times, when it was a river-crossing settlement. The Jewry Wall is believed to date from 130. The Norman castle, built on the site of a Saxon fortification, was dismantled in 1645, but the great hall is still in use. Adjoining the castle is the Norman Church of St Mary de Castro. Older still is St Nicholas's Church, whose origins certainly date back to at least Saxon times. The Augustinian abbey was founded in 1143 by Robert Bossu, Earl of Leicester (see Robert de BEAUMONT (the younger)), and dedicated to St Mary. It was dissolved in 1538 and all that remains are a few fragments of the precinct wall.

Novels: Huon de DOMVILLE held manors in Shropshire, Cheshire, STAFFORD and Leicester. February 1145: in thick woodland south of Leicester the five-strong party from SHREWSBURY, on their way to RAMSEY ABBEY, were ambushed and robbed by 'eleven or twelve' armed men; the countess (see AMICIA, Countess of Leicester) remained in Leicester while the earl, Robert de Beaumont, travelled first to HUNCOTE and then to Shrewsbury.

Refs: **5** (1); **19** (4–5, 7, 9, 11–13); **20** (1).

Leicester, Countess of. See AMICIA, Countess of Leicester.

Leif (b. *c.*1129) (fict.). **Novels:** Born in DUBLIN of a Welsh mother and Danish father, Leif could fluently speak the Welsh of Gwynedd. Able to pass as a Welshman, he often went among the Welsh trefs and the fishing villages spying on behalf of the Danes. His talent for acquiring information reaped many a useful harvest. He was among the raiding party under TURCAILL (*fl.* 1144) which captured CADFAEL and HELEDD near NONNA's hermitage, south-west of BANGOR. Before joining Turcaill in the night raid to abduct CADWALADR, he pinpointed the Welsh prince's whereabouts in OWAIN GWYNEDD's camp.

Refs: **18** (7–11, 13).

Leighton (Shropshire, England). DB – Lestone: in Wrockwardine Hundred; a holding of Reginald the Sheriff under Roger de MONTGOMERY. Some 9 miles south-east of SHREWSBURY, Leighton is an attractive village bounded to the north by the wooded slopes of the WREKIN and to the south by the River SEVERN. Inside St Mary the Virgin's Church, rebuilt in 1714, is a late 13th C. armoured effigy of a member of the Leighton family, brought from BUILDWAS Abbey.

Novels: In 1142 the manor of Leighton belonged to Fulke ASTLEY. When young Richard LUDEL was abducted in November, he was taken to the manor and 'married' to Hiltrude ASTLEY by Cuthred, who was not a priest at all (see BOURCHIER, Renaud).

Refs: **14** (1–3, 10–12).

Leofric (d. 1057), Earl of Mercia (hist.). Son of Leofwine, earldorman of the Hwicce, and husband of Godiva (or Godgifu), he succeeded his father in the earldom of Mercia at some date between 1024 and 1032, and became one of the most powerful magnates in England, rivalled only by Godwine, Earl of Wessex, and Siward, Earl of Northumbria. As his principal residence was at CHESTER, he was sometimes referred to as the Earl of Chester. On the death of Canute (or Cnut), King of England, in 1035, Leofric supported Harold I. A generous benefactor of numerous religious houses, including EVESHAM Abbey, Leofric, together with his wife, founded COVENTRY Abbey in 1043. He was succeeded by their son Aelfgar.

Novels: 'Approaching the city [of COVENTRY in November 1145] from the north, they found Earl Leofric's old defences still in timber, but sturdy enough.'

Refs: **20** (2).

Leominster (Hereford & Worcester, England). Situated on the west bank of the River Lugg, a tributary of the Wye, the busy market town of Leominster is some 12 miles north of HEREFORD and 11 miles south of LUDLOW. Merwald, King of West Mercia, founded a religious house at Leominster in *c.*660. It was destroyed by the Danes in the 9th C., replaced by a collegiate church, later re-founded as a nunnery and suppressed in 1046. The manor was granted to READING ABBEY by HENRY I, who in *c.*1125 founded a Benedictine priory, dedicated to St Peter and St Paul, on the site of the old nunnery. Leominster priory belonged to its mother-house at Reading until the Dissolution. The present parish Church of St Peter and St Paul, remarkable for its three naves, was the former priory church.

Novels: In December 1139 Olivier de BRETAGNE returned to GLOUCESTER from Ludlow by way of Leominster. Brother ADAM (*fl.* 1141) of Reading Abbey arrived at SHREWSBURY on 17 June 1141; he was on his way to Reading's daughter-house of Leominster on a mission for his abbot. In December 1145, on his way back to Shrewsbury from CIRENCESTER, CADFAEL 'stayed over two nights at the priory to rest Hugh [BERINGAR]'s horse.'

Refs: **6** (15); **10** (3, 16); **20** (15–16).

Leonard, Prior (*fl.* 1139) (fict.). **Novels:** 'And striding out of the shadows across the court came Prior Leonard himself, a long, loose-jointed heron of a man, pointed back anxiously advanced, arms flapping like wings.' Prior of BROMFIELD Priory and former Benedictine monk of SHREWSBURY ABBEY, Leonard 'had been a man of the cloister from puberty, serenely content and blissfully innocent'. An old friend of CADFAEL, he sent an urgent message to SHREWSBURY in November 1139, requesting Cadfael's help in doctoring Brother ELYAS. He looked after Yves HUGONIN with kindness and benevolence.

Refs: **6** (2, 4–5, 7–8, 10, 12, 14–15).

Leper of Saint Giles. See MASSARD, Guimar de.

Lethe (myth.). In Greek mythology, Lethe, in Hades, is the river of forgetfulness. Once its waters have been tasted the souls of the dead are no longer able to remember anything of their past life. In another sense it means a mental state of oblivion.

Novels: 'By Hugh's account she (Donata BLOUNT) was now shrunk to a dry wand, her every movement effort, her every moment pain. At least the poppies of Lethe could procure for her some interludes of sleep, if only she would use them. And somewhere deep within his mind CADFAEL could not help wondering if she abstained in order to invite her death the sooner and be free.'

Refs: **17** (11).

Lichfield (Staffordshire, England). DB – Licefelle or Lecefelle: in Offlow Hundred; land of the Bishop of CHESTER. The ancient city of Lichfield is some 40 miles due east of SHREWSBURY and 14 miles north-east of Birmingham city centre. Before the Norman Conquest it was the ecclesiastical centre of the Anglo-Saxon kingdom of Mercia. The first cathedral church to be erected at Lichfield was consecrated in 700 to enshrine the bones of St CHAD, the first Bishop of Lichfield, who died in 672. Bishop ROGER DE CLINTON instigated the building of a Norman, stone cathedral on the site in 1135. The present cathedral was built of red sandstone between 1195 and 1325. Dedicated to St Mary and St Chad, the cathedral is the only one in England with three spires, which are known as the Ladies of the Vale. Housed within the 13th C. Chapter House is the priceless Lichfield Gospels, an illuminated manuscript dating from the early 8th C. which came to the cathedral from Wales about one thousand years ago. Where it originated, or who wrote it, remains a mystery. The hospital of St John the Baptist was founded just outside the walls of Lichfield in *c.*1135, probably by Bishop Roger de Clinton, and refounded in 1495 by Bishop William Smyth. St Chad's Church, at the north-eastern end of Stowe Pool, stands by an ancient spring where, in the 7th C., the saint is said to have founded a monastery.

Novels: 'Bishop de Clinton and his deacon, SERLO, were on their way back to COVENTRY, where one of Roger's predecessors in office had transferred the chief seat of his diocese, though it was still more often referred to as Lichfield than as Coventry, and both churches considered themselves as having cathedral status.' 'CADFAEL went out before Compline into the chill of the dusk, and turned southward from the close to where the burnished surfaces of the minster pools shone with a sullen leaden light in the flat calm, and the newly cleared space where the Saxon church had stood showed as yet a scar slow to heal. Roger de Clinton, continuing work on foundations begun years before, had approved the choice of a more removed and stable site for a projected weight far greater than St Chad, the first bishop, had ever contemplated. Cadfael turned at the edge of the holy ground blessed by the ministry of one of the gentlest and most beloved of prelates, and looked back to the massive bulk of the new stone cathedral, barely yet finished, if indeed there could even be an end to adorning and enlarging it.' After LILIWIN and RANNILT were married at Shrewsbury in May 1140, they set out together on the road to Lichfield. Among the guests at SHREWSBURY ABBEY who were robbed in June 1141 was a yeoman from Lichfield. Cadfael accompanied Brother HALUIN on his penitential pilgrimage to ELFORD in March 1143, and on the way they rested for one night with 'the clerics of Lichfield'. Deacon MARK from Lichfield arrived at Shrewsbury Abbey in May 1144 on an errand into Wales for Bishop Roger de Clinton. The pectoral cross, given as a gift to Bishop GILBERT, was made by a Lichfield silversmith and blessed at the shrine of St Chad . The diocese of Lichfield lost a third of its territory in 1144, when Archbishop THEOBALD OF BEC revived the diocese of ST ASAPH. In November 1145 Cadfael and Hugh BERINGAR stopped overnight at Lichfield, where they found Yves HUGONIN, and, from there, together, they rode to the conference at Coventry.

Refs: **7** (1, 14); **10** (1, 6); **14** (2); **15** (2, 4, 10); **16** (5, 15); **18** (1–2, 5–6, 12); **20** (1–3).

Lichfield, Bishop of. See ROGER DE CLINTON, Bishop of Coventry and Lichfield.

Lidyate (Shropshire, England) (fict.). Although it never existed, the manor of Lidyate lay in the north-east of the county, close to the border with Cheshire; it was most probably, in the vicinity of Shavington Park and Cloverly Hall, 5 miles south-east of WHITCHURCH and 3 miles north-west of Market Drayton.

Novels: 'Hamo FITZHAMON of Lidyate held two fat manors in the north-eastern corner of the county, towards the border of Cheshire.' Hamo FitzHamon arrived at SHREWSBURY ABBEY, from Lidyate, on the morning of Christmas Eve 1135 with Lady FITZHAMON, her maid ELFGIVA, and their two grooms, MADOC and SWEYN.

Refs: **RB** (2).

Liliwin (b. *c.*1119) (fict.). **Novels:** Also known as the Sanctuary Sparrow. Liliwin – 'A name strangely right for a vagabond player, very young and solitary and poor, and yet proud of his proficiency in his craft, tumbler, contortionist, singer, juggler, dancer, purveying merriment for others while he found little cause to be merry himself' – was of obscure origins. He was found while a baby by three wandering mummers and, as soon as he could walk, they trained him to be a fairground entertainer. He ran away from his harsh masters when he was 'half-grown'. In May 1140 he arrived at SHREWSBURY and was employed by the AURIFABERS to perform at Daniel AURIFABER's wedding feast. While in the house he met RANNILT. During his act, he accidentally broke a pitcher and was thrown out into the street. He was later accused of assaulting Walter AURIFABER and robbing his strongbox. Pursued by an angry mob of townsmen, Liliwin took refuge in SHREWSBURY ABBEY church. He was granted forty days' sanctuary by Abbot RADULFUS, but it was understood that if he stepped outside the abbey enclave he would be arrested. During a visit by Rannilt, Liliwin persuaded her to hide in the dark recess behind the altar. While there together they made love. At great risk to himself, Liliwin left the safety of the abbey enclave to escort Rannilt back into the town. He managed to return without serious incident. As soon as it became clear that Susanna AURIFABER and IESTYN had robbed Walter of his treasury, Liliwin was allowed to leave the abbey without fear of arrest. He helped rescue Rannilt from the hands of Susanna and Iestyn. Liliwin and Rannilt were married at the parish altar of Shrewsbury Abbey church in May 1140 and, afterwards, set out together on the road to LICHFIELD.

Refs: **7** (1–14); **19** (1).

Lilleshall (Shropshire, England). DB – Linleshelle: in Wrockwardine Hundred; a holding of ST ALKMUND'S CHURCH in SHREWSBURY. The village of Lilleshall lies some 16 miles east of Shrewsbury and 2 miles south-west of Newport. St Michael and All Angels' Church dates from the 13th C. and was built on the site of a Saxon church. In the fields 1 mile to the south of the village, set against a backdrop of woodland, are the ruins of the Augustinian abbey of St Mary. It was founded in *c.*1148 by Richard de Belmeis as a monastery of the Arrouasian order, which was later absorbed by the Augustinians. The abbey was dissolved in 1538.

Novels: In June 1139, on a pilgrimage to WALSINGHAM, BENED THE SMITH OF GWYTHERIN took the road from SHREWSBURY towards Lilleshall.

Refs: **1** (12).

Lincoln (Lincolnshire, England). Some 131 miles north of LONDON, Lincoln is an ancient city, built 200 ft. above sea level on a limestone ridge, overlooking the flat, Lincolnshire plain. There are a number of Roman remains in Lincoln, of which the most remarkable is the 11 mile long artificial waterway (known as the Fossdyke) constructed to link the Witham with the Trent. After more than eighteen centuries, it is still navigable, making it the oldest man-made canal in Britain. In 1068 WILLIAM I built a motte-and-bailey castle on the ridge, incorporating some of the defences of a Roman fortress. By 1115 the timber stockade had been replaced by a stone curtain wall. Lincoln Castle is unusual in that it has two mottes or mounds: one crowned with an Observatory Tower, built in about 1149 (the round observatory turret on top of the Norman structure was built in the 19th C.); and the other, probably the original motte, topped with a late 12th C. circular stone keep, known as the Lucy Tower. A third two-storey tower, Cobb Hall, was added to the castle in the 13th C. and used as a prison. After 1216, when it was besieged by King Louis VIII of France, the castle played no further part in medieval military history. In *c.*1072 the first Norman bishop, Remigius, started to build a church, opposite the castle, on a site dominating both the city and the skyline for miles around. It was consecrated in 1092, but was damaged by a fire in 1141 and an earthquake in 1185. The rebuilding and enlarging of the church was started by Bishop Hugh of Avalon in 1192. Work continued throughout the following centuries. The upper stage of the central tower, with its immense spire, was erected in 1311,

L

but it collapsed in 1549 during a violent storm. At the southern side of the cathedral, beyond Minster Yard, are the ruins of the 13th C. Bishop's Palace. The city received its first charter from HENRY II in 1154 and, during the Middle Ages, it was an important centre of the cloth industry, particularly famed for the type of cloth known as Lincoln Green. There are a number of interesting buildings in the city, but the two that are most noteworthy are Aaron the Jew's House on Steep Hill and the Jew's House in the Strait, both built in the late 12th C. and probably the oldest domestic buildings in Britain. The battle of Lincoln, in which King STEPHEN was taken captive by ROBERT of Gloucester, took place on 2 February 1141.

Novels: In November 1140 Canon ELUARD of Winchester persuaded King Stephen to pay a diplomatic visit to RANULF of Chester and William of ROUMARE at Lincoln. Stephen took his advice and, in return for their pledges of unshakable loyalty, he officially made both brothers earls. On the 21 December, however, a messenger rode in haste into SHREWSBURY from the Lord Bishop of Lincoln. He urged the sheriff to call up the king's knight-service, for Ranulf and Roumare had taken Lincoln Castle by subterfuge. At the battle of Lincoln, fought on 2 February 1141, Stephen was captured by Robert of Gloucester. Although Hugh BERINGAR managed to return to Shrewsbury with his battered Shropshire force, Gilbert PRESTCOTE the elder was taken hostage by the Welsh under CADWALADR.

Refs: **4** (4:1); **8** (3, 8–10, 12–13); **9** (1–3, 5, 9– 10); **10** (1–2, 7); **11** (1, 5); **12** (1); **14** (1–2); **15** (1); **16** (1); **17** (9, 11); **20** (2).

Lincoln, Earl of. See ROUMARE, William of, Earl of Lincoln.

Linde (Shropshire, England) (fict.). Although it never existed, the manor of Linde was situated on the fringes of the LONG FOREST some 4 miles south-east of SHREWSBURY on the southern bank of the Cound Brook, a small tributary of the River SEVERN. The general location of the manor seems to have been near the village of Cantlop.

Novels: 'The three old neighbour-manors of Linde, ASPLEY and FORIET guarded this eastern fringe, half wooded, half open.' The manor of Linde belonged to Wulfric LINDE. It was the home of his wife, before her death, and their two children, Janyn LINDE and Roswitha (see ASPLEY). After Nigel ASPLEY's marriage to Roswitha in December 1140, it seemed that in time he would inherit the manor.

Refs: **8** (5, 11–13).

Linde, Janyn (b. 1118) (fict.). **Novels:** 'A young gentleman, very light of foot and light of heart.' Son of Wulfric LINDE and twin brother of Roswitha (see ASPLEY). Janyn's mother died while he was a child. He and his sister were raised 'together from pups' with Nigel and Meriet ASPLEY and also Isouda FORIET. In 'midsummer' 1140 Janyn accompanied Nigel to view the Aspley manor near NEWARK and, while in the north, persuaded his 'bosom friend' to join, with him, the rebellion being plotted by William of ROUMARE. Janyn murdered Peter CLEMENCE in October to prevent him from reaching CHESTER and discovering that Roumare and RANULF of Chester were planning to seize King STEPHEN's castle at LINCOLN. On 21 December, before he could be accused or arrested for the murder, Janyn fled north from SHREWSBURY. His horse went lame south-west of STAFFORD and when Nigel caught up with him, Janyn 'dispassionately' knifed him from behind and stole his horse. He escaped the pursuit of the sheriff's men to join Roumare at Lincoln.

Refs: **8** (5–6, 10–13).

Linde, Roswitha. See ASPLEY, Roswitha.

Linde, Wulfric (b. *c.* 1095) (fict.). **Novels:** 'A silly kind man, competent at getting good value out of a manor, and reasonable with his tenants and villeins, but seldom looking beyond, and always the last to know what his children or neighbours were about.' Father of Janyn LINDE and Roswitha (see ASPLEY), Wulfric's wife died while their children were young. He and Leoric ASPLEY planned 'long ago' the match between Roswitha and Nigel ASPLEY. Wulfric gave his daughter away in marriage to Nigel at SHREWSBURY ABBEY on 21 December 1140.

Refs: **8** (5, 10–12).

Little Ness. See NESSE.

Llanarmon or Llanarmon Dyffryn Ceiriog (Clwyd, Wales). Set among the BERWYN mountains, high in the valley of the River CEIRIOG, and some 11 miles south-west of CHIRK, Llanarmon is an attractive village of whitewashed stone houses with a church rebuilt in 1846. St Garmon, to whom the church is dedicated and from whom the name of the village is derived, is reputed to be buried under a grass mound by the entrance to the churchyard.

Novels: In February 1141 it was rumoured that OWAIN GWYNEDD was patrolling the Welsh border with England, and on one occasion might be 'encamped near Llanarmon'.

Refs: **9** (3).

Llanbadarn or Llanbadarn Fawr (Dyfed, Wales). Just over a mile east of ABERYSTWYTH, Llanbadarn Fawr, formerly a village, is now part of the town's sprawling suburbs. During the 6th C. St Padarn founded a Celtic monastery, on land to the north of the River Rheidol. There is a strong tradition that Padarn was the first bishop of what may have been the bishopric of Llanbadarn Fawr. Between 1115 and 1135 the monastery became a Benedictine priory dependent on GLOUCESTER Abbey. The present church stands on the early monastic site.

Novels: HYWEL AB OWAIN and GWION travelled in haste to Llanbadarn in May 1144 to instruct Rhodri FYCHAN (*fl.* 1144), on CADWALADR's orders, to pay the sum of 2,000 marks needed to release his lord from Danish captivity.

Refs: **18** (12–13).

Llanbadarn Castle (or Aberystwyth Castle) (Dyfed, Wales). CADWALADR's castle of Llanbadarn was burnt by HYWEL AB OWAIN in 1143. According to the *Brut y Tywysogyon*, it was situated on a small hill opposite Llanbadarn Fawr, near the estuary of the River Ystwyth. Lloyd pinpoints it more accurately: stating that it could be inferred with certainty that the original fortress of ABERYSTWYTH stood on the hill 'at the back of the farm of Tanycastell which lies in the Ystwyth valley a mile and a half to the south of the town'.

Novels: 'OWAIN GWYNEDD in outraged justice had sent his son Hywel to drive Cadwaladr bodily out of every furlong of land he held in CEREDIGION, and burn his castle of Llanbadarn, and the young man, barely past twenty, had accomplished his task with relish and efficiency.' In retribution for the murder of ANARAWD AP GRIFFITH in 1143, Cadwaladr was driven out of Ceredigion by Hywel ab Owain and his castle of Llanbadarn burnt.

Refs: **18** (2).

Llandeiniolen (Gwynedd, Wales). Midway between BANGOR and CARNARVON, this tiny village is just over a mile inland of the MENAI STRAIT. The church is dedicated to St DEINIOL.

Novels: In May 1144 CADFAEL and Deacon MARK received word of HELEDD's whereabouts from the priest at St Deiniol's Church: 'She came to Llandeiniolen from inland, out of the hills and through the forest.'

Refs: **18** (6).

Llanelwy. See SAINT ASAPH.

L

Llanfaes (Gwynedd, Wales). On the north-eastern peninsula of ANGLESEY, one mile north of Beaumaris, Llanfaes was during medieval times the royal manor of the commote of Tindaethwy, with a port and ferry. In the 13th C., under the patronage of Llywelyn the Great, it became a Welsh borough town of about 120 dwellings. After the death of his wife, Joan, in 1237, Llywelyn founded the Franciscan Friary at Llanfaes on the site of her grave. In the early 19th C. her coffin was discovered in a farmyard being used as a watering-trough. Complete with lid, it is now preserved in the church at Beaumaris.

Novels: Llanfaes on Anglesey was the royal burial-place.

Refs: **18** (4).

Llangollen (Clwyd, Wales). Some 9 miles north-west of OSWESTRY and 9 miles south-west of WREXHAM, this small town straddles the River DEE at the narrow, western end of the Vale of Llangollen. There has been a bridge across the fast-flowing river since the reign of HENRY I. The present stone bridge probably dates from *c.*1500, and is known as one of the 'Seven Wonders of Wales'. The church, largely rebuilt in the 19th C., is dedicated to St COLLEN. On the summit of the conical hill to the north of the town are the remains of the 13th C. Welsh fortress, Castell Dinas Bran. Traces can also be found of an earlier, Iron Age fortification. Some 2 miles north-west of the town are the ruins of Valle Crucis Abbey, founded for Cistercian monks in 1201. Nearby stands Elisegs Pillar, erected in the 9th C. by Cyngen, a prince of Powys, in memory of his grandfather, Eliseg. Since 1947 Llangollen has been the home of the International Musical Eisteddfod, held every July.

Novels: 'They emerged into the green, undulating meadows and bushy coverts along the riverside, the Dee beside them reflecting back orange gleams from the west. Beyond the water a great grassy hill soared, crowned with the manmade contours of earthworks raised ages ago, and under the narrow wooden bridge the Dee dashed and danced over a stony bed. Here at the church of Saint Collen they asked and found a lodging for the night with the parish priest.' CADFAEL and Deacon MARK, on the journey from SHREWSBURY to ST ASAPH, lodged overnight with the parish priest of Llangollen in May 1144.

Refs: **18** (2).

Llanrwst (Gwynedd, Wales). Just outside the eastern border of Snowdonia National Park and some 11 miles south of CONWY, Llanrwst is a small market town in the upper CONWAY valley. It is named after St Grwst's Church, which stands on the eastern bank of the river.

Novels: In May 1137 Prior ROBERT led an expedition into North Wales to procure the sacred relics of St WINIFRED for SHREWSBURY ABBEY. On their way from BANGOR to GWYTHERIN, they passed through Llanrwst.

Refs: **1** (1–2).

Llansantffraid Glyn Ceiriog. See GLYN CEIRIOG.

Llansilin (Clwyd, Wales). Some 5 miles west of OSWESTRY and 20 miles north-west of SHREWSBURY, Llansilin is a small village lying on rising ground above the valley of the River CYNLLAITH. St Silin's Church, from which the village takes its name, dates from the 13th C., but was later remodelled and, during the 19th C., heavily restored. The damage to the south door of the church, which is pockmarked with holes, is reputed to have been caused by bullets fired during the English Civil War. The enormous yew trees in the churchyard are of great antiquity and would certainly have been standing when SHREWSBURY ABBEY was founded in 1083.

Novels: 'It was little more than a mile into Llansilin, and the sun was up, veiled but bright. The village was wide awake, and full of people, converging on the timber church. Every house in the neighbourhood must have given shelter overnight to friends and kin from other parts of the commote, for the normal population of this hamlet could be no more than a tenth part of those met here on this day.' In December 1138 CADFAEL attended the commote court at Llansilin, held in the church, for Llansilin was 'the central seat of the commote of Cynllaith'. While at the court, he heard MEURIG voice his claim to the manor of MALLILIE.

Refs: **3** (8–11); **9** (12).

Lleyn Peninsula (Gwynedd, Wales). Also called Llyn or Lleyn. Situated between Cardigan Bay and CARNARVON Bay in north-west Wales, the Lleyn Peninsula is some 16 miles long and between 3 and 10 miles wide, with YNYS ENLLI lying 2 miles off its southernmost tip. At Caernarvon, in the north, the castle and town walls were built during the reign of Edward I (1272–1307). During medieval times, countless pilgrims journeyed to the peninsula, en route to the holy island of Ynys Enlli. Among the places they visited on the way were St Beuno's Church at CLYNNOG Fawr, and ABERDARON.

Novels: 'The remotest tip of Wales.'

Refs: **10** (4–5).

Llywarch, Griffri ap (b. *c.* 1091) (fict.). **Novels:** 'A lean, sinewy man, perhaps fifty years old, balding and bearded, with a hillman's gait, and the weathered face and wrinkled, far-seeing eyes of the shepherd. His clothing was plain and brown, but good homespun.' Griffri ap Llywarch was a Welsh wool-trader from close by MEIFOD. By his wife, he was the father of Griffri ap GRIFFRI (hanged in 1139) and, by a SHREWSBURY maid-servant, Anion ap GRIFFRI. Griffri ap Llywarch admitted his natural son, Anion, into his kinship in March 1141 and introduced him to OWAIN GWYNEDD at TREGEIRIOG.

Refs: **9** (4, 10–11).

Llywarch ap Trahaearn (d. 1129?), Prince of Arwystli (hist.). Son of Trahaearn ap Caradog and father of GWLADUS, Llywarch was induced by Richard of Beaumais, Bishop of London, to join a crusade against Cadwgan ap Bleddyn and his son, Owain. He invaded CEREDIGION in 1109 and forced Owain to flee to Ireland. However, in 1115, in the service of HENRY I, he joined forces with Owain against Gruffydd ap Rhys. After Owain had been killed by the Flemings, Llywarch abandoned the enterprise and returned home to ARWYSTLI. He is last heard of in 1123 and is thought to have died in *c.* 1129, when fighting broke out between his kin. His nephew, Hywel ab Ieuaf ab Owain ap Trahaearn, eventually succeeded to Arwystli, holding the district until his death in 1185. Hywel's overlord was MADOG AP MEREDITH, King of Powys. Llywarch had four sons: Iorwerth (d. 1130), Maredudd (d. 1129), Madog, and Robert (d. 1171).

Novels: The Prince of Arwystli was father of OWAIN GWYNEDD's wife.

Refs: **18** (4).

Lombardy (Italy). The region of northern Italy bounded to the north by the ALPS and to the south by the River Po. Lombardy takes its name from the Lombards, a Germanic people who invaded northern Italy in 568. They established a kingdom in the Po Valley, and separate principalities further south. By the mid-8th C. the pagan Lombards had been converted to Catholicism. No longer divided by the barrier of religion, the Lombards and the native Romans were drawn closer together and, increasingly, the papacy felt itself threatened with relegation to the status of a mere Lombard bishopric. Although the Lombards seized Ravenna in 751 and threatened to advance towards ROME, they were forced to withdraw when the pope sought aid from the Franks. In 774 CHARLES THE GREAT became King of the Lombards as well as the Franks. Lombardy ceased to exist as an independent kingdom, but many of the traditions and achievements of its people have made a lasting contribution to Italian history, particularly in the fields of art, language and law. The capital city of the present-day region of Lombardy is Milan.

Novels: In 1143 Canon GERBERT warned Abbot RADULFUS about the malignant growth of heresy in regions like FLANDERS, France and Lombardy and on the RHINE.

Refs: **16** (5).

London (England). Situated at the lowest convenient crossing point of the River THAMES, the city and port of London was founded by the Romans in the middle of the 1st C., and called *Londinium*. They built a bridge across the river, probably of wood, only a few hundred yards from the site of the present London Bridge. The town was destroyed in 60 by Icenian tribesmen under Queen Boudicca (or Boadicea), and to prevent further attacks the Romans encircled the city with a stone wall, complete with towers and gates. By the 3rd C. London had become the capital of Roman Britain and the sixth largest city in the Roman Empire. Covering 330 acres with the entire south side a waterfront, the city remained more or less confined within the limits of the Roman walls until the 16th C. London Bridge, lined with houses and shops, was the only access to the city from the south until the 17th C. Little is known about London between the withdrawal of the Roman legions in the 5th C. and the establishment of the Saxon port of *Lundenwic* in the 7th C. According to Bede, Ethelbert, King of Kent, founded a church in London dedicated to St Paul, presumably on the site of the present cathedral. During the 9th C., London was occupied by the Danes. By 886, however, Alfred the Great had recaptured and refortified London, ceding to the Danes the area of England, north and east of the city, known as the Danelaw. Towards the end of the 10th C., London suffered a fresh wave of attacks from Scandinavia and by 1016 the country was under Danish rule. In 1042 EDWARD THE CONFESSOR, the surviving son of the English King ETHELRED II, was offered the crown by popular agreement. Towards the end of his reign, Edward devoted much of his energy and money to the building of an abbey and palace at WESTMINSTER, nearly 2 miles upstream from the walled city. WILLIAM I was crowned king at the abbey in 1066 and soon after began to build castles, including the TOWER OF LONDON, to control the restless inhabitants. London's royal centre, however, remained at Westminster. Like their Anglo-Saxon predecessors, the Norman kings had no one capital and at first a number of cities, like WINCHESTER and GLOUCESTER, vied for prominence. During medieval times London was a divided city with two centres of authority: Westminster, where the power rested in the hands of the king, and later parliament; and the City, which came under the control of the powerful merchant guilds. In the civil war for the throne of England between King STEPHEN and the Empress MAUD, it was the Londoners who determined one major outcome: in June 1141 they expelled the empress from the city and, with the support of Queen MATILDA's army, drove her west to OXFORD.

Novels: In December 1138 Abbot HERIBERT attended a legatine council at Westminster for the reform of the Church and was removed from his office at SHREWSBURY ABBEY. He was replaced by Abbot RADULFUS. In October 1140 Canon ELUARD OF WINCHESTER went to London to urge King Stephen to pay a diplomatic visit to LINCOLN. After Stephen's capture at the battle of Lincoln on 2 February 1141, the Empress Maud entered London. Before she could be crowned, however, the citizens drove her out and allowed Queen Matilda in. On 7 December 1141 RADULFUS attended Bishop HENRY OF BLOIS' legatine council at Westminster, held to justify Bishop Henry's swing back to Stephen. In September 1144 the coffined body of Geoffrey de Mandeville was placed in a pit outside the churchyard of the TEMPLE in London.

Refs: **2** (8); **3** (1, 8); **4** (1:1); **5** (1); **8** (3, 10); **9** (12); **10** (1–2, 10, 16); **11** (1, 7); **12** (1); **14** (4, 9, 13); **15** (1); **16** (1); **17** (3); **19** (Prologue); **20** (1); **RB** (2).

Long Forest (Shropshire, England). DB – The Long Forest, according to Anderson in *Shropshire: Its Early History and Antiquities* (1864), 'involved within its regard nearly the whole of the Domesday Hundred of Condover, besides a number of manors belonging to other Hundreds'. The Long Forest stretched in a broad swath south and south-west of SHREWSBURY. Its eastern limit was a line drawn roughly from Bayston Hill (see BEISTAN) in the north to WENLOCK Edge and the STRETTON Hills in the south. Broken by clearings, hamlets, high, desolate heaths, sheep pastures and wild scrubland, the forest – reaching westward to Wales – embraced all the country between the Lyth Hills and the Long Mynd. Its western extremity was somewhere in the vicinity of PONTESBURY, MINSTERLEY and the Rea Brook valley (see MEOLE BROOK). Up until 1180, jurisdiction of the Long Forest was strict and, apart from a few favoured exceptions, there were very few assarts or manors allowed. By 1235, however, there were only three royal preserves left intact within the forest: Lythwood, Bushmoor and Haycrust. Further encroachment continued and, by the beginning of the 14th C., the woodland was finally broken up. Only isolated fragments of the once great forest remain today.

Novels: 'The woods were thick and well grown, the ground so shadowed that herbal cover was scant, but the interlacing of boughs above shut out the sky. Sometimes the path emerged for a short way into more open upland, for all this stretch of country was the northern fringe of the Long Forest, where men had encroached with their little assarts and their legal or illegal cutting of timber and pasturing of pigs on acorns and beech-mast. But even here settlements were very few.' In August 1138 Hugh BERINGAR and CADFAEL rode south together to the 'old grange . . . [SHREWSBURY ABBEY] used to maintain in the Long Forest, out beyond PULLEY'. The road south to the manor of STANTON COBBOLD 'lay through the more open and sunlit stretches of the Long Forest'. In June CIARAN headed into the Long Forest intent on reaching the Welsh border. He and Matthew (see MEVEREL, Luc) were attacked by Simeon POER and his fellow outlaws. In March 1145 BÉNEZET was captured by the sheriff's men in the 'thick woodland' of the Long Forest. Places in or on the outskirts of the Long Forest included: the neighbouring manors of LINDE, ASPLEY and FORIET; GODRIC'S FORD; Pulley; BRACE MEOLE; THORNBURY; Beistan; Huon de DOMVILLE's Hunting Lodge; SUTTON STRANGE; Pontesbury; HANWOOD; and Minsterley.

Refs: **2** (7); **4** (5:3); **5** (5–11); **8** (5); **9** (1–2, 4, 8–9, 13); **10** (13); **13** (11); **19** (13).

Longner (Shropshire, England). DB – Languenare: in Wrockwardine Hundred; land held by the Bishop of CHESTER. Longner is situated in an isolated position, within a broad loop of the River SEVERN, just over 2 miles south-east of SHREWSBURY and 1½ miles north-west of ATCHAM.

Novels: 'The Longner lands were a fair holding, but not great enough to support two families, even if such sharing had ever promised well, and a younger son would have to work out an independent life for himself, as younger sons had always had to do.' Hugh BERINGAR rode to Longner in October 1143 in order to speak to young Eudo BLOUNT, lord of the manor. CADFAEL later rode out to Longner himself. In February 1145 Cadfael escorted Sub-Prior HERLUIN and Brother TUTILO to Longner to see Sulien BLOUNT (the younger). On a number of occasions over the following weeks, Tutilo went to the manor to play and sing to the dying Donata BLOUNT. Cadfael also visited Longner to talk to GREGORY and LAMBERT about the disappearance of St WINIFRED's reliquary.

Refs: **17** (1, 3–5, 7–14); **19** (1–12).

Longwood, (now Upper Longwood) (Shropshire, England). Upper Longwood is a small village lying on the south-western slopes of the WREKIN, nearly 8 miles south-east of SHREWSBURY and less than 1 mile north-east of EATON Constantine. Lower Longwood, not marked on the OS map, lies along the B4380 just south of Watchoak, between Eyton-on-Severn (see EYTON-BY-SEVERN) and Eaton Constantine. It consists of only a few houses.

Novels: In 1142 John of LONGWOOD was the steward of the manor of Eaton.

Refs: **14** (1–3, 8–9).

Longwood, John of (b. 1092) (fict.). **Novels:** 'A burly, bearded man of fifty, with a balding crown and neat, deliberate movements.' John of Longwood was the steward of the manor of EATON, formerly under Richard LUDEL the elder, who died in October 1142. He was responsible for the upkeep of the manor until young Richard LUDEL came to manhood. John arrived at SHREWSBURY ABBEY on 20 October, presented himself to Abbot RADULFUS and delivered a message from his mistress, Dame Dionisia LUDEL: a request that young Richard should be returned to Eaton. He himself had taken no part in the boy's abduction.

Refs: **14** (1–3, 8–9).

Lothair (b. *c.*1088) (fict.). **Novels:** 'CADFAEL had not been deceived in their relationship, for this one was clearly father to the other, a tough, square-set man in his fifties, close-mouthed like his son, broader in the shoulders, more bowed in the legs from years spent as much on horse-back as on his own two feet. The same cold, unconfiding eyes, the same bold and powerful shaven jaws . . .' Father of LUC, Lothair was the Norman servant of Bertrand de CLARY and, after his lord's death in *c.*1131, the faithful servant of Adelais de CLARY of HALES. He had been a crusader and fought with his lord in the HOLY LAND. In March 1143 he rode with his mistress, Luc and GERTA to ELFORD. Either Lothair or Luc, or both, murdered EDGYTHA in the woods between VIVERS and Elford. When they revealed their crime to Adelais, she sent them far away.

Refs: **15** (4–6, 12–14).

Louis VI (1081–1137), King of France (1108-37) (hist.). Also called Charles the Fat. Father of LOUIS VII, his greatest achievement was in bringing the feudal nobles in his domains firmly under royal control. His biographer and most trusted adviser, Abbot Suger of ST DENIS, depicted him as the archetypal Christian monarch, upholding the values of the Church, while protecting the poor against oppression. He fought wars against HENRY I, King of England, in 1104–13 and 1116–20, which ended in Louis having to accept a definitive peace. In 1124 he was able to muster sufficient forces to prevent a threatened invasion by HENRY V, Holy Roman Emperor. Louis supported William Clito, son of ROBERT, Duke of Normandy, in his claim to the duchy of NORMANDY.

Novels: 'It was long ago, after the old king [Henry I] had conquered and settled Normandy, until King Louis came to the French throne, and started the struggle all over again.'

Refs: **20** (15).

Louis VII (*c.*1120–80), King of France (1137–80) (hist.). Son of LOUIS VI. In the same year as his accession he married Eleanor, daughter of William X, Duke of Aquitaine. Louis was a friend and supporter of STEPHEN, King of England, and spent much of his reign pursuing a long rivalry, marked by intrigue and recurrent warfare, with GEOFFREY of Anjou and, more particularly, his son, HENRY II, King of England. Louis and Emperor CONRAD III joined the Second Crusade in 1146, having been stimulated by the preaching of BERNARD OF CLAIRVAUX, and many others all over Europe followed their example. In 1153, after rumours of Eleanor's misconduct at ANTIOCH, Louis and his wife were divorced. Shortly afterwards, Eleanor married Henry Plantagenet (the future Henry II). Louis VII was succeeded by Philip II, his son by his third wife, Adela of Champagne, daughter of THEOBALD OF NORMANDY.

Novels: In September 1140 Bishop HENRY OF BLOIS went to France to try and win the support of Louis VII and Count Theobald of Normandy. He hoped they would endorse some plan that would bring about a peaceful settlement to the conflict in England between Stephen and the Empress MAUD.

Refs: **8** (1, 3); **19** (11).

Louis, Lay Brother (*fl.* 1138) (fict.). **Novels:** 'Brother Louis . . . was small and wiry and agile, and in this solitude kept a dagger by him, and knew how to use it.' Lay brother of SHREWSBURY ABBEY, born in England but of French descent, Louis was once a groom in the household of ROBERT of Gloucester. In August 1138 Louis and Lay Brother ANSELM looked after an old abbey grange in the LONG FOREST. At CADFAEL's request, they hid Hugh BERINGAR's horses. They also helped Godith Adeney (see BLUND) and Torold BLUND get safely away with William FITZALAN's treasury.

Refs: **2** (7, 9–10).

Lowe. (See LAI).

Luc (b. *c.*1113) (fict.). **Novels:** 'Adelais de CLARY's groom was waiting for them in the porch, as she had promised, leaning indolently with one shoulder propped against the jamb of the door, as though he had been waiting for some time, but with immovable patience.' Norman son of LOTHAIR, Luc was the faithful servant of Adelais de Clary of HALES. In March 1143 he accompanied his father, GERTA and mistress to ELFORD. Either Luc or Lothair, or both, murdered EDGYTHA, mistakenly thinking it would please their mistress. Once she became aware of their crime, however, she sent them both away.

Refs: **15** (4–6, 12–14).

Lucius II (d. 1145), Pope (1144–5) (hist.). Born in Bologna as Gherardo Caccianemici, he was made cardinal priest of Santa Croce by Pope Calixtus II in 1124 and papal chancellor and librarian by INNOCENT II in 1141. Among his powerful friends were BERNARD OF CLAIRVAUX and PETER THE VENERABLE. He succeeded Celestine II as pope on 12 March 1144. Roger II, King of Sicily, invaded the papal states, and Lucius was forced to accept an armistice under which he agreed to allow Roger to retain his newly won territories in return for a cessation of further hostilities. To add to the pope's troubles, Giordano Pierleoni, brother of the antipope Anacletus II, encouraged the citizens of ROME to demand independence from papal control. Lucius led an unsuccessful assault against the rebels, and on 15 February 1145 he died from injuries received in the conflict. He was succeeded by Eugenius III.

Refs: **18** (6); **19** (Prologue).

Lucy, Sir Alan (*fl.* 1139) (fict.). Lord of two manors on the Hereford borders, he was the father of Joscelin LUCY. Alan sent his son as a page to Huon de DOMVILLE in 1131, when the boy was fourteen. Sometime before 1139, Alan made the pilgrimage to COMPOSTELA, to the shrine of St JAMES.

Refs: **5** (1–3).

Lucy, Iveta (née de Massard) (b. 1121) (fict.). **Novels:** 'She was sumptuously arrayed in cloth of gold and dark blue silks, and within the burden of her finery her slight form seemed cramped and straightened, like a body coffined. Her face gazed ahead, beneath a gilded net heavy with dark-gold hair, into emptiness. A softly rounded face, with delicate features and great iris-grey eyes, but so pale and subdued that she might have been a pretty doll rather than a living woman.' Iveta Lucy was the wife of Joscelin LUCY, daughter and heiress of Hamon FitzGuimar de MASSARD, granddaughter of Guimar de MASSARD, and niece of Sir Godfrid and Lady Agnes PICARD. Her mother died in 1121, when she was born. After her father's death in 1131, she was placed under the guardianship of the Picards. She arrived at SHREWSBURY in October 1139 to marry Huon de DOMVILLE. A reluctant bride, she was accompanied by the Picards, who had not only arranged the marriage, but who also kept a close watch on her every movement in case she

L

refused to comply with their plans. Iveta was in love with Joscelin Lucy. While lodged at SHREWSBURY ABBEY, she managed to evade her guards to meet Joscelin in the abbey gardens. They made plans to escape, but were seen together in CADFAEL's workshop by Agnes. In consequence, Joscelin was dismissed from Domville's service. On the day of their wedding, Domville was found murdered. Iveta drugged MADLEN with a draught of Cadfael's poppy syrup and slipped away to meet Joscelin. They were surprised and cornered by the sheriff's men. When it was revealed that the Picards had been using Iveta to further their own ends, she was taken under the guardianship of Abbot RADULFUS. She spent a short while in the care of a manor or nunnery, possibly White Ladies Priory (see BREWOOD NUNNERY). Sometime before October 1140, Iveta and Joscelin were married. They took BRAN into their household.

Refs: **5** (1–11); **8** (6)

Lucy, Joscelin (b. 1117) (fict.). **Novels:** Also called Joss. 'The big, tow-headed youngster in the middle actually turned full-face to the two on the ground, flashed them a dismayed stare from eyes as blue as cornflowers, and rode with his chin on his shoulder until both his fellows elbowed him back to caution and his duty.' Son and heir of Sir Alan LUCY, husband of Iveta LUCY and former squire of Huon de DOMVILLE, Joscelin Lucy was educated by monks, and could write and read Latin. He entered the service of Domville as a page in 1131, when he was fourteen. In October 1139 he arrived at SHREWSBURY in the company of his lord and two fellow squires, Simon AGUILON and Guy FITZJOHN. He loved Iveta de Massard (see LUCY) and, although Domville was about to marry her himself, Joscelin had not given up hope of winning her. Iveta managed to slip away from her guards to meet Joscelin in the abbey gardens. They were seen together in CADFAEL's workshop by Lady Agnes PICARD and, shortly after, Joscelin was dismissed from Domville's service. Although entirely innocent, he was arrested for the theft of a gold collar, but managed to escape by leaping from the English Bridge into the River SEVERN. After being carried downstream by the fast-moving floodwater, Joscelin hauled himself out of the water and vanished into the woods beyond the orchards of the GAYE. He was found by Simon and persuaded to hide in a hut in the grounds of Bishop ROGER DE CLINTON'S HOUSE. Deciding to leave the hay-store, Joscelin was pursued by soldiers towards ST GILES. Lazarus (see MASSARD, Guimar de), however, helped to conceal him. Disguised beneath a hooded cloak and veil, Joscelin found refuge amongst the lepers. He was befriended by BRAN. When Domville was found murdered, Joscelin became the prime suspect. He slipped out of the hospice and managed to get a message to Simon, who passed it on to Iveta. When Joscelin and Iveta tried to escape across the MEOLE BROOK together they were cornered by the sheriff's men. With evidence from Brother MARK and Cadfael, Joscelin was proved innocent of Domville's murder. He persuaded Abbot RADULFUS to take Iveta into his guardianship. Sometime before October 1140, Joscelin and Iveta were married. They took Bran into their household.

Refs: **5** (1–11); **8** (6).

Ludel, Dame Dionisia (b. *c.*1087) (fict.). **Novels:** 'The lady's smile was honey, but her eyes were sharp and cold as knives.' Mother of Richard LUDEL the elder and grandmother of Richard LUDEL the younger, Dame Dionisia Ludel was a strong-willed and domineering woman. Her son placed his own son in school at SHREWSBURY ABBEY to keep him away from her influence. In October 1142, on her son's death, Dionisia determined to get her grandson away from the abbey and marry him to Hiltrude ASTLEY. She set Cuthred (see BOURCHIER, Renaud) up in a disused hermitage and persuaded HYACINTH to cause disruption in the abbey's part of the forest. In November, after various requests and threats were refused by

Abbot RADULFUS, she forcibly abducted the boy. He was taken to Fulke ASTLEY's manor at LEIGHTON and 'married' to Hiltrude by Cuthred, who was not a priest. After seeing Cuthred's dead body, she abandoned all her plans involving Richard and asked Radulfus to hear her confession. Having shed her sins and been given absolution, she made peace with her grandson and returned to EATON without him.

Refs: **14** (1–5, 7–14).

Ludel, Richard (the elder) (1107–42) (fict.). **Novels:** He was lord of the manor of EATON, son of Dame Dionisia LUDEL and father of young Richard LUDEL. His wife died in *c.*1137, and shortly after he sent his son to school at SHREWSBURY ABBEY. In 1138 he made Abbot RADULFUS the boy's guardian. Richard was badly wounded at the battle of LINCOLN on 2 February 1141, and 'It was on the eighteenth day of October of that year 1142 that Richard Ludel, hereditary tenant of the manor of Eaton, died of a debilitating weakness, left after wounds received at the battle of Lincoln, in the service of King STEPHEN.' He was buried at Eaton, three days later, by Father ANDREW.

Refs: **14** (1–2).

Ludel, Richard (the younger) (b. 1132) (fict.). **Novels:** '"Sharp – venturesome . . . A very fetching imp, truth to tell, but as often in trouble as out of it. Bright at his letters, but he'd rather be out at play."' Son and heir of Richard LUDEL the elder and grandson of Dame Dionisia LUDEL, the young Richard Ludel became the new lord of the manor of EATON after his father's death on 18 October 1142. At the age of five, shortly after his mother's death in *c.*1137, he was sent to school at SHREWSBURY ABBEY. Abbot RADULFUS became his guardian in 1138. Richard attended his father's funeral in the company of CADFAEL, Brother PAUL and Brother ANSELM. Curious about what was happening at Eaton, Richard ambushed HYACINTH in the abbey enclave. They became allies and friends. Trying to slip into the church without being seen, Richard overheard Brother JEROME inform Drogo BOSIET that the runaway villein he was seeking might be Hyacinth. Richard immediately set out on his pony for EYTON FOREST to warn his friend. He found Hyacinth with ANNET at EILMUND THE FORESTER's cottage. On his way back to the abbey, Richard was abducted by Fulke ASTLEY's men and taken to LEIGHTON, where his grandmother forced him to 'marry' Hiltrude ASTLEY. He had learnt beforehand from Hyacinth, that Cuthred, who performed the ceremony, was an imposter (see BOURCHIER, Renaud). Richard managed to escape, hotly pursued by Astley. Once he was safely back at the abbey, he revealed the truth about Cuthred, and his marriage to Hiltrude was found to be invalid. Despite his treatment, Richard held no grudges.

Refs: **14** (1–14).

L

Ludgershall (Wiltshire, England). Some 6 miles north-west of ANDOVER, on the main road to DEVIZES, this small market town has the remains of a castle dating back to the reign of HENRY I. A popular royal hunting castle during the 13th C. and 14th C., by the mid-16th C. it was in ruins. The Norman St James's Church, built of flint and rubble, has been altered over the centuries. The name Ludgershall is thought to mean 'secluded place of the trapping spear' – a spear set as a trap to impale wild animals.

Novels: In September 1141, after the 'Rout of WINCHESTER', the Empress MAUD fled with the remnant of her army into GLOUCESTER, by way of Ludgershall and Devizes.

Refs: **11** (8).

Ludlow (Shropshire, England). DB – Ludlow is not mentioned, but the origin of the town is thought to have been in Stanton (Lacy): in Culverstone Hundred; land held by Roger de Lacy (see LACY FAMILY). Situated in the south of Shropshire, close to the

Hereford & Worcester border, and some 22 miles south of SHREWSBURY, Ludlow is an attractive market town with a mixture of ancient and modern buildings. It grew up in the shadow of LUDLOW CASTLE and was designed in the late 11th C. on the grid-iron pattern of most medieval settlements. The arrangement of its streets and narrow connecting lanes at right angles to each other can still be traced. By the early 12th C. the town was fortified and large sections of the perimeter walls are still intact, hidden behind houses and gardens. Broad Gate, at the foot of Broad Street, is the only original gateway to survive, although it has been incorporated into an 18th C. building. Ludlow was granted its first market charter in 1189 and prospered, primarily on the wool trade. Dominating the town is St Laurence's Church, the largest parish church in the county with a massive high tower. The church dates from the late 12th C., but there is little surviving evidence of work before 1300 and the present building is mainly 15th C.

Novels: In December 1139 CADFAEL, Yves HUGONIN, Hugh BERINGAR and a few of his men headed back towards Ludlow from TITTERSTONE CLEE. Josce de DINAN was castellan of Ludlow Castle. He supplied a force for Hugh's attack on Alain le GAUCHER's robber fortress. After the outlaws had been defeated, the prisoners were taken to Ludlow together with their plunder.

Refs: **6** (1–6, 8–11, 14–15); **10** (7); **20** (16).

Ludlow Castle (Shropshire, England). This castle, built from the outset of stone, was erected on a rocky cliff, near the confluence of the Rivers CORVE and TEME, most probably by Roger de LACY in the late 11th C. Hugh de Lacy eventually inherited the castle from his brother and, after his death without heirs sometime before 1122, it became the property of the Crown. Both HENRY I and STEPHEN entrusted the fortress to their constables, or castellans. In 1139 Josce de DINAN was castellan at LUDLOW and was reputed to have considered transferring his allegiance from Stephen to the Empress MAUD. By 1158 Gilbert de Lacy had managed to acquire the castle from HENRY II. During his lifetime, Gilbert made various alterations to the building, including the addition of the outer ward. In 1306 the powerful Roger Mortimer married Joan de Geneville, the heiress to the Lacy estates which included the castle and, as soon as the property became his, he set about turning the fortress into a palace. Ludlow Castle was a major stronghold of the Welsh Marches until the end of the 17th C. By the middle of the 18th C., the castle had fallen into extensive decay. In 1811 it was purchased from the Crown by the Earl of Powis, who began a programme of preservation and selective repair which continues to this day. See also LACY FAMILY.

Novels: In December 1139 Hugh BERINGAR had three men with him at BROMFIELD and twenty-two more 'quartered on Josce de Dinan in Ludlow castle'.

Refs: **6** (1, 3–4, 8, 11).

Luke, Brother (*fl.* 1142) (fict.). **Novels:** Benedictine monk of SHREWSBURY ABBEY, he cut a pair of crutches for Brother HALUIN in January 1142.

Refs: **15** (3).

Luke the Evangelist, Saint (*fl.* 1st C.) (hist.) (f.d. 18 October). Generally accepted as the author of the third Gospel and also of the Acts of the Apostles. A Gentile and Greek physician, Luke accompanied St PAUL THE APOSTLE on parts of his second and third missionary journeys and also on the voyage to ROME when they were shipwrecked at Malta. It is said that he died unmarried in Greece at the age of eighty-four. Luke is the patron saint of physicians and surgeons as well as artists.

Novels: In March 1145, during the *sortes Biblicae* conducted at SHREWSBURY ABBEY, Sub-Prior HERLUIN received Luke 13:27: '"I tell you, I know you not, whence you came. Depart from me, ye workers of iniquity."'

Refs: **19** (9).

Lythwood (Shropshire, England). DB – Lythwood is not mentioned, but its origin may have been in PULLEY: in Condover Hundred; a holding of Theodulf under Roger de MONTGOMERY. Lythwood, represented today by Lythwood Hall (*c.*1782), Lythwood Farm and Lythwood View, was situated 3 miles south-west of SHREWSBURY on the northern fringes of the LONG FOREST. To the south the ground rises to the summit of Lyth Hill, approximately 500 ft. above sea level. See also BEISTAN.

Novels: William of LYTHWOOD and his nephews, Girard and Jevan of LYTHWOOD, were respected merchants of SHREWSBURY.

Refs: **16** (2).

Lythwood, Girard of (b. 1096) (fict.). **Novels:** '"And I thought Girard would have been home before this. I hope nothing has happened to him." "Nothing will have happened," Jevan assured her firmly, "but some matter of business to his profit. You know he can take very good care of himself, and he has excellent relations all along the border. If he meant to be back for the festival, and has missed his day, it will be because he's added a couple of new customers to his tally. It takes time to strike a bargain with a Welsh sheepman. He'll be back home safe and sound in a day or so."' Girard of Lythwood was the husband of Margaret of LYTHWOOD, fosterfather of FORTUNATA, elder brother of Jevan of LYTHWOOD and nephew of William of LYTHWOOD. Girard and Jevan took over their uncle's business in 1136, when William set out for the HOLY LAND with ELAVE. A SHREWSBURY merchant trading in wool, Girard also acted as a middleman and agent for a number of other sheep-farmers. He was out of town in June 1143 when Elave arrived at Shrewsbury with William's corpse and a dowry for Fortunata. Returning home, Girard found that Elave was locked in a SHREWSBURY ABBEY cell, ALDWIN was dead, and CONAN was suspected of his murder. He opened Fortunata's box and discovered that it contained 570 silver pennies. On 25 June he went with Fortunata to see Abbot RADULFUS to try and secure Elave's release. Although Girard promised to act as Elave's guarantor, volunteering his foster-daughter's dowry as bail, Radulfus was unable to accept. Even before Elave had been cleared of the charges of heresy, Girard offered him Aldwin's place in the household and a part of the business.

Refs: **16** (2–15).

Lythwood, Jevan of (1103–43) (fict.). **Novels:** 'He had not been formally educated in boyhood, but by reason of taking early to the craft of vellum-making he had come to the notice of lettered men who bought from him, monastics, clerks, even a few among the lords of local manors who had some learning, and being of very quick and eager intelligence he had set himself to learn from them, aroused their interest to help him forward, and turned himself into a scholar, the only person in this house who could read Latin, or more than a few words of English. It was good for business that the seller of parchments should measure up to the quality of his work, and understood the uses the cultured world made of it.' Jevan of Lythwood was the younger brother of Girard of LYTHWOOD, nephew of William of LYTHWOOD and fosteruncle of FORTUNATA. A vellum-maker and self-educated scholar, he lived in Girard of LYTHWOOD'S HOUSE in SHREWSBURY. Jevan and Girard took over their uncle's business in 1136. In June 1143 he secretly stole THEOFANU's priceless psalter from inside FORTUNATA's box and replaced it with 570 silver pennies. On 22 June, thinking that ALDWIN had seen the original contents of the box, Jevan killed him. Fortunata later gave Jevan her carved box to house one of his books. He took the box to his workshop beyond FRANKWELL and hid it, with the psalter inside, in the thatch of the roof. On 26 June, after Aldwin's funeral,

L

Jevan discovered Fortunata searching his workshop. She accused him of taking the contents of her box and murdering Aldwin. While they were talking, Hugh BERINGAR and CADFAEL arrived. Jevan held her at knife-point until ELAVE set fire to his workshop. Casting his hostage aside, Jevan rushed into the blazing inferno, grabbed the box and, enveloped by flames, threw himself into the River SEVERN. His dead and blackened body was later found caught up in a chain under the English Bridge. In order to protect the family name, the fact that Jevan had murdered Aldwin was not made public.

Refs: **16** (2–4, 6–8,11–15).

Lythwood, Margaret of (b. 1098) (fict.). **Novels:** 'It was Girard's wife who kept the house for the whole family.' Margaret of Lythwood was the wife of Girard of LYTHWOOD and fostermother of FORTUNATA. Having no children of her own, she adopted FORTUNATA and cared for her like her own child. Margaret attended William of LYTHWOOD's funeral on 21 June 1143.

Refs: **16** (3–8, 11–13).

Lythwood, William of (1064–1143) (fict.). **Novels:** Uncle of Girard and Jevan of LYTHWOOD and former fosterfather of FORTUNATA, William of Lythwood was a merchant of SHREWSBURY trading in wool and vellum. He was a generous patron to SHREWSBURY ABBEY and a close friend of Abbot HERIBERT. In 1134 William entertained Deacon SERLO and a preaching canon from OSYTH to supper at his house. During the meal it became clear that his views were 'misguided', possibly heretical, and he was counselled to go on a pilgrimage. Two years later, he left for the HOLY LAND with ELAVE, his apprentice. They journeyed by land to JERUSALEM, pausing in CONSTANTINOPLE 'to see the great collection of relics'. They returned to Europe by way of TRIPOLI (where William purchased FORTUNATA's dowry), CYPRUS and THESSALONIKA. William was taken ill in France and, in April 1142, forced to rest for one whole month in the monastery of ST MARCEL. There he and Elave met Pierre ABELARD. In early May they made the pilgrimage to ST JAMES at COMPOSTELA. William died at VALOGNES in the following year, and Elave transported his coffined body back to England. Despite questions about his beliefs, he was buried at Shrewsbury Abbey on 21 June 1143. 'The loss of William, old, fulfilled, and delivered from this world in a state of grace and to the resting-place he had desired, was not a tragedy, but the completion of an altogether satisfactory life, the more easily and readily accepted because he had been gone from this household for seven years, and the gap he had left had closed gently, and had not now been torn open again by his recovered presence.'

Refs: **16** (1–6, 8–13, 15).

(Girard of) Lythwood's House (near St Alkmund's Church, Shrewsbury, Shropshire) (fict.). Although it never existed, the house of Girard of LYTHWOOD was situated near ST ALKMUND'S CHURCH. Among the streets of interest in the vicinity are Fish Street, St Alkmond's Square and St Alkmond's Place. Formerly called Chepynstrete, Fish Street received its name towards the end of the 14th C. when its shops and stalls traded primarily in the sale of fish and, later, meat. Part of the present St Alkmond's Square and St Alkmond's Place was, in medieval times, known as Old Fish Street. In 1261 the market place, which had previously been in St Alkmund's churchyard, was moved to St Alkmond's Square. Linking St Alkmond's Place with Fish Street are a flight of covered stone steps, known as the Bear Steps. The name is derived from the Bear Inn, which stood on the corner of Grope Lane and Fish Street. It is now the collective name for a group of medieval timber-framed buildings, restored in 1972. It is thought that there was once an arcaded range of shops on the site.

Novels: 'The house of Girard of Lythwood, like so many of the merchant burgages of SHREWSBURY, was in the shape of an L, the short base directly on the street, and pierced by an arched entry leading through to the yard and garden behind. The base of the L was of only one storey, and provided [Jevan of LYTHWOOD'S SHOP] . . . The upright of the L showed its gable end to the street, and consisted of a low undercroft and the living floor above, with a loft in the steep roof that provided extra sleeping quarters. The entire burgage was not large, space being valuable within so enclosed a town, in its tight noose of river.' FORTUNATA had a small room above the master bedchamber on the main floor; her room was closed off from the larger part of the loft where the menservants had their beds.' Jevan of LYTHWOOD 'slept in a small chamber over the entry from the street into the yard, where he kept his choicest wares and his chest of books'.

Refs: **16** (2–4, 12).

(Jevan of) Lythwood's Shop (near St Alkmund's Church, Shrewsbury, Shropshire) (fict.). Although it never existed, the shop of Jevan of LYTHWOOD occupied part of his elder brother's house (see Girard of LYTHWOOD'S HOUSE).

Novels: 'The base of the L [of the house] was of only one storey, and provided the shop where Jevan . . . stored and sold his finished leaves and gatherings of vellum and the cured skins from which they were folded and cut to order.' 'Everything in his shop was in immaculate order, the uncut skins draped over racks, the trimmed leaves ranged on shelves in their varied sizes, and the knives with which he cut and trimmed them laid out in neat alignment in their tray, ready to his hand. The shop was small, and open on to the street in this fine weather, its shutters laid by until nightfall.'

Refs: **16** (3, 8, 12).

(Jevan of) Lythwood's Workshop (Frankwell, Shrewsbury, Shropshire) (fict.). Although it never existed, the workshop of Jevan of LYTHWOOD was situated near ULF's farm, within a gentle loop of the River SEVERN, to the north-west of FRANKWELL. The place is marked as a Danger Area on the OS map.

Novels: 'The workshop where Jevan of Lythwood treated his sheepskins lay well beyond the last houses of the suburb of Frankwell, solitary by the right bank of the river, at the foot of a steep meadow backed by a ridge of trees and bushes higher up the slope. Here the land rose, and the water, even at its summer level, ran deep, and with a rapid and forceful current, ideal for Jevan's occupation.' It was on 26 June 1143, after ALDWIN's funeral, that Jevan discovered FORTUNATA searching his workshop. The dramatic consequences included the death of Jevan and the burning of the workshop.

Refs: **16** (2, 12–14).

M

Madlen (*fl.* 1139) (fict.). **Novels:** 'A hard-faced elderly maid', Madlen was the maidservant of Lady Agnes PICARD. In October 1139 she arrived at SHREWSBURY with her mistress for the wedding of Iveta de Massard (see LUCY) and Huon de DOMVILLE. Madlen was drugged by Iveta with a draught of CADFAEL's poppy syrup.

Refs: **5** (2–6, 8, 10).

Madlyn (*fl.* 1143) (fict.). **Novels:** Maidservant of Emma and Cenred VIVERS, Madlyn alerted her mistress to EDGYTHA's disappearance in March 1143.

Refs: **15** (8–9).

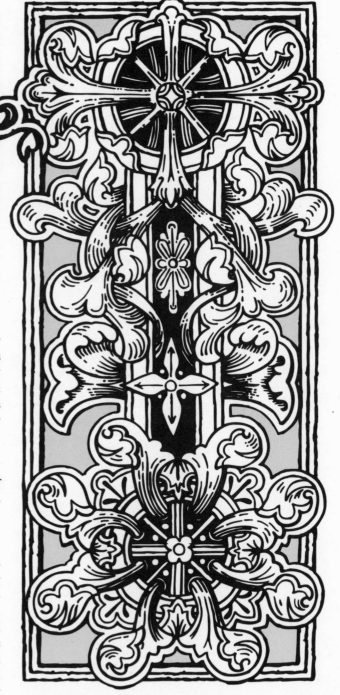

Madoc (b. 1115) (fict.). **Novels:** 'And a very well-looking fellow he was . . . a strapping lad barely twenty years old, with round, ruddy cheeks and merry, guileless eyes, long in the legs, wide in the shoulders, everything a country youth should be.' Groom and villein of Hamo FITZHAMON of LIDYATE, Madoc arrived at SHREWSBURY ABBEY with his master and mistress on Christmas Eve 1135. CADFAEL discovered Madoc and Lady FITZHAMON making love together in his workshop. He did not disturb them. The FitzHamon party, including Madoc, left SHREWSBURY for Lidyate on 26 December.

Refs: **RB** (2).

Madog ap Maredudd. See MADOG AP MEREDITH.

Madog ap Meredith (d. 1160), King of Powys (hist.). Son of Meredith ap Bleddyn, Madog ap Meredith (or Maredudd) married Susanna, daughter of GRIFFITH AP CYNAN, King of Gwynedd, and his wife, ANGHARAD (d. 1162). He succeeded his father in 1132. With an army of Welshmen, Madog fought alongside CADWALADR and RANULF of Chester at the battle of LINCOLN on 2 February 1141. He was the last of his dynasty to rule the whole of Powys and spent much of his reign, particularly between 1149 and 1157, defending his domain against OWAIN GWYNEDD, who was his wife's brother. He captured OSWESTRY from William FITZALAN in 1149, occupying and fortifying the castle for a time. Having lost his lands in Ial to the King of Gwynedd, Madog retrieved them by joining forces with Cadwaladr and HENRY II against Owain. Madog's support was influential in Henry's victory over Owain, who was eventually forced to pay homage to the English king. When Madog died, he was still on the best of terms with Henry. He was buried at MEIFOD.

Novels: '"Things are quiet enough up there," Hugh BERINGAR agreed. "In any event, Madog, whatever else he may be, is a pious soul where churchmen are concerned, however he may treat the English laiety. And for the moment he has all the lesser lads of POWYS FADOG on a tight rein."' Madog ap Meredith was with Cadwaladr at the battle of Lincoln in February 1141. They captured Gilbert PRESTCOTE (the elder) and took him with them into Wales. Madog was with the Welsh raiding party which attacked GODRIC'S FORD. From his base in CAUS CASTLE, Madog and the Welsh of Powys attacked, burned and looted farmsteads along the MINSTERLEY VALLEY. In March he led a revenge assault on Godric's Ford, but was driven away by Hugh Beringar and his men. Hugh was unwilling to stay long at COVENTRY in late 1145, in case Madog began '"casting covetous eyes at Oswestry again. He's never stopped hankering after it."'

Refs: **9** (1, 8–12, 14); **18** (1); **20** (6).

Madog of the Dead-Boat (*fl.* 1140) (fict.). **Novels:** 'A squat, muscular, hairy Welshman, without kith or kin and in no need of either, for he was sufficient to himself and had been since childhood, he yet had an open welcome for his friends. He heeded no one, but if others needed him he was at their disposal.' 'There was very little about the ways of the SEVERN that Madog did not know, it was his life, as it had been the death of many of his generation in its treacherous flood-times. Given a hint as to where an unfortunate had gone into the stream, Madog would know where to expect the river to give him back, and it was to him everyone turned to find what was lost.' Welsh waterman, ferryman and fisherman of SHREWSBURY, Madog of the Dead-Boat's primary means of livelihood was salvaging dead bodies from the River Severn. Among those he pulled from the river, not all dead, were: William REDE, Baldwin PECHE and ALDWIN. In September 1141 Madog ferried Brother HUMILIS and Brother FIDELIS (see CRUCE, Julian) to SALTON. On the return journey, his boat capsized during a heavy rainstorm and Humilis was drowned. Madog took Fidelis to GODRIC'S FORD.

Refs: **3** (8–9); **7** (6–7, 11); **11** (10, 12–14); **12** (9); **13** (6–9); **16** (7–8); **RB** (3).

Madog of the Dead-Boat's Hut (Shrewsbury, Shropshire) (fict.). Although it never existed, Madog of the Dead-Boat's hut was tucked under the lee of the Welsh Bridge in SHREWSBURY. The present bridge, built of Grinshill stone in 1795, is sited a few yards downstream from the earlier medieval bridge, which was approached down Mardol (see MAERDOL). During the reign of HENRY II, it was known as St George's Bridge, because of its proximity to St George's Hospital in FRANKWELL. In the 16th C. the bridge had six stone arches, with gate houses at both ends – one being a 'Great Tower' – and a small row of shops in the centre. Traces of the old bridge can still

M

be found on Frankwell Quay, to the east of the present Welsh Bridge, which is 226 ft. long.

Novels: 'He had a hut tucked under the lee of the western bridge that opened the road into his native Wales, and there he made coracles, or timber boats if required, fished in season, ferried fares on request, carried goods for a fee, anything to do with transport by water.'

Refs: **13** (7); **16** (7).

Maelgwn ab Owain (*fl.* 1144) (hist.). He was the son of OWAIN GWYNEDD by his first wife, GWLADUS, and brother of IORWERTH AB OWAIN. After his father's death in 1170, Maelgwn inherited ANGLESEY. He was driven out of the island in 1173 by his half-brother, Dafydd, whose ambition was the conquest of all Gwynedd. After a period of exile in Ireland, Maelgwn returned the following year to reclaim his lands, but was seized by Dafydd and imprisoned.

Novels: 'The two young boys who came leaping down the steps from the hall door after her were hers, lithe dark imps of about ten and seven years, shrilling with excitement and with a flurry of dogs wreathing round their feet.' Maelgwn of Owain was the son of Owain Gwynedd and was born in *c.*1137. CADFAEL saw him at ABER in May 1144.

Refs: **18** (4).

Maelienydd (Powys, Wales). The medieval Welsh cantref of Maelienydd in Rhwng gwy a Hafren lay immediately north of ELFAEL. It was bounded to the east by the River TEME and the Radnor Forest, and to the west by the River Ithon (downstream from near Penybont) and its western tributary, the Clywedog Brook. The cantref was divided into three commotes, which took their names from the principal royal residences within them: Rhiwlallt, Buddugre and Dinieithon. In 1144 the Norman Marcher lord, Hugh Mortimer of Wigmore, reconquered the region from the Welsh. Its ownership, however, was disputed by both sides until the English finally conquered Wales at the end of the 13th C. The name is retained in the small, upland area of Maelienydd, some 24 miles west of LUDLOW and just over 2 miles south-east of Llanbister.

Novels: On 4 August 1139 Rhodri ap HUW suggested to CADFAEL that OWAIN GWYNEDD should keep away from RANULF of Chester's borders and aim to enlarge his rule in Maelienydd and Elfael.

Refs: **4** (5:2).

Maelor (Clwyd, Wales). The medieval Welsh region of Maelor in Powys Fadog was bounded to the south and east by the River DEE. Apart from its eastern border with England, Maelor – with WREXHAM as its centre – was surrounded by the commotes of Yr Hob, Ial, Nanheudwy and Maelor Saesneg. It was intersected, however, by the line of OFFA'S DYKE and was often occupied by the English. In 1177, for example, it was temporarily conquered by Hugh, Earl of Chester. The present district of Maelor (or Wrexham Maelor) is administered from the town of Wrexham which it surrounds entirely. It borders the counties of Shropshire to the south and Cheshire to the east; and the districts of Ayln and Deeside to the north and Glyndwr to the west. Its western extremity lies in the mountains of Esclusham and Ruabon, descending eastward into the broad levels of the Cheshire plain.

Novels: ENGELARD was 'a Cheshire man from the borders of Maelor, on the run from the bailiffs of Earl RANULF of Chester'.

Refs: **1** (3).

Maerdol (now Mardol) (Shrewsbury, Shropshire). Formerly called Mardefole or Mardeval, Mardol runs from Claremont Street to Smithfield Road in SHREWSBURY, on the east bank of the River SEVERN. It used to be the main approach from the town centre down to the medieval Welsh Bridge, leading to FRANKWELL and Wales. But in 1795 the old bridge was replaced by a new and shorter one, sited a few yards downstream and some distance away from the lower end of Mardol. There are a number of timber-framed houses in the street, including the King's Head Inn, dating from the 15th C. and heavily restored in the early 20th C. Mardol Quay, now a public garden, was constructed in 1610 for the use of river barges. At the upper end of Mardol, running between Shoplatch and Pride Hill, is a short stretch of road known as Mardol Head (formerly called Mardifoldshedde). In medieval times the south side of Mardol Head was called Le Glover Row and the north side Le Stalls.

Novels: 'The burgage of the VESTIER family occupied a prominent place at the head of the street called Maerdol, which led downhill to the western bridge (see VESTIER'S HOUSE AND SHOP). In June 1143 CONAN returned to the LYTHWOOD household 'only a little tipsy after celebrating the end of the day . . . with half a dozen boon companions at the alehouse in Mardol'.

Refs: **13** (3, 6, 9, 12); **16** (6).

Maesbrook. See MERESBROOK.

Maesbury (Shropshire, England). DB – Meresberie: in Merset Hundred; land held by Roger de MONTGOMERY himself (Reginald the Sheriff held the manor from Roger and built the castle of OSWESTRY there). Just over 2 miles south-east of Oswestry and 14 miles north-west of SHREWSBURY, Maesbury is a scattered village, spread over low-lying ground. To the south-west is Maesbury Hall. The Shropshire Union Canal runs past the south-eastern end of the village and, in the early 19th C., a settlement grew up around the canal bridge. Called Maesbury Marsh, it has a small church and chapel, a number of boatmen's cottages, two taverns (one of which is called the Navigation Inn), a warehouse and a restored wharf. Less than 1 mile south-east of Maesbury Marsh is the hamlet of Woolston, once a place of pilgrimage. It is alleged that, while the relics of St WINIFRED were being carried from GWYTHERIN to Shrewsbury in 1137, a spring miraculously appeared at the spot where they were put down to rest. Today St Winifred's Well is housed beneath the projecting gabled porch of a timber-framed cottage, built in *c.*1600 as a courthouse. The waters still emerge from beneath the building, flow through a number of stone basins, in which the faithful once bathed, and into a small stream. The water in the well is reputed to heal wounds, bruises and fractured bones, while the small spring below the well is alleged to relieve sore eyes.

Novels: 'This extreme border castle of Oswestry, with its town, was the king's, but the manor of Maesbury, of which it had become the head, was Hugh's own native place, and there was no man here who did not hold with him and trust him.' Hugh BERINGAR held the manor of Maesbury, in addition to his town house in Shrewsbury. It was usual for the family to spend the summers there. CADFAEL and Deacon MARK, returning to Shrewsbury from North Wales, lodged overnight with the Beringars at Maesbury in May 1144.

Refs: **2** (1); **3** (7–8); **4** (1:1, 5:6); **5** (7); **7** (3); **8** (1); **9** (10); **11** (1); **12** (1); **13** (2); **18** (1, 14).

M

Magdalen, Sister (b. 1095) (fict.). **Novels:** Formerly called Avice of Thornbury. 'Sister Magdalen had formerly been, for many years, the constant mistress of a certain nobleman, and on his death had looked about her with a single-minded resolution for another field in which to employ her undoubted talents. No question but the choice of the cloister had been coolly and practically made. What redeemed it was the vigour and loyalty she had devoted to it since the day of her entry, and would maintain, without question, until the day of her death.' Sub-prioress of GODRIC'S FORD and formerly the constant mistress and whore of Huon de DOMVILLE, Avice of Thornbury was the daughter of ULGER the elder and sister of ULGER the younger. Domville took her away from THORNBURY in c.1118 and established her in a Cheshire manor as his mistress. While there, Avice used the time to educate herself, becoming 'lettered and numerate'. In October 1139 she was at Huon's hunting lodge in the LONG FOREST and spent the night before his wedding day with him. Hearing that Huon had been murdered on his way back to SHREWSBURY, Avice left the lodge to take the veil at the Benedictine nunnery of GODRIC'S FORD; not as a vocation, but as a career. She changed her name to Sister Magdalen. CADFAEL met her there, in pursuit of Domville's murderer, and in her he found someone he could respect and completely trust. In February 1141 Magdalen arrived at SHREWSBURY ABBEY with four sturdy countrymen, including John MILLER. She told Hugh BERINGAR, Abbot RADULFUS and Cadfael that Godric's Ford had been attacked by a Welsh raiding party. Elis ap CYNAN, who had been captured during the skirmish, was handed over to the sheriff. Magdalen returned to Shrewsbury in March 1141 to escort a great-niece of Mother MARIANA to Godric's Ford. In September 1141 she helped Fidelis shed the habit of a monk and re-emerge into the world as Julian CRUCE. By June 1142 she was subprioress of Godric's Ford, having taken on much of the responsibilities of her ailing superior. She helped Judith PERLE return home after her abduction, without causing a scandal.

Refs: **5** (7–11); **9** (1–2, 8, 12–15); **11** (14); **13** (1, 3, 6, 8, 11–14).

Maine (France). This ancient province of north-western France is roughly encompassed by the modern départements of Mayenne and Sarthe in Loire Valley West. Its ancient capital, Le Mans, on the River Sarthe, was the birthplace of HENRY II, King of England. Compressed between ANJOU and NORMANDY, Maine fell to the Angevin empire in the 12th C. and then, at the beginning of the 13th C., to Philip II, King of France.

Novels: '"And what will you do,"' ALARD [THE CLERK] asked CADFAEL in November 1120, '"now the King's got everything he wanted, married his son to ANJOU and Maine, and made an end of fighting?"'

Refs: **RB** (1).

Malcolm III (c.1031–93), King of Scotland (1058–93) (hist.). Also called Malcolm Canmore. Son of Duncan I, King of Scotland (1034–40), father of MATILDA (1080–1118) and of three kings of Scotland (Edgar (d. 1107), Alexander I (d. 1124), and DAVID I), he ascended to the throne after killing Macbeth and the latter's stepson, Lulach. In 1070 he married his second wife, St Margaret of Scotland, granddaughter of Edmund II Ironside, King of England. Malcolm's reign was marked by almost constant warfare, in which he sought not only to consolidate his kingdom, but to extend it southward into northern England. Although he was forced to pay homage to WILLIAM I in 1070 and to WILLIAM II in 1091 he was killed, together with his eldest son, near Alnwick in the last of his five invasions of England.

Novels: Matilda, wife of HENRY I, was daughter to the king of Scots.

Refs: **20** (4).

Mallilie (Clwyd, Wales) (fict.). Although it never existed, the manor of Mallilie lay in the valley of the CYNLLAITH, just over 1 mile north-east of LLANSILIN and in the approximate vicinity of Derwen-deg.

Novels: 'After the hamlet of CROESAU BACH he would come to a cross roads, and turn right, and from that point he would see how the hills were cleft ahead of him, and making straight for that cleft he would come to Mallilie, beyond which the track continued westward to LLANSILIN, the central seat of the commote of CYNLLAITH.' 'The hall was lofty and strongly beamed. CADFAEL passed through it to the solar. This must be where BONEL had intended to install the panelling commissioned from Martin BELLECOTE, the transaction which had first caused him to set eyes and heart on Richildis Gurney (see BONEL) . . . Martin had done good work, and fitted it into place here with skill and love.' The manor of Mallilie, on the Welsh side of OFFA'S DYKE, was acquired by the Bonels during the reign of WILLIAM II. They held it under the Earl of CHESTER. In December 1138 Gervase Bonel granted the manor to SHREWSBURY ABBEY in return for a messuage at the abbey. The agreement, however, could not be ratified because Abbot HERIBERT had been suspended from office. After Bonel's death, the future of Mallilie was uncertain. The question as to whether the manor was in Wales or England was brought up at a meeting of the commote of Cynllaith at Llansilin. After it became clear that the manor did not belong to the abbey, Mallilie passed to Bonel's stepson, Edwin GURNEY. It was managed by an abbey steward until Edwin reached manhood. Early in January 1138, the newly-widowed Richildis Bonel, together with the remainder of her household, left SHREWSBURY to return to Mallilie.

Refs: **3** (1–11).

Malmesbury (Wiltshire, England). Some 11 miles south-west of CIRENCESTER and 14 miles west of Swindon, this ancient market town stands on a defensive hilltop site, almost entirely surrounded by water: the River Avon and its tributary, the Ingleburn. Malmesbury lays claim to being the oldest borough in England, having received its charter from Edward the Elder in 924. The Benedictine abbey, dedicated to St Aldhelm and the Blessed Virgin Mary, stands on the site of an Anglo-Saxon monastery founded in the 7th C. The present building, only a fraction of the abbey's original size, dates from either the reign of STEPHEN (1135–54) or the reign of HENRY II (1154–89). William of Malmesbury, the English historian and abbey librarian, says nothing about the building of a new abbey, so a date *after* his death, in 1143, is suggested. It is known, however, that the dedication was being discussed in *c.*1177. The nave became the parish church in 1541, while the rest of the abbey fell into decay. The south porch, which survives, is considered to be the finest example of Norman decorative stonework in England. A stained-glass window inside the abbey church commemorates Elmer, a monk at Malmesbury, who in 1010 tried to fly with wings fastened to his hands and feet. He launched himself off the summit of the abbey tower, achieving a flight (or glide) of some 200 yards, before crash-landing and breaking both legs. Although he attributed his failure to the lack of a tail, his abbot forbade further experiments. All that survives of the former parish church, dedicated to St Paul, is the west tower and spire. The Market Cross, an ornate crown-like structure, dating from *c.*1500, was built – according to John Leland – 'for poor market folks to stand dry when rain cometh'. The medieval town, noted for its weaving mills, was built within the pre-Conquest fortress, of which nothing remains. The Norman castle, 'an impregnable work of skill' (*Gesta Stephani*, ed. Potter, 1976), surrendered to King Stephen in 1139, but fell to Henry Plantagenet (later Henry II) in 1153.

Novels: 'In the desultory but dangerous and explosive battlefield of the THAMES valley Philip [FITZROBERT], the empress's castellan of CRICKLADE, had been plagued by damaging raids by the king's men garrisoned in OXFORD and Malmesbury.' The castle at Malmesbury was one of a ring of fortresses, centred on Cricklade, and held by King Stephen in December 1145 (see BAMPTON, FARINGDON and PURTON). Philip FitzRobert, who had changed his allegiance, apologised to King Stephen for arriving late at the conference at COVENTRY on 30 November 1145, having been delayed at Malmesbury.

Refs: **20** (1–2, 4, 6–7, 14).

Mandeville, Ernulf de (*fl.* 1144) (hist.) Also spelled Ernald. Eldest, and possibly illegitimate, son of Geoffrey de MANDEVILLE (d. 1144) and brother (or half-brother) of Geoffrey de MANDEVILLE (d. 1166) and William de Mandeville (d. 1189). Ernulf served in his father's household troops and also supported his

M

father in his rebellion against King STEPHEN. After his father's death in 1144, Ernulf was exiled and stripped of his inheritance, as were his descendants.

Novels: In August 1144 the 'eldest son' of Geoffrey de Mandeville was partner in his father's rebellion, and 'excommunicate with him'.

Refs: **19** (Prologue).

Mandeville, Geoffrey de (d. 1144), Earl of Essex (hist.). Father of Ernulf de MANDEVILLE (*fl.* 1144), Geoffrey de MANDEVILLE (d. 1166) and William de Mandeville (d.1189). Hereditary constable of the TOWER OF LONDON and bitter enemy of the citizens of LONDON, he was notorious for his cruelty and lawlessness during the reign of STEPHEN. Mandeville rose to prominence in 1140 when the king made him the 1st Earl of Essex as a reward for his support. But after Stephen's capture at the battle of LINCOLN in February the following year, Geoffrey crossed over to the side of the Empress MAUD, who bestowed further offices, lands and money on him. After the Londoners had driven Maud out of the capital, Queen MATILDA persuaded him to rejoin the royalist cause with more concessions, which were confirmed with interest on Stephen's release from prison. Geoffrey's main importance to both rivals to the throne was his position as constable of the Tower, which virtually gave him control of the capital. The Londoners, however, resented this control. He was arrested at ST ALBANS in 1143 for treason against Stephen, and chose to surrender his offices and castles in return for his freedom. He immediately took his revenge on the innocent inhabitants of the Cambridgeshire FENS, ruthlessly killing and torturing those who stood in his way. He seized RAMSEY ABBEY, driving out the monks, and converted it into a military fortress from which he plundered the surrounding countryside. When Stephen tried to capture him, Geoffrey withdrew into the heart of the watery wastes and defied attack. By chance, Mandeville was mortally wounded by an arrow while laying siege to BURWELL in August 1144. He died on 16 September at MILDENHALL, 'stricken by the sword of excommunication and unabsolved, and as guilty of sacrilege he could not be put in the earth' (*Gesta Stephani,* ed. Potter, 1976). His body was taken to the Old TEMPLE in London by certain KNIGHTS TEMPLAR, where, according to one account, it was sealed in a box and thrown into a pit outside the churchyard, remaining there unburied for almost twenty years. Another account says that his body was wrapped in lead and hung on a tree in the Temple's orchard. Mandeville was eventually given absolution by Pope Alexander III and allowed a Christian burial, after his son, Geoffrey, had given money to Ramsey Abbey in atonement.

Novels: '"Easy going Stephen may be, meek he is not. And there were rumours that the Earl of Essex was bargaining again with the empress while she was in OXFORD, but changed his mind when the siege went against her. He's been back and forth between the two of them times enough already. I think he's near the end of his rope."' At ST ALBANS in September 1143, Geoffrey de Mandeville was accused of having traitorous dealing with Maud, and plotting Stephen's overthrow. He was forced to surrender his constableship of the Tower of London. By way of revenge, he immediately gathered a force about him and sacked CAMBRIDGE. On 30 September he threw the monks out of Ramsey Abbey and turned it into an island fortress. In November Hugh BERINGAR was summoned by Stephen to supply a company of men to try and quell the anarchy in the Fens. However, he returned to SHREWSBURY at the end of the month without a great deal of success: '"What I wanted," said Hugh feelingly, "was de Mandeville's hide, but he wears it still, and devil a thing can Stephen do about it until we can flush the rat out of his hole."' While besieging Burwell castle in late August 1144 Mandeville was struck in the head by an arrow, and died of the wound at Mildenhall on 16 September, 'still excommunicate, still unabsolved'. His coffined body was taken to London by certain Knights Templar, who were 'forced to let him lie in a pit outside the churchyard of the TEMPLE, in unhallowed ground'.

Refs: **16** (1); **17** (3–6, 8–11); **18** (1); **19** (Prologue).

Mandeville, Geoffrey de (d. 1166), 2nd Earl of Essex (hist.). Second son of Geoffrey de MANDEVILLE (d. 1144) by his wife Rohese, daughter of Aubrey de Vere, and brother of William de Mandeville and Ernulf de MANDEVILLE (possibly half-brother). Geoffrey was with the Empress MAUD while his father was wreaking havoc in the FENS. He was recognised as the 2nd Earl of Essex not later than 1147. In 1163, after Geoffrey had agreed to compensate the monks at RAMSEY ABBEY for the damage caused by his father's occupation of the monastery in 1143–44, Pope Alexander III granted Geoffrey (the elder) absolution and, in consequence, his remains were allowed a Christian burial at the New TEMPLE. Geoffrey (the younger) was succeeded by his brother William, who became 3rd Earl of Essex in 1166. Against his mother's wishes, Geoffrey was buried in the church at Walden Abbey, founded by his father in *c.*1141.

Novels: In September 1144 Geoffrey was with the Empress Maud, 'and recognised by her as earl of Essex, for what such an acknowledgement was worth without lands or status'.

Refs: **19** (Prologue).

Manes (216–*c.*276) (hist.). Also called Mani or Manichaeus. He was born in southern Babylonia and died in captivity, after being attacked by Zoroastrian priests. Manes was a Persian prophet who founded the Manichean religion, which combined elements of Zoroastrian, Christian and Gnostic thought. Manes taught a dualistic religious philosophy which was based on the fusion of the two conflicting principles of good and evil: salvation lay in the release of the spirit, or light, which was imprisoned in matter, or darkness. A missionary faith, spreading east to China and west to Spain, Manicheism was suppressed as a heresy by the Roman Catholic Church.

Novels: In June 1143 Canon GERBERT warned Abbot RADULFUS that '"In PROVENCE, in LANGUEDOC, there are regions where a fashion of Manichean heresy has grown so strong it is become almost a rival church."'

Refs: **16** (5).

Marared (*fl.* 1093) (fict.). **Novels:** She was the wife of Ifor ap MORGAN, youngest sister of Brother RHYS, mother of ANGHARAD (1093–1127) and grandmother of MEURIG. In 1138 it was said that Marared died 'years ago'.

Refs: **3** (7–8).

Marared (*fl.* 1137) (fict.). **Novels:** 'The old woman, long widowed and her own sons grown, preened herself at having a strapping young fellow to keep her company, and CADFAEL reflected that [Brother] JOHN might well be favoured with the best bits before the meal ever came to table.' Welsh widow and neighbour of Father HUW of GWYTHERIN, Marared fetched food, water and wine for Prior ROBERT and his party in May 1137. Her sons had grown up and left.

Refs: **1** (2, 4).

Marchmain, John (b. 1122) (fict.). He was a cousin, on his mother's side, of Hugh BERINGAR. In February 1141 John and CADFAEL set out north-west from SHREWSBURY to find OWAIN GWYNEDD. They located him at Tudur ap RHYS's manor of TREGEIRIOG. John remained at the manor as surety for the safe return of the Welsh prisoner Elis ap CYNAN. He returned to Shrewsbury the following month with a message to Hugh from Owain Gwynedd: he 'rode into the castle stiff with the dignity of the embassage with which he was entrusted, and reported himself ceremoniously to Hugh'.

Refs: **9** (3, 9)

Mardol. See MAERDOL.

M

Marescot, Godfrid. See HUMILIS, Brother.

Margery (*fl.* 1137) (fict.). **Novels:** Daughter of a SHREWSBURY draper, she broke her relationship with Brother JOHN when her father became bailiff of Shrewsbury. It was because of her that John took the cowl.

Refs: **1** (7).

Mariam (d. 1127) (fict.). **Novels:** 'The town came back to him now vividly, the lush green of the river valley, the narrow, grateful shade of the streets, the babel of the market. And Mariam, selling her fruit and vegetables in the Street of the Sailmakers, her young, fine-boned face honed into gold and silver by the fierce sunlight, her black, oiled hair gleaming beneath her veil. She had graced his arrival in the east, a mere boy of eighteen, and his departure, a seasoned soldier and seafarer of thirty-three. A widow, young, passionate and lonely, a woman of the people, not to everyone's taste, too spare, too strong, too scornful. The void left by her dead man had ached unbearably, and drawn in the young stranger heart and soul into her life, to fill the gap. For a whole year he had known her, before the forces of the Cross had moved on to invest JERUSALEM.' Saracen widow of ANTIOCH, mother of Olivier de BRETAGNE and former lover of CADFAEL, Mariam first met Cadfael in 1098. Their relationship lasted 'a whole year', and they were briefly reunited in *c.*1113. She gave birth to their son Olivier in 1113, calling him Daoud.

Refs: **1** (1, 9); **3** (4); **6** (1, 8, 12, 15); **10** (16); **20** (1–2, 4, 8–9, 13).

Mariana, Mother (*fl.* 1139) (fict.). **Novels:** 'Mother Mariana, small, wizened and old, presided over a sisterhood of such model devotion as to disarm fate.' Benedictine nun and superior of GODRIC'S FORD, Mother Mariana allowed CADFAEL to speak privately with Avice of Thornbury (see MAGDALEN, Sister) in October 1139. In February 1141 she was 'old and frail'. During the first attack on Godric's Ford by the Welsh of Powys, she shut herself in the chapel, together with the elder sisters and their valuables. During the second attack, she helped heat water and bandage minor injuries. By June the following year, she was bedridden, and Sister Magdalen had taken over many of her responsibilities.

Refs: **5** (8–9); **9** (1, 8, 13–15); **11** (14); **13** (1, 11–12)

Marisco, Godfrid de. See MARESCOT, Godfrid.

Mark, Brother. See MARK, Deacon.

Mark, Deacon (b. 1120) (fict.). **Novels:** 'A little man, of slender bones and lean but wiry flesh, diminutive as a sixteen-year-old boy, and looking very much like one, until the discerning attention discovered the quality and maturity of the oval, beardless face. A Benedictine like these his brothers, tonsured and habited, he stood erect in the dignity of his office and the humility and simplicity of his nature, as fragile as a child and as durable as a tree. His straw-coloured ring of cropped hair had an unruly spikiness, recalling the child. His grey eyes, formidably direct and clear, confirmed the man. A small miracle! CADFAEL found himself suddenly presented with a gift he had often longed for in the past few years, by its very suddenness and improbability surely miraculous. Roger de Clinton had chosen as his accredited envoy into Wales not some portly canon of imposing presence, from the inner hierarchy of his expensive see, but the youngest and humblest deacon in his household, Brother Mark, sometime of SHREWSBURY ABBEY, and assistant for two fondly remembered years among the herbs and medicines of Cadfael's workshop.' Mark was first a Benedictine monk of Shrewsbury Abbey, and then a deacon of LICHFIELD Cathedral, under Bishop ROGER DE CLINTON. A cottar's orphan, he was forced by his neglectful uncle to take the cowl in May 1137, becoming Cadfael's assistant in the herb-gardens. In December 1138 Mark helped Edwin GURNEY escape capture by throwing a pebble at the horse of the captain of the guard, making him rear and almost spill his rider. He took his final vows some time in the first half of 1139. By October Mark had gone to the Hospital of ST GILES to serve a year with the lepers. Although he noticed the fugitive Joscelin LUCY hiding under hood and veil among the inmates, Mark did not give him away. He was able to confirm Joscelin's innocence of Huon de DOMVILLE's murder. In September 1140 Meriet ASPLEY was sent to serve under Mark at the hospice. In November Meriet and Mark found the charred body of Peter CLEMENCE in the charcoal-burner's hearth. Leoric ASPLEY, hearing from his son of Mark's wish to become a priest, offered to be his patron. Mark left SHREWSBURY to join Bishop Roger de Clinton's household at Lichfield, and begin his studies for the priesthood. By June 1141 he had been ordained deacon. In April 1144 Mark was sent on a diplomatic mission to ST ASAPH and BANGOR by Bishop Roger de Clinton. He obtained permission to take Cadfael with him. They found themselves involved in CADWALADR's bid, using Danish mercenaries, to regain the lands taken from him by HYWEL AB OWAIN.

Refs: **1** (12); **3** (1–2, 4–9, 11); **4** (1:1–2, 3:1–2, 4:3–5, 5:5); **5** (1, 6–11); **6** (2); **8** (6–13); **10** (1, 8); **11** (1); **13** (1); **18** (1–14).

Mark the Evangelist, Saint (d. *c.*75) (hist.) (f.d. 25 April). Author of the second Gospel, he is generally thought to have been: the young man who fled naked when Christ was arrested (Mark 14:51–52); the 'John, whose surname was Mark' (Acts 12:25); and, therefore, the son of the householder, Mary, who lived in JERUSALEM (Acts 12:12). He went with PAUL THE APOSTLE and Barnabas on their first missionary journey, turning back alone at 'Perga in Pamphylia' to return to Jerusalem (Acts 13:13). Barred by Paul from accompanying him on his second missionary journey, Mark went with Barnabas to preach in CYPRUS. He was with Paul in ROME, however, and it is there that Mark probably wrote his Gospel. He was also the disciple and interpreter of PETER THE APOSTLE. Tradition says that he went to ALEXANDRIA where he established himself as the first bishop and died a martyr. His relics are reputed to have been translated to VENICE in the 9th C., and enshrined in the original church of St Mark, destroyed in 976. They are now in the cathedral (or basilica) of St Mark.

Novels: 'The Gospels were turning back, out of JOHN into LUKE, out of Luke into Mark . . . and beyond.'

Refs: **19** (9).

Marsh, Godfrid of the. See MARESCOT, Godfrid.

Martel, William (*fl.* 1142) (hist.). He was King STEPHEN's steward and close friend. William had held the strategic stronghold of SHERBORNE CASTLE since 1139. He fought alongside the king at the battle of WILTON in 1143 and, with the men under his command, heroically resisted ROBERT of Gloucester's soldiers in order to cover Stephen's retreat. William was eventually overwhelmed by the odds, captured, taken to BRISTOL as a prisoner and only released because Stephen agreed to surrender Sherborne Castle to Robert.

Novels: William Martel, Stephen's steward – 'long in experience of death by steel through many campaigns' – was captured at the battle of Wilton in 1143 while covering the king's retreat. He was 'bought free by Stephen at the cost of a valuable castle'. On 30 November 1145 he attended the conference at COVENTRY with Stephen.

Refs: **17** (1, 3); **20** (3–5).

Martial, Saint (*fl.* 3rd C.), Bishop of Limoges (hist.) (f.d. 30 June). Reputed to have been one of seven missionary bishops sent from ROME to preach the Gospel in Gaul. He became the first bishop of Limoges (France), and from his diocese in Limousin evangelised neighbouring Aquitaine. According to medieval legend Martial was baptised by St PETER THE

APOSTLE, was a disciple of Christ and should be counted among the apostles. In Limousin his memory is still held in great veneration.

Novels: 'The cadence changed in an instant, the secret words passed magically into: "Ave mater salvatoris . . ." and they were back with the liturgy of Saint Martial before they realised.'

Refs: **19** (1).

Martin (*fl.* 1145) (fict.). **Novels:** Journeyman-mason and a 'tough Shropshire lad'. In February 1145 Martin offered to go to RAMSEY ABBEY to 'seek work in rebuilding the gutted barns and storehouses'. Bound for Ramsey, he was travelling with JAMES, PAYNE, NICOL and ROGER through thick woodland near ULLESTHORPE, when they were ambushed by 'eleven or twelve' armed villains and their wagon and team of horses stolen. Martin was 'clubbed senseless and slung in the bushes'. Suffering from a 'broken head', he returned to SHREWSBURY on foot with James more than a week after they had left. He was older than Payne, and 'built more lightly, and younger' than James.

Refs: **19** (2-4).

Mary, Saint (*fl.* 10) (hist.) (f.d. 15 August). Also called Mary the Blessed Virgin, Mother of God, Our Lady or Virgin Mary. As the mother of Jesus Christ, Mary is the most venerated of all the saints, and is honoured with a special cult, described by St Thomas Aquinas as 'hyperdulia', which considers her to be the highest of all God's creatures. Traditionally of the family of King DAVID, Mary was a virgin living at Nazareth and betrothed to Joseph, when an angel appeared to her and told her that by the power of the Holy Ghost she would conceive a son, Jesus, who would be known as the Son of God. It is believed that she remained a virgin throughout her life. Joseph married Mary and, while they were visiting Bethlehem for a census, Jesus was born. Although she is occasionally mentioned during the public ministry of Jesus, it seems that she was not actively involved in teaching or preaching. Nothing is known of the closing years of her life or where she died; but claims have been made for both Ephesus and JERUSALEM. It has long been explicitly believed, without denying her natural death, that at the end of her life Mary was preserved from corruption and taken into Heaven, both body and soul. The feast of her assumption into Heaven is celebrated on 15 August, but many other feast days are held in honour of St Mary throughout the year.

Novels: BROMFIELD Priory was dedicated to St Mary. In December 1135 Hamo FITZHAMON gave a pair of silver candlesticks to SHREWSBURY ABBEY. They were placed on St Mary's altar. Brother JORDAN, whose eyesight was failing, mistook ELFGIVA for Our Lady. Among the treasury of relics amassed over the years by SHREWSBURY ABBEY was a 'drop of the Virgin's milk' and 'a shred of her robe'.

Refs: **6** (2); **19** (2, 8); **RB** (2).

Mary Magdalen, Saint (*fl.* 1st C.) (hist.) (f.d. 22 July). Having had 'seven devils' cast out of her (Mark 16:9), Mary became one of the most devoted followers of Christ. She was present at his crucifixion and was one of the three women who went to anoint his body at the tomb only to be told that 'he is risen; he is not here' (Mark 16:1–6). According to Mark 16:9, the risen Christ first appeared to Mary; while John 20:11–18 adds that he gave her a message to deliver to his disciples. Many other details and legends about her life have not been generally accepted. In art she is depicted with long unbound hair. Her symbol is a jar of ointment.

Novels: Among the treasury of relics amassed over the years by SHREWSBURY ABBEY was 'a tress from the red hair of Saint Mary Magdalen'.

Refs: **19** (2).

Maserfield or Maserfeld or Maserfelth (Shropshire, England). Thought to be OSWESTRY, Maserfeld is mentioned in *The Anglo-Saxon Chronicle*, when Saint OSWALD, the Christian King of Northumbria, was slain by the pagan King Penda of Mercia, at the battle of Maserfeld in 642. The site of the battle lies to the south-west of the town centre, in the vicinity of the present playing-fields of Oswestry School, Maserfield. Legend says that an eagle picked up one of St Oswald's dismembered arms, flew into the air with it and then dropped it. At the spot where it landed a spring of water bubbled out of the ground. The site is now marked by a plaque on St Oswald's Well nearby.

Novels: In November 1143 St TYSILIO came into CADFAEL's mind. He recalled that 'the saint was reputed to have had military virtues as well as sacred, and to have fought on the Christian side at the battle of Maserfield, by Oswestry, where the royal saint, Oswald, was captured and martyred by the pagans.'

Refs: **17** (10).

Massard, Guimar de (b. 1069) (fict.). **Novels:** Also called Lazarus. Also known as the Leper of Saint Giles. '"He is a wanderer, he goes on perpetual pilgrimage, from shrine to shrine as close as in his condition he may. Seventy years old, he says he is, and I believe him. He will not stay long, I think.' 'He plucked away the facecloth, and uncovered the awful visage left to him, almost lipless, one cheek shrunken away, the nostrils eaten into great, discoloured holes, a face in which only the live and brilliant eyes recalled the paladin of JERUSALEM and ASCALON.' Father of Hamon FitzGuimar de MASSARD and grandfather of Iveta de Massard (see LUCY), Guimar de Massard left his wife and son to join the First Crusade. He was at the storming of Jerusalem in July 1099, but was captured by the Fatimids of Egypt in August at the battle of Ascalon. Although it was rumoured that he had died of his wounds, Guimar had in fact contracted leprosy. At his request, his Saracen physicians made it known that he was dead and established him in a hermitage. His helm and sword were sent back to England. In 1131, hearing that Iveta was orphaned, he set out on an eight-year pilgrimage to England. Calling himself Lazarus, he arrived at the Hospital of ST GILES in SHREWSBURY in October 1139. While watching Huon de DOMVILLE's party arrive, he was struck by the baron's whip. He watched Domville ride out of Shrewsbury on the eve of his wedding, but did not see him return. When Joscelin LUCY was being chased by the sheriff's men, Lazarus helped him to hide inside St Giles, bringing him a hooded leper cloak and veil. Joscelin told him about Iveta and her ill-treatment at the hands of Sir Godfrid and Lady Agnes PICARD. While Godfrid Picard was hunting Joscelin Lucy in the LONG FOREST, Lazarus challenged the former to single combat and killed him with his bare hands. Once he was satisfied that Iveta's future happiness was secured, Guimar disappeared without anyone, except CADFAEL, knowing his true identity.

Refs: **5** (1–2, 4–7, 9, 11); **6** (15); **11** (7).

M

Massard, Hamon FitzGuimar de (d. 1131) (fict.). **Novels:** Son of Guimar de MASSARD and father of Iveta de Massard (see LUCY), he married the sister of Sir Godfrid PICARD. Hamon's wife died in 1121, when Iveta was born. When Hamon himself died, he left his 'great honour in lands and titles' to his daughter.

Refs: **5** (2, 5, 7, 10–11).

Massard, Iveta de. See LUCY, Iveta.

Matilda (1080–1118), Queen of England (hist.). Also called Maud. First wife of HENRY I, daughter of MALCOLM III, King of Scotland, mother of the Empress MAUD and WILLIAM THE AETHELING, she was educated at ROMSEY ABBEY, but taken back to Scotland in *c.*1093 by her father, who intended her to marry

Alan, Count of Richmond, rather than allow her to become a nun. By the end of the year, her father and mother, as well as Alan, were dead, and she was driven out of Scotland by King Donald III. Her uncle, Edgar the Aetheling, found her shelter in England. In 1100, after persuading ANSELM, Archbishop of Canterbury, that she had not taken the vows to be a nun, she was married to Henry and crowned queen in WESTMINSTER Abbey. She lived mainly at Westminster, was very pious and devoted herself to good works, including the founding of an Augustinian priory at Aldgate, and the building of a leper hospital at St Giles-in-the-Fields, both in LONDON. She was buried in Westminster Abbey.

Novels: '"He was king unquestioned, undisputed, and by the loss of a brother [William the Aetheling], I [the Empress Maud] was left the sole living child of my father [Henry I] by his lawful wife, Matilda, his queen, herself daughter to the king of Scots."'

Refs: **20** (4).

Matilda (*c.*1103–52), Queen of England (hist.). Also called Matilda of Boulogne. She was the wife of STEPHEN, King of England, and daughter and heiress of Eustace III, Count of Boulogne, and his wife Mary, daughter of MALCOLM III, King of Scotland. Before 1125 Matilda was given in marriage to Stephen, HENRY I's favourite nephew. On the death of her father, shortly before her marriage, Matilda inherited the county of BOULOGNE and considerable estates in England. She became Queen of England in March 1136, after Stephen had seized the English crown on Henry's death in December 1135. When Stephen was taken prisoner at the battle of LINCOLN in February 1141, she rallied a large army, in concert with WILLIAM OF YPRES, and headed for LONDON, where the Empress MAUD had set up court. At the Queen's approach, the Londoners drove the empress out of the city. Matilda established her headquarters in London and, when Bishop HENRY OF BLOIS was besieged in his castle at WOLVESEY by Maud, she in turn besieged the empress. During Maud's retreat from WINCHESTER, ROBERT of Gloucester was captured and, in November 1141, he was exchanged for Stephen. Matilda died after a short illness in 1152, thereby predeceasing her husband, and was buried at Faversham Abbey. Three children survived her: EUSTACE (d. 1153), Count of Boulogne; William (d. 1160), Count of Boulogne; and Mary (d. 1182), who became abbess of ROMSEY, but after papal dispensation married Matthew, son of the Count of Flanders.

Novels: '"She'll move heaven and earth to get Stephen out of hold, by whatever means, fair or foul. She is," said Hugh [BERINGAR] with conviction, "a better soldier than her lord. Not a better fighter in the field – God knows you'd need to search Europe through to find such a one, I saw him at Lincoln – a marvel! But a better general, that she is. She holds to her purpose, where he tires and goes off after another quarry."' After Stephen was captured at the battle of Lincoln in February 1141, Queen Matilda gathered her army and moved towards London. In April she sent CHRISTIAN to Winchester to address the legatine council and ask that they support Stephen's release. In June, with the support of the Londoners, she forced the Empress Maud to flee the city. In August, she moved her army to Winchester at the request of Bishop Henry of Blois, who was besieged by Maud in his castle at Wolvesey. The queen's army wiped out the empress's raiding party at WHERWELL in September. Eventually, with Winchester completely sealed, Maud was forced to break out of the city. Although the empress managed to escape, ROBERT of Gloucester was captured by the queen's soldiers at STOCKBRIDGE. Matilda negotiated an exchange of prisoners and secured her husband's release in November.

Refs: **9** (1, 15); **10** (1–2, 7, 11, 16); **11** (1–6, 11); **12** (2, 6); **14** (1); **20** (4).

Matilda, Empress. See MAUD, Empress.

Matthew. See MEVEREL, Luc.

Matthew, Brother (*fl.* 1137) (fict.). **Novels:** 'Brother Matthew rolled up his plans with a brisk hand and a satisfied countenance. It was his part to keep a strict eye upon the property and funds of the house, to reckon up land, crops, gifts and legacies in the profits they could bring to the monastery of Saint Peter and Saint Paul, and he had assessed the POTTER'S FIELD with professional shrewdness, and liked what he saw.' Benedictine monk and cellarer at SHREWSBURY ABBEY from at least 1136, Brother Matthew had formerly lived for some years in FLANDERS and could speak Flemish. He was often called on to help the Flemish merchants who attended the annual St Peter's Fair. In 1143 he helped negotiate the exchange of land between Shrewsbury Abbey and HAUGHMOND ABBEY in which the former acquired the Potter's Field. During the chaos caused by rising floodwaters invading the abbey church in February 1145, Matthew helped BÉNEZET carry what they thought was St WINIFRED's reliquary upstairs to the safety of the north porch. Among those who worked under Matthew were: Brother AMBROSE, Brother EUTROPIUS and William REDE.

Refs: **1** (1); **3** (1, 6–7); **4** (1:1); **6** (1); **16** (12); **17** (1, 6); **18** (1); **19** (3); **RB** (3).

Matthew the Archer (*fl.* 1138) (fict.). **Novels:** Archer in the service of Hugh BERINGAR, he helped his lord take William FITZALAN's treasury from Godith Adeney (see BLUND) and Torold BLUND at SHREWSBURY ABBEY grange in the LONG FOREST in August 1138.

Refs: **2** (10).

Matthew the Evangelist, Saint (*fl.* 1st C.) (hist.) (f.d. 21 September). Originally called Levi. A tax-collector (or 'publican', Matthew 10:3) for the Romans, before being called by Christ to be an apostle, Matthew is regarded as the author of the first Gospel. Details of his life are sparse and unreliable. It is not known where he preached or whether he died a martyr.

Novels: At their respective consecrations the *sortes Biblicae* sent to: Roger of Salisbury (see ROBERT, Bishop of Salisbury) '"Bind his hands and feet, and cast him into outer darkness."' (Matthew 22:13); and Henry of Winchester (see HENRY OF BLOIS) '"something from Matthew, concerning the latter days when false prophets would multiply among us. Something to the effect that if any man should claim: Here is Christ! Do not believe him"' (see Matthew 24:23–24). When CADFAEL consulted the Biblical fates himself in March 1145 he received Matthew 10:21: 'And the brother shall deliver up the brother to death.' Later, during the *sortes* held by SHREWSBURY ABBEY, the pages of the Gospels, turning by themselves, came to rest on the same page, with a single bud of blackthorn pointing out the same verse – Matthew 10:21. Abbot RADULFUS received: 'The last shall be first, and the first last' (Matthew 20:16).

Refs: **19** (7–10).

Maud (*fl.* 1139), Countess of Chester (hist.). Daughter of ROBERT of Gloucester, wife of RANULF of Chester and sister of Philip FITZROBERT.

Novels: Maud was in CHESTER in June 1139. In January 1141 in LINCOLN Ranulf left her 'walled up in the castle with the Earl of Lincoln (see ROUMARE, William of) and his wife, and the whole town in arms and seething round them.' '"Philip [FitzRobert]'s sister is wife to Ranulf of Chester."'

Refs: **4** (3:2, 4:1); **8** (1, 3); **9** (1); **20** (1).

Maud (1102–67), Empress (hist.). Also called Matilda, Mold, Aethelic, Aaliz, or Adela. Born in LONDON, she was the only daughter of HENRY I, King of England, and his first wife MATILDA (1080–1118). In 1110, at the age of eight, Maud was betrothed to Emperor HENRY V, whom she married in 1114. After his death in 1125, her father summoned her back to his own court. Her brother WILLIAM THE AETHELING's death in 1120 made her the king's only legitimate heir. In 1127 Henry forced the barons to accept her as his successor to the English throne. She was married to the fifteen-year-old GEOFFREY of Anjou in 1128 at Le Mans. They soon quarrelled, and Geoffrey sent her to ROUEN, out of his domains. It was not until 1131 that he repented and summoned her back. Their

M

first child, Henry Plantagenet (see HENRY II), was born at Le Mans on 5 March 1133, and Henry I immediately made his barons swear fealty to Maud for the third time. She nearly died while giving birth to their second child, Geoffrey (1134–58), who became Count of Nantes. Their third child was William (1136–64), who became Count of Poitou. On the death of Henry on 1 December 1135, Maud entered NORMANDY to claim her inheritance, but found that her cousin, STEPHEN, had seized the English throne. Although the Church and the majority of the barons supported Stephen, Maud's claims were upheld by her uncle DAVID I, King of Scotland, and her half-brother ROBERT of Gloucester. On 30 September 1139 she and Robert landed with their army at ARUNDEL, and for a short while she was besieged in ARUNDEL CASTLE. But Stephen soon allowed her to join Robert at BRISTOL and even provided her with an escort. She eventually made GLOUCESTER her main headquarters, and gathered much support from the west country barons. In February 1141 Stephen was captured at LINCOLN and imprisoned in Bristol Castle. On 8 April, at a clerical council held at WINCHESTER, Bishop HENRY OF BLOIS acknowledged Maud as the 'Lady of the English'. She entered London in June and established her court at WESTMINSTER. But her arrogant and overbearing manner towards the citizens of London provoked them to drive her out of the city before she could be crowned queen. She fled to OXFORD, and soon after besieged Bishop Henry of Blois in his castle at Winchester. Queen MATILDA's forces in turn blockaded the besiegers, and on 14 September 1141, in danger of starvation, Maud and her troops were forced to break out of the cordon. In the rout which followed, Robert of Gloucester was captured. Maud fled to LUDGERSHALL, DEVIZES and finally Gloucester, before returning to Oxford in Spring 1142. On 26 September, Stephen stormed the city and besieged the empress in the castle. After nearly three months, just before Christmas, Maud managed to slip out of the castle unseen, fled on foot to ABINGDON, and by dawn the following day she was safe in WALLINGFORD. Although her cause was effectively lost, she remained in England, maintaining a steadily weakening resistance in the west country, until 1148 when she returned to Normandy. Her husband died in 1151 and her son, Henry, was crowned King of England in 1154. She spent the rest of her life in Normandy, assisting her son in the management of his continental dominions. She died at Nôtre-Dame des Prés, near Rouen, and was buried in the abbey at Bec. In 1847 her remains were translated to Rouen Cathedral.

Novels: '"I ask only that truth be recognised as truth," she said inflexibly. "I am lawful queen of England by hereditary right, by my father's royal decree and by the solemn oaths of all his magnates to accept and acknowledge me. If I wished, I cannot change my status, and as God sees me, I will not. That I am denied my right alters nothing. I have not surrendered it."' '"I would not say she is a wise woman," said RADULFUS carefully. "She is all too well aware how many swore allegiance to her at her father's order, and then swung to King Stephen, and now as nimbly skip back to her because she is in the ascendant. I can well understand she might take pleasure in pricking into the quick where she can, among these. It is not wise, but it is human. But that she should become lofty and cold to those who never wavered – for there are some," said the abbot with respectful wonder, "who have been faithful throughout at their own great loss, and will not waver even now, whatever she may do. Great folly and great injustice to use them so high-handedly, who have been her right hand and her left all this while." You comfort me, thought Hugh, watching the lean, quiet face intently. The woman is out of her wits if she flouts even the like of Robert of Gloucester, now she feels herself so near the throne.' The Empress Maud was the granddaughter of WILLIAM I, daughter and heir of Henry I and Queen Matilda, sister of William the Aetheling, first wife of Emperor Henry V and then of Geoffrey of Anjou, mother of Henry II, half-sister of Robert of Gloucester and cousin of King Stephen. She was betrothed to Emperor Henry V, in 1110, and they were married four years later. She was forced to marry Geoffrey of Anjou in 1128, and in 1133 she gave birth to their son Henry. Before she could claim her right to the throne of England in December 1135, Stephen seized the throne. On 30 September 1139 she landed near Arundel with Robert of Gloucester and 140 knights, and established herself in Arundel Castle. Shortly after, Stephen arranged for her to be escorted to Bristol. After Stephen's capture at the battle of Lincoln in February 1141, Maud prepared for her coronation. She was admitted to London in June, but her arrogant and overbearing manner towards the citizens provoked them into driving her out of the city. She fled west to Oxford. During the 'Rout of Winchester' on 14 September 1141, she managed to escape to Gloucester. But Robert was taken prisoner and Maud was forced to release Stephen in exchange for her champion. In 1142 she moved her headquarters to Oxford and sent Robert to Normandy to try and get her husband to support her cause. Geoffrey, however, was far more concerned with gaining possession of Normandy than helping Maud win the crown of England. Instead of sending the army she requested, Geoffrey sent over their son, Henry. In September, Maud was besieged in OXFORD CASTLE. She managed to escape unseen in December and fled to Wallingford. In August 1143 she was with her ten-year-old son in Bristol. By May 1144 she was securely established in the south-west and 'maintained her own court unmolested in Devizes'. 'Tall and erect against the dimness within the hall, splendidly apparelled and in her proud prime, there stood old King Henry's sole surviving legitimate child, Empress Maud by her first marriage, countess of Anjou by her second, the uncrowned Lady of the English . . . She was regally handsome, her hair dark and rich under the gilded net of her coif, her eyes large and direct, as unnerving as the straight stare of a Byzantine saint in a mosaic, and as indifferent. She was past forty, but durable as marble.' On 30 November 1145 she attended the conference at COVENTRY, where she confessed to Yves HUGONIN that she would not be greatly grieved to see the traitor and renegade, Brien de SOULIS, dead. From Gloucester in December of the same year, the empress rode with her army to attack La MUSARDERIE, vowing to hang the traitor, Philip FITZROBERT, once the garrison had been captured.

Refs: **2** (1–5, 8, 10, 12); **3** (1); **4** (1:1–2, 5:3, 5:5–6); **5** (1, 7); **6** (1, 3, 5, 8–9, 12, 15); **7** (1); **8** (1); **9** (1, 4, 9); **10** (1–2, 7, 10–11, 15–16); **11** (1–8, 10, 14); **12** (1–2, 4, 6–10, 13); **13** (1); **14** (1, 4, 9, 13–14); **15** (1); **16** (1); **17** (1, 3); **18** (1); **19** (Prologue, 4, 9, 11); **20** (1–16).

Mauduit, Arnulf (d. 1116) (fict.). **Novels:** Father of Roger MAUDUIT of SUTTON MAUDUIT, Arnulf Mauduit granted the manor of ROTESLEY, near STRETTON, to SHREWSBURY ABBEY. The abbey granted it back to him as tenant for life, and Arnulf spent the remaining years of his life there. It was understood that on his death, the manor and village should be restored to the abbey. This agreement, however, was disputed by his son.

Refs: **RB** (1).

Mauduit, Lady Eadwina (*fl.* 1120) (fict.). **Novels:** 'It needed only a single day of watching the Lady Eadwina in action to show who ruled the roost here. Roger MAUDUIT had married a wife not only handsome, but also efficient and masterful. She had had her own way here for three years, and by all the signs had enjoyed her dominance. She might, even, be none too glad to resign her charge now, however glad she might be to have her lord home again.' Lady Eadwina Mauduit was the wife of Roger MAUDUIT of SUTTON MAUDUIT, and the mother of their son, born in *c.*1113. In 1117, when her husband departed overseas, she was left to manage the household. During his long absence she took GOSCELIN as her secret lover. On Roger's return in November 1120, she suggested that he ambush Prior (later Abbot) HERIBERT

M

and his party to stop them from reaching WOODSTOCK. She also planned that Goscelin should murder her husband.

Refs: **RB** (1).

Mauduit, Roger (*fl.* 1120) (fict.). **Novels:** Son of Arnulf MAUDUIT, husband of Lady Eadwina MAUDUIT and Lord of SUTTON MAUDUIT, he left England to support HENRY I in NORMANDY in 1117 and returned by ship from BARFLEUR to SOUTHAMPTON in November 1120. He asked CADFAEL and ALARD THE CLERK to remain in his service until his lawsuit with SHREWSBURY ABBEY over the manor and village of ROTESLEY was resolved. Both agreed. He was persuaded by his wife to abduct Prior (later Abbot) HERIBERT to prevent him from giving testimony at the court of WOODSTOCK. Although GOSCELIN, unrecognised, attacked Roger on the journey to Woodstock, Cadfael intervened and saved his life. After judgement had been given in favour of the abbey, Cadfael dismissed himself from Roger's service. Before he left, however, he warned Roger to be on his guard for further attacks on his personage by someone in his employ.

Refs: **RB** (1).

Maurice, Brother (*fl.* 1138) (fict.). Benedictine monk of SHREWSBURY ABBEY and custodian of Saint Mary's altar in December 1138.

Refs: **3** (1).

Mechain (Powys, Wales). The medieval Welsh cantref of Mechain (except for its short, four-mile border with England) was surrounded by the commotes of CYNLLAITH, Mochnant, Caereinion, Ystrad Marchell and Deuddwr. The River Tanat, between its confluences with the rivers CYNLLAITH and VYRNWY, formed Mechain's eastern boundary with England. The Vyrnwy formed its southern extremity, but its western limit stopped just short of Lake Vyrnwy, which was in Mochnant. Its northern border lay in the hills south of the Tanat Valley. In medieval times the cantref was divided by a great forest into the commotes of Mechain Uwch Coed and Mechain Is Coed (Above and Below the Wood). It was an agriculturally fertile region, rich in fish and game. The two main towns were MEIFOD and Llanfyllin. Mechain received its name from the River Cain.

Novels: Griffri ap GRIFFRI was '"A young fellow who used to trade in fleeces to the town market from somewhere in Mechain."'

Refs: **9** (8).

Meifod (Powys, Wales). Nearly 6 miles north-west of Welshpool (see POOL) and 15 miles south-west of OSWESTRY, the village of Meifod lies on the River VYRNWY, in the Vale of Meifod (or Dyffryn Meifod). The Meifod church, founded by St TYSILIO, was the holiest place in Powys and, until the foundation of the Cistercian abbeys of Strata Marcella (1170) and Valle Crucis (1201), was the favoured burial-place of its kings. Dedicated to St Tysilio and St MARY, Meifod parish church stands on the site of the ancient Celtic monastic church and dates from the latter half of the 12th C. Parts of the building have been altered and rebuilt over the succeeding centuries. One of the carved tombstones inside the church is thought to belong to MADOG AP MEREDITH, who was buried on the site in 1160.

Novels: 'Saint Tysilio . . . had a rather special significance here on the borders of Powys, and his influence spilled over the frontier into the neighbouring shires. For the centre of his ministry was the chief church of Powys at Meifod, no great way into Wales.'

Refs: **17** (10).

Meilyr (*fl.*. 1060) (fict.). **Novels:** Welshman of Gwynedd, he was the father of CADFAEL and son of DAFYDD.

Refs: **18** (3); **RB** (1).

Meilyr, Griffith ap (*fl.* 1141) (fict.). **Novels:** He was the father of Eliud ap GRIFFITH, and uncle and foster-father of Elis ap CYNAN. Griffith ap Meilyr's wife was distant kin to OWAIN GWYNEDD, amongst whose officers Griffith ranked high. Griffith arranged the childhood match between Elis ap Cynan and CRISTINA.

Refs: **9** (2, 10).

Meirion, Canon (*fl.* 1144) (fict.). **Novels:** '"My name is Meirion, I have served this church for many years. Under the new dispensation I am a canon of the chapter. If there is anything wanting, anything we can provide you, during your stay, you have only to speak, I will see it remedied." He spoke in formal English, a little hesitantly, for he was obviously Welsh. A burly, muscular man, and handsome in his own black fashion, with sharply cut features and a very erect presence, the ring of his cropped hair barely salted with grey.' Meirion was a Welsh priest, the father of HELEDD and a canon of ST ASAPH under Bishop GILBERT. Meirion's wife died at Christmas 1143. He was an ambitious man, intent on advancement in the Church, but the fact that he had been married and had a daughter was frowned upon by Bishop Gilbert, who expected his priests to be celibate. The presence of Heledd at St Asaph served only as a reminder of Meirion's former marriage. He therefore arranged to remove her from Llanelwy by marrying her to Ieuan AB IFOR of ANGLESEY. He and Canon MORGANT set out in May 1144 to escort the reluctant bride to BANGOR to meet her bridegroom but, while at ABER, Heledd ran away. Although he went in search of her, Meirion failed to find her. Nor did he see her again.

Refs: **18** (2–9, 11, 14).

Melangell. See MEVEREL, Melangell.

Melangell, Saint (d. *c.*590) (hist.) (f.d. 27 May). Also called Monacella. Melangell is thought to have been the daughter of an Irish king, who fled to Wales to avoid her father's plans for her marriage. It seems that she lived as a recluse in the remote BERWYNS for some fifteen years before being discovered by Brocwael (or Brochwel Ysgythrog), King of Powys, who reputedly had a palace at Pengwern (now SHREWSBURY). According to legend, while praying at Pennant in Powys, the saint protected a hare which was being hunted by the king. But, after he had tried unsuccessfully to set his dogs on the animal, Brocwael gave Melangell the land and the rights of sanctuary. Shortly after, she founded the monastery of Pennant Melangell on the north bank of the Afon Tanat, nearly 2 miles west of Llangynog. The present St Melangell's Church, dating from the late 12th C., stands on the site. Her Romanesque shrine, built to enclose her supposed remains, was reconstructed in 1958–9.

Novels: '"Named for some outlandish Welsh saint, she is, Melangell, if ever you heard the like!"' See MEVEREL, Melangell. '"Any creature in peril of death or harm, be it man, woman, plough horse, or Saint Melangell's hare, could draw him through moss or quicksand."'

Refs: **10** (3); **18** (6).

Menai Strait (Wales). This 15-mile-long sea channel separates ANGLESEY from the mainland of North Wales. It varies in width from a few hundred yards to over a mile, and is spanned by two 19th C. bridges: Thomas Telford's suspension road bridge; and Robert Stephenson's tubular railway bridge, Britannia Bridge, rebuilt in 1970 to include a road deck. At the

M

north-eastern end of the strait are Beaumaris, LAVAN SANDS and BANGOR; while at the south-western end are CARNARVON and ABERMENAI.

Novels: 'The anchorage at the mouth of the Menai was separated from the broad sandy reaches of the bay to southward by a long spit of shingle beyond which the water of two rivers and their tributaries wound its way to the strait and the open sea, in a winding course through the waste of sands.' In May 1144 OTIR established the Danish camp on the mainland peninsula at the mouth of the Menai Strait, opposite ABERMENAI. TURCAILL (*fl.* 1144) anchored his dragon-ship in the strait while making a foray into ARFON, and captured HELEDD and CADFAEL.

Refs: **18** (4, 6–10, 14).

Meole, Nicholas of (*fl.* 1138) (fict.). **Novels:** A SHREWSBURY merchant, he was one of the witnesses for the town to the charter of 1138, which granted Judith PERLE's house in the ABBEY FOREGATE to SHREWSBURY ABBEY. See also John RUDDOCK and Henry WYLE.

Refs: **13** (2).

Meole Brace. See BRACE MEOLE.

Meole Brook (now Rea Brook) (Shropshire, England). The waters of the Rea Brook rise on the hills flanking the MINSTERLEY VALLEY. Its source lies in the vicinity of Marton and, from there, the stream winds north-eastward, past MINSTERLEY, PONTESBURY, HANWOOD, Bayston Hill (see BEISTAN) and Meole Brace (see BRACE MEOLE). Beyond SUTTON it forms a narrow loop and then changes direction to head north to ST GILES, on the eastern outskirts of SHREWSBURY. From St Giles it flows north-west to SHREWSBURY ABBEY, where it joins the River SEVERN. During medieval times, the waters of the brook – just before its confluence with the Severn – were diverted by an artificial stream which fed the abbey fish-ponds and powered the abbey mill.

Novels: 'Sanicle, ragwort, moneywort, adder's tongue, all cleansing and astringent, good for old, ulcerated wounds, were all to be found around the hedgerows and the meadows close by, and along the banks of the Meole Brook.' 'The Meole Brook had still a few visible shoals, but was no longer a mere sad, sluggish network of rivulets struggling through pebble and sand.' The waters of the Meole Brook, Severn and abbey mill pond, flooded the nave of Shrewsbury Abbey church in February 1145, and not for the first time.

Refs: **1** (1); **2** (1); **3** (1, 7); **4** (1:1, 3:2); **5** (4–5, 7); **7** (4, 6); **8** (10); **9** (8); **10** (8); **11** (3, 14); **12** (2–3, 5–7, 9, 11–12); **13** (11); **14** (1); 15 (3); **19** (1–2).

Meresbrook (now Maesbrook) (Shropshire, England). DB – Meresbroc: in Merset Hundred; a holding of Reginald the Sheriff under Roger de MONTGOMERY. Maesbrook is 5 miles south of OSWESTRY and 14 miles north-west of SHREWSBURY. The village is divided into two distinct parts: the upper part being on higher and drier ground than the lower part, which is subject to flooding when the nearby rivers Morda and VYRNWY burst their banks. The watery nature of lower Maesbrook is reflected in the names of houses like the Ark and the Moat. The surrounding land, lying in the flood plain, is fertile and has been farmed for centuries. Many of the farms have Welsh names, serving as a reminder that the village was once a part of Wales.

Novels: In November 1143 BRITRIC THE PEDLAR crossed the Welsh border into England. Just short of the village of Meresbrook he was arrested by the sheriff's men.

Refs: **17** (7).

Meulan, Count of. See BEAUMONT, Waleran de, Count of Meulan.

Meulan (France). Forty or so miles north-west of Paris city centre, the ancient town of Meulan stands on the north bank of the Seine, 5 miles down river from Poissy. Very little remains of the Norman castle, but the church of St Nicolas contains a 12th C. choir.

Novels: On the death of his father, Robert de BEAUMONT (d. 1118), Waleran de BEAUMONT inherited 'BEAUMONT, BRIONNE and PONTAUDEMER in

NORMANDY, and the county of Meulan in France'. Waleran's line was '"bound up in the title. Without Meulan he'd be nameless."'

Refs: **19** (4–5).

Meurice, Uncle (*fl.* 1137) (fict.). **Novels:** '"And Uncle Meurice is a gentle creature who knows about running a manor, but nothing about anything else, and wants no trouble and no exertion."' Welshman and 'man of substance' in GWYTHERIN, Meurice was SIONED's uncle and RHISIART's steward and brother-in-law. After Rhisiart's death in May 1137, Meurice became Sioned's guardian. He did not stand in the way of her marriage to ENGELARD.

Refs: **1** (3, 5–6, 8–9, 10).

Meurig (b. *c.*1113) (fict.). **Novels:** '"You have branded me murderer, why should I draw back now from murder? You have ruined me, shamed me, made me a reproach to my own kin, taken from me my birthright, my land, my good name, everything that made my existence worth calling a life, and I will have your life in recompense. I cannot live now, I cannot even die, until I have been your death, Brother CADFAEL."' Illegitimate son of ANGHARAD (1093–1127) and Gervase BONEL, grandson of Ifor ap MORGAN and great-grandson of Brother RHYS, Meurig, a Welshman, was born and brought up at Bonel's manor of MALLILIE. His main employment was working with horses. In December 1138 he was journeyman to Martin BELLECOTE. He helped move the Bonel household into the messuage of SHREWSBURY ABBEY. In order to try and claim the manor of Mallilie for himself, he poisoned his father with a dose of monk's-hood. He helped Edwin GURNEY escape from the sheriff's men and gave him a token to carry to Ifor ap Morgan. Shortly after, he went north to join Edwin and spend Christmas with his kin. At the commote court at LLANSILIN, Meurig offered irrefutable proof of his right under Welsh law to Mallilie. After being accused by Cadfael of murdering Bonel, he fled into the nearby woodland. He later confronted Cadfael at knife-point, but was unable to kill him. Laying his life in Cadfael's hands, Meurig was given a lifelong penance: to live, to make amends and to devote his life to serving others. Before they parted, Cadfael made Meurig promise to make his confession to a priest and also to send it in writing to the sheriff at SHREWSBURY. The last report of Meurig was from the monastery of BEDDGELERT, where he left his horse, asking the brothers to return it to RHYDYCROESAU. From there he vanished.

Refs: **3** (1–5, 7–11).

Meurig (*fl.* 1144) (fict.). **Novels:** 'A shaggy dark boy and kitchen servant of OWAIN GWYNEDD at ABER, Meurig saw Cuhelyn ab EINION leave Bledri ap RHYS's room on the night he was murdered.

Refs: **18** (5).

Meurig (d. 1162), Bishop of Bangor (hist.). Also called Maurice. Welshman of Gwynedd and Bishop of BANGOR, Meurig succeeded Bishop DAVID to the see in 1139. However, at first he refused to swear fealty to King STEPHEN on the advice of his archdeacon, Simeon of Clynnog. His eventual capitulation incurred the displeasure of OWAIN GWYNEDD and CADWALADR. Meurig not only swore fealty to STEPHEN but also made full submission to CANTERBURY and was consecrated by Archbishop THEOBALD OF BEC in 1140. All that remained in his favour with the Princes of Gwynedd was that he was Welsh and not Norman.

Novels: 'A small, round, bustling cleric in his forties, voluble of speech but very much to the point, rapid of movement and a little dishevelled and shaggy, with a sharp eye and a cheerfully pouncing manner, like a boisterous but businesslike hound on a scent.' Born in Wales in *c.*1100 and non-English-speaking Bishop of Bangor, Meurig was consecrated in 1140. At first he refused to swear fealty to Stephen or acknowledge the dominance of Canterbury. Although his eventual capitulation cost him the support of Owain Gwynedd, they finally agreed to work together to reduce Archbishop Theobald of Bec's influence in Gwynedd. Deacon MARK was sent on a diplomatic mission to ST ASAPH and Bangor by Bishop ROGER DE CLINTON in Spring 1144. It was Bishop Roger de Clinton's

M

intention to pay the same courtesy to Bishop Meurig as to the new Norman Bishop of St Asaph, GILBERT, and treat them both alike. With the approach of the Danish fleet, Meurig arranged for NONNA to be escorted into safety at Bangor. St DEINIOL was 'Meurig's founder and patron'.

Refs: **18** (1–2, 4, 6).

Meverel, Luc (b. 1117) (fict.). **Novels:** Also known as the Pilgrim of Hate. Pseudonym Matthew. '"There is no one, man or woman, in that manor but agrees he was utterly devoted to Dame Juliana. But as to the manner of his devotion . . . There are many who say he loved her far too well, by no means after the fashion of a son. Again, some say he was equally loyal to Rainald, but their voices are growing fainter now. Luc was one of those with his lord when Rainald was stabbed to death in the street. And two days later he vanished from his place, and has not been seen since."' Husband of Melangell MEVEREL, distant cousin of Juliana BOSSARD and heir of Rainald BOSSARD, Luc Meverel, without lands himself, entered the Bossard household in 1140. He saw CIARAN murder Rainald on 8 April 1141 at WINCHESTER. Following him into the Old Minster, he overheard Bishop HENRY OF BLOIS banish the murderer to DUBLIN and condemn him to go barefoot every step of the way carrying a heavy cross around his neck. Calling himself Matthew, Luc waited for Ciaran near NEWBURY, warned him that he would kill him if he broke the terms of his penance and became his shadow. South of WARWICK they joined Melangell, RHUN and Dame Alice WEAVER. Matthew was attracted to Melangell, helped carry her few goods and saved her from being trampled by some mad horsemen. The party arrived at SHREWSBURY ABBEY on 18 June 1141. On 22 June, the day of St WINIFRED's festival, Matthew and Melangell joined the procession from ST GILES to the abbey. Realising later that Ciaran had slipped away from him, Matthew abandoned Melangell to go in pursuit. In the LONG FOREST he helped protect Ciaran from Simeon POER and his fellow outlaws. With his enemy at his mercy, Luc was unable to kill Ciaran. He threw away his knife and ran into the forest. Olivier de BRETAGNE followed him and eventually persuaded him to return to SHREWSBURY. Luc found Melangell waiting for him. They were married on 25 June 1141 at the abbey church. Afterwards, Luc took his new wife with him back to the manor of Juliana Bossard.

Refs: **10** (3–16); **20** (1).

Meverel, Melangell (b. 1123) (fict.). **Novels:** 'The pearly morning light became her, softened the coarseness of her linen gown, and smoothed cool lilac shadows round the childlike curves of her face. She had gone to great pains to prepare herself fittingly for the day's solemnities. Her skirts were spotless, crisped out with care, her dark-gold hair, burning with coppery lustre, braided and coiled on her head in a bright crown, its tight plaits drawing up the skin of her temples and cheeks so strongly that her brows were pulled aslant, and the dark-lashed blue eyes elongated and made mysterious. But the radiance that shone from her came not from the sun's caresses, but from within. The blue of those eyes burned as brilliantly as the blue of the gentians CADFAEL had seen long ago in the mountains of southern France, on his way to the east. The ivory and rose of her cheeks glowed. Melangell was in the highest state of hope, happiness and expectation.' Half-English, half-Welsh wife of Luc MEVEREL, elder sister of Brother RHUN and niece of Dame Alice WEAVER, Melangell was named 'for some outlandish Welsh saint' [MELANGELL]. She was orphaned in 1134, at the age of eleven, and left Wales to go and stay with her aunt at CAMPDEN. In June 1141 she walked with Alice and Rhun to SHREWSBURY ABBEY from the COTSWOLDS for St WINIFRED's festival. On the way they joined company with CIARAN and Matthew (see MEVEREL, Luc). She fell in love with Matthew. When Ciaran asked her not to tell Matthew that he had left SHREWSBURY, she willingly complied. Together Melangell and Matthew joined the procession from ST GILES to the abbey. Inside the abbey church they witnessed the miracle of Rhun's healing, and saw him walk unaided. Matthew later realised that Ciaran was missing. Melangell confessed to having known that he had gone. She was unable to stop Matthew from abandoning her. It was later disclosed that Matthew was in fact Luc Meverel. He eventually returned to Shrewsbury to find her waiting for him. They were married on 25 June 1141 at the abbey church.

Refs: **10** (3–6, 8–12, 15–16).

Milburga, Saint (d. 715) (hist.) (f.d. 23 February). Also spelled Milburh or Mildburga. The daughter of Merewald (or Merewalh), King of Mercia, and Ermenburga, a princess of Kent, Milburga was the sister of St Mildred of Thanet and St Mildgyth. After Merewald had founded WENLOCK PRIORY in *c.*680, Milburga became the first abbess and, by the time of her death, it had become the wealthiest in the whole of West Mercia. Her reputed tomb and remains were discovered in 1101, some twenty years after the house had been refounded for Cluniac monks.

Novels: In 1137 Prior Robert was much concerned with a campaign to secure the relics and patronage of a powerful saint for SHREWSBURY ABBEY. 'The prior had had it on his mind . . . ever since the Cluniac house of Wenlock had rediscovered, with great pride and jubilation, the tomb of their original foundress, Saint Milburga, and installed her bones triumphantly on their altar. An alien priory, only a few miles distant, with its own miracle-working saint, and the great Benedictine house of Shrewsbury as empty of relics as a plundered almsbox! It was more than Prior Robert could stomach.'

Refs: **1** (1); **10** (1).

Mildenhall (Suffolk, England). Some 20 miles north-east of CAMBRIDGE and 12 miles north-west of BURY St Edmunds, the market town and former river port of Mildenhall lies on the north bank of the River Lark at the edge of the FENS. The church is noted for its elaborately carved angel roof, depicting biblical scenes, which was peppered with small shot by Puritan zealots in the 17th C. The 'Mildenhall Treasure', a hoard of 4th C. Roman silver tableware, was discovered at nearby Thistley Green in the 1940s and is now in the British Museum, LONDON.

Novels: 'A long way from Mildenhall to ROME for a man dying in terror of hellfire.' Geoffrey de MANDEVILLE died, excommunicate, at Mildenhall on 16 September 1144. Certain KNIGHTS TEMPLAR, who were in Mildenhall at the time, took his coffined body back with them to London.

Refs: **19** (Prologue).

M

Miles (d. 1143), Constable of Gloucester (hist.). Son and heir of Walter de Gloucester and his wife Berta, Miles was hereditary constable of GLOUCESTER and sheriff of Gloucestershire. He was granted the hand of Sibyl, daughter of Bernard de Neufmarché, in 1121 and succeeded to his father's estates in or before 1129. From 1128 he was sheriff of Gloucestershire and Staffordshire and, according to the *Gesta Stephani* (ed. Potter, 1976), together with Payne (or Pain) FitzJohn, sheriff of Herefordshire and Shropshire, they ruled 'from the River SEVERN to the sea, all along the border between England and Wales'. Having sworn allegiance to King STEPHEN early in 1136, Miles was confirmed in his offices of sheriff and castellan of Gloucester. He was not only HENRY I's royal constable, but also Stephen's. In that capacity, he attended the king's Easter court at WESTMINSTER in March 1136 and, later the same year, the council at OXFORD. He was with Stephen at the siege of SHREWSBURY in August 1138, but defected to the side of the Empress MAUD after she landed at ARUNDEL on 30 September 1139. She immediately gave him St Briavel's castle and the Forest of Dean. The

Empress's most trusted supporter, after Brian FITZCOUNT and ROBERT of Gloucester, Miles was one of the most powerful barons of the west country. By the close of 1139 he had relieved FitzCount at WALLINGFORD, attacked and burnt WORCESTER, and captured the castles of South Cerney (near CIRENCESTER), Winchcombe (near Cheltenham) and HEREFORD. After helping to defeat Stephen at the battle of LINCOLN in February 1141, Miles later accompanied Maud to Westminster and was with her when she fled from LONDON to Oxford. He was made Earl of Hereford on 25 July 1141. On 14 September he managed, with extreme difficulty, to escape from the 'Rout of WINCHESTER', in which Robert of Gloucester was captured. Miles was accidentally killed by an arrow while hunting deer on 24 December 1143, and was succeeded by his son and heir, ROGER (d. 1155).

Novels: 'Miles, the constable of Gloucester,' was among those who joined the Empress Maud when she landed at Arundel on 30 September 1139. Father of Roger of Hereford, Miles was 'killed by mishap, out hunting'.

Refs: **5** (7); **20** (2).

Miller, John (*fl.* 1141) (fict.). **Novels:** 'The gentle giant could not only heft sturdy young men as lightly as babies, he also had a deft and reassuring hand with injuries.' Miller at GODRIC'S FORD and trusted ally of Sister MAGDALEN, John Miller helped defend the nunnery from two attacks by Welsh raiders in February and March 1141. He kept Elis ap CYNAN under lock and key, and looked after him when he was injured. In June 1142 he accompanied Magdalen and Judith PERLE to SHREWSBURY.

Refs: **9** (1, 13–15); **13** (12).

Minchinbarrow Priory (now Barrow Gurney) (Avon, England). Some 5 miles south-west of the centre of BRISTOL, Minchinbarrow Priory was founded before 1212 by a member of the Gurney family and dedicated to St Mary and St EDWARD, King and Martyr. The site of the Benedictine nunnery, dissolved in 1536, is now occupied by the manor house of Barrow Court. Although the church was rebuilt during the 19th C., it is thought that the south aisle was the original nuns' church. Fragments of the small medieval convent can be found in the churchyard wall.

Novels: In August 1139 Ivo CORBIÈRE pretended to Aline BERINGAR and Emma Vernold (see CORVISER) that his sister, Isabel CORBIÈRE, was about to enter the Benedictine priory at Minchinbarrow.

Refs: **4** (5:1–2).

Minsterley (Shropshire, England). DB – Menistrelie: in Rhiwset Hundred; land held by Roger de MONTGOMERY himself. Some 9 miles south-west of SHREWSBURY, Minsterley is a large and expanding village lying on the western slopes of Callow Hill. From its source, high in the hills, a small stream flows down through the village before joining the Rea Brook (see MEOLE BROOK) near Malehurst. On the summit of Callow Hill are the earthwork remains of an Iron Age hill-fort, which was adapted, probably in the 13th C., into CAUS CASTLE.

Novels: 'The first thing that happened was a lightning raid from Caus along the valley towards Minsterley, the burning of an isolated farmstead and the driving off of a few cattle. The raiders drew off as rapidly as they had advanced, when the men of Minsterley mustered against them, and vanished into Caus and through the hills into Wales with their booty. But it was indication enough that they might be expected back and in greater strength, since this first assay had passed off so easily and without loss. Alan HERBARD sweated, spared a few men to reinforce Minsterley, and waited for worse.'

Refs: **9** (9, 11–13).

Minsterley Valley (Shropshire, England). The Minsterley Valley runs south-eastward along the valley of the Rea Brook (see MEOLE BROOK) from HANWOOD towards the Welsh border and MONTGOMERY. It is flanked by the Long Mountain to the west and the range of hills, which includes Pontesford Hill, Callow Hill, Luckley Hill and Rorrington Hill, to the east. During the Middle Ages, and even as far back as Roman times, the Minsterley Valley was a major trade route between SHREWSBURY and Wales.

Novels: In March 1141 MADOG AP MEREDITH led the Welsh of Powys on a series of raids to plunder the 'fat farms' in the Minsterley valley.

Refs: **9** (9, 11–12).

Miserden (Gloucestershire, England). See GREENHAMSTED.

Moel Wnion (Gwynedd, Wales). The hill overlooks LAVAN SANDS, the MENAI STRAIT and ANGLESEY. At 1,903 ft. above sea level, Moel Wnion dominates the landscape between ABER and BANGOR. The Carneddau hills to the south, however, rise even higher, with the summit cairn on Carnedd Llewelyn reaching nearly 3,500 ft.

Novels: 'Not merely a brief sally over the border into Powis, this time, but several days riding, in the very fellowship he would have chosen, right across the coastal regions of Gwynedd, from ST ASAPH to CARNARVON, past Aber of the princes, under the tremendous shoulders of Moel Wnion.'

Refs: **18** (1).

Mold or Yr Wyddgrug (Clwyd, Wales). Some 9 miles west of CHESTER and 10 miles north-west of WREXHAM, this busy market town is the administrative capital of Clwyd. Situated on the south bank of the River Alyn (or Afon Alun), the settlement grew up around a motte-and-bailey castle built by Robert de Monte Alto on Bailey Hill in the 12th C. The restored 15th C. Parish Church of St Mary is built on the site of an earlier church. The name Mold is derived from the Old French *mont hault*, meaning 'high hill': a reference to the ancient castle mound. Its Welsh name, Yr Wyddgrug, means 'the burial mound'. An obelisk north-west of the town, erected in 1736, commemorates the 5th C. battle known as the Alleluia Victory, in which the Christian Britons defeated the pagan Picts and Scots.

Novels: Rhodri ap HUW, from Mold, came by river barge to St Peter's Fair at SHREWSBURY in August 1139.

Refs: **4** (1:2).

Montford (Shropshire, England). DB – Maneford: in Baschurch Hundred; a holding of Roger (possibly Roger de Lacy (see LACY FAMILY) rather than Roger, Son of Corbet) under Roger de MONTGOMERY. (It is known that soon after the survey Roger de Lacy was in possession of the manor for he gave it to SHREWSBURY ABBEY before 1091, a gift that seems to have reverted back to the Lacys within a short time.) Some 4 miles north-west of SHREWSBURY and 1 mile south-west of MONTFORD BRIDGE, the village of Montford lies on the north bank of the River SEVERN. The red sandstone church of St CHAD, sited on the top of a hill in Montford, serves both villages and dates from the 13th C. Just over 1 mile west of Montford is Shrawardine (or Shraden), where there are the remains of a Norman castle, probably built by Rainald the Sheriff at the end of the 11th C. It was a royal fortress when it was repaired in 1165, and continued to belong to the crown until 1215 when it was destroyed by the Welsh. The castle was rebuilt from 1220 onwards by John FitzAlan, and it remained in the possession of his descendants until 1583 when it was sold to Sir Thomas Bradley. In 1645 the castle was captured by the Parliamentarians and destroyed. All that remains above ground today are a few standing fragments thought to belong to the medieval keep. On the opposite bank of the Severn at Little Shrawardine are the earthwork remains of a motte-and-bailey castle. Both were probably originally built to guard a crossing.

Novels: 'The sun was high, and the pearly mist of morning all dissolved when they crossed the river at Montford. The road was good, some stretches of it with wide grass verges where the going was comfortable and fast, and Giles demanded an occasional canter.' In March 1141 the injured Gilbert PRESTCOTE (the elder) was taken in easy stages to Shrewsbury. He spent the last night at Montford, 'where Welsh princes and English earls used to meet for parley'.

CADFAEL, Deacon MARK and the BERINGARS crossed the Severn at Montford in May 1144, on their journey north-west from Shrewsbury.

Refs: **9** (3–6); **18** (1); **19** (2).

Montford Bridge (Shropshire, England). DB – see MONTFORD. The village of Montford Bridge grew up around the bridge which carries the main road from SHREWSBURY to OSWESTRY over the River SEVERN. There has been a bridge at Montford since ancient times, when it was chosen by Welsh princes and English nobles as a place for their ambassadors to meet to discuss terms of truce or the exchange of prisoners. In 1283 David ap Gruffudd, the last Welsh prince of Wales, was betrayed by his own countrymen and handed over to the English at Montford Bridge. He was hanged, drawn and quartered in Shrewsbury. In 1485 the army of Henry Tudor (later Henry VII) took Montford Bridge and nearby FORTON before the town of Shrewsbury finally allowed him to enter its walls without bloodshed. Soon afterwards, he defeated and slew Richard III at the battle of Bosworth. The present three-arched bridge was constructed of stone by Thomas Telford in 1792.

Novels: '"Turn back but a mile or more, back across the bridge at Montford, and then you'll find a well-used cart-track that bears off west, to your right hand it will be. Bear a piece west again where the paths first branch, it's no direct way, but it does go on. It skirts Shrewsbury a matter of above four miles outside the town, and threads the edges of the forest, but it cuts across every path out of Shrewsbury. You may catch your men yet. And I wish you may!"' 'Olivier came for the second time to the bridge over the SEVERN, one bank a steep, tree-clad escarpment, the other open, level meadow.'

Refs: **9** (3); **10** (13).

Montgomery or Tre Faldwyn (Powys, Wales). DB – Montgomeri: probably not regarded as part of any Hundred, although its dependencies lay in Wittery Hundred; land held by Roger de MONTGOMERY himself (Montgomery was once in Shropshire, England). Montgomery is a small market town situated at the foot of the Welsh mountains, some 19 miles south-west of SHREWSBURY and 7 miles south of Welshpool (see POOL). It used to be the capital town of the old county of Montgomery, but as a regional centre it has now been superseded by Welshpool. Montgomery was named after Roger de Montgomery, who built a castle sometime between 1070 and 1074 at Hen Domen, 1 mile north-west of the present town. After Roger's death in 1094, Hugh de Montgomery succeeded to his father's estates in England and became 2nd Earl of Shrewsbury. Hugh was killed in a battle at ANGLESEY four years later, and his elder brother, Robert de Bellême, acquired the castle along with the English estates of the house of Montgomery. In 1102, because of treason, HENRY I banished Robert from England and his lands, castles and properties were forfeited to the crown. Montgomery Castle was granted to Baldwin de Bollers (or Boulers), whose family owned it until 1214–15 when it was sold to Thomas de Erdington. However, in 1216, King John gave it to Gwenwynwyn, Prince of Powys, and almost immediately it was captured by Llywelyn the Great. Henry III built a second castle at Montgomery in 1223 and three years later the town was granted a royal charter. The castle was captured by the Parliamentarians during the English Civil War and, in 1649, it was abandoned and subsequently demolished. The earthwork remains of an Iron Age hill-fort, Ffridd Faldwyn, stand above the town, on the same hill as the castle. About a mile to the east of Montgomery is OFFA'S DYKE.

Novels: In August 1138, fleeing with William FITZALAN's treasury into Wales, Godith Adeney (see

BLUND) and Torold BLUND were made aware of the ford at Montgomery.

Refs: **2** (9).

Montgomery, Adeliza de (*fl.* 1083), Countess of Shrewsbury and Arundel (hist.). Daughter of Ebrard de Puiset, she was the second wife of Roger de MONTGOMERY, Earl of Shrewsbury and Arundel, and the mother of their son, Ebrard. Being gentle and religious (in contrast to the character of Roger's first wife), Adeliza supported him in his foundation of SHREWSBURY ABBEY in 1083. It is said that Roger founded the collegiate church at Quatford, near Bridgnorth (see BRIGGE), to commemorate Adeliza's escape from being shipwrecked.

Refs: **17** (9).

Montgomery, Roger de (d. 1094), Earl of Shrewsbury and Arundel (hist.). Son of Roger the Great, he was not only the cousin of WILLIAM I, but also of Ralph de Mortimer and of William FitzOsbern. Roger was the brother of Hugh, Robert, William and Gilbert, who all served Duke William in the disorders of NORMANDY. As Lord of Montgomery and Viscount of L'Hiemois, Roger increased his influence and power by marrying Mabel (or Mabil), daughter of William Talvas de Bellême, Alençon and SEEZ. He was one of William I's most trusted supporters and, having contributed sixty ships to the Norman invasion of England in 1066, he also distinguished himself at Senlac, near Hastings, in the decisive battle. While in England, William left Roger and Mabel in Normandy as joint guardians of the duchy. Soon after, in 1067, Roger returned to England, and was made Earl of Chichester and Arundel, and, in *c.*1071, Earl of Shrewsbury. He is described as being 'wise, and moderate, and a lover of justice, and delighted in the company of wise and modest persons' (Owen and Blakeway, *A History of Shrewsbury*, 1825). His properties in Shropshire were vast; it is estimated that of 406 manors in the county, Roger held all but forty-nine. He became one of the greatest of the powerful Marcher lords, building castles along the Welsh Border from which he conquered a large portion of the territory belonging to the princes of Powys. His wife was assassinated in 1082 by Hugh de la Roche d'Ige at Bures-sur-Dives. After her murder, Roger married Adeliza who, according to Ordericus Vitalis, 'was very different from her predecessor, and by her religious example brought her husband to the love of monks and the relief of the poor' (see MONTGOMERY, Adeliza de, Countess of Shrewsbury and Arundel). In 1083 Roger founded SHREWSBURY ABBEY. After William I's death in 1087, he secretly supported the cause of ROBERT of Normandy, which had been taken up by three of his own sons. But he took no part in the rebellion of 1088, and was eventually won over to the side of WILLIAM II. After garrisoning his castles against Robert in Normandy, Roger eventually returned to England. Although some early historians claim that he was killed fighting in Wales, it is more generally accepted that he died in Shrewsbury Abbey. He was taken ill at SHREWSBURY CASTLE and, sensing that his end was near, he became a monk at the abbey in 1094. He died a few days afterwards and was buried in the church between the two altars. He was a great benefactor of religious foundations, both in England and in Normandy. He was the father of five sons by Mabel: Robert de Bellême, Hugh de Montgomery, Roger, Philip and Arnulf. She also bore him four daughters: Emma, Matilda, Mabel and Sybil, who was the mother of Matilda, the wife of ROBERT of Gloucester. He had one son by Adeliza: Ebrard, who became a royal chaplain in the court of HENRY I.

Novels: '"The great earl, who founded this house, and sleeps there between the altars, he, too, left his lady and put on the habit before he died." Only three days before he died, actually, and with his wife's consent, but no need at this moment to say any word of that.' Earl Roger de Montgomery, founder of Shrewsbury Abbey, was buried between the altars in the abbey church. He originally held the manors of FORIET, ASPLEY and LINDE.

Refs: **8** (1, 12); **12** (11); **15** (1); **17** (9).

M

Montors, Aubrey de (*fl.* 1118) (fict.). **Novels:** Husband of Jovetta de MONTORS, and a knight in the following of William of WARENNE (d. 1138), he fought with his lord in NORMANDY, leaving Jovetta on her own for two years, during which time he was unaware that she had been unfaithful. Theirs was a childless marriage. He died at an unknown date long before 1145.

Refs: **20** (3, 15).

Montors, Jovetta de (née de Redvers) (b. *c.*1085) (fict.). **Novels:** 'Closer than any to her liege lady: the widow of a knight in the earl of Surrey's following, and herself born a de Redvers, from a minor branch of the family of Baldwin de REDVERS, the empress's earl of Devon. Impeccably noble, fit to serve an empress. And old enough and wise enough to be a safe repository for an empress's secrets.' She 'must be sixty, and long widowed, a tall, slender person with the remains of a youthful grace that had lasted well beyond its prime, but was now growing a little angular and lean, as her hair had silvered almost to white.' '"He was my son," she said. "My one sole child, outside a childless marriage, and lost to me as soon as born. It was long ago, after the old king [HENRY I] had conquered and settled Normandy, until King LOUIS [VI] came to the French throne, and started the struggle all over again. Two years away! Love asks no leave, and I was lonely, and Richard de CLARE was kind. When my time came, I was well served and secret, and Richard did well by his own. Aubrey never knew, nor did any other. Richard acknowledged my boy for his, and took him into his own family. But Richard was not living to do right by his son when most he was needed. It was left to me to take his place!" Widow of Aubrey de MONTORS, mother of Geoffrey FITZCLARE by Richard de Clare, and aunt of ISABEAU, Jovetta de Montors was one of the Empress MAUD's gentlewomen. On 30 November 1145 she attended the empress at COVENTRY, where, seeking to avenge the murder of her son, she lured Brien de SOULIS to the north walk of the cloister at St Mary's Priory, and plunged a dagger into his heart: a crime she later confessed to CADFAEL. 'What will be said in the last day of Jovetta de Montors, who also made her judgement when she killed to avenge her son, for want of a father living to lift that load from her? She, also, set the heart's passion for its children before the law of the land or the commandments of the Church. And would she, say: I would do it again? Yes, surely she would. If the sin is one which, with all our will to do right, we cannot regret, can it truly be a sin?' In December 1145 Jovetta attended the empress at GLOUCESTER and at GREENHAMSTED.

Refs: **20** (3-5, 8, 10, 14-16).

Moreton Corbet. See HARPECOTE.

Morgan, Ifor ap (b. *c.*1078) (fict.). **Novels:** 'A venerable old man stood looking at him steadily and silently; a tall old man, white-haired and white-bearded, and eyes as starkly blue as a winter sky beneath them. His dress was the common homespun of the countryman, but his carriage and height turned it to purple.' Welsh husband of MARARED (*fl.* 1093), father of ANGHARAD (1093–1127), grandfather of MEURIG, brother-in-law of Brother RHYS and substitute grandfather of Edwin GURNEY, Ifor ap Morgan lived alone near LLANSILIN. In December 1138 CADFAEL discovered the fugitive, Edwin Gurney, with Ifor.

Refs: **3** (7–9, 11).

Morgant, Canon (b. *c.*1099) (fict.). **Novels:** 'And after him, still silent, stonily expressionless, potentially disapproving, went Canon Morgant, a black recording angel.' Canon of ST ASAPH under Bishop GILBERT, Morgant set out westward from St Asaph to keep a watchful eye on Canon MEIRION and his daughter,

HELEDD. It was his and Meirion's business to see that the reluctant bride reached her bridegroom at BANGOR safely. Heledd, however, gave both of them the slip at ABER.

Refs: **18** (2, 4–6).

Mortain (France). Some 40 miles east of Avranches and 55 miles south of Vire, this small town lies in the upper valley of the River See at the western edge of the Normandy-Maine Regional Nature Park. Mortain was almost totally destroyed during World War II and subsequently rebuilt. The county of Mortain was among the honours held by STEPHEN. It was captured by GEOFFREY of Anjou in 1141 during his conquest of NORMANDY.

Novels: In 1141 the Empress MAUD offended Bishop HENRY OF BLOIS by refusing to allow Stephen's son, Eustace, to 'receive the rights and titles of his father's honours of BOULOGNE and Mortain'.

Refs: **10** (2).

Mortimer, Hugh de (d. 1181) (hist.). Also called Lord of Wigmore. He is thought to be the grandson of Ralph de Mortimer and the great-grandson of Roger de Mortimer (however, some authorities claim that he is the son of Ralph and, therefore, the grandson of Roger). Although one account says that he married Matilda Longespey (who died in 942!) it is thought that he married Matilda la Meschine, who gave him four sons: Roger, Hugh, Ralph and William. It is not certain which side Hugh de Mortimer supported, if any, in the civil war between King STEPHEN and the Empress MAUD. He was an ambitious and powerful baron, taking little part in general politics, and spent much of his life strengthening his position as the chief potentate of the Middle Marches of Wales. He is first mentioned in a royal patent of 1140, which suggests that he had especially reserved rights *sine medio* to the Crown. A few years later Hugh had several severe feuds with MILES, Constable of Gloucester and Earl of Hereford, and the quarrel continued with Miles's son, ROGER (d. 1155). It is said that Hugh was ambushed and imprisoned by Josce de DINAN, Castellan of LUDLOW, and was only released on payment of an extortionate sum of money. In either 1144 or 1145 Hugh captured and imprisoned the Welsh prince Rhys ab Howel and in 1146 killed Maredudd ab Howel, another Welsh chieftain. He became the ruler of MAELIENYDD, took possession of the royal castle at Bridgnorth (see BRIGGE) and resisted HENRY II's attempts to put an end to his power. Although Mortimer's castles at CLEOBURY, Bridgnorth and Wigmore were captured in 1155, the king allowed the rebel baron to retain many of his special privileges and immunities. Thereafter, he played little further part in English politics, except perhaps as a powerful landowner. In *c.*1172 he founded Wigmore Abbey, 7 miles south-west of Ludlow, first founded at Shobden, near LEOMINSTER, in *c.*1140. He died at Cleobury, 'full of good works', and was buried in Wigmore Abbey. He was succeeded by his son and heir, Roger de Mortimer.

Novels: 'And indeed the family was well provided here, keeping Mortimer's little manor prosperous and in good repair, the cleared fields productive, the forest well managed, the small coppice ditched against the invading deer.' Among Hugh de Mortimer's holdings were: PULLEY and a hamlet south of HENLEY. In June 1142 Niall BRONZESMITH made a set of bronze harness ornaments for one of Mortimer's horses. The Mortimers held lands near Ludlow.

Refs: **6** (5); **13** (2–3, 10); **20** (16).

Mosul (Iraq). Situated on the River Tigris, some 200 or so miles north of Baghdad, Mosul is the third largest city in Iraq and capital of the governorate of Ninawa. By the 8th C. this ancient settlement was the principal city of upper Mesopotamia, and in the succeeding centuries was ruled by a number of independent dynasties, including the Hamdanids. In 1098, during the First Crusade, the Atabeg of Mosul, the Turkish general Kerbogha, set out with his huge Moslem army to relieve ANTIOCH. However, while fruitlessly delaying for three weeks to attack BALDWIN I at EDESSA, Kerbogha gave the crusaders enough breathing-space for them to capture Antioch. ZENGHI became Atabeg of Mosul in 1127 and in 1144 seized Edessa from the crusaders. Between 1258, when the

M

Mongols invaded and ravaged the region, and the beginning of the 16th C. there was little effective government in Mosul. It was part of the Ottoman Empire from 1534 to 1918. There are many mosques, shrines and Christian churches in the city, including the Red Mosque. On the east bank of the Tigris, opposite modern Mosul, are the ruins of the ancient Assyrian city of Nineveh.

Novels: 'There were Christian fugitives beginning to drift in then from beyond Edessa, turned out of their monasteries by mamluk raiders from Mosul.' Godfrid Marescot (see HUMILIS, Brother) received his crippling wounds in battle with Atabeg Zenghi and the men of Mosul. William of LYTHWOOD bought THEOFANU's psalter in TRIPOLI from a fugitive monk driven out of his monastery, somewhere beyond Edessa, by raiders from Mosul. The paynims of Mosul captured Edessa at Christmas 1144, and, the following year, were threatening the kingdom of Jerusalem.

Refs: **11** (4); **16** (3, 11); **20** (1).

Mountsorrel Castle (Leicestershire, England). Sited in a commanding position on the top of a high granite crag overlooking the valley of the River Soar, 7 miles north of LEICESTER, the castle at Mountsorrel – a small market town – was built by Hugh d'Avranches, Earl of Chester, in 1080. It was granted (or confirmed) to RANULF of Chester by King STEPHEN. In 1145/6, 'in the fields between Leicester and Mountsorrel', Ranulf gave the castle to Robert de BEAUMONT (the younger) in order to purchase his support: all Ranulf asked in return was that he could lodge in the castle whenever he was in the district. In 1217 the castle, which belonged to Saher (or Saer) de Quincey, Earl of Winchester – a supporter of Louis (later Louis VIII, King of France) – was destroyed by Ranulf III, Earl of Chester. Nothing remains of the castle today, except the granite crag.

Novels: In 1145 the castle at Mountsorrel belonged to Ranulf of Chester. 'Even the earl of Chester's small timber castle within the town [of COVENTRY] had its scars to show, and would hardly be suitable for his occupation with the kind of retinue he intended to bring to the conference table, much less for entertaining his newly appeased and reconciled king. He would prefer the discreet distance of Mountsorrel in which to continue his careful wooing.'

Refs: **20** (1–2).

Much Wenlock. See WENLOCK

Musard, Hascoit (*fl.* 1070) (hist.). After helping WILLIAM I in his conquest of England, Hascoit Musard, a Breton, was rewarded with great estates in Berkshire, Oxfordshire, Derbyshire, Warwickshire and Gloucestershire. His principal seat was at Miserden (see GREENHAMSTED). Described by William Dugdale as 'a good man', renowned for his 'virtue and piety', Hascoit eventually became a Benedictine monk in the monastery at ELY. He was succeeded by his son and heir, Richard Musard.

Novels: King WILLIAM I gave the village of Greenhamsted to Hascoit Musard 'some time before the Domesday survey was taken'. He was the great-grandsire of Robert MUSARD, and built the castle of La MUSARDERIE.

Refs: **20** (6–7).

Musard, Robert (*fl.* 1145) (hist.). Presumably a descendant of Hascoit MUSARD, he was out hunting in 1145, having left his castle at La MUSARDERIE, and was captured by Philip FITZROBERT. Robert surrendered the castle to FitzRobert after the latter had put a halter around his neck and repeatedly threatened to hang him. *The Chronicles of Brother Cadfael* refer to Robert as the great-grandson of Hascoit Musard. According to Samuel Rudder in *A New History of Gloucestershire* (1779) Hascoit's son and heir was Richard; who was succeeded by a second Hascoit (d. 1187) who was succeeded by Ralph (d. 1230) who was succeeded by Robert, who died without issue.

Novels: 'Musard . . . had foolishly gone forth hunting, and ridden straight into Philip's ambush, and been forced to surrender his castle in order to regain his freedom, and possibly also to keep himself man alive; though threats against life in order to gain possession of a fortress were more likely to remain threats than to be put into action, and often met with obstinate defiance even with neck nooses and hangmen ready, in the assurance that they dared not be carried out. Family loyalties and complex intermarriages had baulked a great many such attempts. But Musard, not having a powerful relative on [King] STEPHEN's side, of greater importance to the king than Philip himself, had been less confident of his safety, and given in.' Great-grandson of Hascoit Musard, Robert was ambushed by FitzRobert, while out hunting in Autumn 1145, and, in order to regain his freedom, was forced to surrender his castle of La Musarderie. It was suggested that 'a Musard might yet come back to Greenhamsted. Four generations had left the family still acceptable to their neighbours.'

Refs: **20** (6–10).

(La) Musarderie (Gloucestershire, England). The remains of the Norman motte-and-bailey castle of La Musarderie stand beside the River FROME in the private woodland of Misarden Park (see GREENHAMSTED). The fortress was built shortly after the Conquest by Hascoit MUSARD, and abandoned in the 13th C. It was surrendered to Philip FITZROBERT in 1145, after he had ambushed Robert MUSARD and threatened to hang him. Samuel Rudder, in *A New History of Gloucestershire* (1779), says that the castle was built by Ralph Musard in the reign of King John (1199–1216). He was succeeded in 1230 by his son Robert, 'who entering upon his lands without suing forth livery, his castle of Musarden and all his lands were seized into the king's hands, but were shortly after restored upon composition.' The 17th C. mansion at Misarden Park is said to have been built with stone from the castle.

Novels: 'By all accounts there had been a castle there at La Musarderie ever since King WILLIAM [I] gave the village to Hascoit Musard some time before the Domesday survey was taken.' CADFAEL 'crossed [the River Frome], and began the climb out of the valley. Light and air showed suddenly between the trees, and he emerged from forest into cleared land, bare even of bushes; and there before and above him, at perhaps a half-mile distance, on a level promontory, stood the castle of La Musarderie. He had been right, four generations of the same family in unchallenged possession had afforded time to build in local stone, to enlarge and to strengthen. The first hasty palisades thrown up in timber seventy-five years ago [in 1070], to establish and assure ownership, had vanished long since. This was a massive bulk, a battlemented curtain wall, twin gate-towers, squat and strong, fronting this eastward approach, and the serrated crests of other flanking towers circling a tall keep within. Beyond, the ground continued to rise steeply in complex folds and levels to a long crest above, where Cadfael could just distinguish above the trees the . . . village of Greenhamsted. A rising causeway, stripped of all cover and dead straight, led up to the castle gates. No one was to be allowed to approach La Musarderie unseen. All round it the ground had been cleared of cover.' Named after the Musard family, the fortress was surrendered to Philip FitzRobert by Robert Musard in Autumn 1145. Olivier de BRETAGNE and also Yves HUGONIN were imprisoned in the dungeons by FitzRobert. Both were released because of Cadfael. Yves managed to steal in and out of the castle by climbing the great vine that grew against the wall on the eastern side. 'Every castle ward has a multifarious life of its own,

M

that goes on without fuss, in wellhouse, bakery, armoury, store and workshops, in two parallel disciplines, one military, one domestic. Here in a region of warfare, however desultory the dangers might be, the domestic side of castle life in La Musarderie seemed to have been scaled down to a minimum, and almost womanless. Possibly Philip's steward had a wife somewhere, in charge of such women servants as might be kept here, but the economy within was starkly military and austerely male, and functioned with a ruthless efficiency that surely stemmed from its lord. Philip was unmarried and without children, wholly absorbed into the demonic conflict that no one seemed able to end. His castle reflected his obsession.' In December 1145, after being besieged, the garrison surrendered to the forces of the empress, and, apart from FitzRobert, were allowed to leave safely.

Refs: **20** (6–15).

Nadafan, River (Wales). Untraced. It is most likely, however, that this river was in Glamorgan, South Wales. The River Nadafan is mentioned in connection with the celebrated Welsh saint, ILLTUD, who died early in the 6th C. A 12th C. Latin composition states that Illtud went to live with his wife, TRYNIHID, in a reed hut by the River Nadafan.

Novels: St Illtud 'had a wife, a noble lady, willing to live simply with him in a reed hut by the River Nadafan'.

Refs: **17** (9).

Nan (*fl.* 1145) (fict.). **Novels:** Fictional sister of REINOLD the miller, she was supposed to have a son serving under Guy CAMVILLE at La MUSARDERIE in 1145.

Refs: **20** (14).

Nene, River (Northamptonshire, Cambridgeshire and Lincolnshire, England). The river rises on the rolling uplands south of Daventry, Northamptonshire, and meanders east to NORTHAMPTON before sweeping north past Wellingborough and Oundle. From PETERBOROUGH it is channelled north-east across the FENS to Wisbech before heading north across lonely marshland to the Wash. Roughly 100 miles long, the river is navigable from a junction with the Grand Union Canal near Northampton to the North Sea. Its course has changed considerably since medieval times and the Nene is now part of the inland waterway network.

Novels: In November 1143, after Hugh BERINGAR had withdrawn his men from the Fens, he rode north to Peterborough: 'He had not paused to consider, until he rode over the bridge of the Nene and up into the town, what he expected to find there.'

Refs: **17** (10).

Nesse (now Little Ness) (Shropshire, England). Also spelled Ness. DB – Nesse: in Baschurch Hundred; a holding of Reginald the Sheriff under Roger de MONTGOMERY. Little Ness is a small village, just over 6 miles north-west of SHREWSBURY and 9 miles south-east of OSWESTRY. The red sandstone church, with its Norman doorway, lies on what is probably the outer bailey of an ancient motte-and-bailey castle. At Great Ness, 1 mile to the south-west, is St Andrew's Church dating from the early 14th C. and built of red sandstone. The village of Nesscliffe, 1 mile to the north-west of Great Ness, straddles the main Shrewsbury to Oswestry road. It lies in the shadow of the red sandstone cliffs of the wooded Nesscliffe Hill, which has been quarried for its building stone for many centuries. On its summit are the earthwork remains of two Iron Age forts.

Novels: CONAN set out north from Shrewsbury on 20 June 1143 to find Girard of LYTHWOOD. He went as far as FORTON, where he discovered that his master had gone on to Nesse. In May 1144 CADFAEL, Deacon MARK and the BERINGARS journeyed north-west from Shrewsbury. They halted under the hill at Ness, where one of Hugh's tenants lived, to rest their horses and take refreshment.

Refs: **16** (4); **18** (1).

Nest, Eluned (d. 1141) (fict.). **Novels:** '"My lord, there was a girl of this parish – Eluned – very beautiful. Not like other girls, wild as a hare. Everyone knew her. God knows she never harmed a soul but herself, the creature! My lord, she could not say no to men. Time and again she went with this one or that, but always she came back, as wild returning as going, in tears, and made her confession, and swore amendment. And meant it! But she never could keep it, a lad would look at her and sigh . . . Father ADAM always took her back, confessed her, gave her penance, and afterwards absolution. He knew she could not help it. And she as kind a creature to man or child or beast as ever breathed – too kind!"' Daughter of Widow NEST and mother of the illegitimate child Winifred, Eluned, the ABBEY FOREGATE's 'favourite whore', committed suicide after she had been refused absolution by Father AILNOTH in December 1141. Her body was discovered in SHREWSBURY ABBEY mill-pond and buried in ST CHAD's churchyard.

Refs: **12** (3, 7–8, 12).

Nest, Widow (b. *c.*1101) (fict.). **Novels:** She 'must . . . have been comely, some years ago, she had still fine features, though worn and lined now in shapes of discouragement, and her greying hair, drawn back austerely from her face, was still abundant, and bore the shadowy richness of its former red-brown colouring.' Widow of a forester in EYTON, mother of Eluned NEST and grandmother of Winifred NEST. After Eluned's death in December 1141, the Widow Nest looked after Winifred.

Refs: **12** (8, 12).

Nest, Winifred (b. 1141) (fict.). **Novels:** 'The daughter of the outcast and excommunicate, it seemed, was named for the town's own saint, witness enough to the truth of Eluned's undisciplined devotion. And doubtless Saint WINIFRED would know where to find and watch over both the living child and the dead mother.' Daughter of Eluned NEST and granddaughter of Widow NEST, Winifred was born illegitimate in about the second week of November 1141. It was rumoured that Jordan ACHARD was her father. She was christened Winifred by Father ADAM. After her mother committed suicide in December 1141, she was looked after by her grandmother. CADFAEL went to the Widow NEST'S HOVEL and gave the baby some medicine to soothe the pains in its stomach.

Refs: **12** (3, 7–8).

(Widow) Nest's Hovel (Shrewsbury, Shropshire) (fict.). Although it never existed, the hovel of the Widow NEST was located 'along the back lane from the HORSE-FAIR', somewhere in the vicinity of Holywell Street and Horse-fair. It was within the extensive parish of HOLY CROSS.

Novels: 'This one small room was all the house, and its only inlet for light or outlet for smoke was a vent in the roof. In clement weather the door would always be open from dawn to dusk, but frost had closed it, and the dwelling was lit only by a small oil lamp . . . Furnishings were few, a low bench-bed in a corner, a few pots on the firestone, a rough, small table.'

Refs: **12** (8).

New Minster. See HYDE ABBEY.

Newark (now Newark-on-Trent) (Nottinghamshire, England). Some 18 miles north-east of the centre of NOTTINGHAM and 15 miles south-west of LINCOLN, this ancient market town grew up at an important crossroads on the Roman Fosse Way. It was granted to the bishops of LINCOLN in 1055 and remained in their possession until 1549. The ruined shell of the castle – the Key to the North – towers high above the River Trent. Built of stone in *c.*1173, it replaced an earlier fortress erected between 1123 and 1135 by Bishop Alexander of Lincoln. In 1216 King John died there from over-eating (some maintain, however, that he was poisoned) and, during the three sieges of Newark in 1642, 1644 and 1646, it was used as a Royalist stronghold. Although Cromwell ordered the castle's destruction after the Civil War, the impressive remains include the large and elaborate 12th C. gateway.

Novels: Leoric ASPLEY had a northern manor somewhere south of Newark. During Summer 1140, Nigel ASPLEY and Janyn LINDE travelled north to view the lordship.

Refs: **8** (6, 12–13).

Newbury (Berkshire, England). Some 23 miles north of WINCHESTER and 16 miles west of READING, this market town grew up at an important crossing-point on the River Kennet. It is an ancient town, with a history stretching back to prehistoric times. It was occupied by the Romans, the Anglo-Saxons and also the Normans, who erected a castle overlooking the river.

Novels: Luc MEVEREL met CIARAN on the road near Newbury in 1141 and travelled north with him to SHREWSBURY.

Refs: **10** (7, 12, 14).

Newton Stacey. See STACEYS, The.

Nicholas, Saint (d. *c.*350), Bishop of Myra (hist.) (f.d. 6 December). Although he is one of the most popular saints of Christendom, celebrated in the custom and folklore of many countries, nothing is known of him, except that he was a bishop of Myra in Lycia (south-west Turkey), and that his relics are reputed to be enshrined at BARI. Venerated as the saint of sailors, merchants, children, and others, he is the origin of the gift-bringing Father Christmas, and is variously known as Santa Claus, Sinter Klaas, Sanctus Nicolaus and so on. In medieval England 'Old Father Christmas' was a minor character in medieval mumming plays, with no connection with children or presents. All the ingredients of the modern Father

N

Christmas arrived in the country in the 19th C. from America, where he had been long established by Dutch settlers. St Nicholas is the patron saint of Russia.

Novels: On the feast day of St Nicholas, the sixth day of December, Psalm 88 was read at La MUSARDERIE.

Refs: **20** (9).

Nicol (b. *c.*1090) (fict.). **Novels:** 'He was a stout-hearted, even an obstinate man, not to be deterred by a few bruises, and not to surrender his charge without a struggle.' 'Elderly but resolute . . . steward of RAMSEY ABBEY', Nicol was Sub-Prior HERLUIN's most trusted servant. In February 1145 Nicol, ROGER and another unnamed lay servant escorted Herluin and Brother TUTILO to SHREWSBURY ABBEY. Nicol was put in charge of looking after the coffer containing 'SHREWSBURY's gifts' for Ramsey. On their way back to the FENS with the coffer and a wagonload of timber (and unknown to them, St WINIFRED's reliquary), Nicol, Roger, JAMES, MARTIN and PAYNE were ambushed near ULLESTHORPE by about a dozen armed men. Nicol, who kept the key of the coffer safe, tried unsuccessfully to prevent his abbey's goods from being stolen, but was thrown off the wagon. To spread the news of their disastrous encounter, James and Martin went back to Shrewsbury, Roger and Payne continued to Ramsey, while Nicol set out on foot to WORCESTER, knowing that Herluin was likely to be at the cathedral priory there. He arrived at Worcester less than twenty-four hours after the arrival of Hugh BERINGAR and Prior ROBERT from Shrewsbury. Although he was 'battered and tired from a dogged and laborious journey on foot', Nicol, after a moment to wet his throat, led Hugh, Robert, Herluin and Brother TUTILO to the scene of the ambush and robbery. From Ullesthorpe they rode to HUNCOTE, and from there returned to Shrewsbury with Robert de BEAUMONT and the missing reliquary. In early March Nicol accompanied Herluin back to Ramsey, 'well content to be riding instead of walking'.

Refs: **19** (2–5, 12–13).

Nigel (d. 1169), Bishop of Ely (hist.). Nephew of ROGER, Bishop of Salisbury, and brother of Alexander, Bishop of Lincoln, he was a married man and the father of Richard FitzNeale. Educated at the monastery of Laon, northern France, Nigel is first recorded in England in 1126–30, when he witnessed a charter at ABINGDON. He was consecrated Bishop of Ely in 1133, and was present at HENRY I's departure from England for the last time. As the king's treasurer and administrator Nigel spent much of his time in LONDON. In his absence the wealthy see at ELY was left in the charge of Ranulf, who abused his position and alienated the monks. It was not until 1137, when Ranulf was forced to flee, that Nigel and his monks were reconciled. Throughout his rule, however, Nigel plundered many of the see's possessions for his own purposes. Like his uncle and brother, Nigel supported STEPHEN's claim to the throne, and attended the king's coronation in 1135. When Roger and Alexander were arrested in June 1139, Nigel managed to escape to DEVIZES, but was eventually forced to surrender (see ROBERT (d. 1139)). In consequence, Nigel rebelled, embracing the cause of the Empress MAUD when she landed in England later that year. He fled in poverty to GLOUCESTER, after the king had besieged and taken the newly fortified Isle of Ely, and was with the empress at WINCHESTER, READING, WESTMINSTER and OXFORD in 1141. Realising the hopelessness of her cause, Nigel returned to Ely in 1142, where he was restored to his see. After being compelled to make a protracted journey to ROME in 1143–5, where the pope acquitted him of certain charges and confirmed him in all the possessions of his see, Nigel returned to find that, in his absence, Ely had been ravaged by

Geoffrey de MANDEVILLE. During 1145 Nigel and Stephen made peace at Ipswich, and he may have been restored to some position in the king's central administration. Nigel rose to prominence after the accession of HENRY II, when, because of his unrivalled administrative experience, he was employed to restore the exchequer system that was in operation during the reign of the young king's grandfather, that is before the civil war. He also purchased the office of treasurer for his son, Richard. In 1166 Nigel was struck down by paralysis, and retired to Ely, where he spent the remainder of his life.

Novels: 'Nigel, bishop of Ely, newly reconciled to the king after some years of disfavour, and no doubt wishful to keep his recovered place among the approved.' He was one of the three bishops (see HENRY OF BLOIS and ROGER DE CLINTON) who presided over the conference between Stephen and Maud at COVENTRY on 30 November 1145. Afterwards, he returned to his diocese.

Refs: **20** (3, 5).

Noetus of Smyrna (d. *c.*200) (hist.). He was a native of SMYRNA and is thought to have been the first to teach the Patripassian heresy, which held that God the Father was the only God, and that in the Incarnation this one God was born, suffered and died. It was the earliest form of Sabellianism (named after SABELLIUS), which denied the dogma that there are three Persons in 'One God'. Noetus was excommunicated for preaching the heresy by an assembly of presbyters at Smyrna. One of his disciples, Epigonus, brought the Patripassian teaching from Asia Minor to ROME, where it received the approval of the Roman Church.

Novels: An outraged Canon GERBERT pointed out that Noetus of Smyrna had preached the Patripassian heresy to his ruin, and that Sabellius had been excommunicated for it and other errors.

Refs: **16** (2).

Nonna (*fl.* 1144) (fict.). **Novels:** '"Our holy women do not gather in communities, like yours, but set up their cells in the wilds, alone. Such anchoresses would not settle near a town. More likely far to withdraw into the mountains. There is one we know of here, who has her hermitage by this same Menai water, some miles west from here, beyond the narrows."' Welsh anchoress, Nonna lived alone in her hermitage overlooking the MENAI STRAIT. She had named herself after St NONNA. In May 1144, after Bishop MEURIG had warned her of the threat of a Danish invasion, she allowed herself to be escorted into shelter in BANGOR.

Refs: **18** (6–7).

Nonna, Saint (*fl.* 6th C.) (hist.) (f.d. 3 March) Also called Non or Nonnita. She was the mother of DEWI SANT (or St David). According to legend, Nonna, a nun at Ty Gwyn, near ST DAVID'S, Dyfed, was raped by Sant, a Welsh chieftain. Their son was born in *c.*520. She lived for a while at Altarnun in Cornwall, where there is a church dedicated in her honour, and died in Brittany. Her relics were reputed to have been at Altarnun (Non's altar) until the Reformation.

Novels: '"Saint Nonna," said CADFAEL didactically . . . "was the mother of Saint David. She has many sacred wells about the country, that give healing, especially to the eyes, even to curing blindness."' NONNA the Welsh anchoress named herself after the saint.

Refs: **18** (6).

Normandy (France). This region of France is located directly across the English Channel from southern England. The coastline is over 370 miles in length and stretches from Mont-St-Michel, near Avranches, to Le Tréport, near Dieppe, and includes the busy ports of Cherbourg and Le Havre. ROUEN and Caen are the capitals of Upper and Lower Normandy, respectively. The Duchy of Normandy was created in 911 when the Viking chieftain, Rollo, was granted the territory around Rouen and the mouth of the River Seine by Charles III, King of France. Many of his fellow countrymen settled in the region and, having adopted the French language, religion and customs, they became known as Normans. During a series of wars, the Norman dukes extended their authority over the lords of neighbouring territories, until their power almost rivalled that of the French Crown. By 1100 they had not only conquered England, but also ruled the southern part of the Italian peninsula and Sicily. After the death of William, Duke of Normandy (see WILLIAM I), in 1087, his sons quarrelled over the succession, and the union of England and Normandy was temporarily broken. The two empires were reunited in 1106 by HENRY I, King of England, after the battle of Tinchebrai, when his brother ROBERT, Duke of Normandy, was defeated. In 1135, on Henry's death, Normandy passed to his son-in-law, GEOFFREY of Anjou. In 1150 Geoffrey ceded the duchy to his son, who four years later became HENRY II, King of England. Normandy, thereafter, became the centre of Angevin power in Europe. It was conquered by Philip II, King of France, in 1204, but it was only with the Treaty of Paris in 1259 that England formally surrendered its claim to the duchy. Normandy was reconquered by England in the early 15th C., during the Hundred Years' War and, although it was recovered by France, the French did not achieve permanent control of the province until 1450.

Novels: By December 1120 Henry I was master of both England and Normandy. In 1138 Godith Adeney (see BLUND) and Torold BLUND escaped from SHREWSBURY and took William FITZALAN's treasury safely to Normandy. In July 1139 ROBERT of Gloucester was in Normandy with the Empress MAUD. Alain le GAUCHER served in France for some years, 'for Normandy against ANJOU'. In October 1140 Bishop HENRY OF BLOIS was 'in Normandy, soliciting the help of every powerful man he can get hold of, to try and produce some plan that will save England from being dismembered utterly.' In June 1142 Robert of Gloucester went to Normandy to try and persuade Geoffrey of Anjou to send an army to England to help Maud. Robert de BEAUMONT had 'a large honour in Normandy brought to him by his marriage with the heiress of BRETEUIL'. (See AMICIA, Countess of Leicester.) In February 1145 Waleran de BEAUMONT was in Normandy protecting not only his own interests, but also those of his brother, Robert.

Refs: **2** (2); **4** (1:1); **6** (11); **8** (3); **10** (2); **12** (4, 6); **14** (1, 14); **15** (3); **16** (1); **19** (4–5, 11–12); **20** (11, 15); **RB** (1).

Norreys, John (*fl.* 1139) (fict.). '"A big, sturdy young fellow . . . with tow-coloured hair."' On 31 July 1139 John Norreys helped his friend, Philip CORVISER, escape from the clutches of the sheriff's men.

Refs: **4** (4:2, 4:4–5).

Northampton (Northamptonshire, England). Situated on the River NENE and Grand Union Canal, just over 40 miles west of CAMBRIDGE, Northampton is a large industrial town, noted for its shoe and leather industry. Although it was designated a new town in 1965, it has a long and eventful history stretching back to Anglo-Saxon times. The Normans erected a castle by the river in *c.*1100, and the walled town was granted its first market charter in 1189. After the Civil War, Charles II ordered the castle to be razed to the ground and the town walls to be demolished. The railway station now occupies the castle site. A building of particular interest in association with the novels is Holy Sepulchre Church, built in *c.*1100 in the pattern of the original at JERUSALEM. In addition to NORTHAMPTON PRIORY, there were eight other monastic houses in Northampton: an Augustinian abbey; an Augustinian friary; a Carmelite friary; a Dominican friary; a Franciscan friary; a Sack friary; a Franciscan nunnery; and the Cluniac Delapré Abbey, founded by Simon II de SENLIS, Earl of Northampton.

Novels: In November 1120 Roger MAUDUIT held the manor of SUTTON MAUDUIT somewhat south-east of Northampton. In November 1142 Drogo BOSIET held the manor of BOSIET on 'the far side of Northampton, some miles south-east of the town' and also a fair bit of the county. Robert de BEAUMONT, 'lord of half Leicestershire', also owned 'a good slice of Warwickshire and Northampton, and a large honour in Normandy.'

Refs: **14** (4); **19** (4); **RB** (1).

Northampton, Earl of. See SENLIS, Simon II de, Earl of Northampton.

Northampton Priory (Northamptonshire, England). The Cluniac priory was founded in 1093 by Simon I de Senlis, Earl of Northampton, and dedicated to St Andrew. It was dissolved in 1538 and today there are no remains. It is thought that the priory church stood near the junction of Priory Street and Harding Terrace.

Novels: Brand (see HYACINTH), villein of Drogo BOSIET, bound the missal of 'the sub-prior of CLUNY at NORTHAMPTON'. Renaud BOURCHIER met the runaway villein at the priory in Autumn 1142. Brand stole a habit from the priory store for Bourchier.

Refs: **14** (6, 9, 13).

Northumbria (Northumberland, Cumbria, Durham, North and West Yorkshire, Lancashire, Merseyside and Humberside, England; Strathclyde, Lothian, Dumfries & Galloway, and Borders, Scotland). The Anglo-Saxon kingdom of Northumbria encompassed a massive area, stretching – coast to coast – from the rivers Clyde and Firth in the north to the Mersey and Humber in the south. During its height in the 7th and 8th C., Northumbria was renowned for the culture and learning of its monasteries, notably Jarrow, where the Venerable Bede wrote his Latin *Ecclesiastical History of the English People* (731), and Lindisfarne, Hexham and Whitby. Northumbria ceased to exist as a separate kingdom in 954, when – much reduced in size – it became an earldom within a unified England, ruled by Eadred, formerly King of Wessex. Today Northumbria is another name for the county of Northumberland.

Novels: 'Contention in England was no bad news to a monarch [DAVID I, King of Scotland], whose chief aim was to gain a stranglehold on Northumbria, and push his own frontier as far south as the [River] TEES.'

Refs: **20** (10).

Nottingham (Nottinghamshire, England). Some 30 miles north-east of LICHFIELD and 17 miles south-west of NEWARK, this prosperous industrial centre is noted among other things for the manufacture of bicycles, cigarettes and tobacco, pharmaceutical products, textiles and traditional lace. Known as the Queen of the Midlands, Nottingham originated as an Anglo-Saxon hill settlement, guarding an important crossing-point of the River Trent. The name is derived from Snotengham, meaning 'the homestead of Snot's people'; but, although recorded in the Domesday Book as Snotingeham, the 'S' had been dropped by 1130. The town was occupied by the Danes in the 9th C. and, after the Conquest, the Normans built a castle on the sandstone hill. It was severely damaged during the reign of STEPHEN and rebuilt by HENRY II in 1154, who eventually gave it to his son, John. The legendary outlaw of Sherwood Forest, Robin Hood, is said to have existed at around this time. The castle was demolished by the Parliamentarians in 1651, and little survives except the much restored gatehouse. Until *c.*1300 Nottingham was a divided town, consisting of two separately administered boroughs: one Saxon and the other Norman.

Novels: On their marriage, Avota ASPLEY brought Leoric ASPLEY a manor 'somewhere to the north, beyond Nottingham'. From SHREWSBURY, in June 1141, Olivier de BRETAGNE intended to go north-east to STAFFORD, DERBY and Nottingham.

Refs: **8** (1); **10** (7)

Nyall, Rychart (*fl.* 1139) (fict.). **Novels:** Lay servant at SHREWSBURY ABBEY, he discovered the bottle of spirits abandoned by Turstan FOWLER at St Peter's Fair in 1139.

Refs: **4** (5:2).

Offa's Dyke (Hereford & Worcester, and Shropshire, England; Gwent and Powys and Clwyd, Wales). In the latter half of the 8th C. Offa, King of Mercia, ordered the construction of a huge earthwork mound and ditch to mark the boundary between England and Wales. It stretched, with some gaps, from the River SEVERN, near Chepstow, in the south to the mouth of the River DEE, near Prestatyn, in the north. Although the distance of the boundary was about 150 miles, Offa's Dyke accounted for only 80 miles of the total. It consisted of a bank some 60 ft. high with a ditch some 12 ft. deep on the Welsh side. After 1,200 years sections of the dyke are still in evidence. In 1971 Offa's Dyke Path – a long-distance footpath totalling 176 miles – was opened, following about 60 miles of the best-preserved stretches of the ancient earthwork.

Novels: 'Along the border, English fugitives made for Wales, Welsh fugitives for England. The two laws baulked and held off at the dyke, though trade crossed back and forth merrily enough.' 'The ancient dyke that marked the boundary, somewhat broken and disregarded in these parts but still traceable.' RHYDYCROESAU was 'a good mile or more the Welsh side of the old boundary dyke'. In March 1141 Hugh BERINGAR and OWAIN GWYNEDD met 'on the great dyke at Rhyd-y-Croesau by Oswestry. BRITRIC THE PEDLAR was arrested in November 1143 near MERESBROOK after he had crossed over the ancient dyke into England. Hugh Beringar's manor at MAESBURY lay between Offa's Dyke and WAT'S DYKE.

Refs: **3** (8–9); **9** (3, 8–10); **10** (11); **16** (6); **17** (7); **18** (1).

Oili II, Robert d' (*fl.* 1142) (hist.). It is not certain that he was Sheriff of Oxfordshire in 1142. He was the son of Robert d'Oili I, who was the first Norman sheriff of OXFORD and who built OXFORD CASTLE. The younger Robert married Editha Forne and, in 1129, founded Osney Priory which became an abbey in *c.*1154.

Novels: In late 1142, Hugh BERINGAR said: '"Thanks be to God, I am not sheriff of Oxfordshire! Our troubles here are mild enough, a little family bickering that leads to blows now and then, a bit of thieving, the customary poaching in season."'

Refs: **14** (4).

Old Minster. See WINCHESTER CATHEDRAL.

Olives, Mount of (Israel). Lying at 2,652 ft. above sea-level, it is the southernmost and highest summit on the limestone range of hills just east of JERUSALEM. The Mount of Olives is mentioned in both the Old and New Testaments and is the traditional site of the Garden of Gethsemane and of Christ's ascension. Originally in Jordan, the Mount came under Israeli rule following the Six-Day War of 1967. It is sacred to both Judaism and Christianity.

Novels: Among the 'somewhat dubious' relics amassed by SHREWSBURY ABBEY over the years were: 'Stones from CALVARY and the Mount of Olives – well, stones are stones, every hill has a scattering of them, there is only the word of the purveyor as to the origin of any particular specimen.'

Refs: **19** (1).

Olwen (myth.). Daughter of Yspaddaden Penkawr, she was celebrated for her beauty and charm. Olwen is featured in the story of 'Kilhwch and Olwen' (or 'Twrch Trwyth'), one of eleven Welsh tales translated from the 14th C. Welsh manuscript, *The Red Book of Hergest* by Lady Charlotte Guest in 1838–49. They were published, with the addition of a twelfth tale, under the title *The Mabinogion* (which strictly refers to the first four tales). Kilhwch (or Culhwch) was the cousin of King Arthur and the 'son of Kilydd, the son of Prince Kelyddon, by Goleuddyd the daughter of Prince Anlawdd'. With Arthur's blessing he set out to seek Olwen and eventually found her at her father's castle. He asked for Olwen's hand and was set an enormous number of Herculean tasks which, with Arthur's help, were successfully accomplished. Olwen and Kilhwch were married, and she remained his wife for the rest of her life. Olwen is described as follows: 'Whoso beheld her was filled with love. Four white trefoils sprung up wherever she trod. And therefore was she called Olwen.' Another translation refers to the trefoils as 'four white clover flowers'.

Novels: 'Small miracles followed wherever [St] WINIFRED passed, as flowers sprang in the footsteps of Welsh Olwen in the legend.'

Refs: **16** (1).

O

Onny, River (Shropshire, England). This river has two official sources: the River West Onny rises on the hills to the west of the Stiperstones on the slopes of Stapeley Hill; the River East Onny rises to the east of the Stiperstones on the north-western extremities of the Long Mynd. The two streams flow in a southerly direction to meet near the small hamlet of Eaton, 3 miles west of Bishop's Castle and 4 miles south-west of Church STRETTON. From Eaton the River Onny winds south-eastward past Plowden, Horderley and Cheney Longville, with its much restored 14th C. castle, to the small market town of Craven Arms, which takes its name from the early 19th C. inn. To the north of Craven Arms the Onny is joined by the waters of the various brooks which flow south-west down Ape Dale. About 1 mile south of Craven Arms the River Onny passes Stokesay Castle, dating from the late 13th C. At the time of the Domesday Book survey the manor of Stoke belonged to Roger de Lacy (see LACY FAMILY), but by 1115 it had been granted to

Theodoric de Say, whose ancestor Picot de Say was lord of Clun in 1086. Throughout their ownership, the family gave parts of Stokesay to HAUGHMOND ABBEY, including the church and the mill. The property passed to John de Vernon in the mid 13th C. and in about 1281 the whole manor became the property of a wealthy wool merchant, Laurence de Ludlow (d. 1296). He built a mansion on the site of an earlier building and, under licence from Edward I, he turned it into a fortified manor house. Although it was besieged during the English Civil War, the royal garrison quickly surrendered and the castle suffered little damage. Across the moat, St John the Baptist's Church, with its Norman doorway, was badly damaged during the Civil War. From Stokesay Castle the Onny flows south-east past the villages of Onibury and Wootton to BROMFIELD. A short distance downstream of BROMFIELD the waters of the Onny enter the River TEME.

Novels: CADFAEL set out south from SHREWSBURY for Bromfield in December 1139: 'It was dark by the time he reached the gatehouse of Bromfield, crossing the foot-bridge over the little River Onny.'

Refs: **6** (2).

Orderic, Brother (*fl.* 1120) (fict.). **Novels:** Benedictine monk of SHREWSBURY ABBEY and clerk to Prior (later Abbot) HERIBERT, he accompanied the prior to the king's court at WOODSTOCK in November 1120. On the way they were attacked and Heribert was abducted. Orderic, who carried the documents, was among the brothers who escaped.

Refs: **RB** (1).

Origen (*c.*185–*c.*254) (hist.). Also called Oregenes Adamantius. Probably born in ALEXANDRIA, Origen was a great Christian writer and scholar, a Greek Father of the Church, and the head of the Catechetical School in Alexandria. He was much in demand as a preacher and went to Palestine (see HOLY LAND) in 215. However, being a layman he aroused the anger of Bishop Demetrius of Alexandria, and was instructed to return and resume his role of a teacher. Despite the edict, Origen returned to Palestine in 230 and was ordained a priest. In consequence, Demetrius exiled him, deprived him of his chair and removed him from the priesthood. Origen established himself at Caesarea, where he founded a school which attracted many pupils. In 250, during the persecution under the Emperor Decius, he survived imprisonment and torture, to die at Tyre, Phoenicia. His tomb at Tyre (now Sour, Lebanon) still existed at the time of the crusades. The greatest of his many works is the *Hexapla*, an interpretation of Old Testament texts. His teachings were finally condemned by the Council of CONSTANTINOPLE in 553. He was considered by some to be the 'greatest Christian between [St] PAUL and AUGUSTINE'.

Novels: '"There was a father of the Church, once, as I heard tell, in ALEXANDRIA, who held that in the end everyone would find salvation. Even the fallen angels would return to their fealty, even the devil would repent and make his way back to God."' Although ELAVE did not know the name of the father of the Church who wrote that in the end everyone would find salvation, it was a theme he accepted and believed.

Refs: **16** (4–5, 10, 15).

Osbern, Lame (*fl.* 1138) (fict.). **Novels:** 'He had his little wagon backed well into the lee of a clump of half-grown trees, close to the guard-post, where he might come in for a crust of bread or a drink, and could enjoy the glow of the field-fire at night. Even summer nights can strike chill after the heat of the August day, when you have only a few rags to cover you, and the fire was doubly welcome.' Lame Osbern was a cripple of SHREWSBURY who begged by the castle gates. During the siege of August 1138, Osbern saw Giles SIWARD stealthily enter the king's camp at around midnight, although he did not know the stranger's name. A few days later, CADFAEL presented Osbern with Giles's cloak. The beggar recognised the bronze dragon clasp at the neck. He told Cadfael that he had seen the former owner of the cloak enter and leave the king's camp on the night before the assault on the castle.

Refs: **2** (1, 4, 11).

Osburg, Saint (d. *c.*1018), Abbess at Coventry (hist.) (f.d. 30 March). Also called Osburga. Little is known about this saint, except that she was the one-time abbess of a nunnery at COVENTRY, destroyed by the Danes under Canute (or Cnut) in 1016 (William Dugdale, *The Antiquities of Warwickshire*, 1730). Although tradition says that she founded the nunnery in the late 10th C., Leland, the 16th C. antiquary, credits Canute with its foundation. The saint's name has long been vaguely connected with Coventry: Pool Meadow, for example, was sometimes known as St Osburg's pool. During medieval times her shrine was venerated by pilgrims.

Novels: 'Coventry possessed the relics of its own St Osburg.'

Refs: **20** (2).

Ostia (Italy). Located at the mouth of the River Tiber, some 15 miles downstream from ROME, Ostia was an ancient Roman port. It reached the height of its prosperity in the 2nd C. and was abandoned as a port when the harbour became unsuitable for large vessels because of silting and sandbars. During the first half of the 9th C., Pope Gregory IV ordered the construction of Gregoriopolis, now the site of modern Ostia Antica. Two thirds of the Roman town has been uncovered by archaeological excavation.

Novels: ALBERIC was Cardinal-Bishop of Ostia.

Refs: **3** (8).

Ostia, Cardinal-Bishop of. See ALBERIC, Cardinal-Bishop of Ostia.

Oswald, Brother (*fl.* 1135) (fict.). **Novels:** 'In the villages people shivered and starved, and Brother Oswald the almoner fretted and grieved the more that the alms he had to distribute were not enough to keep all those bodies and souls together.' Benedictine monk of SHREWSBURY ABBEY, Brother Oswald was the almoner from December 1135, at least, until Winter 1141. He was 'a skilled silversmith when he had time to exercise his craft'. On 26 December 1135 Oswald was overjoyed with the basket of money donated anonymously by ELFGIVA to help the poor and needy. In August 1138 Oswald repaired Giles SIWARD's broken dagger.

Refs: **1** (1); **2** (1, 5, 12); **5** (8); **16** (2); **RB** (2).

Oswald, Saint (d. 992), Bishop of Worcester (961–92) (hist.) (f.d. 28 February). Also Archbishop of York (972–92). Oswald, who came from a noble Danish family, was nephew of Odo, Archbishop of Canterbury, under whom he received his education. A secular canon of WINCHESTER, and later dean, he was persuaded by Odo (or Oda) in *c.*952 to enter the Benedictine monastery at Fleury (now St-Benôit-sur-Loire) in France. Returning to England as a priest sometime after his uncle's death in 958, Oswald was consecrated Bishop of Worcester by Dunstan, who had vacated the see to become Archbishop of Canterbury in 960. Oswald gradually transformed his cathedral chapter into a monastic priory (see WORCESTER ABBEY). Vigorously supporting Dunstan's and Ethelwold's efforts to revive monastic life and ecclesiastical discipline in England, Oswald found favour with King Edgar and both he and his monastery were granted considerable privileges. While retaining the diocese of Worcester, Oswald became Archbishop of York. He died suddenly at Worcester on 28 February 992 and was buried in the cathedral, his shrine becoming a place of pilgrimage. In addition to the establishment of many new monasteries, he was a benefactor of RAMSEY ABBEY, and in 974, with Dunstan, was present at the newly completed stone church's dedication to St MARY, St BENEDICT and All Virgins.

Novels: In February 1145 Hugh BERINGAR and Prior ROBERT attended Vespers at Worcester cathedral priory to 'do reverence to the saints of the foundation, Saints Oswald and WULSTAN'.

Refs: **19** (4).

Oswald of Northumbria, Saint (604–42) (hist.) (f.d. 9 August). Son of Ethelfrith, King of Northumbria, he fled to Scotland in 616, when Edwin, Ethelfrith's brother-in-law, seized the kingdom. During his exile Oswald was baptised at Iona. Oswald married Cyneburga, daughter of the Christian King Cynegils of Wessex. In 635, in a battle near Hexham, he defeated Cadwaladr (or Cadwalla or Cadwallon), King of Gwynedd, who had slain Edwin the previous year. Oswald became King of Northumbria and, when he was killed at the battle of MASERFIELD by the heathen King Penda of Mercia, he was venerated as a martyr. Although his body was sacrificially dismembered, the parts were recovered and dispersed in different places. It is said that his head was buried at Lindisfarne in Northumberland (to be discovered in 1827 in the tomb of St Cuthred at Durham); his hands and arms were buried at Bamburgh in Northumberland; while the rest of his body was enshrined at Bardney in Lincolnshire. Many other places, however, claimed to possess some of his relics, including: ELY, GLOUCESTER, Hildesheim in Germany, and Bergues in northern France.

Novels: 'At the battle of Maserfield, by OSWESTRY . . . the royal saint, Oswald, was captured and martyred by the pagans.'

Refs: **17** (10); **18** (1).

Oswestry (Shropshire, England). DB – although Oswestry is not mentioned in the survey it originated in MAESBURY: in Merset Hundred; land held by Roger de MONTGOMERY (Reginald the Sheriff held the manor from Roger and built a castle, called L'Oeuvre, which was almost certainly Oswestry Castle). The border market town of Oswestry nestles in the foothills of Wales, some 16 miles north-west of SHREWSBURY. Built by Reginald the Sheriff prior to 1086, little now survives of Oswestry Castle except a high mound and fragments of stonework, enclosed by a small park in the centre of the town, near Horsemarket. During the reign of STEPHEN the castle seems to have been held by the Welsh, for Anderson in *Shropshire: Its Early History and Antiquities* (1864) quotes Powel who wrote in 1811: 'At the close of the year 1148, Madoc [see MADOG AP MEREDITH], the son of Meredith ap Blethyn, did build the castle of Oswestrie, and gave his nephews, Owen and Meyric, the sonnes of Gruffyth ap Meredyth, his part of Cyvelioc.' The castle later came into the possession of William FITZALAN and the FitzAlan family. A royal stronghold during the Civil War, it was captured in 1644 by the Parliamentarians and demolished. To the north of the town are the extensive earthwork remains of an Iron Age hill-fort, covering around 40 acres. Old Oswestry hill-fort, dating from the 5th C. BC, was abandoned after the Roman Conquest and, except for a brief period during the Dark Ages and perhaps in the Middle Ages, it remained unoccupied. The town of Oswestry was a Saxon settlement and took its name from St OSWALD, King of Northumbria, who was killed at the battle of MASERFIELD (thought to be near Oswestry) in 642. The large parish church, which dates from Norman times, is dedicated to the saint. Being a frontier town, Oswestry was fought over for centuries by the Welsh and the English. It was destroyed by fire on a number of occasions, sometimes deliberately, sometimes accidentally, and during the latter half of the 16th C. one third of the inhabitants were wiped out by plague. In 1536 Henry VIII's Act of Union of Wales with England placed Oswestry officially on the English side of the border.

Novels: Torold BLUND came from a hamlet by Oswestry. SHREWSBURY ABBEY had a sheepfold 'near RHYDYCROESAU by Oswestry'. Hugh BERINGAR came from Maesbury near Oswestry. CADFAEL rode from SHREWSBURY towards Oswestry in December 1138. In March 1141 Hugh went north to meet OWAIN GWYNEDD and reinforce the king's castles along the

Cheshire border, including Oswestry. Cadfael was in the town later that month. It was said that St TYSILIO fought on the Christian side 'at the battle of MASERFIELD, by Oswestry', where St Oswald was captured and martyred. In May 1144 Cadfael and Deacon MARK travelled from Shrewsbury to ST ASAPH by way of Oswestry and CHIRK. Hugh Beringar was unwilling to stay long at COVENTRY in late 1145, in case Madog ap Meredith began '"casting covetous eyes at Oswestry again. He's never stopped hankering after it."'

Refs: **2** (5); **3** (7, 8, 11); **4** (1); **9** (2–3, 5, 9–10, 12); **10** (11–14); **17** (9–10); **18** (1); **20** (6).

Oswin, Brother (b. 1120) (fict.). **Novels:** 'Brother Oswin, who had worked with him among the herbs for more than a year, and was now on his way to put his skills into practice among the most needy. Oswin was sturdy, well-grown, glowing with enthusiasm. Time had been when he had cost plenty in breakages, in pots burned beyond recovery, and deceptive herbs gathered by mistake for others only too like them. Those times were over. All he needed now to be a treasure to the hospital was a cool-headed superior who would know when to curb his zeal. The abbey had the right of appointment, and the lay head they had installed would be more than proof against Brother Oswin's too exuberant energy.' Benedictine monk at SHREWSBURY ABBEY, Brother Oswin was CADFAEL's assistant from around August 1139 to August 1140, when he went to spend a year serving the lepers at the Hospital of ST GILES. Oswin gave Iveta de Massard (see LUCY) the draught of poppy syrup which she used to drug MADLEN. He attended the wedding of LILIWIN and RANNILT in May 1140 and took his final vows in about October. In Spring 1144 he was still at St Giles, having been there far longer than the customary year.

Refs: **5** (1–3, 5–7, 10); **6** (1); **7** (1, 3, 5, 7, 14); **8** (1, 11); **9** (2, 4, 15); **10** (7–8, 10, 12); **11** (1, 3, 5); **12** (2); **13** (1); **14** (11); **15** (3); **17** (6); **18** (1); **RB** (3).

Otir (*fl.* 1144) (hist.). Irish Dane from DUBLIN and son of Otir, Otir was promised 2,000 head of cattle by CADWALADR if he would invade Gwynedd and restore his lost lands. He was the leader of the fleet which landed at ABERMENAI in 1144, but Cadwaladr made peace with OWAIN GWYNEDD and refused to pay the contracted fee. The Danes seized Cadwaladr and forced him to settle his promise in full. Once his brother, Cadwaladr, was free, Owain attacked Otir and his followers and forced them to flee.

Novels: 'This formidable man before them could overrule all other authorities.' Irish Dane from DUBLIN, Otir was born in *c.*1091. He was a kinsman of the two TURCAILLS. In May 1144 he led the Danish force which invaded Gwynedd to try and help Cadwaladr regain his lands. Although the Welsh prince reneged on his promise to pay the Danes the sum of 2,000 marks for their services, Otir took Cadwaladr prisoner and forced him to honour their agreement in full. After Cadwaladr's release, Otir returned to Dublin with his fee and his fleet.

Refs: **18** (7–14).

Otmere, Giles (*fl.* 1143) (fict.). **Novels:** 'Father of Pernel OTMERE, he held the manor of WHITTINGTON, a crown tenant these days, since [William] FITZALAN's lands were seized'. He had a wife and four children, the eldest being Pernel. The others, in November 1143, were two boys of twelve and eight, and a girl of five or six.

Refs: **17** (8, 11).

Otmere, Pernel (b. 1125) (fict.). **Novels:** 'The perfect picture of a young woman conforming to every social sanction imposing rules upon her bearing and movements, with her maid for guardian and companion, and her grooms for escort. Pernel was ensuring that this venture out of her usual ambience should be too correct in every detail to attract comment. She might he the eldest of the brood at WITHINGTON, but she was still very young, and it was imperative to temper her natural directness and boldness with caution. It had to be admitted that she did it with considerable style and grace, and had an admirable abettor in the experienced GUNNILD.' Pernel Otmere was the eldest child of Giles OTMERE of Withington. When Gunnild happened into the manor in December 1142, Pernel took a liking to the 'minstrel' and kept her on as her tirewoman. Pernel met Sulien BLOUNT when he came to Withington enquiring after Gunnild. She was attracted to him and when she heard that he was suspected of GENERY's murder, she was determined to prove his innocence. She was with Sulien at church on 22 November 1143 at SHREWSBURY ABBEY. Her first visit to LONGNER to meet Donata BLOUNT was at the end of the month. While Sulien went back with CADFAEL to SHREWSBURY, Pernel stayed over the night. She told Donata everything about Sulien and the mystery woman's body found in the POTTER'S FIELD. The next day Pernel accompanied her to Shrewsbury, where Donata made her confession. In February 1145 Pernel and Sulien were shortly to marry.

Refs: **17** (8, 10–14); **19** (1–2, 8).

Otto I (912–73), Holy Roman Emperor (962–73) (hist.). Son of Henry I, King of Germany, and his second wife Matilda, he married firstly Edith, daughter of Edward the Elder, King of England and secondly Adelaide, widow of Lothair, King of Italy. After his father's death, Otto was elected King of Germany at AACHEN in 936. After a period of warfare, he not only strengthened his kingdom, but also managed to extend its frontiers. His main achievement was to found the first Reich, which consolidated Germany and much of Italy into one empire. He was crowned Holy Roman Emperor in 962. In the following year, he deposed Pope John XII and, thereafter, made sure the elected popes were in favour of the imperial cause. After his death, Otto was succeeded by his son, OTTO II.

Novels: In June 1143 Brother ANSELM examined the priceless book which William of LYTHWOOD had given to FORTUNATA for her dowry. On the dedication page it said in Latin that the psalter had been made '"at the wish of Otto, King and Emperor, for the marriage of his beloved son, Otto, Prince of the Roman Empire, to the most Noble and Gracious THEOFANU, Princess of Byzantium, this book is the gift of His Most Christian Grace to the Princess. DIARMAID, monk of SAINT GALL, wrote and painted it."' Otto I was in St Gall with his son the year that the prince was married.

Refs: **16** (15).

Otto II (955–83), Holy Roman Emperor (973–83) (hist.). Son of OTTO I by his second wife Adelaide, he was crowned co-regent of Italy and Germany with his father in 961 at the age of six. He became co-regent emperor in 967 and married the Byzantine princess THEOFANU in 972. On his father's death, he succeeded as Emperor and spent the early years of his reign quelling revolts in Lorraine and the duchy of Bavaria. By 980 Otto had secured his German dominions, but was forced by the French to renounce his claim to Lorraine. An attempted invasion of southern Italy failed in 982. After his death, he was succeeded by his three-year-old son, Otto III, who died in 1002.

Novels: 'Otto, Prince of the Roman Empire,' was the recipient of the priceless psalter on his marriage to Theofanu (see OTTO I). The year that the prince was married, he was with his father in ST GALL where the book was written and painted: 'It is recorded in the chronicle. The young man was seventeen, and knew how to value manuscripts. He took several away with him from the library. Not all of them were ever returned.'

Refs: **16** (15).

Our Lady. See MARY, Saint.

Outremer, Kingdoms of (parts of Israel, Jordan and Egypt). During medieval times, those in Western Europe referred to the crusader states in PALESTINE as Outremer, meaning the 'land overseas'. See HOLY LAND.

Novels: 'The fabled world of Outremer, once familiar to him [CADFAEL], where Olivier de BRETAGNE had grown up to choose, in manhood, the faith of his unknown father.' 'Beyond the fabled Midland Sea, into the legendary Frankish kingdoms of Outremer.'

Refs: **20** (1, 8).

Owain, Elis ab (*fl.* 1139) (fict.). **Novels:** Elder son of Owain ap RHYS and nephew of Cynfrith ap RHYS, he married in Spring 1139.

Refs: **3** (8).

Owain, Rhys ab (*fl.* 1142) (fict.). **Novels:** Welsh farrier, smith and 'notability' of the ABBEY FOREGATE in SHREWSBURY, he attended the funeral of Father AILNOTH at SHREWSBURY ABBEY on 1 January 1142.

Refs: **12** (11).

Owain ap Griffith. See OWAIN GWYNEDD.

Owain Gwynedd (*c.*1100–70), Ruler of Gwynedd (hist.). Also called Owain ap Griffith or Gruffudd. Son of GRIFFITH AP CYNAN, King of Gwynedd, and his wife ANGHARAD (d. 1162), he married first GWLADUS, daughter of LLYWARCH AP TRAHAEARN, by whom he had two sons who survived him, IORWERTH AB OWAIN and MAELGWN AB OWAIN. Despite the condemnation of the Church, he later married his cousin Christina (or Cristin), daughter of Gronw ap Owen, by whom he had Dafydd and Rhodri. Among his other children were: Angharad, Gwenllian, RHUN AB OWAIN, HYWEL AB OWAIN by an Irish woman called Pyfog, and Cynan. Towards the end of his father's lifetime Owain fought alongside his younger brother, CADWALADR, to conquer the Welsh regions of Meirionydd, RHOS, Rhufoniog and DYFFRYN CLWYD, all of which were added to the kingdom of Gwynedd. On his father's death in 1137, he succeeded to the kingship, and became known as Owain Gwynedd to distinguish himself from another Owain ap Griffith (or Owain Cyfeiliog). In 1146, despite opposition from MADOG AP MEREDITH and RANULF of Chester, he conquered MOLD, and three years later the cantrefs of Tegeingl and Ial were added to his domain. Although he took advantage of the political anarchy in England during STEPHEN's reign to expand and consolidate his kingdom, he was unable to stop HENRY II from invading North Wales in 1157. Having lost Tegeingl and Ial, Owain was forced to return the lands and possessions of his exiled brother, Cadwaladr, and pay homage to Henry. He also agreed to call himself Prince instead of King. During the general Welsh uprising of 1165, Owain forced the English army to retreat and destroyed the royal castles in Tegeingl (Basingwerk, RHUDDLAN and Prestatyn) and extended his territory westward to the River DEE. It proved to be the climax of his long military career. After his death, he was buried in the cathedral church at BANGOR.

Novels: '"A wise prince – and Owain Gwynedd seems to me very wise – will let well alone."' 'Though there was every indication that the prince of Gwynedd needed no other man's wits to fortify his own, but had been lavishly endowed by God in the first place.' 'Owain Gwynedd, the formidable lord of much of Wales, withheld his hand courteously from interfering in England's fratricidal war, and very cannily looked after his own interests, host to whoever fled his enemy, friend to whoever brought him useful information. The borders of SHREWSBURY he did not threaten. He had far more to gain by holding aloof. But his own firm border he maintained with every severity.' Owain Gwynedd was the son of Griffith ap Cynan by his wife Angharad, grandson of RAGNHILD, brother of Cadwaladr, and father of Hywel ab Owain and Rhun ab Owain. In May 1137, when he was 'Prince Owain . . . regent of Gwynedd owing to the illness of the old king, his father', he granted his consent to Prior ROBERT and his party to remove the bones of St WINIFRED from GWYTHERIN to Shrewsbury. Griffith ap RHYS was his bailiff. In

August 1138 Owain Gwynedd and William FITZALAN were friends. FitzAlan gave Torold BLUND his commendation to Owain. Rhodri ap HUW went to St Peter's Fair in August 1139 to gather intelligence for Owain. In February 1141 CADFAEL met Owain at TREGEIRIOG and enquired whether his brother, Cadwaladr, held Gilbert PRESTCOTE (the elder) prisoner. Discovering that Prestcote was indeed in Wales, Owain agreed to an exchange of prisoners. Hugh BERINGAR later met Owain on the border, and they agreed to form an alliance against Ranulf of Chester. In June 1143 Canon GERBERT rode north to make a cautious gesture of peace and goodwill to Ranulf. In return for Ranulf's support, Stephen offered to help him hold off Owain and his Welshmen. In 1143 Owain sent Hywel south to drive Cadwaladr out of CEREDIGION in retaliation for the killing of ANARAWD AP GRIFFITH, to whom his daughter was betrothed. Despite Cadwaladr's invasion of Gwynedd with a Danish fleet from DUBLIN in May 1144, he and Owain were reconciled.

Refs: **1** (2–7, 9–11); **2** (5, 9–10); **3** (11); **4** (5:2); **7** (12); **9** (1–6, 9–12, 14–15); **11** (1); **12** (6); **16** (1, 15); **17** (7); **18** (1–14); **19** (11).

Oxford (Oxfordshire, England). Some 49 miles west of LONDON and 42 miles east of GLOUCESTER, the university city of Oxford lies between the River THAMES and its tributary the Cherwell, just north of their confluence. Originally a Saxon river-crossing settlement, the town was first mentioned in *The Anglo-Saxon Chronicle*, when it was occupied by Edward the Elder in 912. Although sacked and burnt by the Danes in 1002, Oxford soon recovered. After the Norman Conquest the market town became an important military centre with town walls and a castle on the east bank of the Thames. Oxford Cathedral stands on the site of a nunnery, founded in *c.*727 by Didan for his daughter, Frideswide. It was destroyed during the Danish invasion of 1002 and rebuilt soon after by ETHELRED II. Although the monastery fell into disuse, the canons of St Frideswide are briefly mentioned in the Domesday Book. Oxford Priory, dedicated to St Frideswide, was refounded by Bishop Roger of Salisbury (see ROBERT) in the 1120s and completed in *c.*1180. In 1525 Cardinal Wolsey began building Cardinal College, on the site of the Augustinian Priory. Before his ambitious plans could be completed, Wolsey fell from power and in 1530 he died. The building became the Cathedral Church of Christ in Oxford, or Christ Church, in 1546. In the 12th and following centuries numerous religious houses were founded in and around Oxford: the Augustinian Osney Abbey in 1129; the Benedictine Godstow Abbey in *c.*1133; the Dominican Oxford Friary in 1221; the Franciscan Oxford Friary in 1224; the Carmelite Oxford Friary in 1256; the Augustinian Oxford Friary in *c.*1266; the Cistercian Rewley Abbey in 1281; the Benedictine Gloucester College in *c.*1283; the Trinitarian Oxford Friary in *c.*1286; the Crutched Oxford Friary in 1342; the Benedictine Canterbury College in *c.*1370; the Benedictine Durham College in *c.*1381; the Augustinian St Mary's College in 1435; and the Cistercian St Bernard's College in 1437. Many were established as places of learning during the evolution of Oxford into a university town, which began during the reign of HENRY II, when all English scholars in Europe, particularly PARIS, were ordered to return to home. Although the first reference to a Chancellor was in 1214, the University was in existence by the end of the 12th C. Friction between the townspeople and scholars led to riots, the most violent of which was the Massacre of St Scholastica's Day in 1355. Backed by royal and ecclesiastical approval, the University received many privileges at the expense of the city merchants. University College was founded in 1249, Balliol in 1263–8 and Merton in 1264. Many others followed including New College, Queen's, Lincoln, All Souls and Magdalen.

Novels: 'Round Oxford men have other things to do this autumn besides scour the woods for a dead man. There are dead men enough to bury after the looting and burning of Oxford town.' In June 1141 the Empress MAUD withdrew to Oxford while the long negotiations with the city of LONDON over her coronation went on. On his way north in search of Luc MEVEREL, Olivier de BRETAGNE passed through ABINGDON and Oxford. In Spring 1142 Maud had cautiously moved her headquarters to Oxford. In September it was rumoured that William FITZALAN was back in England and had joined the empress in Oxford. In the same month Maud was besieged in OXFORD CASTLE by King STEPHEN. Just before the king 'shut his iron ring around the castle', Renaud BOURCHIER escaped carrying money, jewels and a letter from Maud to Brian FITZCOUNT. In December Maud managed to slip out of the castle unseen and get safely away to WALLINGFORD. Among those on Stephen's side at the siege were: Eudo BLOUNT (the elder) and Audemar de CLARY. After the conference at COVENTRY on 30 November 1145, King Stephen and HENRY OF BLOIS went to Oxford.

Refs: **3** (2); **7** (4); **10** (2, 7); **11** (5); **12** (6); **13** (1); **14** (1, 4, 14); **15** (1, 3); **16** (1); **17** (1); **20** (1–2, 5–7).

Oxford Castle (Oxfordshire, England). Oxford Castle was built in the 1070s, beside the River THAMES, by the father of Robert d'OILI II. The Empress MAUD made the castle one of her headquarters during the reign of STEPHEN and was besieged in it for three months in 1142, until she managed to secretly escape across the frozen river. It was rebuilt during the Middle Ages and belonged to the Crown until 1611. The site is now occupied by Oxford Prison. Among the remains are: the motte, known as Castle Mound, which stands just outside the walls of the prison, and the defensive tower of St George's Church, which stands within.

Novels: 'And here was September ended . . . The iron grip of siege tightened steadily round Oxford castle, and for once Stephen showed no sign of abandoning his purpose. Never yet had he come so close to making his cousin and rival his prisoner, and forcing her acceptance of his sovereignty.' From September 1142, for three months, Maud was besieged in Oxford Castle by Stephen's forces. She slipped secretly out of the castle in December, crossed the Thames and reached safety at WALLINGFORD. In Summer 1145 those castles in the Thames valley belonging to the empress, including CRICKLADE under Philip FITZROBERT, were 'plagued by damaging raids by the king's men garrisoned in Oxford and MALMESBURY.'

Refs: **14** (1); **15** (1); **20** (1).

Oxfordshire, Sheriff of. See OILI II, Robert d'.

P

Padrig (*fl.* 1137) (fict.). **Novels:** Travelling Welsh poet and harpist, he stayed for a while in GWYTHERIN at RHISIART's Hall in May 1137. Having visited the village for many years, Padrig knew all the inhabitants.
Refs: **1** (3–4, 6–7, 11).

Palestine. See HOLY LAND.

Palladius (*c.*365–*c.*425) (hist.). Born in Galatia, Asia Minor, he became a monk on the Mount of OLIVES in *c.*385 and, thereafter, spent a number of years in Egypt, where he was a pupil of Evagrius Ponticus. Palladius became Bishop of Helenopolis in Bithynia in 400, but – because of his support of St JOHN CHRYSOSTOM – was imprisoned for almost a year in *c.*403 and exiled in 406. He returned to Asia Minor in *c.*412 and was accused of Origenism (see ORIGEN) by St Jerome and St Epiphanius, even though the charges were groundless. Although famous as an historian of early monasticism (*Historia Lausiaca*), Palladius wrote a book on gardening (mainly derived from Columella), with tips on what to do each month throughout the calendar. Copies of the work, written in the late 12th C. and 13th C., were in use in a number of English monasteries, including Byland, CANTERBURY and WORCESTER.

Novels: Referring to Meriet ASPLEY, Brother PAUL commented to CADFAEL: '"I think the only thing that frets him is having no work to do, so I have taken him the sermons of Saint AUGUSTINE, and given him a better lamp to read by, and a little desk he can set on his bed. Better far to have his mind occupied, and he is quick at letters. I suppose you would rather have given him Palladius on agriculture," said PAUL, mildly joking. "Then you could make a case for taking him into your herbarium, when OSWIN moves on."'

Refs: **8** (6).

Papal Legates. See ALBERIC, Cardinal-Bishop of Ostia; HENRY OF BLOIS, Bishop of Winchester; WILLIAM OF CORBEIL, Archbishop of Canterbury.

Paris (France). Inland port 233 miles upstream from the English Channel and capital city of France, Paris began as a settlement on an island in the River Seine (now Île de la Cité), inhabited by the Gallic Parisii tribe. During Roman times the town, known as Lutetia, spread to the south bank of the river. By the 4th C. the area, concentrated on the walled island, became known as Paris. At the end of the 5th C. it became the capital city of Gaul, under Clovis, first Christian king of the Salian Franks. During the Carolingian Empire (751–987) the city ceased to be a major capital, coming under the control of the counts of Paris. It became a seat of power again, when Hugh Capet, King of France (987–96), made the city his royal capital. Expansion quickly followed, and during the reign of Philip II Augustus (1180–1223) the city walls were enlarged and the streets paved. Among the many buildings dating from medieval times are: the cathedral of Notre Dame; several royal palaces, including the Louvre, built on the site of a *c.*1200 fortress, and the Conciergerie; the churches of St-Germain-l'Auxerrois and St-Germain-des-Prés; the Sainte-Chapelle, built in the 13th C. to house the 'Crown of Thorns'; and a number of private mansions such as the Hôtel de Cluny, beneath which are the remains of Roman baths, and the Hôtel de Sens. The Sorbonne, now part of the University of Paris, was founded in *c.*1257. See also ST DENIS.

Refs: **4** (1:4); **20** (6).

Partholan (myth.). Son of Sera and husband of Queen DAALNY, he murdered his father and mother, hoping to inherit their kingdom. Failing to accomplish this goal, Partholan led his followers to Ireland from beyond the western seas and, finding the land inhabited by the FOMORIANS, drove them out of the country. He and his race were wiped out by plague on the great plain of Senmag, leaving the land empty for the people of Nemed, who were to come from the west some time later. Partholan is credited with the introduction of agriculture into Ireland.

Novels: The first hero of the Irish people '"came into Ireland out of the western seas, from the land of the happy dead, which they call the land of the living. His name was Partholan . . . And Daalny was his queen. There was a race of monsters then in the land, but Partholan drove them northward into the seas and beyond. But in the end there was a great pestilence, and all the race of Partholan gathered together on the great plain, and died, and the land was left empty for the next people to come out of the western sea. Always from the west. They come from there, and when they die they go back there."'

Refs: **19** (2, 11–13).

Patrice, Mother (b. *c.*1098) (fict.). **Novels:** 'A dumpy round loaf of a woman, perhaps in her middle forties, with a plump russet face and shrewd brown eyes that weighed and measured in a glance, and were confident of their judgement. She sat uncompromisingly erect on an uncushioned bench in a small and Spartan parlour, and closed the book on the desk before her as CADFAEL came in. Abbess of FAREWELL, Mother Patrice was brought from COVENTRY in *c.*1140 by Bishop Roger de CLINTON to direct his new foundation at Farewell. She received Brother HALUIN and Cadfael in March 1143.

Refs: **15** (10–11, 13).

Patrick (d. 1168), Earl of Salisbury (hist.). Son of Walter of Salisbury (sheriff of Wiltshire under STEPHEN (d. 1147)), he was originally a supporter of the king, but is thought to have been persuaded to change sides by his rival for power in Wiltshire, John FITZGILBERT, who married Patrick's sister, Sibyl. The Empress MAUD rewarded Patrick by making him Earl of Wiltshire (usually styled Earl of Salisbury) at some time between 1142 and 1147. He was also sheriff of Wiltshire, with his main stronghold at Old Sarum (see SALISBURY). In 1149 and again in 1153 he supported Henry Plantagenet (later HENRY II) when he was in England. After Henry's accession, Patrick continued to act as sheriff, and was frequently at court. In 1167 he was in charge of the king's forces in the troublesome province of Poitou (western France), and the following year he was helping Eleanor, Queen of England, govern the region. While returning from a pilgrimage to COMPOSTELA (or while escorting the queen between castles), Patrick was ambushed by the members of the rebellious Lusignan family and killed. He was buried in the abbey of St Hilaire at Poitiers. William FitzPatrick, his son, succeeded to the earldom.

Novels: One of the Empress Maud's most powerful adherents, Patrick of Salisbury attended the conference at COVENTRY on 30 November 1145. The following month he was among the great army that besieged and took La MUSARDERIE.

Refs: **20** (10–11).

Paul, Brother (b. 1092) (fict.). **Novels:** 'Brother Paul, who could discover an angel within every imp he taught, was nevertheless a sceptic concerning their elders.' '"I cannot regard a simple mistake in letters," retorted Brother Paul, up in arms for lads no older than his own charges, "as an offence. Offence argues a will to offend, and these children answer as best they know, having no will but to do well." "The offence," said JEROME pompously, "is in the neglect and inattention which caused them to be imperfect in answering. Those who attend diligently will be able to answer without fault." "Not when they are already afraid," snapped Brother Paul, and fled the argument for fear of his own temper. Jerome had a way of presenting his pious face as a target, and Paul, who like most big, powerful men could be astonishingly gentle and tender with the helpless, like his youngest pupils, was only too well aware of what fists could do to an opponent of his own size, let alone a puny creature like Jerome.' Brother Paul was a Benedictine monk and priest of SHREWSBURY ABBEY and master of the novices from at least 1137. Among those he taught were: Brother MARK, Richard LUDEL (the younger), Brother RHUN, Brother RUALD, and Sulien BLOUNT. Melangell [see MEVEREL] and Luc MEVEREL were married by Paul in May 1141.

Refs: **1** (1); **2** (1, 8); **3** (1, 7); **8** (1–2, 6–7, 10); **9** (8); **10** (1, 3, 16); **11** (3–4); **12** (1, 3); **14** (1–2, 4, 7, 10–12); **17** (2–6, 9); **19** (3, 5, 9, 13).

Paul the Apostle, Saint (*c.*3–*c.*65) (hist.) (f.d. 29 June, with St Peter). Formerly called Saul of Tarsus. Born at Tarsus in Cilicia (now Turkey), Saul was a Jew of the tribe of Benjamin, a Roman citizen and a Pharisee. He was sent by his parents as a young man to JERUSALEM, where he trained as a rabbi and learned the trade of a tent-maker. He took part in the stoning of St STEPHEN and became a zealous opponent of Christianity. On his way to DAMASCUS Saul experienced a vision of Christ which transformed his life. He accepted the call to take the Christian faith to the Gentiles, changed his name to Paul and, after being baptised, retired to Arabia for a while before returning to Damascus. Having been forced to escape from the city by the hostility of his Jewish enemies, Paul went to Jerusalem, where he visited St PETER THE APOSTLE and St JAMES THE GREATER. After spending some time in ANTIOCH and its vicinity, he began his three missionary journeys that took him to CYPRUS, Asia Minor and Greece. On his return to Jerusalem Paul was arrested and imprisoned. As a Roman citizen he appealed to the emperor for a trial in ROME, was shipwrecked at Malta and, after reaching the city in 60, was under house-arrest for two years. During this time he wrote several letters. According to ancient tradition, Paul was beheaded in Rome under Nero at Tre Fontane and buried where the basilica of St Paul Outside the Walls now stands. His conversion is celebrated on 25 January.

Novels: SHREWSBURY ABBEY was dedicated to St Peter and St Paul.

Refs: **1** (1, 11); **2** (2–3); **3** (1); **4** (1:1); **5** (1, 7); **6** (1); **8** (1–2, 5, 12); **10** (2); **11** (1, 3, 14); **12** (1); **14** (2); **15** (1, 10–11, 13); **16** (4, 14); **17** (1, 5–6, 9); **19** (3); **20** (15–16); **RB** (3).

Payne (*fl.* 1145) (fict.). **Novels**: Journeyman mason from Shropshire, possibly SHREWSBURY, Payne offered to go to RAMSEY ABBEY to help 'rebuild the gutted barns and storehouses' in February 1145. Bound for Ramsey, he was travelling with JAMES, MARTIN, NICOL and ROGER through thick woodland near ULLESTHORPE, when they were ambushed by about a dozen armed men and their wagon and team of horses stolen. He chose to go on to Ramsey with Roger to report their loss and to find more steady work. Payne was younger than Martin.

Refs: **19** (2–4).

Peche, Baldwin (*c.*1088–1140) (fict.). **Novels:** 'The locksmith was a man in his fifties; short, sturdy, but beginning to grow a round paunch, a noted fisherman along the SEVERN, but a weak swimmer, unusually for this river-circled town. He had, truly enough, a long nose that quivered to every breath of scandal, though he was cautious in the use he made of it, as though he enjoyed mischief for its own sake rather than for any personal profit. A cold, inquisitive merriment twinkled in his pale-blue eyes, set in a round, ruddy smiling face.' Widower without children and SHREWSBURY locksmith, Baldwin Peche occupied part of the wing of Walter AURIFABER'S BURGAGE. He was a guest at the wedding feast of Daniel AURIFABER in May 1140. A few days later, he told CADFAEL that Daniel and Cecily CORDE, wife of Ailwin CORDE, were having an affair. After GRIFFIN had discovered a silver coin in the bucket of Walter AURIFABER's well, Baldwin suspected Susanna AURIFABER of having robbed her father's strong-box. Baldwin tried to blackmail her, but she struck him on the head with a stone and held him in the Severn until he drowned. His corpse was discovered by Cadfael in the river. John BONETH was Baldwin's journeyman locksmith and, after his death, inherited the business.

Refs: **7** (1–3, 5–9, 11, 13).

(Baldwin) Peche's Shop (Castle Street, Shrewsbury, Shropshire) (fict.). Although it never existed, the shop of Baldwin PECHE occupied part of the wing of Walter AURIFABER'S BURGAGE. It was situated on the southern side of CASTLE STREET, near ST MARY'S WATER-LANE.

Novels: WALTER 'had divided off the wing [of his house] and let it as a shop and dwelling to the locksmith Baldwin Peche . . . who found it convenient and adequate to his needs.'

Refs: **7** (2–3).

P

Penelope (myth.). In Greek mythology, she was the wife of Ulysses and the mother of Telemachus. In Ulysses's absence, according to Homer, she was pestered by suitors and, in order to forestall their attentions, she promised to submit to one of them as soon as she had finished making a shroud. Each night, however, she unravelled what she had worked during the day. When Ulysses returned he slew the suitors.

Novels: 'Iveta (see LUCY] rose submissively and went back with her to the guest-hall, and sewed unenthusiastically at the piece of embroidery that had been her cover for weeks, even though her needle was not so industrious that she need unpick at night what she worked during the day, like a certain Dame Penelope, of whom she had once heard tell from a passing jongleur in her father's house, long ago.'

Refs: **5** (10).

Penllyn (Gwynedd, Wales). The medieval Welsh cantref of Penllyn was in Powys Fadog. Forming part of the extreme eastern boundary of present-day Gwynedd, Penllyn lies to the west of the commotes of Dinmael, Edeyrnion and CYNLLAITH, and is almost bisected by the upper River DEE with Bala Lake (or Llyn Tegid) at its centre.

Novels: 'As for the fugitive MEURIG, cried through Powys for murder, the hunt had never set eyes on him since, and the trail was growing cold. Even the report of his voluntary confession, sent by a priest from a hermitage in Penllyn, did not revive the scent, for the man was long gone, and no one knew where.'

Refs: **3** (11).

Penmachmo (now Penmachno) (Gwynedd, Wales). Some 4 miles south of Betws-y-Coed and 7 miles south of LLANRWST, Penmachno lies in the little valley of the River or Afon Machno. Surrounded by mountains, it was formerly a slate quarrymen's village and many of its cottages are constructed of grey stone. The church was built in 1859 on the site of an earlier church founded in the 6th C. by St Tudclyd, to whom the present building is dedicated. Inside the church are the oldest Christian gravestones in Wales, dating from the late 5th and the early 6th C. IORWERTH AB OWAIN is reputed to have been buried at Penmachno and it is thought that, during the 12th C., it was an important ecclesiastical centre.

Novels: After leaving GWYTHERIN in May 1137 with the sacred relics of St WINIFRED, Prior ROBERT's party stopped overnight 'at Penmachmo, in the shelter of the church, where there was hospitality for travellers'. It was there that Brother JEROME claimed that a traveller in great pain from a malignant illness had been eased of his pain by the miracle-working saint.

Refs: **1** (11).

Pennant, Prior Robert. See ROBERT PENNANT.

Peredur (*fl.* 1137) (fict.). **Novels:** 'He's a very gay, lively, well-looking young fellow, spoiled as you please, being the only one.' 'The parents were ordinary enough, comfortable people grown plump from placid living, and expecting things to go smoothly still as they always had. CADWALLON had a round, fleshy, smiling face, and his wife was fat, fair and querulous. The boy cast back to some more perilous ancestor. The spring of his step was a joy to watch. He was not above middle height, but so well-proportioned that he looked tall. His dark hair was cut short, and curled crisply all over his head. His chin was shaven clean, and all the bones of his face were as bold and elegant as his colouring was vivid, with russet brushings of sun on high cheekbones, and a red, audacious, self-willed mouth. Such a young person might well find it hard to bear that another, and an alien at that, should be preferred to him. He proclaimed in his every movement and glance that everything and everyone in his life had responded subserviently to his charm until now.' Peredur was a Welshman of GWYTHERIN, and the son and sole heir of Cadwallon by his wife, Dame BRANWEN. In May 1137 Peredur was 'fathoms deep in love' with SIONED, whom he had grown up with from a child. Although Sioned's father, RHISIART, wanted her to marry Peredur, she preferred ENGELARD. Peredur discovered Rhisiart dead in the forest, and thrust one of his rival's arrows into the wound to implicate Engelard in the murder. At Sioned's request, he reluctantly attended the funeral of Rhisiart. When asked to place a silver cross on the breast of the dead man, Peredur shrank back in horror and confessed to his deed.

Refs: **1** (3–11).

Perle, Edred (d. 1138) (fict.). **Novels:** '"He was a very comely man . . .' said CADFAEL, shaking his head mildly over the vulnerability of beauty, "I saw him pared away to the bone in a searing fever, and had no art to cool him. A man remembers that."' Edred Perle was the husband of Judith PERLE, whom he married in 1135.

Refs: **13** (1–3, 5–6).

Perle, Judith (née Vestier) (b. 1115) (fict.). **Novels:** 'She was not a beautiful woman, Judith Perle, born Judith Vestier, and sole heiress to the biggest clothiers' business in the town. But she had a bodily dignity that would draw the eye even in a market crowd, above the common height for a woman, slender and erect, and with a carriage and walk of notable grace. The great coils of her shining light-brown hair, the colour of seasoned oak timber, crowned a pale face that tapered from wide and lofty brow to pointed chin, by way of strong cheekbones and hollow cheeks, and an eloquent, mobile mouth too wide for beauty, but elegantly shaped. Her eyes were of a deep grey, and very clear and wide, neither confiding nor hiding anything. CADFAEL had been eye to eye with her, four years ago now, across her husband's death-bed, and she had neither lowered her lids nor turned her glance aside, but stared unwaveringly as her life's happiness slipped irresistibly away through her fingers.' 'As heiress to the clothier's business for want of a brother, she had learned all the skills involved, from teasing and carding to the loom, and the final cutting of garments, though she found herself much out of practice now at the distaff.' Judith Perle was cousin of Miles COLIAR, niece of Agatha COLIAR, daughter of Richard VESTIER, and widow of Edred PERLE, whom she married in 1135. She was sole heiress to the rich Vestier clothier's business in SHREWSBURY. Having lost her husband and unborn child in 1138, within twenty days of each other, Judith granted her house in the ABBEY FOREGATE to SHREWSBURY ABBEY (see Judith PERLE'S HOUSE). The terms demanded the annual rent of one white rose from the bush in her old garden to be paid on 22 June, the day of St WINIFRED's translation. Although many of the town's merchants proposed marriage, Judith was determined to remain single. In June 1142 she considered taking the veil. On the morning of 18 June, Judith set out for the abbey to draw up a new charter, removing the need for the rose-rent and making the contract unconditional. On the way, she was abducted by Vivian HYNDE and hidden in William HYNDE'S COUNTING-HOUSE. Judith eventually persuaded Vivian to set her free. To avoid a scandal, he secretly escorted her to GODRIC'S FORD. After they had parted, she was attacked by Miles Coliar, but was rescued by Niall BRONZESMITH. He took her to the safety of the Benedictine cell, where Sister MAGDALEN gave them shelter for the night and agreed to find a way to cover her disappearance. The following day, Judith was escorted to Shrewsbury Abbey by Magdalen and John MILLER. On 22 June Niall delivered the rose-rent to Judith, taking his daughter, Rosalba, with him. Just as they were about to leave, Judith called him back. It is highly likely that Judith and Niall were married, possibly during the latter half of 1142.

Refs: **13** (1–14).

(Judith) Perle's House (Abbey Foregate, Shrewsbury, Shropshire) (fict.). Although it never existed, the house of Judith PERLE was in the ABBEY FOREGATE, on the opposite side of the road to SHREWSBURY ABBEY, somewhere in the vicinity of HORSE-FAIR and Holywell Street.

Novels: 'My house in the Monks' Foregate, between the abbey forge and the messuage of THOMAS THE FARRIER. From June 1138 Judith Perle received from Shrewsbury Abbey 'one rose every year for the rent of the house and garden in the Foregate, where her man died. The only gesture of passion and grief and loss she ever made, to give away voluntarily her most valuable property, the house where she had been happy, and yet ask for that one reminder, and nothing more.' The abbey, in turn, rented the house to Niall BRONZESMITH. See also Niall BRONZESMITH'S HOUSE AND SHOP.

Refs: **13** (1–2).

Perronet, Jean de (b. *c.*1117) (fict.). **Novels:** 'There was nothing clandestine or secretive, certainly, about Jean de Perronet's arrival, though nothing ceremonious or showy, either. He came with one body-servant and two grooms, and with two led horses for the bride and her attendant, and pack-horses for the baggage. The entire entourage was practical and efficient, and de Perronet himself went very plainly, without flourishes in his dress or his manner, though CADFAEL noted with appreciation the quality of his horse-flesh and harness. This young man knew where to spend his money, and where to spare.' Jean de Perronet was the son and heir of the lord of a BUCKINGHAM manor. In 1141 he formally asked Cenred VIVERS for the hand of his supposed half-sister, Helisende VIVERS. Two years later, in March, Jean travelled from Buckingham to VIVERS for the wedding, even though his bride did not love him. The marriage was thwarted when Adelais de CLARY announced that Roscelin VIVERS and Helisende were not related, and that Brother HALUIN was Helisende's father. Helisende was, therefore, able to marry Roscelin.

Refs: **15** (7–9, 12–13).

Pershore (Hereford & Worcester, England). Some 6 miles west of EVESHAM and 9 miles south-east of WORCESTER, this Georgian town lies on the north bank of the River Avon. It is an ancient market town, situated at the western edge of the fertile Vale of Evesham and in the heart of a fruit-growing area, particularly noted for its plums. Pershore Abbey was first founded in *c.*689 by Oswald, nephew of Ethelred, King of Mercia, and refounded for Benedictine monks in 972 by Edgar, King of England, and Egelward, Duke of Dorset. Dedicated to St MARY and St EADBURGA, the abbey (which was also called Holy Cross) lost much of its land when EDWARD THE CONFESSOR granted it to WESTMINSTER Abbey. The monks retaliated by closing the abbey church to Westminster's tenants in the town. In order not to aggravate the situation further, the monks of Westminster built St Andrew's Church. The abbey possessed the relics of St Eadburga, which had been brought 'at great expense' from WINCHESTER. It was dissolved in 1540, and the nave was given to the parishioners. The townspeople, however, exchanged the nave for the choir and transepts, and the rest of the building was demolished. All that now remains of the monastery are the choir, tower and south transept of the church and the almonry, nearby.

Novels: In the severe winter of 1139, Brother ELYAS of Pershore travelled to BROMFIELD Priory with a sacred finger-bone of St Eadburga. He was sent on the 'errand' by his abbot, WILLIAM. On his way back to Pershore Abbey, Elyas was attacked and left for dead.

Refs: **6** (2); **19** (1–2).

Peter the Apostle, Saint (d. *c.*64) (hist.) (f.d. 29 June, with St Paul). Formerly called Simeon, Simon or Simon Peter. The son of John, younger brother of St ANDREW and married, Simon was a fisherman from Bethsaida on the Sea of Galilee. Like his brother, he was a disciple of St JOHN THE BAPTIST before he was chosen by Christ to become an apostle. Jesus immediately gave him the Aramaic name Kephas meaning 'rock'; hence Peter, from the Greek *petros* and the Latin *petra*. Christ said: 'Thou art Peter, and upon this rock I will build my church . .. And I will give unto thee the keys of the kingdom of heaven' (Matthew 16:18–19). Peter had a unique position among the apostles and was recognised in the early Christian Church as the leader of the disciples. He was one of the three disciples privileged to witness the raising of Jairus's daughter, the transfiguration of Christ and his agony in the garden of Gethsemane. In spite of being warned by Jesus beforehand, Peter denied him three times. After Christ's ascension Peter became the leader of the Christian community. He was the first of the apostles to perform miracles, took a prominent part in the council of JERUSALEM, and may have been the first bishop of ANTIOCH. According to tradition, Peter eventually went to ROME, where he was martyred on Vatican Hill under Nero. He was buried where the St Peter's Basilica now stands, and his relics are enshrined beneath the high altar of the present church. Peter is symbolised in art by two crossed keys. The subsidiary feast of St Peter ad Vincula, or St Peter's Chains, held on 1 August, commemorates his escape from prison by divine intervention.

Novels: '"At the beginning of this year his Grace King STEPHEN . . . confirmed also our right to this three-day fair on the feast of our patron Saint Peter, at the same fee we have paid before, and on the same conditions."' 'Subsistence goods they grew, or bred, or brewed, or wove, or span themselves, the year round, but once a year they came to buy the luxury cloths, the fine wines, the rare preserved fruits, the gold and silver work, all the treasures that appeared on the feast of Saint Peter ad Vincula, and vanished three days later.' SHREWSBURY ABBEY was dedicated to St Peter and St PAUL. The annual St Peter's Fair was held on the first three days in August.

Refs: **1** (1, 11); **2** (2–3); **3** (1–2, 4, 9); **4** (1:1, 3:1); **5** (1, 5, 7); **6** (1); **8** (1–2, 5, 12); **10** (2); **11** (1, 3, 14); **12** (1); **14** (2); **15** (1, 10–11, 13); **16** (4, 14); **17** (1, 5–7, 9); **19** (3); **20** (15–16); **RB** (3).

Peter the Groom (*fl.* 1145) (fict.). **Novels:** One of Philip FITZROBERT's grooms at La MUSARDERIE, Peter showed CADFAEL to the stables. 'The groom Peter was easy and talkative about helping Cadfael unsaddle and unload, groom and water the horse and settle him in a stall.'

Refs: **20** (7).

Peter the Venerable (*c.*1092–115t) (hist.). Also called Blessed Peter of Montbossier. Born at Montbossier in Auvergne, France, Peter became a monk at CLUNY in 1109. Some three years later, he became prior of Vézelay, in Burgundy, and in 1122 was appointed Abbot of Cluny. He was one of the most eminent churchmen of the time, and under his abbacy the Cluniac monastery retained its position as one of the greatest and most influential religious houses in Europe. After Pierre ABELARD had been convicted of heretical writings at the Council of SENS in 1140, Peter received him at Cluny and arranged his reconciliation with BERNARD OF CLAIRVAUX and Pope INNOCENT II. Peter was the first to have the Koran translated into Latin, so that it could be refuted.

Novels: '"There was one of the brothers died there," said ELAVE, standing up sturdily for the sanctity and wisdom of Cluny, "who had written on all these things, and taught in his young days, and he was revered beyond any other among the brothers, and had the most saintly name among them. He saw no wrong in pondering all these difficult matters by the test of reason, and neither did his abbot, who had sent him there from Cluny for his health."' Abbot Peter of Cluny sent Pierre Abelard to the Cluniac priory at St MARCEL for his health.

Refs: **16** (2).

P

Peterborough (Cambridgeshire, England). Some 14 miles north of HUNTINGDON and 30 miles north-west of CAMBRIDGE, this industrial city is situated on the River NENE. Although excavations have revealed evidence of prehistoric habitation, the ancient market town grew up around the 7th C. Saxon monastery dedicated to St Peter. It owed its expansion to the coming of the railways in the 19th C., together with the draining of the FENS. Further expansion occurred in the mid-20th C., and today it is an important centre for warehousing and distribution. Priestgate lies to the south of the 15th C. Church of St John the Baptist, a short distance south-west of the cathedral. It runs east from Bourges Boulevard to the Town

Hall, built in the 1930s, and contains some fine Georgian houses.

Novels: Fleeing from RAMSEY ABBEY, Sulien BLOUNT lodged overnight with John HINDE, the silversmith of Peterborough. In October 1143 Sulien told Abbot RADULFUS that he had got GENERY's ring from 'a jeweller in Peterborough'. In November, on his way home from the Fens, Hugh BERINGAR questioned Hinde about the ring: 'The road from the bridge brought him up into the marketplace, which was alive and busy. The burgesses who had elected to stay were justified, the town had so far proved too formidable to be a temptation to [Geoffrey] de MANDEVILLE while there were more isolated and defenceless victims to be found. Hugh found stabling for his horse, and went afoot to look for Priestgate', where he found (John) HINDE'S SHOP.

Refs: **17** (5–6, 10, 12).

Peterborough, Minster of (Cambridgeshire, England). First founded in 655 by Peada, King of Mercia, the monastery was destroyed by the Danes in 870. Athelwold, Bishop of Winchester, refounded the house for Benedictine monks in 960, and in 1116 it was destroyed by fire. The first Norman abbot, Thorold, built the small motte-and-bailey castle on the north side of the church, the remains of which can be still seen today. The Norman part of the present cathedral, dedicated to St Peter, was begun by Abbot John de Sais in 1116. The new church laid out to the north of the old one was consecrated in 1238. Although Peterborough Abbey was dissolved in 1539, there are numerous monastic remains, including the 12th C. west gate, and the 14th C. abbot's gatehouse. The abbey church became the cathedral in 1541. It contains the Anglo-Saxon Hedda Stone, and was the burial place of Catherine of Aragon and Mary, Queen of Scots (the latter's body was removed by James I to WESTMINSTER).

Novels: The shop of John HINDE the PETERBOROUGH silversmith was 'not far from the minster'.

Refs: **17** (6).

Petrus, Brother (*fl.* 1138) (fict.). **Novels:** 'Before High Mass, CADFAEL went to the abbot's kitchen. He was one of a dozen or so people within these walls who were not afraid of Brother Petrus. Fanatics are always frightening, and Brother Petrus was a fanatic, not for his religion or his vocation, those he took for granted, but for his art. His dedicated fire-tinted black hair and black eyes, scorching both with a fiery red. His northern blood boiled like his own cauldron. His temper, barbarian from the borders, was as hot as his own oven. And as hotly as he loved Abbot HERIBERT, for the same reasons he detested Prior ROBERT.' Benedictine monk of SHREWSBURY ABBEY and the cook of both Abbot Heribert and Abbot RADULFUS, Brother Petrus vehemently objected to having to serve Prior Robert while Heribert was away in December 1138. Petrus prepared the dish which, after MEURIG's tamperings, poisoned Gervase BONEL.

Refs: **3** (1–3, 5, 11); **5** (10); **8** (10); **10** (1); **11** (2); **14** (5); **17** (5).

Picard, Lady Agnes (*fl.* 1139) (fict.). **Novels:** 'On the other side rode a lady of about the same years, thin and neat and sharply handsome, dark like her lord, and mounted on a roan mare. She had a pursed, calculating mouth and shrewd eyes, beneath brows tending to a frown even when the mouth smiled. Her head-dress was of the most fashionable, her riding habit had the LONDON cut, and she rode with grace and style, but the very look of her struck with a coldness.' Wife of Sir Godfrid PICARD and aunt of Iveta de Massard (see LUCY), Lady Agnes Picard aided and abetted her husband in the exploitation of Iveta's inheritance. In October 1139 Agnes and Godfrid arrived at SHREWSBURY ABBEY for the arranged marriage of Iveta to Huon de DOMVILLE. While lodging at the abbey, she kept her niece under close guard. After discovering Iveta with Joscelin LUCY in CADFAEL'S

WORKSHOP she contrived with Godfrid to get Lucy dismissed from Domville's service. Discovering that her husband had been killed in the LONG FOREST, Agnes accused Simon AGUILON of both his and DOMVILLE's murder.

Refs: **5** (1–11).

Picard, Sir Godfrid (1094–1139) (fict.). **Novels:** 'A dark, sinewy, olive-faced man perhaps five and forty years old, very splendidly dressed in sombre, glowing colours, and well mounted on a light, fast grey, surely part Arab, thought CADFAEL. The man had plenteous black hair coiling under a plumed cap, and a clipped black beard framing a long-lipped mouth. It was a narrow, closed face, subtle and suspicious.' Sir Godfrid Picard was the husband of Lady Agnes PICARD, and uncle and guardian (from 1131) of Iveta de Massard (see LUCY). He exploited Iveta's inheritance and lands for his own ends and, in order to gain advancement with King STEPHEN through Huon de DOMVILLE's influence, he forced Iveta into a marriage contract with the baron. Picard arrived at SHREWSBURY in October 1139 for Iveta's wedding, but Huon was murdered before the ceremony could take place. He caused Domville to dismiss Joscelin LUCY from his service. After Lucy's escape from the sheriff's men, Godfrid hunted the youth with 'savage determination'. Cadfael discovered Picard's body in the LONG FOREST. He had been challenged to single combat and killed by Guimar de MASSARD, Iveta's grandfather and avenger.

Refs: **5** (1–11).

Pilgrim of Hate. See MEVEREL, Luc.

Plantagenet, Geoffrey. See GEOFFREY, Count of Anjou.

Plantagenet, Henry. See HENRY II, King of England.

Poer, Simeon (*fl.* 1141) (fict.). **Novels:** 'A big man, but so neatly and squarely built that his size was not wholly apparent, he stood with his thumbs in the belt of his plain but ample gown, which was nicely cut and fashioned to show him no nobleman, and no commoner, either, but a solid, respectable, comfortably provided fellow of the middle kind, merchant or tradesman.' Self-styled merchant of GUILDFORD, trickster, gambler and thief, Simeon Poer arrived at SHREWSBURY ABBEY on 19 June 1141, supposedly on a pilgrimage 'for his soul's sake'. He was, in fact, one of a gang of tricksters, who took money and valuables by various means including gambling with loaded dice, picking pockets and cutting purses. It is most likely that Poer had fled north because of some misdemeanour in the south. On 21 June he stole CIARAN's ring and sold it later to Daniel AURIFABER. While gambling under the English Bridge, Poer and his associates (Walter BAGOT, William HALES and John SHURE) were surprised by Hugh BERINGAR and his men. He managed to evade capture and fled into the LONG FOREST with Bagot and Shure. They attacked CIARAN and Matthew (see MEVEREL, Luc), but were captured and taken back to SHREWSBURY. Under lock and key in SHREWSBURY CASTLE, they were brought to trial to answer for more 'than a little cheating in the marketplace'.

Refs: **10** (5–8, 13–15).

Polesworth (Warwickshire, England). Located between Tamworth and Atherstone, this small coal mining town is some 9 miles south-east of LICHFIELD. It lies within a bend of the River Anker, just to the east of the Coventry Canal. Much of the ancient town has now disappeared, although a few half-timbered buildings remain. The vicarage, built in 1868, stands on part of the site of POLESWORTH ABBEY and incorporates segments of the Elizabethan manor house, built by Sir Henry Goodyer after the Dissolution.

Polesworth Abbey (Warwickshire, England). First founded in 827 by King Egbert, the monastery at Polesworth was re-established in *c.* 980 for Benedictine nuns. Shortly after the Norman Conquest, the nuns moved to Oldbury near Atherstone, having been forced to leave Polesworth by Robert Marmion. His son, or possibly grandson, also Robert Marmion, together with his wife, Milicent, refounded the nunnery at Polesworth in *c.*1130. It was dedicated to St Edith (or Editha), who died in *c.*925 at Polesworth and who was probably abbess and certainly the widow of a Northumbrian king. The abbey was dissolved in 1539. The remains include: part of the Abbey Church of St Editha; the 14th C. stone and timber gatehouse; and the effigy of an abbess, dating from *c.*1200, which now rests on a tomb-chest.

Novels: '"Mother MARIANA regularly receives letters from the prioress of our mother house at Polesworth."' The Benedictine nunnery at GODRIC'S FORD was a cell of Polesworth Abbey. CADFAEL predicted in early 1141 that Sister MAGDALEN would become the superior at GODRIC'S FORD first and the prioress of Polesworth after. Bertrade VIVERS took the veil at Polesworth after her husband's death in 1135. Bishop ROGER DE CLINTON sent Sister URSULA and Sister BENEDICTA from Polesworth to FAREWELL for a season, to instruct the novices.

Refs: **5** (8); **9** (1, 8); **11** (14); **13** (3); **15** (7, 10, 13)

Pontaudemer (France). Also spelled Pont-Audemer. Some 30 miles south-east of Le Havre and 14 miles south-west of ROUEN, Pontaudemer is an ancient port on the River Risle, noted for its tanneries in medieval times. Despite World War II damage, much of the old town, built over a network of little waterways, has survived, including the church of St-Ouen, dating from the 11th C. The Norman castle, on a hill to the north of the town, was destroyed by cannon in the 14th C.

Novels: Waleran de BEAUMONT inherited BEAUMONT, BRIONNE and Pontaudemer in NORMANDY on the death of his father, Robert de BEAUMONT (the elder) (d. 1118).

Refs: **19** (4).

Pontesbury (Shropshire, England). DB – Pantesberie: in Rhiwset Hundred; a holding of Roger, Son of Corbet, under Roger de MONTGOMERY. Some 6 miles south-west of SHREWSBURY and 10 miles east of Welshpool (see POOL), this village has expanded rapidly since the mid-1950s owing to housing developments. Once a small agricultural settlement clustered around the medieval manor and church, it became a thriving mining and quarrying community during the Industrial Revolution. The large red sandstone church of St George, dating from the 13th C., was rebuilt in 1829, after the tower had collapsed. Near the church there was once a castle, probably built by the Corbets who owned the manor at the time of the Domesday Book survey. It was destroyed by fire in *c.*1300 and abandoned. *The Anglo-Saxon Chronicle* mentions that in 661 'Cenwalh fought at Pontesbury; and Wulfhere, the son of Penda, laid the country waste as far as Ashdown [in Berkshire]'.

Novels: 'When the company rode out of the town they aimed towards Pontesbury itself, prepared to swerve either northward, to cut across between the raiders and SHREWSBURY, or south-west towards GODRIC'S FORD, according as they got word on the way from scouts sent out before daylight.' In March 1141 the Welsh of Powys, fired by their success at the battle of LINCOLN, began to make further incursions into Shropshire from their advanced outpost at CAUS CASTLE. Led by MADOG AP MEREDITH, they raided and burned the farmsteads in the MINSTERLEY VALLEY, reaching as far as Pontesbury.

Refs: **9** (9, 11, 13).

Pontesbury Hills (Shropshire, England). The Pontesbury Hills (consisting of the volcanic outcrops of Callow Hill, Pontesbury Hill, Pontesford Hill and Earl's Hill) are situated some 7 miles south-west of SHREWSBURY, to the east of MINSTERLEY and immediately south of PONTESBURY and Pontesford. Lead has been mined on the hills for centuries, and it is thought that some of the old workings date back at least to Roman times. Pontesford Hill and Earl's Hill are each crowned by the earthwork remains of an Iron Age hill-fort.

Novels: Among the valuables taken by Julian CRUCE supposedly to the convent at WHERWELL in 1138 was 'a necklet of polished stones from the hills above Pontesbury'.

Refs: **11** (7, 9).

Pool (now Welshpool or Y Trallwng) (Powys, Wales). Just over 16 miles west of SHREWSBURY, Welshpool is an important market town on the west bank of the River SEVERN. Originally called Pool after a nearby lake, the town was given its prefix to show that it was on the Welsh rather than the English side of the border. It was first granted a market charter in 1263. During the 17th C. it was a busy inland port, with goods being transported by barge up the Severn from as far away as BRISTOL. The parish church of St Mary and St Cynfelyn, dating from the 13th C., stands on a hill overlooking the town. Outside, near the porch, is a large stone reputed to have been used as an altar by the Druids and later as a throne by the abbots of Strata Marcella (see below). About a mile south of the town is Powis Castle, built of red sandstone on the site of an earlier fortress known as Y Castell Coch (the Red Castle), which was destroyed by Llywelyn ap Gruffudd in 1275. Powis Castle was the medieval stronghold of the princes of Powys and was rebuilt in stone by Owain (Llywelyn's brother), who adopted the Norman surname of de la Pole. In 1587 the castle was purchased by Sir Edward Herbert, whose descendants became the earls of Powis. After the Restoration the medieval castle and Elizabethan house were transformed into a mansion. It now belongs to the National Trust. There are a number of ancient motte-and-bailey sites in and around Welshpool. Some 2 miles north-east of the town is the site of the Cistercian abbey of Strata Marcella (or Ystrad Marchell), founded in 1170 and dissolved in 1536. The earthwork remains of the medieval abbey are in a field to the east of the A483. In a lay-by, on the opposite side of the road, is a commemorative stone to the now vanished abbey. It was featured in Edith Pargeter's historical trilogy *The Heaven Tree* (1960–63).

Novels: '"This ride that crosses us here is a fine, straight road the old Romans made. Eastward, here to our left, it would bring us to the Severn bridge at ATCHAM. Westward, to our right, it will take you two straight as an arrow for Pool and Wales, or if you find any obstacle on the way, you may bear further south at the end for the ford at MONTGOMERY."' In August 1138 Godith Adeney (see BLUND) and Torold BLUND set out from Shrewsbury with William FITZALAN's treasury, aiming for Pool and eventually France. In February 1145 Hugh BERINGAR warned Abbot RADULFUS that he had received word from Pool of heavy floodwaters coming down the Severn from Wales, and that SHREWSBURY ABBEY could be threatened.

Refs: **2** (9–10); **11** (10); **19** (2).

Popes. See Popes INNOCENT II; LUCIUS II.

Porter, Brother (*fl.* 1138) (fict.). **Novels:** 'The porter was a lay brother, a little surprised at being roused to let in two horsemen at such an hour.' 'The porter was sitting in the doorway of his lodge in the mild sweet air, taking the cool of the evening very pleasurably, but he also had an eye to his duties and the errand he had been given.' 'Brother Porter was not an exclaiming man, and scarcely recognised a crisis when he blundered into one.' A number of monks and lay brothers at SHREWSBURY ABBEY served as porter, being generally responsible for security at the gatehouse and for admissions during both day and night. It was the porter's duty to hand on visitors, once he had established the nature of their business, to the appropriate superior or obedientiary. The chief porter had a lodge in the gatehouse, where he lived. At Shrewsbury Abbey it was a rule that all visitors had to leave their weapons with the porter, to be reclaimed when they departed. See also Brother ALBIN.

Refs: **2** (1, 3, 7, 9–10); **3** (6, 11); **9** (8); **10** (6, 8, 10–11); **11** (1, 3, 6–7); **12** (2–3, 5); **13** (2, 4–5, 10); **14** (1, 5–7); **16** (1, 5–7, 13); **19** (1, 3, 11–13); **20** (16); **RB** (2, 3).

Porter, Brother (*fl.* 1139) (fict.). **Novels:** 'The wicket was lofty, to admit mounted men, and Brother Porter was short and slight, and stooping to shake his skirts clear.' Brother Porter was a Benedictine monk and porter of BROMFIELD Priory.

Refs: **6** (7–8).

Potter's Field (Longner, Shropshire, England) (fict.). DB – Languenare: in Wrockwardine Hundred; land held by the Bishop of CHESTER. (In the mid-12th C. the land was held by Geoffrey, son of Reginald, under the Bishop of COVENTRY and he gave about 15 acres to HAUGHMOND ABBEY.) Although it never existed, the Potter's Field was situated within a loop of the River SEVERN, on its east bank, 2 miles south-east of SHREWSBURY. It lay immediately to the west of the hamlet of PRESTON and at the north-western edge of the extensive grounds of LONGNER Hall.

Novels: '"It has the Severn along the one flank . . . but the bank is high, and the meadow climbs gradually from it, to a headland and a windbreak of trees and bushes along the ridge . . . There were two or three claypits along the river bank, but I believe they are exhausted. The field is known as the Potter's Field."' In September 1143 the Potter's Field became the property of SHREWSBURY ABBEY, after an exchange of land with Haughmond Abbey. Formerly belonging to Eudo BLOUNT (the elder) of Longner, the field passed to Haughmond in October 1142. It was tenanted by RUALD until May 1142, when the potter took the cowl. While ploughing the field in September 1143, the unidentifiable remains of GENERYS were unearthed, buried in a corner under the headland.

Refs: **17** (1–8, 10–14); **19** (1).

Powis Fadog (Clwyd, Wales). The medieval Welsh territory of Powys Fadog is represented today by southern Clywd and a small part of eastern Gwynedd, which includes Bala Lake (or Llyn Tegid). It was subdivided into the commotes of Dinmael, Endeyrnion, CYNLLAITH, Nanheudwy, Ial, Yr Hob and Ystrad Alun, and the cantref of PENLLYN. It also included MAELOR and Maelor Saesneg. Separating Powis Fadog from Powys Wenwynwyn in the south were the BERWYNS.

Novels: In 1144 MADOG AP MEREDITH had 'all the lesser lads of Powys Fadog on a tight rein'.

Refs: **18** (1).

Prees (Shropshire, England). DB – Pres: in HODNET Hundred; land held by the Bishop of CHESTER, who also held it in Anglo-Saxon times. Prees is an ancient hill village, some 13 miles north-east of SHREWSBURY and 4 miles north-east of Wem. There was a settlement at Prees in Saxon times and also a collegiate foundation of monks. The 14th C. parish church of St CHAD stands on the site of a Saxon church. The tower was erected in 1758 and the chancel was rebuilt in 1864, when the entire church was extensively restored. Prees was once surrounded by extensive heathland and this is reflected in the names of neighbouring farms and villages: Heathgates, Heath Farm, Prees Heath, Prees Higher Heath, Prees Lower Heath and Ightfield Heath.

Novels: In 1141 the CRUCE family held several manors in the north-east of Shropshire from the Bishop of Chester, including Prees.

Refs: **11** (4).

Prestcote, Gilbert (the elder) (*c.*1087–1141) (fict.). **Novels:** 'Prestcote was a quiet, laconic knight past fifty, experienced and formidable in battle, cautious in counsel, not a man to go to extremes, but even he was arguing for severity.' Sheriff of Shropshire, husband of Lady Sybilla PRESTCOTE (his second wife), father of Melicent PRESTCOTE (by his first wife) and Gilbert PRESTCOTE (the younger) (by Sybilla), Gilbert Prestcote owned six manors in the Shropshire border region. He was chief aide and liegeman of King STEPHEN and was with him at the siege of SHREWSBURY in August 1138. After the fall of SHREWSBURY CASTLE he was made sheriff of Shropshire. In December Prestcote spent Christmas at WESTMINSTER with the king. He also attended the king's court at Easter 1139 and at Michaelmas. Wounded at the battle of LINCOLN on 2 February 1141, Prestcote was captured by CADWALADR and taken into Wales. In March, after both sides had agreed to an exchange of prisoners, the ailing sheriff was escorted to Shrewsbury. While in SHREWSBURY ABBEY infirmary, Prestcote was murdered by Eliud ap GRIFFITH. He was buried in a tomb in the transept of the abbey church: 'And whatever personal enemies Gilbert Prestcote might have had, he had been a fair and trusted sheriff to this county in general, and the merchant princes were well aware of the relative security and justice they had enjoyed under him, where much of England suffered a far worse fate.' He was succeeded as sheriff of Shropshire by Hugh BERINGAR.

Refs: **2** (1–4, 6, 8, 10–12); **3** (2–10); **4** (1:1–4, 2:1–3, 3:1–2, 4:1–5, 5:1–2, 5:5–6); **5** (3–11); **6** (1–14); **7** (1–3, 12); **8** (1, 3, 5, 9–10, 12); **9** (1–14); **12** (1, 6).

Prestcote, Gilbert (the younger) (b. 1134) (fict.). **Novels:** 'Gilbert the younger, a little bewildered but oblivious of misfortune, played with the child oblates and the two young pupils, and was tenderly shepherded by Brother PAUL, the master of the children. At seven years old he viewed with untroubled tolerance the eccentricities of grown-up people, and could make himself at home wherever his mother unaccountably conveyed him.' Son and heir of Gilbert PRESTCOTE by his second wife, Sybilla, and half-brother of Melicent PRESTCOTE, young Gilbert Prestcote was in SHREWSBURY with his mother and half-sister in February 1141. Gilbert visited his injured father's bedside at SHREWSBURY ABBEY infirmary in March. After his father's burial, Gilbert was taken to his mother's favourite border manor.

Refs: **9** (2, 5–6, 8–9).

Prestcote, Melicent (b. 1123) (fict.). **Novels:** 'She was the very opposite of small, sharp and dark, being tall and slender like a silver birch, delicately oval of face, and dazzlingly fair. The sun in her uncovered, waving hair glittered as she hesitated an instant on the doorstone, and shivered lightly at the embrace of the frosty air.' Melicent Prestcote was the daughter of Gilbert PRESTCOTE (the elder) by his first wife, stepdaughter of Sybilla PRESTCOTE and half-sister of Gilbert PRESTCOTE (the younger). While staying at SHREWSBURY CASTLE in February 1141, Melicent met and fell in love with the Welsh prisoner ELIS AP CYNAN. Realising that she would never see Elis again when her father returned to SHREWSBURY, she was determined to find a way out of their dilemma. What made matters worse was that her father hated the Welsh. After her father had been murdered, Melicent mistakenly accused Elis of the crime. Shortly after, intent on taking the veil, she asked Sister MAGDALEN to take her to the nunnery at GODRIC'S FORD. At the battle of Godric's Ford in March, Melicent witnessed Elis's bravery in facing his fellow countrymen alone. After he had been wounded, she rushed to his side and they were reconciled. She and Elis drugged Eliud ap GRIFFITH and arranged an escort to take him to TREGEIRIOG. Melicent returned to her step-mother, until such time as Elis could formally ask for her hand in marriage.

Refs: **9** (2, 4–6, 8–11, 13–15).

Prestcote, Lady Sybilla (b. *c.*1107) (fict.). **Novels:** 'Her lord was dead, his overlord the king a prisoner; there was no one to force her into an unwelcome match. She was many years younger than her lost husband, and had a dower of her own, and good enough looks to make her a fair bargain. She would live, and do well enough.' Second wife of Gilbert PRESTCOTE (the elder), mother of Gilbert PRESTCOTE (the younger) and step-mother of Melicent PRESTCOTE, Lady

P

Sybilla Prestcote arrived at SHREWSBURY in February 1141 to await her husband's return from captivity in Wales. She was widowed in March, when Gilbert was murdered. Shortly after she returned to her favourite manor somewhere close to the Welsh border. It seemed that she would not stand in the way of Melicent's marriage to Elis ap CYNAN.

Refs: 9 (2, 4–6, 8–9, 14).

Preston (Shropshire, England). DB – although Preston is not mentioned in the survey it was part of the manor of UPTON: in Wrockwardine Hundred; a holding of Reginald the Sheriff under Roger de MONTGOMERY. Formerly called Preston Boats or Preston on Severn. According to Eyton's *Antiquities of Shropshire* (1860): 'There was a Weir or Fishery here from a very remote period, and which to this day occupies and commands the principal Channel of the Severn by the prescription of more than seven centuries. The said Weir or Fishery being in the demesne of the first William FITZALAN, was granted to him about the year 1135 to the support of Fulk, Prior of Haughmond, and his Brethren.' Eyton also mentions that in *c.* 1240-50 Richard de Preston 'gave to HAUGHMOND ABBEY an acre of land in the field of Preston, whence the Canons might take and draw marl for the improvement of their land at UFFINGTON'. By 1255 Preston was a distinct manor of half a hide in Bradford Hundred called Preston juxta le Goord; held by Stephen de Stanton under John FitzAlan. The village is some 3 miles east of SHREWSBURY and ½ mile north of LONGNER.

Novels: ADLHELM owned 'a half yardland by Preston'. CADFAEL visited the 'tiny hamlet' in February 1145 to talk to Aldhelm, but found that he was not at home. A servant of the parish priest at UPTON visited 'his brother's family at Preston once a week'.

Refs: **19** (2–6, 8, 10, 12).

Priest of Saint Chad's (*fl.* 1141) (fict.). **Novels:** In December 1141 an unnamed priest of ST CHAD'S CHURCH buried Eluned NEST in the churchyard.

Refs: **12** (3).

Priest of Saint Mary's (*fl.* 1140) (fict.). **Novels:** In May 1140 an unnamed priest of ST MARY'S CHURCH took the last confession of Dame Juliana AURIFABER.

Refs: **7** (10–11).

Priestgate. See PETERBOROUGH.

Provence (France). Situated in the extreme south-east corner of France, this ancient region was bounded in general by the Mediterranean in the south, the Lower Rhone in the west, and the ALPS in the east; however, in the early Middle Ages the region extended further westward and northward. Provence became a separate kingdom in 855 under Charles, the third son of the Frankish emperor Lothair I. On Charles' death in 863, Provence was seized by his elder brother, the emperor Louis II, King of Italy. In 934 Rudolf II of Jurane Burgundy was elected King of Provence, and in 1032 Burgundy–Provence, the Kingdom of Arles, became part of the Holy Roman Empire. It was the local counts of Arles and later Provence, however, who dominated the region, successfully repelling an Arab invasion in 983. By 1113 Provence had passed to the House of Barcelona and was ruled by the Spanish from Catalonia until well into the 13th C. Provence became part of France in 1481.

Novels: In June 1143 Canon GERBERT warned Abbot RADULFUS about the malignant spread of Manichean heresy in regions like Provence and LANGUEDOC. See also MANES. RÉMY of Pertuis, 'a genuine troubadour', came to SHREWSBURY ABBEY in February 1145 from the 'heart of Provence', with his two attendants, BÉNEZET and DAALNY.

Refs: **16** (5); **19** (1–2, 11–13).

Pulley (Shropshire, England). DB – Polelie: in Condover Hundred; a divided manor: one part held by Theodulf under Roger de MONTGOMERY; the other held by Edith under Ralph of Mortimer (it is thought that Edith was Queen Edith, wife of EDWARD THE CONFESSOR; her manor was probably in the parish of Meole Brace [see BRACE MEOLE] in which Mortimer also had a manor). Pulley is a small hamlet, just under 2 miles south of SHREWSBURY, between Bayston Hill (see BEISTAN) and Meole Brace.

Novels: 'The talk of SHREWSBURY found its way out here softened and distanced into a kind of folk-tale, hardly bearing at all on real life. The reality here was the demesne, its fields, its few labourers, the ditched coppice from which the children fended off the goats at pasture, the plough-oxen, and the enshrouding forest.' SHREWSBURY ABBEY used to maintain an old grange in the LONG FOREST, out beyond Pulley. In August 1138, it was looked after by Lay Brothers LOUIS and ANSELM. CADFAEL took Hugh BERINGAR there, and later Godith Adeney (see BLUND) and Torold BLUND. John and Cecily STURY lived in 'the hamlet of Pulley, a minor manor of the Mortimers' (see MORTIMER, Hugh de). John farmed the demesne as steward. In June 1142 Niall BRONZE-SMITH visited the family. On his way home, Niall came across Judith PERLE and Vivian HYNDE, and followed them towards GODRIC'S FORD.

Refs: **2** (6, 9); **13** (2–4, 10–11).

Purton Castle (Wiltshire, England). This large village lies some 4 miles north-west of Swindon and 4 miles south of CRICKLADE. St Mary's Church dates from the 12th C. and is unusual in that it has two towers, one with a spire and the other with pinnacles. Inside are medieval wall paintings. The castle named 'Burtuna', held by King STEPHEN and mentioned in the *Gesta Stephani* (ed. Potter, 1976), is thought to be Purton. Ringsbury Camp, south-west of the town, is an Iron Age hill-fort.

Novels: Purton Castle was one of a circle of castles, centred on Cricklade, and held by King Stephen in December 1145. It was one of Philip FITZROBERT's garrisons.

Refs: **20** (6, 10, 14).

R

Radulfus, Abbot (d. *c.* 1148) (hist.). Also called Ranulph or Ralph. Radulfus succeeded HERIBERT as abbot of SHREWSBURY ABBEY some time after 1137. On his death in *c.* 1148 he was succeeded by Prior ROBERT PENNANT.

Novels: 'They had to amend their ways . . . since Abbot Radulfus had taken over the rudder of this cloistral vessel, for he was a man who brooked no slipshod dealings, and would have all his crew as meticulous as himself.' 'The abbot was a man of the world and of the Church, of wide experience, but not so wide as to include those manifestations of violence which were an open book to Brother CADFAEL who had been soldier and sailor besides. Rare among men of wide experience, Radulfus knew precisely the gaps that were left, and was willing to be instructed. The honour and integrity of his house was his prime concern, and in that criterion pure justice was implied.' 'Radulfus was tall, erect, vigorous, with strong, austere features, magisterially calm. When needed he could blaze, and those scorched drew back advisedly, but his fire was always in control.' Radulfus was a Benedictine monk and abbot of Shrewsbury Abbey.

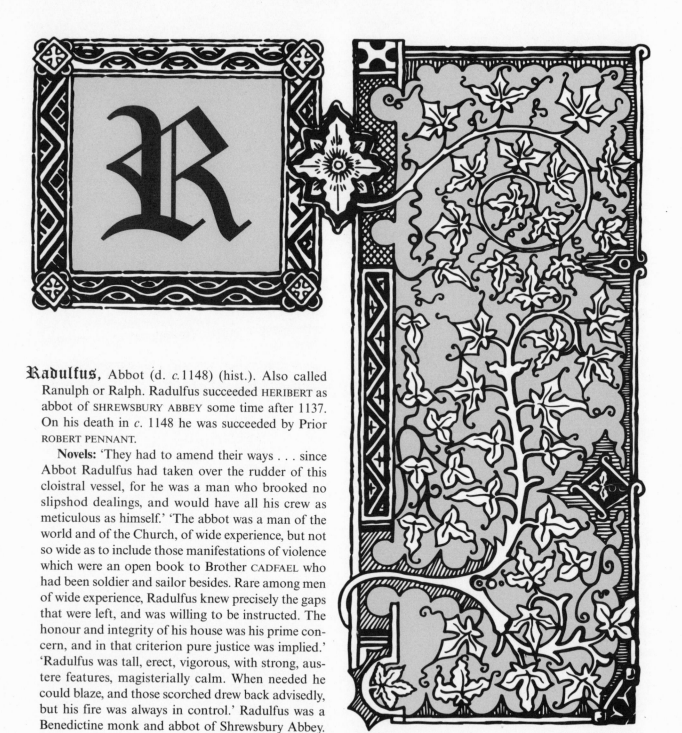

He was appointed abbot by the legatine council under Cardinal-Bishop ALBERIC of Ostia, and replaced Heribert in late December 1138. On 30 July 1139 a delegation from the Guild Merchant asked Radulfus to allocate a proportion of the abbey's rent from St Peter's Fair for the repair of the town walls and streets. Radulfus was unhappy about taking any more children as oblates into the cloister. In April 1141 he attended a legatine council at WINCHESTER and another, in December, at WESTMINSTER. Returning from the latter, Radulfus brought Father AILNOTH, the new parish priest of HOLY CROSS, with him. In October 1142 he refused to return young Richard LUDEL to the custody of his grandmother, Dame Dionisia LUDEL. Among those under Radulfus's guardianship were: Edwin GURNEY, Iveta de Massard (see LUCY), and Richard Ludel. In November 1145 Radulfus gave Cadfael leave to go with Hugh BERINGAR to COVENTRY, saying: '"If you go further and delay longer, then you go as your own man, none of mine. Without my leave or blessing."' Cadfael's penance ended when the abbot said: '"It is enough!"'

Refs: **3** (11); **4** (1:1–3, 2:1, 2:3, 3:1, 4:1, 4:4, 5:3, 5:5); **5** (1, 3–6, 10–11); **6** (1–2); **7** (1–4, 7, 11, 13–14); **8** (1–8, 10–13); **9** (1–2, 4–9, 15); **10** (1–2, 5–13, 15); **11** (1–3, 5, 7, 10, 12–14); **12** (1–3, 5–13); **13** (1–7, 9–12, 14); **14** (1–14); **15** (1–4, 6); **16** (1–7, 9–10, 12–15); **17** (1–9, 11–14); **18** (1, 14); **19** (1–13); **20** (1–2, 6, 14, 16); **RB** (3).

Ragnhild (*fl.* 1055) (hist.). Also spelled Ragnhildr or Rhagnell. Mother of GRIFFITH AP CYNAN and grandmother of OWAIN GWYNEDD and CADWALADR, she was the grand-daughter of SITRIC SILKBEARD, King of Dublin. Ragnhild married Cynan ap Iago while he was in exile in the Danish Kingdom of DUBLIN.

Novels: Owain Gwynedd's 'grandmother had been a princess of the Danish kingdom of Dublin, more Norse than Irish'.

Refs: **9** (3); **18** (1, 9).

Ramsey (Cambridgeshire, England). Some 8 miles north-east of HUNTINGDON and 19 miles north-west of CAMBRIDGE, this small fenland town grew up around the Anglo-Saxon abbey. After the Dissolution the town declined in importance, and in 1665 the population was decimated by the plague. Due to several major fires in the 17th and 18th C. most of the buildings are no older than the 19th C. During the Middle Ages a watercourse, serving the abbey dock, ran down the middle of the wide main street, or the Great Whyte. The town is linked to the River NENE and Great Ouse by the Middle Level Navigations. Ramsey derives its name from the Old English words *hramsa*, meaning 'wild garlic', and *eg*, meaning 'island'.

Novels: 'CADFAEL could not imagine that this confrontation would be over easily or quickly. He had never seen Ramsey, but Sulien [BLOUNT]'s description of it, an island with its own natural and formidable moat, spanned by only one narrow causeway, defensible by a mere handful of men, held out little hope of an easy conquest. And though de Mandeville's marauders must sally forth from their fortress to do their plundering, they had the advantage of being local men, used to all the watery fastnesses in that bleak and open countryside, and able to withdraw into the marshes at any hostile approach.' Geoffrey de MANDEVILLE and his followers seized Ramsey on 30 September 1143 and turned it into an island fortress. Only after de Mandeville's death in September 1144 did life in the town return to 'any kind of normality'.

Refs: **17** (3–4, 9); **19** (4).

R

Ramsey Abbey (Cambridgeshire, England). Founded in 969 by Aylwyn (or Ailwyn), Ealdorman of East Anglia and foster-brother of the English King Edgar, Ramsey Abbey became the tenth wealthiest house in England and flourished as a centre of learning. On his death in 986, Aethelstan Mannsonne left substantial estates to the monastery. His son, Eadnoth, was the first abbot (*c.*1000–6) and founded a nunnery at Chatteris, 7 miles to the east, where his sister, Alfwenna, became the first prioress. English abbots continued to be appointed until 1113, forty-seven years after the Norman Conquest. In *c.*1143 Abbot WALTER was replaced by the monks, who were themselves expelled from the abbey by Geoffrey de MANDEVILLE. He converted it into an unassailable island fortress from which his followers ravaged and plundered the FENS. After Mandeville's death in 1144, Walter regained control of the abbey, which had been badly damaged and impoverished by Mandeville's marauders. The fortunes of the Benedictine abbey were restored over the succeeding centuries, and at the Dissolution in 1539 the mother-house with its cells at Modney and St Ives was valued at £1,716 12*s*. 3*d*. Although most of the abbey was demolished for its stone, part of the remains have been incorporated into the 16th C. house which now occupies the site, including the 13th C. Lady Chapel. The ornate, late-15th C. gatehouse is in the care of the National Trust. St Thomas à Becket's Church is thought to have originally been the abbey infirmary, built in *c*.1185. It became a church in the early 13th C. and the parish church in *c*.1875. The embattled west tower was added in 1672.

Novels: 'They drove us out into the court and out of the gate, seizing everything we had but our habits. Some part of the enclave they fired. Some of us who showed defiance, though without violence, they beat or killed. Some who lingered in the neighbourhood though outside the island, they shot at with arrows. They have turned our house into a den of bandits and torturers, and filled it with weapons and armed men, and from that stronghold they go forth to rob and pillage and slay. In August 1143 Sulien BLOUNT of LONGNER was a novice at Ramsey Abbey under Abbot Walter. On 30 September Geoffrey de Mandeville seized the town, drove the monks out of the abbey and turned it into a fortress. Abbot Walter ventured alone into their camp the following day and excommunicated Mandeville and his followers. He was allowed to leave unharmed and took most of the brothers to one of their distant manors. Before the end of 1144, news reached Abbot Walter that Mandeville's deathbed charter had given his monastery back to him. On his return to Ramsey, Walter found the 'monastic buildings were a mere shell, the lands untilled, the manors the house had formerly possessed handed out to thieves and vagabonds, all its treasures stripped away. The walls they said bled for very grief.' Immediately the abbot and his brothers set to work on the restoration of the house and church, sending out 'an urgent appeal for help in alms, material and labour to speed the work of rebuilding and refurnishing the sacred place.' To that end Sub-Prior HERLUIN and Brother TUTILO, escorted by three lay servants, two of which were NICOL and ROGER, journeyed to SHREWSBURY in February 1145. The 'two emissaries from Ramsey' also went to EVESHAM and WORCESTER.

Refs: **17** (1, 4, 6); **19** (Prologue, 1–13).

Rannilt (*fl.* 1140) (fict.). **Novels:** 'A skinny little girl laboured at feeding a sluggish fire and heaving a great pot to the hook over it. CADFAEL had caught a glimpse of the child once before, all great dark eyes in a pale, grubby face, and a tangle of dark hair. Some poor maidservant's by-blow by her master, or her master's son, or a passing guest. For all the parsimony in this household, the girl could have fallen into worse hands. She was at least fed, and handed down cast-off clothing, and if the old matriarch was grim and frightening, Susanna was quiet and calm, no scold and no tyrant.' Welsh wife of LILIWIN, singer, illegitimate child of some poor maidservant, and former servant of Susanna AURIFABER and the AURIFABER household in SHREWSBURY, Rannilt was unschooled and half-wild. She met and fell in love with Liliwin at Daniel AURIFABER's wedding feast in May 1140. Susanna found Rannilt in the kitchen crying over Liliwin and allowed her to go to SHREWSBURY ABBEY to see him. While in hiding inside the church, Rannilt and Liliwin made love. She returned home late that evening, secretly escorted by Liliwin. Rannilt overheard the bitter exchange between Susanna and Dame Juliana AURIFABER over Walter AURIFABER's valuables, which had been stolen. Realising that her maid had seen the bundle containing the stolen valuables, Susanna decided to take Rannilt with her to FRANKWELL, where she planned to meet IESTYN and flee with him and their booty into Wales. Although Rannilt helped carry the goods, she was unaware that her mistress planned to kill her. Before Susanna and Iestyn could leave, however, they were surrounded by the sheriff's men and Rannilt was held hostage at knife-point. She was rescued by Liliwin. Aline BERINGAR welcomed the maidservant into her care, 'and undertook to provide and instruct her in everything a bride should possess and know'. A week later, in May 1140, Rannilt and Liliwin were married by Father ADAM at the parish altar of HOLY CROSS. Afterwards, they set out together on the road to LICHFIELD.

Refs: **7** (1–14); **19** (1).

Ranulf (*c.*1100–53), Earl of Chester (hist.). Also spelled Rannulf, Randulf or Ralph. Ranulf de Gernons was the son and heir of Ranulf le Meschin, Earl of Chester, whom he succeeded as the 4th Earl in *c.*1129. At the height of his power he ruled over a realm that covered almost a third of England, represented by a great triangle between CHESTER, LINCOLN and COVENTRY. He was a key participant in the long fratricidal civil war, which broke out after the death of HENRY I, between King STEPHEN and the Empress MAUD. He initially took the side of the empress for two reasons: his father's honour of Carlisle, which he had vowed to recover, had been granted by Stephen to the son of the King of Scotland; and he had married MAUD, the daughter of ROBERT of Gloucester, the empress's half-brother. In 1140, with his half-brother William of ROUMARE, Ranulf seized and occupied LINCOLN Castle, and, at the battle of Lincoln on 2 February 1141, helped Robert of Gloucester take Stephen captive. Although he claimed allegiance to the empress, it is more likely that Ranulf was trying to fulfil his ambition of becoming the powerful magnate of a kingdom, fortified by a chain of castles, which stretched right across England from coast to coast. Ranulf was arrested by Stephen at NORTHAMPTON in 1146 and forced to surrender all his castles. On his release, like Geoffrey de MANDEVILLE before him, Ranulf plunged into an orgy of violence and destruction, attacking Coventry in 1147. When the empress's son, Henry Plantagenet (see HENRY II), landed in England in 1149, Stephen bought Ranulf's allegiance by granting him the city and castle of Lincoln, besides several other castles, towns and estates. In his *Antiquities of Shropshire* (1860) Eyton wrote: 'Between the years 1151 and 1152 Ranulf, Earl of Chester . . . confirmed the Monks of SHREWSBURY in the possession of all their lands between the Ribble and the Mersey.' Ranulf died on 16 December 1153, poisoned it was believed by William Peverel of NOTTINGHAM. He was buried in St Werburg's Abbey at Chester.

Novels: 'Earl Ranulf of Chester, was certainly one of the most powerful men in the kingdom, virtually king himself of an immense palatine where his writ ran, and no other. But for that very reason he was less likely to feel the need to declare for either side in the contention for the throne. Himself supreme, and unlikely ever to be threatened in his own possessions by either Maud or Stephen, he could afford to sit back and watch his own borders, not merely with a view to preserving them intact, rather to extending them. A land at odds with itself offers opportunities, as well as threats.' Just before Christmas 1140 Stephen officially recognised Ranulf as Earl of Chester 'in name as well as in fact'. In return the earl pledged the king his 'unshakeable loyalty'. Two days later, Ranulf and William of Roumare seized the king's castle at Lincoln, entering it by subterfuge. Early the following year, Stephen marched north with his army to retrieve his garrison. Ranulf slipped out of the castle to seek the support of Robert of Gloucester. On 2 February, at the battle of Lincoln, Stephen was captured. In 1143, Ranulf and Stephen agreed to a truce: 'An agreement to put off contention to a more convenient time'. 'Seeking to inveigle himself back into the king's favour,' Ranulf met Stephen in October 1145, at STAMFORD, where he pledged his allegiance. The following month, 'all complacent smiles', he attended the conference at Coventry.

Refs: **1** (3); **3** (8); **4** (1:1, 4:1, 5:2–3, 5:6); **8** (1, 3, 10, 12); **9** (1–3, 9–10, 12); **10** (1); **11** (1); **12** (1, 6); **14** (1); **15** (3); **16** (1, 15); **17** (4, 9–10); **19** (2, 5, 11); **20** (1–2, 4).

Raven in the Foregate. See AILNOTH, Father.

Rea Brook. See MEOLE BROOK.

R

Rea Valley. See MINSTERLEY; MINSTERLEY VALLEY.

Reading (Berkshire, England). Some 36 miles west of the centre of LONDON and 30 miles north-east of WINCHESTER, this ancient market town lies on the rivers THAMES and Kennet. It was occupied by the Danes in 871, and during STEPHEN's reign it possessed a castle, the only remains of which is a mound in Forbury Gardens, near the ruins of READING ABBEY. Due essentially to its famous and powerful abbey, Reading became an important centre, favoured by kings, often chosen as a meeting place for Parliament, and noted for its cloth. The town suffered during the Civil War and expanded rapidly in the 19th C. Today, in addition to being a large university town, Reading is an important industrial and market centre.

Novels: The Empress MAUD did not attend the legatine council at WINCHESTER in early April 1141, but moved around the region, 'to Reading and other places'. In September, after the sack of WHERWELL Abbey, the abbess and some of the nuns fled to a manor near Reading.

Refs: **5** (4, 6); **8** (4, 6); **10** (2); **11** (6).

Reading Abbey (Berkshire, England). Founded in 1121 by HENRY I, who was buried in the church, the Benedictine abbey at READING was dedicated to St Mary and St John the Evangelist. It stood on the site of an Anglo-Saxon nunnery and had connections with CLUNY until the mid-12th C. LEOMINSTER Priory was among its dependencies and remained so until the Dissolution. The abbey became one of the most powerful and wealthiest houses in England and it was here, on a number of important occasions, that Parliament met. It was dissolved in 1539 by Henry VIII, and the last abbot executed. All that now survives of the monastery are parts of St Lawrence's Church, remnants of the cloistral buildings and the much restored inner gate-house. In addition to the Benedictine abbey there was a Franciscan friary, founded in 1233. After the Dissolution the friary church became partly the town hall and partly an almshouse. Having been almost entirely rebuilt, it is once again in use as a church.

Novels: Brother ADAM, Benedictine monk of Reading, arrived at SHREWSBURY on 17 June 1141. He had been sent by his abbot with a mission to their daughter house of Leominster.

Refs: **10** (3, 16).

Recordine (now Wrockwardine) (Shropshire, England). DB – Recordine: in Wrockwardine Hundred; land held by Roger de MONTGOMERY himself. Some 8 miles east of SHREWSBURY and about 2 miles north of the WREKIN, Wrockwardine is thought to derive its name from Wrekin Worthen or the 'village under the Wrekin'. Originally a Saxon foundation, St Peter's church was given to Shrewsbury Abbey by Roger de Montgomery. The present church dates from the 12th C. By the beginning of the following century a new crossing tower, transepts and chancel had been added and early in the 14th C. the top of the tower was embattled and the west end rebuilt. The north chapel was constructed in the late 14th C. and the south chapel in the 15th C. The church is a prominent landmark on the flat plain between Shrewsbury and Wellington. Less than a mile south-east of the village is Orleton Hall, a late Georgian house built on a much earlier core. The timber-framed gatehouse was erected in 1588, but altered later. The manor was held by Earl Roger de Montgomery.

Novels: At Shrewsbury Abbey, in Spring 1140, Jacob of BOULDON brought William REDE's attention to an erasure in the 'leiger' book, referring to a carucate of land in Recordine. It was disputed land for a while, when the heir tried to reclaim it from the abbey.

Refs: **RB** (3).

Red Sea (Egypt, Sudan, Ethiopia, Yemen, and Saudi Arabia). Linking the Mediterranean to the Indian Ocean, by way of the Straits of Bab el-Mandeb and the Gulf of Aden in the south, and the Gulf of Suez and the Suez Canal in the north, the Red Sea separates north-east Africa from the Arabian Peninsula. Some 1,300 miles long, the sea's maximum width is 190 miles. It is remarkable in the fact that it does not receive the waters of a single river. In biblical history the Red Sea is chiefly connected with Exodus, when the waters miraculously parted to allow Moses and the children of Israel to cross on dry land. The pursuing Egyptians were drowned when the two walls of water collapsed upon them.

Novels: 'But the congestion was miraculously stricken apart like the Red Sea when [King] STEPHEN came striding through.'

Refs: **20** (4).

Rede, Edward (b. 1118) (fict.). **Novels:** also called Eddi. 'A tall, shock-haired, dark-eyed youth, hunched of shoulder just now, and grim of face, but admittedly very quiet in movement, and low-voiced.' Son of William and Mistress REDE, Edward Rede was named after EDWARD THE CONFESSOR. In Spring 1140, he was in debt from gambling. He was also fined for brawling in the street. After his father had been knocked on the head and thrown into the River SEVERN, Eddi visited him in SHREWSBURY ABBEY infirmary. Pretending to be Rhodri FYCHAN the Less, Eddi was attacked by Jacob of BOULDON in Roger CLOTHIER's loft. He managed to overpower his assailant and force him to confess to robbery and attempted murder.

Refs: **RB** (3).

Rede, Mistress (*fl.* 1140) (fict.). **Novels:** Wife of William REDE and mother of Edward REDE, Mistress Rede was a 'brisk birdlike' woman.

Refs: **RB** (3).

Rede, William (b. *c.*1085) (fict.). **Novels:** Also called Will. 'He was a querulous, argumentative man in his fifties, who, if you said white to him, would inevitably say black, and bring documentary evidence to back up his contention.' Father of Edward REDE and husband of Mistress REDE, William Rede was the elder of the abbey's lay servants, who collected their rents and the tolls due from merchants and craftsmen bringing their goods to the annual fair and Brother MATTHEW's chief steward at SHREWSBURY ABBEY. In Spring 1140, while collecting the town rents, he was attacked, robbed and thrown unconscious into the River SEVERN by Jacob of BOULDON. Within moments, William was fished out of the river by MADOG OF THE DEAD-BOAT and taken to the abbey infirmary, where he made a full recovery. The Redes lived in the vicinity of ST MARY'S WATER-LANE in the parish of St Mary's (see ST MARY'S CHURCH).

Refs: **17** (7); **RB** (3).

Redvers, Baldwin de (d. 1155), Earl of Devon (hist.). Eldest son and heir of Richard de Redvers (or Reviers) and husband of Adeliza, he never accepted STEPHEN's claim to the English throne, and was consistently loyal to the Empress MAUD. After rebelling against the king in 1136, he and his men were besieged in Exeter Castle, but eventually negotiated terms and were allowed to leave. Baldwin and his family fled to the Isle of Wight, from where they were driven into exile, to be warmly received by GEOFFREY, Count of Anjou. In 1138, while attacking Stephen's adherents in NORMANDY, Baldwin was captured by Ingelram de Say. The following year, just before the Empress Maud's arrival in England, Baldwin landed with a strong force at WAREHAM, and successfully held Corfe Castle against the king. He became the Earl of Devon at some time before June 1141, and was with the empress at the siege of WINCHESTER in August and September, when he was styled the Earl of Exeter (*Gesta Stephani*, ed. Potter, 1976). He was buried in Quarr Abbey on the Isle of Wight, which he founded in 1132, and was succeeded by his son, Richard.

Novels: Earl of Devon and a distant relative of

R

Jovetta de MONTORS, he was a powerful adherent of the Empress Maud. In December 1145 Baldwin was with the empress in GLOUCESTER, and also at the siege of La MUSARDERIE.

Refs: **20** (3, 10–11).

Reginald, Brother (*fl.* 1138) (fict.). **Novels:** Benedictine monk of SHREWSBURY ABBEY, Brother Reginald, 'who was old and deformed in the joints', was in the abbey infirmary in August 1138.

Refs: **2** (7).

Reinold (b. *c.*1095) (fict.). **Novels:** 'A thickset, bearded, well-fleshed man of about fifty, in dark homespun and a shoulder cape and capuchon of green, but all their colours faintly veiled and dusted over from long professional days spent in an air misty with the milling of grain.' Miller at WINSTONE, and brother of NAN, Reinold helped Olivier de BRETAGNE get Philip FITZROBERT out of La MUSARDERIE, by pretending that the unconscious man was his dead nephew. Having been given permission to take the body away for burial 'among his own people', Reinold loaded FitzRobert onto his cart. A few miles from CIRENCESTER, Reinold returned to 'his business and his family', leaving Olivier to take FitzRobert to safety at CIRENCESTER ABBEY. His cart was later returned.

Refs: **20** (13–15).

Remigius, Saint (*c.*438–533) (hist.) (f.d. 1 October). Also called Remi or Remy, and Apostle of the Franks. Born near Laon (now in Picardy, France) of Gaulish parentage, Remigius was appointed Bishop of Reims while in his early twenties. He is famous for the conversion and baptism of Clovis I, King of the Franks, in *c.*496. An eloquent preacher, Remigius is said to have also baptised the king's family and three thousand of his followers.

Novels: 'Brother ELYAS was lying mute and still, while a young brother read to him from the life of Saint Remigius.'

Refs: **6** (4).

Rémy of Pertuis (b. *c.*1093) (fict.). **Novels:** 'Rémy of Pertuis was a man of fifty or so, of striking appearance, a gentleman who valued his looks and presentation. CADFAEL . . . had not so far had occasion to pay him much attention, but if [Brother] ANSELM respected him and approved his musical conscience he might be worth studying. A fine, burnished head of russet hair and clipped beard. Good carriage and a body very handsomely appointed, fur lining his cloak, gold at his belt.' '"But what," wondered Cadfael, "is a minstrel from the heart of PROVENCE doing here in the heart of England? And plainly no mere jongleur, but a genuine troubadour. He's wandered far from home, surely?" And yet, he thought, why not? The patrons on whom such artists depend are becoming now as much English as French, or Norman, or Breton, or Angevin. They have estates both here and overseas, as well seek them here as there. And the very nature of the troubadour, after all, is to wander and venture, as the Galician word *trobar*, from which they take their name, though it has come to signify to create poetry and music, literally means find. Those who *find* – seek and find out the poetry and the music both, these are troubadours. And if their art is universal, why should they not be found everywhere?' Rémy was a Provençal troubadour, 'obviously of some wealth and repute'. In February 1145, in search of a powerful patron, he was on his way north to CHESTER with his two servants, BÉNEZET and DAALNY, when he was delayed at SHREWSBURY ABBEY by a lame horse. He was given some medicine for his 'hoarse and dry' throat by Cadfael. His horse having recovered, Rémy was about to leave Shrewsbury when the providential arrival of Robert de BEAUMONT caused him to think again: 'Such a patron would be complete protection, a life of comparative luxury, and a very congenial employment.' 'Why abandon an opportunity present and promising, to go after a distant and unproven one?' Playing 'his cards cleverly', Rémy persuaded the earl to find 'room in his household for so good a poet and maker of songs'. Although Rémy was forced to leave for Leicester without either Daalny or Bénezet, Robert promised that he should have the means to find 'others as gifted'. Among Rémy's instruments was a Saracen *ud*, brought back by his father from the Crusade.

Refs: **19** (2–3, 5, 7–8, 11–13).

Renfred (b. *c.*1111) (fict.). **Novels:** '"The Saxon pair are clever and subtle, but clever enough to know when they have a good lord, and loyal enough to be grateful for him."' Saxon brother of WULFRIC, Renfred was bowman and servant to both Humphrey and Reginald CRUCE at LAI. Renfred, together with Wulfric, John BONDE and Adam HERIET, escorted Julian CRUCE south to ANDOVER in August 1138. He was taller than his brother and 'used the new long-bow, drawn to the shoulder'.

Refs: **11** (4, 6–8,10–11).

Renold, Walter (b. *c.*1097) (fict.). **Novels:** Also called Wat. '"For every mass of ours they'll be celebrating the Gamblers' Mass elsewhere. And by all means let the fools throw their money after their sense, so the odds be fair. But Wat knows a loaded throw when he sees one."' Taverner at the ABBEY FOREGATE in SHREWSBURY, with at least one son, Walter Renold had been a rover in his younger days. He sold Turstan FOWLER a quart flask of strong geneva spirits in August 1139. In June 1141 he alerted Hugh BERINGAR to the presence of the crooked gamblers: Simeon POER, William HALES, John SHURE and Walter BAGOT. During St Peter's Fair in August 1143, Wat allowed BRITRIC THE PEDLAR to store his goods in his loft. See also WAT'S TAVERN.

Refs: **4** (2:2–3, 4:5, 5:1–2); **10** (5, 7); **17** (7).

Reynald, Fulke (*fl.* 1139) (fict.). **Novels:** '"There is a lay superior, who lives in the Foregate, a decent man and a good manager."' Steward of SHREWSBURY ABBEY and lay superior of the hospital of ST GILES, Fulke Reynald lived in the ABBEY FOREGATE.

Refs: **5** (1, 5–6, 9); **8** (7); **11** (1).

Rhine, River (Switzerland, Germany, Netherlands). Rising in the Swiss ALPS as two small headstreams, the 820-mile-long Rhine flows north-west through Germany to Arnhem in the Netherlands, where it splits into a number of branches each of which eventually enter the North Sea. Its two headwaters, the Vorderrhein and Hinterrhein, unite near Chur to form the Rhine proper, which enters Lake Constance before meandering west and then north to Strasbourg. From the inland port, the river passes through cities such as Bonn, Cologne and Düsseldorf before heading west along the Nieuwe Maas River, one of its tributaries, to the Dutch seaport of Rotterdam. The longest river in western Europe, much of the river is navigable and is linked by a network of canals to the valleys of the Maas, Rhône-Saône, Marne and Danube. The Rhineland is an historical region lying along the river, east of the modern German frontier with France, Luxembourg, Belgium and the Netherlands.

Novels: In 1143 Canon GERBERT warned Abbot RADULFUS about 'malignant wandering preachers' active on the Rhine, and in FLANDERS, France and LOMBARDY, 'who cry out against Holy Church and her priesthood, that we are corrupt and greedy, that the Apostles lived simply, in holy poverty'.

Refs: **16** (5).

Rhisiart (*c.*1087–1137) (fict.). **Novels:** '"He speaks his mind. An open-hearted, open-natured man, with a temper soon up and soon down, and never a grudge in him, but try and move him when his mind's made up, and you're leaning on SNOWDON."' 'He had the voice that might have been expected from him, large melodious and deep, a voice that sang what it felt, and waited for thought afterwards, to find that the thought had been there already in the feeling.' Welsh lord in GWYTHERIN, Rhisiart was a widower and father of SIONED. MEURICE was his steward and brother-in-law. Rhisiart took ENGELARD, an outlander, into his service in 1135 and set him up in his croft. He vehemently and openly opposed Prior ROBERT's plans to remove the relics of St WINIFRED from Gwytherin. He was murdered by Brother COLUMBANUS in May 1137 and buried in the same grave as the saint at Gwytherin.

Refs: **1** (3–12); **10** (1).

Rhiwlas (Clwyd, Wales). Some 2 miles south-east of TREGEIRIOG, this small hamlet of stone-built houses lies at the foot of the 1,490-ft-high, grass- and bracken-covered Foel Wylfa. Near the stone bridge over the fast flowing stream is a small chapel.

Novels: In February 1141 OWAIN GWYNEDD was patrolling the fringes of Cheshire. Early informants, 'encountered near Rhiwlas, were positive that he had crossed the BERWYNS and come down into GLYN CEIRIOG'.

Refs: **9** (3).

Rhos (Clwyd, Wales). The medieval Welsh cantref of Rhos in ancient Gwynedd Is Conwy (or Gwynedd below Conwy) was bounded by the rivers CONWY, ELWY and CLWYD and the Irish Sea. In the south it extended along the east bank of the Conwy to Capel Garmon, some 4 miles south-east of LLANRWST. The Llandudno peninsula, which formed the commote of Creuddyn, was also included in the region. Rhos was bordered by the cantrefs of Tegeingl and Rhufoniog to the east and the cantref of ARLLECHWEDD and the commote of Nant Conwy to the west. It should not be confused with Rhos, in Dyfed, at the south-western extremity of Wales. Rhos was subdivided into the commotes of Creuddyn, Rhos Uwch Dulas and Rhos Is Dulas.

Novels: Griffith ap RHYS was OWAIN GWYNEDD's bailiff in Rhos.

Refs: **1** (2, 7).

Rhuddlan (Clwyd, Wales). Midway between ST ASAPH and Rhyl, the small town of Rhuddlan lies on the east bank of the River CLWYD. From the 10th C. it was a residence of Welsh princes. In 1063 Harold Godwinson (later HAROLD II) captured and burned the royal palace. The Normans built a motte-and-bailey castle at Twt Hill in 1073 and thereafter the settlement became an English borough. It was captured by the Welsh during the first half of the following century and thereafter became alternately English and Welsh. Between 1277 and 1282, Edward I erected a new fortress a short distance north-west of Twt Hill. The castle was captured by the Parliamentarians in 1646 and subsequently fell into ruin. In 796, at the battle of Rhuddlan Marsh, the Welsh were defeated by the Saxons under Offa, King of Mercia.

Novels: 'Before the sun had stooped towards setting they came down into the narrowing tongue of land between the CLWYD and the ELWY, before the two rivers met above Rhuddlan, to move on together into tidal water. And there between lay the town of Llanelwy and cathedral of ST ASAPH.'

Refs: **18** (2).

Rhun. See RHUN, Brother.

Rhun, Brother (b. 1125) (fict.). **Novels:** 'So Rhun had arrived at the last frontier of belief, and fallen, or emerged, or soared into the region where the soul realises that pain is of no account, that to be within the secret of God is more than well being, and past the power of the tongue to utter. To embrace the decree of pain is to translate it, to shed it like a rain of blessing on others who have not yet understood.' 'That warm, clear call, that was Brother Rhun, the youngest of the novices, sixteen years old, only two months since received into probation, and not yet tonsured, lest he should think better of his impulsive resolve to quit a world he had scarcely seen. But Rhun would not repent of his choice. He had come to the abbey for Saint WINIFRED's festival, a cripple and in pain, and by her grace now he went straight and tall and agile, radiating delight upon everyone who came near him.' Benedictine monk of SHREWSBURY ABBEY, nephew of Alice WEAVER and brother of Melangell MEVEREL, Rhun and his sister were orphaned in 1134. Thereafter, they were looked after by their aunt at CAMPDEN. The family travelled to SHREWSBURY to celebrate St Winifred's festival, arriving on 18 June 1141. The journey took three weeks and Rhun, his right leg twisted and feebled from a child, walked the whole way on foot, supported by crutches. On 22 June on St Winifred's day, as he approached the saint's altar, Rhun's crippled leg was miraculously straightened. In lifelong gratitude to the saint, Rhun asked to be allowed to take the cowl. He was immediately taken in by Shrewsbury Abbey, and received the tonsure to become the novice, Brother Rhun, in August. He befriended Brother Fidelis (see CRUCE, Julian) and helped protect him from Brother URIEN's approaches. Rhun's novitiate ended in August 1142, when he became a full brother and choir monk. He devoted himself to St Winifred, making himself the custodian of her altar, her page and her squire.

Refs: **10** (3–6, 8–12, 15–16); **11** (2–5, 7, 9–10, 14); **13** (1, 9); **14** (9); **15** (2); **16** (4); **17** (9); **18** (4); **19** (2–4, 9–10).

Rhun ab Owain, (d. 1146) (hist.). He was the son of OWAIN GWYNEDD by an unknown woman and half-brother of HYWEL AB OWAIN, IORWERTH AB OWAIN and MAELGWN AB OWAIN. Rhun is described as being tall, with white skin, large flashing blue eyes and curly flaxen hair. On the news of his early death, his father was heartbroken.

Novels: 'All radiance and clarity, all openness and serenity in the face. No wonder his father, recognising a prodigy, loves him better than all others.' Most beloved son of Owain Gwynedd, by a woman other than his wife, Rhun ab Owain was born in *c.*1128. CADFAEL and Deacon MARK saw him at ABER in May 1144.

Refs: **18** (4).

Rhydycroesau (or Rhyd-y-Croesau) (Clwyd, Wales; Shropshire, England). Some 19 miles north-west of SHREWSBURY and 3 miles west of OSWESTRY, the village of Rhydycroesau straddles the border between England and Wales formed by the River CYNLLAITH. OFFA'S DYKE is about a mile to the east. To the south of the village is a standing stone (marked on the OS map). Sometimes called hoar stones, these single upright stones are thought to have been erected to define the limits of territory. There is another near Carreg-y-big, about a mile to the north-east, known as Carreg-y-big or the Pointed Stone.

Novels: 'The mountain sheep had not the long, curly wool of the lowlands, but they brought a very thick, short fleece that carried almost as much wool of a somewhat less valuable kind, and they converted handsomely the pasture their spoiled lowland cousins could not make use of. Their cheeses alone were worth their keep.' SHREWSBURY ABBEY ran two hundred mountain sheep on the remote hills near Rhydycroesau, all looked after by just two lay brothers: BARNABAS and SIMON. In December 1138 a messenger from the sheepfolds arrived at SHREWSBURY with news that Barnabas had been taken ill. CADFAEL rode north to doctor him. After denouncing MEURIG as a murderer, Cadfael helped him escape by giving him one of the horses stabled at Rhydycroesau. It was later returned. In March 1141, Hugh BERINGAR met OWAIN GWYNEDD on the great dyke at Rhydycroesau.

Refs: **3** (7–11); **9** (9); **15** (1).

Rhys, Bledri ap (d. 1144) (fict.). **Novels:** 'It was plain, as soon as the bishop's steward brought the petitioner into the hall, that he had not come straight from travel to ask for this audience. Somewhere about the bishop's enclave he had been waiting at ease for his entry here, and had prepared himself carefully, very fine and impressive in his dress and in his person, every grain of dust from the roads polished away. A tall, broad-shouldered, powerful man, black-haired and black-moustached, with an arrogant beak of a nose, and a bearing truculent rather than conciliatory. He swept with long strides into the centre of the open space fronting the dais, and made an elaborate obeisance in the general direction of prince and bishop. The gesture seemed to CADFAEL to tend rather to the performer's own aggrandisement than to any particular reverence for those saluted. He had everyone's attention, and meant to retain it.' Liegeman of CADWALADR and Welshman of CEREDIGION, Bledri ap Rhys was among those who ambushed and killed ANARAWD AP GRIFFITH in 1143. In May 1144, at ST ASAPH, he petitioned OWAIN GWYNEDD to make peace with Cadwaladr. He was obliged to accompany Owain to ABER. There, in his lodgings, he told GWION that he was considering transferring his allegiance to Owain. In order to prevent Bledri from betraying him, Gwion stabbed him through the heart. His body was taken back to his wife in Ceredigion for burial.

Refs: **18** (3–6, 8, 11, 14).

Rhys, Brother (b. *c.*1078) (fict.). **Novels:** Formerly called Rhys ap Griffith. 'Prior ROBERT looked round for the few Welshmen among the brothers, passed somewhat hurriedly over Brother CADFAEL, who had never been one of his favourites, perhaps by reason of a certain spark in his eye, as well as his notoriously worldly past, and lit gladly upon old Brother Rhys, who was virtually senile but doctrinally safe, and had the capacious if capricious memory of the very old.' Benedictine monk of SHREWSBURY ABBEY, Brother Rhys was a Welshman and brother of MARARED (b. *c.*1093), uncle of ANGHARAD (1093–1127), great-uncle of MEURIG, and cousin of Owain and Cynfrith ap RHYS. Brother Rhys came from a village between RHYDYCROESAU and LLANSILIN. He had no children and lost his wife early. By December 1138 he was confined to the infirmary, suffering from old age and mild senility, plus creaks and pains in his shoulders, back and joints. By February 1141 he was almost blind and confined to his bed.

Refs: **1** (1); **3** (1–4, 7–8, 11); **9** (4–5, 7–8).

Rhys, Cynfrith ap (b. *c.*1058) (fict.). **Novels:** 'A solid, thick-set, prominent-boned Welshman was Cynfrith, with wiry black hair now greying round the edges and balding on the crown, and quick, twinkling eyes set in the webs of good-humoured creases common to outdoor men.' Elder brother of Owain ap RHYS and cousin of Brother RHYS, Cynfrith ap Rhys had a holding half a mile or so west of MALLILIE. CADFAEL visited him in December 1138.

Refs: **3** (7–9).

Rhys, Griffith ap (*fl.* 1137) (fict.). **Novels:** 'And that experienced and sceptical officer soon proved himself not only a quick and agile listener, but a very shrewd dissector of feelings and motives, too. He was, after all, Welsh to the bone, and Welsh bones were at the heart of this tangle.' OWAIN GWYNEDD's royal bailiff in RHOS and cousin of DAVID (*fl.* 1137), Griffith ap Rhys came to GWYTHERIN in May 1137 to investigate RHISIART's murder. PEREDUR passed on CADFAEL's word about Brother COLUMBANUS's guilt and ENGELARD's innocence to the bailiff. After Prior ROBERT's party had left GWYTHERIN, Griffith 'let it be known that all was well, and should be let well alone'.

Refs: **1** (5–12).

Rhys, Owain ap (*fl.* 1138) (fict.). **Novels:** Younger brother of Cynfrith ap RHYS, father of Elis ab OWAIN and cousin of Brother RHYS, Owain ap Rhys, a Welshman, had a 'good wife, and grown sons'. In December 1138, at the commote court at LLANSILIN, he was fined for moving a whole length of Hywel FYCHAN's fencing by a 'cautious yard'.

Refs: **3** (7–9).

Rhys, Tudur ap (*fl.* 1141) (fict.). **Novels:** 'A short, square man, very powerfully built, with a thick thatch of brown hair barely touched with grey, and a loud, melodious voice that ranged happily up and down the cadences of song rather than speech.' Welsh lord of TREGEIRIOG and close friend and ally of OWAIN GWYNEDD, Tudur ap Rhys married a woman of Gwynedd and was the father of CRISTINA. In February 1141 he was with Owain patrolling the fringes of RANULF of Chester's territory.

Refs: **9** (2–3, 10–12, 15).

Richard, Brother (*fl.* 1137) (fict.). **Novels:** 'Brother Richard the sub-prior was the last man to presume; large, good-natured and peace-loving to the point of laziness, he never exerted himself to advance even by legitimate means.' Benedictine monk of SHREWSBURY ABBEY and sub-prior from at least early 1137, Brother Richard went, in May 1137 with Prior ROBERT's party to GWYTHERIN to acquire the sacred bones of St WINIFRED for Shrewsbury Abbey. In September 1143, 'secure in the experience of his farming stock', Richard recommended the exchange of abbey land with HAUGHMOND for the POTTER'S FIELD. In October, he was present when the coulter of the plough unearthed GENERYS's body.

Refs: **1** (1–11); **3** (1–2, 4–5, 7); **8** (1); **12** (1, 11); **13** (2, 4–6); **16** (5); **17** (1–3); **19** (2–3, 5, 10); **RB** (3).

Robert (d. 1139), Bishop of Salisbury (hist.). While this bishop appears as Robert in most of the novels, his name was really Roger. Originally a humble priest near Caen in NORMANDY, Roger became the steward and chaplain of the future King HENRY I, when by chance the prince attended Mass at his chapel. In 1101, after Henry had become King of England, Roger was made his chancellor, and in the following year he became Bishop of Salisbury. However, the Archbishop of Canterbury, ANSELM, refused to consecrate him owing to the Crown's interference in matters of the Church. The dispute between the king and the archbishop was formally settled in 1107, when Roger was finally consecrated by Anselm. Shortly after, he was appointed the king's justiciar, and was responsible for administering the country while Henry was absent in Normandy. It was through Roger's influence that WILLIAM OF CORBEIL was consecrated Archbishop of Canterbury in 1123. Roger swore allegiance to Henry's daughter, the Empress MAUD, in 1126, recognising her as heir to the throne of England. But when King STEPHEN seized the crown in December 1135, Roger took his side, abandoning his previous oath. He attended Stephen's coronation and was retained as the new king's justiciar. Being in charge of the administration of the kingdom in the king's absence, Roger was extremely powerful; his son, Roger, was chancellor; his nephew, NIGEL, was Bishop of Ely; and another nephew, Alexander, was Bishop of Lincoln. Waleran de BEAUMONT, Count of Meulan, however, turned Stephen against Roger, his son and nephews and, in consequence, in June 1139 they were arrested and their castles confiscated. Although Nigel managed to escape to DEVIZES, he too was eventually forced to surrender. Stephen was summoned before a Church council on 29 August, by Bishop HENRY OF BLOIS, to answer for his violent treatment of the bishops, and was forced to do penance. The incident greatly damaged Stephen's relationship with the clergy, and is said to have led to the civil war. Roger did not survive to take part in the conflict, for he died a broken man on 11 December 1139 and was buried in Salisbury Cathedral.

Novels: In August 1138 Bishop Robert of Salisbury, Stephen's justiciar, arrived at SHREWSBURY. He was befriended by Abbot HERIBERT. Later, having been stripped of his power by Stephen, Robert died 'naturally from old age, bitterness and despair'. At the consecration of Roger of Salisbury, 'who fell into Stephen's displeasure . . . and died disgraced', the *sortes Biblicae* sent: '"Bind his hands and feet, and cast him into outer darkness."' (Matthew 22:13.)

Refs: **2** (11); **10** (1); **19** (7).

Robert (1065–1111), Count of Flanders or Robert II (1093–1111) (hist.). He joined the First Crusade in 1096 and became one of the most celebrated of crusaders. After his return from the HOLY LAND in 1100, he fought alongside Louis VI, King of France, against the English. Robert was succeeded by his son, Baldwin VII.

Novels: ALARD THE CLERK 'had seen, he said, Italy as far south as ROME, served once for a time under the Count of Flanders, crossed the mountains into Spain, never abiding anywhere for long'.

Refs: **RB** (1).

Robert (*c.*1054–1134), Duke of Normandy as Robert II (1087–1106) (hist.). Also called Robert Curthose or Robert Gambaron. Eldest son of WILLIAM I, King of England, he was given the name Curthose because of his short, fat stature. In 1067, during his father's absence in England, Robert became co-regent of NORMANDY with his mother. He was betrothed to Margaret, heiress of Herbert II, Count of Maine, but she died before they could be married. Although William, on at least one occasion, called his son by the title of Count of Le Mans, he refused to grant MAINE and Normandy to Robert and ruled both provinces himself. Quarrelling with his father and brothers (the future Kings of England, WILLIAM II and HENRY I), Robert attempted to seize ROUEN. WILLIAM I ordered his arrest, but Robert fled and was eventually driven out of Normandy. In 1078 he established himself at Gerberoi, where, in the following year, he was besieged by William, but was allowed to withdraw to FLANDERS. Soon after, Robert was reconciled with his father and was once again acknowledged as heir to Normandy. By 1081, however, he had been banished for causing further trouble. However, on William's death in 1087, Robert became the Duke of Normandy. As William's eldest son, Robert expected to receive the crown of England, and was surprised to find that his brother, William II, was established on the throne by common consent. In 1088 Robert made a half-hearted attempt at invasion, which inevitably failed. Further conflict followed, but in 1091 Robert and William joined together to drive their youngest brother, Henry, out of Normandy and divide his lands between them. Having pledged his duchy to William for five years, Robert joined the First Crusade in 1096. In 1097 he was at the siege of Nicaea and at the battle of Dorylaeum, and, between 1097 and 1098, at the siege of ANTIOCH. He established himself and his forces at Laodicea for a while, before being forced to rejoin his fellow crusaders under threat of excommunication. It is said that after the capture of JERUSALEM in 1099 he was offered the crown, but refused, saying that he intended to return to his duchy. Leaving the HOLY LAND later that year, he reached Normandy in 1100, having married Sibyl, daughter of Geoffrey, Count of Conversana, in Italy. On William II's death in the same year, Henry seized the English crown. The following year Robert invaded, landing at Portsmouth; many of the great Norman barons rallied to his side. The two armies met at Alton, near WINCHESTER, but, instead of fighting, a peaceful treaty was negotiated, allowing Henry to retain the crown of England in return for paying Robert an annual pension. Once his brother had left England, Henry set about strengthening his realm, and in 1105 he landed in Normandy at the head of an army. Robert was captured at the battle of Tinchebrai in 1106, taken to England and imprisoned for the rest of his life. It is generally agreed that he died in Cardiff Castle on 10 February 1134.

Novels: CADFAEL was a crusader 'with Robert of Normandy's company, and a mongrel lot we were, Britons, Normans, Flemings, Scots, Bretons – name them, they were there!' They were at the storming of Jerusalem in 1099. In 1120 Robert was a prisoner in DEVIZES Castle.

Refs: **6** (12, 15); **8** (2); **10** (7); **15** (4); **RB** (1).

Robert (*c.*1090–1147), Earl of Gloucester (hist.). Illegitimate son of HENRY I and half-brother to the Empress MAUD, he married Mabel (or Matilda or Sybil), daughter of Robert FitzHamon, and came into properties in NORMANDY, the lordship of Glamorgan in Wales, and considerable estates in England. He was the father of William FITZROBERT and Philip FITZROBERT. HENRY made Robert Earl of Gloucester in 1122. After the death of his father and STEPHEN's seizure of the crown of England in 1135, Robert became the leader of the party loyal to Maud, the rightful heir to the throne. On 30 September 1139 he landed at ARUNDEL, with the empress and 140 knights. As commander-in-chief of her forces, with his headquarters at BRISTOL, Robert won from Stephen most of western England and southern Wales. He captured Stephen at the battle of LINCOLN on 2 February 1141 and imprisoned him in Bristol. In the same year he accompanied Maud in triumph to WINCHESTER and LONDON, and fled with her to OXFORD after the Londoners had driven her out. He was captured himself at STOCKBRIDGE on 14 September 1141, covering Maud's retreat from Winchester, and was later exchanged for the king. The following year Maud sent Robert overseas to try and persuade her husband, GEOFFREY of Anjou, to come to her assistance in England. Geoffrey, preoccupied with his conquest of Normandy, forced Robert to join him in a campaign. Robert eventually returned to England in Autumn 1142, with his young nephew Henry Plantagenet (see HENRY II), and laid siege to WAREHAM Castle. Before Christmas he rejoined Maud at WALLINGFORD after her escape from Oxford. Robert continued to support Maud throughout the civil war. He fell sick and died at Bristol on 31 October 1147 and was buried in St James's Church, which he founded. One of his daughters, MAUD (*fl.* 1139), married RANULF of Chester.

Novels: 'A man of fifty, broad built, plain in his clothing and accoutrements, a lacing of grey in his brown hair, lines of weariness in his comely face. Grey in his short beard, too, accentuating the strong lines of his jaw in two silver streaks.' '"A good man," agreed Hugh [BERINGAR], doing his opponent generous justice, "one of the few on either side not grasping for what he himself can get."' 'There was not a man of the first-rank on Stephen's side to match the quality of her half-brother, Earl Robert of Gloucester.' Earl Robert of Gloucester was half-brother and loyal champion of the Empress Maud, father of Philip and William FitzRobert, and half-brother of Reginald FITZROY. One of his daughters was married to Ranulf of Chester. Robert was in Normandy with Maud in Summer 1139, making plans to bring her to England to challenge Stephen's right to the throne. They landed with 140 knights near Arundel on 30 September and installed themselves in ARUNDEL CASTLE. From there, Robert went to Bristol, where Maud's faction was already firmly established. On 2 February 1141 Robert took Stephen prisoner at the battle of Lincoln. He was with MAUD when she was driven out of LONDON in June, and in August he was at the siege of Winchester. On 14 September he was captured by the forces of Queen MATILDA at Stockbridge, covering the empress's retreat. He was taken to ROCHESTER Castle, being freed in November in exchange for Stephen. In June 1142 Robert sailed from Wareham for Normandy to try and persuade Geoffrey of Anjou to help in the empress's cause. Instead, Robert found himself detained in Geoffrey's service, but finally returned to England in Autumn 1142 with Henry Plantagenet. In 1143, at the battle of WILTON, Robert almost recaptured Stephen. At the close of 1143, he was busy turning the south-west into a fortress for the empress. In 1145 Robert built the castle at FARINGDON, then handed it over to Philip, his younger son. When the castle was besieged by Stephen's forces, the earl refused to send reinforcements despite plea after plea from Philip. 'The sudden and violent breach between

Robert, earl of Gloucester, the Empress Maud's half-brother and loyal champion, and his younger son Philip, in the heat of midsummer, had startled the whole of England, and still remained inadequately explained or understood.' Robert attended the conference at COVENTRY on 30 November 1145. The following month, travelling from HEREFORD, he was reconciled with Philip at CIRENCESTER ABBEY.

Refs: **2** (10); **4** (1:1–2, 1–4; 4:1, 5:3, 5:6); **5** (1, 7); **8** (1, 3); **9** (1); **10** (1, 16); **11** (1, 6–8, 10); **12** (1); **13** (1); **14** (1, 4); **15** (1, 3); **16** (1); **17** (1, 3); **18** (1); **20** (1–11, 14–16).

Robert Pennant, Prior (d. 1167) (hist.). Prior of SHREWSBURY ABBEY during the first half of the 12th C., he wrote a *Life* of St WINIFRED, which ended with the account of his journey to GWYTHERIN in 1137, accompanied by a party of SHREWSBURY monks, to obtain the relics of the saint for the abbey. Owen and Blakeway in *A History of Shrewsbury* (1825) thought that he was a member of 'the ancient family still subsisting at Downing in the immediate neighbourhood of HOLYWELL'. On the death of RADULFUS in *c.*1148, Robert became abbot. When Robert died he was succeeded by Abbot Adam I.

Novels: 'Prior Robert Pennant, of mixed Welsh and English blood, was more than six feet tall, attenuated and graceful, silver-grey of hair at fifty, blanched and beautiful of visage, with long, aristocratic features and lofty marble brow. There was no man in the midland shires would look more splendid in a mitre, superhuman in height and authority, and there was no man in England better aware of it, or more determined to prove it at the earliest opportunity. His very motions, sweeping across the chapter-house to his stall, understudied the pontificate.' 'For whatever virtues might be found in Prior Robert, humility was not one, nor magnanimity. He was invariably sure of his own rightness, and where it was challenged he was not a forgiving man.' 'Prior Robert Pennant, who had looked to be abbot by this time, and been sorely disappointed at having a stranger promoted over his head, maintained a silvery, ascetic calm, appeared to move his lips in prayer, and shot sidelong looks at his superior between narrowed ivory lids, wishing him irredeemable error while appearing to be compassionate and bless.' 'The precise letter of canon law was sacred to Robert, and the influence of an archbishop, distilled through his confidential envoy, hung close and convincing at his elbow, stiffening a mind already disposed to rigidity.' Prior and Benedictine monk of Shrewsbury Abbey, Robert Pennant was born into an aristocratic Norman family in 1087. In May 1137 Prior Robert led an expedition into Wales to acquire the sacred bones of St Winifred. He tried to bribe RHISIART into persuading the parish of Gwytherin to agree to the saint's removal. After the questionable translation of Winifred's relics to Shrewsbury, Robert wrote a *Life* of the saint. He had the most comprehensive knowledge of the riches of the house. He also knew the pedigree of every lord of a manor in Shropshire and beyond, for 'thirty years back and more'. In February 1145 Robert accompanied Hugh BERINGAR to WORCESTER to ask Sub-Prior HERLUIN and Brother TUTILO if they knew anything about the disappearance of St Winifred's reliquary. From there, he was among the party that rode to ULLESTHORPE and HUNCOTE, returning to Shrewsbury with Robert de BEAUMONT and the 'errant saint'. During the *sortes Biblicae*, conducted at the abbey in March, Prior Robert received: '"Ye have not chosen me, but I have chosen you."' (John 15:16.) 'Prior Robert disapproved of any departure from the strict Rule, and had for years disapproved of what he considered privileges granted to Brother CADFAEL, in his freedom to move among the people of the [ABBEY] FOREGATE and the town when there was illness to be confronted.'

Refs: **1** (1–12); **2** (1–3, 6–8, 10, 12); **3** (1–8, 10–11); **4** (1:1–2, 2:1); **5** (1–7, 10–11); **6** (1); **7** (1–7,14); **8** (1–4, 10, 12); **9** (4, 6–9); **10** (1, 3, 6, 8–9, 12–13, 15); **11** (2–3, 13); **12** (1–5, 7–12); **13** (1–4, 9, 12); **14** (1, 3–7, 11–14); **16** (1–2, 4–7, 10–11, 13–14); **17** (1, 5, 7, 9–10); **18** (1); **19** (2–10, 13); **20** (2); **RB** (2, 3).

Robert the Forester. See BRETAGNE, Olivier de.

Robin (b. *c.* 1129) (fict.). **Novels:** 'The boy, perhaps sixteen years old, pert and lively, had waited their pleasure with stretched ears and eyes bright with curiosity when their errand was mentioned. Some younger son from among Leicester's tenants, placed by a dutiful father where he could readily get advancement.' Robin was a member of Robert de BEAUMONT's household at HUNCOTE.

Refs: **19** (4).

Robin (*fl.* 1143) (fict.). **Novels:** A manservant at LONGNER under Eudo BLOUNT the younger.

Refs: **17** (3).

Rochester (Kent, England). Some 32 miles south-east of the centre of LONDON, this ancient cathedral city lies on the lower reaches of the River Medway and stands on the site of a walled Roman town, which had previously been a Celtic settlement. The cathedral-priory was founded in 1080 for Benedictine monks by Gundulf (or Gundolf), Bishop of Rochester. It occupies the site of St Andrew's Church, built in 604 by Ethelbert (or Aethelberht), king of the Jutish kingdom of Kent. The Norman building was severely damaged by fires in 1137 and 1179. Most of Rochester's older buildings can be found in the vicinity of the cathedral, around which grew the medieval walled city. The oldest parts of the present cathedral, one of the smallest in England, are Gundulf's Tower and part of the crypt. The scant remains of the monastery include two 14th C. gatehouses (the third is a later replica) and sections of the precinct wall. Towering above the river is the massive keep of Rochester Castle, built largely of Kentish ragstone between 1127 and 1139, and considered to be one of the finest and best preserved in Britain. The first Norman castle at Rochester was built by Gundulf to defend the strategic river-crossing. The outer walls follow the line of the old Roman fort. It was besieged by King John in 1215 and rebuilt in 1226. Further sieges followed, in 1264 and 1381, and in the early 17th C., having fallen into disrepair, the castle was partly dismantled.

Novels: In September 1141, ROBERT of Gloucester was imprisoned in Rochester Castle.

Refs: **11** (7).

Roden, River (Shropshire, England). The River Roden rises on the Meres, to the south-east of ELLESMERE, and flows south-east towards WEM. Skirting the south of the town, it heads east to form a series of wide loops before meandering south to Stanton-upon-Hine-Heath. On the opposite bank of the river to the village are the ruins of Moreton Corbet Castle (see HARPECOTE). Beyond Morton Mill the river flows south-west to Shawbury, an ancient village straddling an old Roman road. There was once a fort beside the river, but all that now remains of the stronghold is a mound and a moat. The site is now preserved, the moat being regarded as the finest in Shropshire. From Shawbury the river winds south, past Poynton Green, Poynton, Roden and RODINGTON, to Walcot where it merges with the River TERN.

Novels: The River Roden is not mentioned by name in *The Chronicles of Brother Cadfael*, but it is marked on the 'Shrewsbury and Eastern Environs' map in *The Potter's Field.*

Rodington (Shropshire, England). DB – Rodintone: in Wrockwardine Hundred; a holding of Reginald the Sheriff under Roger de MONTGOMERY. Rodington, a small village on the banks of the River RODEN, is 6 miles east of SHREWSBURY and just over a mile north-east of WITHINGTON. Roger de Montgomery gave the church (mentioned in DB) to SHREWSBURY ABBEY. The church (now dedicated to St George) was rebuilt in the 18th C. and again in 1851.

Novels: In November 1143 Giles OTMERE and his wife went to Rodington, where they had 'business with the miller's wife'.

Refs: **17** (8).

Roger, Bishop of Salisbury. See ROBERT, Bishop of Salisbury.

Roger (d. 1155), Earl of Hereford (hist.). Also called Roger FitzMiles or Roger of Gloucester. Son of MILES, Constable of Gloucester, and a supporter of the Empress MAUD, he succeeded to the earldom of Hereford on his father's death in 1143. His newly built castle at Winchcombe, near Cheltenham, was besieged and taken by King STEPHEN in 1144. Towards the close of Stephen's reign, Roger formed alliances with RANULF of Chester, William FITZROBERT, William de Beauchamp and Robert de BEAUMONT (the younger). He was knighted with Henry Plantagenet (later HENRY II) at Carlisle on 22 May 1148, in the presence of Ranulf of Chester and Prince Henry of Scotland. The following year Roger helped Henry Plantagenet escape from DEVIZES and return to NORMANDY. It seems he made a secret pact of loyalty and friendship with Stephen in 1152, provided the king helped him recover William de Beauchamp's castle at WORCESTER. After Henry's accession in 1154, Roger quarrelled with the king over GLOUCESTER castle, and the following year appears to have become a monk at Gloucester abbey. After Roger's death the earldom was suppressed, but his son, William, inherited his estates and was sheriff of both Gloucestershire and Herefordshire.

Novels: '"Roger of Hereford . . . the new earl. He whose father was killed by mishap, out hunting, a couple of years ago."' A loyal supporter of the Empress Maud, Roger attended the conference at COVENTRY on 30 November 1145. In December he entertained ROBERT of Gloucester in HEREFORD.

Refs: **20** (2–3, 5, 10–11).

Roger, Master (*fl.* 1143) (fict.). **Novels:** A retainer at the manor of ELFORD, under Audemar de CLARY.

Refs: **15** (5).

Roger de Clinton (d. 1148), Bishop of Coventry and Lichfield (hist.). The Norman soldier, Roger de Clinton, was ordained a priest on 21 December 1129 and the following day consecrated Bishop of COVENTRY and LICHFIELD at CANTERBURY. It is said that he purchased the see from HENRY I for 3,000 marks. Nephew of Geoffrey de Clinton, Henry's chamberlain and treasurer, Roger de Clinton was noted for his prowess with arms during the civil war of STEPHEN's reign. It is reputed that he was among those bishops who, 'girt with swords and wearing magnificent suits of armour, rode on horseback with the haughtiest destroyers of the country and took their share of the spoil' (*Gesta Stephani*, ed. Potter, 1976). Despite his reputation as a soldier, Roger de Clinton was a generous benefactor to the Church. He instigated the building of Lichfield Cathedral in 1135 and, on its completion in *c.*1140, dedicated it to St Mary and St CHAD. He is credited with having founded, among others: BUILDWAS Abbey in 1135; St John's Hospital, Lichfield, about the same time; FAREWELL Abbey in *c.*1140; and possibly BREWOOD NUNNERY at an uncertain date. He also established a dean and chapter on Norman lines at Lichfield, in addition to fortifying the Close around the cathedral. Roger de Clinton eventually joined the Second Crusade and died at ANTIOCH on 16 April 1148. See also CHESTER, Bishops of.

Novels: 'And Roger de Clinton was a man of good repute, devout and charitable if austere, a founder of religious houses and patron of poor priests.' 'A man austere, competent, and of no pretensions because he needed none, there was something about him, CADFAEL thought, of the warrior bishops who were becoming a rare breed these days. His face would have done just as well for a soldier as for a priest, hawk-featured, direct and resolute, with penetrating grey eyes that summed up as rapidly and decisively as they saw.' Bishop of Coventry and Lichfield, Roger de Clinton built Lichfield cathedral on 'a more removed and stable site', founded the abbeys of Buildwas and Farewell, and also granted the church at UPTON to SHREWSBURY ABBEY. Sisters URSULA and BENEDICTA and Mother PATRICE were all sent by him to serve at Farewell. In June 1143, at Shrewsbury Abbey, the case of ELAVE's heresy was heard by Roger de Clinton in person. After he had found Elave not guilty of the charge, FORTUNATA gave the bishop THEOFANU's psalter to take back to Coventry for his 'church treasury'. In Spring 1144 Roger de Clinton sent Deacon MARK to ST ASAPH and BANGOR on a diplomatic mission. He was one of the three bishops (see HENRY OF BLOIS and NIGEL) who presided over the conference between Stephen and Maud at COVENTRY on 30 November 1145. At the time, however, he 'had Christendom heavy on his mind, and was already away in the spirit to the HOLY LAND'.

Refs: **1** (12); **5** (1); **10** (1); **14** (2); **15** (6–7, 10–11); **16** (5–7, 13, 15); **17** (8); **18** (1–6, 12, 14); **20** (1–8, 10).

Roger de Clinton's House (Abbey Foregate, Shrewsbury, Shropshire) (fict.). Although it never existed, Bishop ROGER DE CLINTON's house stood in the ABBEY FOREGATE, half-way between SHREWSBURY ABBEY and ST GILES. To the north of the Abbey Foregate, facing Whitehall Street, is a large red sandstone mansion called Whitehall. Built for a lawyer, Richard Prince, in 1578–82, using stones from Shrewsbury Abbey, it has an arched gateway and a crenellated tower. The long outbuilding at the rear is reputed to have been an abbey barn.

Novels: 'It was a large house, well walled round, with garden and orchard behind, and it belonged to Roger de Clinton, Bishop of COVENTRY, though he rarely used it himself.' Roger de Clinton loaned his house to Huon de DOMVILLE for the latter's marriage to Iveta de Massard (see LUCY) in October 1139. In the same month Joscelin LUCY, evading the sheriff's men, hid in the grounds of the bishop's house.

Refs: **5** (1, 4–5, 8).

Roger of Ramsey (*fl.* 1145) (fict.). **Novels:** Lay servant at RAMSEY ABBEY, Roger, together with NICOL and an unnamed lay servant, escorted Sub-Prior HERLUIN and Brother TUTILO to SHREWSBURY ABBEY in February 1145. On his return to Ramsey, with a wagon full of the alms collected at SHREWSBURY (including St WINIFRED's reliquary), Roger was accompanied by NICOL, MARTIN, PAYNE and JAMES. A 'good enough hand with horses and wagons', Roger was driving when they were ambushed near ULLESTHORPE by about a dozen armed men. Despite laying into their attackers with his whip and leaving 'the print of it on two of the rogues', Roger was overpowered and bound by its thong. He chose to go on home to Ramsey, taking Payne with him.

Refs: **19** (2-4).

R

Rome (Italy). The ancient city of Rome, built on and around seven hills, lies on the River Tiber, 15 miles inland from the Tyrrhenian Sea. Capital of Italy and of the Latium region, Rome was founded, according to legend, by Romulus in 753 BC and named after him. As the centre of the Roman Empire, Rome reached the peak of its grandeur during the late 1st C. and early 2nd C. AD. The city was sacked by the Visigoths in 410 and the Vandals in 455. Although imperial power shifted to Ravenna, the papacy remained at Rome, and by the end of the 6th C. civil authority and the responsibility for the protection of the city was entirely in the hands of the Church. The Byzantine emperor, Justinian (reigned 527–65), attempting to reconquer the western provinces of the Roman Empire from the Germanic kingdoms, captured Rome in 552. In 568, shortly after his death, the Lombards invaded northern Italy, and set up powerful principalities in the south (see LOMBARDY). CHARLES THE GREAT conquered the Lombard kingdom in 774, and in 800 he was crowned emperor by Pope Leo III. After the Arabs sacked Rome in 846, Pope Leo IV built a wall around the Vatican, creating the suburb which came to be known as the Leonine City. OTTO I, who became Holy Roman Emperor in 962, united Germany and much of Italy into one empire. Bitter factional strife after Otto III's death in 1002 led to the reform of the papacy in 1046. Although Rome was sacked by the Normans in 1084, and underwent the Roman Revolution of 1143, control of the city gradually reverted to the papacy. By 1420 it was under absolute papal rule, which lasted until 1870, when Italian troops regained the city from the French and Rome was made the capital of a united Italy. In 1929 the Lateran Treaty between the papacy and the Italian government established Vatican City as an independent state. Today Rome – the Eternal City – is not only the spiritual and administrative capital of the Roman Catholic Church, but also one of the world's great cultural and tourist centres.

Novels: 'The Benedictines had very little hold in Wales, Welshmen preferred their own ancient Celtic Christianity, the solitary hermitage of the self-exiled saint and the homely little college of Celtic monks rather than the shrewd and vigorous foundations that looked to Rome.' 'The monks of CLUNY have hospices all across France and down through Italy, even close by the emperor's city they have a house for pilgrims.' After St WINIFRED had been miraculously restored to life, she went on a pilgrimage to Rome, where she 'attended at a great synod of saints' and was appointed prioress at GWYTHERIN. After King STEPHEN's seizure of the English throne in 1135, the Empress MAUD protested strongly to the pope in Rome. In 1136 William of LYTHWOOD and ELAVE left SHREWSBURY on a pilgrimage to the HOLY LAND, and on the journey visited Rome.

Refs: **1** (1); **3** (1, 8); **16** (3–4, 9–11); **19** (Prologue); **RB** (1).

Romsey (Hampshire, England). Some 9 miles southwest of WINCHESTER, this ancient market town stands on the east bank of the River TEST. It lies on the edge of the New Forest and King John's House, near ROMSEY ABBEY church, was used as a royal hunting lodge in the early 13th C.

Romsey Abbey (Hampshire, England). Romsey Abbey was first founded in *c.*907 by King Edward the Elder, whose eldest daughter, Ethelflaeda, is thought to have been the head of the community. It was refounded for Benedictine nuns in 967 by King Edgar and dedicated to St Mary and St Ethelflaeda. The monastery was badly damaged by the Danes in *c.*993, while the nuns fled to WINCHESTER. It is thought that the present building was begun in the reign of HENRY I, probably in *c.*1120, some two years after the death of his wife, MATILDA, who in childhood had been educated at the abbey. Mary, daughter of King STEPHEN, was abbess until 1160 when she left the order to marry Matthew, son of the Count of Flanders. At the Dissolution of 1539 the 12th C. abbey church was purchased by the town and saved from destruction. It is still in use, and is considered to be one of the finest Norman churches in England. Among its treasures is the Romsey Psalter, an illuminated manuscript of 1440.

Novels: 'Nicholas rode the twelve miles or so to ROMSEY . . . He came to the abbey gatehouse, in the heart of the small town, in the late evening, and rang the bell at the gate.' In September 1141 Nicholas HARNAGE travelled to Romsey Abbey to speak to the prioress of WHERWELL, who was in refuge there.

Refs: **11** (6).

Rotesley (Staffordshire) (fict.). Although it never existed, Rotesley lay in the vicinity of STRETTON in Staffordshire, and was a small hamlet 2 miles north of Brewood and 25 miles east of SHREWSBURY. It stood on a Roman road, near its intersection with the ancient Watling Street.

Novels: In November 1120 Roger MAUDUIT was in dispute with SHREWSBURY ABBEY over the manor of Rotesley, near Stretton, 'demesne, village, advowson of the church and all'. Roger's father, Arnulf MAUDUIT, gave the manor to the abbey in 1094, but the abbey granted it back to him as tenant for life. After his death, Roger claimed the manor as part of his inheritance; while the abbot claimed that it should be restored to the abbey. The dispute was brought before HENRY I's court at WOODSTOCK and judgement was given for the abbey.

Refs: **RB** (1).

Rouen (France). Some 70 miles north-west of Paris and 50 miles east of Le Havre, the ancient city of Rouen lies on the River Seine, and is one of France's largest ports and an important industrial centre. Rouen was conquered by the Normans in 876 and, after the Norman Conquest of England in 1066, became subject to Anglo-Norman rule. The city was captured by the French in 1204, but was recaptured by the English, under Henry V, in 1419, during the Hundred Years' War. Joan of Arc, patron saint of France, was imprisoned at Rouen and, after being condemned for heresy, was burned at the stake by the English in 1431. After the French recaptured the city in 1449, Rouen prospered until the religious wars in the late 16th C. After 1685, when the Edict of Nantes was revoked – depriving French Protestants of their religious and civil liberties – more than half of the population of Rouen emigrated. The city declined until the textile trade in the 19th C. regenerated its prosperity. Rouen was occupied by the Germans in 1870 and it was extensively damaged during World War II. Since then much of the city has been rebuilt.

Novels: '"There are malignant wandering preachers active even now in FLANDERS, in France, on the RHINE, in LOMBARDY, who cry out against Holy Church and her priesthood, that we are corrupt and greedy, that the Apostles lived simply, in holy poverty. In ANTWERP a certain TACHELM has drawn deluded thousands after him to raid churches and tear down their ornaments. In France, in Rouen itself, yet another such goes about preaching poverty and humility and demanding reform."' In June 1143 Canon GERBERT warned Abbot RADULFUS about 'malignant wandering preachers' active in Europe. Among them was one in Rouen who 'goes about preaching poverty and humility and demanding reform'. His name was EUDES DE L'ÉTOILE.

Refs: **16** (5).

Roumare, William of (*fl.* 1140), Earl of Lincoln (hist.). He was the son of Roger Fitzgerald and his wife Lucy, a great heiress, who possibly had previously been the wife of Ivo de Taillebois. After Roger's death, Lucy married Ranulf le Meschin, Earl of Chester, and through this marriage William became the half-brother of Ranulf's son, RANULF of Chester. William remained loyal to HENRY I, despite the rebellion of Hugh de Gournay in 1118–19, and supported the king at the battle of Bremule on 20 August 1119. He sailed to England from BARFLEUR with the king's fleet in 1120, having decided not to sail in the *White Ship* because it was overladen (see BLANCHE NEF). When, in 1122, Henry I refused to allow him to claim the English lands of his mother, which had been surrendered to the crown by his step-father, William rebelled and joined William Clito, ROBERT of Normandy's son, in NORMANDY in his war against the English king. Reconciliation followed shortly after the death of Clito in 1128, and Henry I granted William the hand in marriage of Hawisia (or Matilda), daughter of Richard de Redvers. By *c.* 1130 William had recovered his family estates in England. He supported King STEPHEN after Henry I's death in 1135 and was made Earl of Lincoln in *c.* 1138. Towards the close of 1140, William and Ranulf of Chester seized and occupied LINCOLN Castle. In the battle of Lincoln which followed on 2 February 1141, Stephen was captured. Although William may have

R

been reconciled with the king in 1142, his earldom was given to Gilbert de Gand, the husband of one of Ranulf of Chester's sisters. In 1142 William founded, with his wife and son, the Cistercian abbey at Revesby, Lincolnshire. Towards the end of his life he went on a pilgrimage to COMPOSTELA. He ended his days as a monk at Revesby and probably died in *c.*1153, but certainly before 1168. He was buried before the high altar; his tomb was discovered in 1870.

Novels: 'Rumours flew, but news was in very poor supply. Yet word had filtered through that Chester and Lincoln, long lurking in neutrality between rival claimants for the crown, having ambitious plans of their own in defiance of both, had made up their minds in short order when menaced by King Stephen's approach, and sent hotfoot for help from the champions of his antagonist, the Empress MAUD. Thus committing themselves for the future, perhaps, so deep that they might yet live to regret it.' Half-brother of Ranulf of Chester, William of Roumare had large holdings in Lincolnshire. In December 1140 Stephen paid William a diplomatic visit and officially granted him the title of Earl of Lincoln. On 18 December a messenger arrived at SHREWSBURY with news of Ranulf of Chester's and William of Roumare's treachery. Both earls, entering the royal castle at Lincoln by a subterfuge, had taken it by force. It was a move that had been planned earlier, in September, at CHESTER. For their support, William had promised Janyn LINDE and Nigel ASPLEY 'advancements, castles and commands'. At the battle of Lincoln on 2 February 1141, with help from the champions of the Empress Maud, Stephen was taken prisoner. It was a move which committed William and Ranulf to the side of the empress.

Refs: **4** (4:1); **8** (1, 3, 9–10, 12–13); **9** (1); **20** (2, 6).

Ruald, Brother (b. *c.*1103) (fict.). **Novels:** 'A slight, quiet, grave man, with a long, austere face, very regular of feature, of an ageless, classical comeliness, he still went about the devout hours of the day like one half withdrawn into a private rapture, for his final vows were only two months old, and his desire for the life of the cloister, recognised only after fifteen years of married life and twenty-five of plying the potter's craft, had burned into an acute agony before he gained admittance and entered into peace. A peace he never seemed to leave now, even for a moment. All eyes might turn on him, and his calm remained absolute. Everyone knew his story, which was complex and strange enough, but that did not trouble him. He was where he wanted to be.' Benedictine monk of SHREWSBURY ABBEY and widower of GENERYS, Brother Ruald was formerly a potter, who had a croft in the POTTER'S FIELD which he rented from Eudo BLOUNT at LONGNER. Ruald met Generys in Wales and married her in 1127. He abandoned her in May 1142, after a revelation of God, to take the cowl at Shrewsbury Abbey, and took his final vows in June 1143. In October he was unable to identify the remains of his wife that had been found buried in the Potter's Field.

Refs: **17** (1–14).

Ruddock, John (*fl.* 1138) (fict.). **Novels:** A merchant of SHREWSBURY, he was one of the witnesses for the town to the charter signed in 1138 between Judith PERLE and SHREWSBURY ABBEY, which granted her house in the ABBEY FOREGATE to the monks for an annual rent of one white rose. See also Nicholas of MEOLE and Henry WYLE.

Refs: **13** (2).

Rufus (fict.). **Novels:** 'A tall, high-spirited chestnut beast with a paler mane and tail, and a white blaze', Rufus was the horse of Gervase BONEL. Rufus carried Edwin GURNEY to freedom in December 1138. Pretending that he was the fugitive, Edwy BELLECOTE, riding Rufus, led the sheriff's men on a wild-goose chase through the countryside south-east of SHREWSBURY. He was eventually captured when Rufus tired and stumbled in the woods beyond ACTON.

Refs: **3** (6–7).

Ruiton (now Ruyton-XI-Towns or Ruyton-of-the-Eleven-Towns) (Shropshire, England). DB – Ruitone: in Baschurch Hundred; a holding of Odo under Roger de MONTGOMERY. Some 9 miles north-east of SHREWSBURY and 8 miles south-east of OSWESTRY, Ruyton is a long village built along two streets at right angles to each other. Situated on the River Perry, it became a borough town in 1301 and remained as such until 1883. The eleven 'towns', which were united into one manor and from which Ruyton gets its name, are: Ruyton, Coton, Eardiston, Shelvock, Shotatton, Wykey, West Felton, Haughton, Rednal, Sutton and Tedsmore. Ruyton Castle dates from the early 12th C. and was destroyed by Fulk Fitz Warine in 1148. It was later rebuilt and in 1212 it was again destroyed, this time by the Welsh. It was rebuilt by Edmund FitzAlan, Earl of Arundel, in the early 14th C., but was abandoned soon after 1364. The remains, mainly fragments of the keep, lie in the churchyard to the west of the parish Church of St John the Baptist. The red sandstone church dates from the early 12th C. and was probably originally in the castle precinct.

Novels: '"If luck serves," said Hugh, "we may pick him up before then. I know Ruiton, it lies barely eight miles from Shrewsbury. He'll time his journeys to bring him round by all those Welsh villages and bear east through KNOCKIN, straight for home. There are many hamlets close-set in that corner, he can go on with his selling until the weather changes, and still be near to home. Somewhere there we shall find him."' BRITRIC THE PEDLAR's mother lived at Ruiton. In the winter he made his way back there to avoid the 'hard frosts and snow'. In November 1143 one of Hugh BERINGAR's men waited at Ruiton for Britric to arrive.

Refs: **17** (6–7).

Russet. See BARBARY.

Ruthin or Rhuthun (Clwyd, Wales). Some 12 miles south-east of ST ASAPH and 12 miles north-west of LLANGOLLEN, the old market town of Ruthin lies on elevated ground at the southern end of the fertile Vale of CLWYD. Markets and fairs are still held in St Peter's Square. According to legend, King Arthur beheaded Huail, brother of Gildas, on the great stone block, known as Maen Huail or Huail's Stone. St Peter's consisted originally of two churches: the parochial church; and the collegiate church, founded in 1310. After the monastic college was dissolved at the Reformation, the collegiate church fell into ruin. It is said that the present carved oak roof of the parochial church was a gift from Henry VII. South of the town centre is Ruthin Castle, begun in 1277 after Edward I's conquest of the region and completed in 1296. It stands on the site of an earlier stronghold. In 1400 it came under attack by Owain Glendower (or Glyndwr), who failed to take the castle but sacked and burned the town. The red sandstone fortress was demolished after the Civil War, reconstructed into a castellated mansion during the 19th C., and is now a hotel.

Novels: In May 1144, on their journey from SHREWSBURY to ST ASAPH, Deacon MARK and CADFAEL passed through 'Ruthin, under the outcrop of red sandstone crowned with its squat timber fortress, and into the vale proper, broad, beautiful, and the fresh green of young foliage everywhere'.

Refs: **18** (2).

S

Sabellius (*fl.* 218) (hist.). Sabellius, a theologian of the Monarchian school, was probably a Libyan who came to ROME in the 3rd C. His teachings, known as Sabellianism, denied the dogma that there are three Persons in 'One God'. The earliest form of the heresy was Patripassianism, first taught by NOETUS OF SMYRNA, which held that God the Father was the only God, and that in the Incarnation this one God was born, suffered and died. Sabellius, about whom very little is known, was condemned as a heretic by Pope Calixtus I and excommunicated.

Novels: An outraged Canon GERBERT pointed out that Sabellius had been excommunicated for the Patripassian heresy and other errors, and that Noetus of Smyrna had preached it to his ruin.

Refs: **16** (2).

Saint Albans (Hertfordshire, England). Some 20 miles north-west of LONDON, this cathedral city lies in the valley of the River Ver. It stands to the east of the walled, Roman town of Verulamium, sacked by Queen Boudicca (or Boadicea) in 61. In *c.*209, Alban, a Romano-Briton who had been converted to Christianity, was arrested and executed on

Holmhurst Hill on the east bank of the river. He was venerated as the first Christian martyr in Britain, and in 793, on the site of his beheading, King Offa II of Mercia founded a monastery, dedicated to the saint. It was refounded in *c.*970 by St OSWALD, Bishop of Worcester, and Edgar, King of England, for Benedictine monks, and in *c.*1077 the church was rebuilt by the Norman abbot, Paul of Caen, using stone from the ruins of Verulamium. The town which grew up around the abbey became known as St Albans. Geoffrey de MANDEVILLE was arrested at St Albans in 1143 and charged with treason. Having been given the choice of the gallows or the surrender of the TOWER OF LONDON and his Essex castles, he chose the latter. The abbey, which had close associations with SOPWELL PRIORY, was severely damaged during the second battle of St Albans in 1461. After the Dissolution in 1539, most of the buildings were demolished. The abbey church became the parish church, and in 1877 it was dedicated a cathedral. Apart from the church, all that remains of the abbey is the massive 14th C. gatehouse.

Novels: '"At St Albans there's been the devil to pay. Half the lords at court, it seems, accused the Earl of Essex of having traitorous dealings with the Empress yet again, and plotting the king's overthrow, and he's been forced to surrender his constableship of the Tower, and his castle and lands in Essex. That or the gallows, and he's by no means ready to die yet."' In September 1141 Sister MAGDALEN delivered a letter to Hugh BERINGAR at SHREWSBURY from Julian CRUCE, saying that she had been living at Sopwell Priory by St Albans. In October 1143 news reached Shrewsbury of Geoffrey de Mandeville's arrest at St Albans.

Refs: **11** (14); **17** (3).

Saint Alkmund's Church (St Alkmond's Square, Shrewsbury, Shropshire). (While the Church is spelt 'Alkm*u*nd', the square is spelt Alkm*o*nd.) The Church dates from Saxon times, and is thought to have been founded by Ethelfleda, the 'Lady of the Mercians'. Dedicated to Alkmund (also spelled Alcmund or Alchmund) – who died in *c.*800 and was a younger son of Alchred, King of Northumbria – it became a collegiate church during the reign of King Edgar (957–75). In the 12th C. HENRY I granted the church to Richard de Belmeis. But, when he and his brother Philip founded LILLESHALL Abbey in *c.*1148, much of the wealth of St Alkmund's went towards the building and maintenance of the abbey. After the collapse of ST CHAD'S CHURCH in 1788, it was decided to pull down and rebuild the medieval St Alkmund's, except for the 184 ft. high spire dating from the 15th C. The new building, completed in 1795, was designed by Carline and Tilley. The east window, representing 'Faith', was designed by Francis Eginton of Birmingham. The parish of St Alkmund's is one of four in central SHREWSBURY; the others being St Chad's, ST JULIAN'S and ST MARY'S.

Novels: The family of Aline Siward (see BERINGAR) on her mother's side had a tomb at St Alkmund's Church. In August 1138 Giles SIWARD was interred in the tomb of his maternal grandfather. The priest of the parish, from at least 1136, was Father ELIAS. He buried ALDWIN in the graveyard of the church on 26 June 1143. Before the month was out, Jevan of LYTHWOOD was also buried there.

Refs: **2** (3); **13** (7); **16** (2–3, 12, 15).

S

Saint Asaph (Clwyd, Wales). Also called Llanelwy. Some 5 miles north of Denbigh (or Dinbych) and 2 miles south of RHUDDLAN, the small cathedral city of St Asaph straddles the River ELWY, near its confluence with the River CLWYD. It grew up around the monastery said to have been founded by St KENTIGERN in the 6th C. The church and city are named after his successor, a scholar named Asaph, who became both abbot and bishop. The first recorded mention of the place as St Asaph was not until 1100, for it was originally called Llanelwy, meaning 'the church beside the Elwy river'. The double-naved parish Church of St Kentigern and St Asaph dates from 1524, but was restored in 1872. Some 2 miles south-west of the city are the Cefn Caves, inside which were discovered the bones of animals extinct in Britain: bear, bison, rhinoceros, reindeer and hyena.

Novels: 'And there between lay the town of Llanelwy and the cathedral of SAINT ASAPH, comfortably nestled in a green, sheltered valley . . . Hardly a town at all, it was so small and compact. The low wooden houses clustered close, the single track led into the heart of them, and disclosed the unmistakable long roof and timber bell-turret of the cathedral at the centre of the village. Modest though it was, it was the largest building to be seen, and the only one walled in stone.' CADFAEL and Deacon MARK arrived in Llanelwy in May 1144 to find that OWAIN GWYNEDD had set up his camp on the surrounding hills. Mark had been sent by Bishop ROGER DE CLINTON to deliver a letter and gift to the Norman bishop, GILBERT, who had been newly installed in the diocese. HELEDD's mother and Canon MEIRION's wife died in Llanelwy at Christmas 1143.

Refs: **18** (1–7, 9, 11, 14).

Saint Asaph, Cathedral of (Clwyd, Wales). The Cathedral of St Asaph, the smallest in England and Wales, stands on the site of the Celtic clas said to have been founded by St KENTIGERN in *c.*560. The ancient bishopric fell into abeyance, but was revived by Archbishop THEOBALD OF BEC in 1143 under Bishop GILBERT. Almost nothing survives of the cathedral begun in 1180 and destroyed by the soldiers of Edward I in 1282. The present building was started by Bishop Anian II (1268–93), but over the centuries it has undergone much rebuilding and restoration. It was damaged during the revolt of Owain Glendower (or Glyndwr) in 1402 and by the Parliamentarians during the Civil War. The tower, completed in 1385, collapsed in 1715 and was rebuilt. Restoration work was carried out by Sir George Gilbert Scott in 1869–75, and again in 1929–32. The former Bishop's Palace nearby was built in 1791. A monument outside the cathedral commemorates the translation of the Bible into Welsh by Bishop William Morgan (1601–4). The cathedral is the venue for the North Wales Music Festival held every September.

Novels: 'The location of the see, with a foot either side the border, and all the power of Gwynedd to westward, had always made it difficult to maintain. The cathedral stood on land held by the Earl of CHESTER, but all the CLWYD valley above it was in GWYNEDD's territory. Exactly why Archbishop THEOBALD had resolved on reviving the diocese at this time was not quite clear to anyone, perhaps not even the archbishop. Mixed motives of Church politics and secular manoeuvring apparently required a firmly English hold on this borderland, for the appointed man was a Norman. There was not much tenderness towards Welsh sensitivities in such a preferment, CADFAEL reflected ruefully.' The cathedral of St Asaph, with its long roof and timber bell-turret, stood in the centre of Llanelwy (see ST ASAPH). Although the church had remained in use, the diocese, the fourth in Wales, had been dormant since *c.*1074. Originally, it had been founded by St Kentigern on the monastic principle of the old Celtic clas, a college of canons under a priest-abbot, and with one other priest or more among the members. In 1144 Bishop GILBERT was installed in the newly revived see. MORGANT and MEIRION were both canons at St Asaph.

Refs: **18** (1–2, 4).

Saint Chad's Church (now Old St Chad's) (Belmont, Shrewsbury, Shropshire). Situated near the junction of Belmont (formerly called St Chad's Lane), Princess Street (formerly Candlelane Street) and Milk Street, the remains of St Chad's Church stand on the site of a church reputed to have been founded in the late 8th C. by Offa, King of Mercia. It is said that it was formerly the palace of Brocwael, King of Powys, but was converted into a collegiate church, dedicated to Ceadda (now CHAD), when Pengwern (now SHREWSBURY) fell to the Mercians. In the Domesday Book survey of 1086, St Chad's was recorded as holding one and a half hides of land (*c.*180 acres) in the town, in addition to other land and tithes in Shropshire. The collegiate church was not dissolved until the reign of Edward VI (1547–53). It continued to be used as a parish church until 1788, when the tower and north side of the building collapsed. Although large sections of the church remained standing, the building was demolished in 1789, except for the Lady Chapel, which still survives. A new parish Church of St Chad's was erected on a site to the west, on the hill above the quarry and river. Designed by George Steuart with an unusual circular plan, the church was built by John Simpson using pale Grinshill stone and consecrated in 1792.

Novels: 'Parochially, the situation of the whole demesne of LONGER was peculiar, for it had belonged earlier to the bishops of CHESTER, who had bestowed all their local properties, if close enough, as outer and isolated dependencies of the parish of Saint Chad in Shrewsbury.' Eluned NEST was buried in the churchyard of St Chad's in December 1141. The VESTIER house and Ralph GIFFARD the elder's house both lay in the town parish of St Chad.

Refs: **11** (2); **12** (3–4); **13** (9, 13); **17** (3).

Saint Cross, Hospital of. See HENRY OF BLOIS, Bishop of Winchester.

Saint David's See (Dyfed, Wales). The cathedral city of St David's (Tyddewi), the smallest in Britain, lies at the extreme south-western corner of Wales and within the Pembrokeshire Coast National Park. Since the first monastery was founded by DEWI SAINT in the 6th C., St David's has been the seat of a bishop. It became the chief ecclesiastical centre of Wales until the end of the 11th C., when it lost its independence and surrendered to CANTERBURY. Today the see embraces the whole of Dyfed.

Novels: '"I have heard," said MARK [in 1144], "that formerly, a long time ago, St David's was the metropolitan see of Wales, with its own archbishop not subject to Canterbury. There are some Welsh churchmen now who want that rule restored."'

Refs: **18** (1).

Saint Denis (Paris, France). The town of St Denis (now part of the northern suburbs of PARIS) grew up around the Benedictine abbey church, founded in the 7th C. by Dagobert I, King of the Franks. For twelve centuries it was the burial place of the kings and queens of France – from Dagobert I (reigned 629–39) to LOUIS XVIII (reigned 1814–24). During the Revolution of 1792–3 the monastery was dissolved and the graves desecrated, but the tombs were saved. The present basilica, incorporating parts of a Carolingian church built in the 8th–10th C., was started in 1137 by Abbot Suger. The first major building marking the transition from the Romanesque to the Gothic style, it transformed Western architecture, and served as a model for Chartres and other late-12th C. French cathedrals. The abbey's possessions in England included the monastery at DEERHURST, and the village of Coln St. Dennis in the COTSWOLDS.

Novels: 'At Deerhurst there was an alien priory belonging to St Denis in Paris.'

Refs: **20** (6).

Saint Eata's Church. See ATCHAM; ATTINGHAM.

S

Saint Edmundsbury. See BURY.

Saint Gall (Switzerland). Situated just south of Lake Constance, St Gallen is the capital of Sankt Gallen canton, north-eastern Switzerland. In 612 St GALLUS established a hermitage in the Steinach Valley around which the town which now bears his name grew up. In *c.*720 a Benedictine abbey was founded on the site of the hermitage under Abbot Otmar. It became an important monastic school and its library was world famous; many of its manuscripts, dating from the Carolingian and Ottoman Empires, still survive. The town was ruled by the abbots from 1206 until the Reformation of 1524, and in 1803 it became the capital of the newly-formed canton of Sankt Gallen. The abbey, dedicated to St Gall, survived until 1805 and the Baroque church is now the Catholic cathedral.

Novels: Emperor OTTO I and his son, the future OTTO II, were in St Gall in 972. The teenage prince took several manuscripts away with him from the library, but did not return them all. The psalter given to FORTUNATA for her dowry by William of LYTHWOOD in 1143 was written and painted by DIARMAID, the Irish monk of St Gall. St TUTILO was also a monk of St Gall.

Refs: **16** (15); **19** (1).

Saint Giles, Church and Hospital of (Wenlock Road, Shrewsbury, Shropshire). All that remains of the Hospital of St Giles are parts of the present church, situated beyond the eastern end of the ABBEY FOREGATE, in a green island between London Road, St Giles Road and Wenlock Road. The exact date of the foundation of St Giles is uncertain, but it is thought to have been built during the 12th C. Some authorities, however, claim that it was founded by Roger de MONTGOMERY in the late 11th C. It is known that St Giles's Church formed part of a hospital for lepers in the reign of HENRY II. Up until 1857, when it became a separate parish, St Giles was part of the parish of HOLY CROSS and until the Dissolution it was almost certainly served by one of the monks from SHREWSBURY ABBEY. In the early 18th C. the church was in a bad state of repair and in the 19th C. it was extensively restored and enlarged; alterations included the rebuilding of the north aisle, the lengthening of the nave, the construction of the north transept and the building of a new chancel. The church was re-opened in 1895. The oldest parts of the present church building are the south wall and doorway, built of red sandstone and dating from the early 12th C. or possibly earlier. The wooden porch was built in 1858. The cross in the churchyard was erected in 1957, on the ancient octagonal base which held the original 15th C. cross. Fragments of the old cross can be found inside the church.

Novels: 'Beyond the bishop's house the road opened between trees, leaving the town well behind; and at the fork, a bow-shot ahead, the long, low roof of the hospice appeared, the wattled fence of its enclosure, and beyond again, the somewhat higher roof of the church, with a small, squat turret above. A modest enough church, nave and chancel and a north aisle, and a graveyard behind, with a carven stone cross set up in the middle of it. The buildings were set discreetly back from both roads that converged towards the town. Lepers, as they may not go among the populous streets of towns, must also keep their distance even to do their begging in the countryside. St GILES, their patron, had deliberately chosen the desert and the solitary place for his habitation, but these had no choice but to remain apart.' In 1137 Prior ROBERT and his party returned to SHREWSBURY from GWYTHERIN with the bones of St WINIFRED. Before the relics were installed in the abbey church, they were taken to the boundary Church of St Giles. The leper hospital of St Giles was located at the far end of the Abbey Foregate, where the town suburbs ended, barely half a mile from the abbey. It sheltered and cared for roughly twenty to thirty inmates at a time. Fulke REYNALD was the hospital superior. Among those who were inmates at St Giles were: Lazarus (see MASSARD, Guimar de), BRAN and WARIN. The brothers who served there included: MARK, OSWIN, Meriet ASPLEY, CADFAEL, HALUIN and SIMON.

Refs: **1** (11); **2** (6–8, 10); **3** (6); **4** (1:1); **5** (1, 4); **6** (2); **8** (6–7, 9, 11); **9** (4); **10** (1, 8); **11** (1, 8); **12** (2); **13** (1); **14** (1, 11); **15** (1, 3); **16** (1, 4, 9); **17** (6); **18** (1, 14); **19** (3, 11–13); **20** (2, 16).

Saint Giles-with-Sutton. See SUTTON.

Saint James at Compostela. See COMPOSTELA.

Saint John, Knights of. See KNIGHTS OF SAINT JOHN.

Saint Julian's Church (Fish Street, Shrewsbury, Shropshire). Situated on the corner of Fish Street and WYLE Cop, in close proximity to ALKMUND'S CHURCH, St Julian's Church was made redundant in the 1970s. Standing on the site of a Saxon foundation, the oldest part of the present building is the lower part of the west tower, which dates from *c.*1200. Its correct dedication is to St Juliana, reputed to have been martyred at Nicomedia in Asia Minor in *c.*305, but more probably at Naples (or Curnae) in Italy. The medieval church was rebuilt in 1749–50 to the design of Thomas Farnolls Pritchard, a local architect, and in 1846 the south side, facing the end of the High Street, was decorated and embellished. It is now in use as a craft centre.

Novels: In June 1143 Father ELIAS, parish priest of ST CHAD'S, went to St Julian's to enquire about ALDWIN.

Refs: **16** (8).

Saint Marcel (France). Situated just east of CHALONS ON THE SAÔNE, this small town grew up around the monastery, founded in the 6th C. by Gontram (or St Gunthramnus), King of Orleans and Burgundy. In the 11th C. the priory became a dependency of CLUNY, and is particularly noted for being the place where Pierre ABELARD died on 21 April 1142.

Novels: In April 1142 ELAVE, and William of LYTHWOOD were forced to stay a whole month in the monastery at St Marcel. There they met and spoke to Pierre Abelard before he died.

Refs: **16** (2).

Saint Mary Magdalene Church (Woodstock, Oxfordshire). Founded in the reign of HENRY II as a chapel-of-ease to the parish Church of St Martin at the nearby village of Bladon, St Mary Magdalene's Church was often used by the king when he was in residence at his royal manor of WOODSTOCK. The only surviving feature of the original church is the Norman south door decorated with a zig-zag pattern which, dispensing with the usual capitals, goes round the arch and down both sides to the ground. Over the centuries the church was altered and enlarged, and in 1878 it was extensively restored. Preserved inside the church, on the south arcade, are over twenty beautifully carved stone heads thought to be portraits of people living in the 13th century, including a man wearing a coronet said to be Henry III.

Novels: With the conclusion of Roger MAUDUIT'S suit against SHREWSBURY ABBEY at Woodstock in November 1120, CADFAEL was released from his service. Still carrying his weapons, he immediately went to Vespers in the parish church at Woodstock. After the service, in response to the stern reproof of a child, he removed his sword and 'laid it down, flatling, on the lowest step under the altar'. It was the last time he bore arms.

Refs: **RB** (1).

Saint Mary's Church (St Mary's Place, Shrewsbury, Shropshire). In *c.*970, after King Edgar had made it a royal chapel, with a dean, seven prebends and a parish priest, St Mary's Church was rebuilt on the site of probably two earlier Saxon churches. It remained a collegiate church, with the King as its patron, until the Dissolution when in 1547–8 it became a parish church. It continued, however, to be the royal chapel until 1846. The Saxon church was demolished during the reign of HENRY II, and in its place a cruciform Norman church without aisles was constructed of red sandstone. The Trinity Chapel was added in *c.*1360, the central tower removed in *c.*1471 and a clerestory built from the east end of the church to the west. The octagonal stone spire, reaching a height of over 138 ft., partly collapsed in 1894 and was rebuilt. St Mary's was extensively restored in Victorian times and is the largest church in SHREWSBURY, measuring 185 ft. in length. The stained glass in the Jesse window is thought to have originally belonged to the Franciscan friary in Shrewsbury. After the Dissolution, it was installed in ST CHAD'S CHURCH but, when the latter collapsed in 1788, it was given to St Mary's. Of further interest is the glass depicting scenes from the life of St BERNARD OF CLAIRVAUX, which was originally made in the early 16th C. for the Cistercian abbey of Altenberg, near Cologne.

Novels: Daniel and Margery AURIFABER were married at St Mary's Church in May 1140. Hugh BERINGAR had a town house near the church. In March 1141 Elis ap CYNAN slipped out of SHREWSBURY CASTLE, and sheltered the night in St Mary's churchyard. The blind beggar, Rhodri FYCHAN the Less, held the pitch outside the west door of the church. It was the envy of the beggars of SHREWSBURY.

Refs: **7** (4); **8** (1); **9** (11); **10** (7); **11** (7, 10, 13); **12** (4); **13** (7); **15** (3); **17** (1); **RB** (3).

Saint Mary's Close (now St Mary's Place) (Shrewsbury, Shropshire). Lying to the east of St Mary's Street, St Mary's Place surrounds the graveyard and parish Church of St Mary. The timber-framed Draper's Hall, at 10 St Mary's Place, was built in *c.*1560 as the guildhall for the powerful drapers' guild. Although there are several timber-framed houses in the close, none are older than the Hall. St Mary's Street is thought to have originally been called Upper Dogpole. When the Drapers' Almshouses (now replaced by a modern office block) were erected in the 16th C., it became known as St Mary's Almshouse Street .

Novels: Hugh BERINGAR had a town house in St Mary's Close.

Refs: **16** (9).

Saint Mary's Water-Lane (Shrewsbury, Shropshire). A steep passage, between high stone walls, running from the junction of St Mary's Place and Castle Street down to the River SEVERN. It passes through one of the outer gates of the medieval town wall, beside the river.

Novels: "'I came from the house, along the passage towards Saint Mary's, above the water-gate. The door of the tanner's yard was standing open, I know – I'd passed it . . . But I never heard a step behind me. As if the wall had fallen on me! I recall nothing after, except sudden cold, deadly cold.'" In August 1138 a fisherboy at SHREWSBURY CASTLE saw Adam COURCELLE come down alone from the water-gate and throw a knife into the Severn. In Spring 1140 William REDE was attacked and robbed in the passage above the water-gate.

Refs: **2** (11); **13** (7); **RB** (3).

Saint Maurice's Church See HIGH STREET (Winchester).

Saint Osyth (Essex, England). (Formerly called Chich). Situated some 10 miles south-east of Colchester, between Brightlingsea and Clacton-on-Sea, the village of St Osyth is noted for its Augustinian priory. Set amidst small creeks and marshland, the monastery was first founded in the 7th C. as a nunnery by St Osyth, the wife of Sighere, King of the East Saxons. It was destroyed by the Danes in 653, when, according to legend, the saint, who was the first abbess, was beheaded and martyred. It is said that her body was translated to Aylesbury, but by *c.*1000 it had been returned to Chich and enshrined. Dedicated to St Peter, St Paul and St Osyth, the convent was refounded in 1121 for Augustinian canons by Richard de Belmeis, Bishop of London. WILLIAM OF CORBEIL, was prior at St Osyth's before he became Archbishop of Canterbury in 1123. The house became an abbey in *c.*1161 and rapidly prospered, gaining a reputation for piety and learning. It was dissolved in 1539 and today the remains, including the great gatehouse of *c.*1475, are incorporated into a private house, set in extensive grounds. St Osyth's Priory is open to the public throughout the summer months.

Novels: In 1134 Archbishop WILLIAM OF CORBEIL sent out a preaching mission to many towns in England, 'and thought fit to use preaching canons from his own house at St. Osyth's'. It was one of these preachers who suggested that William of LYTHWOOD should go on a pilgrimage to the HOLY LAND.

Refs: **1** (2–3).

Saint Peter and Saint Paul's Abbey (or Church, Monastery, etc.) See SHREWSBURY ABBEY.

Saint Symeon (Turkey). Formerly called Seleucia Pieria; now called Suadiye. Situated at the mouth of the River Orontes (now Asi), St Symeon was the ancient port of ANTIOCH, some 18 miles upriver. It was from here that St PAUL THE APOSTLE embarked on his first missionary journey, and during the crusades it was an important supply point, particularly during the siege of Antioch in 1097/8. Today the ruins of the port lie some 2 miles inland near the village of Magaracik.

Novels: '"It was St Symeon I favoured myself. There were good craftsmen in the shipyards there, a fine harbour, and Antioch only a few miles upriver."' CADFAEL sailed from St Symeon in 1113, when he left Antioch and the HOLY LAND for the last time.

Refs: **6** (1, 15); **20** (1).

Saint Winifred's Grave. See GWYTHERIN.

Saint Winifred's Well. See HOLYWELL.

Salisbury (Wiltshire, England). Some 20 miles west of WINCHESTER and 17 miles south-west of ANDOVER, this ancient city stands on the River Avon, at its confluences with the Bourne and Nadder. Its origins lie at Old Sarum, nearly 2 miles to the north, where an early Iron Age fort became a Roman hill-top settlement. It was an important town in Saxon times, and after the Conquest the Normans erected a castle on the mound. The see was transferred from SHERBORNE, near Yeovil, in 1075 and the town became a bishopric. Conflict between the clerics and the military, together with a position that was found to be too windy and waterless, led to the see being moved from Old Sarum to the site of the present city of Salisbury. The foundations for the new cathedral were laid in 1220 and the main building was consecrated in 1258. The 404 ft. high spire, the tallest in England, was added in the 14th C. A new city quickly grew up around it, laid out on the medieval grid pattern, and during the Middle Ages Salisbury prospered on the cloth and wool trade. There were two monastic houses in the city: a Dominican friary, founded in 1281, possibly by Archbishop Kilwardby of CANTERBURY; and a Franciscan friary, founded before 1230 by Bishop Richard le Poer (or Poore) and Henry III.

Novels: In October 1139 it was rumoured that one EUDO DE DOMVILLE, a canon of Salisbury, was to perform the marriage ceremony between Huon de DOMVILLE and Iveta de Massard (see LUCY). After the battle of WILTON in 1143, the body of Eudo BLOUNT (the elder) was brought back to LONGNER from Salisbury. See also ROBERT, Bishop of Salisbury.

Refs: **5** (1); **17** (13); **19** (7).

Salisbury, Bishop of. See ROBERT, Bishop of Salisbury.

S

Salton (now Shelton) (Shropshire, England). DB – Saltone: in Shrewsbury Hundred; land held by the Bishop of Chester. Shelton, now almost part of the western suburbs of SHREWSBURY, lies on the south side of the River SEVERN some 2 miles west of the town centre.

Novels: 'Up the green slope and through the windbreak of trees they carried their burden, and there in the fields of the demesne, small but well husbanded, was the manor-house of Salton in its ring fence lined with byres and barns. A low, modest house, no more than a hall and one small chamber over a stone undercroft, and a separate kitchen in the yard. There was a little orchard outside the fence, and a wooden bench in the cool under the apple-trees.' Godfrid Marescot was born in 1094 at the manor of Salton, the only property his father held in Shropshire. The manor was held formerly by the Bishop of CHESTER, and granted to ST CHAD'S CHURCH, SHREWSBURY. They in turn let it to the Marescots. Godfrid returned there, as Brother HUMILIS, in September 1141. The tenant of Salton was AELRED.

Refs: **11** (2, 10, 12–14).

Sanctuary Sparrow. See LILIWIN.

Saône, River (France). Rising in the Vosges mountains, near Viomenil, south-west of Épinal in north-eastern France, the River Saône flows in a southwesterly direction for some 300 miles to Lyon, where it joins the Rhône. Among the towns on its course are Auxonne, CHALONS ON THE SAÔNE, Tournus, Mâcon and Villefranche. It is navigable for some 230 miles, and is connected by canal to the Rivers RHINE and Seine.

Novels: 'SAINT MARCEL is close by Chalons on the Saône. It is a daughter house of CLUNY.'

Refs: **16** (2).

Savigny (France). After he had established a hermitage in the Forest of Savigny in Normandy in 1105, Vitalis of Mortain obtained from Rudolf, Count of Fougères, a grant of land to build a monastery. The new Savigniac house, founded in 1112, prospered, especially under abbots Geoffrey (1122–38) and Serlon (1140–53), and daughter-houses were founded in France, Britain and Ireland, among other places. The first Savigniac house in England was Furness Abbey in Cumbria, founded in 1123. By the time the order was absorbed by the Cistercians in 1147, there were over a dozen houses throughout England and Wales, including BUILDWAS, founded in 1135.

Novels: In 1142 the Savigniac house had been at Buildwas for some seven years, and was a foundation of Bishop ROGER DE CLINTON.

Refs: **14** (2, 12).

Seez (now Sées) (France). Some 42 miles north of Le Mans, the ancient cathedral town of Sees in Normandy lies at the north-eastern edge of the great Forest of Ecouves. During the 5th C. the town was a bishopric, but after the Norse invasions in the 9th C. the old cathedral was destroyed. In 1083 Benedictine monks from the monastery of St Martin were brought over to England to supervise the building of SHREWSBURY ABBEY; among them were Abbot FULCHERED, Rainald and Frodo. Sées became an Anglo-Norman stronghold under HENRY I, and on his death in 1135 the castle was handed over to his heir, the Empress MAUD. The cathedral, dedicated to St Latrium, dates from the 12th C. Its twin spires dominate the market square and surrounding buildings.

Novels: In *c.* 1083 Roger de MONTGOMERY brought monks over from Seez to supervise the building of Shrewsbury Abbey. Brother CONRADIN, as a boy, was among the brothers who worked under them.

Refs: **15** (1).

Senlis, Simon II de (d. 1153), Earl of Northampton (hist.). He was the son of Simon I de Senlis (or Saintliz), Earl of Northampton, and his wife, Maud (or Matilda), daughter of Waltheof, Earl of Huntingdon. Simon I fought with WILLIAM I at Senlac, Hastings, and founded NORTHAMPTON PRIORY. Simon II was a minor when his father died in 1109 and in 1113, on his mother's remarriage to the future DAVID I, King of Scotland, he was excluded from his inheritance. In 1136 he was witness to the Easter charter of King STEPHEN at OXFORD, and sometime before 1141 the king restored him to the earldom of Northampton. Simon fought at the battle of LINCOLN in 1141, and was one of only three earls who remained loyal to the king throughout his captivity. In 1152 he was rewarded with the earldom of Huntingdon. He died the following year and was succeeded by his son Simon III de Senlis. Simon II married Isabel, daughter of Robert de BEAUMONT (the younger), Earl of Leicester. He was the founder of the Cistercian, Sawtry Abbey, near HUNTINGDON, and the Cluniac, Delapré Abbey at NORTHAMPTON.

Novels: In order to get some favour out of the Earl of Northampton, Drogo BOSIET forced Brand (see HYACINTH) to make a book cover to give him as a present.

Refs: **14** (9).

Sens (France). Some 70 miles south-east of Paris, the ancient town of Sens stands beside the River Yonne on the site of the Gallic capital of the Senon tribe, from whom it derives its name. It became a Roman provincial capital, later a bishopric and during medieval times it was an important ecclesiastical centre with five abbeys. In 1140 the writings of Pierre ABELARD were condemned as heretical at the Council of Sens. The Gothic Cathedral of St Étienne, dating from the 12th C., contains many treasures including some magnificent medieval stained-glass windows.

Novels: Pierre Abelard was convicted of heretical writings at the Council of Sens in 1140, and was 'condemned to have his works destroyed and end his life in perpetual imprisonment'.

Refs: **16** (2).

Serlo, Deacon (*fl.* 1143) (fict.). Novels: 'This Serlo was, as Hugh had said, a meek little fellow with a soft, round, ingenuous face, much in awe of Gerbert. He might have been in his forties, smooth-cheeked and pink and wholesome, with a thin, greying ring of fair hair, erased here and there by incipient baldness. No doubt he had suffered from his overpowering companion along the road, and was intent simply on completing his errand as soon and as peaceably as possible.' Serlo was one of Bishop ROGER DE CLINTON's deacons. In 1134 Serlo was sent to SHREWSBURY to look after a preaching canon from ST OSYTH. They were entertained to supper by William of LYTHWOOD. Serlo returned to Shrewsbury in June 1143, with Canon GERBERT. He had been lent by Roger de Clinton to Gerbert as a guide through the diocese. During chapter, he mentioned, in innocence, that in 1134 the preaching canon had suggested that William go on a pilgrimage to the HOLY LAND. It led to questions about William's beliefs, and whether or not they were heretical. After ELAVE had been accused of heresy, Serlo went to COVENTRY to fetch Roger de Clinton. By the end of June, Serlo and Roger de Clinton had returned to Coventry.

Refs: **16** (1–3, 5–6, 9, 13, 15)

Severn, River (or Afon Hafren) (Shropshire, Hereford & Worcester, Gloucestershire and Avon, England; Powys and Gwent, Wales). The longest river in Britain, the Severn rises on Plynlimon in the mountains of central Wales to flow, in a huge semicircular curve for some 200 miles, to the Bristol Channel and the Atlantic Ocean. Among the towns on its course are: Newtown, Welshpool (see POOL), SHREWSBURY, Bridgnorth (see BRIGGE), Stourport-on-Severn, WORCESTER, TEWKESBURY, GLOUCESTER and BRISTOL. The first English town on the river is Shrewsbury, and from there the Severn winds south across the Shropshire plain, past the WREKIN and through the Ironbridge Gorge to Bridgnorth. During the 19th C. barges, travelling from as far away as Bristol, could reach Welshpool. But today the recommended upper limit for navigation is Stourport-on-Severn, about 17 miles down river from Bridgnorth. At the port of Gloucester the river becomes tidal and, near Chepstow, it is spanned by the Severn Road Bridge, linking South Wales and England, with a main span of 3,240 ft. It was opened in 1966. The Severn is also noted for its Bore, a large wave surging upstream at flood tides, which has been known to exceed 9 ft in height at the popular vantage point of Stonebench, near Elmore.

Novels: 'They had circled the whole of the town in their early passage, for the Severn, upstream from the abbey, made a great moat about the walls, turning the town almost into an island, but for the neck of land covered and protected by the Castle. Once under Madog's western bridge, that gave passage to the roads into Wales, the meanderings of the river grew tortuous, and turned first one cheek, then the other, to the climbing, copper sun . . . Beyond the suburb of FRANKWELL, outside the town walls and the loop of the river, they were between wide stretches of water-meadows, still moist enough to be greener than the grass on high ground, and a little coolness came up from the reedy shores, as though the earth breathed here, that elsewhere seemed to hold its breath. For a while the banks rose on either side, and old, tall trees overhung the water, casting a leaden shade. Heavy willows leaned from the banks, half their roots exposed by the erosion of the soil. Then the ground levelled and opened out again on their right hand, while on the left the bank rose in low, sandy terraces below and a slope of grass above, leading up to hillocks of woodland.' 'Sunlit and peaceful, the Severn landscape lay somnolent in the afternoon light, denying the existence of murder, malice and abduction in so lovely a world.' 'MADOG OF THE DEAD-BOAT, in addition to his primary means of livelihood, which was salvaging dead bodies from the River Severn at any season, had a number of seasonal occupations that afforded him sport as well as a living. Of these the one he enjoyed most was fishing, and of all the fishing seasons the one he liked best was the early Spring run up-river of the mature salmon, fine, energetic young males which had arrived early in the estuary, and would run and leap like athletes many miles upstream before they spawned.' In February 1145 the Severn, swollen by thaw-water from Wales, burst its banks and, backed up by the waters of the MEOLE BROOK and mill pond, flooded parts of the enclave of SHREWSBURY ABBEY, including the nave of the church.

Refs: **1** (1); **2** (5–7, 9, 12); **3** (1, 6); **4** (1:2–4, 2:2, 3:1, 4:3); **5** (3); **7** (1, 5–7, 11); **8** (2, 4); **9** (9); **10** (5); **11** (8, 10, 12–14); **12** (4–5, 9, 11); **13** (6, 8); **14** (1–2, 11); **15** (3); **16** (7, 9); **17** (1, 6–8, 11, 13–14); **18** (1); **19** (1–4, 8, 11–13); **20** (1, 7, 10); **RB** (3).

Shelton. See SALTON.

Sherborne (Dorset, England). Situated in the valley of the River Yeo, some 5 miles east of Yeovil, this ancient town is noted for its abbey, public school (first founded in the 8th C.), and two castles. The see of Sherborne was created in 705 by Ine, King of Wessex, and the first cathedral was built near the site of the present abbey church, by Aldhelm, the first Bishop of Sherborne. It became a Benedictine monastery in 998, and in *c.*1050 work began on building a new cathedral church. In 1070, however, the see was transferred to Old Sarum (see SALISBURY). Stephen Harding (d. 1134), a major force in the foundation of the Cistercian Order, was educated in the monastery. After the Dissolution, the abbey church of St Mary the Virgin (rebuilt in the 12th C. and much reconstructed in the 15th C.) became the parish church. It is particularly celebrated for its ornate fan-vaulted ceiling and medieval sculpture. The Almhouses of St John the Baptist and St John the Evangelist were built in 1437/8. The Norman castle (known as Sherborne Old Castle) was built in the early 12th C. by ROGER, Bishop of Salisbury. Roger was forced to surrender the keys of the castle to King STEPHEN in 1139. William MARTEL held the castle on behalf of the king in 1142, but when William was captured at WILTON the following year, he was only released after Stephen had surrendered the castle to ROBERT of Gloucester. The ruins are now in the care of English Heritage. The second castle at Sherborne was built by Sir Walter Raleigh in 1594.

Novels: After William Martel's capture at Wilton, he had been 'bought free by Stephen at the cost of a valuable castle'.

Refs: **20** (3).

Sheriffhales. See HALES.

Shotwick (Cheshire). This small village on the edge of the River marshes in the Wirral is 5 miles north-west of CHESTER. Before the Norman Conquest, Shotwick belonged to the secular canons of St Werburgh at Chester. In 1093 they were succeeded by Benedictine monks. The village is named after the Norman family of Shotewyk (or Shotwike), who held the manor under the abbots. The Shotewyk line came to an end during the reign of Edward I (1272–1307), and the manor passed by marriage to the Hockenhulls (or Hokenhull). During the Middle Ages, Shotwick Ford was a major assembly point for English assaults against the Welsh. Among the kings who led their armies from here across the border into Wales were: Henry III in 1245; and Edward I in 1278 and 1284. Shotwick was also a port, formerly on the Dee, until the river silted up and the marshland took over. All that is left of the royal stronghold at Shotwick is a grassy mound. St Michael's Church, standing on the site of a Saxon foundation, dates from the 12th C. It was mainly rebuilt during the 15th C., when the embattled tower was erected, and restored in 1869.

Novels: Euan of SHOTWICK, the glover, came from the village.

Refs: **4** (5:1).

Shotwick, Euan of (d. 1139) (fict.). **Novels:** '"That's Euan of Shotwick, the glover, and an important man about Earl Ranulf's court at CHESTER, I can tell you." "For his skill at his trade?" asked CADFAEL dryly, observing the lean, fastidious, high-nosed figure with interest. "That and other fields, brother, Euan of Shotwick is one of the sharpest of all Earl Ranulf's intelligencers, and much relied on, and if he's setting up a booth here as far as SHREWSBURY, it may well be for more purposes than trade."' Glover and one of RANULF of Chester's intelligencers, Euan of Shotwick worked alone, trusting no one, armed and well able to take care of himself. He arrived at St Peter's Fair, Shrewsbury, on 31 July 1139. Expecting to collect a secret letter from Thomas of BRISTOL to pass on to Ranulf, he was murdered by Turstan FOWLER and EWALD THE GROOM in the early hours of 3 August. In the struggle Euan wounded Ewald with his dagger. He never received the expected message.

Refs: **4** (1:2, 1:4, 3:2, 4:1–5, 5:1–3, 5:6).

Shrewsbury (Shropshire, England). Formerly called Pengwern or Scrobbesbyrig. DB – Sciropesberie: in Shrewsbury Hundred; during the reign of EDWARD THE CONFESSOR there were 252 houses in Shrewsbury, with a burgess residing in each house; the king had three moneyers, or minters, in the town; the population was nearly 1,000; among those who held land in Shrewsbury were: the churches of St Alkmund, St Chad, St Julian, St Mary, and St Milburga, as well as the Bishop of Chester and Ediet. Strategically situated within a tight loop of the River SEVERN, close to the Welsh border, the ancient town of Shrewsbury dates back to at least Saxon times. In the 6th C. the settlement was known by its Welsh name of Pengwern, meaning 'hill of alders', and Brocwael, King of Powys, reputedly had a palace on the hill where the remains of Old ST CHAD'S CHURCH now stand. By the 9th C. Shrewsbury was part of the kingdom of Mercia, and was called by the Anglo-Saxon name of Scrobbesbyrig, probably meaning the 'town on the shrub-covered hill'. Some authorities, however, have suggested that Scrobbes is a personal name. Towards the end of the 9th C., Alfred the Great granted Mercia to his son-in-law, Ethelred, and on Ethelred's death in 911 his widow, Ethelfleda, ruled as the 'Lady of the Mercians'. By this time Shrewsbury was an important administrative centre in the Severn valley, and was guarded by a timber fortification at the narrow neck of land where SHREWSBURY CASTLE now stands. According to tradition, Ethelfleda frequently visited Shrewsbury, where she founded ST ALKMUND'S CHURCH. During the 10th C., the town was allowed to mint coins (see SHREWSBURY MINT). Within the town walls there were four principal churches: St Alkmund's, St Chad's, ST JULIAN'S and ST MARY'S. The wooden Church of St Peter's, later SHREWSBURY ABBEY, stood outside the loop of the Severn. After the Norman Conquest in 1066, WILLIAM I allowed Edwin, Earl of Mercia, to retain his Midland kingdom, which included Shrewsbury. After Edwin's death, William I conferred the earldom of Shrewsbury upon Roger de MONTGOMERY, who was succeeded by his son, Hugh de Montgomery. When Hugh was killed in a battle against Danish invaders in 1098, his brother, Robert de Bellême, became the 3rd Earl of Shrewsbury. In 1101 HENRY I forced Bellême to surrender the town and castle and, after confessing to treason, he was banished from the country. Richard of Belmeis (or Beaumais), who became Bishop of London in 1108, resigned the overlordship of Shropshire in *c.*1125. He was succeeded by Pain FitzJohn, who held the lordship of both Shropshire and Herefordshire until 1137, when he was killed fighting the Welsh. Control of the county then passed to William FITZALAN, but in August 1138, during King STEPHEN's siege of Shrewsbury, he fled to NORMANDY. There is no record as to the identity of the sheriff between 1138 and 1154, when FitzAlan was reinstated. Shrewsbury was granted its first market charter by Henry I, but the terms have been lost. Several old streets in the town were named after those who traded in them: BUTCHER ROW, Milk Street and Fish Street all survive today. Other names, however, have disappeared: Corviser's or Shoemaker's Row is now known as Pride Hill, while Baker's or Baxter's Row has been swallowed by the HIGH STREET. Between the main streets in medieval times there existed a warren of shuts and passages, and, despite the enormous changes that have taken place in the town throughout the intervening centuries, many have survived. Although the origins of their names are often obscure, among those that have been preserved are: Bear Steps, Plough Shut, Compasses Passage, St Mary's Shut, Grope Lane and Gullet Passage. The town has many buildings of interest, including: the Market Hall, built in 1595; the Abbot's House, dating from *c.*1500; the Bear Steps, dating from the late 15th C.; Owen's Mansion, dated 1592; Clive House, formerly part of the college of St Chad; the late 16th C. Ireland's Mansion; and the 16th C. timber-framed Rowley's House. Charles Darwin (1809–82) was born and educated in the town.

Novels: 'Across the broad river the hill of Shrewsbury rose in a great sweep of green, that wore the town wall like a coronet. Two or three small wickets gave access through the wall to gardens and grass below. They could easily be barred and blocked in case of attack, and the clear outlook such a raised fortress commanded gave ample notice of any approach. The vulnerable neck unprotected by water was filled by the Castle, completing the circle of the wall. A strong place, as well as a very fair one, yet King Stephen had taken it by storm, four years ago, and held it through his sheriffs ever since. . . . But all this stretch of our land, CADFAEL thought, brooding over its prolific green, is overlooked by hundreds of houses and households there within the wall. How many moments can there be in the day when someone is not peering out from a window, this weather, or below by the riverside, fishing, or hanging out washing, or the children playing and bathing?' Shrewsbury was given to Roger de Montgomery 'almost as soon as Duke William became king'. There were four parishes within the walls: St Alkmund's, St Chad's, St Julian's and St Mary's. The town was a charter borough, 'where the unfree may work their way to freedom in a year and a day'. In August 1138 Shrewsbury was besieged and captured by King Stephen and his army. The sheriff, William FitzAlan, managed to escape. He was replaced by Gilbert PRESTCOTE (the elder). Within the town walls Shrewsbury Abbey held 'some thirty or more messuages'. Geoffrey CORVISER was Provost of Shrewsbury from at least 1139. In August 1139 Abbot RADULFUS gave a tenth of the fruits of St Peter's Fair to the town for 'the repair of the walls and repaving of the streets'. The merchants and tradesmen of the town included: ARNALD THE FISHMONGER, Reginald of ASTON, Walter AURIFABER, Edred BELE, Martin BELLECOTE, Roger CLOTHIER, Ailwin CORDE, Geoffrey CORVISER, Edric FLESHER, Godfrey FULLER, Eward GURNEY, William HYNDE, Girard of LYTHWOOD, Baldwin PECHE, Judith PERLE, Richard VESTIER and Henry WYLE. The beggars included: Rhodri FYCHAN the Less and Lame OSBERN. For further information on Shrewsbury see: ABBEY FOREGATE; CASTLE FOREGATE; Walter AURIFABER'S BURGAGE; Martin

BELLECOTE'S HOUSE AND SHOP; Martin BELLECOTE'S WOOD-YARD; Hugh BERINGAR'S TOWN HOUSE; BONEL'S MESSUAGE; Niall BRONZESMITH'S HOUSE AND SHOP; CASTLE STREET; Roger CLOTHIER'S CART-HOUSE AND CART-YARD; CORVISER'S HOUSE AND GARDEN; FRANKWELL; Godfrey FULLER'S HOUSE; Godfrey FULLER'S DYE-HOUSE, FULLING-WORKS AND TENTER-GROUND; GAYE; Ralph GIFFARD THE ELDER'S HOUSE; HIGH CROSS; HIGH STREET; HOLY CROSS, Parish Church of; HOLY CROSS, Parish of; William HYNDE'S COUNTING-HOUSE; William HYNDE'S WAREHOUSE; Girard of LYTHWOOD'S HOUSE; Jevan of LYTHWOOD'S SHOP; Jevan of LYTHWOOD'S WORKSHOP; MADOG OF THE DEAD-BOAT'S HUT; MAERDOL; Widow NEST'S HOVEL; Baldwin PECHE'S SHOP; ROGER DE CLINTON'S HOUSE; ST ALKMUND'S CHURCH; ST CHAD'S CHURCH; ST GILES, Church and Hospital of; ST JULIAN'S CHURCH; ST MARY'S CHURCH; ST MARY'S CLOSE; ST MARY'S WATER-LANE; SHREWSBURY ABBEY; SHREWSBURY CASTLE; SHREWSBURY MARKET; THREE-TREE SHUT; VESTIER'S HOUSE & SHOP; WAT'S TAVERN; WYLE.

Ref: **1** (1–6, 8–11); **2** (1–3, 6–8, 12); **3** (1–4, 6, 8, 11); **4** (1:1, 2:1, 4:2, 5:5); **5** (3); **6** (15); **7** (1–4, 6, 8, 11–12, 14); **8** (2, 9, 12–13); **9** (9, 11); **10** (5, 7–8); **11** (1, 10, 12–13); **12** (1); **13** (2–3, 6–10); **14** (1, 4); **15** (1–6, 10–14); **16** (3, 6, 8); **17** (9); **18** (1–3, 6, 9); **19** (1–7, 9–13); **20** (2–3, 5–6, 14, 16); **RB** (1–3).

Shrewsbury Abbey (Shropshire, England). Occupying a spur of high, dry land at the eastern end of the English Bridge, outside the loop of the River SEVERN, Shrewsbury Abbey stands on the site of a small wooden Saxon church, dedicated to St Peter. In 1082 its priest, Odelirius, the father of Ordericus Vitalis, made a pilgrimage to ROME. On his return he vowed to replace his wooden church with one built of stone, in honour of the two apostles St PETER and St PAUL. Roger de MONTGOMERY, Odelirius's master, received the idea of building a new and grander church with great enthusiasm. The Benedictine abbey was founded by Roger in 1083, and monks were brought over from SEEZ in NORMANDY to supervise its construction. Work began immediately and continued for many years. The first abbot, FULCHERED, was appointed in 1087. In 1137 Prior Robert obtained the relics of St WINIFRED, whose shrine in the abbey church survived for some 400 years. After its dissolution in 1540 many of the monastic buildings were destroyed. All that remains today of the abbey church, originally 302 ft. from east to west and 133 ft. across the transepts, is the nave and western tower, which served as the parish Church of HOLY CROSS. A wall was built between the pillars at the eastern end and, in the mid-1880s, the church was restored and extended eastward (though not to its original size) to create the present Choir and Lady Chapel. The few remaining monastic buildings, which managed to survive the Dissolution and escape major damage during the Civil War, were demolished in 1836 when Thomas Telford constructed a new road linking LONDON to Holyhead (see CAERGYBI). One structure to remarkably escape destruction is the 14th C. Refectory Pulpit, now situated in a small, railed garden to the south of the abbey church and across the main road. Other monastic houses in medieval SHREWSBURY were: an Augustinian friary, founded *c.*1254; a Dominican friary, founded before 1232 and dedicated to St Mary; and a Franciscan friary, founded in 1245 and possibly dedicated to St Francis.

Novels: 'In the dim space of the choir, partially shut off from the nave of the church by the parish altar, the brothers in their stalls showed like carven copies, in this twilight without age or youth, comeliness or homeliness, so many matched shadows. The height of the vault, the solid stone of the pillars and walls, took up the sound of Brother ANSELM's voice, and made of it a disembodied magic, high in air. Beyond, where the candle-light reached and shadows ended, there was darkness, the night within, the night without. A benign night, mild, still and silent.' 'Abbot RADULFUS had been speaking for some time, slowly, with the high, withdrawn voice of intense thought, every word measured. In the choir it was always dim, a parable of the life of man, a small, lighted space arched over by a vast shadowy darkness, for even in darkness there are degrees of shadow. The crowded nave was lighter, and with so many people in attendance not even notably cold. When choir monks and secular congregation met for worship together, the separation between them seemed accentuated rather than softened. We here, you out there, thought Brother CADFAEL, and yet we are all like flesh, and our souls subject to the same final judgement.' Shrewsbury Abbey was founded by Roger de Montgomery for Benedictine monks in 1083. He brought over monks from Seez to supervise the building work. They replaced the small wooden church with one of stone. The couples married in the abbey included: Nigel and Roswitha ASPLEY; Luc and Melangell MEVEREL; and LILIWIN and RANNILT (at the parish altar). Among those buried inside the abbey church were: Nicholas FAINTREE and Gilbert PRESTCOTE (the elder). Those buried in the abbey graveyard included: Father ADAM, Father AILNOTH, Gervase BONEL, Brother ELURIC, GENERYS and William of LYTHWOOD, as well as sixty-six victims of the siege of Shrewsbury. In February 1145 the floodwaters of the River Severn, backed up by the swollen waters of the MEOLE BROOK and the mill pond, invaded much of the abbey enclave, including the nave of the church; the latter having 'been known to float a raft now and again over the years, once even a light boat'. See also Abbots FULCHERED, GODEFRID, HERIBERT and RADULFUS; Brothers ADAM; ADRIAN; AELFRIC; ALBIN; AMBROSE; ANDREW; ANSELM; ATHANASIUS; AYLWIN; BENEDICT; BERNARD; CADFAEL; COLUMBANUS; CONRADIN; DAFYDD; DENIS; EDMUND; ELURIC; EMMANUEL; EUTROPIUS; EVERARD; Fidelis (see CRUCE, Julian); FRANCIS; HALUIN; HENRY; HUMILIS; JEROME; JOHN; JORDAN; LEONARD; LUKE; MARK; MATTHEW; MAURICE; MERIET; ORDERIC; OSWALD; OSWIN; PAUL; PETRUS; PORTER (*fl.* 1138); REGINALD; RHUN; RHYS; RICHARD; RUALD; SIMEON; SIMON; Sulien (see BLOUNT, Sulien); URIEN; VITALIS; WILFRED; WINFRID; WOLSTON; Lay Brothers ANSELM; BARNABAS; LOUIS; SIMON; PRIOR LEONARD; ROBERT PENNANT; Sub-prior Richard (see RICHARD, Brother).

Ref: **1** (1, 11); **2** (3–5, 7–10); **3** (1–2, 5–7); **4** (1:1, 1:4, 2:3, 3:2, 4:1, 5:5); **5** (1–2, 4, 6, 8–10); **6** (1); **7** (1, 5); **8** (1–2, 4, 7, 9, 12); **9** (1, 4–5, 7–8); **10** (2–5, 8, 10); **11** (2, 5, 8–9, 13); **12** (1–5, 8–11); **13** (1, 6); **14** (1, 7, 9); **15** (1); **16** (1–2, 4, 9–11); **17** (14); **18** (1, 14); **19** (Prologue, 1–7, 9–13); **20** (1–2, 9, 11, 13–16); **RB** (1–3).

Shrewsbury Castle (Shropshire, England). Shrewsbury Castle was originally an Anglo-Saxon timber fortification, guarding the only dry-shod approach to the town. The Norman castle, built of red sandstone, was founded by Roger de MONTGOMERY in *c.* 1070. During Summer 1138 King STEPHEN laid siege to and captured the fortress, which was held by William FITZALAN for the Empress MAUD. Apart from the gateway, very little of the Norman building survives. Much of it was demolished during the rebuilding and strengthening of the castle by Edward I in *c.* 1300, when an outer bailey was also added. It was never used as a fortress after this date and, over the centuries, was allowed to fall into disrepair. Elizabeth I gave the castle to the bailiffs and burgesses of SHREWSBURY in 1586 and little was done to the building until the Civil War, when further alterations were made. The interior of the great hall was partitioned and extra floors were constructed, including an upper floor lit by a row of square mullioned windows on the south side. The doors of the main gateway date from this time. It was captured by the Parliamentarians in 1645, and it was not until 1660, when Charles II was restored to the throne, that it was surrendered to the Crown. The king granted the castle to Sir Francis Newport of High Ercall, Shropshire, in 1663, and it remained in private hands until 1924, when it was acquired by the Corporation of Shrewsbury. It was restored as much as possible to its Edwardian condition and opened to the public in 1926. It now houses the Shropshire Regimental Museum. Laura's Tower, standing on top of the original Norman motte, was built in 1790 by Thomas Telford, who also converted the castle into a private residence for Sir William Pulteney, MP for Shrewsbury.

Novels: 'Across the stream, so silent and so fast, the walls of Shrewsbury loomed, at the crest of a steep green slope of gardens, orchards and vineyard, and further downstream fused into the solid bulk of the king's castle, guarding the narrow neck of land that broke Shrewsbury's girdle of water.' 'The apartments in the castle tower, when the best had been done to make them comfortable, remained stony, draughty and cold, no place to bring a young family, and it was exceptional indeed for Sybilla PRESTCOTE and her son to come to Shrewsbury, when they had six far more pleasant manors at their disposal.' In August 1138 Stephen besieged and captured Shrewsbury Castle. William FitzAlan and Fulke ADENEY managed to escape by swimming across the River SEVERN. Arnulf of HESDIN, however, was captured and hung from the battlements, along with ninety-three other prisoners. Among those who spent some time in the castle cells were: Elis ap CYNAN, Eliud ap GRIFFITH, HARALD and Adam HERIET. Gilbert PRESTCOTE (the elder), the sheriff, lived in apartments at the castle.

Refs: **2** (1–3, 8, 10–11); **3** (3, 7–8); **4** (2:2, 2:3, 4:3); **5** (3); **6** (1, 15); **7** (1, 6); **8** (9); **9** (2, 4, 9, 11); **10** (2); **11** (12–13); **12** (6–7, 11–12); **13** (6–8, 10); **16** (6, 12); **17** (1, 6, 9); **19** (1, 3, 5–8, 11, 13); **20** (1–3, 15–16); **RB** (3).

Shrewsbury Market (Shropshire, England). By the end of the 12th C. SHREWSBURY was the most important market centre in the region, attracting business from the Welsh as well as the English side of the border. It received its first market charter from HENRY I, at some time during the early 12th C. Further charters, in 1209 and 1266, gave the town a virtual monopoly in the trade of hides and wool in Shropshire. By the mid-14th C. this monopoly had extended to include almost the whole of the northern half of Wales. There have been a number of market sites within the town walls, despite the fact that many medieval traders occupied stalls in the streets: BUTCHER ROW, Fish Street and Corvisor's Row, for example. One of the early market places was centred round ST ALKMUND'S CHURCH. It was transferred to the Square (formerly called Corn Market) in *c.*1269, which quickly became the commercial hub of the town. The Old Market Hall, probably designed by Walter Hancock, was built in 1596. On its walls are two items of interest: a carved angel from the town gate near SHREWSBURY CASTLE; and a statue of Richard, Duke of York, which was formerly on the old Welsh Bridge. It is most likely that HIGH CROSS was also a medieval market site. The most important medieval market place outside the town walls was the HORSE-FAIR, on the north side of the ABBEY FOREGATE. Although there are a wealth of shops in Shrewsbury, general markets are still held weekly in the town; while the Cattle Market (previously held from the mid-18th C. on the Raven Meadows, between CASTLE STREET and the River SEVERN) lies to the north at the junction of Battlefield Road and Harlescott Lane.

Novels: 'The news went round, as news does, from gossip to gossip, those within the town parading their superior knowledge to those without, those who came to market in town or Foregate carrying their news to outer villages and manors.' 'By chance it was Welsh woollen cloth, patterned in a regular array of crude four-petalled flowers in a dim blue; many of its kind found their way into English homes through the market of Shrewsbury.'

Refs: **3** (1, 4); **4** (4:5); **5** (7); **8** (9); **16** (1); **17** (8); **19** (3).

Shrewsbury Mint (Pride Hill, Shrewsbury, Shropshire). The first mint at SHREWSBURY was established during the reign of Aethelstan (924–39), King of Wessex and Mercia, when in 925 he passed a law to unify the coinage throughout his empire. The Domesday Book survey of 1086 records that there were three recognised minters in the town during the reign of EDWARD THE CONFESSOR, one of whom was GODESBROND. When Parliament seized the Royal Mint in LONDON in 1642, a mint was established in Shrewsbury, among other places, to provide Charles I with money to pay his army. No further coins have been minted in the town since then. The 13th C. sandstone remains of the Shrewsbury Mint, or Bennet's Hall, were incorporated into a shop in Pride Hill during redevelopment in 1962. All that is left of the medieval building, including part of the great hall, an undercroft and a flight of steps leading to an arched doorway, can only be seen from inside the store, and not from the street. Originally John Colliers and now Evans, the shop stands next door to Lloyds Bank at the junction of Mardol Head, High Street and Pride Hill.

Novels: In May 1140 Hugh BERINGAR showed CADFAEL a silver penny, which had been found wedged in the bucket in Walter AURIFABER's well: 'a beautiful piece minted in this town' by Godesbrond. In the same month Walter Aurifaber gave LILIWIN another silver penny, also minted in Shrewsbury by Godesbrond.

Refs: **7** (4, 8, 11).

Shure, John (*fl.* 1141) (fict.). **Novels:** 'Lean-jowled and sedate, with lank hair curtaining a lugubrious face.' John Shure, claiming to be a tailor, appeared at SHREWSBURY ABBEY on 17 June 1141 in the company of Walter BAGOT and William HALES. He had, however, the 'long, well-tended nails of a fairground sharper, hardly suitable for a tailor's work'. Shure and his companions (along with Simeon POER) were surprised by Hugh BERINGAR and his men while gambling with loaded dice under the arch of the English Bridge. All, except Hales, managed to evade capture and fled west towards Wales. Attacking CIARAN and Matthew (see MEVEREL, Luc) in the LONG FOREST, the footpads were foiled by CADFAEL, Olivier de BRETAGNE, Hugh and his men. Shure and the others were captured and taken back to SHREWSBURY CASTLE 'to answer for more, this time, than a little cheating in the marketplace'.

Refs: **10** (4, 7–8, 13–15).

Sigebert (*fl.* 1142) (hist.). He was an Oxford moneyer, or minter, who struck coins, bearing his name and the head of the Empress MAUD, during the period when she was in the city. Examples of his coinage still survive.

Novels: The coin, which Rafe of COVENTRY had intended to place in the alms box of SHREWSBURY ABBEY in November 1142, was 'a silver penny like other pennies, the universal coin. Yet not quite like any he [CADFAEL] had seen before in the alms boxes. It was bright and untarnished, but indifferently struck, and it felt light in the hand. Clumsily arrayed round the short cross on the reverse, the moneyer's name appeared to be Sigebert, a minter Cadfael never remembered to have heard of in the midlands. And when he turned it, the crude head was . . . unmistakably a woman's, coifed and coroneted. It hardly needed the name sprawled round the rim: "Matilda Dom. Ang." The empress's formal name and title. It seemed her mintage was short-weight.' The coin was struck in OXFORD.

Refs: **14** (9, 14).

Simeon, Brother (*fl.* 1142) (fict.). **Novels:** Benedictine monk of SHREWSBURY ABBEY, he chopped jagged holes in the frozen pools to let in air to the fish below, in December 1142.

Refs: **15** (1).

Simon, Brother (b. *c.*1096) (fict.). Novels: Benedictine monk of SHREWSBURY ABBEY, Brother Simon 'was a comfortable, round man in his forties'. He served for a term at the Hospital of ST GILES, initially under Brother MARK. In August 1141 he was joined by Brother OSWIN. In November 1142 Simon cut a pair of crutches to EILMUND THE FORESTER's measure.

Refs: **11** (1); **14** (8).

Simon, Lay Brother (b. *c.*1098) (fict.). **Novels:** 'A thin, wiry, dishevelled brother, some forty years old but still distrait as a child when anything went wrong with other than sheep.' Benedictine monk and lay brother of SHREWSBURY ABBEY, Brother Simon served at the abbey sheepfolds, near RHYDYCROESAU. In December 1138 he sent a message to the abbey saying that Lay Brother BARNABAS had been taken ill.

Refs: **3** (7–10).

Sioned (b. *c.*1119) (fict.). **Novels:** '"The greatest match anywhere in this valley, is Sioned, and young men after her like bees. But God willing, she'll be a contented wife with a son on her knee long before Rhisiart goes to his fathers."' Sioned was the Welsh wife of ENGELARD, mother of CADFAEL (b. 1139) and daughter and heiress of RHISIART of GWYTHERIN. In May 1137, despite her father's wishes, she refused to marry PEREDUR. She was in love with the outlander and ox-caller, Engelard, and it was during secret meetings with him that she learned to speak English. After her father's murder, Sioned allowed her holding to be used to confine Brother JOHN, promising that she would neither go near the prisoner nor hold the key to his prison herself. While Brother COLUMBANUS was watching the night through alone in St WINIFRED's chapel, Sioned tricked him into confessing to the murder of her father while pretending to be an avenging St Winifred. Realising finally that she was merely flesh and blood, Columbanus slashed at her with his knife, slightly grazing her left forearm. Making his escape, Columbanus was accidentally killed by Engelard. She helped Brother Cadfael cover up the death: placing the monk's corpse in the saint's reliquary; reburying the saint in her grave alongside Rhisiart; and collecting petals of may blossom to scatter in the church. With the death of her father, Sioned became Engelard's lord. By dividing all his goods with her, he became a free man. She in turn endowed him with half her goods. They were married and, in March 1139, Sioned gave birth to their son, Cadfael.

Refs: **1** (2–12); **10** (1).

Sitric Silk-Beard (d. 1042), King of Dublin (hist.). Also spelled Sihtric or Sigtryggr; also called Sitric Silki-Skegg. Grandson of Sitric (d. 927) and son of Olaf Sitricson (d. 981) by Gormflaith (or Kormlada) (d. 1030), Sitric Silk-Beard was grandfather of RAGNHILD. King of the Danish kingdom of DUBLIN, he was driven out of the city in 995 by Imhar of Waterford, but returned the following year. In 1000 Sitric was defeated by Brian Boroimhe (or Brian Boru), King of Ireland (1002–14) and forced to accept a treaty which resulted in two marriages: that of his sister Maelmuire to Maelsechlain II; and that of himself to Brian's daughter. After Brian's death in 1014, Sitric was involved in several forays into neighbouring territories, but suffered a major defeat at Delgany in Wicklow in 1019. He went on a pilgrimage to ROME in 1028 and in 1035 he left Ireland, probably to become a monk. His son having died, he was succeeded by his nephew, Eachmarcach Ragnallsson. He is reputed to be the founder of Holy Trinity Church (now Christ Church) DUBLIN.

Novels: OWAIN GWYNEDD's grandmother, Ragnhild, was granddaughter of Sitric Silk-Beard, King of the Danish kingdom of DUBLIN.

Refs: **18** (2).

Siward, Aline. See BERINGAR, Aline.

Siward, Giles (1114-38) (fict.). **Novels:** '"No, I never knew him as sister should know brother. Giles was always for his own friends and his own way, and five years my elder. By the time I was eleven or twelve he was for ever away from home, and came back only to quarrel with my father. But he is the only brother I have, and I have not disinherited him. And they're saying there's one there more than they counted, and unknown."' Brother of Aline Siward (see BERINGAR), Giles Siward was away from home in *c.*1131. After returning, he quarrelled with his father, a supporter of King STEPHEN, and left to join the party of the Empress MAUD. He was besieged in SHREWSBURY CASTLE in August 1138, but managed to slip secretly out of the fortress to betray William FITZALAN's plans for his treasury to Adam COURCELLE. Although Courcelle promised him his life and freedom in exchange for the information, he ordered the Flemings to hang Giles from the castle battlements. Siward died vehemently protesting that he had been promised his life. After his corpse had been identified by Aline, he was interred in the tomb of his maternal grandfather in ST ALKMUND'S CHURCH.

Refs: **2** (1–4, 7–8, 10–12).

Smyrna (now Izmir, Turkey). Capital of the province of Izmir, the city and port of Smyrna is located at the head of the Gulf of Izmir, on the Aegean Sea. Dating back to at least 3,000 BC, the city prospered to become one of the major cities of Asia Minor under Alexander the Great and later the Romans. Homer, the supposed author of the Greek epics the *Iliad* and the *Odyssey*, is reputed to have been born beside the River Meles (now Kizilcullu). The old city of Smyrna, with its citadel 'the velvet fortress', was built on Mount Pagus (or Kadifekale), which lies to the south of the modern commercial centre. It was one of the early centres of the Christian church and the location of one of the seven churches of the Apocalypse (Revelation 1:11). After it had been conquered by the crusaders and later by the Turkish-Mongol Tamberlaine (or Timur), Smyrna became part of the Ottoman Empire in *c.*1425. The city was occupied by the Greeks in 1919, but the Turks recaptured it in 1922, and today it is Turkey's third largest city with a thriving port.

Novels: NOETUS OF SMYRNA was a native of the city.

Refs: **16** (2).

Snowdon, Mount (Gwynedd, Wales). Also called Yr Wyddfa. The highest mountain in England and Wales, at 3,560 ft above sea level, Snowdon lies in the north-western corner of the Snowdonia National Park. Although the summit is a popular goal for walkers, it can also be reached from Llanberis, some 6 miles south-east of CARNARVON, by the Snowdon Mountain Railway. The mountainous block which stretches south-west from the mouth of the River CONWAY and includes Snowdon, was known as Eryri, 'the haunt of the eagles'. It was said that the pastures of Eryri could graze all the sheep and cattle in Wales.

Novels: 'They came over the crest of a high ridge before noon, and there below them the valley of the CONWY opened, and beyond, the ground rose at first gently and suavely, but above these green levels there towered in the distance the enormous bastions of Eryri, soaring to polished steel peaks against the pale blue of the sky.' CADFAEL and Deacon MARK saw the distant peaks of Eryri on their expedition into North Wales in May 1144.

Refs: **1** (3); **3** (7); **18** (4, 6).

Solomon (d. *c.*922 BC), King of Israel (bib.). The son of King DAVID and Queen Bathsheba, Solomon succeeded his father to become the third King of Israel.

Almost all that is factually known about Solomon comes from the Bible (notably I Kings 1–11, and II Chronicles 1–9). After his succession, he quickly established his dominion by military strength and, from his capital of JERUSALEM, 'reigned over all kingdoms from the river unto the land of the Philistines, and unto the border of Egypt' (I Kings 4:21). Although he married the daughter of an Egyptian pharaoh, he is reputed to have had a harem of 700 wives and 300 concubines. Among many accomplishments, his most famous was the building of the Temple at Jerusalem. Solomon is particularly noted for his wisdom: 'which excelled the wisdom of all the children of the east country, and all the wisdom of Egypt' (I Kings 4:30). He was also famous as a poet, and is traditionally regarded as the author of the Song of Solomon. King of Israel for forty years, after his death he was buried in Jerusalem, the 'city of David'. He was succeeded by his son, Rehoboam, who soon found himself king of a hostile and divided kingdom.

Novels: 'A judgement of Solomon, thought CADFAEL, well content with his abbot.'

Refs: **16** (5).

Sopwell Priory (Hertfordshire, England). Located on the southern outskirts of ST ALBANS, the priory was founded in 1140 for Benedictine nuns by Prior GEOFFREY, and dedicated to St MARY. Until their move to Sopwell, the nuns were originally part of the double monastery at St Albans. The priory remained a dependency of St Albans abbey until it was dissolved in 1537. The buildings were demolished and a number of houses built in succession on the site. Although excavations were carried out between 1963 and 1966, nothing now remains of the priory.

Novels: In September 1141 Sister MAGDALEN delivered a letter to Hugh BERINGAR at SHREWSBURY from Julian CRUCE, who was reputedly at POLESWORTH ABBEY. The letter said: '"I have been living retired and serviceable, but have taken no vows as a nun. At Sopwell Priory by St Albans a devout woman may live a life of holiness and service short of the veil, through the charity of Prior Geoffrey."'

Refs: **11** (14).

Soulis, Brien de (*c.*1110–45) (fict.). **Novels:** 'A very personable man, trimly built and moving with an elegant arrogance, his fair head uncovered, a short cloak swinging on one shoulder. Thirty-five years old, perhaps, and well assured of his worth.' Castellan of FARINGDON Castle under Philip FITZROBERT, and a follower of the Empress MAUD, Brien de Soulis was as close to FitzRobert as 'twin to twin, at all times in his councils'. In Summer 1145 de Soulis 'sold out Faringdon to the king, and made prisoner all the knights of the garrison who refused to change sides', including Olivier de BRETAGNE. He ordered the murder of one of his captains, Geoffrey FITZCLARE, claiming the cause was accidental, and added FitzClare's forged seal to the five others on the document of surrender. Traitor to Maud and supporter of King STEPHEN, de Soulis attended the conference at COVENTRY on 30 November. He was lured to the north walk of the cloister of St Mary's Priory, where he was murdered by FitzClare's mother, Jovetta de MONTORS. De Soulis's belongings were delivered to his younger brother in WORCESTER, who also looked after the arrangements for his burial.

Refs: **20** (1–10, 15).

S

South Downs (East Sussex and West Sussex, England). Like the HAMPSHIRE DOWNS, the South Downs are an expanse of rolling, grassy uplands in southern England, composed mainly of chalk. The name comes from the Old English *dun*, meaning 'hill'. Once cloaked by extensive woodland, the low, rounded summits of the South Downs are notable for numerous prehistoric remains. In medieval times vast flocks of sheep grazed on the open downland, providing wool for the cloth industry. Today, most of the lower slopes have been ploughed. The South Downs stretch from Beachy Head and the Seven Sisters, westward along the south coast, passing to the north of Brighton and Worthing, to the Hampshire border. Where they meet the sea, the crumbling chalk has produced sheer white cliffs up to 500 ft. high.

Novels: On the ship from NORMANDY to England in November 1120, CADFAEL had his 'eyes fixed on the shore that began to show the solidity of land and the undulations of cliff and down'.

Refs: **RB** (1).

Southampton (Hampshire, England). This city and seaport lies at the head of Southampton Water, on a broad peninsula between the estuaries of the rivers TEST and Itchen. Its origins date back to ancient times: the Romans had a town and naval base at nearby Bitterne; while the Anglo-Saxon settlement was sacked on several occasions by the Danes. The Normans built a castle on the site, of which little now remains. Many crusaders sailed from the port at the start of their journey to the HOLY LAND. Although the city was extensively damaged during World War II, and has since been rebuilt, many ancient buildings have survived. Among them are: God's House (or Maison Dieu) a pilgrim hospice founded in 1185; Bargate, dating from the late 12th C.; St Michael's Church, dating from 1070; the Medieval Merchant's House, dating from *c.*1290; and sections of the medieval town walls.

Novels: In November 1120, CADFAEL and ALARD THE CLERK disembarked at Southampton, having set sail from BARFLEUR in the service of Roger MAUDUIT. They spent the night in the town before travelling north to SUTTON MAUDUIT. William HYNDE's wool clip was taken by barge to BRISTOL, and then overland to Southampton where it was shipped to Europe.

Refs: **13** (10); **RB** (1).

Staceys, The (Hampshire, England). The two villages of Barton Stacey and Newton Stacey lie to the south of the rivers TEST and Dover, some 4 miles south-east of ANDOVER. The smaller of the two, Newton Stacey, sited just to the west of a Roman road, is now essentially a farming manor with a small cluster of cottages. It once had a chapel, dependent on Barton Stacey Church, which seems to have been destroyed in *c.*1635. Barton Stacey was known as Bertune in the 11th C., meaning 'a place for threshing corn'. In 1086, according to DB, the hundred of Barton Stacey covered 5,026 acres and stretched south-eastward almost to WINCHESTER. It was a royal demesne until 1206, when the manor was granted to Roger de Stacey – from whom both villages get the second part of their name. The advowson of the church was granted to Lanthony Priory, GLOUCESTER, in 1136 by MILES, Constable of Gloucester. In 1792 much of Barton Stacey was destroyed by an accidental fire.

Novels: '"There was a beggar, able bodied but getting old, who came in three days ago, and stayed only overnight to rest. He was from the Staceys' near Andover."' In August 1141 a beggar from the Staceys – 'a queer one, perhaps a mite touched in his wits, who can tell?' – brought news to SHREWSBURY about the burning of WINCHESTER.

Refs: **11** (1).

Stafford (Staffordshire, England). Some 28 miles north-east of SHREWSBURY and 15 miles north-west of LICHFIELD, the county town of Stafford lies on the River Sow near its confluence with the Penk. It is an ancient market town and was fortified in the 10th C. by Ethelfleda, eldest daughter of Alfred the Great. It also had a mint until the reign of HENRY II. Recorded as Stadford (or Statford) the town is mentioned as a borough in the Domesday Book survey of 1086, and contained thirteen prebendary canons. WILLIAM I built a castle (now disappeared) at Tenter Banks in the town; while Robert de Stafford, one of his barons, built another about a mile to the west. The latter was rebuilt in the 14th C., destroyed by the Parliamentarians in 1643, and partly rebuilt once more in the early 19th C. The remains of Stafford Castle stand on a hill overlooking the M6 motorway. A Franciscan friary was established by 1274, and in 1344 Ralph de Stafford founded an Augustinian friary; nothing remains of either. During medieval times Stafford prospered on the wool and cloth trade, while from the late 18th C. onwards its main industry was shoemaking. Among the buildings of interest are: St Mary's Church, dating from the 12th C., with its 13th C. octagonal tower; and St Chad's church dating from the 12th C.

Novels: Huon de DOMVILLE held manors in Shropshire, Cheshire, Stafford and LEICESTER. In December 1140 the fugitives Janyn LINDE and Nigel ASPLEY met in the heathland to the south-west of Stafford. After stabbing Nigel, Janyn took his fellow conspirator's horse and headed towards the town. The CRUCE family had manors in Stafford and the north of Shropshire. During autumn 1142, Aymer BOSIET went to Stafford in search of the runaway villein Brand (see HYACINTH).

Refs: **5** (1); **8** (13); **10** (7); **11** (4); **14** (4).

Stamford (Lincolnshire, England). Close to the borders of Leicestershire, Cambridgeshire and Northamptonshire, this ancient market town lies on the River Welland, 12 miles north-west of Peterborough and 29 miles east of LEICESTER. A river-crossing settlement, Stamford grew up at the convergence of numerous ancient roads, including Ermine Street (the latter also passed through the Roman town of Great Casterton, a few miles north-west). Stamford was one of five major towns within Danelaw (the area settled by the Danes in the 10th C.), the others being LEICESTER, DERBY, LINCOLN and NOTTINGHAM. After the Conquest, the Danish fortress was replaced by a Norman motte-and-bailey castle. The town was also walled. It was at Stamford in 1145 that RANULF of Chester made peace with King STEPHEN. The importance of the medieval town (where in the 14th C. students from OXFORD briefly set up an alternative college), is reflected in the wealth of its religious foundations: a Benedictine priory, first founded in the 7th C. (parts of the medieval monastery survive); a Franciscan friary, founded before 1230; a Dominican friary, founded before 1241; a Carmelite friary, founded before 1268 (some remains); a Sack friary, founded before 1274; and an Augustinian friary, founded in 1343. Churches of interest include St Mary's, All Saints', and St Martins. Burghley House, on the south-eastern outskirts of the town, was built by William Cecil, 1st Lord Burghley, in 1587.

Novels: Ranulf of Chester pledged his allegiance to King Stephen at Stamford in October 1145. 'So Stamford was no surprise, and Chester is reconciled and accepted.'

Refs: **20** (1).

Stanton Cobbold (Shropshire, England) (fict.). The manor of Stanton Cobbold was situated in the south of the shire, beyond Church STRETTON, a 'good' 17 miles from SHREWSBURY. The Bishop of Hereford held land at Onibury during the Domesday Book survey of 1086 and, although it never existed, the location of Stanton Cobbold seems to have been somewhere in the region bounded by Craven Arms, Onibury and Stanton Lacy.

Novels: '"Not my most amiable home," said Ivo with a grimace, "but in these Welsh borders we built for defence, not for comfort."' Although the main part of his honour lay in Cheshire, under RANULF of Chester, Ivo CORBIÈRE held a manor at Stanton Cobbold in Shropshire. Having tricked Emma Vernold (see CORVISER) into accompanying him there in August 1139, Corbière forcibly attempted to take the letter she was secretly carrying. Emma overturned the lighted brazier and the manor, including Corbière, went up in flames.

Refs: **4** (1:3, 2:2, 5:1–5).

S

Stephen (*c.*1097–1154), King of England (1135–54) (hist.). Also called Stephen of Blois. He was the third son of Stephen, Count of Blois, by ADELA, daughter of WILLIAM I, and brother of HENRY OF BLOIS and THEOBALD OF NORMANDY. Stephen was brought up and educated by his uncle, HENRY I, who knighted him and granted him vast lands in England and NORMANDY. In 1119 Stephen fought alongside his uncle at the siege of Evreux, in Eure, Normandy. Illness, however, prevented him from embarking from BARFLEUR on 25 November 1120 in the ill-fated *White Ship* (see BLANCHE NEF), in which Henry's son and heir, WILLIAM THE AETHELING, was drowned. Thereafter, Henry treated Stephen as if he were his own son, keeping him constantly at his side, and marrying him to MATILDA of Boulogne in 1125. Stephen pledged to acknowledge Henry's daughter, the Empress MAUD, as the successor to the throne of England and Normandy. But when the king died on 1 December 1135, Stephen lost no time, rushed to England, and with the help of his brother, Henry of Blois, Bishop of Winchester, he seized the throne and had himself crowned king at WESTMINSTER within the month. Many of the barons who had sworn fealty to Maud retracted their oaths and declared themselves for him. Stephen's action heralded the start of a long fratricidal civil war for the Crown of England which lasted some nineteen years. With his army of Flemish mercenaries under WILLIAM OF YPRES, Stephen laid siege to and captured many castles, including SHREWSBURY in August 1138, granting them, together with earldoms, to many of his loyal supporters. When his rival and cousin, Maud, landed near ARUNDEL on 30 September 1139, he was persuaded to give her safe escort to BRISTOL, and within a short while she controlled much of south-west England. Stephen was captured at the battle of LINCOLN on 2 February 1141 and taken to Bristol where he was imprisoned in the castle. He was released in November in exchange for ROBERT of Gloucester, Maud's half-brother, who had been captured at STOCKBRIDGE in September. Stephen was formally recognised as king by a legatine council on 7 December 1141 and the restored ruler submitted to a second coronation in CANTERBURY Cathedral on 25 December. During Spring 1142, at NORTHAMPTON, Stephen was seriously ill for many weeks. During the Summer he captured the castle at WAREHAM, and on 26 September he took the city of OXFORD, driving Maud into the castle where for nearly three months he held her under close siege until her escape. Stephen was almost captured for a second time at the battle of WILTON in 1143. During 1143/4, among his other campaigns, Stephen was heavily involved in trying to quell the anarchy in the eastern counties, particularly in the FENS where Geoffrey de MANDEVILLE had established an impregnable stronghold. After the capture of Robert of Gloucester's castle at FARINGDON in 1145, the tide of the war turned in the king's favour, with many of Maud's supporter's losing heart. RANULF of Chester, who had helped Stephen regain Bedford Castle, was arrested at Northampton in 1146 and forced to surrender his castles, including Lincoln where the king spent the Christmas. Eventually, in 1148, Maud withdrew from England and tried unsuccessfully to settle her claim to the crown in the papal court. Her son, Henry Plantagenet (see HENRY II), landed in England with a small force in Spring 1149, but soon returned to Normandy. The following year Stephen attacked WORCESTER but failed to take the castle from Waleran de BEAUMONT, Count of Meulan. After the deaths of his wife and eldest son and heir EUSTACE, Count of Boulogne, Stephen lost heart and at Westminster, in December 1153, he signed a treaty designating Henry Plantagenet as his successor. Stephen was king of a peaceful, undivided realm for less than a year, for on 25 October 1154 he died. He was buried beside his wife and eldest son in the Cluniac monastery which they had founded at Faversham in *c.*1147.

Novels: 'Energy and lethargy, generosity and spite, shrewd action and incomprehensible inaction, would always alternate and startle in King Stephen. But somewhere within that tall, comely, simple-minded person there was a grain of nobility hidden.' 'King Stephen, big, flaxen-haired, handsome.' 'King Stephen's tenacity, in any undertaking, had always been precarious. Not want of courage, certainly, not even want of determination, caused him to abandon sieges after a mere few days and rush away to some more promising assault. It was rather impatience, frustrated optimism and detestation of being inactive that made him quit one undertaking for another. On occasion, as at OXFORD, he could steel himself to persist, if the situation offered a reasonable hope of final triumph, but where stalemate was obvious he soon wearied and went off to fresh fields.' Stephen was the elder brother of Henry of Blois, younger brother of Theobald of Normandy, and cousin of the Empress Maud. Stephen seized the crown of England in December 1135. In August 1138 he besieged and captured SHREWSBURY CASTLE. Arnulf of HESDIN was one of the ninety-four prisoners hung from the battlements on the king's orders. Among those who swore fealty to the king at this time were: Hugh BERINGAR and Aline Siward (see BERINGAR). After he had slain Adam COURCELLE in a trial by combat, Beringar was appointed deputy sheriff of Shropshire by Stephen. In December 1138 the king made Abbot HERIBERT the scapegoat for 'Shrewsbury's offence in holding out against his claims'. Heribert was replaced by Abbot RADULFUS. In early 1139 Stephen confirmed the ancient charter of SHREWSBURY ABBEY, 'with all its grants of lands, rights and privileges', and also the right to hold the three-day fair of St Peter's. In October 1139, through 'misplaced generosity' or 'the dishonest advice of some of his false friends', Stephen allowed the Empress Maud to reach Bristol. Two months later, Stephen and his army went to Worcester. In December 1140 the king paid a diplomatic visit to Lincoln and granted Ranulf of Chester and William of ROUMARE the titles of Earl of Chester and Earl of Lincoln, respectively. After the two half-brothers had seized the royal castle, Stephen rode north with his army. He was captured at the battle of Lincoln on 2 February 1141, taken to Bristol and imprisoned in the castle. By December 1141 Stephen was released in exchange for Robert of Gloucester, who had been captured at Stockbridge in September. At the end of December, Stephen confirmed Beringar in office as sheriff of Shropshire. The king was seriously ill in early 1142. By June, he had recovered, and managed to capture both town and castle at Wareham. In September 1142 he besieged Maud in OXFORD CASTLE, while in Winter 1143 he led an army into the Fens to try and quell the rebellion of Geoffrey de Mandeville. The death of Mandeville in September 1144 relieved Stephen of 'the most dangerous and implacable of his enemies, and instantly eased him of the necessity of immobilising the greater part of his forces in one region'. By February the following year the king was 'master of the Fens again'. He besieged and took Faringdon Castle in Summer 1145, and was reconciled with Ranulf of Chester at STAMFORD in October. On 30 November, together with the Empress Maud, Stephen attended the conference at COVENTRY, where he refused to make concessions, or give up anything he had won.

Ref: **2** (1–12); **3** (1, 3, 7–9); **4** (1:1–2, 2:1, 4:1, 5:3, 5:6); **5** (1–3, 7, 9, 11); **6** (1, 3, 5, 8, 10–11, 13–14); **7** (1–3, 6–7, 13); **8** (1, 3, 8–10, 13); **9** (1, 6, 9–10, 14); **10** (1–2, 7, 16); **11** (1, 3, 5–8, 10–11, 13–14); **12** (1–4, 6–7, 10–13); **13** (1, 6–7); **14** (1–2, 4, 8–9, 14); **15** (1, 3–4, 9); **16** (1, 4); **17** (1, 3–14); **18** (1); **19** (Prologue, 1–7, 9–13); **20** (1–11, 15–16).

Stephen, Saint (d. *c.*35) (hist.) (f.d. 26 December). Also called Stephen the Deacon. Chosen by the apostles as the first of the seven deacons, Stephen was 'a man full of faith and the Holy Ghost' (Acts 6:5). A Greek-speaking Jew, who was also a zealous preacher, he was stoned to death by the Jews to become the first Christian martyr. St PAUL took an active part in his execution.

Novels: In 1135, at midnight of the day of St Stephen's, ALARD THE SILVERSMITH became a free man.

Refs: **RB** (2).

S

Stockbridge (Hampshire, England). Some 8 miles north-west of WINCHESTER and 7 miles south of ANDOVER, the ancient market town of Stockbridge lies on the River TEST. Most of the buildings run along each side of the wide, irregular main street, which crosses the river by a low bridge. Essentially, there are very few side streets in the town. For centuries, until the coming of the railways, Stockbridge was on the Welsh cattle drovers' route to the fairs and markets of the south-east, and one of the inns (now a private house) still bears the sign in Welsh: 'Worthwhile grass – pleasant pasture – good beer – and – a comfortable shelter'. It was here, on 14 September 1141, while fleeing from the 'Rout of WINCHESTER', that ROBERT of Gloucester was surrounded and captured.

Novels: Nicholas Harnage 'halted, staring in sick wonder at such a spectacle, while the flight and pursuit span forward into the distance under its shining cloud, towards the Test at Stockbridge'. On 14 September 1141 the army of the Empress MAUD, in headlong flight from Winchester, was attacked by William de WARENNE and his Flemings. Robert of Gloucester was caught while trying to ford the River Test at Stockbridge.

Refs: **11** (6).

Stoke. See GODSTOKE.

Stoke St Milborough. See GODSTOKE.

Stratford (now Stratford-upon-Avon) (Warwickshire, England). Some 8 miles south-west of WARWICK and 13 miles north-east of EVESHAM, this ancient market town – at the intersection of 7 main roads – originated as a prehistoric river-crossing settlement. It became the site of a Romano-British village, and also an Anglo-Saxon monastery. By 1196 the town, on the west bank of the River Avon, had been granted the right to hold a weekly market, and in 1214 it was allowed to hold a three-day fair. The Guild Chapel was built in *c.*1269, but rebuilt in the 15th C. The adjoining half-timbered guildhall and almshouses were built in 1417–18. After the guild was suppressed, the guildhall became part of King Edward VI Grammar School. Clopton Bridge, spanning the Avon, was erected in *c.*1485. Stratford, with its many half-timbered buildings, is famed throughout the world for its associations with William Shakespeare (1564–1616). Among Shakespearian properties which survive are: the Birthplace; Nash's House; Hall's Croft; Mary Arden's House (Wilmcote); and Anne Hathaway's Cottage (Shottery). Shakespeare was buried in the chancel of the 13–15th C. Holy Trinity Church.

Novels: 'At the approach to Stratford the merchant and his man turned off to make for the town, and CADFAEL rode on alone once again.'

Refs: **20** (6).

Stretton (now Church Stretton) (Shropshire, England). DB – Stratun: in Culvestone Hundred; land held by Roger de MONTGOMERY himself. The holding probably also included All Stretton and Little Stretton. Some 12 miles south-west of SHREWSBURY, the small market town of Church Stretton lies in the heart of Stretton Dale between the volcanic ridge of the Stretton Hills and the moorland plateau of the Long Mynd. St Lawrence's Church dates from Norman times. The tower, chancel and transepts were built in the 13th C. and, between 1867 and 1883, the western aisles of the transepts were added, including a vestry and organ loft. Over the north doorway is an ancient fertility figure, known as a 'Sheela-na-gig'. Towards the end of the 19th C., after the arrival of the railway, Church Stretton became a fashionable health resort and spa town. The village of All Stretton is just over a mile north-east of the town, while Little Stretton, also in the valley, is about the same distance to the south-west.

Novels: In August 1139 Philip CORVISER, in pursuit

of Ivo CORBIÈRE and Emma Vernold (see CORVISER), headed towards Stretton and STANTON COBBOLD.

Refs: **4** (5:2).

Stretton (Staffordshire, England). DB – Estretone: in Cuttlestone Hundred; land of Robert of Stafford. Stretton is a small village 6 miles west of Cannock (see CHENET) and some 24 miles east of SHREWSBURY. It lies on a minor Roman road just north of the ancient highway of Watling Street. The Norman Church of St John was partly rebuilt in 1860. At Stretton Mill on Watling Street there was a Roman fort, built on the site of an earlier fort, both probably dating from the middle and latter half of the 1st C. AD.

Novels: In November 1120 Roger MAUDUIT was in dispute with SHREWSBURY ABBEY over 'a manor by the name of ROTESLEY, near Stretton, demesne, village, advowson of the church and all'. In March 1143 Adelais de CLARY and her servants possibly lodged overnight at the manor of Stretton on their journey to ELFORD from HALES.

Refs: **15** (4); **RB** (1).

Stury, Cecily (*fl.* 1142) (fict.). **Novels:** 'Fair and benign, happy in her husband and a born hand with children', Cecily Stury was the wife of John STURY and mother of two sons and a daughter. She was also the sister of Niall BRONZESMITH and aunt of his daughter, Rosalba BRONZESMITH. Cecily lived with her family at PULLEY and looked after Rosalba until June 1142.

Refs: **13** (2–4, 10–11).

Stury, John (*fl.* 1142) (fict.). **Novels:** Husband of Cecily STURY and father of two sons and a daughter, he was a steward of the MORTIMERS, farming the demesne at PULLEY.

Refs: **13** (2–4, 10–11).

(John) Stury's House and Demesne (Pulley, Shropshire) (fict.). Although it never existed, the house and demesne of John STURY lay in the hamlet of PULLEY, on the edge of the LONG FOREST.

Novels: 'Late after supper that night, in the small manor-house of Pulley, in the open scrubland fringes of the Long Forest, Niall [BRONZESMITH] opened the outer door of his brother-in-law's timber hall, and looked out into the twilight that was just deepening into night.'

Refs: **13** (3, 11).

Sulien, Brother. See BLOUNT, Sulien.

Sulien, Saint. See TYSILIO, Saint.

Surrey, Earl of. See WARENNE, William de.

Sutton (Shropshire, England). DB – Sudtone: in Shrewsbury Hundred; a holding of St Milburga's Church (see WENLOCK PRIORY). Nearly 2 miles southeast of SHREWSBURY and close to the Rea Brook (see MEOLE BROOK), Sutton is now almost part of the town's southern suburbs. It was once a small village with a Norman church, a mill and even its own spa: the church was abandoned in the mid-19th C. and the remains form part of a barn at the southern end of the modern Sutton Farm Estate; the mill has also disappeared; Spa Cottage, however, still exists. In the 1980s, a decade after Shrewsbury and Atcham Borough Council was formed, the parishes of Sutton and neighbouring St Giles were united under the new name of St Giles-with-Sutton.

Novels: 'The ride out through Sutton into the

Long Forest, dense and primitive through all but the healthy summits of its fifteen square miles, was like a sudden return visit to aspects of his past, night raids and desperate ambushes once so familiar to him as to be almost tedious, but now, in this shadowy elderly form, as near excitement as he wished to come.' In August 1138, on their way to the abbey grange near PULLEY, CADFAEL and Hugh BERINGAR headed south to Sutton. From there they headed west into the LONG FOREST. The lord of the manor of Sutton granted the right of collecting wood on his land to the Hospital of ST GILES. Huon de DOMVILLE was murdered on the forest ride from Shrewsbury to Sutton and BEISTAN in October 1139. The old widow at LONGNER used to live with her husband at the smithy in Sutton.

Refs: **2** (6–7, 10); **5** (6–7); **17** (7).

Sutton Mauduit (Northamptonshire, England) (fict.). Although it never existed, the manor of Sutton Mauduit lay some 8 miles south-east of NORTHAMPTON, near YARDLEY CHASE. There is, however, a village called Easton Maudit, situated a few miles to the north, between Castle Ashby and Bozeat (see BOSIET).

Novels: In November 1120 Roger MAUDUIT held the manor of Sutton Mauduit, 'which was the head of . . . [his] scattered and substantial honour [and] lay somewhat south-east of Northampton'.

Refs: **RB** (1).

Sutton Strange (now Betton Strange) (Shropshire, England). DB – Betune: in Condover Hundred; land held by the Bishop of Chester (the holding of BETTON is now represented by Betton Strange and Betton Abbots). The isolated hamlet of Betton Strange lies 2 miles south-east of SHREWSBURY between BAYSTON HILL (see BEISTAN) and the River SEVERN. It takes the latter part of its name from the le Strange family who granted lands here to HAUGHMOND ABBEY in the 12th C. Betton Abbots, one mile to the south, is essentially a farm.

Novels: 'At Sutton Strange the woods fell back before fields. CADFAEL, exchanged the time of day with a cottar whose children he had once treated for a skin rash, and enquired if the news of [Huon de] DOMVILLE's death had reached the village. It had, and was the chief gossip for miles around, and already the inhabitants were expecting that the hunt for the murderer might reach as far as their homes and byres the next day.'

Refs: **5** (7).

Sweyn the Groom (*fl.* 1135) (fict.). **Novels:** 'An older man, lean and wiry with a face like the bole of a knotty oak', Sweyn was the older groom, body-servant and villein of Hamo FITZHAMON of LIDYATE. Sweyn arrived at SHREWSBURY ABBEY with his master, Lady FITZHAMON, MADOC and ELFGIVA on the morning of Christmas Eve 1135. They left to return to Lidyate on 26 December.

Refs: **RB** (2).

Sweyn the Herdsman (b. *c.*1096) (fict.). **Novels:** 'A thickset, grizzled man of middle age, with a ragged brown beard and a twinkling glance', Sweyn was the herdsman of Sanan BERNIÈRES' household and her 'willing and devoted slave'. He helped her escape from SHREWSBURY with Ninian BACHILER. In December 1141 Sweyn went into Shrewsbury to fetch a pair of his wife's shoes from Geoffrey CORVISER. He lent Ninian his coat and capuchon so that he could attend Father AILNOTH's funeral unrecognised.

Refs: **12** (10–12).

Swithun, Saint (d. 862) (hist.) (f.d. 15 July). Also spelled Swithin. Very little is known for certain about Swithun, except that he was Bishop of Winchester from 852 to 862 and that he had close connections with the Wessex Kings Egbert and Ethelwulf. According to tradition, he had been chaplain to

Egbert and tutor to young prince Ethelwulf. After his death, Swithun was buried in the cemetery, just outside the west door of the old Minster at WINCHESTER. But when his relics were translated to a new shrine inside the cathedral in 971, many miracles occurred. A heavy downpour of rain at the time gave rise to the popular saying that if it rains on St Swithun's Day, it will rain for forty days thereafter. His cult flourished throughout the Middle Ages and his shrine at Winchester became a centre of pilgrimage. It was destroyed at the Reformation, but restored in 1962.

Novels: At Winchester there was 'the golden shrine of Saint Swithun'.

Refs: **11** (8).

Syria A country located at the eastern end of the Mediterranean Sea, Syria is bordered by Turkey, Iraq, Jordan, Israel and Lebanon. It has a long and eventful history stretching back to at least 9,000 BC. Syria was a Roman province by the end of the 1st C. BC, and became part of the Byzantine Empire in *c.*300 AD. It was invaded by the Muslims in 634, and in the following year DAMASCUS surrendered. The country came under the control of various Arab dynasties, and in 877 it was annexed by the Tulunids of Egypt. They managed to retain a political connection with Syria for over 600 years, except for periods of occupation by the Seljuk Turks in the 11th C., and the crusaders in the late 11th and 12th C. The Mamluks of Egypt conquered part of the Syrian kingdom in the 13th C., and between 1516 and 1918 the country was a province of the Ottoman Empire. The capital of modern Syria is Damascus.

Novels: CADFAEL went to Syria during the First Crusade and met MARIAM in ANTIOCH. Their son, Olivier de BRETAGNE, was born there in 1113. Thomas of BRISTOL traded in fancy wares from the east, brought by the Venetians from CYPRUS and Syria.

Refs: **4** (1:2); **6** (8, 15); **13** (1); **20** (1, 9).

Tachelm (d. *c.*1115) (hist.). Also spelled Tanchelm. Tachelm, a revivalist, lived in ANTWERP and preached that the Church was so corrupt that it was pointless to take the eucharist from the hands of a priest. Instead, his followers drank his bath-water. Although he did not claim to be Christ, he was said to be possessed of the Holy Spirit, which to his followers meant that he was like Christ and, therefore, God. He was murdered by an enraged priest.

Novels: In June 1143 Canon GERBERT warned Abbot RADULFUS about malignant wandering preachers active in Europe. Among them was a certain Tachelm, who had 'drawn deluded thousands after him to raid churches and tear down their ornaments'.

Refs: **16** (5).

Tame, River (West Midlands and Staffordshire, England). A tributary of the River Trent, the River Tame rises in the northern suburbs of Birmingham, among a complex network of navigable canals. The 8-mile-long Tame Valley Canal, built in 1844 to connect Salford Junction with the Walsall Canal, follows the river for part of its journey. Some 36 miles long, the River Tame winds its way southeastward through the industrial city to Gravelly Hill where it heads east to Water Orton. Near Blyth End the river sweeps north to Tamworth and from there meanders further north, past ELFORD, to join the River Trent near Alrewas, 5 miles north-east of LICHFIELD.

Novels: 'There before them lay the sleek curves of the River Tame, the steep-pitched roof of a mill, and the close cluster of the houses of Elford, beyond the water.' CADFAEL accompanied Brother HALUIN on his journey of expiation to HALES in March 1143. At Elford they crossed the River Tame.

Refs: **15** (4).

Tancred (Prince of Antioch) (d. 1112) (hist.). Son of Tancred de Hauteville, a Norman baron from near Coutances in NORMANDY, by his second wife Fredesendis, Tancred became a Norman lord of southern Italy. He was the nephew of BOHEMOND, and joined his uncle as one of the leaders of the First Crusade. He took part in most of the major battles and, after the conquest of JERUSALEM in 1099, received the title Prince of Galilee. When Bohemond, Prince of ANTIOCH, was a prisoner of the Turks between 1100 and 1103, Tancred acted as regent of Antioch. He succeeded to the princedom in 1104, when Bohemond returned to Europe. Tancred also became the Prince of Odessa in the same year. He was an aggressive leader and engaged in almost constant warfare, not only with his Muslim neighbours, but also with the Byzantines.

Refs: **5** (11).

Tees, River (Cumbria, Durham, North Yorkshire, and Cleveland, England). Rising on Cross Fell, the highest peak in the Pennines at 2,930 ft., the river flows eastward for some 70 miles to enter the North Sea, south of Hartlepool. Towns on its course include Barnard Castle, Stockton-on-Tees, Thornaby-on-Tees and Middlesbrough. Before the revision of county boundaries in 1974, the river separated Yorkshire and Durham.

Novels: 'Contention in England was no bad news to a monarch [DAVID I, King of Scotland] whose chief aim was to gain a stranglehold on NORTHUMBRIA, and push his own frontier as far south as the Tees.'

Refs: **20** (10).

Teme, River (Shropshire and Hereford & Worcester, England; Powys, Wales). From its source high on the Kerry Hills in mid-Wales to its confluence with the River SEVERN near WORCESTER, the River Teme runs through three counties for a distance of almost 70 miles. It rises on the hills 4 miles south of Newtown (or Y Drenewydd) to flow south-east to the market town of Knighton (or Trefyclawdd). Within 5 miles of its source, the river (sometimes its valley) forms the boundary between England and Wales, a 14-mile stretch that ceases 4 miles downstream of Knighton. Settled in Saxon times, Knighton was situated on OFFA'S DYKE and parts of the great earthwork boundary remain to the north and south of the town. At Bryn y Castell the Normans built a timber fortification, and later, on a nearby hill, another of stone. Some 7 miles east of Knighton, at Leintwardine – a small village at the confluence of the rivers Teme and Clun – is the site of a Roman settlement. Passing Brandon Camp, an ancient hill-top fortress, the river meanders south-east, and within a few miles turns north-east to BROMFIELD. Just outside the village, the Teme is joined by the River ONNY and, at LUDLOW 2 miles downstream, by the River CORVE. From the medieval town of Ludlow the river flows south to Ashford Carbonell, and from there sweeps east to the small market town of Tenbury Wells, once a fashionable spa. The six-arched bridge spanning the river at Tenbury Wells, and also the Shropshire and Hereford & Worcester border, is thought to date from the 14th C., but only three of the arches are medieval. The rest are probably 18th C. The bridge was widened under Thomas Telford's supervision in 1815, widened probably again in the mid-19th C., and yet again in 1908. At Burford House Gardens the Teme receives the waters of the LEDWYCHE BROOK and at Newnham, some 3 miles downstream of Burford, the waters of the River Rea. From Newnham in Hereford & Worcester the river meanders south-east for another

30 miles, through wooded hill-sides and lush water-meadows, to merge with the Severn just south of the city of Worcester.

Novels: 'They came to the manor of LEDWYCHE over a slight ridge and emerged from woodland to look down an equally gentle slope towards the Ledwyche Brook, into which all the others drained before it flowed on, mile after mile, southward to join the River Teme.'

Refs: **6** (6).

Temple (London). Modelled on the Church of the Holy Sepulchre (or possibly the Dome of the Rock) in JERUSALEM, the 'round church' known as the Temple (or Old Temple) was built by the KNIGHTS TEMPLAR in *c.*1128. Although it no longer exists, it was situated in what is now High Holborn. Records state that in 1144 Geoffrey de MANDEVILLE's body was taken from MILDENHALL to the Temple, but, being excommunicate and unabsolved, he was not allowed a Christian burial in the churchyard. In 1162 the Templars moved their headquarters to a site further south and nearer the River THAMES, where a second round church, known as the New Temple, was consecrated in 1185. In 1312, when the Order was suppressed, the property, including the church, passed to the KNIGHTS OF ST JOHN, who leased part of it to the lawyers, whose successors became the barristers of the Inner and Middle Temples (two of four legal societies forming the Inns of Court, the others being Lincoln's Inn and Gray's Inn). After the Dissolution the property was appropriated by the Crown. In 1609 James I granted it to the Inner and Middle Temples, who did not formally divide the property until 1732. The New Temple (or Temple Church), essentially a private chapel, still survives, but has been much restored, particularly after severe bomb damage during World War II. On the floor of the nave are the effigies of several Knights Templar, including one of William Marshall, Earl of Pembroke, (*c.*1147–1219).

Novels: In September 1144 the coffined body of Geoffrey de Mandeville, 'still excommunicate, still unabsolved', was taken by 'certain Knights Templar' from Mildenhall to LONDON, 'where for want of any Christian relenting they were forced to let him lie in a pit outside the churchyard of the Temple, in unhallowed ground'.

Refs: **19** (Prologue).

Ten Eyck, Captain. See TEN HEYT, Willem.

Ten Heyt, Willem (b. *c.*1111) (fict). **Novels:** Also spelled Ten Eyck. Ten Heyt – 'a huge, well-favoured man with reddish-fair hair and long moustaches, barely thirty years old but a veteran in warfare' – was captain of the Flemish mercenaries under King STEPHEN. He was with the king at the siege of SHREWSBURY in August 1138. He tortured Arnulf of HESDIN, but failed to get him to divulge the whereabouts of William FITZALAN and Fulke ADENEY. The Flemings under Ten Heyt hanged ninety-four prisoners, including Arnulf, from the battlements of SHREWSBURY CASTLE. On 2 February 1141, along with many others, Ten Heyt fled from the battle of LINCOLN, leaving Stephen to be captured.

Refs: **2** (1–2, 8, 10–11); **9** (1).

Tern, River (Staffordshire and Shropshire, England). This river rises to the south of the Maer Hills, on the open hillside between the villages of Ashley and Maer in Staffordshire. On its 30-mile journey to the River SEVERN in Shropshire, the Tern sweeps south-west in a huge arc, passing to the south of Market Drayton and to the east of HODNET. Beyond Hodnet the river meanders in a southerly direction to Crudgington, where it swings south-east. At Longdon-upon-Tern, in 1794, Thomas Telford constructed an aqueduct to carry the Shropshire Union Canal over the river. It was the earliest cast-iron aqueduct to be built. Near WITHINGTON the Tern is joined by the River RODEN and, within 3 miles, enters the grounds of ATTINGHAM

Hall. At the south-eastern extremity of the deer park the waters of the Tern enter the Severn.

Novels: In October 1142 HYACINTH left Richard LUDEL the younger at SHREWSBURY ABBEY and set off back to CUTHRED'S HUT in EYTON FOREST. At ATTINGHAM he 'waded the watery meadows' of the River Tern. In the four years between 1136 and 1140, fresh grants to Shrewsbury Abbey included a new mill on the Tern. In November 1143 the lord of the manor of UPTON granted the abbey a fishery on the Tern, which bordered his land. Sulien BLOUNT rode from LONGNER along the bank of the Tern almost to Upton, before heading for WITHINGTON.

Refs: **14** (3); **17** (7–8, 11); **RB** (3).

Test, River (Hampshire, England). Rising on the HAMPSHIRE DOWNS near Overton, some 5 miles west of Basingstoke, the River Test flows in a southerly direction for some 40 miles before entering the English Channel beyond SOUTHAMPTON. The Test passes WHERWELL, STOCKBRIDGE, ROMSEY and Southampton before finally debouching into Southampton Water and the Solent.

Novels: In September 1141 ROBERT of Gloucester was captured trying to ford the River Test at Stockbridge.

Refs: **11** (5–6, 8).

Tevyth (*fl.* 7th C.) (hist.). Also spelled Teuyth, Tefydd, Temic or Tybyt. Father of St WINIFRED (his only child), Tevyth is reputed to have been a Welshman of high estate and the son of Eiludd (or Eylud), a chieftain in Clwyd, North Wales. His wife, Gwenlo, who was the mother of Winifred, was the daughter of Insi, King of Powys, and the sister of St BEUNO. It is said that Tevyth, who lived in the cantref of Tegeingl, asked Beuno to undertake the education of his daughter and, in return, he granted the holy man some land at Sychnant, meaning 'dry valley', where Beuno built a church. After the miraculous appearance of St Winifred's Well close by, the place became known as HOLYWELL, or Treffynnon, meaning the 'town of the fountain'.

Novels: '"St Winifred," declaimed the old man, beginning to enjoy his hour of glory, "was the only child of a knight named Tevyth, who lived in those parts when princes were yet heathens. But this knight and all his household were converted by St Beuno, and made him a church there, and gave him houseroom."'

Refs: **1** (1).

Tewkesbury (Gloucestershire, England). Some 15 miles south of WORCESTER and 11 miles south-west of EVESHAM, this ancient town is situated on the River Avon, near its confluence with the River SEVERN. The first monastery was founded in 715, but was twice ravaged by Danish invaders in the 9th C., and declined to such an extent that in 980 it became a cell of the newly founded Benedictine monastery at Cranborne in Dorset. Tewkesbury Abbey was founded by Robert FitzHamon and Giraldus, Abbot of Cranborne, in 1092. It was occupied in 1102, and consecrated in 1121. After the Dissolution the abbey church of St Mary was saved by the townspeople. The massive 12th C. Norman tower once supported a lead-covered wooden spire, which collapsed in 1559 and was never replaced. The pinnacles were added in 1660. Among the remains of the wealthy medieval monastery are the Gatehouse, and the Abbot's House, both 15th–16th C. The Domesday survey records two mills in the town, and the tradition of milling flour is maintained today by Healing's Mill.

Novels: 'CADFAEL crossed the ford, climbed the green track up through the woods on the other side, and rode eastward through the village of WINSTONE towards the great highroad [see ERMIN WAY]. But

T

when he reached it he did not turn left towards Tewkesbury and the roads that led homeward, but right, towards CIRENCESTER.'

Refs: **20** (6, 15).

Thame (Oxfordshire, England). Some 14 miles south-east of OXFORD and 19 miles north of READING, the ancient market town of Thame lies on the east bank of the River Thame, a tributary of the THAMES. It received its first charter during Anglo-Saxon times, and today its extremely wide High Street reflects its importance as a centre for markets and fairs. The Cistercian abbey at Thame, dedicated to St Mary, was refounded in 1140 by Alexander, Bishop of Lincoln, and Robert Gait. It was first founded in 1137 at Otley, 8 miles north-east of Oxford, but the land proved to be unsuitable. The site of the medieval abbey is now occupied by the house, Thame Park, which incorporates some of the monastic buildings, including the 16th C. abbot's lodging. The abbey church has been completely destroyed.

Novels: In September 1142, while searching for the runaway villein Brand (see HYACINTH), Drogo and Aymer BOSIET 'lodged overnight with the white monks at their new Abbey' at Thame. There Drogo played chess with Renaud BOURCHIER.

Refs: **14** (9, 13–14).

Thames, River (Gloucestershire, Wiltshire, Oxfordshire, Berkshire, Buckinghamshire, Surrey, Greater London, Essex and Kent, England). The second longest river in Britain, the Thames rises in the COTSWOLDS near Thames Head, a few miles south-west of CIRENCESTER, to flow in an easterly direction to LONDON and the North Sea. On its 210-mile journey, the river meanders past OXFORD (where it is known as the Isis), ABINGDON, READING, Henley-on-Thames, Maidenhead, Windsor and Hampton Court, before snaking its way, through the extensive suburbs of London, to WESTMINSTER and Tower Bridge. Some 10 miles downstream from the City of London, at Woolwich, is the world's largest movable flood barrier, designed to protect the capital from a dangerous tidal surge. Some 15 miles further east, beyond Gravesend and Tilbury (on the south and north banks respectively), the Thames begins to widen, before debouching into the sea beyond Canvey Island and Southend-on-Sea. The river has been navigable since ancient times. During the early 17th C. barges could reach as far as Oxford; while today, with the addition of locks, pleasure craft can travel 190 miles upstream from the Thames estuary to a place 20 miles west of Oxford.

Novels: In May 1141 Queen MATILDA moved her army closer and closer to London, tightening her cordon south of the River Thames. It was first thought that the body of Renaud BOURCHIER might have ended up in the river near Oxford. In December 1142, the Empress MAUD, with two or three of her men, slipped secretly out of OXFORD CASTLE. '"Ah, but she did, CADFAEL! She did both! She got out of the castle unseen, and passed through some part at least of STEPHEN's lines. To the best they can guess, she must have been let down by a rope from the rear of the tower towards the river, she and two or three of her men with her. There could not have been more. They muffled themselves all in white to be invisible against the snow. Indeed by all accounts it was snowing then, to hide them the better."' In late 1145 King Stephen held a number of castles along the 'dangerous and explosive battlefield' of the Thames valley, including Oxford, FARINGDON and CRICKLADE.

Refs: **10** (1); **14** (14); **15** (1); **20** (1, 6).

Theobald of Bec (*c.*1090–1161), Archbishop of Canterbury (hist.). Also called Tedbaldus. Born near Bec (or Le Bec Hellouin) in NORMANDY, Theobald entered the great Benedictine abbey of Bec at some time before 1124, and became prior in 1127 and abbot in *c.*1137. On 24 December 1138 he was elected Archbishop of Canterbury and was consecrated on

8 January the following year. However, under pressure from HENRY OF BLOIS, Bishop of Winchester, who had wanted the primacy for himself, Pope INNOCENT II granted the office of papal legate to Henry, giving him powers superior to the archbishop. The appointment meant that Theobald was overshadowed by Henry until the pope's death on 24 September 1143, when the bishop's legatine authority ceased. After King STEPHEN's capture at LINCOLN in 1141, Theobald was persuaded by Henry to support the Empress MAUD: he was with her at OXFORD in July; and he was also among those who fled with her from WINCHESTER in September; but he returned to Stephen's side in November, when the king was released from captivity. Theobald opposed Stephen in Spring 1152, when Pope Eugenius III forbade him to crown Stephen's son EUSTACE, Count of Boulogne, and in consequence the archbishop was forced to flee to FLANDERS. Under threat of excommunication, Stephen recalled Theobald, who returned to CANTERBURY in September. Theobald played a leading role in negotiating the treaty at WESTMINSTER which brought Henry Plantagenet (see HENRY II) to the English throne, and performed the coronation ceremony in 1154. Theobald, Archbishop of Canterbury and papal legate, was buried in Canterbury Cathedral; later his body was removed and re-buried before St Mary's altar in the nave. He was succeeded by Thomas à Becket.

Novels: 'Bishop Henry had taken good care to keep the direction of events in his own hands. Calling all the prelates and mitred abbots to Winchester early in April, and firmly declaring the gathering a legatine council, no mere church assembly, had ensured his supremacy at the subsequent discussions, giving him precedence over Archbishop Theobald of Canterbury, who in purely English church matters was his superior. Just as well, perhaps. CADFAEL doubted if Theobald had greatly minded being outflanked. In the circumstances a quiet, timorous man might be only too glad to lurk peaceably in the shadows, and let the legate bear the heat of the sun.' Archbishop of Canterbury, Theobald, a Benedictine, was sympathetically inclined to the Cistercian Order. In purely English church matters Theobald was the superior of Bishop Henry of Blois. But in papal matters Henry took precedence, a situation which led to ill feeling between the two of them. The enmity dated back to 1138, to the time when Pope Innocent II made Theobald Archbishop of CANTERBURY instead of Henry. By way of consolation, Henry was made papal legate in England, 'thus making him in fact superior to the archbishop, a measure hardly calculated to endear either of them to each other'. In 1144 Theobald decided to revive the diocese of ST ASAPH and appointed Bishop GILBERT, a Norman, to the Welsh see.

Refs: **10** (1); **16** (1–2, 4–7, 10); **18** (1–3, 6).

Theobald of Normandy (1093–1152), Count of Blois as Theobald IV (1102–52) (hist.). Eldest son of Stephen, Count of Blois, by Adela, daughter of WILLIAM I, King of England, Theobald was the brother of STEPHEN, King of England, and HENRY OF BLOIS, Bishop of Winchester. In addition to being Count of Blois and Chartres from 1102, he was Count of Champagne from 1125. He preferred to stay in France rather than compete against Stephen for the throne of England. After reuniting Champagne and Blois in 1125, Theobald became the second most powerful person in France next to the King. After his death, Champagne and Blois were divided between his sons and the countship declined. LOUIS VII, King of France, married Theobald's daughter, Adela of Champagne, in 1160.

Novels: In September 1140, on King Stephen's behalf, Bishop HENRY OF BLOIS was 'bound away into France . . . after the backing of the French King [Louis VII] and Count Theobald of Normandy'.

Refs: **8** (1).

Theofanu (d. 991), Princess of Byzantium (hist.). A Greek princess of Byzantium (see CONSTANTINOPLE), she became the wife of Emperor OTTO II in ROME in 972. She gave birth to their son, the future Emperor Otto III in 980. After her husband's death in 983, Theofanu served as regent for her son. On her death in 991, Otto's grandmother, Adelaide, assumed the regency until he came of age in 994. Although both women took the title Augusta, Theofanu sometimes used the masculine title Imperator Augustus. Otto III died in 1002, at the age of twenty-two.

Novels: Before his death in 1143, William of LYTHWOOD bequeathed to FORTUNATA for her dowry a carved wooden box containing Theofanu's priceless psalter, which had been made at the wish of Emperor OTTO I for the marriage of his son, Otto, to the princess. DIARMAID, a monk of ST GALL, had written and painted the psalter.

Refs: **16** (15).

Thessalonika (Greece). Also spelled Thessaloniki. The industrial and commercial city of Thessaloniki is situated in the north-east corner of Greece. It is second only to Athens in size, and is one of the country's major seaports. The city, named after a sister of Alexander the Great, was founded in *c.*315 BC, and less than two hundred years later it was the capital of the Roman province of Macedonia. St PAUL delivered two epistles to the inhabitants, and one of his companions, Gaius, became the city's first bishop. Thessaloniki became part of the Byzantine Empire and prospered; but, over succeeding centuries, it suffered from the hostilities of the Bulgarians, Normans and Turks, among others. It was eventually conquered by the Ottomans and remained a part of their empire until 1912, when it was captured by the Greeks.

Novels: '"There are plenty of Greek and Italian merchant ships plying as far as Thessalonika, some even all the way to BARI and VENICE."' On their homeward journey from the HOLY LAND, William of LYTHWOOD and ELAVE took a ship from TRIPOLI to CYPRUS and Thessalonika.

Refs: **16** (3).

Thomas the Farrier (*fl.* 1138) (fict.). **Novels:** In June 1142 Thomas the Farrier lived next door to Niall BRONZESMITH'S HOUSE AND SHOP (see THOMAS THE FARRIER'S MESSUAGE).

Refs: **13** (2, 4,13).

Thomas the Farrier's Messuage (Abbey Foregate, Shrewsbury, Shropshire) (fict.). Although it never existed, the house of Thomas the Farrier was in the ABBEY FOREGATE. It stood on the opposite side of the road to SHREWSBURY ABBEY, somewhere in the vicinity of HORSE-FAIR and Holywell Street.

Novels: Thomas the Farrier lived in the Abbey Foregate, next door to and on the eastern side of NIALL BRONZESMITH'S HOUSE AND SHOP. He rented the premises from Shrewsbury Abbey and, on 22 June 1138, witnessed the charter granting Judith PERLE's house to the abbey for an annual rent of one white rose.

Refs: **13** (2, 4, 13).

Thornbury (Shropshire, England) (fict.). Although it never existed, Thornbury was situated on the fringes of the LONG FOREST, and stood in the general vicinity of Hook-a-Gate, about a mile west of Bayston Hill (see BEISTAN) and some 2 miles south-west of SHREWSBURY. The hamlet lay on the south bank of the Rea Brook (see MEOLE BROOK), in a clearing of meadows and ploughland.

Novels: In October 1139 CADFAEL set out from SHREWSBURY ABBEY to try and trace Avice of THORNBURY (see MAGDALEN, Sister). At Thornbury he spoke to Avice's brother, ULGER the younger, the village wheelwright.

Refs: **5** (7–8, 10–11).

Thornbury, Avice of. See MAGDALEN, Sister.

Three-Tree Shut (Shrewsbury, Shropshire) (fict.). Although it never existed, Three-Tree Shut led to a secluded close, somewhere off the upper end of WYLE Cop, in the near vicinity of ST JULIAN'S CHURCH.

Novels: 'There was a small tavern in a narrow, secluded close off the upper end of the steep, descending Wyle. It was sited about midway between the house near SAINT ALKMUND'S CHURCH and the town gate, and the lanes leading to it were shut between high walls, and on a feast day might well be largely deserted.'

Refs: **16** (8).

Thurstan (b. *c.*1099) (fict.) **Novels:** 'A sturdy, squat husbandman no more than forty years old, in good brown homespun and leggings of home-tanned leather.' Husbandman, cottar and forester, Thurstan lived with his wife in an assart in CLEE FOREST (see THURSTAN'S ASSART). In December 1139 he gave shelter to Yves HUGONIN.

Refs: **6** (3–4, 6, 10).

Thurstan's Assart (Shropshire, England) (fict.). Although it never existed, the assart of THURSTAN was located at the eastern fringes of the CLEE FOREST to the west of Stoke St Milborough (see GODSTOKE) and Upper LEDWYCHE, about half a mile east of the village of Hopton Cangeford.

Novels: 'Before him [CADFAEL] the trees drew apart, restoring an hour of the failing day. Someone had carved out an assart, a clearing of narrow garden and field about a low cottage . . . He had made a good job of his lonely holding, and stood erect to face the traveller as soon as he had penned his goats.'

Refs: **6** (3).

Titterstone Clee (Shropshire, England). Titterstone Clee is situated 5 miles east of LUDLOW, between CLEE HILL and BROWN CLEE HILL. Together, they form the Clee Hills, the highest hills in Shropshire. On the summit of Titterstone Clee, 1,749 ft. above sea level, are the earthwork remains of a large Iron Age hill-fort, which has been partly destroyed by extensive quarrying and the construction of a modern radar establishment. The small hamlet of Dhustone, on its southern slopes, is named after the local name for dolerite, the hard volcanic layer of rock that caps all the Clee Hills. There is a legend that the massive boulders found scattered on Titterstone Clee were caused by a battle of giants.

Novels: 'Beyond the watered valley the ground rose again, and there, directly before them in the distance, hung the vast, bleak outline of Titterstone Clee, its top shrouded in cloud.' In December 1139 the outlaw band of Alain le GAUCHER had a fortress on Titterstone Clee. John DRUEL'S HOLDING was situated high on the north-eastern slopes of the hill; the village of CLEETON lay some distance below; the manor of CALLOWLEAS stood to the north; while FOXWOOD lay on its eastern slopes.

Refs: **6** (3, 5–6, 9–11, 13–15); **10** (7); **11** (5).

Todenham (Gloucestershire, England). Some 3 miles north-east of Moreton-in-Marsh and 12 miles west of Banbury, this ancient hill-top village lies close to the borders of Oxfordshire and Warwickshire. Todenham, together with HARDWICKE, Sutton-under-Brailes and Bourton-on-the Hill, was recorded in the Domesday survey as an outlier of the manor of DEERHURST. The 14th C. octagonal spire of the church of St Thomas à Becket collapsed in 1772, and was re-erected.

Novels: FORTHRED came from Todenham, '"which is an outlier of this manor of DEERHURST"'.

Refs: **20** (7).

Torsten (*fl.* 1144) (fict.). **Novels:** He was one of the Irish Danes from DUBLIN who invaded Gwynedd for CADWALADR in May 1144. Torsten was reputed to be able to throw a lance to split a sapling at fifty paces. He captained the watch at OTIR's camp on the Welsh mainland and helped TURCAILL (*fl.* 1144) take Cadwaladr prisoner.

Refs: **18** (7, 9–13).

Tower of London (Tower Hill, London). After the Norman Conquest of 1066, WILLIAM I promised the citizens of LONDON that they could retain the same laws they had enjoyed under EDWARD THE CONFESSOR. At the same time, to control the city, he began the construction of a number of castles, first in wood and later in stone. All traces of these have disappeared except for the fortress at the south-east corner of the city, just outside the walls, known as the Tower of London. Built of Caen limestone, Kentish ragstone and local sandstone, the castle was added to by successive monarchs. Its central stronghold was the keep, or White Tower, a 90 ft. high, squarish building with sides varying in length from 107 to 118 ft., and walls ranging in thickness from 11 to 15 ft. Designed by Gundulf, Bishop of Rochester, the keep was not mentioned in the Domesday Book survey of 1086. Some authorities maintain that it was completed during WILLIAM II's reign; others argue for a date in HENRY I's reign. The Tower of London was first used as a royal residence by King STEPHEN in 1140. The following year, Geoffrey de MANDEVILLE, the Constable of the Tower, was driven out of the fortress by Londoners supporting Stephen.

Novels: In 1143 Stephen forced Geoffrey de MANDEVILLE to surrender his constableship of the Tower.

Refs: **17** (3).

Trefriw (Gwynedd, Wales). Situated on the western side of the broad vale of the River CONWAY, at its confluence with the Afon Crafnant, the large village of Trefriw is just over a mile north-west of LLANRWST and some 8 miles south of CONWY. Nestling beneath the wooded hillside, it was once a busy inland port and a resort noted for its mineral waters. The Chalybeate Wells and Baths, which were extremely popular in late Victorian times, are about a mile to the north, on the CONWY road. The springs are said to yield the richest sulphur and iron waters in the world. St Mary's Church was founded in the 13th C. by Llywelyn the Great, allegedly to save his wife the climb up the steep hill to the original church at Llanrhychwyn, about a mile to the south (which is reputed to contain the oldest font in Britain).

Novels: '"My name is CADFAEL, a Welsh brother of this house, born at Trefriw."'

Refs: **3** (8); **4** (1:2); **5** (2); **6** (4); **8** (5); **18** (3); **RB** (1).

Tregeiriog (Clwyd, Wales). On the River CEIRIOG, between GLYN CEIRIOG and LLANARMON, Tregeiriog is 9 miles south-west of CHIRK and 8 miles north-west of OSWESTRY. The hamlet consists of a cluster of houses and a chapel on rising ground to the north of the river, with a stone-built farm and a few dwellings near the bridge.

Novels: 'All the colours had changed since last he rode down the steep hillside into Tregeiriog. Round the brown, timbered warmth of maenol and village beside the river, the trees had begun to soften their skeletal blackness with a delicate pale-green froth of buds, and on the lofty, rounded summits beyond the snow was gone, and the bleached pallor of last year's grass showed the elusive tint of new life. Through the browned and rotting bracken the first fronds uncurled. Here it was already Spring.' Tudur ap RHYS, a man of Powys, was the lord of Tregeiriog in CYNLLAITH. On occasions, during February and March 1141, OWAIN GWYNEDD lodged at Tudur's maenol. In those same months, CADFAEL journeyed there twice. Hugh BERINGAR rode into Tregeiriog with a company of twenty men to see Owain.

Refs: **9** (2–3, 10, 12, 14–15).

Tripoli (Lebanon). This ancient city and port lies at the eastern end of the Mediterranean Sea, some 40 miles north of Beirut. It has been occupied, among others, by the Phoenicians, the Seleucids, the Romans and, from *c.*638, the Muslims. During the First Crusade, the city was taken by Raymond de Saint

Gilles, who declared himself Count of Tripoli. It became one of the four crusader states: the Kingdom of JERUSALEM, the Principality of ANTIOCH, and the Counties of Tripoli and EDESSA. The two states of Tripoli and Antioch were united in 1187 by Bohemond IV, who became Prince of Antioch and Count of Tripoli. In 1289 Tripoli was conquered by the Mamluks, a Muslim dynasty of Egypt and Syria. It became part of the Ottoman Empire in 1516, was occupied by the Egyptians in the 19th C., and fell to the British during World War I. By the end of 1946 Tripoli was part of Lebanon, and today is the country's second largest city.

Novels: On his return to England from the HOLY LAND, Laurence d'ANGERS sailed from the port of Tripoli. Olivier de BRETAGNE went with him. CADFAEL knew the port while he was in the Holy Land. William of LYTHWOOD bought FORTUNATA's dowry in a market in Tripoli from some fugitive monks.

Refs: **6** (1, 15); **16** (3, 11).

Trynihid (*fl.* 5th C.) (hist.). She was the wife of St ILLTUD. According to tradition, Trynihid was deserted suddenly by her husband after an angel had warned him to leave her.

Novels: Illtud 'had a wife, a noble lady, willing to live simply with him in a reed hut by the River NADAFAN. An angel told him to leave his wife, and he rose up early in the morning, and drove her out into the world alone, thrusting her off, so we are told, very roughly, and went to receive the tonsure of a monk from St DYFRIG.'

Refs: **17** (10, 14).

Turcaill (*fl.* 1124) (hist.). An Irish Dane from DUBLIN, Turcaill is briefly mentioned in the *Brut y Tywysogyon*. His unnamed son was among the Danish fleet which landed at ABERMENAI in 1144 to try and restore CADWALADR to his Welsh lands.

Novels: Turcaill was the father of TURCAILL (*fl.* 1144), kinsman to OTIR and an Irish Dane from Dublin.

Refs: **18** (7–8).

Turcaill (*fl.* 1144) (hist.). Turcaill is briefly mentioned in the *Brut y Tywysogyon*, but not by name. He is referred to as the 'son of TURCAILL [*fl.* 1124]' and was one of the leaders of the Danish fleet from DUBLIN which landed at ABERMENAI in 1144 to try and restore CADWALADR to his Welsh lands. After receiving two thousand head of cattle for Cadwaladr's release, they were attacked by OWAIN GWYNEDD and forced to flee back to Dublin.

Novels: 'He spoke a loose mixture of Erse, Danish and Welsh, very well able to make himself understood in these parts. Not all the centuries of fitful contact between Dublin and Wales had been by way of invasion and rapine, a good many marriages had been made between the princedoms, and a fair measure of honest commerce been profitable to both parties. Probably this youth had a measure of Norman French in his tongue, no less. Even Latin, for very likely Irish monks had had him in school. He was plainly a young man of consequence. Also, happily, of a very open and cheerful humour, by no means inclined to waste what might turn out a valuable asset.' Son of Turcaill, kinsman to OTIR, an Irish Dane from Dublin and an adventurer, Turcaill spoke a mixture of languages. He was one of the Danish mercenaries, under Otir, who invaded Gwynedd in 1144 on promise of payment by Cadwaladr. He captured CADFAEL and HELEDD in the woods north-east of CARNARVON and took them back with him to Otir's camp. He led the party which successfully snatched Cadwaladr away from OWAIN GWYNEDD's camp and made him their prisoner. After the main Danish fleet had left Wales, Turcaill returned in his dragon-ship to find Heledd waiting for him. He took her back with him to Dublin, where they were married, probably that year.

Refs: **18** (7–10, 12–14).

Tutilo (b. *c.*1125) (fict.). **Novels:** Also known as the Holy Thief. '"It irked him to be a menial in the same house as a loathsome old satyr who liked him far too well. A third son to a poor man – he had to look out for himself."' 'About twenty years old, perhaps even less; a lightly built lad, notably lissome and graceful in movement, a model of disciplined composure in stillness. His crown only just topped Herluin's shoulder, and was ringed with a profusion of light brown curls, the crop grown during a lengthy journey. No doubt they would be clipped austerely close when Herluin got him back to Ramsey, but now they would have done credit to a painted seraph in a missal, though the face beneath this aureole was scarcely seraphic, in spite of its air of radiant devotion. At first glance a lovely innocent, as open as his wide eyes, and with the silken pink and whiteness of a girl, but a more penetrating study revealed that this child-like colouring was imposed upon an oval face of classic symmetry and sharp incisive moulding. The colouring of roses on those pure marble lines had almost the air of disguise, behind which an engaging but slightly perilous creature lurked in possibly mischievous ambush.' '"And where did he get that outlandish name of his?" "Tutilo! Yes," said [Brother] ANSELM, musing. "Not at his baptism! There must be a reason why they chose that for him."' Named after St TUTILO because he was 'immensely talented' in music, Brother Tutilo was a novice of RAMSEY ABBEY and, in February 1145, 'close to the end of his novitiate'. He had been a 'harper to his father's lord at the manor of BERTON for a year or more' before he had taken the cowl. '"Listening to that pure, piercingly sweet thread, delivered so softly, falling on the ear with such astonishment, no one could doubt it. There was no way of subduing that voice into anonymity among the balanced polyphony of a choir. CADFAEL wondered if it might not be equally shortsighted to try and groom its owner into a conforming soul in a disciplined brotherhood."' Tutilo walked all the way to SHREWSBURY ABBEY with Sub-Prior HERLUIN, escorted by NICOL, ROGER and an unnamed lay servant. Visiting LONGNER with Herluin and Cadfael, he played at the bedside of the dying Donata BLOUNT, 'singing not in English, not even in Norman-French as England knew it, but in the *langue d'oc* . . . of the Provençal troubadours'. Hearing someone, possibly Herluin, open the door, Tutilo – 'with the wild perceptions of a fox' – switched 'magically' from his love song into 'liturgical piety'. Donata asked Herluin if he would let his 'songbird' sing for her again, when she was in need of consolation; to which the sub-prior agreed. During the chaos caused by the abbey flood and believing that he was doing St WINIFRED's will, Tutilo secretly stole her reliquary for the 'future glory' of his monastery, tricking ALDHELM into helping him hoist it on the wagon bound for Ramsey. He went with Herluin to PERSHORE, and then to WORCESTER; from where he accompanied the sub-prior, Hugh BERINGAR, Prior ROBERT and NICOL to ULLESTHORPE and HUNCOTE, returning to Shrewsbury with Robert de BEAUMONT and the missing reliquary. When DAALNY warned the young Benedictine novice that Aldhelm was on his way to the abbey to identify him as the Holy Thief, Tutilo hid with her in the HORSEFAIR stable. After Daalny had returned to the abbey, Tutilo stumbled across Aldhelm's dead body on the path from the Longner ferry. He immediately went to SHREWSBURY CASTLE to report his discovery. Back at the abbey, in an attempt to forestall the accusation of murder, he confessed to being the Holy Thief and was promptly locked in one of the penitentiary cells, charged with theft. After a plea from Sulien BLOUNT, Tutilo was released to go and sing at Donata's deathbed, on his 'honour to return, and under escort'. He came back well before Prime, with a psaltery bequeathed to him by Donata, and delivered 'himself dutifully back into captivity'. Cleared of murder, but faced with 'a clerical hell' on his return to Ramsey, Tutilo was freed by Daalny and urged to 'go westward, into Wales'. Unbeknown to her he hid in the abbey church, and when the opportunity presented itself he persuaded Daalny to flee with him. It is possible that he came across CONRADIN and found a change of clothes in the horse's saddlebag. Before she died, Donata had told his fortune: '"A troubadour, she said, needs three things, and three things only, an instrument, a horse, and a ladylove. The first she gave him, an earnest for the rest. Now, perhaps, he has found all three."'

Refs: **19** (1–13).

Tutilo, Saint (d. *c.*915) (hist.) (f.d. 28 March). Benedictine monk of SAINT GALL, who became head of the cloister school. Described by Alban Butler in his *Lives of the Saints* (1756–9) as being 'handsome, eloquent and quick-witted . . . a universal genius . . . a poet, an orator, an architect, a painter, a sculptor, a metal worker and a mechanic', as well as being a brilliant musician. The Holy Roman Emperor, CHARLES III, a great admirer of Tutilo, is said to have regretted that such a genius should have become a monk.

Novels: '"Tutilo you'll find among the March saints, though we don't pay him much attention here [at SHREWSBURY ABBEY]. He was a monk of Saint Gall, two hundred years and more ago he died, and by all accounts he was master of all arts, painter, poet, musician and all."' '"Great pity, said . . . Charles the Fat . . . that ever such a genius should be made a monk. He called down a malediction on the man that did it."' Brother TUTILO was named after the saint.

Refs: **19** (1).

Tysilio, Saint (*fl.* 7th C.) (hist.) (f.d. 8 November). Also called Tyssel, Tyssilo, Sulien or Suliau. This Welsh saint was a pupil of Gwyddfarch (or Guimarchus) at MEIFOD, and later spent seven years at a hermitage in Llandysilio, near Four Crosses, Powys. The centre of his ministry was at Meifod, where he is said to have become abbot. It is reputed that he was also a warrior, and fought at the battle of MASERFIELD in 642. Tysilio is known as Sulien in Brittany, where many traditions of the saint have been preserved.

Novels: 'Now that CADFAEL came to consider the early part of the November calendar, it seemed to be populated chiefly by Welsh saints . . . Saint Tysilio, whose day came on the eighth, had a rather special significance here on the borders of Powys, and his influence spilled over the frontier into the neighbouring shires. For the centre of his ministry was the chief church of Powys at Meifod, no great way into Wales, and the saint was reputed to have had military virtues as well as sacred, and to have fought on the Christian side at the battle of Maserfield by OSWESTRY, where the royal saint, OSWALD, was captured and martyred by the pagans.' Tysilio is also said to have gone over to Brittany to fly from a woman's persecution. There they knew him by the name of Sulien.

Refs: **17** (10).

U

Uffington (Shropshire, England). DB – Ofitone: in Wrockwardine Hundred; a holding of Helgot under Roger de MONTGOMERY. Some 3 miles north-east of SHREWSBURY and on the eastern banks of the River SEVERN, Uffington is a small linear village with a mixture of old and newer properties. Across the fields, about a mile north-east of Uffington, are the ruins of HAUGHMOND ABBEY. On the summit of the wooded Haughmond Hill, to the east of the village, are the remains of an Iron Age hill-fort and an earthwork called Queen Eleanor's Bower.

Novels: In December 1138, Edwy BELLECOTE led the sheriff's men on a wild-goose chase around the countryside east of Shrewsbury. The fugitive was first spotted beyond the ford at Uffington.

Refs: **3** (6).

Ulf (*fl.* 1138) (fict.). **Novels:** 'Ulf was busy gleaning after carrying his corn, and not at first disposed to be talkative to an unknown monk, but the mention of Torold's name, and the clear intimation that here was someone Torold had trusted, loosened his tongue.' Farmer and distant relative of Torold BLUND on his mother's side, Ulf had a holding to the west of FRANKWELL (see ULF'S HUT). In August 1138 he exchanged a fresh horse for Nicholas FAINTREE's, lamed by a caltrop.

Refs: **2** (5–6).

Ulf's Hut (near Frankwell, Shropshire) (fict.). Although it never existed, ULF's holding was situated within a gentle loop of the River SEVERN to the north-west of FRANKWELL. Ulf's hut lay a short distance away, on the southern side of the most northerly of the three roads leading west from SHREWSBURY to Wales.

Novels: CADFAEL visited Ulf in his hut in the early summer of 1138.

Refs: **2** (6).

Ulger (the elder) (*fl.* 1094) (fict.). **Novels:** '"My father in his time was also Ulger, and also wheelwright to this and many another hamlet round here. Belike you had him in mind. God rest him, he died some years back."' Father of ULGER the younger and Avice of Thornbury (see MAGDALEN, Sister), Ulger was a freeman and the village wheelwright of THORNBURY.

Refs: **5** (8).

Ulger (the younger) (b. *c.*1094) (fict.). **Novels:** 'The wheelwright, a thickset fellow of about forty-five years, bearded and muscular, was working away with an adze on a length of well-curved ash for the felloes, shaping with the grain of the wood.' Ulger the younger was the son of ULGER the elder, and was the village wheelwright of THORNBURY like his father. Ulger, a freeman, was the brother of Avice of THORNBURY. He disowned her, however, when she left the village to become the mistress of Huon de DOMVILLE. Ulger's wife gave birth to their son in *c.*1125. CADFAEL visited him in October 1139, while searching for Avice.

Refs: **5** (7–8).

Ullesthorpe (Leicestershire, England). Some 12 miles south-west of LEICESTER city centre and 12 miles north-east of COVENTRY, Ullesthorpe is a small compact village with a brick windmill (lacking its sails), and several inns. In the fields between Manor Farm and Lodge Farm, just south of the village, are substantial manorial earthwork remains, dating from *c.*1300, with evidence of fish-farming ponds and a moat. The name Ullesthorpe means Ulf's settlement, or hamlet.

Novels: NICOL, MARTIN, ROGER, JAMES and PAYNE, escorting the wagon carrying 'SHREWSBURY's gifts' for RAMSEY ABBEY, were ambushed in the forest, not far from the village of Ullesthorpe. See also ULLESTHORPE, Reeve of.

Refs: **19** (4, 13).

Ullesthorpe, Reeve of (b. 1100). **Novels:** 'The reeve of ULLESTHORPE was a canny forty-five-year-old, wiry and spry, and adroit at defending not only himself and his position, but the interests of his village.' Although unnamed, in February 1145, the reeve did what he could for the injured JAMES and MARTIN, before setting them back on the road to SHREWSBURY. He showed Hugh BERINGAR, Prior ROBERT, Sub-Prior HERLUIN, Brother TUTILO and NICOL where the timber bound for RAMSEY ABBEY had been dumped. He also explained to Hugh that, having discovered St WINIFRED's reliquary hidden among the logs, he had taken it to his lord, Robert de BEAUMONT (the younger), at HUNCOTE.

Refs: **19** (4).

Upper Ledwyche. See LEDWYCHE.

Upper Longwood. See LONGWOOD.

Uppington (Shropshire, England). DB – Opetone: in Wrockwardine Hundred; a holding of Gerard de Tornai under Roger de MONTGOMERY. Some 7 miles south-east of SHREWSBURY and 3 miles south-west of Wellington, Uppington is a small village lying on rising ground to the north-west of the WREKIN. The

Norman Church of Holy Trinity was extensively restored in 1885 by J.P. Pritchard. The Roman altar by the south porch was dug up close by.

Novels: On their journey to HALES in March 1143, CADFAEL and Brother HALUIN lodged the night at the manor of Uppington.

Refs: **15** (3).

Upton (now Upton Magna) (Shropshire, England). DB – Uptune: in Wrockwardine Hundred; a holding of Reginald the Sheriff under Roger de MONTGOMERY. The village of Upton Magna, with several half-timbered, black-and-white houses round the green, is situated 4 miles east of SHREWSBURY and a mile to the north of ATTINGHAM Park. The Norman church, with a rare dedication in England to St Lucy, was restored in 1856 by George Edmund Street, who also added the north aisle, vestry, south porch and east buttresses. The village smithy is traditionally sited under the shade of a large chestnut tree.

Novels: 'The way was by open fields as far as the village of Upton, climbing very gently.' Upton was a crown tenancy. The small church was granted to SHREWSBURY ABBEY by Bishop ROGER DE CLINTON. In December 1138 Edwy BELLECOTE led the sheriff's men on a wild-goose chase through the Shropshire countryside, including Upton. In November 1143 the lord of the manor at Upton granted Shrewsbury Abbey a fishery on the River TERN, which bordered his land. In February 1145 Cadfael journeyed to the manor of Upton to speak to ALDHELM, who 'worked with the sheep' there. He found the young shepherd a further mile away, at 'a fold high and dry above the water-meadows'. In March Aldhelm was buried 'among his people' by the parish priest of Upton.

Refs: **3** (6); **17** (7–8, 10–11); **19** (3, 5–6, 8, 10).

Urien (*fl.* 1137) (fict.). **Novels:** 'A compact, neat, well-shaven personage, handsomely dressed and mounted, more of an ambassador than a clerk', Urien was the English-speaking Welsh clerk and chaplain of OWAIN GWYNEDD. In May 1137 he escorted Prior ROBERT's party from ABER to GWYTHERIN, and commended them and their errand to Father HUW.

Refs: **1** (2).

Urien, Brother (*fl.* 1141) (fict.). **Novels:** 'A dark, passionate, handsome man, one who should never have shut himself in within these walls, one who burned, and might burn others before ever he grew cool at last.' Benedictine monk of SHREWSBURY ABBEY, Urien had been a body-servant and groom before becoming a monk. Tortured by the loss of his wife, who had spurned him, and burning with an inward desire, Brother Urien saw her remembered face in those of both Brother RHUN and Brother Fidelis. To Urien, they even began to look like the woman. But each time he tried to find comfort in them, his advances were rebuffed. Urien overheard the list of Julian CRUCE's valuables and realised that Fidelis wore a similar chain around his neck. Plunging his hand into the bosom of the boy's habit to drag out the silver chain, Urien made the startling discovery that Fidelis was a woman. He gave her three days to give herself to him or he would reveal her secret and destroy her. After the news that Fidelis had drowned in the River SEVERN, Urien was overcome with grief, blaming himself for her death. Rhun found him huddled in the muddy grass among the bushes at the edge of the MEOLE BROOK. Urien promised Rhun that he would keep Fidelis's secret to the grave. He later learned that Fidelis was alive and well as Julian Cruce. In December 1142 Urien was among those brothers who helped repair the abbey guest-hall roof. In February 1145 Urien helped Rhun to wrap St WINIFRED's reliquary, before it was moved for safety from the altar to one of the two rooms over the north porch.

Refs: **11** (3–5, 7, 9–10, 14); **15** (1); **17** (2); **19** (3).

Ursula, Sister (b. *c.*1093) (fict.). **Novels:** 'Sister Ursula the hospitaller was a tall, thin woman perhaps fifty years old, with a lined, experienced face at once serene, resigned and even mildly amused, as if she had seen and come to terms with all the vagaries of human behaviour, and nothing could now surprise or disconcert her. If the other borrowed instructress measures up to this one, CADFAEL thought, these green girls of Farewell have been fortunate.' Benedictine nun of POLESWORTH ABBEY and hospitaller of FAREWELL Abbey, Sister Ursula, together with Sister BENEDICTA, was sent from Polesworth by Bishop ROGER DE CLINTON to the new foundation at Farewell to instruct the novices. In March 1143 she thought that she would return to Polesworth when the timber housings were replaced in stone. If she was offered a choice, however, it seemed her preference was to stay at Farewell.

Refs: **15** (10–11).

V

Valognes (France). Some 12 miles south-east of Cherbourg and 16 miles south-west of BARFLEUR, this ancient town in Normandy was formerly the capital of the Cotentin peninsula area. During the 18th C. it was known as the 'Versailles of Normandy'.

Novels: William of LYTHWOOD died at Valognes in 1143.

Refs: **15** (2–3).

Vaughan, Richildis. See BONEL, Richildis.

Venice (Italy). Situated off the north-east coast of Italy, this world-famous city and seaport lies almost in the centre of a 32-mile-long, crescent-shaped lagoon which is separated from the Adriatic Sea by a barrier of islands and peninsulas. Venice is built on about one hundred and twenty alluvial islands, mostly separated by a network of narrow canals crossed by some four hundred bridges. Founded in the 5th C., by the 13th C. it had become an important trading centre with a maritime empire that extended throughout the eastern Mediterranean.

Novels: In his roving youth, CADFAEL travelled as far afield as Venice, CYPRUS and the HOLY LAND.

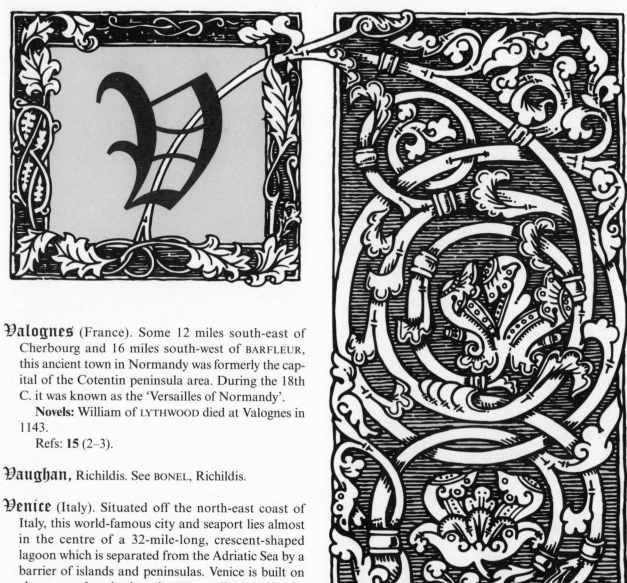

Thomas of BRISTOL traded in a small way in fancy wares from the east, such as sweetmeats, spices and candies, which were brought from Cyprus and SYRIA by the Venetians.

Refs: **1** (1); **4** (1:2, 3:1); **16** (3).

Vere, Robert de (d. *c.*1151), King's Constable (hist.). He was a loyal supporter of King STEPHEN and seldom left his side.

Novels: King Stephen's constable, Robert de Vere attended the conference at COVENTRY on 30 November 1145.

Refs: **20** (4).

Vernold, Emma. See CORVISER, Emma.

Vestier, Judith. See PERLE, Judith.

Vestier, Richard (*fl.* 1115) (fict.). **Novels:** Father of Judith PERLE, he built up a wealthy clothier's business in SHREWSBURY: 'The Vestiers were the biggest and best-known clothiers in Shrewsbury.' Richard and his wife died some years before 1142.

Refs: **13** (1–2).

Vestier's House and Shop (Mardol Head, Shrewsbury, Shropshire) (fict.). Although it never existed, the house and shop of the VESTIERS stood in Mardol Head, the short section of street between Pride Hill and Shoplatch.

Novels: 'The burgage of the Vestier family occupied a prominent place at the head of the street called MAERDOL, which led downhill to the western bridge. A right-angled house, with wide shop-front on the street, and the long stem of the hall and chambers running well back behind, with a spacious yard and stables. There was room enough in all that elongated building, besides the living rooms of the family, to house ample stores in a good dry undercroft, and provide space for all the girls who carded and combed the newly dyed wool, besides three horizontal looms set up in their own outbuilding, and plenty of room in the long hall for half a dozen spinsters at once. Others worked in their own homes, and so did five other weavers about the town.' The house and shop of the Vestiers stood in the town parish of ST CHAD'S.

Refs: **13** (3, 6, 9, 12).

Virgin in the Ice. See HILARIA, Sister.

Vitalis, Brother (*fl.* 1139) (fict.). **Novels:** 'Brother Vitalis had lived so long with documents and accounts and legal points that nothing surprised him, and about nothing that was not written down on vellum did he retain any curiosity. The errands that fell to his lot he discharged punctiliously but without personal interest.' Benedictine monk of SHREWSBURY ABBEY and the chaplain and secretary of Abbot RADULFUS, Brother Vitalis accompanied Radulfus to WINCHESTER in early April 1141. They returned to SHREWSBURY on 3 June. He was with the abbot at the legatine council at WESTMINSTER in December 1141, from which they returned with Father AILNOTH, Benet (see BACHILER, Ninian), and Dame Diota HAMMET.

Refs: **4** (5:5); **10** (2, 8); **12** (2, 13); **13** (2–3); **17** (4, 13); **19** (6).

Vivers (Staffordshire, England) (fict.). Although it never existed, the manor of Vivers was situated on the old Roman road of Ryknild Street to the north-east of LICHFIELD. It lay between ELFORD and FAREWELL in the vicinity of Hilliard's Cross.

Novels: 'He walked the width of the enclave to the gate, to see the full extent of the house. There were windows in the steep roof above the solar, probably two retired rooms were available there . . . Beyond the pale of the stockade the soft, undulating landscape extended in field and copse and sparsely treed upland, all the greens still bleached and dried with winter, but the black branches showed here and there the first nodules of the leaf-buds of spring. Returning to SHREWSBURY from Elford in March 1143, CADFAEL and Brother HALUIN lodged at the manor of Vivers. Cenred VIVERS took his name from the manor and held it under Audemar de CLARY of Elford.

Refs: **15** (6–13).

Vivers, Bertrade (née de Clary) (b. 1107) (fict.). Later called Sister Benedicta. 'There was one of the sisters standing beside the stone bowl in the centre, very slender and erect and composed, feeding the birds. She crumbled bread on the broad rim of the bowl, and held fragments of it out on her open palm, and the flurry and vibration of hovering wings span fearlessly about her. The black habit became her slenderness, and her bearing had a youthful grace that stabbed piercingly into CADFAEL's memory. The poise of the head on its long neck and straight shoulders, the narrow waist and elegant, long hand offering alms to the birds, these he had surely seen before, in another place, by another and deceptive light.' Daughter of Bertrand and Adelais de CLARY of HALES, sister of Audemar de CLARY, second wife of Edric VIVERS and mother of Helisende VIVERS, Bertrade de Clary fell in love with HALUIN and in 1125, at the age of eighteen, she became pregnant with his child. Her mother rejected Haluin's suit and, after he had left Hales to become a monk at SHREWSBURY, she quickly married Bertrade to Edric VIVERS. When the child was born, the old lord believed her to be his own, and she was christened Helisende VIVERS. After Edric's death in 1135, Bertrade entered POLESWORTH ABBEY as a Benedictine nun, taking the name of Benedicta. She was sent to FAREWELL Abbey by Bishop ROGER DE CLINTON to instruct the novices in *c.*1140. There, in March 1143, she and Haluin met after eighteen years of separation. He learned both that Bertrade had not died and that Helisende was his daughter. They were able to talk privately to each other and make their peace. Bertrade and Haluin parted as sister and brother, asking nothing more, and returned to their duties blessedly whole and content.

Refs: **15** (2–7, 10–14).

Vivers, Cenred, (b. *c.*1105) (fict.). **Novels:** 'A fair man, long-boned and sparsely fleshed, with a short trimmed beard the colour of wheat straw, and a thick cap of hair of the same shade. Perhaps in his late thirties, CADFAEL thought, of a ruddy, open countenance in which the blue Saxon eyes shone almost startlingly bright, candid and concerned.' Son of Edric VIVERS, husband of Emma VIVERS and father of Roscelin VIVERS, Cenred Vivers, lord of the manor of VIVERS, was tenant and vassal to Audemar de CLARY of ELFORD. He married Emma in *c.*1123, and Roscelin was born in 1124. Aware that Helisende VIVERS, his supposed half-sister, and Roscelin were growing perilously close to each other, Cenred separated them. He sent Roscelin away to Elford in the service of his overlord. In March 1143 he arranged for Helisende to marry Jean de PERRONET, asking Brother HALUIN to perform the ceremony. He learned later from Adelais de CLARY that Helisende was not his half-sister. More importantly, as Helisende and Roscelin were unrelated, there was no barrier to their marriage. As her uncle, Audemar placed Helisende in Cenred's fosterage. EDRED THE STEWARD was Cenred's steward.

Refs: **15** (5–13).

Vivers, Edric (1077–1135) (fict.). **Novels:** '"A decent, kind man he was, but old, old!"' Father of Cenred VIVERS and grandfather of Roscelin VIVERS, Edric Vivers married his second wife, Bertrade de Clary (see VIVERS), in 1125. He was deceived by Adelais de CLARY into believing that he was the father of Bertrade and HALUIN's child, Helisende VIVERS. After his death he was succeeded by Cenred.

Refs: **15** (6–8, 10–13).

Vivers, Emma (*fl.* 1143) (fict.). **Novels:** '"My lady Emma could never be harsh to any young thing. Too soft, indeed, the pair of them could always get their will of her."' Wife of Cenred VIVERS and mother of Roscelin VIVERS, Emma married Cenred in *c.*1123, and gave birth to Roscelin in 1124. When Bertrade VIVERS left to become a nun at POLESWORTH ABBEY in 1135, Emma cared for Helisende VIVERS as if she were her own daughter.

Refs: **15** (6–10, 13).

Vivers, Helisende (b. *c.*1125) (fict.). **Novels:** 'And in the hush the half-open door of the solar opened fully upon the pale gold candle-light within, and a woman stepped into the doorway. For that one instant she was sharply outlined as a shadow against the soft light within, a slender, erect figure, mature and dignified in movement, surely the lady of the house and Cenred's wife. The next moment she had taken two or three light, swift steps into the hall, and the light of the nearest torch fell upon her shadowy face and advancing form, and conjured out of the dim shape a very different person. Everything about her was changed. Not a gracious chatelaine of more than thirty years, but a rounded, fresh-faced girl, no more than seventeen or eighteen, half her oval countenance two great startled eyes and the wide, high forehead above them, white and smooth as pearl.' Helisende Vivers was the daughter of HALUIN and Bertrade de Clary (see VIVERS), granddaughter and heiress of Adelais de CLARY, and niece of Audemar de CLARY. Helisende was brought up believing she was the child of Edric VIVERS, the half-sister of Cenred VIVERS and the aunt of Roscelin VIVERS. Helisende and Roscelin grew up in the manor of VIVERS together, like brother and sister. As they grew older, they came to love each other and were, therefore, forcibly separated: Helisende remained at Vivers, while Roscelin was sent to ELFORD. In March 1143 Cenred arranged for Helisende to marry Jean de PERRONET, planning that the bridegroom would take her far away to his home at BUCKINGHAM. Although it was not what her heart desired, Helisende was in full agreement to the match. On the eve of their wedding, however, Helisende changed her mind and ran away from Vivers to join her mother at FAREWELL Abbey. There she discovered that she was not Edric's daughter, but Haluin's. In consequence, there was nothing to stop Helisende and Roscelin from marrying each other. She was placed under the fosterage of Cenred, and probably married Roscelin in the latter half of 1143.

Refs: **15** (2, 6–14).

Vivers, Roscelin (b. 1124) (fict.). **Novels:** 'The young squire had remained standing to watch his lord cross to the lady's door, Audemar's cloak flung over his shoulder, his bare head almost flaxen against the dark cloth. He had still the coltish, angular grace of youth. In a year or two his slenderness would fill out into solid and shapely manhood, with every movement under smooth control, but as yet he retained the vulnerable uncertainty of a boy.' Son and heir of Cenred and Emma VIVERS, and squire of Audemar de CLARY, Roscelin Vivers believed himself to be the nephew of Helisende VIVERS. In danger of forming an incestuous relationship with Helisende, whom he loved, Roscelin was sent away to ELFORD in the service of Audemar de Clary. As soon as he heard of EDGYTHA's murder and his father's plans to marry Helisende to Jean de PERRONET, Roscelin sped to VIVERS. Once there, he found that Helisende had run away to her mother at FAREWELL Abbey. Roscelin later learned that he and Helisende were unrelated and that there was nothing to stand in the way of their marriage. It is most probable that they married in the latter half of 1143.

Refs: **15** (5–14).

Vrnwy (now Vyrnwy), River (Shropshire, England; Powys, Wales). Also called Afon Efyrnwy. The headwaters of the River Vyrnwy rise on the Cambrian Mountains in North Wales to enter Llyn Efyrnwy (or Lake Vyrnwy), a 5-mile-long reservoir surrounded by woodlands which supplies water to Liverpool 70 miles away. At the south-eastern end of the lake is a large dam and beside it is the village of Llanwddyn. Most of the old village lies under the water, including the church, two chapels, forty houses and the school. The Vyrnwy flows in a south-easterly direction from Llanwddyn, through the Welsh mountains, to Newbridge where it is joined by the Afon Banwy. Here it turns sharply north-east to enter the Vale of Meifod (or Dyffryn Meifod), passing to the south of MEIFOD and along the valley to Llansantffraid-ym-Mechain, near the confluence of the Vyrnwy and the Afon Cain. Within a mile the river is also joined by the Afon Tanat, which rises on the southern heights of the BERWYNS, 4 miles north of Lake Vyrnwy. At Llanymynech the river leaves the Welsh hills and enters the broad Shropshire plain, meandering in an easterly direction through rich water-meadows to merge with the River SEVERN at Crewgreen. Between Llanymynech and Crewgreen the Vyrnwy forms the county boundary between Powys and Shropshire. From source to SEVERN, the river is approximately 40 miles in length.

Novels: Rhodri ap HUW, from MOLD, came by river barge to St Peter's Fair at SHREWSBURY in August 1139. He 'brought a great load up the DEE, and ported it over to Vrnwy and Severn, which must have cost him plenty'.

Refs: **4** (1:2).

W

Waleran, Earl. See BEAUMONT, Waleran de, Count of Meulan.

Walkelin, (d. 1098), Bishop of Winchester (hist.). Also spelled Walchelin. Reputed to have been a kinsman of WILLIAM I, Walkelin was appointed the first Norman Bishop of WINCHESTER in 1070, after the deposition of Stigand, Archbishop of Canterbury. He soon headed a movement to replace the monks in the cathedral churches by canons, to which the king agreed. But Archbishop LANFRANC, who strongly opposed the notion, persuaded Pope Alexander II to ban any such change in both CANTERBURY and Winchester. In 1079 Walkelin began the construction of a new cathedral at Winchester to replace the Old Minster. At the Council of Winchester in 1097, he supported WILLIAM II in the dispute with ANSELM, Archbishop of Canterbury. Walkelin and Ranulf Flambard were appointed joint regents when the king left England the following month. It is reputed that on Christmas Day Walkelin received an order from the king to send him a large sum of money. Unable to pay, he prayed for deliverance. Nine days later, on

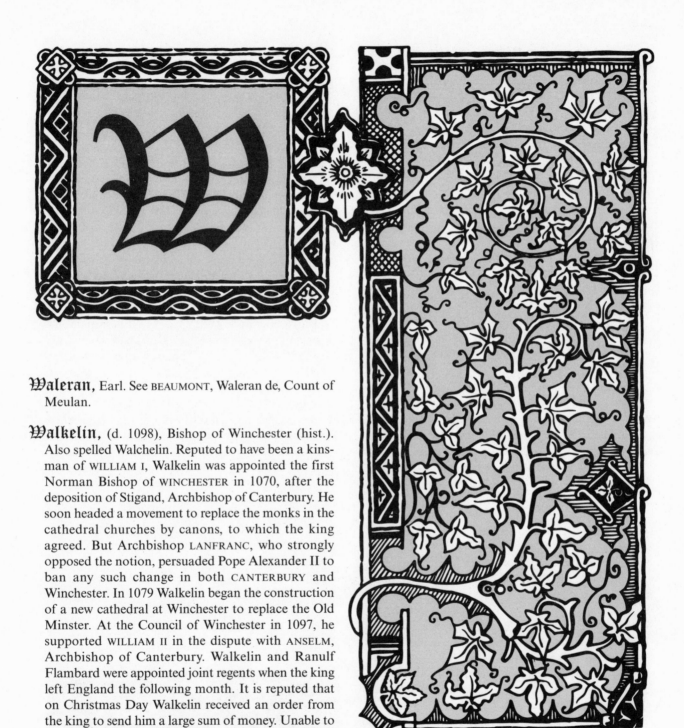

3 January 1098, he died. He was buried inside his new cathedral church.

Novels: Adam HERIET 'launched into a very full and detailed account of Bishop Henry's city . . . He could describe in detail the frontages of the steep High Street, the golden shrine of St SWITHUN, and the magnificent cross presented by Bishop HENRY [OF BLOIS] to his predecessor Bishop Walkelin's cathedral.'

Refs: **11** (8).

Wallingford (Oxfordshire, England). Some 12 miles south-east of OXFORD, the market town of Wallingford lies on the west bank of the River THAMES. Built on the site of a prehistoric settlement, later occupied by the Romans, it was an important Saxon town – greater than OXFORD or READING – with a fortress guarding the ford. Nevertheless, the town was sacked by the Danes in 1006. The Norman castle (the stronghold of Brian FITZCOUNT during the civil war between King STEPHEN and the Empress MAUD) was demolished in 1652 by the Parliamentarians. Although there are a few remains of the castle, all signs of the Benedictine priory, founded in *c.* 1088, have long disappeared: the stone being used to build many houses in the town. Wallingford received its first market charter in 1153, after HENRY II's right to the English throne was confirmed in the Treaty of Wallingford. St Leonard's Church is essentially medieval, while the medieval seventeen-arched bridge (five of which span the Thames) was widened in 1809.

Novels: Among those who rallied to the support of Maud in October 1139 was Brian FitzCount, the castellan and lord of Wallingford. In December 1142 Maud managed to slip unseen out of OXFORD CASTLE, under siege by Stephen's army, and make her way to safety at Wallingford.

Refs: **5** (7); **12** (1); **14** (4, 14); **15** (1).

Walsingham (Norfolk, England). Great and Little Walsingham lie midway between Wells-next-the-Sea and Fakenham, some 25 miles north-west of Norwich. The larger and most important of the two villages is Little Walsingham, noted for the ruins of its Augustinian Priory, founded in *c.* 1153 by Geoffrey de Favarches. It was once a leading centre of pilgrimage, containing a shrine to 'Our Lady of Walsingham' – originally built in 1061 by Lady Richeldis de Favarches who was commanded to do so in a vision. The last of the wayside shrines on the journey to Walsingham was at Houghton St Giles, just over a mile south-west of the village. Here can be found the Slipper Chapel (now a Roman Catholic church), where many of the pilgrims removed their shoes to walk the final stage barefoot. Walsingham also contains the ruins of a Franciscan Friary, founded in 1347 despite strong opposition from the Augustinians. It was always, however, overshadowed by its famous and much wealthier neighbour (which incorporated the shrine in its church). The shrine, the priory and the friary were all destroyed at the Dissolution. The pre-Reformation pilgrimage was revived in the late 19th C. and a new shrine (Anglo-Catholic) completed in 1937. The remains of the priory include a 15th C. gatehouse and two ancient healing wells.

Novels: In 1139 BENED THE SMITH, of GWYTHERIN, went on a pilgrimage to the shrine of Our Lady of Walsingham. While on a pilgrimage to Walsingham, Gervase BONEL bought what he supposed was a piece of Our Lady's mantle, from the hem.

Refs: **1** (11–12); **3** (5).

Walter (*fl.* 1139) (fict.). **Novels:** Servant of Sir Godfrid and Lady Agnes PICARD, Walter went to SHREWSBURY ABBEY with his master in October 1139 for the wedding of Iveta de Massard (see LUCY) and Huon de DOMVILLE. He was given orders to keep watch on the parish door of the church in case Iveta should try to leave the enclave.

Refs: **5** (1).

Walter, Abbot (d. 1161) (hist.). Abbot of RAMSEY ABBEY from 1133 to 1161, Walter is described very differently by chroniclers: one states that he was a man of gentle and pious habits; while another suggests that he misused his power, particularly his control of abbey property, for the benefit of his relations, thereby arousing the animosity of the brothers. In consequence, there seem to be two alternatives for the temporary loss of his abbacy in 1143: either he was replaced by Abbot DANIEL because of his unpopularity; or he was induced by Daniel to resign his office. Whatever the cause, it is known that Walter went to ROME, where he succeeded in gaining a bill of restitution from the Pope. It is said that while he was there he 'won all hearts by his dove-like simplicity'. On his return to RAMSEY, however, he found that the monks, including Abbot Daniel, had been driven out of the monastery by Geoffrey de MANDEVILLE and his soldiers. Apparently, Walter seized a torch, marched into Mandeville's camp and set fire to the marauders' tents. Somehow he managed to escape unhurt. In 1144, after Mandeville's death, Walter regained control of the badly damaged abbey. He is credited with the rebuilding of the great tower of the abbey church, completed in 1154. After his death in 1161, Walter was succeeded by Abbot William.

Novels: '"Abbot Walter is a valiant man indeed."' Abbot of Ramsey Abbey, Walter gave up his office for a time to Brother Daniel. At the end of September 1143, after the sack of the abbey by Geoffrey de Mandeville, Abbot Walter ordered Brother Sulien (see BLOUNT, Sulien) to go to SHREWSBURY and report to Abbot RADULFUS. On 31 September Walter went alone into the aggressors' camp, pronounced excommunication against them all, and set fire to their tents. Although he was mocked, they allowed him to go unharmed. Walter sought refuge, with most of the brothers, at one of the abbey's distant manors. At the end of 1144 Walter was back in possession of Ramsey Abbey, and, together with those brothers who had returned from exile, he set about the restoration of their house and church. To this end, in February 1145, Walter sent Sub-Prior HERLUIN and Brother TUTILO to Shrewsbury and beyond to 'appeal for help in alms, material and labour'.

Refs: **17** (4–6, 9–10, 12); **19** (Prologue, 1, 12).

Walter the Cooper (*fl.* 1141) (fict.). **Novels:** 'It seemed that Walter had a full quiver of helpers in his business, for they were all alike, and all plainly sons of one father, and he the small, spry, dark man who straightened up from his shaving-horse, knife in hand.' Norman cooper of BRIGGE, Walter had three sons: ADAM (b. 1124) and two others (b. *c.*1125 and *c.*1131). His wife, Elfrid HERIET, was the sister of Adam HERIET. Enquiring after Adam Heriet, Hugh BERINGAR went to Brigge to see Walter in September 1141.

Refs: **11** (8, 13).

Walter the Cooper's Shop (Bridgnorth, Shropshire) (fict.). Although it never existed, the shop of WALTER THE COOPER was situated in an alley below the castle walls at Bridgnorth. Part of his premises made use of a cave within the cliff as some of the houses and shops do today. The most likely site for the shop is on the eastern side of Castle Hill, above Underhill Street and between Cartway in the north and New Road in the south. The cave, Lavington's Hole, forms part of a small landscaped garden with public seating.

W

Novels: 'Walter the cooper had a shop in the hilltop town of BRIGGE, in a narrow alley no great way from the shadow of the castle walls. His booth was a narrow-fronted cave that drove deep within, and backed on an open, well-lit yard smelling of cut timber, and stacked with his finished and half-finished barrels, butts and pails, and the tools and materials of his craft. Over the low wall the ground fell away by steep, grassy terraces to where the SEVERN coiled, almost as it coiled at SHREWSBURY, close about the foot of the town.'

Refs: **11** (8).

Warden, William (b. *c.* 1093) (fict.). **Novels:** Also called Will. 'A big, bearded, burly man of middle age, grizzled and weatherbeaten, and with a solid conceit of himself that sometimes tended to undervalue others. He had taken Hugh for a lightweight when first the young man succeeded to the sheriff's office, but time had considerably tempered that opinion, and brought them into a relationship of healthy mutual respect.' Sergeant at SHREWSBURY CASTLE under Gilbert PRESTCOTE (the elder) and also Hugh BERINGAR, William Warden was the oldest, most experienced and longest-serving of the sheriff's officers. In December 1138, he investigated the murder of Gervase BONEL. He followed CADFAEL north towards LLANSILIN and arrested Edwin GURNEY at Ifor ap MORGAN's house. With Warden's invaluable experience to support him, Alan HERBARD was left in charge of the garrison while Beringar and Prestcote went to fight at the battle of LINCOLN in February 1141. Warden led the search for Ninian BACHILER in December 1142. He was among those looking for Richard LUDEL (the younger) and HYACINTH in November 1142. He remained behind at SHREWSBURY in November 1143 while Beringar went with his muster to the FENS. Warden was among those who captured BÉNEZET in the LONG FOREST in March 1145.

Refs: **3** (3–5, 7–9); **9** (1, 9); **12** (6–7, 12); **13** (10); **14** (8); **16** (7–8); **17** (8–9); **19** (13).

Wareham (Dorset, England). This ancient market town, some 34 miles south-west of SALISBURY, lies on a low platform above the flood plains of the rivers Frome and Piddle (or Trent). Protected by massive earthwork ramparts (originally built by the ancient Britons), Wareham was an Anglo-Saxon settlement and a river port of great strategic importance. Between the 9th and 11th C., it suffered from attacks by the invading Danes, who sailed up the Frome from the English Channel by way of Poole Harbour. The Normans built a castle at Wareham, shortly after the Conquest, which was used to hold ROBERT of Normandy, after his capture in 1106, and also Robert de Bellême, son of Roger de MONTGOMERY. During the civil war between King STEPHEN and the Empress MAUD, Wareham was a stronghold of ROBERT of Gloucester and often the centre of conflict. In 1142, for example, Stephen captured the castle while Robert was in NORMANDY. On his return to England, Robert landed his ships at the port, and retook the harbour and town and, after a short siege, the castle. During the Middle Ages the Frome gradually silted up, destroying Wareham's viability as a port. Inside the Church of Lady St Mary, overlooking the river, is a Purbeck marble coffin thought to have held the body of EDWARD THE MARTYR before his translation to Shaftesbury. The small Anglo-Saxon Church of St Martin has been restored. Although the site of the royal castle can be discerned, nothing now remains above ground.

Novels: Maud and her army landed near ARUNDEL on 30 September 1139. Instead of seizing her, Stephen gave her an escort to Robert of Gloucester's fortress at Wareham. Stephen captured the town, harbour and castle at Wareham in June 1142, ten days after Robert had embarked from there for Normandy. In November Robert landed at Wareham and retook the town, but not the castle. By January 1143, however, he was also in possession of the castle.

Refs: **12** (1); **13** (1); **14** (1, 4); **15** (3).

Warenne, William de (d. 1138), Earl of Surrey (hist.). Eldest son of William de Warenne by his wife Gundrada, and father of William de WARENNE (d. 1148), he succeeded to the earldom of Surrey on his father's death in 1088. It is thought that his early hatred of HENRY I was due to the fact that he had failed to win the hand of MATILDA (1080–1118), later queen. William joined the army of ROBERT, Duke of Normandy, when he invaded England in 1101, and, in consequence, was stripped of his earldom. After his title had been restored by Henry in 1103, William became the king's loyal supporter and trusted friend. In 1106 he fought at the battle of Tichebrai in which Robert was captured, and from thereon, until 1120, he was in various other royal campaigns in France and NORMANDY. He married Elizabeth (or Ysabel), widow of Robert de BEAUMONT (the elder), by whom he had three sons and two daughters. William was with Henry when he died at Lyons-la-Fôret in 1135, became governor of ROUEN, and attended King STEPHEN's court at WESTMINSTER in 1136. After his death he was buried at Lewes Priory, Sussex, founded by his father and mother in 1077. One of his daughters, Gundrada, married Roger de BEAUMONT, Earl of Warwick; while the other, Ada (or Adeline), married Henry, son of DAVID I, King of Scotland.

Novels: Warenne's forces were with Henry I, helping to defend his conquest in Normandy.

Refs: **20** (3, 14).

Warenne, William de (d. 1148), Earl of Surrey (hist.). Eldest son of William de WARENNE, Earl of Surrey, he was half-brother of the twins, Robert de BEAUMONT, Earl of Leicester, and Waleran de BEAUMONT, Count of Meulan. William fought with King STEPHEN at Lisieux, NORMANDY, in June 1137. After his father's death the following year, William became the 3rd Earl of Surrey. He fled, together with Waleran de Beaumont, from the battle of LINCOLN on 2 February 1141; but during Stephen's imprisonment he remained loyal to Queen MATILDA. In the company of WILLIAM OF YPRES and his Flemings, he helped capture ROBERT of Gloucester at STOCKBRIDGE in September 1141. He may also have assisted in the arrest of Geoffrey de MANDEVILLE at ST ALBANS in September 1143. William joined the Second Crusade in 1146, setting out with the army in June the following year. He was killed by the Turks in January 1148, either during a fight or after a short captivity. By his wife Adela, William had one daughter and heir, Isabel, who married William, the second son of King Stephen, before 1153.

Novels: '"Did we not say, last time, that the empress must try to break out from WINCHESTER soon, or starve where she was? She has so tried . . . Three days ago they marched out westward, towards Stockbridge, and William de Warenne and the Flemings fell on them and broke them to pieces."' In September 1141 William de Warenne and the Flemings captured Robert of Gloucester at Stockbridge.

Refs: **11** (6).

Warin (b. *c.*1129) (fict.). **Novels:** 'Brother SIMON . . . came out to meet them at the porch, with a gangling boy of about twelve by the hand. The child's eyes were white with the caul of blindness, but otherwise he was whole and comely, by no means the saddest sight to be found here.' A blind child, Warin was an inmate at the Hospital of ST GILES in August 1141.

Refs: **11** (1).

Warin the Groom (*fl.* 1142) (fict.). **Novels:** 'A meagre but wiry fellow, turning grey, in faded homespun of a dull brown, and a rubbed leather coat. He slid one sidelong glance at CADFAEL and nodded a silent greeting, so inured to being wary of all men that even a Benedictine brother was to be avoided rather than welcomed.' Warin was the groom of Drogo BOSIET from the manor of BOSIET, where he had a wife and children. In November 1142 Warin accompanied his master to SHREWSBURY ABBEY in the search for the runaway villein Brand (see HYACINTH). CADFAEL dressed a festering wound at the corner of the groom's mouth, which had been inflicted earlier by Drogo. Warin returned home with Aymer BOSIET, shortly after his master's death.

Refs: **14** (4, 6, 8–9, 13).

Warin the Porter (b. *c.*1089) (fict.). **Novels:** 'Warin was a leathery, middle-aged man, who had clearly been in his present service many years, and was probably completely trusted within his limits, but had not the ability ever to rise to the position Roger Dod now held.' Servant and porter of Thomas of BRISTOL, Warin arrived at SHREWSBURY by barge for St Peter's Fair on 30 July 1139. He was one of three men in Thomas's service: the other two being GREGORY and Roger DOD. He slept in the booth to mind the goods. On the night of 1 August, he was attacked inside the booth by Turstan FOWLER and EWALD THE GROOM. The following morning, he was discovered tightly bound and gagged, but he was unable to give a description of his two assailants.

Refs: **4** (1:3–4, 2:1–2, 3:1, 4:1).

Warren, Maidservant of Widow (b. *c.*1123) (fict.). **Novels:** 'At the second house the door was opened to them by a pretty slattern of about eighteen, with a mane of dark hair and bold inquisitive eyes. The tenant was merely a high, querulous voice from the inner room, demanding why the door stood open to let in the cold. The girl whisked away for a moment to reassure her, speaking in a loud screech and perhaps with much gesture, for the complaint sank to a satisfied mumble.' Maidservant of Widow WARREN, she lived with the old dame in one of the abbey cottages by the mill-pond. On 24 December 1141 she spent the night with Jordan ACHARD.

Refs: **12** (5, 9–10, 12).

Warren, Widow (*fl.* 1141) (fict.). **Novels:** 'The old woman in one cot was stone deaf, and would not have heard even the loudest screams, but generally old people sleep lightly and fitfully, and also, being no longer able to get about as actively as before, they have rather more than their share of curiosity, to fill up the tedium of their days. It would be a bold or a desperate man who attempted violence under their windows.' Old, infirm, stone deaf and house-bound during the winter frosts, the Widow Warren was looked after by a pretty maidservant (see WARREN, Maidservant of Widow). She was a tenant in one of the cottages by the abbey mill-pond, next door to the miller.

Refs: **12** (5, 9–10, 12); **13** (6).

Warwick (Warwickshire, England). Some 27 miles east of WORCESTER and 38 miles north-west of OXFORD, Warwick stands on a rocky cliff above the River Avon. Although there is evidence of Neolithic occupation, the name Warwick is Saxon in origin, meaning 'the dwellings by the weir'. In 914 Ethelfleda, Alfred the Great's daughter, built a fortress on the rock. The large mound inside the present castle is still known as Ethelfleda's Mound. By the 11th C. the Normans had built a wooden motte-and-bailey castle on the site, which was replaced by one of stone in the 12th and 13th C. Guy's Tower and Caesar's Tower were built in the 14th C. Warwick was by far the most famous of the Midland castles, and its powerful earls have been involved in most of the influential events in the nation's history: they fought in the Hundred Years' War at Agincourt, Crécy and Poitiers; they were prominent in the wars of King STEPHEN and of Edward II, the Wars of the Roses and the Civil War. Warwick Castle, billed as one of the finest medieval castles in the land, was purchased by Madame Tussaud's in 1978.

Novels: On his way home from WINCHESTER in May 1141, Abbot RADULFUS passed through Warwick. RHUN, Melangell (see MEVEREL, Melangell), and Dame Alice WEAVER met CIARAN and Matthew (see MEVEREL, Luc) on the road south of Warwick. On 24

June 1141 a courier from Warwick carried the news to SHREWSBURY of the Empress MAUD's flight from LONDON. In November 1142 Drogo and Aymer BOSIET separated near Warwick to search for their runaway villein Brand (see HYACINTH).

Refs: **10** (1, 4, 16); **14** (4, 14).

Warwick, Earl of. See BEAUMONT, Roger de, Earl of Warwick.

Wat the Groom (*fl.* 1138) (fict.). **Novels:** Groom of SHREWSBURY ABBEY, Wat was one of the abbey grooms who discovered Edwin GURNEY, disguised as a monk, hiding in the barn at the corner of the HORSE-FAIR in December 1138.

Refs: **3** (6).

Wat the Taverner. See RENOLD, Walter.

Wat's Dyke (Shropshire, England; Clwyd, Wales). East of OFFA'S DYKE, extending for some 40 miles from the River DEE estuary near Flint in the north to MAESBURY in the south, are traces of an earlier and shorter earthwork known as Wat's Dyke. Defining the frontier between England and Wales, it is thought to have been constructed by Offa's predecessor, Aethelbald (or Ethelbald), King of Mercia (716–57). The best-preserved section of the ancient dyke can be seen at Old Oswestry hill-fort, just north of OSWESTRY.

Novels: 'Hugh [BERINGAR] lived between the two great dykes the princes of Mercia had constructed long ago, to mark where their holding and writ began, so that no force should easily encroach, and no man who crossed from one side to the other should be in any doubt under which law he stood. The lower barrier lay just to the east of the manor of Maesbury, much battered and levelled now, the greater one had been raised to the west, when Mercian power had been able to thrust further into Wales.'

Refs: **18** (1).

Wat's Tavern (Horse-Fair, Shrewsbury, Shropshire) (fict.). Although it never existed, Wat's Tavern was located, on the southern side of the road, at the north-west corner of the street called HORSEFAIR.

Novels: 'The door stood propped wide on the warm, luminous twilight, and the traffic in and out was brisk. Youngsters came with jugs and pitchers to fetch for their elders, maids tripped in for a measure of wine for their masters, labourers and abbey servants wandered in to slake their thirst between spells of work.' Situated in the ABBEY FOREGATE, at the north-west corner of Horse-Fair, the tavern was run by Walter RENOLD. Among those who frequented the inn were: Turstan FOWLER, EWALD THE GROOM, Philip CORVISER, Simeon POER, John SHURE, Walter BAGOT and William HALES.

Refs: **4** (2:2, 4:5, 5:2); **10** (5); **17** (7).

Weaver, Dame Alice (b. *c.*1091) (fict.). **Novels:** 'And there she stood, filling the doorway, shoulders squared, hands folded at her waist, head braced and face full forward. Her eyes, wide and wide-set, were bright blue but meagrely supplied with pale lashes, yet very firm and fixed in their regard.' Widow, aunt of Melangell (MEVEREL) and Brother RHUN, and sister of their mother, Dame Alice Weaver ran her late husband's weaving business at CAMPDEN. In 1134, after Melangell and Rhun were orphaned, Alice brought them out of Wales to live with her. They arrived at SHREWSBURY ABBEY on 18 June 1141 for St WINIFRED's festival, having walked from the COTSWOLDS. On 22 June she witnessed Rhun's miraculous healing in the abbey church, something she had hoped and prayed for. Alice set out on the return journey home without her niece and nephew on 26 June: for Rhun remained behind at the abbey, and Melangell married Luc MEVEREL.

Refs: **10** (3–4, 6, 8–11, 15–16).

Weaver, John (*fl.* 1143) (fict.). **Novels:** 'The sergeant shook his head. "If he killed his man there, under the arch or in the bushes, he'd clean the knife in the edge of the water and take it away with him. Why waste a good knife? And why leave it lying about for some neighbour to find, and say: I know that, it belongs to

John Weaver, or whoever it might be, and how comes it to have blood on it? No, we shan't find the knife."' John Weaver, who lived in SHREWSBURY, is named at random – the sergeant might have said: "I know that, it belongs to my neighbour so-and-so."

Refs: **16** (8).

Welsh Marches (Hereford & Worcester and Shropshire, England; Gwent, Powys and Clwyd, Wales). The Welsh Marches, with ill-defined western and eastern boundaries, extends from the mouth of the Wye at Chepstow to the River DEE estuary. In this context the word march simply means a tract of land bordering two countries. The Welsh Marches, therefore, refers to the broad swath of land on each side of the English-Welsh border. After the Norman Conquest, WILLIAM I gave some of his more rapacious barons wide-ranging powers along the border, and with their private armies these Marcher Lords carved out petty kingdoms for themselves: Hugh of Averanche, known as Hugh the Wolf because of his cruelty, was granted the northern Marches to be controlled from CHESTER; Roger de MONTGOMERY was given control of the middle Marches from SHREWSBURY; and William FitzOsbern was posted to HEREFORD to subjugate the southern Marches. The border line, however, was seldom static, and advanced and receded according to the strength of Welsh resistance. The independent status of the Marches was finally abolished by the Acts of Union in the mid-16th C.

Novels: In September 1140 Hugh BERINGAR, on behalf of his superior Sheriff Gilbert PRESTCOTE (the elder), went to see King STEPHEN at WESTMINSTER 'for his half-yearly visit . . . to render account of his shire and its revenues. Between the two of them they had held the county staunch and well-defended, reasonably free from the disorders that racked most of the country, and . . . [SHREWSBURY] ABBEY had good cause to be grateful to them, for many of its sister houses along the Welsh Marches had been sacked, pillaged, evacuated, turned into fortresses for war, some more than once, and no remedy offered. Worse than the armies of King Stephen on the one hand and his cousin the empress on the other – and in all conscience they were bad enough – the land was crawling with private armies, predators large and small, devouring everything, wherever they were safe from any force of law strong enough to contain them. In Shropshire the law had been strong enough, thus far, and loyal enough to care for its own.'

Refs: **1** (3); **8** (1).

Welshpool. See POOL.

Wem (Shropshire, England). DB – Weme: in Hodnet Hundred; a holding of William Pantulf (or Pandulph) under Roger de MONTGOMERY. (In 1086 Aelmer, a free man, held ALKINGTON under William Pantulf, lord of Wem.) Some 11 miles north-east of SHREWSBURY and 8 miles south of WHITCHURCH, Wem is a small market town on the River RODEN. It was almost destroyed by fire in 1667 and, consequently, there are few really ancient buildings. The 14th C. church of St Peter and St Paul survived but was rebuilt and altered during the 19th C. There was a castle near the church in the 12th C., probably founded by the Pantulfs. It was possibly rebuilt in *c.*1200 by Hugh Pantulf and, after it had fallen into ruin at the end of the 13th C., was rebuilt again by the le Botilers. It was acquired by the de Audley family in 1459 and later dismantled. The town was fortified with earth and timber by the Parliamentarians during the Civil War.

Novels: The tenant at Alkington held the manor under the Lord of Wem. A merchant's widow from Wem, on her way to WENLOCK 'for her daughter's lying-in', lodged overnight at SHREWSBURY ABBEY in February 1145.

Refs: **8** (3); **16** (6); **19** (5).

Wenlock (now Much Wenlock) (Shropshire, England). Formerly called Llan Meilen. DB – Wenloch: in Patton Hundred; held by St Milburga's Church (see WENLOCK PRIORY). The small market town of Much Wenlock, at the north-eastern tip of Wenlock Edge, is 12 miles south-east of SHREWSBURY and 7 miles north-west of Bridgnorth (see BRIGGE). Dating back to Saxon times, the town grew up around the monastery founded towards the end of the 7th C. by Merewald (or Merewalh), King of Mercia, whose daughter MILBURGA was the first abbess. The large church of Holy Trinity dates from the middle of the 12th C. and contains a chapel dedicated to St Milburga. Much Wenlock was granted borough status in 1468 by Edward IV.

Novels: At Wenlock, in February 1145, the pregnant daughter of a merchant's widow from WEM was about to give birth.

Refs: **19** (5).

Wenlock Priory (Shropshire, England). Although Wenlock Priory was originally founded towards the end of the 7th C., little is known about the monastery until the Norman Conquest when it was granted to Roger de MONTGOMERY, who refounded it as a Cluniac priory sometime between 1079 and 1082. The priory church was rebuilt and enlarged in the 1220s by Prior Humbert and, when completed, it was over 350 ft. in length. At the end of the 15th C. large cracks appeared in the vaulting over the high altar, and the church had to be extensively repaired. The Lady Chapel was rebuilt probably at about this time. After the Dissolution Wenlock Priory was stripped of its valuables, including the lead from the roofs, and its buildings and estates sold. All that remains of the once great monastery are ruins, except for the Prior's House – lavishly rebuilt in *c.*1500 – which survived and is now a private residence. Wenlock Priory is managed by English Heritage.

Novels: In 1137, after hearing of the rediscovery of St Milburga's tomb at Wenlock Priory, Prior ROBERT mounted a campaign to secure the relics and patronage of a powerful saint for SHREWSBURY ABBEY. The lands at GODSTOKE, to the north of TITTERSTONE CLEE, belonged to Wenlock Priory.

Refs: **1** (1); **6** (2–3); **10** (1).

West Felton. See FELTON.

Westbury (Shropshire, England). DB – Wesberie: in Rhiwset Hundred; a holding of Roger, Son of Corbet, under Roger de MONTGOMERY. Some 8 miles west of SHREWSBURY and 8 miles east of Welshpool (see POOL), the village of Westbury lies on the old Roman road from Shrewsbury through Yockleton to Wales. The Norman Church of St Mary was considerably altered and lengthened in the 13th C., the aisle widened in the 15th C. and a new tower built in 1753. The north porch and vestry were added during the restoration of 1878. Less than 2 miles to the south-west are the ruins of CAUS CASTLE, high up on the eastern foothills of the Long Mountain. At Yockleton, 3 miles to the east of Westbury, the tithes were granted to SHREWSBURY ABBEY by Roger, Son of Corbet, Baron of Caus, in *c.*1093.

Novels: In March 1141 CADFAEL, Hugh BERINGAR and a company of twenty men tried to prevent the Welsh raiders of Powys from getting back to their base at Caus. They set out from TREGEIRIOG and headed down the border to LLANSILIN. From there they passed to the east of the BREIDDEN Hills and down by Westbury to MINSTERLEY.

Refs: **9** (12–13).

W

Westminster (London, England). Also called Palace of Westminster, or Houses of Parliament. Situated on the north bank of the River THAMES, near Westminster Bridge, Westminster has been the seat of British government for hundreds of years. EDWARD THE CONFESSOR was the first monarch to build a palace on the site (although King Canute may have had a residence here in 1035) and beside it he built a Benedictine monastery, consecrated in 1065. Westminster Abbey was rebuilt by Henry III, commencing in 1245, and contains the tombs of many kings and queens as well as the Coronation Chair made for Edward I in 1300 to enclose the legendary Stone of Scone. After the Norman Conquest, WILLIAM I made Westminster Palace his home and it remained the main residence of the English monarchs until the reign of Henry VIII (1509–47), when the king moved the court to Whitehall Palace. Before 1099, WILLIAM II added Westminster Hall, which is the only part of the original palace to survive the disastrous fire of 1834. St Stephen's Chapel, traditionally founded by King STEPHEN, was used from 1547 for meetings of the House of Commons, previously held in the chapter house of the abbey. The present Houses of Parliament, designed in Gothic Revival style by Charles Barry and assisted by Augustus Pugin, were constructed between 1837 and 1868. Big Ben, the world-famous bell named after Sir Benjamin Hall, is housed in the 329 ft. Clock Tower. The buildings were damaged during World War II and rebuilt by Giles Gilbert Scott between 1945 and 1950.

Novels: '"All overturned in a day", said Hugh [BERINGAR]. "There'll be no coronation. Yesterday as they sat at dinner in Westminster, the Londoners suddenly rang the tocsin – all the city bells. The entire town came out in arms, and marched on Westminster. They're fled . . . she [the Empress MAUD] and all her court, fled in the clothes they wore and with very little else, and the city men have plundered the palace and driven out even the last hangers-on."' In December 1138 Abbot HERIBERT was summoned by Cardinal-Bishop ALBERIC of Ostia to attend a legatine council at Westminster. While there he was removed from office and replaced by Abbot RADULFUS. Gilbert PRESTCOTE (the elder) went to Westminster in September 1140 to render account of his shire and its revenues. After Stephen's capture in 1141, Maud managed to inveigle herself into Westminster. She was driven out of the palace by the enraged citizens of LONDON in June 1141. Radulfus attended a legatine council held at Westminster on 7 December 1141. On his return to SHREWSBURY, he reported that the discussions and decisions there had 'brought the Church back into full allegiance to King Stephen'.

Refs: **3** (1); **8** (1, 3); **10** (1–2, 10, 16); **11** (1); **12** (1–2); **13** (1); **15** (1); **RB** (1).

Weston (now Weston-under-Lizard) (Staffordshire, England). DB – Westone: in Cuttlestone Hundred; land of Reginald (de Balliol) the Sheriff. Some 20 miles east of SHREWSBURY and 4 miles north-east of Shifnal, Weston-under-Lizard is situated to the north of Weston Park on the old Roman road of Watling Street. Almost on the Shropshire – Staffordshire border, the estate village takes the latter part of its name from the Lizard Hill, across the border in Shropshire, 2 miles to the south-west. During the Middle Ages the estate belonged to the de Weston family, followed by the Myttons.

Novels: On his penitential journey to HALES in March 1143, Brother HALUIN, accompanied by CADFAEL, stopped overnight with a cottar and his wife a mile or so to the east of the hamlet of Weston.

Refs: **15** (4).

Wharton, Will (*fl.* 1139) (fict.). **Novels:** A man of SHREWSBURY, he frequented WAT'S TAVERN. In August 1139 Will witnessed the death of EWALD THE GROOM, brought down from his horse with a bolt loosed by Turstan FOWLER, and helped to pick up the body.

Refs: **4** (4:5).

Wherwell (Hampshire, England). This village, with its small green, 19th C. church and attractive half-timbered thatched cottages, lies on a tributary of the River TEST some 4 miles south-east of ANDOVER. The abbey, dedicated to the Holy Cross and St Peter, was founded in *c.*986 by Queen Elfrida, widow of King Edgar, for Benedictine nuns – reputedly in penance for the murder of her step-son, EDWARD THE MARTYR. In 1141 a body of the Empress MAUD's soldiers, attempting to establish a base at Wherwell, were surprised by the enemy. Many fled the inevitable massacre and took refuge inside the abbey church. It was destroyed when King STEPHEN's forces, attempting to drive them out, put the building to the torch. Wherwell Abbey subsequently prospered to become one of Hampshire's most important nunneries. It was dissolved in 1539. There are no remains above ground, but 'The Priory' may incorporate parts of the building.

Novels: '"The empress has made an attack on the town of Wherwell, a disastrous attack. Her force is wiped out by the queen's army. But in the fighting the abbey of Wherwell was fired, the church burned to the ground."' Julian CRUCE left the manor of LAI in August 1138, supposedly to enter the nunnery at Wherwell. In September 1141 Maud sent out a three- or four-hundred-strong force from WINCHESTER CASTLE to seize the town of Wherwell, and try to secure a base there and open a way to bring in supplies. They were attacked and cut to pieces at the edge of the town by WILLIAM OF YPRES and Queen MATILDA's men. The remnant of the empress's force swarmed into the abbey church and turned it into a fortress. The Flemings, under William, set the building alight and burnt it down to the ground. Immediately on hearing the news, Nicholas HARNAGE went to the town to search for Julian Cruce.

Refs: **11** (4–6, 10).

Whitbache (now Whitbach) (Shropshire, England). DB – Although not mentioned Whitbach was later, almost certainly, held in demesne by the monks of BROMFIELD Priory. Whitbache is a small farm, lying in partly wooded countryside, less than 2 miles north of LUDLOW and 2 miles east of Bromfield.

Novels: Josce de DINAN was overlord of the manor at Whitbache. When Yves HUGONIN was captured in December 1139 by Alain le GAUCHER, he pretended that he was Jehan, a shepherd's lad from Whitbache. Gaucher knew that he was lying because his outlaws had just attacked, plundered and burnt the manor. When Olivier de BRETAGNE returned to GLOUCESTER with Yves and Ermina Hugonin (see BRETAGNE), he took with him a boy orphaned at Whitbache.

Refs: **6** (9–10, 15).

Whitchurch (Shropshire, England). Formerly called Weston. DB – Westune: in Hodnet Hundred; a holding of William of Warenne under Roger de MONTGOMERY. Some 18 miles north of SHREWSBURY and 10 miles north-east of ELLESMERE, Whitchurch is a busy market town lying on the Shropshire plain, close to the Welsh and Cheshire border. It was founded in 55 by the Romans who called it Mediolanum, meaning 'the place in the Middle of the plain'. In the Domesday Book survey of 1086 it is recorded that in Saxon times the estate was held by Earl HAROLD, who became King of England in January 1066. Shortly after 1086, a large church was built of white limestone at Weston and, because of it, the town changed its name to Album Monasterium – Blancminster or, in English, White-church (OSWESTRY was also once called Album Monasterium or Blancminster for the same reason). The medieval Church of St Alkmund collapsed in 1711 and a new church, built of red sandstone, was erected in 1712–13 designed by John Barker. There were two castles at Whitchurch in Norman times, strategically sited to guard the Welsh Marches: one on Castle Hill near the town centre; the other, Pan Castle, just over a mile to the south-west. The remains of the former have completely disappeared. Whitchurch developed as a market town during the Middle Ages and was famous for its cheese-making. Some 4 miles north-east of Whitchurch stood Combermere Abbey, founded in 1133. The site is now occupied by a house, begun in the 16th C.

Novels: On 9 September 1140 Peter CLEMENCE, on his way to CHESTER, disappeared between the manor of ASPLEY and Whitchurch. His horse, BARBARY, was found wandering on the peat-hags nearby. Hugh

BERINGAR reinforced the fortress at Whitchurch in March 1141, to discourage raids by RANULF of Chester along the Cheshire-Shropshire border.

Refs: **8** (3–5); **9** (9–10,12); **16** (6)

White Ladies Priory. See BREWOOD NUNNERY.

White Ship. See BLANCHE NEF.

Whittington (Shropshire, England). DB – Wititone: in Merset Hundred; land held by Roger de MONTGOMERY himself (it was formerly held by EDWARD THE CONFESSOR). Some 16 miles north-west of SHREWSBURY and 2 miles north-east of OSWESTRY, Whittington is a large village dating back to Anglo-Saxon times. It grew up around WHITTINGTON CASTLE, built by the Normans on the site of an earlier fortress. Opposite the castle there was once a medieval chapel, which was replaced by the red-brick St John the Baptist's Church in 1747. The nave was constructed in 1804, and the entire church was restored by Eustace Frere in 1894.

Novels: The church at Whittington, previously in the diocese of LICHFIELD, became part of the diocese of ST ASAPH in 1144.

Refs: **9** (10); **18** (1).

Whittington Castle (Shropshire, England). The ruins of the castle are situated on low-lying ground in the village of WHITTINGTON. It was once surrounded and protected by marshland and, although the land has since been drained, the wide moat still contains water. At the end of the 11th C., Roger de MONTGOMERY may have built a castle on the site of the present ruins. The manor remained in the possession of the Montgomerys until the estates of Roger's eldest son, Robert de Bellême, were confiscated by the Crown in 1102. HENRY I granted the manor to William Peverel and in 1138 the castle was held by his nephew (also called William Peverel), who supported the Empress MAUD against King STEPHEN. Whittington Castle was given to Geoffrey de Vere in 1164 by HENRY II, but in the following year the king granted it to Roger de Powys. At the beginning of the 13th C. it belonged to Fulk Fitz Warin, who rebuilt and enlarged the earlier fortress. It was attacked by the Welsh on a number of occasions and in 1223 it was reputedly captured by Llywelyn the Great. The castle was soon retaken, however, and remained the property of the Fitz Warin family until the 15th C. when it was given by Henry VI to the Earl of Stafford. By the middle of the following century, the castle was in a bad state of repair and subsequently fell into ruin. In about 1760, much of the stone was used to repair part of the road between WHITTINGTON and ELLESMERE. The outer gateway was repaired with stone from one of the towers in 1809. Near the restored 13th C. gatehouse, with its two drum towers and broad archway, is a small timber-framed house.

Novels: Hugh BERINGAR reinforced his northern border fortress at Whittington in March 1141. 'Delivered of the baggage and the womenfolk, they rode on at a brisker pace the few miles to Whittington, where they halted under the walls of the small timber keep.' In 1144 CADFAEL and Deacon MARK halted on their journey from SHREWSBURY to ST ASAPH under the walls of the timber keep at Whittington.

Refs: **9** (10); **18** (1).

Wilfred, Brother (*fl.* 1141) (fict.). **Novels:** Benedictine monk of SHREWSBURY ABBEY, he was lame from a young man and walked with a stick.

Refs: **9** (7).

Will the Groom (*fl.* 1138) (fict.). **Novels:** 'A stout-hearted man', Will was head groom at SHREWSBURY ABBEY. In December 1138 he was one of the grooms who discovered Edwin GURNEY, disguised as a monk, in the abbey barn at the corner of the HORSE-FAIR.

Refs: **3** (6).

William, Abbot (*fl.* 1138) (hist.). Abbot of PERSHORE Abbey from 1138 to 1140, he was succeeded by Thomas, who was abbot until 1162.

Novels: The Abbot of PERSHORE sent Brother ELYAS to BROMFIELD Priory in November 1139 to deliver a finger-bone of St EADBURGA.

Refs: **6** (2).

William I (*c.* 1028–87), King of England (1066–87) (hist.). Also called William the Conqueror, William the Bastard or William of Normandy. The illegitimate son of Robert I, Duke of Normandy, and Herleva (or Arlette), daughter of a tanner of Falaise, William succeeded to the dukedom after his father's death in 1035 whilst returning from a pilgrimage to JERUSALEM. Many of the nobles despised him for being a bastard, and the subsequent breakdown in law and order saw the murder of three of his guardians and various attempts on his own life. William was protected by his mother, however, and eventually managed to regain control of his duchy by great determination and skill. In *c.* 1052 he married Matilda, daughter of Baldwin V, Count of Flanders, despite the match being condemned by Pope Leo IX as incestuous. She gave him four sons: ROBERT, Duke of Normandy; Richard, who died young; WILLIAM II; and HENRY I. One of their daughters, ADELA, became the mother of King STEPHEN. In 1066 William landed at Pevensey with his army and, at the battle of Senlac Hill, near Hastings, defeated HAROLD II to become the first Norman King of England. He strengthened his power and established order in the country by a systematic policy of castle-building, ruthless harrying and the confiscation of estates belonging to those who offered resistance. Within five years he had finally quelled English and Anglo-Danish rebellions. In 1072 he invaded Scotland forcing MALCOLM III to pay him homage, and in 1081 he invaded Wales. In order to secure his English frontiers, William created defensive 'marcher' counties along the borders of Scotland and Wales (see WELSH MARCHES). Throughout his reign he spent long periods in NORMANDY, putting down rebellions and French invasions. In 1086 he ordered the written survey of English landowners and their estates which came to be known as the Domesday Book. He died after receiving an internal injury while campaigning in France, and was buried in St Stephen's Church, Caen. Instead of allowing his eldest son, Robert, to succeed to the whole inheritance, William compromised: Robert received Normandy and MAINE; while William II became King of England.

Novels: 'What the Conqueror had misguidedly dealt out in two separate parcels to his two elder sons, his youngest son had now put together again and clamped into one.' 'SHREWSBURY had been given to the great Earl Roger [de MONTGOMERY] almost as soon as Duke William became king, but many a manor in the outlying countryside had remained with its old lord, and many a come-lately Norman lordling had had the sense to take a Saxon wife, and secure his gains through blood older than his own, and a loyalty not due to himself.' King William gave the village of GREENHAMSTED to Hascoit MUSARD 'some time before the Domesday survey was taken'.

Refs: **2** (1); **7** (8); **8** (12); **10** (2); **15** (4); **20** (6–7); **RB** (1).

William II (*c.* 1056–1100), King of England (1087–1100) (hist.). Also called William Rufus. Third son and favourite of WILLIAM I, William received his nickname 'Rufus', or 'the Red', from his ruddy complexion. In 1079, during the fighting which followed the rebellion by his elder brother, ROBERT of Normandy, against his father, William – who fought on his father's side – was wounded. After the death of William I in 1087, William inherited England and was crowned king by LANFRANC, Archbishop of Canterbury. The following year, Odo, Bishop of Bayeux, who was William I's half-brother, led a plot to dethrone William and set Robert in his place. William gained the support of the native English by making false promises and the rebellion was put down. From 1090, having secured England, the king's main goal was to take NORMANDY from his elder brother. A treaty, however, between the two brothers in 1091 led to a co-operative venture to drive their youngest brother, the future HENRY I, out of Normandy and divide his lands between them. In the same year William returned to England, and later forced MALCOLM III, King of Scotland, to acknowledge his overlordship. When Malcolm invaded Northumberland (see NORTHUMBRIA) in 1093, he was killed by William's forces. In 1094 the king resumed the war against Robert in Normandy, imposing heavy taxes on the English not only to hire mercenaries but also to pay bribes. Requiring money to join the First Crusade in 1096, Robert pledged his duchy to William for five years in return for 10,000 marks. The king quarrelled with ANSELM, Archbishop of Canterbury, over the question of investitures and in 1097 Anselm left the country for ROME. In 1100, while hunting in the New Forest, William was hit by an arrow and killed. Although his death was widely held to have been an accident, later speculation said that he had been assassinated by order of his younger brother, Henry, who had promptly seized the throne. William, who never married, was buried without ceremony in WINCHESTER Cathedral.

Novels: It was said that Henry I was not 'without a hand in removing from the light of day' William II, who after his death 'had been shovelled into a hasty grave under the tower at Winchester'.

Refs: **3** (7); **RB** (1).

William of Corbeil (*c.*1060/80–1136), Archbishop of Canterbury (hist.). Born probably at Corbeil (also spelled Corbail or Corbeuil) in France, he was educated at Laon, in Picardy. Entering the priory of Augustinian canons at Aldgate, LONDON, he eventually became the prior of ST OSYTH, in Essex. He was consecrated Archbishop of Canterbury in 1123, after a long conflict with Thurstan, Archbishop of York, and three years later was appointed papal legate. In 1135 he crowned STEPHEN King of England at WESTMINSTER. He died on 21 November 1136 at CANTERBURY.

Novels: 'The enmity [between Bishop HENRY OF BLOIS and THEOBALD OF NORMANDY] dated back five years, to the time when the archbishopric of CANTERBURY had been vacant, after William of Corbeil's death, and King Stephen's younger brother, Henry, had cherished confident pretensions to the office, which he certainly regarded as no more than his due.' In 1126, at Henry I's Christmas court, William of Corbeil, Archbishop of Canterbury, swore allegiance to the Empress Maud. As papal legate he was concerned for the wellbeing of the Church and, in 1134, sent out a preaching mission from St Osyth to many of the towns in England, including SHREWSBURY.

Refs: **16** (1–2); **20** (4).

William of Ypres (d. *c.*1165) (hist.). Also called William of Loo. He was the son (possibly illegitimate) of Philip, Count or Viscount of Ypres. Although he inherited his father's estates at Loo (near Furnes in West FLANDERS), William did not receive his rank or title. After the murder at BRUGES of his first cousin Charles, Count of Flanders, on 2 March 1127, William seized YPRES and the towns in the neighbourhood, and claimed that he had been granted Flanders by its overlord Louis VI, King of France. Louis, however, granted the country to William Clito, son of ROBERT of Normandy. The choice was against the interests of the English King HENRY I, Clito's uncle. Henry, therefore, despatched his nephew, the future King STEPHEN, to Flanders to form a league with the nobles to oppose Clito, which William joined. After attempting and failing to make peace with Ypres, Louis – together with Clito – attacked William on 26 April 1127. He was captured and imprisoned, and was only released in March the following year when Clito – who had been expelled from Bruges and Ghent by a new rival, Thierry of Alsace – needed his support. Clito was killed in battle on 22 August 1128 and William, who was somehow related to Thierry's wife Swanhild, remained in Flanders until 1133, three years after her death. Forced eventually to leave his castle at Sluys, William sought refuge with Stephen in England. When Stephen became king in December 1135, he put William in charge of his army of Flemish mercenaries. After campaigning for Stephen in NORMANDY, William returned to England and was at the siege of DEVIZES in June 1139. Although he fled during the battle of LINCOLN on 2 February 1141, he remained loyal to the king throughout the latter's captivity. William joined Queen MATILDA in Kent and was with her army at the siege of WINCHESTER in July. In September he and his Flemings captured some two hundred of the Empress MAUD's forces at WHERWELL, setting fire to the abbey church. On 14 September, after the 'Rout of Winchester', he was party (with William de WARENNE) to the capture of ROBERT of Gloucester at STOCKBRIDGE. This action secured Stephen's eventual release. But, despite the fact that he was rewarded with lands in Kent, William did not, as some authorities claim, become Earl of Kent. He is said to have been 'a fear and a terror to all England', but after becoming blind he used some of his wealth for good works – founding, for example, a Cistercian Abbey at Boxley, Kent, in *c.*1146. On the accession of HENRY II in 1154, Stephen's foreign mercenaries were banished from England. William, however, remained in the country until *c.*1157 when he returned to Flanders. He died at the monastery of St Peter in Loo, where he had spent the last seven years of his life, and was buried in the church.

Novels: William of Ypres was among the Flemish captains who fled from the battle of Lincoln on 2 February 1141, leaving Stephen to be captured. William was at the siege of Winchester in September 1141. He and his Flemings attacked a three- to four-hundred-strong force belonging to Maud outside Wherwell: "'William of Ypres cut them to pieces outside the town, and the remnant fled into the nunnery and shut themselves into the church. The place was burned down over them.'" With Stephen, William attended the conference at COVENTRY on 30 November 1145.

Refs: **9** (1); **11** (4–6); **20**(3).

William the Aetheling (1103–20), Prince (hist.). Also called Prince William or Duke of Normandy. He was the only legitimate son of HENRY I by his wife MATILDA of Scotland, and the brother of the Empress MAUD. Recognised by the English as the Aetheling, the lawful heir to the realm, he received the homage of the Norman barons in 1115. In June 1119 at Lisieux, NORMANDY, William married Matilda, daughter of FULK, Count of Anjou. Later the same year he fought alongside his father at the battle of Brémule against LOUIS VI, King of France, and William Clito, son of ROBERT of Normandy. In 1120 Henry and Louis made peace, and Prince William was invested with the duchy of Normandy. On the night of 25 November 1120, William sailed for England from BARFLEUR in the *White Ship* (see BLANCHE NEF). Shortly after leaving the harbour the vessel struck a rock and sank. According to the sole survivor, William managed to get aboard a small boat but, attempting to rescue his half-sister still aboard the stricken vessel, it was swamped by the weight of others.

Novels: "'His only lawful son, recently married in splendour, now denied even a coffin and a grave, for if ever they found those royal bodies it would be by the relenting grace of God, for the sea seldom puts its winnings ashore by Barfleur. Even some of his unlawful sons, of whom there were many, gone down with their royal brother, no one left but the one legal daughter to inherit a barren empire.'" Prince William was lost at sea on 25 November 1120, when the *Blanche Nef* struck a rock and foundered with all hands.

Refs: **2** (8); **10** (2); **20** (3–4); **RB** (1).

Wilton (Wiltshire, England). Some 3 miles west of SALISBURY, this market town – once the capital of Saxon Wessex – stands at the confluence of the rivers Wylye and Nadder. In 830 King Egbert founded a nunnery in the town and in 890 it was refounded by Alfred the Great. Dedicated to St Mary, St Bartholomew and St Edith, Edgar's daughter, the church was rebuilt in stone by Edith, wife of EDWARD THE CONFESSOR, and consecrated in 1065. Wilton was granted its first market charter in 1121 by HENRY I. In

1143 King STEPHEN and his army were in the process of fortifying the castle at Wilton, when they were surprised by a force under ROBERT of Gloucester. In the battle which followed, Stephen was forced to withdraw into the abbey precincts. Robert set fire to the town and in the ensuing confusion Stephen was almost taken prisoner. He was saved by the heroic rearguard action of William MARTEL and the men under his command. Although the Benedictine abbey was destroyed, it was rebuilt. After the Dissolution the monastery was granted to William Herbert, 1st Earl of Pembroke, by Henry VIII. Today the site is occupied by Wilton House, the home of the Earls of Pembroke. Wilton Friary was founded in 1245 for Dominican friars, but was abandoned in 1281 when the community moved to Salisbury. The ruins of the medieval parish church of St Mary stand near the market place and, although the chantry has been restored, it has been replaced by the church of St Mary and St Nicholas.

Novels: Eudo BLOUNT (the elder) was killed at the battle of Wilton in March 1143. (According to some authorities, the battle of Wilton took place on 1 July 1143 and not in March as stated in *The Chronicles of Brother Cadfael*. Ellis Peters says: 'Maud escaped from Oxford Castle shortly before Christmas 1142, the garrison surrendered as soon as they knew she was safely away. The *Gesta Stephani* says that Stephen installed his own garrison and secured the country round Oxford. Then, the *Gesta* says "after a short interval" he laid siege to Wareham, and failing there, went to attack Wilton. It all suggests an early date in 1143.')

Refs: **17** (1, 9); **20** (3).

Winchester (Hampshire, England). Lying in the valley of the River Itchen, 12 miles north of the port of SOUTHAMPTON, Winchester increased in size and importance after the Roman Conquest to become one of two capitals of the region. Winchester was the capital of Wessex during the reign of Alfred the Great (871–99) and, with his kingdom's rise in prominence, it became the capital of the nation. A number of kings were buried in the city, including Alfred. Even after the Norman Conquest, partly because of its proximity to Southampton and the sea-route to NORMANDY, Winchester was joint capital with LONDON for many years and maintained close links with the Crown until the reign of Charles II. In 1141 the Empress MAUD besieged HENRY OF BLOIS in WOLVESEY CASTLE; he retaliated by setting fire to the city. She in turn was besieged by the forces of Queen MATILDA. On 14 September Maud was forced to retreat and, in what came to be known as the 'Rout of Winchester', ROBERT of Gloucester was captured. During medieval times Winchester prospered on the wool trade and even today, as the county town of Hampshire, it remains an important market centre. There were a number of monastic orders in the town. Nunnaminster (or Nunminster) was first founded in *c.*900 for Benedictine nuns by Alfred the Great and his wife. Dissolved in 1539, today there are no remains. Its site lay between High Street and Colebrook Street. The town also contained: a Dominican Friary, founded before 1234; a Franciscan Friary, founded in 1237; a Carmelite Friary, founded before 1268; and an Augustinian Friary, founded before 1300. See also HYDE ABBEY. Among the wealth of medieval buildings of interest are: the remains of Wolvesey Castle and Hyde Abbey; WINCHESTER CATHEDRAL; the Hospital of St Cross, founded in 1136 by Bishop Henry of Blois; the Great Hall (all that remains of WINCHESTER CASTLE); Westgate, one of the main gateways into the walled city, and now a museum; the tiny church of St Swithun-upon-Kingsgate, standing on another gateway; and Winchester College, founded by Bishop William of Wykeham in 1382.

Novels: 'He [Adam Heriet] launched into a very full and detailed account of Bishop Henry's city, from the north gate, where he had entered, to the meadows of St Cross, and from the cathedral and the castle of Wolvesey to the north-western fields of Hyde Mead. He could describe in detail the frontages of the steep High Street, the golden shrine of Saint SWITHUN, and the magnificent cross presented by Bishop Henry to his predecessor Bishop WALKELIN's Cathedral.' 'In the streets of Winchester the stinking, blackened debris of fire was beginning to give place to the timid sparks of new hope, as those who had fled returned to pick over the remnants of their shops and households, and those who had stayed set to work briskly clearing the wreckage and carting timber to rebuild. The merchant classes of England were a tough and resilient breed, after every reverse they came back with fresh vigour, grimly determined upon restoration and willing to retrench until a profit was again possible. Warehouses were swept clear of what was spoiled, and made ready within to receive new merchandise. Shops collected what was still saleable, cleaned out ravaged rooms and set up temporary stalls. Life resumed, with astonishing speed and energy, its accustomed rhythms, with an additional beat in defiance of misfortune. As often as you fell us, said the tradesmen of the town, we will get up again and take up where we left off, and you will tire of it first.' Bishop Henry of Blois held a legatine council at Winchester on 7 April 1141. On 9 April Rainald BOSSARD was killed by CIARAN in the street near the Old Minster. At the end of July, Maud marched with her army to Winchester and besieged Bishop Henry in Wolvesey Castle. In August, after Bishop Henry had set fire to the city and destroyed Hyde Mead Priory, Brother HUMILIS and Brother Fidelis (see CRUCE, Julian) fled north to SHREWSBURY. The empress, in turn, was besieged in the royal castle at Winchester by Queen Matilda. In September Maud sent a three- or four-hundred-strong force out of the castle to try to secure a base at WHERWELL. They were cut to pieces by the queen's Flemings under WILLIAM OF YPRES. Nicholas HARNAGE visited the city a number of times in his search for Julian Cruce. At the silversmith's shop in High Street he found her ring, sold by Adam HERIET on 20 August 1138. On 14 September 1141 Maud and her followers were forced by starvation out of the castle. Their retreat became a headlong flight, during which Robert of Gloucester was captured. In 1141, King STEPHEN spent Christmas with Bishop Henry at Winchester.

Refs: **8** (8, 10); **10** (1–2, 5–7, 10–11, 14–16); **11** (1–6, 8, 11, 13); **12** (1); **15** (1); **16** (1); **20** (1, 3, 5); **RB** (1).

Winchester, Bishop of. See HENRY OF BLOIS, Bishop of Winchester.

Winchester Castle (Hampshire, England). After the Norman Conquest, WILLIAM I built a royal palace in the vicinity of the present St Lawrence's Church and a castle in the south-western corner of WINCHESTER. The palace was destroyed when Bishop HENRY OF BLOIS set fire to the city in August 1141. The royal castle was occupied by the Empress MAUD until she was forced to flee on 14 September. HENRY II started a programme of rebuilding and modernisation on the 4-acre site which was not completed until the reign of Henry III (1216–72). The castle continued to be a royal residence up until 1302 when the royal apartments, containing Edward I and his queen, caught fire. On occasions, between 1330 and 1449, the main hall was used by Parliament. During the Civil War, Parliamentarian troops besieged the castle and, after the execution of Charles I in 1649, it was demolished. All that now remains is the 13th C. Great Hall, which is considered to be one of the finest medieval halls in England, second only to WESTMINSTER. On the western wall hangs 'King Arthur's Round Table', probably dating from the 13th C. It was repainted in 1522.

Novels: '"The empress entered Winchester towards the end of July, I do not recall the date, and took up her residence in the royal castle by the west gate."' In July 1141, having been driven out of LONDON, Maud

W

took up residence in the royal castle at Winchester. From there, in August, she besieged Bishop Henry of Blois in WOLVESEY CASTLE. She, in turn, was besieged by Queen MATILDA and fled the city on 14 September.

Refs: **11** (1–2, 4–6).

Winchester Cathedral (Hampshire, England). The first cathedral at Winchester, known as the Old Minster, was built by the Saxon King Cenwalh in *c.*645 and dedicated to St Peter. Its foundations lie just to the north of the present cathedral. The first Norman Bishop of Winchester, WALKELIN, began the construction of the present cathedral in 1079. It was consecrated in 1093 and, shortly after, the Old Minster was demolished. Winchester Cathedral, 556 ft. from east to west, is the second longest in Europe (the longest being St Peter's in ROME). The Perpendicular arches and vaulting of the nave are the work of the 14th C. bishop, William of Wykeham, who continued the transformation from Norman to Gothic started by his predecessor William of Edington. Inside the cathedral are a number of monuments to Saxon kings and queens, as well as the tomb of the Norman King, WILLIAM II. See also HYDE ABBEY.

Novels: Winchester Cathedral was built by Bishop Walkelin. In March 1141 Bishop HENRY OF BLOIS let the Empress MAUD into the cathedral, 'where the crown and the treasure are guarded'.

Refs: **9** (9); **10** (2); **11** (8).

Winfrid, Brother (*fl.* 1142) (fict.). **Novels:** 'Brother Winfrid had so much energy in him that it had to find constant outlet, or it would probably split him apart.' Benedictine monk of SHREWSBURY ABBEY, Brother Winfrid, not long out of his novitiate, became CADFAEL's assistant in the herb garden in October 1142. He was still there in December 1145.

Refs: **14** (1, 4, 9, 13); **15** (1, 3); **16** (1, 12, 15); **17** (2, 5, 10); **18** (1); **19** (5, 12); **20** (1–2, 16).

Winifred (Daughter of Eluned Nest). See NEST, Winifred.

Winifred Saint (d. *c.*655) (hist.) (f.d. 3 November). Also called Gwenfrewi or Guinevra; also spelled Winefred, Winefride or Wenefrida. Much of the information about Winifred, who lived at HOLYWELL in the 7th C., is based on medieval legend. She was the niece of St BEUNO and the only child of a knight called TEVYTH. When Prince CRADOC tried to seduce her, she fled, and he cut off her head with his sword. After Beuno had restored her to life, Winifred went on a pilgrimage to ROME, returning to Wales to become the prioress of a convent at GWYTHERIN under the direction of St ELERIUS. Another tradition claims that she was the abbess of a nunnery at Holywell. Nevertheless, she was buried in the churchyard at Gwytherin and in 1137 her relics were taken to SHREWSBURY by Prior ROBERT: first to the church of ST GILES and then to SHREWSBURY ABBEY. Her translation is celebrated on 22 June.

Novels: 'Brother CADFAEL kneeled. It may even have been a significant omen that at this moment he alone was kneeling. He judged that he was at the feet of the skeleton. She had been there some centuries, but the earth had dealt kindly, she might well be whole, or virtually whole. He had not wanted her disturbed at all, but now he wanted her disturbed as little as might be, and delved carefully with scooping palms and probing, stroking finger-tips to uncover the whole slender length of her without damage. She must have been a little above medium height, but willowy as a seventeen-year-old girl. Tenderly he stroked the earth away from round her. He found the skull, and leaned on stretched arms, fingering the eye-sockets clear, marvelling at the narrow elegance of the cheek-bones, and the generosity of the dome. She had beauty and fineness in her death. He leaned over her like a shield, and grieved.' St Winifred was the daughter of Tevyth, niece of St Beuno and abbess of Gwytherin. In May 1137 Brother JEROME claimed that he had had a miraculous dream in which he was visited by St Winifred. She told him that if Brother COLUMBANUS bathed in the water of her spring at

Holywell he would be healed and restored at once to his senses. St Winifred, it was revealed, had been miraculously brought back to life by St Beuno, after Prince Cradoc had struck off her head with his sword. She went on a pilgrimage to Rome, where she attended 'at a great synod of saints, and was appointed to be prioress over a community of virgin sisters at Gwytherin'. She was buried in the village, in a grave that had long been neglected. In May 1137 Prior Robert's party travelled to Gwytherin to acquire her bones for Shrewsbury Abbey. After the villagers had withdrawn their opposition to the translation, Winifred was removed from her grave and placed in an ornate wooden reliquary. Cadfael later replaced her remains with the corpse of Columbanus, and reburied her with RHISIART in her original grave. It was Columbanus, therefore, who was taken back to Shrewsbury in the reliquary and not St Winifred. During the flood of February 1145 Brother TUTILO attempted to steal the reliquary for 'the future glory' of RAMSEY ABBEY. It was fortunate for Cadfael that, despite its eventful journey from Shrewsbury to HUNCOTE and back, the lid was never removed and the contents revealed. Through the *sortes Biblicae*, which took place at her altar in Shrewsbury Abbey, St Winifred revealed to Prior Robert: 'Ye have not chosen me, but I have chosen you' – '"a warning rather than an acknowledgement. She chose you, and she can as well abandon you if she chooses, and you had better be on your guard in future, for she won't put up with another such turmoil upsetting her established rule."'

Refs: **1** (1–4, 6–12); **5** (1); **7** (10); **10** (1, 3, 6–12, 15–16); **11** (3, 5, 14); **12** (8); **13** (1, 9, 12); **14** (2); **15** (2–3); **16** (1, 3–4, 9); **17** (9–10); **18** (1, 4); **19** (2–13); **20** (1, 4, 16).

Winstone (Gloucestershire, England). Some 7 miles north-west of CIRENCESTER, this COTSWOLD stone hamlet of scattered farmsteads lies on a bleak hill-top site to the west of the valley of the River FROME and Miserden (see GREENHAMSTED). St Bartholomew's Church is partly Saxon and partly Norman, probably dating from around the time of the Conquest. The porch and saddleback tower were added in the 14th C. and later. In the churchyard are the remains of a 14th C. cross.

Novels: In December 1145 CADFAEL rode through Winstone on his way to and from La MUSARDERIE. REINOLD had a mill by the village. After the surrender of La Musarderie, Guy CAMVILLE 'led his garrison away eastward, over the river and through Winstone to the Roman road [see ERMIN WAY], heading, most likely, for CRICKLADE.'

Refs: **20** (7, 13–15).

Withington (Shropshire, England). DB – Wientone: in Wrockwardine Hundred; a holding of Fulcuius (or Fulcwy) under Roger de MONTGOMERY. After Fulcuius's death, presumably without heirs, the manor reverted to the Crown; one half was made a serjeantry (a tenure dependent upon certain specified services), and the other was granted to William FITZALAN. However, it was one tenant, a member of the Haughton family, who held both halves of the estate. Eventually the serjeantry became extinct and the whole manor passed to the FitzAlans, with the Haughtons remaining as tenants. Withington is a small village with a number of timber-framed buildings. It is situated in a broad valley, some 5 miles east of SHREWSBURY and about a mile from the confluence of the Rivers TERN and RODEN. Like many villages, within easy reach of a major town, Withington has its fair share of modern building development. It is recorded that there was a church at Withington in at least 1159, and possibly ten years earlier. Originally a chapel of UPTON Magna, the advowson belonged to SHREWSBURY ABBEY. In the Middle Ages much of the land around Withington was granted to nearby HAUGHMOND ABBEY.

Novels: 'There was a well-used track . . . to Withington, through flat land, rich and green. Two brooks threaded their gentle way between the houses of the village, to merge on the southern edge and flow on to empty into the River Tern. The small church that sat in the centre of the green was a property of the abbey, like its neighbour at Upton . . . On the far side of the village, drawn back a little from the brook, the manor lay within a low stockade, ringed round with its barns and byres and stables. The undercroft was of timber beams, one end of the living floor of stone, and a short, steep flight of steps led up to the hall door, which was standing open at this early working hour of the day, when baker and dairymaid were likely to be running busily in and out.' In December 1142 GUNNILD was welcomed to the manor of Withington by Giles OTMERE, 'a crown tenant these days, since FitzAlan's lands were seized'. CADFAEL and Sulien BLOUNT, on different occasions, visited the manor during November 1143. Father AMBROSIUS was the parish priest at Withington.

Refs: **17** (8, 10–11).

Wolstan, Brother (*fl.* 1140) (fict.). **Novels:** He was a Benedictine monk of SHREWSBURY ABBEY. In October 1140 Brother Wolstan, then 'the heaviest and most ungainly of the novices', fell from one of the apple trees in the GAYE orchards and landed on a sickle. His injuries looked worse than they were.

Refs: **8** (2, 7, 10).

Wolverhampton. See HAMPTON.

Wolvesey Castle (Winchester, Hampshire). To the south-east of WINCHESTER CATHEDRAL are the remains of Wolvesey Castle, a great fortified palace built in 1138 by Bishop HENRY OF BLOIS on the site of an earlier Anglo-Saxon palace. It also incorporated the stone residence now known as the West Hall, built by the Norman Bishop William Giffard in *c.*1107. In Summer 1141, during the fratricidal war between King STEPHEN and the Empress MAUD, the latter and her forces besieged Bishop Henry in his castle. He retaliated by setting fire to the city, and was only relieved when the army, weakened by disease and starvation, decided to retreat. ROBERT of Gloucester was captured and, after much bargaining, was freed in return for the release of Stephen who had been taken prisoner at LINCOLN in February. Wolvesey Castle was virtually abandoned in the 17th C. and in the early 1680s Bishop George Morley decided to build a new palace in its place. The house was again neglected in the following century and, in 1786, the building was demolished except for the west wing. It was used for a number of purposes until 1928, when it became once again the residence of the Bishops of Winchester. The remains of the medieval palace are now in the care of English Heritage.

Novels: In August 1141 Bishop Henry of Blois was besieged by the forces of the empress 'in his new castle of Wolvesey, in the south-east corner of the city, backed into the wall'. He set fire to Winchester in retaliation, and was only relieved on 14 September, when Maud fled the city.

Refs: **11** (1–2, 5, 8, 11).

Wombridge Priory (Shropshire, England). It was founded for Augustinian canons in *c.*1130–5 by William de Hadley (a vassal of William FITZALAN), together with his wife Seburga and their son Alan. However, Wombridge Priory never attained the wealth or the influence of abbeys like HAUGHMOND, BUILDWAS, LILLESHALL and SHREWSBURY, all within 12 miles of Wombridge. At its dissolution in 1536, among the items surrendered to the Crown was an iron forge and a coal-mine. The site of the priory was granted by Henry VIII to James Leveson, who also acquired the lands of Lilleshall Abbey in 1539. Today Wombridge, 12 miles east of SHREWSBURY, has been swallowed by the sprawling western suburbs of modern Telford. The slight remains of the medieval priory can be found below the churchyard.

Novels: On 5 March 1143 CADFAEL and Brother HALUIN lodged overnight with the Augustinian canons at Wombridge Priory.

Refs: **15** (3).

Woodstock (Oxfordshire, England). Some 7 miles north-west of OXFORD and on the north-eastern edge of Blenheim Park, the former market town of Woodstock was once renowned for the manufacture of gloves. According to tradition, Woodstock was the royal residence of Alfred the Great, King of Wessex (871–*c.*899). Woodstock means 'a place in the wood' and, in the 10th C., it is known that ETHELRED II built a timber hunting-lodge in the forest. Woodstock is mentioned in the Domesday Book survey of 1086 as one of the demesne forests of WILLIAM I in Oxfordshire. HENRY I built or rebuilt the Manor House at Woodstock and enclosed the royal park with a stone wall some 7 miles in circumference, stocking it with lions, leopards, camels and other wild animals, including a porcupine. A village grew up outside the walls, first at Old Woodstock, on the hillside above the River Glyme, and later, in the late 13th C., on the other side of the river at New Woodstock. The Manor House, badly damaged in the Civil War, was demolished in 1709. The site of the manor, marked by a small mound beside the great lake, lies in what are now the landscaped grounds of Blenheim Palace built by John Vanbrugh for John Churchill, 1st Duke of Marlborough, in 1705.

Novels: In November 1120 Roger MAUDUIT retained ALARD THE CLERK and CADFAEL in his service until his lawsuit with SHREWSBURY ABBEY was resolved. HENRY I intended to preside over the case himself at Woodstock on 23 November. The tragic death of his son in the BLANCHE NEF, however, meant that the court sat in his absence. Henry 'makes his forest lodges the hub of his kingdom, there's more statecraft talked at Woodstock, so they say, than ever at WESTMINSTER. And he keeps his beasts there – lions and leopards – even camels.' The hunting chase was 'many miles in extent'.

Refs: **12** (1); **RB** (1).

Woodstock, Church of. See ST MARY MAGDALENE CHURCH.

Worcester (Hereford & Worcester, England). Standing on high ground near the confluence of the rivers TEME and SEVERN, some 24 miles north of GLOUCESTER, the cathedral city and industrial town of Worcester dates back at least to Roman times. Because of its strategic importance as a crossing-point of the Severn, the town has been the scene of numerous battles: the most important being the Civil War battle of 1651, in which the Parliamentarians finally defeated the Royalist army. During the fratricidal war between King STEPHEN and the Empress MAUD, the town was sacked twice: first by the forces of the empress, and later by those of the king. According to Florence of Worcester, the city, cathedral and Norman castle were destroyed by fire in 1113. Although the castle was subsequently rebuilt and became the stronghold of Waleran de BEAUMONT, Count of Meulan, by the early 16th C. it was in ruins. John Leland wrote in *c.*1139: 'The castle stood hard on the south part of the Cathedral Church, almost on Severn. It is now clean down, and half the base court or area of it is now within the wall of the close of the Cathedral Church of Worcester. The dungeon-hill of the castle is a great thing, overgrown at this time with brush-wood. The castle fell to ruin soon after the Conquest, and half the ground of it was given to the augmenting of the close of the priory.' The great motte of the castle was levelled in 1833 and is now part of the grounds of King's School. Edgar's Tower, at the entrance to College Green, was once the gate to the abbey: before that, it may have been part of the castle. Worcester is noted for the manufacture of fine bone china and porcelain, the making of gloves and, of course, Worcester sauce. Among the buildings of interest are: Worcester Cathedral (see WORCESTER ABBEY); the Commandery, founded in the 11th C. as the Hospital of St WULSTAN, now a museum and Civil War Centre; Tudor House, also a museum; Greyfriars, the 15th C. timber-framed home of a wealthy brewer; and the 18th C. Guildhall.

Novels: 'It was early in November of 1139 that the tide of civil war, lately so sluggish and inactive, rose suddenly to sweep over the city of Worcester, wash away half its livestock, property and women, and send all those of its inhabitants who could get away in time scurrying for their lives northwards away from the marauders, to burrow into hiding wherever there was manor or priory, walled town or castle strong enough to afford them shelter.' In August 1138, after the siege of SHREWSBURY, Stephen moved his army south towards Worcester, to 'attempt inroads into the western stronghold of Earl ROBERT of Gloucester'. In November 1139, the city of Worcester was sacked and burned by men from Gloucester. Many of the inhabitants, including Sister HILARIA, Yves HUGONIN and Ermina Hugonin (see BRETAGNE), fled north into Shropshire. The city was regarrisoned in December by Stephen's forces. In 1145 Brien de SOULIS had a brother in Worcester.

Refs: **2** (10); **4** (5:2, 5:6); **5** (7); **6** (1, 3); **8** (9); **10** (1, 6); **13** (10); **19** (2–5, 7, 11–12); **20** (1, 5).

Worcester, Earl of. See BEAUMONT, Waleran de, Count of Meulan.

Worcester Abbey (Hereford & Worcester, England). Standing on the east bank of the River SEVERN, overlooking the grounds of the county cricket club, Worcester Cathedral was first founded in 680 for secular canons. In 743 an adjacent house was established for monks and nuns. The church was refounded for Benedictine monks in *c.*964 by St OSWALD, Bishop of Worcester, later Archbishop of York. It was severely damaged by the Danes in 1041 and rebuilt from 1084 by Bishop WULSTAN, who was the only Saxon bishop allowed to retain his see after the Norman Conquest. The monastic chronicler, Florence of Worcester, was educated at the abbey and remained there until his death in 1118. The building was damaged by fire in 1113, 1189 and 1203. In 1216 King John was buried in the cathedral, at his own request. His Purbeck marble effigy is flanked by the smaller figures of St Oswald and St Wulstan. The present cathedral, although it has been heavily restored, is an amalgam of styles from Norman to Tudor. Among the remains of the monastic buildings are: the conventual church with its Early Norman crypt; the circular Chapter House, dating from 1120; the Cloisters, built 1374 and restored; the 14th C. gateway, Edgar's Tower; and the Refectory (now part of King's School), founded in 1548. Other religious houses in the city included: a Franciscan Friary, founded in *c.*1226; a Sack Friary, founded before 1272; and a Dominican Friary, founded in 1347. Half a mile north of the city centre was Whistones Priory (or White Ladies Nunnery), founded before 1240 for Cistercian nuns by Bishop Walter de Cantilupe.

Novels: Brother HERWARD, 'sub-prior of the Benedictine monastery of Worcester', arrived at SHREWSBURY ABBEY on 29 November 1139. He was searching for Yves HUGONIN and Ermina Hugonin (see BRETAGNE), who had gone missing after the sack of WORCESTER. Yves had been in the care of the monks, while Ermina had been looked after by their sister convent close by. In February 1145 Sub-Prior HERLUIN and Brother TUTILO, accompanied by an unnamed lay brother, rode from Shrewsbury to Worcester to ask for help in the restoration of RAMSEY ABBEY. They were followed, over a week later, by Hugh BERINGAR and Prior ROBERT, who were investigating the disappearance of St WINIFRED's reliquary. NICOL, having travelled on foot from ULLESTHORPE, arrived at the 'cathedral priory of Worcester' less than a day after Hugh and Robert.

Refs: **6** (1, 8–9); **19** (1, 4, 7).

Worthin (now Worthen) (Shropshire, England). DB – Wrdine: in Wittery Hundred; a holding of Roger, Son of Corbet, under Roger de MONTGOMERY. The village of Worthen lies in the valley of the Rea Brook (see MEOLE BROOK), beneath the eastern hills of the Long Mountain, some 11 miles south-west of SHREWSBURY and 6 miles east of Welshpool (see POOL). The watermill, demolished in 1973 to make way for a housing estate, was fed by the Worthen Brook and over the centuries was used not only to grind corn, but also for a number of other purposes, including cider-making and timber production. All Saints' Church dates from the late 12th C. and retains the original south doorway and north tower, although the latter has a 15th C. top and an 18th C. parapet. The nave was built in the 13th C., the south porch with balustraded sides in the 17th C., and the brick chancel in 1761.

Novels: AELGAR had an uncle and cousin, who held a yardland in the manor of Worthin by customary services: 'My father's younger brother, being landless, took the yardland gladly when it fell vacant, and agreed to do service for it, but for all that he was born free, like all my kin.'

Refs: **12** (3).

Wrekin (Shropshire, England). Some 4 miles south-west of Telford and 8 miles east of SHREWSBURY, the volcanic hog-back of the Wrekin rises dramatically from the flat Shropshire plain. Its summit is 1,335 ft. above sea-level and from it there is an extensive view embracing more than twelve counties. During the Iron Age it was the site of a fort built by the ancient Britons, and may have been the administrative capital of the Cornovii tribe, who controlled much of Shropshire in the early 1st C. In addition to the earthwork remains of the hill-fort, there is evidence of Bronze Age occupation. The Wrekin is rich in legends and folklore and some of the tales try to account for the names of its natural features, for example: Hell Gate; Heaven Gate; the Needle's Eye; and the Raven's Bowl.

Novels: 'The land rose on the skyline into the forested ridge of the Wrekin, a great heaving fleece of woodland that spread downhill to the SEVERN, and cast a great tress of its dark mane across LUDEL land and into the abbey's woods of EYTON-BY-SEVERN.

Refs: **14** (1–2, 10); **15** (3); **16** (1, 7); **20** (2).

Wrexham or Wrecsam (Clwyd, Wales). Some 11 miles south-west of CHESTER and 12 miles north of OSWESTRY, Wrexham has been the administrative seat of the Wrexham MAELOR district since 1974. Although it is the industrial and commercial capital of North-East Wales, the town originated as an Anglo-Saxon settlement in Mercia (the English-Welsh boundary of OFFA'S DYKE lies 4 miles to the west). During medieval times Wrexham was an important market centre, noted for its leather industry. From the end of the 18th C. the town derived its wealth from coal-mining, brick-making, quarrying and brewing.

Novels: '"I've left all quiet and every garrison on the alert across the north, and RANULF [of Chester] seems to have pulled back his advance parties towards Wrexham."' In February 1141 OWAIN GWYNEDD was patrolling the Welsh border, 'keeping an eye a close watch on Chester and Wrexham'.

Refs: **9** (2, 12).

Wrockwardine. See RECORDINE.

Wroxall Nunnery (Warwickshire, England). Hugh de Hatton, son of Henry, Earl of Warwick, founded a small priory of Benedictine nuns at Wroxall (5 miles north-west of Warwick) during the reign of King STEPHEN, in thanksgiving to God and St Leonard for a miraculous deliverance after 7 years of chained imprisonment in the HOLY LAND. According to the historian, Sir William Dugdale (1605–86), Hugh vowed that he would 'found at his church a house of nuns of St Benet's Order . . . Which vow was no sooner made, than that he became miraculously carried thence, with his fetters, and set in Wroxhall woods, not far distant from his own house; yet he knew not where he was, until a shepherd of his own, passing through those thickets, accidentally found him.' The priory, dedicated to St Leonard, was dissolved in 1536. Fragments of the convent buildings have survived, including parts of the refectory and chapter house. St Leonard's Church dates from the 14th C.

Novels: In October 1139 Isabel de DOMVILLE, the estranged wife of Huon de DOMVILLE, was in the nunnery at Wroxall.

Refs: **5** (6).

Wroxeter (Shropshire, England). DB – Rochecestre: in Wrockwardine Hundred; a holding of Reginald the Sheriff under Roger de MONTGOMERY. The village of Wroxeter lies on the east bank of the River SEVERN, some 5 miles south-east of SHREWSBURY and about a mile to the south-east of ATTINGHAM Park. Wroxeter grew up near an ancient ford across the river, beside which there is evidence that the Romans built a bridge. Although part of the north wall is Anglo-Saxon, most of the Norman Church of St Andrew was built with reused stone taken from the ruins of WROXETER ROMAN CITY. In 1155, after HENRY II had reinstated his confiscated estates, William FITZALAN gave the church to HAUGHMOND ABBEY and in *c.*1170–80 the chancel was added. It was longer and wider than the original Saxon nave, which itself was lengthened in the 13th C. In the walls of the embattled tower, added in the 16th C. are moulded stones from Haughmond Abbey. During the building of the south wall in 1763 the south aisle, which at some time had been added, was removed. The porch is Victorian. Roman columns and capitals were used to build the churchyard gate and the font is fashioned from the base of a Roman pillar. In the south wall of the nave, placed high up and horizontally, is part of an Anglo-Saxon cross-shaft carved with foliage and a dragon.

Novels: CADFAEL, Brother PAUL and Brother ANSELM accompanied Richard LUDEL the younger to EATON on 21 October 1142. On the way they crossed the ford at Wroxeter. The manor at Wroxeter belonged to Sir Fulke ASTLEY. The following month, Drogo BOSIET asked directions to CUTHRED'S HUT from the villagers in Wroxeter. Fleeing from Astley, Richard was forced to hide near the ford until all was quiet to cross.

Refs: **14** (1–3, 5–6, 8, 10–12).

Wroxeter Roman City (Shropshire, England) (formerly called Viroconium). To the north of the village and church of WROXETER are the remains of ancient Viroconium, the fourth largest city in Roman Britain with defences that enclosed an area of 180 acres. Excavations have revealed that it was also the site of a legionary fortress of the 1st C. Although the Celtic-British tribe of the Cornovii occupied the Iron Age hill-fort on the summit of the nearby WREKIN, there is no evidence to suggest that they had a settlement at Wroxeter, which seems to have been founded entirely by the Romans. In the 1920s archaeologists discovered the shattered pieces of a carved Latin inscription, which when reconstructed was 12 ft. long and 4 ft. high. It stood above the entrance to the forum and, although sections are missing, the inscription states that the building was erected by the Community of the Cornovii in honour of the Emperor Hadrian in 130. Viroconium is in the care of English Heritage and at the site is a small museum.

Novels: 'The groom, a long-legged boy of sixteen, loped cheerfully beside him, and led the pony as they splashed through the ford at Wroxeter, where centuries back the Romans had crossed the SEVERN before them. Nothing remained of their sojourn now but a gaunt, broken wall standing russet against the green fields, and a scattering of stones long ago plundered by the villagers for their own building purposes. In the place of what some said had been a city and a fortress there was now a flourishing manor blessed with fat, productive land, and a prosperous church that maintained four canons.'

Refs: **14** (2).

Wulfnoth, Father (d. 1136) (fict.). **Novels:** In March 1143, on his penitential pilgrimage to HALES, Brother HALUIN expected to find Father Wulfnoth, the parish priest. However, the new parish priest told him: 'Father Wulfnoth is gone to his rest . . . seven years ago now it must be. Ten years back I came here, after he was brought to his bed by a seizure, and three years I looked after him until he died. I was newly priest then, I learned much from Wulfnoth, his mind was clear and bright if the flesh had failed him.'

Refs: **15** (4).

Wulfric (b. *c.*1111) (fict.). **Novels:** 'Two long, fair fellows surely no more than thirty years old, with all the lean grace of their northern kin and eyes that caught the light in flashes of pale, blinding blue.' Saxon brother of Renfred, Wulfric was servant to both Humphrey and Reginald CRUCE at LAI. A swordsman, he was shorter than his brother. Together with John BONDE, RENFRED and Adam HERIET, he escorted Julian CRUCE to ANDOVER in August 1138.

Refs: **11** (4, 6–8, 10–11).

Wulstan (*c.*1008–-95), Bishop of Worcester (1062–95) (hist.) (f.d. 19 January). Also called Saint Wulstan; also spelled Wulfstan, Ulfstan or Wolstan. A Saxon, born at Long Itchington in Warwickshire, Wulstan was educated at the Benedictine monasteries of PETERBOROUGH and EVESHAM. After he had been ordained a priest, he entered WORCESTER ABBEY as a monk, filling the offices of master of the novices, precentor and prior, before becoming Bishop of Worcester in 1062. At his consecration, according to William of Malmesbury, the *sortes Biblicae* sent Wulstan, 'a beautiful and worthy presage, this prognostic: Behold an Israelite indeed, in whom there is no guile' (John 1:47). After the Norman Conquest Wulstan supported WILLIAM I and was allowed to retain his see. In 1084 he began work on demolishing St OSWALD's cathedral at Worcester and replacing it with a new and grander building. Together with LANFRANC, Archbishop of Canterbury, Wulstan preached, persistently and persuasively, against the slave-trade between BRISTOL and Ireland. With less success, he also tried to enforce the discipline of priestly celibacy. Canonised in 1203, Wulstan's shrine at Worcester became a popular place of pilgrimage.

Novels: Bishop Wulstan preached against slavery '"years back . . . and did his best to shame it out of England, if not out of the world."' '"The trade still goes on, and Bishop Wulstan's sermons haven't made it illegal, only frowned upon."' The cathedral priory at Worcester was dedicated to Saints Oswald and Wulstan. At his consecration, the '"good Bishop of Worcester got: 'Behold an Israelite indeed, in whom there is no guile'"' (John 1:47).

Refs: **19** (2–4, 7, 11).

Wulstan, Saint. See WULSTAN, Bishop of Worcester.

Wyle (now Wyle Cop) (Shrewsbury, Shropshire). The steep winding street, known as Wyle Cop, leads from the English Bridge to the junction of High Street, Fish Street and Milk Street. Although Wyle Cop is commonly used to refer to the whole street, it really consists of three sections: Under the Wyle (from the English Bridge to the foot of the hill); the Wyle (the hill itself); and Wyle Cop (the top of the hill from Dogpole to the steps of ST JULIAN'S CHURCH). Since medieval times the street has been widened. To reduce its steepness, the top has also been lowered, and the bottom raised. Among the buildings of interest in the street are: Nag's Head Inn, standing on the site of the earlier Nag's Head Without (so named because it stood outside the city walls); Lion Hotel, dating from the 15th C., formerly the town's main

W

coaching inn; Henry Tudor House, in which Henry VII is reputed to have stayed in 1485 before the Battle of Bosworth; and Mytton's Mansion (Nos. 65–9), dating from the early 15th C. The medieval English Bridge (formerly called Stone Bridge) – which had houses upon it – was replaced by a new seven-arched bridge, designed by John Glynn and completed in 1774. It was reconstructed and lowered (to reduce the gradient of the roadway) by Arthur Walburgh Ward and re-opened in 1927.

Novels: 'They climbed the steep curve of the Wyle in silence, the gradient making demands on their breath.' 'The Wyle, uncoiling eastward, brought them down to the town wall and the English gate.' Among the properties on the Wyle were: Martin BELLECOTE'S HOUSE AND SHOP; and the house of CONSTANCE'S cousin; while ARNALD THE FISHMONGER lived 'under the Wyle'.

Refs: **2** (2–3, 12); **3** (3–4, 8, 11); **4** (2:1–2, 3:2); **7** (3, 5, 7, 10); **9** (9); **10** (5, 7); **11** (13); **12** (4–5); **13** (7, 9); **14** (1); **16** (8); **20** (1).

Wyle, Henry (*fl.* 1138) (fict.). **Novels:** A merchant of SHREWSBURY, he was one of the witnesses for the town to the charter of 1138 between Judith PERLE and SHREWSBURY ABBEY, which granted her house in the ABBEY FOREGATE to the abbey for an annual rent of one white rose. See also Nicholas of MEOLE and John RUDDOCK.

Refs: **13** (2).

Y

Yardley Chase (or King's Chase) (Northamptonshire, England). Yardley Chase – an extensive tract of moorland and woodland, noted for its magnificent oaks – lies between the villages of Yardley Hastings and Denton, some 6 miles east of NORTHAMPTON. After the Norman Conquest it became the hunting preserve of kings, including HENRY I. Today Chase Park is part of the estate of Castle Ashby House, and is connected to it by a 3-mile-long avenue. The Elizabethan mansion, standing on the site of a Norman castle, was built by the 1st Lord Compton in *c.*1574 and enlarged in the early 17th C. by his son, the 1st Earl of Northampton. The grounds, which include a series of ornamental lakes, were landscaped by Capability Brown in the 1760s. The parkland, including the avenue, was planted with trees after a visit by William III in 1695. Castle Ashby belongs to the Marquess of Northampton. The much-restored Church of St Mary Magdalene, near the Orangery, dates from the 13th C.

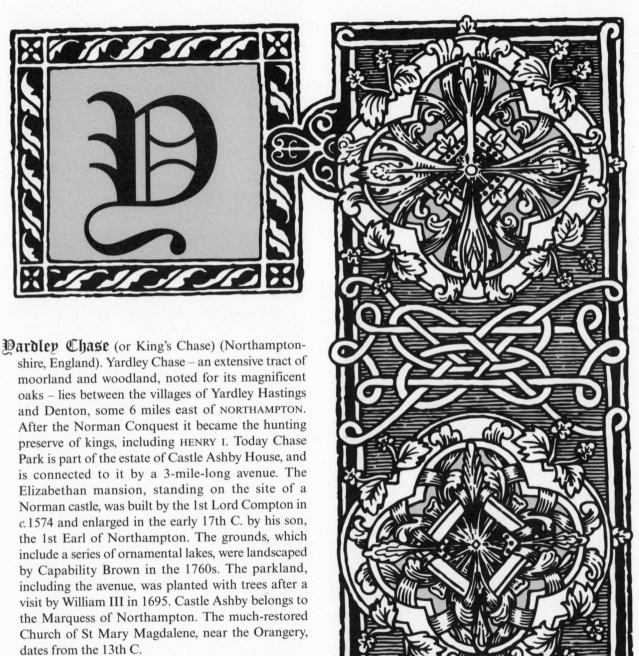

Novels: The manor of SUTTON MAUDUIT which was the head of Roger MAUDUIT's scattered and substantial honour lay somewhat south-east of Northampton, 'comfortably under the lee of the long ridge of wooded hills where the king had a chase, and spreading its extensive fields over the rich lowland between.'

Refs: **RB** (1).

Yockleton. See WESTBURY.

Ynys Enlli (or Bardsey Island) (Gwynedd, Wales). A small island off the tip of the LLEYN PENINSULA, Ynys Enlli is separated from the mainland by the 2-mile channel of Bardsey Sound. Its Welsh name, meaning 'island of tides', refers to the strong tidal race of the Sound. From the 5th C., when St Cadfan founded a Celtic monastery on the island, it became an important ecclesiastical centre and a major place of pilgrimage. Such was Ynys Enlli's reputation for sanctity that it came to be known as the 'Island of 20,000 Saints'. It was thought to be 'the gate of Paradise', and the greatest desire of many a Welsh warrior or poet was to be buried in its soil. During the 13th C. the abbey became Augustinian. Very little now remains of the monastic buildings. Today the island is a nature reserve.

Novels: In Spring 1141 CIARAN let it be known that he intended to walk barefoot on a penitential pilgrimage to ABERDARON, so that after his death he could be 'buried on the holy isle of Ynys Enlli, where the soil is made up of the bones and dust of thousands upon thousands of saints'.

Refs: **10** (3, 5, 14).

Ynys Lanog (Gwynedd, Wales). Also spelled Lannog; also called Priestholm, Puffin Island or Ynys Seiriol. Half-a-mile offshore, beyond the easternmost tip of ANGLESEY, is the tiny island of Ynys Seiriol. It received its original Welsh name of Ynys Lannog from the mythical Glannog, father of Helig Foel. A small colony of puffins inhabiting the island provided its popular English name of Puffin Island. The Celtic monastery, associated with St Seiriol, was destroyed by the Danes in 853. It was occupied by the canons of Priestholm, who were members of no recognised monastic order, and eventually became a priory cell of Augustinian canons, dependent on Penmon Priory, one mile south-west. It is now a ruin. Over the centuries it is reputed that many saints have been buried on the island and possibly one King of Gwynedd, the 6th C. Maelgwn.

Novels: 'Immediately below them a village lay in its patterned fields, beyond it narrow meadowland melting into salt flats and shingle, and then the wide expanse of sea, and beyond that again, distant but clear in the late afternoon light, the coast of Anglesey stretched out northward, to end in the tiny island of Ynys Lanog.'

Refs: **18** (4)

Ypres (Belgium). **Novels:** Some 30 miles south-west of BRUGES and 25 miles south of Ostend, the agricultural and industrial city of Ypres lies on the River Yperlee. During the Middle Ages, together with Bruges, Ghent and other Hanseatic League towns, it was an important centre of the Flemish cloth industry. Between the 15th and 17th C., because of wars and religious struggles, Ypres's prosperity rapidly declined. Finally, in 1794, it was captured by the French.

Refs: **9** (1); **11** (4–6).

Z

Zenghi (1084–1146), Atabeg of Mosul (hist.). The amir Aq Sunqur was executed in 1094 for rebelling against Tutush, Sultan of Aleppo. His Turkish son, Zenghi, then only ten years old, was forced to flee to MOSUL. In 1126 he was appointed Governor of Basra by the Seljuk Sultan, Mahmud II. The following year, he helped the Sultan put down an Abbasid rebellion and was rewarded by being made Lord of Mosul. He immediately extended his authority by taking a number of cities, including Aleppo. Although Zenghi saw himself as the champion of the Muslims, charged with defeating the Christians, he was opposed, not only by the Crusaders, but also by other Muslim princes. One of his main objectives was to take DAMASCUS: a goal he never achieved. Nevertheless, he steadily extended his domain, and on Christmas Eve 1144, he seized the capital of the Crusader state of EDESSA and the territory east of the Euphrates. While besieging the Uqailid ruler of Ja'bar, however, Zenghi was murdered by a group of his servants on 14 September 1146. He founded the Zangid dynasty and was succeeded by his eldest son, Saif al Deen Ghazi.

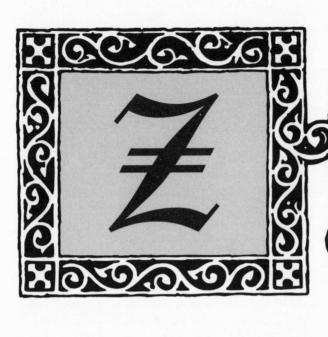

Novels: 'It was very soon made known to all . . . that [SHREWSBURY] ABBEY had acquired a most distinguished son, a crusader of acknowledged valour, who had made a name for himself in the recent contention against the rising Atabeg Zenghi of Mosul, the latest threat to the Kingdom of JERUSALEM.' Godfrid Marescot (see HUMILIS, Brother) was severely wounded in the battle of 1137, when the forces of the King of Jerusalem were defeated by Atabeg Zenghi and the men of Mosul. Nicholas HARNAGE was also at the battle. Atabeg Zenghi and the paynims of Mosul captured Edessa at Christmas 1144.

Refs: **11** (2, 4); **20** (1).

Zephyr or Zephyrus (myth.). **Novels:** In Greek mythology, he loved HYACINTH. Son of Astraeus and Eos, Zephyr is represented by the West Wind of spring – a wind favourable to vegetation.

Refs: **14** (3).

Appendix I

Plants and Herbs mentioned in The Chronicles of Brother Cadfael

Warning: The following plants and herbs should not be used as medicinal or culinary ingredients, without first referring to more specialist sources. The publisher, author or their assignees will not be liable for harm caused to or by persons who ignore this warning.

Note: 'Cul' refers to the Latin identification in *Culpeper's Complete Herbal* where it varies from modern sources.

A

Adder's-Tongue (*Ophioglossum vulgatum*). **Novels:** Used for cleansing and as an astringent, good for old, ulcerated wounds. Found along the banks of the Meole Brook and in the hedgerows and meadows nearby.
Refs: **11** (3).

Alder (*Alnus glutinosa*). **Novels:** A source for withies.
Refs: **7** (7, 11); **16** (6).

Alkanet (also Dyer's Bugloss) (*Alkanna tinctoria*) (Cul: *Anchusa tinctoria*). **Novels:** An ingredient in a bottle of unspecified lotion.
Refs: **5** (1).

Almond (*Prunus dulcis*). **Novels:** Oil extracted from almonds. Mixed with certain herbs, it is used as a lotion for tender frost-nipped hands.
Refs: **12** (7).

Anemone (also Windflower, or Wood Anemone) (*Anemone nemorosa*). **Novels:** An ingredient in a bottle of unspecified lotion.
Refs: **5** (1); **7** (12); **9** (15); **10** (4); **19** (8).

Angelica (*Angelica archangelica*) (Wild Angelica: *Angelica sylvestris*). **Novels:** Angelica water for unspecified use in the abbey infirmary.
Refs: **4** (4:3).

Apple (*Malus pumila* or *Pyrus malus*). **Novels:** Tree in the Gaye orchard, valued for edible fruit.
Refs: **1** (2, 7); **2** (8); **3** (2, 4–6, 8–9); **5** (3, 5); **6** (5); **7** (8); **8** (1–2, 10, 13); **11** (3, 12, 14); **12** (4, 8, 11); **13** (6); **14** (1, 5); **17** (6); **20** (1).

Archangel (also White Deadnettle) (*Lamium album*) (Yellow Archangel: *Lamiastrum galeobdolon*). **Novels:**

Plant in the Potter's Field. Yellow mild nettle: an ingredient in a salve for dressing wounds.
Refs: **6** (6); **17** (1).

Ash (*Fraxinus excelsior*). **Novels:** Wood used to make the curved 'felloes' of the rim of a wheel. A coppice-tree.
Refs: **5** (1, 8); **8** (7); **14** (3, 9).

Aspen (*Populus tremula*). **Novels:** A coppice-tree.
Refs: **14** (3).

B

Barley (*Hordeum vulgare*). **Novels:** Oats used to make gruel, and as an ingredient in an unspecified bottle of lotion.
Refs: **3** (9); **5** (1); **17** (1).

Basil (also Sweet Basil) (*Ocimum basilicum*). **Novels:** A plant in Cadfael's herb garden. Culinary use.
Refs: **1** (1); **3** (1).

Bay (also Sweet Laurel) (*Laurus nobilus*). **Novels:** An ingredient in a mixture for coughs and colds.
Refs: **12** (6); 13 (4).

Bean (also Broad Bean) (*Vicia faba*). **Novels:** A food crop grown on vines. Staple food in monastery. Propagated by seed. Haulms dug back into ground .
Refs: **3** (1–2, 4); **5** (6); **14** (1); **17** (1, 5); **20** (1).

Beech (*Fagus sylvatica*). **Novels:** Ancient and enormous trees in the Long Forest.
Refs: **4** (5:3); **6** (3); **10** (13–14); **14** (3).

Beet (*Beta*) (White Beet: *Beta vulgaris*; Red Beet: *Beta hortensis*). **Novels:** Beet-tops used for fodder.
Refs: **3** (8).

Betony (also Woundwort) (*Stachys officinalis*). **Novels:** Used as an ingredient in healing creams and waxes. An ingredient in a lotion for cleansing wounds and grazes.
Refs: **11** (3); **16** (2).

Betony, Water (also Brown-Wort) (*Betonica aquatica*). **Novels:** Used as an ingredient in healing creams and waxes. An ingredient in a lotion to cleanse wounds and grazes.
Refs: **11** (3); **14** (4).

Betony, Wood (also Common Betony) (*Betonica officinalis*). **Novels:** An ingredient in a lotion for cleansing wounds and grazes. An ingredient in a paste for dressing wounds.
Refs: **11** (3); **12** (5).

Bindweed (*Calystegia sepium*) (Lesser Bindweed, or Cornbine: *Convolvulus arvensis*).
Refs: **13** (2).

Birch (*Betula alba*). **Novels:** A tree.
Refs: **4** (4:5, 5:1); **8** (10); **17** (1).

Blackthorn (*Prunus spinosa*). **Novels:** 'A very fine plant . . . good for almost anything that ailed a man's insides, providing bud and flower and bitter black fruit were all taken at their best. Good in hedges, too, for keeping cattle and sheep out of planted places.' White blossom, just out of bud, used for 'infusing, to make a gentle purge for the old men in the infirmary, who could no longer take the strenuous exercise that had formerly kept their bodies in good trim.' Found along the edges of Shrewsbury abbey's pease-fields and the shore of the mill-pond. Thorny.
Refs: **19** (8–10).

Borage (*Borago officinalis*). **Novels:** An ingredient in mulled wine for a bad chest and throat.
Refs: **3** (8).

Box (*Buxus sempervirens*). **Novels:** Tall box-hedge separating the abbey gardens from the main courtyard.
Refs: **10** (10, 16); **11** (7, 14); **12** (2–4, 7); **14** (1, 4); **16** (1, 3, 15); **19** (2, 5).

Bracken (also Brake) (*Pteridium aquilinum*) (Cul: *Pteris aquilina*). **Novels:** A fern used to cover the logs in a charcoal-burner's hearth. It kept out the earth and ash that goes over all to seal it. Ferns were often represented in illuminated designs and engravings.
Refs: **8** (7); **11** (7, 11); **12** (4); **16** (11).

Bramble (also Blackberry) (*Rubus fruticosus*). **Novels:** Growing wild over St Winifred's grave at Gwytherin. Found also in the Long Forest, on the wasteland near Farewell Abbey, on the headland above the Potter's Field and in the forest near Ullesthorpe.
Refs: **1** (3, 6, 8); **10** (13); **12** (10); **15** (10); **17** (1, 3); **19** (4).

Briar (also Dog Rose or Wild Rose) (*Rosa canina*). **Novels:** Trained to climb on fretwork at Shrewsbury Abbey. Found also on the headland above the Potter's Field.
Refs: **4** (2:3); **14** (3); **17** (10).

Broom (*Sarothamnus scoparius* or *Cytisus scoparius*). (Cul: *Orobanche major*). **Novels:** Broom-bush. Found in the Long Forest near Huon de Domville's hunting lodge, and at the Potter's Field.
Refs: **5** (7); **17** (1–2, 6, 12).

Bryony (also White Briony) (*Bryonia dioica*) (Cul: *Bryonia alba*). **Poisonous**. **Novels:** A plant grown in Cadfael's herb garden.
Refs: **11** (6).

Bugloss (*Lycopsis arvensis*). **Novels:** A plant grown in Cadfael's herb garden.
Refs: **11** (6).

C

Cabbage (*Brassica oleracea capitata*). **Novels:** Edible plant grown by Cadfael in the abbey gardens. Also grown by inmates at St Giles Hospital, Father Huw at Gwytherin, Father Eadmer the younger at Attingham, and the nuns at Godric's Ford.
Refs: **1** (1–2); **2** (1); **3** (1); **5** (8–9); **11** (1); **13** (6); **16** (9).

Carrot (*Daucus carota*). **Novels:** A vegetable grown by Cadfael in the abbey gardens.
Refs: **13** (1).

Centaury (*Centaureum erythraea*) (Cul: *Centaurea cyanus*). **Novels:** An ingredient in a salve or ointment for wounds. A plant grown in Cadfael's herb garden. It was also found growing wild in the Potter's Field.
Refs: **6** (6); **7** (1); **11** (6); **17** (1).

Cherry (*Prunus avium*) (Cul: *Prunus cerasus*). **Novels:** Cadfael made a red wine from sweet cherries and their stones. A tree grown in the Gaye orchards.
Refs: **3** (1); **13** (6, 8).

Chervil (*Anthriscus cerefolium*). **Novels:** A plant grown by Cadfael in the herb garden.
Refs: **1** (1).

Chestnut (also Sweet Chestnut) (*Castanea sativa*) (Cul: *Castanea vesca*).
Refs: **11** (10); **13** (13); **14** (7, 12–14); **15** (5); **20** (7, 14, 16).

Cinquefoil (Silverweed: *Potentilla anserina*) (or Creeping Tormentil: *Potentilla reptans*) (Cul: *Potentilla*). **Novels:** An ingredient in a linctus for sore throats. Kept in a flask in Cadfael's workshop.
Refs: **19** (2).

Cleavers. See GOOSE-GRASS.

Clove-Pink (also Gilly-Flower or Carnation) (*Dianthus caryophyllus*) (Cul: *Motthiala incona*). **Novels:** A flower grown in the abbot's own garden at Shrewsbury Abbey.
Refs: **2** (7).

Clover (also White Clover) (*Trifolium repens*) (Red Clover: *Trifolium pratense*). **Novels:** Dried and stored for fodder. Found growing on Horse-Fair ground. Used as a fragrant ingredient in perfumed oils in altar lamps.
Refs: **2** (6); **11** (1); **12** (8); **16** (10); **20** (9).

Colewort (also Kale) (*Brassica oleracea*) **Novels:** Edible plants grown by Cadfael and monks in the abbey gardens.
Refs: **1** (1); **13** (1, 6).

Coltsfoot (also spelled Colt's-Foot) (*Tussilago farfara*). **Novels:** An ingredient in a syrup for coughs and colds.
Refs: **12** (6).

Columbine (*Aquilegia vulgaris*) (Cul: *Aquilegia*). **Novels:** A flower grown in Cadfael's herb garden.
Refs: **1** (1).

Comfrey (*Symphytum officinale*). **Novels:** An ingredient in a lotion for cleansing wounds and grazes. Soothing preparations were made from the roots and leaves, freshly picked if possible.
Refs: **12** (5); **16** (2, 7).

Corn. See WHEAT.

Cornflower (*Centaurea cyanus*). **Novels:** Flowers often found in a wheat-field.
Refs: **1** (5); **5** (1–2).

Cowslip (*Primula veris*). **Novels:** A flower found in the meadows beyond the abbey enclosure at Shrewsbury.
Refs: **10** (1).

Crab-Apple (*Malus sylvestris*).
Refs: **2** (6).

Crowfoot, Water (*Ranunculus aquatilis*) (Cul: *Ranunculus auricomus*). **Novels:** A plant found growing in the shallows of the River Severn.
Refs: **7** (7, 11); **16** (9).

D

Daisy (*Bellis perennis*) (Cul: *Bellis minor perennis*). **Novels:** An ingredient in a lotion or ointment for cleansing wounds and grazes. A flower growing in the Potter's Field.
Refs: **3** (7); **9** (2); **12** (5); **14** (4); **17** (1).

Damson (*Prunus institia*).
Refs: **1** (2).

Dill (*Anethum graveolens*). **Novels:** A fragrant herb grown in Cadfael's walled garden. An ingredient in a cordial to soothe the stomach of a baby with wind.
Refs: **1** (1); **2** (1); **12** (8).

Dittany (also Burning Bush) (*Dictamnus albus*) (Cul: also called Dittander: *Lepidium sativum*) (Dittany of Crete: *Origanum dictamnus*; White Dittany: *Dictamnus albus*). **Novels:** A plant grown by Cadfael. Was this the same as Aelfric's 'dittanders'?
Refs: **8** (1).

Dock (*Rumex obtusifolius*). **Novels:** An ingredient in a soothing ointment.
Refs: **10** (16).

E

Eglantine (also Sweet Briar) (*Rosa rubiginosa*). **Novels:** Bowers of eglantine.
Refs: **16** (15).

F

Fennel (*Foeniculum vulgare*) (Cul: *Arethum foeniculum*). **Novels:** A fragrant herb grown in Cadfael's walled garden. An ingredient in a cordial for soothing the stomach of a baby with wind.
Refs: **1** (1); **2** (1); **12** (8); **16** (15).

Fern. See BRACKEN.

Fig (*Ficus carica*). **Novels:** Cadfael had grown a fig, brought back with him from the Holy Land, against the sheltering north wall of his walled garden.
Refs: **10** (3).

Figwort (*Scrophularia nodosa*). **Novels:** An ingredient in an unspecified bottle of lotion.
Refs: **5** (1).

Flax (*Linum usitatissimum*). **Novels:** Oil extracted from the seeds used as an ingredient in a medicinal preparation for rheum in the eyes or head. Fibres from the stems were used for making linen.
Refs: **1** (2); **2** (8); **3** (1); **4** (4:1); **7** (2–3); **9** (8); **19** (3); **RB** (3).

Fleur-de-luce. See IRIS.

Fox-Stones. See ORCHIS.

Fungus. Bracket (*Laetioporus sulphureus*, or *Ganoderma adspersum*). **Novels:** Brackets of orange fungus jutted from tree boles in the Long Forest .
Refs: **8** (5).

G

Gentian (*Gentiana verna*) (Several similar species grow in the Alps). (Cul: *Sivertia perennis*). **Novels:** Blue gentians existed in the mountains of southern France.
Refs: **10** (8); **19** (1).

Gilver (also Gillyvor or Gilly-Flower) variously used to describe CLOVE-PINK, white stock, wallflower. **Novels:** A flower grown in Cadfael's herb garden.
Refs: **1** (1).

Ginger (*Zingiber officinale*). **Novels:** A plant grown in Cadfael's herb garden.
Refs: **1** (1).

Goose-Grass (also Cleavers or Catchweed) (*Galium aparine*). **Novels:** 'A queer, creeping thing that grows little hooks to hold fast.' The principal ingredient in a salve or unguent for healing grazes and also green wounds that are stubborn to knit.
Refs: **2** (4, 6, 12); **4** (4:3).

Gooseberry (*Ribes uva-crispa*) (Cul: *Ribes grossularia*). **Novels:** A fruit grown on thorny bushes in the Gaye orchards.
Refs: **13** (6, 8).

Gorse (also Furze) (*Ulex europaeus*).
Refs: **3** (8).

Grape (also Vine) (*Vitis vinifera*). **Novels:** Vines were trained to grow along the north wall of the enclosed abbey garden. Grapes and vine leaves were often represented in illuminated designs, carvings and engravings. An old, crabbed vine grew in Niall Bronzesmith's garden; a great vine grew against the eastern wall of La Musarderie. The abbot's vineyard lay between the town wall and the River Severn, opposite the Gaye.

Refs: **3** (3); **4** (5:3); **5** (3); **7** (6); **11** (3, 7, 9, 11); **12** (9); **13** (4, 9, 13); **14** (1); **16** (3, 11, 15); **20** (9–11, 14).

Gromwell (*Lithospermum officinale*) (Blue Gromwell: *Lithospermum purpurocaeruleum*). **Novels:** The blue creeping gromwell was exceedingly rare, even in Wales. It grew only on chalk or limestone outcrops. At Huon de Domville's hunting lodge in the Long Forest the plant was found growing amidst the branches of a BROOM.

Refs: **5** (6–8, 10).

Groundsel (*Senecio vulgaris*). **Novels:** The plant grew in the crevices of the flooring of Brother Ruald's derelict cottage.

Refs: **17** (1).

H

Harebell (*Campanula rotundifolia*). **Novels:** Found growing among the unreaped grass in the Potter's Field.

Refs: **5** (5); **12** (4, 8, 11); **15** (7); **17** (1, 4).

Hawthorn (*Crataegus monogyna*) (Cul: *Mespilus oxyacantha*). **Novels:** Found growing near St Winifred's chapel at Gwytherin. White flower petals were scattered in the chapel after Brother Columbanus's miraculous disappearance. Tree also found at Ruald's croft.

Refs: **1** (6–7, 10–11); **6** (10); **10** (1, 9); **13** (7); **17** (1); **19** (8–9); **20** (16).

Hay (Grass or other plants, like CLOVER, grown for fodder).

Refs: **2** (5–6, 8); **3** (4–6); **4** (1:1); **5** (4–6); **6** (7, 9–10, 15); **7** (12–13); **11** (1); **12** (10); **13** (3); **14** (8); **15** (4, 14); **16** (1); **17** (1, 6); **19** (8, 11–12); **20** (1); **RB** (1, 3).

Hazel (*Corylus avellana*). **Novels:** Hedges of hazel grew around the abbey enclosure at Shrewsbury. Madog of the Dead-Boat wove hazel withies around the rim of a new coracle. They had been peeled and soaked in the shallows under the Welsh Bridge.

Refs: **2** (9); **3** (7); **8** (2, 7–9); **10** (1); **11** (10); **12** (2, 4); **13** (2); **16** (3, 6, 10–11).

Heather (*Calluna vulgaris*). **Novels:** Found growing on outcrops in the Long Forest, and on the limestone ridge near the track from Shrewsbury Abbey to the Longner ferry.

Refs: **8** (3); **10** (13); **19** (6); **20** (6).

Hemlock (*Conium maculatum*). **Poisonous. Novels:** Used in small doses against pain. It was the main ingredient in a lotion for ulcers, swellings and inflammations. Cadfael did not use the plant because the dangers of poisoning were too great. Generys died after drinking a draught of wine containing hemlock.

Refs: **3** (1); **17** (14).

Hemp (*Cannabis sativa*). **Poisonous. Novels:** The fibres of stem were plaited to form the shell of a litter.

Refs: **17** (13).

Herb of Grace. See RUE.

Honeysuckle (also Woodbine) (*Lonicera periclymenum*) (Cul: *Lonicera caprifolium*). **Novels:** Tendrils of honeysuckle were often represented in illuminated designs, carvings and engravings.

Refs: **16** (15).

Horehound (*Marubium vulgare*). **Novels:** An ingredient in a medicinal preparation for rheum in the eyes or head. An elixir for winter coughs and colds. Also used as a linctus for sore throats.
Refs: **3** (1); **9** (2); **12** (6); **17** (8); **19** (2).

Hound's-Tongue (*Cynoglossum officinale*). **Novels:** An ingredient in a lotion applied to a dog's bite.
Refs: **8** (9).

Houseleek (*Sempervivum tectorum*). **Novels:** An ingredient in an oil for rubbing into the skin to ease aching joints.
Refs: **3** (2).

Hyacinth (*Hyacinthus*).
Refs: **12** (11).

Hyssop (*Hyssopus officinalis*). **Novels:** Both herb and root, dried and powdered, used for chest troubles and yellow distemper or jaundice. In large doses it could procure an abortion. Known to kill.
Refs: **15** (2, 12).

I

Iris (also Fleur-de-luce; also spelled Fleur-de-lys) (*Iris florentina*) (Yellow Iris: *Iris pseudacorus*). **Novels:** An unnamed species of Iris was found growing in the meadow outside the abbey enclosure at Shrewsbury. Fleur-de-luce was an ingredient in a draught meant to procure an abortion.
Refs: **4** (1:1); **5** (3, 5); **6** (4); **10** (1); **11** (4); **13** (11); **15** (2, 12); **16** (15).

Ivy (*Hedera helix*). **Novels:** A 'murderous' plant which clings to trees, like oak. It grew at Huon de Domville's hunting lodge in the Long Forest.
Refs: **5** (4, 7).

Ivy, Ground (*Glechoma hederacea*).
Refs: **8** (7).

J

Jasmine (also spelled Jessamine) (*Jasminum officinale*). **Novels:** Used as a floral essence or perfume.
Refs: **5** (7).

Juniper (*Juniperis communis*). **Novels:** Berries used to flavour gin. Juniper spirit. Geneva spirit was its Dutch equivalent.
Refs: **4** (4:5, 5:1).

K

Kale. See COLEWORT.

L

Lady's Mantle (*Alchemilla vulgaris*). **Novels:** An ingredient in a pot of salve for bed-sores. Also used in an unguent, or ointment, for burns.
Refs: **3** (1); **4** (5:5).

Laurel. See BAY.

Lavender (*Lavandula augustifolia*) (Cul: *Lavandula spica*). **Novels:** A fragrant plant grown in Cadfael's

walled garden. Flowers or flowering-stems were harvested and dried. Used for perfumes. Also useful for all disorders that trouble the head and spirit. Its scent was calming and it was an ingredient in herbal pillows to promote sleep and rest.
Refs: **2** (1, 8); **5** (2); **6** (4); **16** (12); **17** (1); **RB** (2).

Lettuce (*Lactuca sativa*). **Novels:** An edible plant grown in Cadfael's garden and the abbey vegetable plots along the Gaye.
Refs: **1** (1); **13** (8)

Lichen (Plants composed of fungus and algae in close combination). **Novels:** Found growing on rocky outcrops in the Long Forest. Used to produce red, brown and yellow dyes for cloth.
Refs: **8** (7); **13** (3).

Lilac (*Syringa vulgaris*).
Refs: **10** (8); **14** (6).

Lily (*Lilium candidum*) (Lily-of-the-Valley: *Convallaria majalis*). **Novels:** A sweet ingredient in the perfumed oil for altar lamps.
Refs: **10** (16); **12** (8); **19** (1–2).

M

Madder (*Rubia tincorum*). **Novels:** Used to produce a red dye for cloth.
Refs: **13** (3).

Magnolia (*Magnoliaceae*).
Refs: **19** (13).

Mandrake (*Mandragora officinarum*). **Novels:** Fresh leaves bruised to produce a soothing ointment.
Refs: **10** (16).

Marjoram (Sweet Marjoram: *Origanum marjorana*) (Wild Marjoram, or Oregano) (*Origanum vulgare*). **Novels:** A herb grown in Cadfael's walled garden.
Refs: **1** (1); **2** (4).

Marsh Mallow (*Althaea officinalis*) (Cul: *Malva sylvestris*). **Novels:** Leaves and roots freshly prepared to soothe the surface soreness of a wound.
Refs: **16** (7).

Mint (Spearmint: *Mentha spicata*) (Cul: *Mentha viridis*, *Mentha piperita*, *Mentha sylvestris* and *Mentha pulegium*). **Novels:** Plant grown in beds in Cadfael's herb garden. Dried in bunches for storage over winter. Used to brew mint cordials. An ingredient in a bottle of unspecified lotion. A little flask of mint and sorrel vinegar sniffed as a restorative after dizziness and fainting. An ingredient in a mixture for coughs and colds. Also used in a cordial to soothe the stomach of a baby with wind.
Refs: **1** (1); **2** (5); **3** (2); **5** (1–2, 5); **9** (8); **10** (3); **12** (2, 6, 8); **13** (1); **14** (2).

Mistletoe (*Viscum album*) (Cul: *Viscus quercus*). **Poisonous. Novels:** Dried powder from oak mistletoe added to water, wine or milk and drunk after a seizure.
Refs: **7** (2, 9).

Moneywort (also Creeping Jenny) (*Lysimachia nummularia*). **Novels:** Cleansing and astringent, good for old, ulcerated wounds. Found along the banks of the Meole Brook and around nearby meadows and hedgerows.
Refs: **11** (3).

Monk's-Hood (also Wolfsbane or Aconite) (*Aconitum napellus*). **Poisonous. Novels:** Ground root of the plant, mixed with oils, used for rubbing deep into aching joints to relieve pain. Anointing oil of

monk's-hood stored in a great jar. Extremely poisonous if swallowed. A small dose killed Gervase Bonel.
Refs: **3** (1–6, 9).

Mulberry (*Morus nigra*). **Novels:** Leaves used as an ingredient in a paste for burns.
Refs: **4** (5:5).

Mullein (also Aaron's Rod) (*Verbascum thapsus*) (Cul: *Verbascum lychnitis* and *Verbascum nigrum*). **Poisonous. Novels:** An ingredient in an aromatic syrup for coughs and colds.
Refs: **3** (4); **12** (6).

Mushroom (*Agaricus campestris*). **Novels:** An edible fungus found growing in the woods and meadows beyond the Meole Brook.
Refs: **1** (1); **2** (8).

Mustard, Hedge (*Sisymbrium officinale*) (Cul: *Sinapis nigra* and *Sinapis alba*). **Novels:** A plant grown in Cadfael's herb garden. Oil extracted from seeds. Oil, mixed with root of monk's-hood, used as a rub for aching joints. Emetic mixture of mustard swallowed to induce vomiting. Hedge mustard used as an ingredient in a syrup for coughs and colds. Ointment of goose-grease impregnated with mustard and other heat-giving herbs used as a rub for sore chests and throats. The fruits of the plant used as an ingredient in pastes and poultices to fight malignant ulcers.
Refs: **1** (1); **3** (1–2, 4–5, 8); **5** (1); **12** (6).

N

Nettle, Common or Stinging (*Urtica dioica*). **Novels:** Found growing in the crevices of the flooring at Ruald's derelict cottage.
Refs: **3** (1); **17** (1).

O

Oak (*Quercus robur*). **Novels:** A common and ancient tree found growing in the Eaton, Eyton and Long Forests, and the woods near Gwytherin. Wood used for boards, planks, carved panelling, reliquaries and coffins. Cleft heartwood used for spokes of wheels. A host for clinging ivy and parasitic mistletoe.
Refs: **1** (2–3, 5–6, 9); **2** (7); **3** (8); **5** (4–5, 8–9); **7** (2, 9); **8** (5); **9** (13); **10** (3, 8–9); **11** (11, 13); **13** (1); **14** (3, 5–6, 8, 10–12); **19** (3); **20** (14); **RB** (1–2).

Oats (*Avena sativa*) (Wild Oat: *Avena fatua*). **Novels:** Grains of oats, an ingredient in a bottle of unspecified lotion. Oatmeal.
Refs: **5** (1, 6).

Onion (*Allium cepa*). **Novels:** An edible bulb grown in Cadfael's herb garden. A staple food for the monks. Cooked and eaten raw.
Refs: **3** (2); **8** (7); **17** (5).

Orchis (also Fox-Stones) (possibly Early Purple Orchid: *Orchis mascula*) (Cul: *Satyrium*). **Novels:** Found growing on the banks of the River Severn at Shrewsbury.
Refs: **7** (7, 11).

Orpine (also Livelong) (*Sedum telephium*). **Novels:** An ingredient in a soothing syrup for a raging quinsy.
Refs: **RB** (3).

P

Parsley (*Petroselinum crispum*) (Cul: *Petroselinum sativum*). **Novels:** A herb grown in Cadfael's walled garden.
Refs: **1** (1).

Paynim Poppy. See POPPY, Opium.

Pea (also spelled Pease) (*Pisum sativum*). **Novels:** Plant grown in the abbey fields running down to the Meole Brook and along the Gaye. Pods harvested for food. Dried haulms used for fodder and bedding. Two crops a year.
Refs: **2** (1, 7–8); **3** (1); **5** (10); **7** (4, 6); **10** (6, 8, 12–13, 15); **11** (10–11, 13); **12** (2, 6–7); **13** (1); **14** (1); **16** (1).

Pear (*Pyrus communis*) (Cul: *Pyrus sativa*). **Novels:** Tree grown for its edible fruit in the Gaye orchards. Sometimes plagued by winter moth. Cadfael made a wine from the fruit. Wood used to make small reliquary.
Refs: **1** (11); **2** (10); **3** (5, 7); **7** (8); **13** (6); **14** (5); **17** (6).

Pease. See PEA.

Peony (also spelled Paeony) (*Paeonia officinalis*) (Cul: *Paeonia*). **Novels:** Grown in Cadfael's herb garden for their seeds. Used medicinally and also as spices in abbey kitchen.
Refs: **1** (1); **10** (1); **17** (6).

Periwinkle (*Vinca minor*) (Cul: *Vinca major*). **Novels:** A trailing plant often represented in illuminated designs and engravings.
Refs: **7** (1); **9** (2); **11** (11); **15** (7); **16** (15).

Pine (Scots Pine) (*Pinus sylvestris*). **Novels:** Resinous wood used for making flaming torches.
Refs: **6** (8).

Plum (*Prunus domestica*). **Novels:** A tree grown in the Gaye orchards for its edible fruit. Purple-black Lammas plums: eaten fresh, boiled down into a thick preserve, or dried on racks to wrinkle and crystallise into gummy sweetness.
Refs: **2** (6, 9); **5** (1); **11** (1–2); **13** (6); **16** (11).

Pond-Weed. See WATER-WEED.

Poppy, Field (also Corn Rose) (*Papaver rhoeas*). **Novels:** Found growing wild among the unreaped grass in the Potter's Field.
Refs: **13** (13); **17** (1).

Poppy, Opium (also Paynim Poppy or Oriental Poppy) (*Papaver somniferum*). **Novels:** Plants with white or purple-black petals, originally brought as seed from the East and grown in Cadfael's herb garden. He raised and cross-bred them to perfect the plant. Juice used to make sweet syrup to dull pain and promote deep sleep. Seed harvested in heads for following year's crop. Cakes of poppy-seed. An ingredient in a syrup for coughs and colds.
Refs: **1** (1, 9–10); **4** (1:1, 4:3, 5:5); **5** (6, 10); **9** (14–15); **10** (3); **11** (2–3); **12** (6, 8); **15** (2); **17** (7, 11, 14); **RB** (2).

Primrose (*Primula vulgaris*).
Refs: **1** (4); **5** (9); **6** (10); **9** (11); **11** (11); **17** (1, 4, 10); **19** (8); **20** (16).

Pulse (also Lentils) (*Lens esculenta*) (Cul: *Ervum lens*). **Novels:** Grown in the abbey fields running down to the Meole Brook. Staple food of the monks.
Refs: **3** (1–2, 4).

R

Radish (*Raphanus sativus*). **Novels:** An edible root vegetable grown by Cadfael in his walled garden.
Refs: **13** (1).

Ragwort (also Ragweed) (*Senecio jacobaea*). **Novels:** Cleansing and astringent, good for old, ulcerated wounds. Found along the banks of the Meole Brook and in the hedgerows and meadows nearby.
Refs: **11** (3).

Reed (*Glyceria maxima* or *Phragmites communis*). **Novels:** Reed-beds found along the edges of the water-meadows upstream of Frankwell, immediately downstream of the Gaye, in the shallows around the abbey mill pond, and alongside the River Severn near Atcham. Often used as building material for huts.
Refs: **7** (3); **11** (12); **12** (5, 8–10, 12); **13** (8); **16** (9); **17** (9).

Rose (*Rosa*). **Novels:** Grown in the abbot's own garden at Shrewsbury as well as in the cloister garth, Cadfael's walled garden and the rose garden. Pale yellow petals shading into pink at the tips. Rose-beds manured with stable-muck. Used as a fragrant ingredient in perfumed oils for altar lamps. White and very fragrant roses grew on the bush in Judith Perle's old garden in the Abbey Foregate. Climbing roses were often represented in illuminated designs.
Refs: **1** (2, 12); **2** (7); **4** (1:1, 2:3, 3:2, 4:1–2); **5** (2, 5); **8** (5, 13); **10** (1–3); **11** (3, 5, 10); **12** (1–2, 4, 8); **13** (1–7, 9–14); **14** (1, 3, 5, 14); **15** (10); **16** (1–3, 7, 15); **17** (13); **19** (1, 13); **20** (1).

Rose, Dog or Wild. See BRIAR.

Rosemary (*Rosmarinus officinalis*). **Novels:** A herb grown in Cadfael's walled garden. An ingredient in a medicinal preparation for rheum in the eyes or head. Also an ingredient in a cough syrup. The needles were dried and stored.
Refs: **1** (1); **2** (1); **3** (1, 4); **5** (2); **RB** (2).

Rue (also Herb of Grace) (*Ruta graveolens*). **Novels:** A herb grown in Cadfael's walled garden. An ingredient in cough syrup. Used as an aromatic ingredient in perfumed oils for altar lamps.
Refs: **1** (1); **3** (4); **12** (8).

Rush (*Juncus*) (Common Bulrush: *Scirpus lacustris*). **Novels:** Used for rush-lights or rush-candles, for bedding, and for covering floors. The stems were woven into baskets.
Refs: **2** (9); **3** (3, 5); **9** (12); **12** (4); **13** (7); **14** (8); **15** (6–8).

S

Saffron (*Crocus sativus*) (Autumn Crocus: *Colchicum autumnale* – **Poisonous**).
Refs: **10** (7).

Sage (*Salvia officinalis*). **Novels:** A fragrant culinary herb grown in Cadfael's walled garden. Used as an aromatic ingredient in perfumed oils for altar lamps.
Refs: **1** (1); **2** (1, 4); **3** (1); **10** (3); **12** (8).

Saint John's Wort (*Hypericum perforatum*). **Novels:** An ingredient in wine added to a little poppy-syrup and woundwort-syrup to soothe pain. The plant was also used in an ointment for wounds.
Refs: **11** (3); **14** (4).

Sanicle (*Sanicula europoea*). **Novels:** Cleansing and astringent, good for old, ulcerated wounds. Found

along the banks of the Meole Brook and in the hedgerows and meadows nearby. An ingredient in a lotion for cleaning gashes and grazes.
Refs: **11** (3); **14** (4).

Savoury (also spelled Savory) (*Satureia hortensis*). **Novels:** A herb grown in Cadfael's walled garden.
Refs: **1** (1).

Saxifrage (also Burnet Saxifrage) (*Pimpinella saxifraga*). **Novels:** An ingredient in a medicinal preparation for rheum in the eyes or head.
Refs: **3** (1).

Selfheal (*Prunella vulgaris*). **Novels:** A plant found growing among the white stones of a wall near Huon de Domville's hunting lodge in the Long Forest.
Refs: **5** (7).

Snowdrop (*Galanthus nivalis*).
Refs: **17** (3).

Sorrel (*Rumex acetosa*). **Novels:** A little flask of mint and sorrel vinegar sniffed as a restorative after dizziness and fainting.
Refs: **5** (5).

Spikenard (*Nardostachys jatamansi*). **Novels:** Used to anoint the Saviour's feet.
Refs: **RB** (2).

Spruce (*Picea abies*).
Refs: **18** (7).

Stonecrop (also Wall Pepper) (*Sedum acre*). **Novels:** Found growing among the white stones of a wall near Huon de Domville's hunting lodge in the Long Forest.
Refs: **5** (7).

Strawberry (*Fragaria vesca*). **Novels:** A plant grown for its edible fruit along the orchards of the Gaye.
Refs: **13** (8).

Sweet Cicely (*Myrrhis odorata*) (Cul: *Scandix odorata*). **Novels:** An ingredient in a cough-syrup.
Refs: **3** (4).

T

Tansy (*Tannacetum vulgare*). **Novels:** A herb grown in Cadfael's walled garden.
Refs: **1** (1).

Tare (also Hairy Tare) (*Vicia hirsuta*). **Novels:** Found growing like weeds in wheat-fields.
Refs: **16** (5).

Thistle, Sow- (*Sonchus oleraceus*, or *Sonchus asper*). **Novels:** Found growing among the beds of mint in Cadfael's walled garden. Thistledown.
Refs: **2** (8); **11** (1, 10); **13** (1, 5); **19** (1).

Thyme (*Thymus vulgaris*) (Wild Thyme: *Thymus praecox*) (Cul: *Thymus serpyllum*). **Novels:** A fragrant herb grown in Cadfael's walled garden. Wild thyme used to turf over an earth-bench seat in Father Eadmer the elder's garden at Attingham.
Refs: **1** (1); **2** (1, 5); **5** (2); **10** (3); **12** (2); **16** (9); **17** (7).

Toadflax (*Linaria vulgaris*). **Novels:** A plant found growing among the white stones of a wall near Huon de Domville's hunting lodge in the Long Forest.
Refs: **5** (7).

Toadstool (possibly *Panaeolus sphinctrinus*). **Novels:** Frail bluish toadstools found growing in the turf on the edges of the Long Forest.
Refs: **8** (5).

Trefoil, Heart (*Trifolium cordatis*). **Novels:** A decoction of heart trefoil was used to strengthen the heart after a seizure.
Refs: **7** (2).

V

Vetch (*Vicia augustifolia*, *Lathyrus montanus* or *Lathyrus pratensis*). **Novels:** Found growing among the grass and moss-pasture on the banks of the Meole Brook. Grown in Cadfael's walled garden. Tendrils of vetches were often represented in illuminated designs and engravings.
Refs: **2** (9); **11** (6–7, 9, 11, 13).

Vine. see GRAPE.

Violet (*Viola odorata*). **Novels:** Used as a fragrant ingredient in perfumed oils for altar lamps. Violets were sometimes represented in illuminated designs.
Refs: **12** (8); **16** (7).

W

Walnut (*Juglans regia*). **Novels:** Two big walnut trees grew in the orchards of the Gaye.
Refs: **13** (6).

Water-Weed (also Pond-Weed) (*Potamogeton crispus*). **Novels:** Found growing in the Meole Brook and in the stream at Godric's Ford.
Refs: **5** (10); **9** (13).

Wheat (also Corn) (*Triticum aestivum*) (Cul: *Triticum*). **Novels:** Fields of wheat were grown beyond the Gaye, almost opposite the castle. After the crop had been harvested and stored in the barns the sheep and cattle were allowed to graze the stubble. The corn was ground in the abbey mill. Winter wheat was sown in the Potter's Field. Corn was also grown at Ulf's holding near Frankwell, and in the Fens.
Refs: **2** (5–6, 8); **4** (1:1, 4:1); **5** (2, 10); **7** (6); **10** (4); **11** (1); **12** (5); **13** (6); **15** (6); **16** (5, 7); **17** (1, 8); **20** (1).

Willow (*Salix alba*). **Novels:** The tree grew along the banks of the River Severn, around the abbey millpond and beside the brook in Eyton Forest. It was a source for withies. Many of the trees were pollarded (the practice of cutting back the top branches to produce a dense crop of new shoots for fencing, etc.). Long bands of willow were used for binding the staves of a barrel together when it was set up in its truss hoop.
Refs: **2** (9); **7** (6, 11); **11** (8, 12); **12** (5, 9, 12); **13** (7, 11); **14** (3-4, 11); **16** (1, 6); **17** (7, 11); **20** (5, 8).

Willowherb Broad-Leaved (*Epilobium montanum*) (Rose-Bay Willowherb: *Epilobium angustifolium*). **Novels:** Willowherb was found growing among the thyme in Cadfael's herb garden.
Refs: **2** (5).

Windflower. See ANEMONE.

Wintergreen (*Pyrola minor*). **Novels:** Used as an ingredient in healing creams and waxes.
Refs: **11** (3).

Woad (*Isatis tinctoria*). **Novels:** Used as a blue dye for cloth.
Refs: **13** (3).

Wolfsbane. See MONK'S-HOOD.

Wormwood (*Artemisia absynthium*). **Novels:** Used as an aromatic ingredient in perfumed oils for altar lamps.
Refs: **12** (8).

Woundwort. See BETONY.

Y

Yew (*Taxus baccata*). **Novels:** Grown as hedging in the abbey gardens.
Refs: **10** (6).

Appendix II

The Brothers and Officers of Shrewsbury Abbey

Adam, Brother
Adrian, Brother
Aelfric, Brother (illuminator and copyist)
Albin, Brother (porter)
Ambrose, Brother (almoner)
Andrew, Brother
Anselm, Brother (precentor and librarian)
Anselm, Lay Brother
Athanasius, Brother
Aylwin, Brother

Barnabas, Lay Brother
Benedict, Brother (sacristan)
Bernard, Brother (apiarist)

Cadfael, Brother (herbalist)
Columbanus, Brother
Conradin, Brother

Dafydd, Brother
Denis, Brother (hospitaller)

Edmund, Brother (infirmarer)
Eluric, Brother (custodian of St Mary's altar)
Emmanuel, Brother (Abbot Heribert's personal clerk and secretary)
Europius, Brother
Everard, Brother

Fidelis, Brother (formerly of Hyde Mead Priory)
Francis, Brother (custodian of St Mary's altar)
Fulchered, Abbot

Godefrid, Abbot

Haluin, Brother (illuminator)
Henry, Brother
Heribert, Abbot (formerly Prior Heribert; later Brother Heribert)
Humilis, Brother (formerly of Hyde Mead Priory)

Jerome, Brother (Prior Robert Pennant's clerk and chaplain)
John, Brother
Jordan, Brother

Leonard, Brother (later Prior Leonard of Bromfield Priory)
Louis, Lay Brother
Luke, Brother

Mark, Brother (later Deacon Mark of Lichfield)
Matthew, Brother (cellarer)
Maurice, Brother (custodian of St Mary's altar)
Meriet, Brother

Orderic, Brother (Prior Heribert's clerk)
Oswald, Brother (almoner)
Oswin, Brother

Paul, Brother (master of the novices, chief of confessors)
Petrus, Brother (abbot's cook)

Porter, Brother (porter)

Radulfus, Abbot
Reginald, Brother
Reynald, Fulke (steward and lay superior of Hospital of St Giles)
Rhun, Brother
Rhys, Brother
Richard, Brother (sub-prior)
Robert Pennant, Prior (later Abbot Robert)
Ruald, Brother

Simeon, Brother
Simon, Brother
Simon, Lay Brother
Sulien, Brother (formerly of Ramsey Abbey)

Urien, Brother

Vitalis, Brother (Abbot Radulfus's chaplain and secretary)

Wilfred, Brother
Winfrid, Brother
Wolston, Brother

Those brothers and novices who assisted Cadfael in the herb garden were: Haluin, John, Mark, Oswin, Sulien and Winfrid.

In June 1141 there were fifty-four brothers, seven novices and six schoolboys in the house, excluding the abbot. This does not include the numerous lay stewards, lay servants and lay brothers working inside and outside the abbey enclave and in the outlying granges. It should be noted, however, that historical records suggest that there were never more than nineteen brothers in the abbey.

Appendix III

Kings, Emperors, Popes and Archbishops

Kings of England, 975-1189

Edward the Martyr	975–978
Ethelred II the Unready	978–1016
Edmund Ironside	1016
Canute	1017–1035
Harold I	1035–1040
Hardicanute	1040–1042
Edward the Confessor	1042–1066
Harold II	1066
William I the Conqueror	1066–1087
William II Rufus	1087–1100
Henry I	1100–1135
Stephen	1135–1154
Henry II	1154–1189

Kings of France, 1031–1180

Henry I	1031–1060
Philip I	1060–1108
Louis VI	1108–1137
Louis VII	1137–1180

Kings of Jerusalem, 1099–1192

Godfrey of Bouillon	1099–1100
Baldwin I	1100–1118
Baldwin II	1118–1131
Fulk	1131–1143
Baldwin III	1143–1162
Amaury I	1162–1174
Baldwin IV	1174–1185
Baldwin V	1185–1186
Guy de Lusignan	1186–1192

Holy Roman Emperors, 1056–1190

Henry IV	1056–1106
Henry V	1106–1125
Lothair II	1125–1137
Conrad III	1138–1152
Frederick I Barbarossa	1152–1190

Byzantine Emperors, 1056–1180

Michael VI Stratioticus	1056–1057
Isaac I Comnenus	1057–1059
Constantine X Ducas	1059–1067
Romanus IV Diogenes	1067–1071
Michael VII Ducas	1071–1078
Nicephorus III Botaniates	1078–1081
Alexius I Comnenus	1081–1118
John II Comnenus	1118–1143
Manuel I Comnenus	1143–1180

Popes, 1059–1181
Note: Antipopes are not included.

Nicholas II	1059–1061
Alexander II	1061–1073

Gregory VII	1073–1085
Victor III	1086–1087
Urban II	1088–1099
Paschal II	1099–1118
Gelasius II	1118–1119
Calixtus II	1119–1124
Honorius II	1124–1130
Innocent II	1130–1143
Celestine II	1143–1144
Lucius II	1144–1145
Eugenius III	1145–1153
Anastasius IV	1153–1154
Adrian IV	1154–1159
Alexander III	1159–1181

Archbishops of Canterbury, 1052–1170

Stigand	1052–1070
Lanfranc	1070–1089
Anselm	1093–1109
Ralph d'Escures	1114–1122
William of Corbeil	1123–1136
Theobald of Bec	1138–1161
Thomas à Becket	1162–1170

Appendix IV

Glossary

Although some of the following words have alternative meanings, the entry is specifically related to its reference in *The Chronicles of Brother Cadfael*.

Advowson. The right to nominate a clergyman to a vacant BENEFICE or ecclesiastical office.

Alltud (also outlander). Alltud is a Welsh word meaning 'other-country-man'. The foreigner or alien living in exile in Wales was not necessarily an alltud. In essence, an alltud, whether villein or freeman, had no claim upon the land in the district. In order to acquire a stake in the land, he had to place himself under the protection of a landowner and, after three generations, his descendants although villein-bound might themselves become landowners.

Amour de loin. Love at a distance. Chivalrous love. A lot of the troubadour love songs are dedicated to far-distant or even imaginary loves. The phrase 'amour de loin' or 'amour de lonh' appears in the songs.

Arbalest (also spelled arbalist). A crossbow with a special mechanism for drawing and loosing the arrows, bolts, stones and other missiles.

Assart. An arable tract of land created by clearing an area of forest or woodland.

Baileywick (also spelled bailiwick). District under the jurisdiction of a bailiff.

Baldric. Belt hung from shoulder across chest to support a sword.

Banker. A stone bench used by masons to cut stone.

Bannerole. A long, narrow streamer attached to a lance.

Benefice. The property or living held by the vicar of a parish church.

Bliaut. An indoor garment worn over the COTTE, the full-length, sleeved gown. It was close fitted to the hip, full-skirted below, had no sleeves, and was cut low at the neck, and laced at the sides, to show the dress beneath.

Bodice. A laced outer garment worn by a woman over a blouse, or the laced upper part of a dress down to the waist.

Bower. An arbour, a shady place enclosed by foliage.

Brattice. A timber gallery erected on the battlements of a fortress, for use during a siege.

Brychan. A blanket. The home-woven woollen furnishings of a bed and sometimes, by extension, used of the bed itself.

Burgage. A tenure of land in a town held for a yearly rent, or other services, under the king or a lord.

Butts. (1) A strip of land used for target practice, particularly archery; the butt was usually a mound or similar on which the target was set up. (2) A wooden cask. (3) A strip of land in the abbey gardens.

Caltrop (also spelled caltrap). An iron ball with four projecting spikes. It was scattered on the ground to obstruct the advance of cavalry horses.

Cantref (also spelled cantred). The Welsh equivalent of the English HUNDRED. The cantref was subdivided into COMMOTE, MAENOL and TREF. It signified one hundred villages.

Capuchon. A cowl-like hood, the folds of which were wrapped round the neck.

Caput. The chief seat of a noble family's honour, or head manor.

Cariad. Welsh for my dear, darling, beloved.

Carucate. An alternative term for a HIDE, normally used in former Danish areas.

Cassock. A long, usually black, garment, reaching to the feet. It is worn by monks, choristers and clergymen.

Castellan. Governor or lord of a castle.

Chasseours. Hunting hounds. The stag was flushed from cover by a leashed hound called a lymer, and once on the move the pack was loosed to course the animal in relays, first the 'van chasseours', then the middle, and finally the PARFYTOURS, who were in at the kill.

Chatelaine. The lady or mistress of a manor or large house.

Causses. A medieval tight-fitting garment worn by men to cover the legs and feet, similar to tights.

Chevet. The east end of church, behind the high altar, with radiating apses or chapels.

Clas. An important and responsible body in the Celtic Church. Consisting of a community of canons under an abbot, with at least one priest, it received half of the revenues of the church, settled disputes among its members and succeeded to the movable property of the abbot on his death.

Coif. A close-fitting linen cap, usually worn under a veil, especially by nuns.

Collation. Held in the chapter-house after supper, Collations was a short formal reading on the monastic life, usually taken from the Lives of the Saints.

Commote (also spelled commot). Each CANTREF was divided into two, three or more commotes. The main feature of the commote was its court, which was generally used to settle disputes among the free Welshmen. The commote was itself subdivided into TREFS.

Compline (also completorium). A short service, Compline was the last office said before the monks retired for the night. It was held about half past seven during the summer and about half past eight during the winter.

Conversus (plural: conversi). A monk who had voluntarily entered the cloister after being active in the world. (See also OBLATUS).

Coppice. A coppice is produced by periodically cutting back deciduous trees to their base in order to provide a crop of light branches for fuel and other purposes. Coppicing is an ancient craft, dating back to prehistoric times.

Coram Rege. A matter for the king's court.

Cot. A small house or cottage.

Cottar (also spelled cotter). A villein who, in return for his labour, was granted a cottage with a small piece of land.

Cotte. The main garment, coat, tunic or gown: full-length for the nobility; and knee-length for the working men.

Coulter. Iron blade fixed vertically in front of a plough which makes a preliminary cut through the sod or soil.

Creance. A long leash attached to the leg of a hawk to allow it to fly while being trained.

Cresset. A metal vessel containing oil or similar, pitched wood or coal, to be burnt for light. Often mounted on a pole or suspended from a roof. Cresset stones, which may still be found in some churches, are solid slabs of stone hollowed into a number of small bowls in neat rows, often thirteen, to hold oil and burned for warmth rather than light. They simply rested on the floor, wherever most needed.

Croft. A small enclosed piece of pasture or arable land, next to a house.

Currier. A comb for grooming a horse.

Dadanhudd. The provision under Welsh law which enabled the son to obtain temporary possession of his dead father's land while it was being disputed in the court. It meant 'uncovering' and referred to the son's right to uncover his father's hearth.

Dais. Raised platform in a hall used by speakers and dignitaries.

Demesne. Lands retained by the lord of the manor for his own use.

Diocese (also bishopric). The district, with a cathedral, under the jurisdiction of a bishop.

Dortoir (also spelled dorter; also dormitorium). The monks' dormitory or sleeping-place.

Electuary. Medicinal powder mixed with sugar or honey and taken orally.

Eremite. A religious recluse or hermit.

Espringale. A military machine, resembling a large crossbow, used for shooting darts or javelins.

Estampie. A medieval dance measure.

Fealty. The obligation of loyalty owed by a tenant or VASSAL to his feudal lord.

Febrifuge. Medicine used to reduce fever.

Feudal. Medieval system of government based on the relation of a VASSAL to his lord, in which land was held in return for homage and service.

Fiat. An authorisation or order.

Frater (also refectorium). The monastic refectory or common dining-room.

Galanas. The vendetta or blood-feud in medieval Wales, which provoked the unanimous hostility and vengeance of all of the victim's clan, could last for generations. Galanas not only meant the effect of the feud, the blood money or 'wergild', but also its cause, the deed which led to the violent death. It became a means of satisfaction for the slaughter of a kinsman.

Garderobe. A lavatory or toilet. Simple shafts set in the thickness of the wall. One or more chambers entered, for instance, by a lobby ventilated by a window.

Garth. The grassy quadrangle within the monastic cloisters.

Geneth. Welsh for girl or maiden.

Gentle. Person from an honourable, well-born family.

Glebe. A plot of land held by a clergyman, while in office, as part of his BENEFICE.

Grange. The buildings and land of an outlying farm belonging to a monastery.

Greensward. Turf or short grass.

Groat. A small coin.

Gruel. A thin, watery or milky porridge, usually fed to invalids.

Guild. A tradesmen's association, formed to protect its members' interests and maintain standards.

Guildsman. A member of a GUILD.

Gyve. Iron shackle or fetter, especially for the leg.

Hauberk. A long coat of mail Originally armour for the defence of the neck and shoulders.

Headland. A strip of unploughed land at the end of a field, on which the oxen and plough could be turned. In the open field system of farming, the headland was usually shared by the strip-farmers. It was often used as a boundary.

Helm. A helmet; armour protection for the head.

Hide (also CARUCATE, husbandland, ploughland or ploughgate). The measure of land which could be ploughed in one year, using one plough pulled by a team of eight oxen. It varied between 60 and 120 acres, according to the quality of the soil, and was usually enough to support one free family and their dependants. It was used in the Domesday Book survey of 1086 as a measure of tax liability.

Hogget. A yearling sheep.

Horarium. The monastic daily time-table. The horarium was divided into the canonical hours or offices of MATINS, LAUDS, PRIME, TERCE, SEXT, NONE, VESPERS and COMPLINE.

Hundred (also wapentake, lathe, rape, leet, ward or liberty). Administrative division within a county or shire, having its own court which usually met once a month at an open space.

Husbandman. A tenant farmer.

Jess. Short strap fastened round the leg of a hawk in falconry to which a CREANCE may be attached.

Largesse. Money, gifts or favours bestowed freely by an important person on a great occasion.

Lauds. A short office, immediately following MATINS, which ended between one and two in the morning. After Lauds the monks retired to their beds in the DORTOIR.

Leat (also spelled leet). An artificial waterway, cut to divert water from a stream in order to power a mill, mining works and such like.

Liripipe. A long tail or extension to the point of a CAPUCHON.

Litany. An alternating series of phrases in a prayer recited by a clergyman and answered by the congregation.

Llys. The royal court or 'castell' of Welsh princes. All of the buildings of the llys were made of timber.

Lodestar. A star forming a fixed point of reference, usually the Pole Star.

Lodestone. A magnetised piece of magnetite metal ore.

Lungeous. To charge at things like a bull in a china shop.

Lye. A strong alkaline solution used for washing, cleaning and making soap. It is obtained by leaching or straining a solution of water and wood or vegetable ashes.

Maenol. A subdivision of the COMMOTE. The maenol was originally the stone-encircled residence of a Welsh chieftain. It later came to mean a group of villein TREFS.

Mandora. An ancient stringed instrument. Ancestor of the mandolin.

Mangonel. A military machine for hurling bolts, stones and other missiles at the enemy.

Marl. Soil consisting of clay and lime and valuable as a fertiliser.

Matins (formerly called Nocturns). An office held about midnight, Matins was the first and longest service of the monastic day. It was followed, almost immediately, by LAUDS.

Merlon. The solid part of an embattled or crenellated parapet. The open space on each side of the merlon is an embrasure.

Messuage. A house with its adjoining land and outbuildings, usually rented.

Mews. Cages in an enclosed yard or alley used for hawks when they are moulting.

Midden. Dunghill or manure heap.

Minuscule (also spelled miniscule). A small cursive script.

Missal. A prayer book, containing all the services for celebrating Mass throughout the year.

Moguing. A Shropshire word, often used by children, meaning making up, being nice, getting round someone.

Moneyer. A minter of coins.

Mountebank. Charlatan or trickster; also a strolling tumbler or entertainer.

Mullion. The vertical or upright post dividing the lights in a window.

Mummer. An actor or player in a traditional, usually religious, mime or masque.

Murage. The tax levied to pay for building or repairing the walls of a town.

Murrain. An infectious disease in cattle.

Myrmidon. Faithful follower or servant who carries out orders without question.

Nacre. Mother-of-pearl.

Neums. The signs in plainsong used to indicate a note or group of notes to be sung to a single syllable.

None. The short monastic office of None was usually held about three in the afternoon.

Obedientiary. The holder of any office under a superior in a convent or monastery.

Oblatus (also oblate). A monk who had been placed in the monastery from a very early age and who, therefore, had little or no experience of the world outside the cloister.

Orts. Waste food or scraps.

Ostler. A person who takes charge of horses, particularly at an inn.

Outlander. See ALLTUD.

Palfrey. A saddle horse for women.

Pallet. A narrow wooden bed or straw-filled mattress.

Palliative. Something that alleviates rather than cures illness, disease, pain, etc.

Pannikin. Small metal cup or saucepan.

Parfytours. Hunting hounds. The parfytours finish the quarry after it has been chased to exhaustion by the pack, loosed to course the animal in relays. See also CHASSEOURS.

Parole. The word of honour, or promise, given by a prisoner not to escape if he is conditionally given his freedom.

Patten. A wooden sandal or clog with a metal support fixed to the undersole to raise the wearer's foot out of water, mud and the like.

Pavage. The tax levied to pay for the paving of streets in a town.

Penteulu. The Welsh rank of captain of the royal guard.

Ploughland. The equivalent of a HIDE.

Pommel. The saddlebow; the upward-pointing front part of a saddle.

Poniard. A dagger.

Prelate. A bishop, abbot or a person having a similar high status in the church.

Prie-Dieu. A kneeling desk for prayer.

Prime. The monastic office of Prime was usually held at dawn.

Psalter (plural: psalteries). A copy of the Book of Psalms for liturgical use.

Psaltery. A medieval stringed instrument, similar to a dulcimer, usually played by plucking the strings with quills, using both hands.

Pyre. A pile of combustible material, especially used for burning a corpse at a funeral.

Pyx. Small box or casket, usually to contain the consecrated bread.

Quintain. A target mounted on a post and tilted at by horsemen. It usually swung round to strike the less skilful tilter.

Rebec. A medieval three-stringed instrument played with a bow.

Rheum. A watery secretion or discharge from the eyes or nose.

Rood-loft. The singing gallery on the top of the carved wooden 'rood-screen' which separates the nave and choir in a church. The 'rood-beam' supports the 'rood', or Cross of Christ.

Rubric. A chapter or section heading of a book written or printed in red.

Saeson. An Englishman.

Scabbard. The sheath of a dagger or sword.

Sconce. A wall bracket for holding a candle or torch.

Seisin. A legal term meaning possession rather than ownership of a freehold estate.

Sext. The short monastic office of Sext was held about noon.

Sheepfold. An enclosure for penning sheep.

Shriven. The state of someone who has received confession, done penance and been absolved.

Shut. A narrow alleyway or passageway running between the main streets of a town. In Shrewsbury many of these passages are still referred to as shuts.

Skiff. An open flat-bottomed rowing boat, with pointed prow and square stern.

Sortes Biblicae. The ancient custom of reading the future by opening an ancient text at random, in this case the Gospels. Although the *sortes* were often consulted by individuals in private, according to some 12th C. historians, the practice was used officially in the ceremony of the consecration of a bishop. William of Malmesbury in his *Gesta Pontificum Anglorum* records that Wulstan, Bishop of Worcester, received John 1:47. According to the *Trinity MS R.7.5*, compiled in *c.*1123, others were given the following prognostics: Lanfranc (Luke 11:41); Anselm (Luke 14:16–17); William of Corbeil (Luke 1:41 and 44); Roger, Bishop of Salisbury (Matthew 22:13); and Henry of Blois (Matthew 24:23). It is possible that some prognostics were the result of human rather than divine intervention. Not all *sortes* were favourable, some were openly derogatory. (See *Sortes Biblicae in Twelfth-Century England: the List of Episcopal Prognostics in Cambridge, Trinity College MS R.7.5* by George Henderson, published in *England in the Twelfth Century*, The Boydell Press, 1990.)

Sow (or Cat). A long, moveable structure with a strong roof, used to cover and protect a team of men and a heavy ram when advancing to the walls of a besieged fortress.

Specific. A medicinal remedy intended for a specific ailment or disorder.

Springe. A sprung noose for snaring small game.

Stoup. A cup, flagon, tankard or other drinking vessel. Also basin for holy water.

Sumpter. A pack-horse.

Synod. A council or assembly of bishops and other church officials.

Tallow. A mixture of animal or vegetable fat used to make candles, soap and lubricants.

Terce. The short monastic office of Terce was held about nine in the morning.

Tilth. (1) The cultivation or tillage of the land. (2) The condition of the soil with respect to stimulating plant growth.

Tiltyard. An enclosed area for tilting contests.

Timbrel. An ancient instrument similar to a tambourine.

Tithe. A tax of one-tenth part of income from labour or produce from land taken to support the clergy and church.

Tocsin. A bell rung to sound an alarm.

Toft. (1) A plot of land including a house. (2) A plot of land on which a house once stood.

Toper. A heavy drinker or drunkard.

Touchstone. A hard black stone, like jasper or basalt, used to test the quality of gold or silver.

Touchwood. Soft, decayed and readily inflammable wood used as tinder.

Tref. A subdivision of the COMMOTE. Originally a 'house' or 'dwelling-place', the Welsh tref later came to mean a hamlet or village.

Trencher. A wooden platter for food.

Troche. A small circular medicinal pastille or lozenge.

Uchelwr. A class of wealthy landowners who were the nearest Welsh equivalent to the English nobility. The name means 'high man'.

Ud. Also spelled Oud. A form of lute or mandolin played mainly in Arab countries.

Vassal. A holder of land from a feudal lord. In return for his service, homage and FEALTY, the vassal received protection.

Vespers (also Evensong). The monastic office of Vespers took place in the late afternoon, between NONE and COMPLINE.

Villein. A feudal serf or tenant bound to the land and subject to the control of a lord. A villein was above the status of a slave, but could not marry without his lord's consent.

Virelai. Short medieval French lyric poem.

Vittles (also victuals). Food or provisions suitable for human consumption.

Votary. A person bound by vows to follow a certain course, ideal or way of life, usually religious.

Wattle. Sticks interlaced with twigs or branches used in the construction of huts, walls or fences. In buildings the weave was often plastered with mud or clay (wattle-and-daub).

Wicket. A small door or gate built in or beside a larger one.

Wimple. A linen or silk cloth folded round the head and under the chin to frame the face. It was worn by women, especially nuns.

Withy (also spelled withe; plural withies). A long, strong flexible twig of alder, osier, willow, hazel or similar used to bind bundles, or weave baskets, rims of coracles and so on.

Yardland (also virgate). A variable measure relating to the quality of the soil; approximately one quarter of a hide.

Yeoman. A respectable freeman, usually an independent farmer, with a status below that of a gentleman. He was qualified to serve on juries and vote in county elections.

Select Bibliography

Anderson, John Corbet, *Shropshire: Its Early History and Antiquities*, Willis and Sotheran, 1864

Bede, Adam, *A History of the English Church and People* (Sherley-Price, Leo, translator), Penguin Books, Harmondsworth, 1955

Benedictine Monks of St Augustine's Abbey, Ramsgate, comp., *The Book of Saints* (6th edition), Black, London, 1989

Blackwall, Anthony, *Historic Bridges of Shropshire*, Shropshire Libraries, Shrewsbury, 1985

Boston, Noel, T*he Story of Lilleshall Abbey*, Newport Advertiser, 1934

Bottomly, Frank, *The Explorer's Guide to the Abbeys, Monasteries and Churches of Great Britain*, Avenel Books, New York, 1981

Cross, F.L., ed., *Oxford Dictionary of the Christian Church*, Oxford University Press, 1974

Culpeper's Complete Herbal, Foulsham, London, n.d.

Delaney, John J. and Tobin, James Edward, *Dictionary of Catholic Biography*, Hale, London, 1962

Dickinson, J.C., *Monastic Life in Medieval England*, Adam and Charles Black, London, 1961

The Dictionary of Welsh Biography, Blackwell, Oxford, 1959

Evans, Kathleen M., *A Book of Welsh Saints*, Church in Wales Provincial Council for Education, Penarth, 1959

Eyton, Rev. R.W., *Antiquities of Shropshire: Vols. I–XII*, John Russell Smith, London, 1854

Forrest, H.E., *The Old Churches of Shrewsbury*, Wilding, Shrewsbury, 1920

Frend, W.H.C., *Saints and Sinners in the Early Church*, Darton, Longman and Todd, London, 1985

Gabrieli, Francesco, *Arab Historians of the Crusades*, (Islamic World series), Routledge and Kegan Paul, London, 1969

Garner, Lawrence, *Shropshire* (Shire County Guide: 7), Shire, Aylesbury, 1985

Glubb, Sir John, *A Short History of the Arab Peoples*, Dorset Press, New York, 1969

Guest, Lady Charlotte, *The Mabinogion*, Dent, London, 1906

Hallam, Elizabeth, gen. ed. *The Plantagenet Chronicles*, Weidenfeld and Nicolson, London, 1986

Haslam, Richard, *Powys* (The Buildings of England series), Penguin Books, Harmondsworth, 1979

Harvey, John, *Mediaeval Gardens*, Batsford, London, 1981

Henken, Elissa R., *Traditions of the Welsh Saints*, Brewer, London, 1987

Hubbard, Edward, *Clwyd* (The Buildings of England series), Penguin Books, Harmondsworth, 1986

Hunt, Tony, *Plant Names of Medieval England*, Brewer, London, 1989

Jackson, Michael, *Castles of Shropshire*, Shropshire Libraries, Shrewsbury, 1988

Jones, Thomas, translator, *Brut Y Tywysogyon* (*Chronicle of the Princes*), University of Wales, Cardiff, 1952

Knowles, David, *The Monastic Order in England*, Cambridge University Press, Cambridge, 1976

Lloyd, Sir J.E., *A History of Wales: From the Earliest Times to the Edwardian Conquest*, Longmans, Green and Co., London, 1954

McCall, Andrew, *The Medieval Underworld*, Hamish Hamilton, London, 1979

Mee, Arthur, *Shropshire* (The King's England series), Hodder and Stoughton, London, 1939 (revised 1968)

Midmer, Roy, *English Medieval Monasteries 1066–1540*, Heinemann, London, 1979

Owen, H., *Some Account of the Ancient and Present State of Shrewsbury*, Sandford, Shrewsbury, 1808 (republished by Morten, Manchester, 1972)

Owen, H. and Blakeway, J.B., *A History of Shrewsbury* (2 vols.), Harding, Lepard and Co., London, 1825

Parry, David, *The Rule of Saint Benedict*, Darton, Longman and Todd, London, 1984

Peake, Harold, *Historical Guide to Ellesmere* (local guide), Roberts, Ellesmere, 1897

Pevsner, Nikolaus, *Shropshire* (The Buildings of England series), Penguin Books, Harmondsworth, 1958

Pevsner, Nikolaus, *Staffordshire* (The Buildings of England series), Penguin Books, Harmondsworth, 1974

Platt, Colin, *The Abbeys and Priories of Medieval England*, Secker and Warburg, London 1984

Platt, Colin, *The English Medieval Town*, Secker and Warburg, London, 1976

Poole, Austin Lane, *The Oxford History of England: From Domesday to Magna Carta* (2nd edition), Oxford University Press, 1975

Potter, K.R., ed. & translator, *Gesta Stephani*, Oxford Medieval Texts, 1976

Randall, J., *The Severn Valley*, James S. Virtue, London, 1862

Raven, Michael, *A Shropshire Gazetteer*, Raven, Market Drayton, 1989

Runciman, Steven, *A History of the Crusades: The First Crusade*, Cambridge University Press, 1951 (republished by Penguin Books, London, 1978)

Savage, Anne, translator & collator, *The Anglo-Saxon Chronicles*, Heinemann, London, 1982

Scott-Davies, A. and Scars, R.S., *Shuts and Passages of Shrewsbury*, Shropshire Libraries, Shrewsbury, 1986

Shropshire (county guide), The British Publishing Company, Gloucester, 1988

The Shropshire Village Book (compiled by the Shropshire Federation of Women's Institutes), Countryside Books, Newbury, 1988

Stephen, Sir Leslie and Lee, Sir Sidney, *The Dictionary of National Biography*, Oxford University Press, 1917

Thorn, Frank and Caroline, ed., Morris, Jon, gen. ed., *Domesday Book: Shropshire*, Phillimore, Chichester, 1986

Thurston, Herbert J. and Attwater, Donald, ed., *Butler's Lives of the Saints* (4 vols.), Burns and Oates, London, 1926–38

Whitelock, Dorothy, *The Beginnings of English Society* (The Penguin History of England series), Penguin Books, Harmondsworth, 1952

Whitelock, Dorothy, ed. *English Historical Documents: Vol. 1, c.500–1042,* Eyre Methuen, London, 1979